AND HE GAVE PASTORS

EDITOR

Thomas F. Zimmerman, D.D.
General Superintendent
Assemblies of God

ASSOCIATE EDITORS

G. Raymond Carlson, D.D.
Assistant General Superintendent
Assemblies of God

Zenas J. Bicket, Ph.D
Academic Dean
Evangel College

02-0460

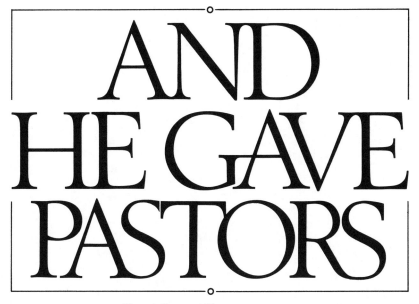

AND HE GAVE PASTORS

Pastoral Theology In Action

Gospel Publishing House/Springfield, Missouri

11th Printing 2004

Library of Congress Catalog Card Number 78-50485
International Standard Book Number 0-88243-460-8

Printed in the United States of America

Preface

For a number of years there has been a need for a book dealing with pastoral theology from the Pentecostal perspective and with a practical emphasis. Pastors and ministerial students have asked for such a volume. College faculty members have requested a textbook for classroom use. The few books in this field with late copyright dates is evidence of the appropriateness of these requests.

In recognition of this need the General Presbytery of the Assemblies of God in 1975 called for the publishing of such a book. This volume is the product of that authorization and the efforts of the editors and ministers who have shared their knowledge and experience in these chapters.

The Executive Presbytery asked Dr. Thomas F. Zimmerman, General Superintendent of the Assemblies of God, to serve as editor of the book. Dr. G. Raymond Carlson, Assistant General Superintendent of the Assemblies of God, and Dr. Zenas Bicket, Dean of Evangel College, were asked to serve as associate editors.

In making plans for the content it was decided the book should emphasize the practical rather than the theoretical aspects of the work of the pastor. To implement this objective 20 ministers who have demonstrated expertise in respective areas of ministry were asked to do the writing. This has made it possible to present ideas that have been proven in the pastorate.

Guidelines for preparing this book were developed on the basis of expressions of leaders from across the Assemblies of God fellowship. The book must be written from a Pentecostal perspective. It must emphasize ethical principles of the Word of God. It must be intensely practical. Every effort has been made to keep these guidelines in constant focus.

We are deeply grateful to God for the privilege of being a part of the Pentecostal revival which has circled the world. With the firm conviction that the greatest days of this revival are not in the past but in the future, we send this book forth with the earnest prayer and fervent desire that it will help pastors meet the challenge of the future by ministering in the best tradition of the Pentecostal revival.

> —*The Executive Presbytery of the Assemblies of God*

Contents

1   The Pastor and His Lord   1
     Hardy W. Steinberg

2   The Pastor and the Church Call   37
     William H. Robertson

3   The Pastor and His Personal Life   61
     Owen C. Carr

4   The Pastor and His Family   103
     Delmer R. Guynes

5   The Pastor and His Denomination   131
     Lowell C. Ashbrook

6   The Pastor and His Preaching-Teaching   157
     Richard E. Orchard

7   The Pastor and Personal Counseling   197
     Richard D. Dobbins

8   The Pastor and Evangelism-Missions   221
     Robert M. Graber

9   The Pastor and Special Ministries   255
     Edward B. Berkey

10 The Pastor and Congregational Services 281
   Thomas E. Trask

11 The Pastor and Christian Education 311
   Robert H. Spence

12 The Pastor and Total Church Leadership 337
   Richard L. Dresselhaus

13 The Pastor and His Community 369
   James K. Bridges

14 The Church and the Community 399
   Edward S. Caldwell

15 The Pastor and Administration 435
   James E. Hamill

16 The Pastor and Official Church Relationships 467
   G. Raymond Carlson

17 The Pastor and Church Finances 503
   R. D. E. Smith

18 The Pastor and Legal Affairs 537
   Joseph L. Gerhart

19 The Pastor and Building Programs 575
   Thomas E. Scruggs

20 The Pastor and Pentecostal Distinctives 591
   Leland R. Keys

Appendix 607

AND HE GAVE PASTORS

1

The Pastor
and
His Lord

HARDY W. STEINBERG

A minister with many years of experience wisely observed: "A pastor is the servant of the people, but they are not his master. There is only one who is his Master, even the Lord Jesus Christ."

In the course of a lifetime the pastor feels pressures from many different directions. Members of the congregation will express how they feel things should be done, and this is often complicated by the fact that these views are divergent and at times even contradictory. A pastor should always try to get new ideas, but if he is not careful he can become a victim of the pressures. He may find himself doing things not because he feels they are right but because he is intimidated.

If pastors are to have effective ministries, they must be leaders. They must have an inner conviction that they are doing what Christ would have them do. This entails great responsibility, but there must be a willingness to accept it along with all the consequences, both pleasant and unpleasant.

There is great significance in the fact that Jesus is referred to as the "chief Shepherd" (1 Peter 5:4). The implication is clear. Because He is Chief, pastors are undershepherds. They must get their instructions from Him. They must have His approval on their work, and in the end they will have to give an account to Him for every day of their ministries. To be what He intends them to be means they must work carefully under His direction.

Hardy W. Steinberg, D.D., is national director of the Assemblies of God Division of Christian Education, Springfield, Missouri.

Recognizing Christ as the Chief Shepherd does not mean that pastors will disregard the thinking of others, including those in the congregation. The Bible teaches that in the multitude of counselors there is safety (Proverbs 11:14). Much can be learned from many different sources, and the pastor who capitalizes on the best thinking of others will enhance his ministry. Eventually, however, the pastor has the lonely responsibility of determining the mind of Christ concerning the leadership in the congregation.

The pastor will be effective only as he recognizes that the pastoral office is created by Christ, that the individual call and guidance come from Christ, and that he is ultimately accountable to Christ.

The Office of the Pastor

THE HEAD OF THE CHURCH

The New Testament makes it clear that Jesus is the Head of the Church. Unfortunately, not everyone recognizes this fact. In the earlier years of the church there was a heretical group that wanted the Christians to believe Christ was less than God, that He was a creature rather than the Creator. Paul had a great concern for those who were being subjected to this heretical teaching. In the letter to the Colossians he wrote that the One through whom believers have redemption is "the image of the invisible God, the firstborn of every creature: . . . and he is the head of the body, the church" (Colossians 1:15, 18).

In writing to the Ephesians concerning the husband-wife relationship, Paul used the Christ-Church relationship as an illustration. Here he again stated the headship of Christ when he wrote, "For the husband is the head of the wife, even as Christ is the head of the church" (Ephesians 5:23).

In Colossae the attempt to discredit Christ was deliberate. These heretics who were vainly puffed up by the fleshly mind were "not holding the Head, from which all the body by joints and bands having nourishment ministered, and knit together, increaseth with the increase of God" (Colossians 2:19).

Committed pastors today will never deliberately reject the headship of Christ. They must be careful, however, lest an overconcern for public opinion should produce the same effect. The work of the church can be seriously impaired, whatever the reason may be for not recognizing the lordship of Christ. There must be a continuing conscious recognition of the fact that Jesus is Lord, that He is the Head of the Church, and that He is the Master of every undershepherd.

THE GIFT OF PASTORAL LEADERSHIP

Sometimes people think of Christ as no longer being in the world. In a sense this is true, but in another sense it is not. In addition to the fact of His omnipresence, the Church as the body of Christ is very much in the world. It touches people in all nations, and every member has a vital role in this relationship. In Ephesians 4:11, however, Paul recognizes people who have been given to the Church for special leadership roles. He writes, "And he gave some, apostles; and some, prophets; and some, evangelists; and some, *pastors* and teachers."

Ministerial leadership is not an idea of human origin. It is the gift to the Church from the Lord Jesus Christ. Any effort to minimize the importance of these servants of the Lord is an affront to the Son of God. On the other hand, pastors must always deport themselves in such a way as to bring no evil reflection on the ministry.

MINISTERIAL RESPONSIBILITIES

The Head of the Church in delegating ministerial leadership has also specified responsibilities. These have been made very clear both through precepts and through the implications of titles given to leaders. Paul wrote that all ministers are placed in the Body "for the perfecting of the saints, for the work of the ministry, for the edifying of the body of Christ" (Ephesians 4:12). *The New International Version* gives a helpful translation when it points out that the ministerial gifts are given "to prepare God's people for works of service, so that the body of Christ may be built up."

The word translated "perfecting" in the King James Version has various shades of meaning. It is used of mending or repairing nets (Matthew 4:21), of restoring in a spiritual or disciplinary sense (Galatians 6:1), and of preparing or furnishing a body (Hebrews 10:5). The word translated "perfecting" then has the sense of preparing and equipping believers for ministry in a general sense, with the idea of restoring or mending where needed.

The pastor should clearly understand the nature of his work. He is not to do everything he can without calling on others. His divinely appointed responsibility is to prepare God's people for service. In some cases this service will be public; in others it may be almost hidden. But until every member of the congregation is ministering in some way, the pastor's work is incomplete.

The titles given to pastors also give insight into the nature of their responsibility. A comparison of Acts 20:17 with verse 28 indicates that those responsible for congregational leadership were referred to as elders, overseers, and shepherds or pastors.

The title translated "elder" in Acts 20:17 is from the Greek word *presbuteros*. It was used in reference to mature men who were known for their experience and wisdom. From this Greek word we get our English word *presbyter*. As can be seen, the emphasis of this title is on the kind of person the pastor should be.

The title translated "overseers" in Acts 20:28 is from the Greek word *episkopas*. It referred to one who supervised and directed workmen in the performance of their duties. The emphasis of this title is on the nature of the pastor's work. It indicates his administrative function. From this we get our English word *bishop*.

The injunction "to feed the church of God" (Acts 20:28) would more accurately be translated "to shepherd the church." The word *shepherd* is from the Greek word *poimainein*, and is the same word (in the noun form) translated "pastors" in Ephesians 4:11. The root from which this word comes means "to protect." There are many implications in the use of this term, but one emphasis would certainly be on the spirit in which the pastor performs his work. It is not a mechanical ministry, but one of faithful, loving concern.

Donald Gee in writing concerning the pastoral ministry states:

> It is easy to grasp the nature of the type of ministers called "pastors" in Ephesians 4:11. They were the recognized shepherds of the flock; and no company of believers can be gathered together for long without feeling the need of such a ministry. There is always the need of wise and competent oversight of the meetings of the assembly, so that all things are done "decently and in order" (1 Corinthians 14:40); so that the doctrine is kept sound and convincing (Titus 1:9); and so that the flock be preserved from wolves in the shape of false teachers (Titus 1:11; 2 Peter 2:1). There will also be the need of personal ministration to the members in times of special individual need (James 5:14) and of a loving care over all the souls for which those spiritual rulers in the Master's household (Matthew 24:45) will have to give an account (He-

brews 13:17). Above all else will be the positive work of feeding the flock (Acts 20:28; 1 Peter 5:2), because a flock well fed is least likely to become unhealthy spiritually or to give any trouble.[1]

According to Acts 20:17, 28, then, a pastor is a shepherd or protector of and provider for the church. He is an overseer or bishop who supervises the ministry of the members of the church. And he is an elder to be recognized for his wisdom and standing in the community.

PASTORAL GOALS

The pastor need not be uncertain concerning the duration or goal of his ministry. His work is to continue "till we all come in the unity of the faith, and of the knowledge of the Son of God, unto a perfect man, unto the measure of the stature of the fullness of Christ" (Ephesians 4:13).

Three key expressions in this passage are important: "unity of the faith," "knowledge of the Son of God," and "perfect man." The work of pastors will not be complete until these objectives have been reached, and it is evident this will not happen until the Church is translated.

As believers increase in the unity of the faith and the full knowledge of Christ, they come closer to perfection or maturity. The word translated "perfect" has an interesting meaning. Its use in Ephesians 4:13, 14 shows that it refers to adulthood as contrasted with infancy. Then, lest believers should adopt their own concept of adulthood, Paul points out the extent of the maturation. It is to be "unto the measure of the stature of the fullness of Christ."

It can be seen from Scripture that the office of the pastor is a demanding one. It is also obvious that as long as the Church is in the world the pastor is indispensable. As demanding as this ministry is, and as tremendous as the goals are, there will always be those who respond to this call of God. They will respond because they know whom God calls He also enables.

The Call of the Pastor

What Scripture says of the priestly ministry can also be said of the

[1]Donald Gee, *The Ministry-Gifts of Christ* (Springfield, MO: Gospel Publishing House, 1930), p. 56. (This book now available as Part 2 of *Now That You've Been Baptized in the Spirit.*)

pastoral ministry: "And no man taketh this honor unto himself, but he that is called of God, as was Aaron" (Hebrews 5:4). While some refer to the ministry as a profession, it is more accurately a divine calling. And no one should attempt to serve as a pastor who is not convinced that he is called of God.

Dr. J. H. Jowett in his Yale Lectures wrote:

> Now I hold with profound conviction that before a man selects the Christian ministry as his vocation he must have the assurance that the selection has been imperatively constrained by the eternal God. The call of the Eternal must ring through the rooms of his soul as clearly as the sound of the morningbell rings through the valleys of Switzerland, calling the peasants to early prayer and praise. The candidate for the ministry must move like a man in secret bonds. "Necessity is laid" upon him. His choice is not a preference among alternatives. Ultimately he has no alternative: all other possibilities become dumb: there is only one clear call sounding forth as the imperative summons of the eternal God.[2]

Because it is imperative that pastors have a sense of call, it will be helpful to understand some of the many implications of the pastor's vocation.

THE MEANING OF A CALL

The idea of the call of God occurs throughout the Bible. The significance in each instance must be determined by the context in which it appears. It is obvious there is a distinction between the general call to salvation, the general call to service, and the specific call to leadership.

General Call to Salvation. The call to salvation is extended to all. Jesus said, "Come unto me, all ye that labor and are heavy laden, and I will give you rest" (Matthew 11:28). This call is from darkness to light (1 Peter 2:9). It is a call to eternal life (1 Timothy 6:12). Those who accept the call of salvation can rejoice in the assurance that they are accepted in Christ Jesus on the basis of the atonement.

General Call to Service. Once the call to salvation has been accepted, the believer immediately receives a call to service. There should be no period in the believer's life when he is exempt from ministry of some kind. He is saved to serve. Jesus recognized this truth

---

[2]J. H. Jowett, *The Preacher, His Life and Work* (New York: Harper and Brothers, 1912), p. 12.

when during His wilderness temptation He said to Satan, "Thou shalt worship the Lord thy God, and him only shalt thou serve" (Matthew 4:10).

When the believers were scattered abroad as the result of the great persecution which resulted in Stephen's death, "they that were scattered abroad went every where preaching the word" (Acts 8:4). It should be noticed that these witnesses who went abroad were not the apostles, but all the believers. At this time the apostles stayed in Jerusalem (Acts 8:1). Again Jesus said, "If any man will come after me, let him deny himself, and take up his cross, and follow me" (Matthew 16:24). This general call to service is as applicable today as when Christ spoke the words. James reinforced the importance of service when he wrote, "Ye see then how that by works a man is justified, and not by faith only" (James 2:24).

Specific Call to Leadership. In addition to the general call to service, there is also the specific call to ministerial leadership. God has *set* some in the Church (1 Corinthians 12:28) to serve as apostles, prophets, evangelists, pastors, and teachers (Ephesians 4:11). These people have not placed themselves in positions of leadership. They have simply responded to Christ's plan for their lives.

Although Paul had to exercise his apostolic authority at times and even defend his apostleship, he did not choose this ministry. He made this clear when he wrote, "And I thank Christ Jesus our Lord, who hath enabled me, for that he counted me faithful, putting me into the ministry" (1 Timothy 1:12). When the Lord gave Ananias instructions concerning his ministry to Saul He said, "Go thy way: for he is a *chosen* vessel unto me, to bear my name before the Gentiles, and kings, and the children of Israel: for I will show him how great things he must suffer for my name's sake" (Acts 9:15, 16).

Thus, while every believer has a ministry to perform, there are special calls to church leadership which believers need to recognize. Those in leadership positions are assigned the task of enlisting, coordinating, and overseeing the total work of the congregation.

R. M. Riggs, late general superintendent of the Assemblies of God, illustrated this when he wrote:

> A large firm places a sign in the window that help is wanted. In response to this, say one hundred people apply at the office to seek employment in this firm. They are employed and told to report to work

the following morning. Upon their arrival in working clothes they present themselves to the foreman to be told just where to work and what to do. They had all been "called" the previous day, but now each must be particularly and especially assigned to his individual task. When a gang of men is hired to erect a building, each must be assigned his specific job by the contractor and his foremen. Different types of workers are needed, from the architect and his draftsman to the contractor, the masons, the carpenters, the plumbers, the electricians, the plasterers and the common laborers. A wide range of work is required to complete the whole job. All phases of construction work must be harmonized and integrated so that there is no overlapping and no great part of the job is left undone.[3]

THE METHOD OF THE CALL

In the earlier years of the minister or ministerial student there is sometimes an interest in learning how others were called of God. In some cases the interest stems from a desire to determine whether one's call compares favorably with that of others.

Here it is important to remember that God is a Being of infinite variety. Just as it is impossible to find exact duplication in the entire realm of nature, it is impossible to find duplication among people. No two are alike and this means no two ministers are identical. While in one sense ministers can always learn from others, in another sense it is unwise to make comparisons (2 Corinthians 10:12). Every person is different because God intended it to be that way. He is not interested in an assembly line production, and it is imperative for all to recognize this principle of individuality.

Variety of Methods. Because each person is a distinctive being, he is approached by God on the basis of his individuality. Every call is original. No one can tell another what the call of God must be like. The conviction of having been called must be personal.

The Bible gives a little indication of the variety of ways in which God called people. Moses was startled by a bush that burned but was not consumed. This was God's way of getting Moses' attention so he could hear the call to leadership. Isaiah had a vision of the Lord, high and lifted up, surrounded by seraphim crying one to another, "Holy, holy, holy, is the Lord of hosts." As he was overwhelmed with his unworthiness he heard God say, "Go, and tell . . ." (Isaiah 6:1-9). The reticent Jeremiah's call came in a revelation of the omniscience and

[3]R. M. Riggs, *The Spirit-filled Pastor's Guide* (Springfield, MO: Gospel Publishing House, 1948), p. 7.

sovereignty of God, followed by visions of direction and encouragement (Jeremiah 1:1-19). Saul of Tarsus was smitten with blindness as he traveled toward Damascus, after which God indicated the plans for Saul's life (Acts 9:1-20).

Not all calls, however, were of an extraordinary nature. Timothy entered the ministry because Paul found him to be a young man of good reputation who could help in spreading the gospel. As a result, he joined Paul and Silas in their missionary journeys and eventually launched out on a ministry of his own (Acts 16:1-3). John Mark is another whose entrance into the ministry was not accompanied by unusual phenomena. He apparently was first chosen as an assistant to Paul and Barnabas (Acts 12:25). At a later time, John was rejected by Paul because he had deserted the ministerial group in Pamphylia (Acts 13:13; 15:37,38). Because of Barnabas' concern and patience, John survived his initial failure and later proved himself to be useful even to Paul (2 Timothy 4:11).

Dr. J. H. Jowett was led to respond to the call of God as the result of a brief conversation with his old Sunday school teacher. He was at the crossroads and trying to decide on a career. It looked as though it would be the legal profession. His father was making all the necessary arrangements for his son to join a firm as a clerk when John met his Sunday school teacher on the street. The conversation shifted to career plans, and when the teacher learned that John was going in for the law, he quietly said, "I always hoped and prayed you would go into the ministry." That was a momentous word for Jowett. It threw all his life into confusion. Following this interchange John had a new encounter with Christ which resulted in his accepting the call of God. After serving the Lord as a minister for 35 years, Jowett said, "I have never regretted my choice."

These illustrations are but examples of the different ways in which God has brought people into places of special ministry. The list of variations could be multiplied by the number of people whom God has called. The message then is this: Do not despise your call because it is different from others; cherish it because it is distinctively yours!

Spiritual Conception. Since a call cannot be validated on the basis of conformity to some standard pattern, it is logical to ask how one can know he is called. Or conversely, how can one know he is not called to a special ministry? R. M. Riggs writes in this regard:

A call to preach is a spiritual conception. "But the natural man receiveth not the things of the Spirit of God: for they are foolishness unto him: neither can he know them, because they are spiritually discerned" (1 Corinthians 2:14). It is one of "the things of the Spirit of God" which the natural man cannot understand but which are nevertheless very real and clear to the regenerate man. The Lord declared in John 10:27, "My sheep hear my voice." This voice is inaudible to the natural ear but is very clear and distinct to the heart of one who is born again. Elijah heard it, and it was called "a still small voice" (1 Kings 19:12). Isaiah said, "Thine ears shall hear a word behind thee, saying, This is the way, walk ye in it" (Isaiah 30:21). There will be a definite whispering in the deepest soul that the child of God will be conscious of, and it will be his clarion call into the Lord's service.[4]

Practical Evaluation. People who are called of God sometimes have handicaps which in the natural seem to disqualify them for the work of God. Moses pleaded to be excused on the basis of the unbelief of Israel and a speech problem he had (Exodus 4:1-13). Jeremiah was overwhelmed with a sense of inadequacy, pleading inability to communicate (Jeremiah 1:6). In these and many instances since, God more than compensated for human inadequacy. Young people who have been considered total failures by some have risen to places of outstanding leadership.

On the other hand, if handicaps that make pastoral leadership impossible are not overcome, one might question whether the call is genuine. The line between faith and presumption can sometimes appear to be very thin. Practical considerations must certainly be one element to consider in the call.

It is said that John Wesley recognized three tests of a call to preach. He wrote: "Inquire of applicants, 1. Do they know God as a pardoning God? Have they the love of God abiding in them? Do they desire and see nothing but God? And are they holy in all manner of conversation? 2. Have they gifts, as well as grace, for the work? Have they a clear, sound understanding? Have they a right judgment in the things of God? Have they a just conception of salvation by faith? And has God given them any degree of utterance? Do they speak justly, readily, clearly? 3. Have they fruit? Are any truly convinced of sin, and converted to God, by their preaching?"

If one indeed has a call from God, there will be that inner conviction that no alternative exists. As in the case of Paul, there will be the

---

[4]*Ibid.*, pp. 12, 13.

strong conviction: "Yea, woe is unto me, if I preach not the gospel!"
(1 Corinthians 9:16).

But if one is called of God there will also be fruit from one's labor.
To be called does not always mean popularity, but it does mean that
salutary results should be in evidence. Dr. Augustus H. Strong wrote:

> Of his call to the ministry, the candidate himself is to be first per-
> suaded (1 Corinthians 9:16; 1 Timothy 1:12); but, secondly, the church
> must be persuaded also, before he can have authority to minister among
> them (1 Timothy 3:2-7; 4:14; Titus 1:6-9).[5]

The Anointing of the Pastor

In Christ's great priestly prayer He said, "As thou hast sent me into
the world, even so have I also sent them into the world" (John 17:18).
Because of this fact, every pastor might spend valuable time studying
the ministry of Christ with the thought of conforming to Christ's pattern as much as possible. It soon becomes obvious that among other
things Jesus was anointed for ministry. In the home of Cornelius, Peter
spoke of "how God anointed Jesus of Nazareth with the Holy Ghost
and with power: who went about doing good, and healing all that
were oppressed of the devil; for God was with him" (Acts 10:38). In
the synagogue in Nazareth Jesus applied to himself the words of Isaiah
61:1 when He said, "The Spirit of the Lord is upon me, because he
hath anointed me to preach the gospel" (Luke 4:18).

The recognition by Pentecostals of the necessity of the anointing in
ministry is in harmony with the teaching of Scripture. If pastors are
going to be sent forth as Christ was sent forth, they must know that
the Spirit of the Lord is upon them for special ministry.

THE SIGNIFICANCE OF ANOINTING

The custom of anointing was very familiar to people in Biblical
times. It had both a secular and a sacred significance.

The cosmetic or ordinary anointing is illustrated by Ruth's anointing of herself before she presented herself to Boaz (Ruth 3:3). Both
men and women anointed themselves in this way. In times of sorrow
or tragedy anointing was omitted (Daniel 10:3). The medical anoint-

---

[5]Augustus Hopkins Strong, *Systematic Theology* (11th ed.; Philadelphia: The Judson
Press, 1907), p. 919.

ing is illustrated by the kindness shown to the man who had been wounded by thieves. The Samaritan poured oil and wine into the wounds (Luke 10:34).

Sacred anointing was also a very important part of Israel's religious life. This anointing included both things, such as the tabernacle (Exodus 30:22-29), and people, such as prophets, priests, and kings.

In this sacred rite the anointing oil was sometimes put into an animal's horn (1 Samuel 16:1) and then poured upon the head of the person being anointed. The Psalmist spoke of "the precious ointment upon the head, that ran down upon the beard, even Aaron's beard: that went down to the skirts of his garments" (Psalm 133:2). Concerning this rite, Samuel Fallows observed:

> The act of anointing appears to have been viewed as emblematical of a particular sanctification; of a designation to the service of God; or to a holy and sacred use. Hence the anointing of the high priests (Exodus 29:29; Leviticus 4:3), and even of the sacred vessels of the tabernacle (Exodus 30:26, etc.); and hence also, probably, the anointing of the king, who, as "the Lord's anointed," and, under the Hebrew constitution, the viceroy of Jehovah, was undoubtedly invested with a sacred character.
>
> The first instance of anointing which the Scriptures record is that of Aaron, when he was solemnly set apart to the high priesthood. Being first invested with the rich robes of his high office, the sacred oil was poured in much profusion upon his head. It is from this that the high priest, as well as the king, is called "the Anointed" (Leviticus 4:3; 4:16; 6:20; Psalm 133:2). In fact, anointing being the principal ceremony of regal inauguration among the Jews, as crowning is with us, "anointed," as applied to a king, has much the same significance as "crowned."[6]

This sacred anointing had a double significance. First, it meant that God had set an individual apart for special service. When God wanted to indicate that Elisha was to be Elijah's successor in the prophetic office, He instructed Elijah to anoint him (1 Kings 19:16). Aaron and his sons were set apart for the priestly ministry in a special ceremony that included anointing (Exodus 40:13-15). Solomon is an example of a man being designated to be king by anointing. When David was advanced in years, Adonijah tried to usurp the throne of Israel. David learned of this in time and instructed Zadok the priest

[6]Samuel Fallows, *The Popular and Critical Bible Encyclopedia* (Chicago: The Howard-Severance Company, 1910), I, p. 110.

and Nathan the prophet to indicate that Solomon was God's choice by anointing him with oil (1 Kings 1:34). Just as people were anointed for offices such as prophet, priest, and king, God anointed Jesus. And while in New Testament times there is neither example nor instruction concerning the use of oil to designate ministerial leadership, God in a spiritual sense anoints or sets apart people for ministry today. This consciousness of the anointing causes pastors to recognize that they have been appointed to special service. They know they have a ministry to perform and no one else can take that place.

The second significance of sacred anointing is that those whom God sets apart He enables and empowers. After Solomon became king he was aware of his need of special endowment. He prayed: "Give me now wisdom and knowledge, that I may go out and come in before this people: for who can judge this thy people, that is so great?" (2 Chronicles 1:10). In 1 Kings 3:5-15 there is an illustration of the way God made Solomon equal to the task.

When we look at the ministry of Jesus, it is clear that in the incarnation He never ceased to be God, but He did surrender the independent exercise of the attributes of deity. He said, "I do nothing of myself" (John 8:28). What He did He did through the anointing or enablement of the Spirit. Peter spoke of "how God anointed Jesus of Nazareth with the Holy Ghost and with power" (Acts 10:38).

Samuel Fallows has called attention to the following significance of anointing:

> The anointing or pouring of sacred oil on the heads of persons set apart to these offices implied the gift of those qualifications from God which could alone fit them for their work; and it was typical of the communication of the gift of the Holy Ghost to Christ, as the prophet, priest, and king of his church. Hence persons set apart to these offices were termed the Lord's anointed; and especially so, because Jesus, of whom they were lively types, was the Lord's anointed, or his Christ. This anointing of Jesus, by which he became Christ, or the anointed one, implied his call and separation to the office of Mediator, and the communication of those gifts of the Spirit beyond measure, which qualified him to be the prophet, priest, and king of his people as well as the recipient of those ineffable communications of love which the Spirit of God, in his office as the Comforter, imparts to him (1 Samuel 2:35; Psalm 84:9; Daniel 9:24). The anointing of Messiah was predicted (Psalm 45:7). He was anointed with the oil of gladness above his fellows; that is, he was called to high offices, and more abundantly filled

with the Holy Spirit than any of his people; "for God giveth not the Spirit by measure unto him" (John 3:34). The unction with which God anointed his Son, and with which he yet anoints all his chosen people, and of which the anointing oil is typical, is the influence of the Holy Spirit. The grace of the Spirit shed abroad in them is that unction from the Holy One by which they know all things (1 John 2:20, 27). By this grace they are separated to service (Romans 1:1); endowed with all graces and comforts, and blessed with all spiritual *activity* and prosperity in the service of God (2 Corinthians 1:21; Psalm 23:5; 92:10).[7]

E. M. Bounds once quoted an old Scottish preacher who said: "There is sometimes somewhat in preaching that cannot be ascribed either to matter or expression, and cannot be described what it is, or from whence it cometh, but with a sweet violence it pierceth into the heart and affections and comes immediately from the Lord."[8]

The significance of the anointing, then, is to be aware that Christ who is the Head of the Church has both set apart and given the enablement of the Holy Spirit to make ministry effective.

THE SECRET OF THE ANOINTING

The secret of being anointed for ministry today is both simple and difficult. Jesus in His incarnation made himself completely available to the Holy Spirit. For this reason John could write, "God giveth not the Spirit by measure unto him" (John 3:34). The degree to which a person makes himself available to the Holy Spirit determines the amount of anointing he will have.

It is said a group of ministers in a community were thinking of inviting D. L. Moody for a union meeting. It seemed all but one were in favor of extending the invitation. Finally, the opposing pastor asked, "Does Mr. Moody have a monopoly on the Holy Ghost?" One of the others answered, "No, but the Holy Ghost seems to have a monopoly on Mr. Moody." That's the secret of the anointing—giving the Holy Spirit a monopoly!

Jesus instructed the disciples, "But tarry ye in the city of Jerusalem, until ye be endued with power from on high" (Luke 24:49). When Peter and the others spent time with God, the power of the Holy Spirit was manifested. The end result was that people were crying out, "What shall we do?" (Acts 2:37). Three thousand souls were born

---

[7]*Ibid.*, p. 111.

[8]E. M. Bounds, *Preacher and Prayer* (Chicago: The Christian Witness, n.d.), p. 88.

again. The same power will be manifested to those who spend time waiting upon God. Waiting upon God in daily meditation and in total surrender is the secret of having the anointing.

THE RESULTS OF THE ANOINTING

When the Holy Spirit comes upon a man in special anointing, God is able to accomplish through that man what could not be done otherwise. Samson was an ordinary man until the Spirit of the Lord moved upon him. Then he rent a lion as he might a kid (Judges 14:6). He slew 30 men of Ashkelon (14:19), easily broke new cords (15:14), slew 1,000 Philistines (15:15,16), and brought a greater blow to the enemy in his death than he did in his entire lifetime (16:30).

When a pastor ministers in the power of the Spirit he becomes a giant who has power with God and with man. It does not mean everyone will respond favorably to his ministry, but it will mean that he has extraordinary power in ministering. There will be a sense of being borne along by the Holy Spirit. There will be manifestations of the gifts of the Spirit as the occasion may require. And the servant of the Lord will have the assurance that God is at work.

Jeff D. Ray wrote concerning the transformation that takes place when spiritual leaders are surrendered to the Lord:

> Renan characterized Paul as an "ugly little Jew," and Paul's own references to his personal appearance seem to justify Renan's scoffing allusion, but when Paul stood before an audience anywhere to speak of Jesus and the resurrection, he spoke like a king on his throne. When with clanking chains he preached to a Roman governor, he was on the throne and Felix, forgetting his royal trappings, was a trembling suppliant at the feet of the royal preacher.
>
> Athanasius was a dwarf—stoop-shouldered, scarcely five feet tall, hook-nosed, with yellowish hair and a short, stubby beard, but he had such exalted conceptions of his calling and so reveled in the royalty of his pulpit that kings were humbled by his preaching and ecclesiastics trembled in his presence. One of his enemies characterized him "a dwarf and no man," but once in the pulpit he was a giant and no dwarf.[9]

Ministering under the anointing will mean the total ministry will be more effective. There is a great truth, however, that every pastor must keep in mind. The anointing is more than a once-in-a-lifetime ex-

---

[9]Jeff D. Ray, *Expository Preaching* (Grand Rapids: Zondervan Publishing House, 1950), p. 18.

perience. In the words of the Psalmist, every pastor should purpose under God to "be anointed with fresh oil" (Psalm 92:10).

The Guidance of the Pastor

Since the pastor is the servant of Jesus Christ, the Lord will provide direction and guidance for him. This should always be a source of encouragement for the pastor.

THE FACT OF GUIDANCE

One of the things that becomes obvious in studying the Word is that God has a plan for every life. He showed Ananias that Saul of Tarsus was to become an apostle to Gentiles, kings, and Israelites. He even pointed out that suffering would be a part of his ministry (Acts 9:15,16).

Jesus also indicated that He had a plan for Peter's life when He said: "When thou wast young, thou girdedst thyself, and walkedst whither thou wouldest: but when thou shalt be old, thou shalt stretch forth thy hands, and another shall gird thee, and carry thee whither thou wouldest not. This spake he, signifying by what death he should glorify God" (John 21:18, 19).

Donald Gee asked, "Does God guide?" Then he proceeded to answer the question:

Most certainly He does guide. The testimony of the Bible is emphatic on this point.

It was not by chance that Noah had the ark ready when the flood came. Abram didn't leave Ur just because he thought emigration worth an experiment. The people of Israel didn't pitch in the wilderness just wherever they happened to be. Gideon didn't trust to luck when he attacked the Midianites, nor Samuel to "gumption" when he anointed one of Jesse's sons to be king. Elijah didn't stage that great duel with the priests of Baal on Carmel just because he loved the dramatic; neither was it an accident that Nehemiah received his mandate to rebuild Jerusalem. Cornelius and Peter did not meet each other with such resultant Pentecostal blessing by sheer chance; neither did Paul and Silas quit Asia for Europe just because they wanted a change. Jude did not alter his purpose (verse 3, R.V.) and write a powerful letter against apostates because of a passing whim; neither did John pen the Book of Revelation and send the letters to the seven churches merely to relieve the monotony of exile on Patmos. In each and every case there was definite guidance from God.[10]

[10]Donald Gee, *This Is the Way* (Springfield, MO: Gospel Publishing House, reprinted 1975), pp. 9, 10.

Since God has a plan for every life, He makes this plan known to His servants. They need not be at a loss as to what God wants them to do. When Moses led Israel in the wilderness, God made His will known by the pillar of a cloud and the pillar of fire (Exodus 13:21). Moses could always be sure when he should move or stay.

Not only does God provide guidance for action, but also a restraining direction when this is necessary. The wise men planned to return to Herod, but God told them to go another way (Matthew 2:12). When David wanted to build the temple, God used Nathan the prophet to check him (2 Samuel 7; 1 Chronicles 17). When David wanted to take a census, the Holy Spirit did not favor this course of action. He used Joab to try to check David (2 Samuel 24; 1 Chronicles 21:1-6).

The pastor can be sure that if as a servant of the Lord he wants guidance, the Lord is more concerned in providing it than the pastor can be in receiving it. A good manager wants to use all his help effectively, and the Lord is the perfect Manager. He will give His servants all the direction they need. It is for them to receive it.

THE AREAS OF GUIDANCE

God is interested in all aspects of the pastor's life including spiritual, mental, physical, and material. Throughout Biblical history there are many illustrations of this fact.

Place of Ministry. Paul knew he was an apostle by the will of God and that he was an apostle to the Gentiles, kings, and Israelites (Acts 9:15). The Lord, however, not only gave general direction, but also specific direction when it was needed. When Paul wanted to go to Asia he was forbidden by the Holy Spirit (Acts 16:6-8). Instead, he was directed to go to Macedonia (16:9-12). Later, when Paul was at Corinth he discovered a situation which made him very fearful. At this time, when it would have been easier to leave, the Holy Spirit instructed Paul to stay (Acts 18:9-11). He did stay—for 18 months—and a church was established.

It is sometimes easy to be too casual about God's will concerning the pastor's place of ministry. When he talks about something being God's will, let him be sure it is. There is nothing more confusing to church boards when they need a pastor than to receive letters from several ministers, all stating they believe it is God's will for them to become the pastor. Speaking of the will of God in a trifling manner will not only hurt the servant of the Lord but it can bring reproach on the cause of Christ.

The Lord is sovereign. He opens and closes doors. And while God uses individuals in bringing His servants to places of ministry, it is Christ, the Head of the Church, who gives the directions.

Content of Ministry. There are many factors that can control the content of the pastor's preaching. Sometimes personal feelings enter in. The unworthy desires of some in the congregation can be a subtle influence. And, being human, the pastor may be tempted at times to impress the people rather than persuade them by the proclamation of God's Word.

When the pastor seeks to please God in his ministry, he will find divine direction concerning the content of his messages is also available. There is, of course, the general mandate to preach the Word (2 Timothy 4:2). But the pastor can expect specific guidance for the various occasions as well.

Jude had the experience of wanting to make one emphasis when another was necessary. He told about this in verse 3, "Beloved, when I gave all diligence to write unto you of the common salvation, it was needful for me to write unto you, and exhort you that ye should earnestly contend for the faith which was once delivered unto the saints." Balaam had one message he wanted to bring. It would have resulted in financial enhancement, social prestige, and political power. But God had another message that needed proclamation (Numbers 23 and 24).

As much as a pastor might mingle with and try to understand the needs of his people he will not always succeed. Buried in the human heart and sometimes hidden by a smile are deep hurts, tormenting doubts, and perplexing anxieties. Often these problems are known only to God. But when the pastor walks in close communion with the Lord, he can have the inner witness that the burden of his message is the one needed. How gratifying it is for the pastor to hear the words, "That message was meant for me. It helped me more than you will ever know."

Selection of Key People. One of the greatest challenges pastors face is in the selection of key people. The right person in the right place at the right time can help a pastor to multiply the effectiveness of his ministry. If leaders ever need divine direction it is when they are appointing people to serve in various capacities.

At a time when Moses was living on the edge of exhaustion and the thousands of people had unmet needs, Jethro offered Moses excellent advice. He suggested the appointment of leaders who would be over 10, 50, 100, and 1,000. Only those problems that had worked up through all levels and were still unresolved finally came to Moses. Two blessings resulted. Moses was able to expand his ministry in other channels, and the needs of the people were met in a more satisfactory manner (Exodus 18).

Since the results of this organization of manpower proved to be so effective, the question might be asked why more pastors do not take advantage of it today. In taking a closer look at Exodus 18, there is a message that must be read between the lines: "Make sure to appoint the right people for the right positions, and then provide them with adequate training."

Simply to appoint people is not enough. Moses had to select people whose qualifications and temperaments matched the levels of responsibility. There were leaders who could comfortably minister to 10, but no more. Had leaders like this been put over 1,000 people, it would have been tragic for the leader and people alike. But when appropriate people were placed in the various positions, harmony and peace prevailed.

Pastors must recognize that God has a place for every member in the body of Christ. Paul wrote, "But now hath God set the members every one of them in the body, as it hath pleased him" (1 Corinthians 12:18). The members are not alike. They are not interchangeable. Like parts of the body each functions normally in the role assigned to it. The head cannot do the work of the eye; the eye cannot do the work of the foot; the foot cannot do the work of the ear.

From the natural vantage point, then, pastors must be careful to select workers on the basis of the demands of the position and the qualifications of the worker. From the divine perspective it must be recognized that God has a place for every member, and pastors under the headship of Christ will seek the guidance needed to help people find their place in the Body.

In the natural it would be impossible to appoint volunteer workers with maximum effectiveness. The pastor, however, can rely on supernatural guidance. It may be manifested through providential discovery of information, through counsel of others, through impressions of the Holy Spirit, and, where needed, through gifts of the Spirit, such as a word of knowledge.

In the guidance process, pastors must recognize the importance of the checks of the Holy Spirit as well as His promptings. The temptation will always be there to look on outward appearances or to judge by human standards. God looks on the heart. He sees that which man cannot see and knows what man cannot know. This knowledge becomes available to the pastor through divine guidance.

When Samuel was sent to the house of Jesse to anoint a king over Israel he could have made a tragic mistake. As Eliab, the oldest son, was brought before Samuel, he must have been impressed with what he saw. He said, "Surely the Lord's anointed is before him." God, however, said, "I have refused him." Seven sons were interviewed before David was finally anointed (1 Samuel 16:6-13). David did not seem to be the logical choice, but he was God's choice.

There are many positions that need to be filled in the church. The task, however, is not just to put anyone in any position. Job descriptions must be prepared so workers can know what is expected of them. Prospective workers need to be evaluated for both present and potential abilities. Time must be taken to train the workers. But when all human care has been taken, pastors will still need the important element of divine guidance.

Leadership of the Church. On his last journey to Jerusalem Paul made a stop at Miletus. While there he asked the pastors from Ephesus to meet with him. There is no way of knowing how many there were or even how many congregations were represented. Ephesus was a large city, believed to have had a population of more than 300,000. Since congregations met primarily in homes at this time, it is logical that quite a few congregations existed. The elders or pastors of these congregations had had their last meeting with Paul in Ephesus.

Among other things, Paul said to them, "Take heed therefore unto yourselves, and to all the flock, over the which the Holy Ghost hath made you overseers" (Acts 20:28). The word translated "overseer" speaks of the administrative function of the pastor. He was to oversee all the work and give the church the direction it might need at any particular time.

It was incumbent upon the pastor to keep in focus the general mission of the Church. He needed to remember the instructions Christ had given as well as the inspired writings of the apostles. All facets of the mission would need proper emphasis at appropriate times. For divine guidance in maintaining balance, it was imperative for the pastor to be sensitive to the Holy Spirit.

The pastor today in his role as overseer must also make sure the congregation remains true to its mission. The Assemblies of God in 1967 appointed a committee to make an in-depth study of the Church. After many months were given to this study, one of the conclusions the committee reached was that the mission of the Church is threefold. On the basis of this Biblical conclusion the following statement was made a part of the Constitution of The General Council of the Assemblies of God.

WE BELIEVE:
That God's purpose concerning man is 1) to seek and to save that which is lost, 2) to be worshiped by man, and 3) to build a body of believers in the image of His Son.
That these believers, saved and called out of the world, constitute the body or church of Jesus Christ built and established upon the foundation of the apostles and prophets, Jesus Christ himself being the chief cornerstone.
That the members of the body, the church (ecclesia) of Jesus Christ, are enjoined to assemble themselves for worship, fellowship, counsel, and instruction in the Word of God, the work of the ministry and for the exercise of those spiritual gifts and offices provided for New Testament church order.
That it is evident the early apostolic churches came together in fellowship as a representative body of saved, Spirit-filled believers who ordained and sent out evangelists and missionaries, and under the supervision of the Holy Spirit set over the church, pastors and teachers.
That the priority reason-for-being of the Assemblies of God is to be an agency of God for evangelizing the world, to be a corporate body in which man may worship God, and to be a channel of God's purpose to build a body of saints being perfected in the image of His Son.
That the Assemblies of God exists expressly to give continuing emphasis to this reason-for-being in the New Testament apostolic pattern by

teaching and encouraging believers to be baptized in the Holy Spirit which enables them to evangelize in the power of the Spirit with accompanying supernatural signs, adding a necessary dimension to worshipful relationship with God, and enabling them to respond to the full working of the Holy Spirit in expression of fruit and gifts and ministries as in New Testament times for the edifying of the body of Christ.

That we are a cooperative fellowship of Pentecostal, Spirit-baptized saints from local Pentecostal Assemblies of like precious faith throughout the United States and foreign lands to be known as The General Council of the Assemblies of God whose purpose is neither to usurp authority over the various local assemblies, nor to deprive them of their scriptural and local rights and privileges; but to recognize and promote scriptural methods and order for worship, unity, fellowship, work, and business for God; and to disapprove unscriptural methods, doctrines and conduct, endeavoring to keep the unity of the Spirit in the bond of peace, "till we all come in the unity of the faith, and of the knowledge of the Son of God, unto a perfect man, unto the measure of the stature of the fulness of Christ" (Ephesians 4:13).[11]

The general threefold mission must be kept in view in the local congregation. The pastor must provide the leadership that will enable the church to understand and fulfill this total mission. If in giving emphasis to one aspect other aspects have been neglected, the pastor should be the first to detect this and lead in bringing about the balance of worship, edification, and outreach.

In addition to leadership in general areas of emphasis the pastor must also provide leadership in specific areas. Often God places resource people right in the congregation who can provide background information. At other times the pastor may need to look elsewhere for help. Ultimately, however, it is the pastor who must lead, whatever the project might be. He must be convinced in his heart that the effort will help fulfill the mission of the church, and he must be convinced as to the proper timing as well. In other words, the pastor must have the assurance that what is being proposed is in the will of God.

Human judgment is essential. But in addition to this there must be assurance that the judgment is being guided by God. The Psalmist called attention to this possibility when he wrote: "The meek will he guide in judgment: and the meek will he teach his way" (Psalm 25:9). At other times, through circumstances or other providential intervention, God will guide the pastor who earnestly desires to be His undershepherd.

[11]Revised Constitution and Bylaws, The General Council of the Assemblies of God, 1975, pp. 73, 74.

Is a new location needed? a new building? Should the congregation
establish an elementary or secondary school? Should the church sponsor a radio or television program? Should a larger auditorium be provided, or should another congregation be sponsored? Questions similar
to these will arise at various intervals. Blessed is the pastor who will
have the mind of Christ when action is taken.

In addition to the above areas where divine guidance is needed,
others will surface. Some will represent corporate concerns, while
others may be personal. Were it not for the assurance of divine guidance pastors might throw up their hands in desperation and exclaim,
"Who is sufficient for these things?" (2 Corinthians 2:16). When the
pastor remembers that the work is the Lord's, that He is building the
Church, and that He will provide the guidance, courage will replace
desperation. The pastor will move forward with confidence, gratitude,
and humility.

THE METHOD OF GUIDANCE

When the pastor becomes engrossed in the many responsibilities of
the church he may wonder at times, "When is the Lord going to guide
me, and how will He do it?" Here again it must be kept in mind that
God is sovereign and a Being of infinite variety. Whether or not He
guides when or how a pastor expects Him to, this one thing is sure—
the time and method will always be right.

Guidance Through the Word. The first priority in guidance is the
Word of God. It must be determined at the outset whether a considered course of action is scriptural. Anyone who trifles with the
clear teaching of God's Word is walking on dangerous ground.
Donald Gee speaks to this point with great conviction:

> On many questions of life and practice, indeed on all big moral ques-
> tions, the Bible gives such clear answers to guide us that they lie right
> on the surface for all. "Wherewithal shall a young man cleanse his
> way? By taking heed thereto according to thy word. . . . Thy word is a
> lamp unto my feet, and a light unto my path" (Psalm 119:9, 105).
>   If the guidance we seek involves matters of truthfulness, honesty, or
> purity the Bible is emphatic. Nothing is more dangerous than seeking
> supposed special "revelations" that will apparently justify us in evading
> the clear commandments of God. On this road we throw ourselves open
> to demonic deception in some of its worst forms. "Revelations" (?) that
> permit dishonesty or adultery or the breaking of any of the command-
> ments stand self-condemned.

God expects honesty with His Word from all who come to Him seeking guidance, and prayers for special guidance are likely to go unanswered if there is a deliberate attempt to twist the plain meaning of the Word of God.[12]

In the incarnation Jesus never ceased to be God, but when He was tempted of the devil He faced the temptation as a man and relied on the written Word to reply. Even though Satan tried to make some of his suggestions seem legitimate, Jesus refused to accept them, and the basis of His decision was Scripture (Matthew 4:1-11).

When the Church in its earlier years faced a doctrinal controversy, leaders carefully evaluated the situation. Then they were careful to make sure their observations and conclusions squared with the Scripture (Acts 15:15-18).

Further evidence of the priority given to the Word can be found in the Epistles. The Holy Spirit honored that which had been written in earlier times by inspiring the New Testament writers to refer to Old Testament passages to support, clarify, or illustrate New Testament teachings. The Psalmist wrote: "For thou hast magnified thy word above all thy name" (Psalm 138:2). Since God has given His Word this exalted position, it is imperative that pastors give it the same status in seeking divine guidance.

In some cases the Bible speaks directly, but in other cases it deals with principles that are applicable to every generation. In those many areas where specific injunctions or prohibitions are not evident, guidance must be sought in the principles stated in the Word. Donald Gee wrote:

> It is in this connection that we need to learn that the Bible is a book of principles, and it should be the purpose of every student of the Word of God to discover those principles that are revealed as underlying all God's will for His children. It is this very quality that makes the Bible capable of affording solid guidance to us today, even though there are multitudinous details in our everyday life, which are the result of modern conditions that did not exist at the time the Bible was written, nor in the land where it originated.
>
> Some of these outstanding principles that serve as a guidepost for many decisions about detail are *God first* ("Seek ye first the kingdom of God, and his righteousness"[Matthew 6:33]); *separation* ("Come out from among them, and be ye separate, saith the Lord" [2 Corinthians

---

[12]Gee, *This Is the Way*, pp. 19, 20.

6:17]); *discipleship* ("If any man will come after me, let him deny himself, and take up his cross, and follow me" [Matthew 16:24]).

Ask yourself on any given question: "Am I putting God first?" "Am I simply going the way of the world just because it is the way of the world?" "Am I doing what I honestly believe the Lord would do in this matter?"[13]

Guidance Through Counsel. Fortunate is the man who has discovered he can learn from others. Sometimes the learning situation will be words of counsel and advice. At other times it may be example. Not only should the pastor profit from excellent advice or example, but he can also learn from the failures of others.

Moses was greatly helped by the counsel of his father-in-law (Exodus 18). Because Moses followed this advice an entire congregation possibly numbering from one-fourth to one-half million was blessed. It is not difficult to imagine what might have happened had God not provided guidance for Moses through Jethro.

When considering the counsel of others, the advice must be carefully evaluated. Sometimes all of it can be accepted; at other times, only a portion or even none at all.

Rehoboam was Solomon's successor to the throne of Israel. He had the opportunity of leading an already great people to higher heights. He even had enough wisdom to ask for counsel. The problem was he received both good and bad counsel, and, regrettably, he chose the bad (1 Kings 12). Instead of unifying the people he divided them. What might have been a ministry of triumph turned out to be one of failure. All because he chose the wrong counsel rather than that which was right.

The easiest thing in all the world is to find someone who will give advice. God will see to it that proper advice is given, but the pastor must make sure he is so yielded to God that he can receive help in selecting proper counsel.

Guidance Through Circumstances. No pastor can isolate himself from the circumstances in which he finds himself. But the circumstances must always be seen and interpreted from the divine perspective. Problems and obstacles may be one method God uses in changing the course of a pastor, but problems may also simply be a challenge and opportunity for God to provide a great victory.

---

[13]*Ibid.*, p. 20.

There are only two kinds of pastors who can expect storms—those out of the will of God and those in the will of God. Jonah found himself in serious difficulty involving jeopardy of life because he disobeyed God. On the other hand, Paul was in an equally serious storm because he was obeying God (Acts 27 and 28).

When circumstances arise that demand action, pastors should look to God to determine how they should interpret the circumstances. There were times when Paul left a situation because of adversity (Acts 9:20-25), but there were also times when he weathered the storm to see the work of God advanced (18:9-11).

A number of years ago, Reinhold Niebuhr wrote a little prayer which has been given visibility in many forms. He prayed, "God grant me the serenity to accept the things I cannot change, courage to change the things I can, and wisdom to know the difference." Pastors will find that in difficult circumstances God will provide the courage, serenity, or wisdom as needed.

Guidance Through Extraordinary Means. The Bible indicates that when it was necessary, God provided guidance in extraordinary ways. While in most cases supernatural guidance will develop in such a natural way that extraordinary intervention is hardly necessary, it is heartening to know that if extraordinary guidance is necessary, God will provide it.

When Philip the evangelist was leading a great meeting in Samaria, God wanted him to leave for the desert where he would lead one soul to Christ. In the natural this must have seemed unwise. If Philip had an impression that he should leave at this time, he might have questioned his own judgment. Whatever the reason, in this case God sent an angel to direct Philip (Acts 8:26).

On some occasions God has used dreams or visions to make His will known. It was through the appearance of an angel in a dream that Joseph was directed to go to Egypt (Matthew 2:13). Ananias was instructed in a vision to go and minister to Saul of Tarsus (Acts 9:10ff). Peter was prepared for his mission to Cornelius by a vision (Acts 10:9-20). Paul was given a vision regarding ministry in Macedonia (Acts 16:9). It is interesting to note that in the vision Paul appeared to be welcomed to Macedonia, but ended up in jail. The important lesson is that Paul correctly interpreted the guidance, and a great church was established.

Another extraordinary way God guides His servants is through the gifts of the Spirit. The prophet Agabus, while in Antioch, indicated there would be a famine throughout the world. The result was the churches sent relief to the brethren in Judea (Acts 11:27-30). As Paul was making his last journey to Jerusalem, he stopped in the home of Philip the evangelist for an extended time. It was while he was there that Agabus was again used to indicate the suffering that awaited Paul (Acts 21:8-13). Two emphases are important in considering this aspect of guidance. First, this guidance is available to believers in right relationship with the Lord. Second, care must be taken in ascertaining whether a manifestation is indeed a manifestation of the Spirit.

A study of the Scriptures indicates there were occasional situations in which the Church and its leaders were guided through the manifestation of gifts of the Holy Spirit. While some hold that this form of guidance ceased with the end of the Apostolic Age, nowhere in Scripture is there any intimation that this is so. The Holy Spirit will intervene in unusual ways today when it is necessary just as He did in the early days of the Church.

Donald Gee, who was used of God in a special way during the earlier years of the Pentecostal revival, has helpful insights concerning spiritual gifts that provided guidance. He writes:

> The outstanding spiritual gift for guidance is undoubtedly the gift of prophecy, judging from its preeminence in the Bible for this purpose, and it would seem to be the will of God that the Church should be largely endowed with it (1 Corinthians 14:31). The dispensational setting of the gift needs to be carefully noted, however.
>
> There are no scriptural illustrations of the gifts of tongues and interpretation of tongues being used for guidance. Their main sphere is declared to be devotional (1 Corinthians 14:2, etc.), and they only become channels for divine guidance when manifested as the equivalent of prophesying.
>
> The gifts of the word of wisdom and the word of knowledge probably play a larger part as directive spiritual gifts than is generally recognized. The "wisdom" of the Bible, especially in the New Testament, is always an *active* thing, proceeding from words to deeds, and will therefore logically include a big share of guidance in its function. Spirit-given knowledge will also obviously provide a basis for making guided decisions "with the understanding." Both these gifts probably supply guidance in the council chamber as their normal sphere of mani-

festation, though the individual may know something of them in
private life also.[14]

Some people today seem to be more concerned with having unusual
manifestations than in being in a right relationship with God. There is
no indication that ministerial leadership in New Testament times un-
duly emphasized seeking gifts. There is ample indication, however,
that they concerned themselves with being the right kind of people.
Philip, Peter, Paul, and those in Antioch were people who wanted to
obey God more than anything else in life.

The lesson to be learned from this is that the minister's concern
should be to stay in unbroken fellowship with God. He must avoid
those attitudes that break this vital relationship. If breaches occur, he
must repair them as soon as they develop. This is undoubtedly one implication of Scripture when it says, "Grieve not the Holy Spirit"
(Ephesians 4:30), and, "Quench not the Spirit" (1 Thessalonians 5:19).

Just because ministers today believe in the extraordinary means of
guidance does not mean that they will be gullible. They recognize that
wherever the genuine exists, counterfeits are certain to occur. And this
possibility exists in the realm of spiritual gifts as well.

It is not irreverent to evaluate unusual manifestations. Scripture
teaches that the church should weigh what seems to be manifestations
of the Spirit. Paul wrote, "Let the prophets speak two or three, and let
the other judge. If any thing be revealed to another that sitteth by, let
the first hold his peace" (1 Corinthians 14:29, 30).

If there is a genuine manifestation of the Spirit, He will bear witness
with the hearts of those in the congregation. This is illustrated by experiences in the Book of Acts. In a time of stress the apostles suggested
by what seems to be a word of wisdom that seven men be appointed
over the business affairs of the congregation. The result was that "the
saying pleased the whole multitude" (Acts 6:5). Concerning the doctrinal decision of Acts 15, James could say, "For it seemed good to
the Holy Ghost, and to us" (v. 28). If, however, a congregation feels
uneasy about guidance through manifestations, this check of the Holy
Spirit must not be disregarded. All manifestations must first be in harmony with the Word of God. Anything contrary to the precepts or
principles of Scripture must be rejected. And in areas where scriptural

---

[14]Gee, *This Is the Way*, pp. 32, 33.

principles do not seem to apply, manifestations must square with the spiritual sensitivity of the corporate body.

THE RESPONSE TO DIVINE GUIDANCE

When Christ provides guidance to those He has placed in the Body as pastors, that direction will be clear. It is unthinkable that a human manager would intentionally give garbled instructions to employees. Christ, the Head of the Church, is not an imperfect manager. He is not confused in His plans or in His instructions. Leaders in the church can know the will of God.

Whether leaders respond affirmatively to divine guidance, however, is another matter. In Biblical times, some did while others did not. It is important for pastors to learn from both the successes and failures of others if they would be the leaders God wants them to be.

People who rejected God's guidance in Biblical days were chastened or judged. Where correction was possible, the reproof was remedial. Jonah did not want to go to Nineveh, but God knew that with appropriate chastening he would be willing to obey. When David was chastened because of his sin of adultery and murder, he repented and God permitted him to continue as king. God's mercy was great, but lest people be tempted to take advantage of God's mercy, it should be remembered that the penalty for deliberate failure can be great. Only David and God knew how thoughts of his failure must have tormented him; and though he died long ago, the blemish of his failure lives to the present day.

In other cases where God in His wisdom deemed best, judgment terminated the ministries of others. Nadab and Abihu were so defiant in rejecting divine direction that fire from the Lord devoured them (Leviticus 10:1,2). King Saul's ministry was terminated on the field of battle because he insisted on his own will, rather than the will of God (1 Samuel 28:18; 31:1-6).

Those who disobey God's guidance determine by their own attitude and response whether they will receive remedial chastening or punitive judgment.

The picture is much happier when the servants of the Lord contemplate the blessing and useful service that follow affirmative responses to the Spirit's guidance. Noah built an ark to the saving of his household when he accepted what must have seemed like unusual guidance (Genesis 6:22; Hebrews 11:7). Jonah, in spite of the personal problems he had, finally went to Nineveh and saw a city turn to God. Paul did not go to Asia as he planned, but when he went to Europe he saw great churches established in such places as Philippi, Thessalonica, Berea, and Corinth. Jude heeded the guidance of the Spirit and left a challenging Epistle that bears his name.

As pastors today yield their personal plans and wishes to Jesus Christ, He will guide them in the great work that needs to be done. There will be eternal rewards for obedience to be sure, but there are present rewards as well. What greater gratification can any minister have than to know that he is in God's perfect will—right now?

The Accountability of the Pastor

When Bishop Gore spoke to candidates for the Anglican ministry in England he made a statement that most of them would remember for years to come. He said, "Tomorrow I will say to you, 'Wilt thou, Wilt thou, Wilt thou?' But there will come a day when Another will say to you, 'Hast thou, Hast thou, Hast thou?' "

Bishop Gore was aware of what every pastor should keep in focus. The call to the ministry is not only a privilege, an opportunity, and an honor, it is also a solemn responsibility for which leaders in the church will have to give an account.

THE FACT OF ACCOUNTABILITY

In writing concerning his ministry, Paul said, "We labor, that, whether present or absent, we may be accepted of him. For we must all appear before the judgment seat of Christ" (2 Corinthians 5:9, 10).

The writer to the Hebrews also had the matter of accountability in view. He wrote, "Obey them that have the rule over you, and submit yourselves: for they watch for your souls, as they that must give account" (Hebrews 13:17). In a sense every person is responsible for his own soul. What he does with Jesus determines his eternal destiny. There is, however, a sense in which leaders are responsible for the souls of others. Ezekiel was brought face to face with this responsibility. He heard God say that failure to warn the wicked would result in the death of the wicked. Then God said, "But his blood will I require at thine hand" (Ezekiel 3:18).

In both the parables of the talents (Matthew 25:14-30) and the pounds (Luke 19:11-27) Jesus also emphasized the fact of accountability. Each servant was given opportunity to serve his master, but finally the time came when an accounting was made.

When Paul wrote about the judgment seat of Christ, he directed the attention of the readers to a familiar scene in both the Grecian and Roman worlds. F. E. Marsh has helpful observations concerning this judgment seat:

> The "Bema" or judgment seat was the raised place where the judge sat, and witnessed the Grecian games, and determined who were the successful competitors, and from it he gave the prizes won. It was also the place of judicial authority, for the word is used to describe the seat where the judge sat when he had to hear cases upon which he had to adjudicate. Its use in the following Scriptures will determine its meaning: Matthew 27:19; John 19:13; Acts 12:21; 18:12, 16, 17; 25:6, 10, 17. The word is only used twice in connection with believers (Romans 14:10; 2 Corinthians 5:10); but from its use it will be seen that it is a place of judicial authority and discrimination, from whence Christ tests the service of His servants, and rewards them according to their faithfulness.[15]

THE PURPOSE OF ACCOUNTABILITY

The purpose for appearing before the judgment seat of Christ is not to determine the question of salvation, but the quality of service for the Master. Salvation is not a matter of human merit, but of the grace of God. Paul made this clear when he wrote, "For by grace are ye saved through faith; and that not of yourselves: it is the gift of God: not of works, lest any man should boast" (Ephesians 2:8, 9). Nothing can be added to what Jesus did to provide salvation whereby believers become children of God. There is much, however, that all believers can do as servants of Jesus Christ. F. E. Marsh has a helpful paragraph on this:

> A simple illustration may further elucidate the meaning. A son who is in his father's business, who has a special department under his control, has to give an account to his father and his father's partners at the end of the year, as to the discharge of the trust committed to him. The reckoning is not to determine whether he is the son of his father, but to see how he has acted as a servant to the firm. Thus we stand before the judgment seat of Christ. It is not to determine whether we are sons or not, but to reckon with us as servants, as we gather from Matthew 25:19, where the Lord comes to reckon with His servants as to their work.[16]

---

[15]F. E. Marsh, *Fully Furnished* (Glasgow: Pickering and Inglis, Ltd., 1924), p. 365.

[16]*Ibid.*, pp. 364, 365.

At the judgment seat of Christ the servant's work and not sin will be made manifest. This judgment will deal not with the quantity, but with the quality of the work, ". . . of what sort it is" (1 Corinthians 3:13). The big question every worker will face is, "Did I do it for the glory of God?"

Jesus taught it is possible to do a good thing in a wrong way. It is possible to be generous for the wrong reason (Matthew 6:1; 1 Corinthians 13:3). It is possible to pray for the wrong reason (Matthew 6:5-7). It is even possible to fast for the wrong reason (Matthew 6:16-18). Because there are those who fail in these areas, it is important for pastors to ask themselves not only what they are doing, but why. The motive for ministry may not always be manifest now, but it will be when God's servants stand before the judgment seat of Christ.

> Paul writes of a day that is coming, called "the day" (that is, the day of Christ's appearing) when our hearts will be x-rayed, turned inside out, and our work will be made "manifest." This word *manifest* means visible, open to sight, appearing in true light. All of our workmen-believers will be uncovered, laid bare, exposed for exactly what they were. Think of it! In one sweeping view, our entire life of service will be revealed. This is that period of judgment which must first begin at the house of God (1 Peter 4:17) when the perishable and the permanent will be separated. Paul adds that "the day shall *declare* it," that is, to announce it. Some of our friends might sing our praises now, but Christ will announce the whole truth. There will be no mistake made then because our work shall be revealed and tried by *fire*. This means that the judgment will be a righteous judgment, "For our God is a consuming fire" (Hebrews 12:29).[17]

THE RESULT OF THE ACCOUNTING

God has not left His servants in doubt as to the possible outcome of the appearance before the judgment seat of Christ. "If any man's work abide which he hath built thereupon, he shall receive a reward. If any man's work shall be burned, he shall suffer loss: but he himself shall be saved; yet so as by fire" (1 Corinthians 3:14, 15). It must be repeated that this passage does not deal with the sin question, but with the service or ministry question. It is possible that some who have been held in high esteem here for their many labors will find

---

[17]Lehman Strauss, *God's Plan for the Future* (Grand Rapids: Zondervan Publishing House, 1965), p. 115. Used by permission.

these deeds all reduced to ashes there. The servant will be saved, "yet so as by fire."

The difference between a servant of God being rewarded or suffering loss of reward is illustrated by F. E. Marsh. He wrote:

> There is all the difference between an Atlantic liner which has weathered the storm, through the ability of the captain, the alacrity of all under him, and the perfect make and working of her machinery, coming triumphantly into port; and the liner which has lost her cargo, which has her deck broken and torn, and her machinery out of order, because of her unseaworthiness and the unskillful action of the captain, and which has to be towed into port by an insignificant tug. They both get in, but what a difference! Similarly, there is all the difference between an out-and-out believer, who has chorused to God's praise in an all round consecrated behavior, and who has the abundant entrance like Paul the apostle; and one who has only the end of his life, like the dying thief, or the half-heartedness of a Christian life, to give to the Lord. There may be *entrance* for such, but *abundant* entrance for the latter there can never be.[18]

One of the figures the Bible uses to describe rewards is the crown. There are five mentioned in the New Testament. The disciplined person will obtain an incorruptible crown (1 Corinthians 9:24-27). Those who love and look for the Lord's glorious appearing will receive a crown of righteousness (2 Timothy 4:5-8). Those who endure testings and trials will receive the crown of life (James 1:12; Revelation 2:10). Soul winners will receive a crown of rejoicing (1 Thessalonians 2:19, 20). Faithful pastors will receive ". . . a crown of glory that fadeth not away" (1 Peter 5:4).

The guidelines for receiving the pastor's crown are clearly spelled out in the Bible. No leadership ministry is given more specific instruction. Peter describes the qualifications and requirements (1 Peter 5:1-4). Paul also gave careful instructions concerning the pastor to Timothy (1 Timothy 3:1-7) and to Titus (Titus 1:5 to 3:11). If pastors are to receive the crown of glory, they should read these divine instructions often and pray that their efforts will be of the gold, silver, and precious stones variety. These will stand the fire of God's testing.

THE MOTIVATION OF ACCOUNTABILITY

The fact of accountability should have a very salutary effect upon

---

[18]Marsh, *Fully Furnished*, p. 375.

those who remind themselves of the judgment seat of Christ. Moses succeeded because he kept the reward in view: "By faith Moses, when he was come to years, refused to be called the son of Pharaoh's daughter; choosing rather to suffer affliction with the people of God, than to enjoy the pleasures of sin for a season; esteeming the reproach of Christ greater riches than the treasures in Egypt: for he had respect unto the recompense of the reward" (Hebrews 11:24-26). Paul triumphed because he kept the reward in view. He wrote, "I press toward the mark for the prize of the high calling of God in Christ Jesus" (Philippians 3:14).

In 2 Corinthians 5:9 Paul wrote, "Wherefore we labor, that, whether present or absent, we may be accepted of him." In the next verse Paul states that the reason for laboring to be accepted of Christ is that all must appear before the judgment seat of Christ. Paul performed his ministry, always remembering that he would have to give an account to Christ.

According to A. T. Robertson, the expression translated "we labor" would be better translated "we are ambitious." This means that Paul's driving ambition was to please Christ.

A. T. Robertson observes that this expression has a noble origin. He writes:

> It means to be fond of honor. One is actuated by a love of honor to strive for noble ends. Paul exhorts the Thessalonians to be ambitious to be quiet (4:11). He is himself ambitious to preach the Gospel where other men have not been so as not to build upon another man's foundation (Romans 15:20). With Paul it is a matter of honor to please Christ. Surely this is a perfectly legitimate ambition. Since he surrendered to Christ that has been the master motive of his life, to be well pleasing to Him. This deep undertone comes to the surface often in his epistles (Romans 12:1ff; 14:18; Ephesians 5:10; Philippians 4:18; Colossians 3:10; Titus 2:9). He is like the musician who cares naught for the applause of the audience if he can watch the eye of approval from the master who taught him. He is under orders and his constant aim is to please his great taskmaster. "He that judgeth me is the Lord" (1 Corinthians 4:4). Paul brought "into captivity every thought to the obedience of Christ" (2 Corinthians 10:5). He stands entranced by the meekness and gentleness of Christ (2 Corinthians 10:1). There is no comfort in Paul for the nerveless, spineless minister who is afraid of his shadow, who runs at a whisper, who lacks virility, who speaks peace when there is no peace, who is satisfied with things as they are, who watches for the praise of the groundlings, who trims his sail to every wind that

blows, who caters to popular taste, however maudlin and sensational.
The minister without ambition will accomplish nothing for God or
man, only let his ambition not be the feverish restlessness to get another
man's place and an unwillingness to do a full man's work where he is.
. . . There are few preachers who do not have a sporadic ambition to
please Christ. The trouble is to hold one's self to this high ideal year in
and year out.[19]

At first thought the pastor might feel it is very difficult to have as a
primary ambition the desire to please his Lord. Actually, this is far
less difficult than trying to satisfy a proliferation of ambitions including the desire to please every pressure group that appears on the
pastoral horizon. This is illustrated by the words of a young man who
had just been installed as the pastor of a congregation. One member
said to the pastor, "I do not understand how you dared attempt the
task of pleasing seven hundred people!" The young man's reply was,
"I did not come to this city to please seven hundred people. I have
come to please only One, and if I please Him all will be well."

As the pastor strives to please his Lord, he will be able to please
more people than otherwise and, furthermore, he will help more too.
He will find that his attitudes and outlook on the ministry will be
what they should be. The total result will then be the overwhelming
consciousness that he is a worker together with his Lord who provides
the direction and enablement for every aspect of the pastoral ministry.

Suggested Reading

Thomas, W. H. *Ministerial Life and Work.* Grand Rapids: Baker Book
House, reprinted 1974.

Marsh, F. E. *Fully Furnished.* Grand Rapids: Kregel Publications,
1924.

Prime, Derek. *A Christian's Guide to Leadership.* Chicago: Moody
Press, 1966.

Riggs, R. M. *The Spirit-filled Pastor's Guide.* Springfield, MO: Gospel
Publishing House, 1948.

Robertson, A. T. *The Glory of the Ministry.* Grand Rapids: Baker
Book House, reprinted 1967.

---

[19]From *The Glory of the Ministry: Paul's Exultation in Preaching* by A. T. Robertson.
Reprinted 1967 by Baker Book House and used by permission.

Sanders, J. Oswald. *Spiritual Leadership.* Chicago: Moody Press, 1967.

Turnbull, Ralph G., ed. *Baker's Dictionary of Practical Theology.* Grand Rapids: Baker Book House, 1967.

_____. *A Minister's Obstacles.* Old Tappan, NJ: Fleming H. Revell Company, 1966.

2

The Pastor
and the
Church Call

WILLIAM H. ROBERTSON

By what right does a man stand before his fellows, Bible in hand, and claim their attention? . . . because he is obeying a "tap on the shoulder." Because God has whispered to him in the ear and conscripted him for the glorious company of those voices crying in the wilderness of life. The preacher is conscious of being *called*, as we say, and that means that he is responding to an inward urge that could not be resisted . . .— an urge that grew into a conviction that only by obeying could he ever find that joy and satisfaction of a life lived according to the plan of God.[1]

These words of the late Peter Marshall aptly describe the call to the ministry.

Paul's testimony, too, is very inspiring: "I am deeply grateful to Christ Jesus our Lord (to whom I owe all that I have accomplished) for trusting me enough to appoint me his minister" (1 Timothy 1:12, *J. B. Phillips*).

The Call to Pastor

When God calls people to pastoral ministry He also arranges for His servants to receive calls from congregations. This may happen in several different ways, but it is always important to remember Christ is the Head of the Church and His leading is involved.

Usually the district superintendent will be active in helping a con-

---

[1]Peter Marshall, *Mr. Jones, Meet the Master* (Old Tappan, NJ: Fleming H. Revell Co. © 1949), p. 28.

gregation find a minister to whom a pastoral call can be extended. At
other times a happy relationship develops as a result of recommendations from people in the congregation. Whatever the process, it is important that all involved should ascertain the mind of Christ. Unless
the most honorable procedures are followed, the ministry can be
brought into disrepute and the work of God suffer. When the church,
the district superintendent, and the prospective pastor all move in the
will of God, the work of the Lord will be strengthened.

Cooperation With the District Office

When a church chooses a pastor, the majority decision is usually
the outcome of much prayer and spiritual evaluation not only on the
part of the membership but also by the district officials. With the
knowledge that God is more concerned than anyone in the selection of
the right shepherd for the Lord's flock, every scriptural means must
be employed to find the right man. The district superintendent has
come to his position in the providence of God and it is proper that
both churches and ministers recognize his responsibility of overseeing
the work of the Lord. He and the other district officials are mature
servants of God, and their spiritual wisdom and knowledge of ministers and their abilities are immensely valuable when a vacant pulpit
needs to be filled.

THE ROLE OF THE DISTRICT SUPERINTENDENT

What responsibilities are usually assumed by a district superintendent in the selection of pastors for churches in his district? He ordinarily maintains in his office a list of ministers who have expressed
their desire to be considered for a pastoral call. Some may be residing
in the district, and some may not. Each potential pastor should have
filed with the superintendent a biographical data sheet with additional pertinent information and a recent photograph of himself. A
photocopy of this can then be sent to an assembly that requests the
superintendent's assistance.

In wisdom and with a strong sense of fairness, a superintendent will
make it known that preference is usually given to ministers who are
currently in his own district. Nevertheless, he will be spiritually sensitive and realize God's will may not be limited to district boundaries.
The matter of most importance is to find God's choice.

THE CHURCH CALL / Robertson

District bylaws usually state that before a pastor leaves a church, he should communicate with the district superintendent so assistance may be offered to the assembly in the selection of a new pastor. When the superintendent is thus notified, he can immediately assure the church (if it is self-governing) that he is in a position to render assistance in the choice of a suitable minister when the present pastor leaves. He will ask the church to inform him by letter when his assistance should be given. Correspondence of this nature will be brought to the daily morning prayer meeting at the district office, where the Lord's help will be sought in the choice of a pastor.

In addition to the work of the superintendent, the district executive officers go before the Lord in prayer and spend time in consultation as they examine the lists of candidates. By so doing they can identify men whom they feel God would have them recommend to the church. The district superintendent will suggest to the church pulpit committee that these recommendations be prayerfully considered and one name be selected from the list.

FILING OF PERSONAL DATA WITH THE DISTRICT OFFICE

The availability of a minister to consider a pastoral call should be made known in writing and addressed to the district superintendent. The applicant should keep in mind the district superintendent does not appoint pastors in any of the self-governing churches. All self-governing assemblies are encouraged to contact the district office for assistance, but this is voluntary on their part. Pastors for home missions assemblies are usually appointed by the district superintendent in consultation with the other officers, by the district presbytery, or the Home Missions Board. A few assemblies have, for particular reasons, asked the district executive committee to serve their churches as a temporary board. In such instances the district executive presbyters appoint pastors to meet specific needs.

The form that follows is adapted from a form used by one district of the Assemblies of God. It can be used by an applicant to make sure all essential data is listed in his notification to the district office that he is available to pastor a church in the district. A completed form provides the district office with sufficient information to introduce a minister to a church board. The application, personal data sheet, and photograph are kept on file in the district office. When an applicant is

recommended to a church, photocopies are made of this information
and sent to the church board for consideration.

PASTORAL INFORMATION

_____ District Council, Inc.
Assemblies of God

If more space is needed, use the other side of the sheet and identify question
answered by a number.

Date _____

1. Name _____ Phone number_____

2. Home address _____

3. Date of birth _____ 4. Personal health _____

5. Married_____ Name of wife _____

6. Number of children _____ Ages _____ Number at home _____

7. Wife's health _____ Health of children _____

8. Major interests of wife_____

    _____

9. Educational background:

10. Licensed____ Date_____ By what district_____

    Ordained____ Date_____ By what district _____

11. Present position_____

    Name of church or organization _____

    Address _____ Telephone_____

11a. Member of _____ District.

11b. What type of ministry are you seeking? _____

12. Current information on church now pastored:

Date Pastorate Began	Member- ship	Total Annual Income	Assemblies of God Missions	Average No. New Converts Per Year	Average No. New Members Per Year

13. Along what lines has your church advanced during your pastorate?

_____

_____

14. List other churches served. Check here ☐ if a personal resumé has more information.

Name of Church	Place	From	To	Membership

If you did not serve as pastor indicate whether you were an associate pastor, Christian education director, youth pastor, music director, or a combination of these.

15. List district or national offices you have held during the past 10 years in the Assemblies of God.

_____

_____

_____

16. Special work experience (business, professional, social service, Christian education, evangelism, etc.)

_____

_____

17. Special interest, hobbies, and musical ability _____

_____

Do you have any outside business interests? _____

18. Please state briefly your present position in relation to the Assemblies of God Statement of Fundamental Truths.

_____

19. Areas of emphasis in your ministry. (Number in order of emphasis; those of equal emphasis, give same number; use 1 for highest emphasis.)

( ) Preaching   ( ) Christian education   ( ) Ministries outside church
( ) Public worship   ( ) Young people's work   ( ) Administration
( ) Pastoral calling   ( ) Missionary promotion   ( ) Community service
( ) Evangelism   ( ) Missionettes   ( ) Charismatic renewal
( ) Royal Rangers   ( ) Other _____

20. Method of preaching (manuscript, notes, without notes) _____

What do you feel is the ideal length of a service? _____

_____

Length of sermon? _____
21. What is furnished in present pastorate?

Cash salary $ _____ Parsonage $ _____ or, Rental

allowance $ _____ Utilities $ _____ Car expenses $ _____

Retirement $ _____ Other benefits _____

_____

22. Do you have a retirement program? _____

Health insurance _____ Social Security _____

23. Have you served in an organization, church, or denomination outside the Assemblies of God? If so, give particulars.

_____

_____

24. Would you promote the district and national Assemblies of God ministries? _____

25. What kind of church do you think you are best fitted to serve?

Downtown _____ Suburban _____ Small city _____ Rural _____

Other (please specify) _____

26. Have you had experience in organizing a church? _____

_____

Experience in church building? _____

27. Please give a list of references and their complete addresses:

An Assemblies of God pastor _____

A district official _____

A secretary or treasurer of current church _____

Two other persons (one layman) (1) _____

_____

(2) _____

_____

28. Credit references:
    Name of bank/address   _____

    _____

    Trade accounts   _____

    _____

    _____

    _____

29. What is your present attitude toward making a pastoral change?

_____

_____

_____

_____

Remarks:

Please send a picture—a family snapshot is acceptable.

SIGNED _____

DATE _____

TO: CHAIRMAN, PULPIT COMMITTEE
     OF LOCAL CONGREGATION—This photocopy of a PERSONAL
     DATA SHEET is being forwarded to
     your committee for consideration ex-
     actly as we have received it. There
     may be other pertinent information at-
     tached hereto from candidate's refer-
     ences, etc., that may be of help to you.

SIGNED _____
                          District Superintendent

_____District Council

Address _____

Telephone _____

It is important for the prospective pastor to keep this file up to date
with current address and telephone number, so he can be reached
promptly if a church board wishes to communicate with him. A photo
of the entire family should be included with the application. All
churches are interested in a prospective pastor's family.

An applicant should be assured that district officers try without
favor or partiality to give each minister an equal opportunity. When
increasing numbers of ministers come into a district, it is virtually impossible to find pastorates for all of them. The more important con-

sideration, however, is for the district officers to seek the will of God earnestly for each vacant pulpit, so the man of God's choice will stand behind it.

Personal Resumé

In some cases a prospective pastor might also wish to prepare a personal resumé to supplement the information given in a questionnaire. The following form suggests items that might be included in a resumé. Because of individual differences the prospective pastor may wish to include other information than that in the suggested form.

RESUME*
John Robert Brown
1234 Lakewood Drive
Highland Park, Illinois 60035
Telephone: 312-831-4321

Personal: Born—April 10, 1936   Cleveland, Ohio
Married—June 18, 1960   Helen Jones Brown
Children—Robert   November 17, 1963
Jill   March 11, 1966

Credentials: Licensed, 1958 _____ District Council
Ordained, 1961 _____ District Council

Educational Background:

Experience: 1971—Senior Pastor
First Assembly of God
City, State
Average Sunday morning attendance has increased from 150 to 475. The church staff has grown from one part-time secretary to two full-time secretaries, a full-time youth minister/Christian education director, and a full-time music director/visitation pastor. A new sanctuary and education building were constructed. Served as district presbyter from 1973.
1964-1971—Pastor
Assembly of God
City, State
Pioneered this church under the auspices of the _____ District. The church grew to an average Sunday morning attendance of 225. It was self-supporting within 15 months and developed a strong missionary budget during the 7 years of my pastorate.

*All names and places are fictitious.

1960-1964—Minister of Christian Education
Central Assembly of God
City, State
Responsible for administration of total Christian
education program of a church of 650, including Sunday school, Missionettes, Royal Rangers, and senior
adults' activities.

Wife's Abilities: Mrs. Brown plays both the piano and organ and has
other musical abilities including experience as a choir director. She is willing to assist in any area of the church
where help is needed but does not feel the need to have a
prominent place of leadership.

References: _____, Superintendent

_____ District of the Assemblies of God
Address
City, State

_____, Sectional Presbyter
Address
City, State

_____, President
First National Bank
Address
City, State

Points of Concern in Considering a Call

It has already been noted that the minister who desires to pastor a
church will come under close scrutiny by district and local church officials. This is as it should be, for the shepherd of the Lord's flock is
required to reveal the will of God to his people not only by his words,
but also by his Christlike manner of life. The church will want to
know if a prospective pastor manifests the spiritual fruit of faithfulness (Galatians 5:22) in all the responsibilities of his calling; and
whether he conducts himself with integrity in dealing with the laity
and also with his fellow ministers.

It is not possible (nor is it wise to try) to ascertain whether the
prospective pastor has these desired and needed characteristics merely
by hearing him preach twice on Sunday. Nor is it possible for the
minister to evaluate his prospective congregation in such a brief exposure. Therefore it is wise to arrange a situation in which both the
congregation seeking a pastor and the potential pastor have adequate
time and opportunity to see each other in both structured and un-
structured activities.

When entering into negotiations concerning a potential pastorate, the minister and the congregation inviting him should have a clear understanding of the process the church will use in selecting a pastor. If there are only certain conditions under which the potential pastor will allow his name to be considered, he should make these clear from the beginning. Such conditions might include the church's official board allowing only one name at a time to be presented to the congregation for a vote.

The congregation seeking a pastor, or at least those members of the congregation given the responsibility of screening pastoral candidates such as a pulpit committee or the official board, will want to get important information about the potential pastor. This can be done by consulting the district superintendent, studying the resumé, and contacting references.

The potential pastor will also want to learn some things about the church before he can agree to consider a call. This can be done by requesting such documents as annual financial reports for the past 2 or 3 years, several back bulletins, a copy of the constitution and bylaws, and a pictorial directory if the church has produced one recently. He can also learn a great deal about the community in which the church is located by requesting information from the chamber of commerce.

Just as it is wise for the church to consult with the district superintendent when searching for a pastor, the potential pastor can learn important information about the church by conferring with the district superintendent. Has the church had serious doctrinal or moral problems? Have there been other situations of which he should be aware? Are there unresolved issues currently causing unrest in the church?

The purpose for asking these questions is not to eliminate the church from consideration by the potential pastor, for certainly there are no perfect churches. However, each individual knows his own strengths and weaknesses, and it is indeed helpful to be able to seek God's will in the matter knowledgeably rather than in ignorance.

Visiting the Church

When the screening process has been completed, the church will extend a formal invitation to the potential pastor to visit the church, speak at two or more services, and meet with the church board. An ideal situation would be for the pastoral candidate to spend as much as a week with the church so he could speak at the midweek service as well as on Sunday. Such a time frame would also allow for an interview to be conducted away from the pressure of Sunday services and would give members of the congregation opportunities to meet him perhaps in a social setting.

What should the minister preach on such a visit? Faris D. Whitesell suggests:

> Preach your best sermons and preach to help the people. Preach not merely to make a good impression but to do the most possible good. If you are never invited back, you can still feel you have done your best. Preach practical sermons rather than heavy doctrinal ones. A sermon on prayer is always in place. People are always interested in this subject, just as they are in faith, love, peace, grace, and spiritual growth.[2]

Jay E. Adams gives the following advice:

> Assuming he will preach twice, he might be wise to do the following (and to let the pulpit committee know his intentions in advance):
> 1. *Morning:* Preach a pastoral sermon typical of the sort that the congregation might expect to receive on any Sunday were he to be called. He might stress the fact that he will take pains not to arouse any false expectations by preaching a one-of-its-kind, special, super hot-shot sermon on that occasion.
> 2. *Evening:* Preach a sermon from a passage that sets forth the work of the minister or of the relationship of a pastor to his people, etc. By this sermon (hopefully) he might indicate something of what the Biblical goals for any future relationship might be as he sees them.[3]

When the prospective pastor is interviewed by the church board, he should be open and honest. He should try to answer questions as thoroughly as possible. In addition to answering all questions in this manner, he should also feel free to ask questions. He can thereby obtain needed information and also open opportunities to share his own philosophies and beliefs about pastoral leadership which the members of the board need to know.

When the pastoral candidate questions the church board about vital issues he should be sure he is getting the consensus of the *group*.

---

[2]Faris D. Whitesell, "Guidelines for Candidating," *Advance Magazine*, April 1971, pp. 34, 35.

[3]Jay E. Adams, *The Pastoral Life*, Vol. 1 of *Shepherding God's Flock* (3 vols.; Nutley, NJ: Presbyterian and Reformed Publishing Co., 1975).

Sometimes one or two vocal individuals will express their personal opinions on a subject which may not be the feeling of the majority of the group. Those who disagree may choose to keep silent rather than appearing to be divisive. When there seem to be conflicting views on an issue, it may be well to probe until the majority's opinion is understood.

Subjects that might be discussed in the prospective pastor/board interview include:

1. *The role of the pastor.* Each church, because of its distinct personality and history of development, has its own unique expectations of its pastor. The prospective pastor should question the members of the board concerning what they are looking for in a pastor. To some, his pulpit ministry may be more important. Inherent in this expectation then must be the understanding that the pastor needs to be allowed adequate time for preparation.

Other churches will place priority emphasis on such areas as the pastor's counseling ability, his administrative ability, or his rapport with youth. While the pastor will be filling all of these roles to a greater or lesser degree, if the prospective pastor knows the expectations of the congregation he will be able to weigh his own strengths and weaknesses as he prays for guidance, should the invitation be extended.

2. *Goals and special objectives of the church.* The prospective pastor should attempt to determine from the board how they see themselves as a church—what they see as their church's reason-for-being. To a great extent this conception of the church by its members will determine its future direction. The prospective pastor should also inquire about plans for the future—does the church plan to enter a building program in the immediate or foreseeable future? If the present facilities are inadequate, he should seek to determine why a building program has not been undertaken. Is there resistance to growth? The answers to these questions may help him evaluate how effective his leadership of this congregation would be.

3. *Staff.* Questions should be asked concerning the church staff. If the church is small, there will most likely not be a multiple staff. But if the church does have, or has had, a staff, the prospective pastor needs some information concerning this area. It is customary for staff members to offer their resignations subsequent to the resignation of

the senior pastor. Have these resignations been tendered? Will the incoming pastor be allowed to name his own staff; build his own team? Who invites the staff members? Who is responsible if for some reason a staff member must be dismissed? To whom are staff members amenable? Understanding these relationships *before* a senior pastor is called or accepts a call may avoid misunderstandings that could arise after the pastor has assumed responsibilities.

4. *Wife.* The potential pastor should discuss his views concerning the role and relationship of his wife with the congregation. In some cases the wife works very closely with her husband and in fact they are a pastoral team. However, if the candidate and his wife view her first place as that of wife and mother this should be communicated during the interview so at a later time demands are not made on her time that she is not prepared to fulfill.

5. *Personal educational goals.* Many ministers feel the need to continue their formal education to improve themselves and keep pace with the increasing demands of the ministry. If a minister plans to take further study while he is pastoring, these plans should be discussed with the board.

6. *Salary and emoluments.* Sometimes ministers are reluctant to ask too many questions regarding salary and benefits lest they appear to place too high a priority on financial considerations in making the decision about accepting a call. However, the pastor and the board should have a clear understanding concerning finances in order to avoid problems and difficulties that could arise later because of misunderstanding or lack of communication. It is wise to go over all the details of what the church offers including cash salary, housing allowance, utilities, pension and health insurance, car allowance, vacation arrangements, secretarial help, and expenses to conferences and conventions. An understanding should also be reached concerning how salary increases are determined.

A member of the board may ask a minister the salary he would ask if he were to be elected pastor. A wise response would be to remind the board they are in a better position to know the living costs of the community, the standard of living they expect their pastor to maintain, and what the church is financially able to offer its pastor.

This list of topics for discussion by the church board and prospective pastor is not intended to be comprehensive. There should be a discussion of any subjects that would affect the influence of a pastor in his leadership of the congregation.

Accepting the Call

A prospective pastor must consider that the church incurs considerable expense when it invites him to visit the church. Travel and entertainment expenses as well as an honorarium are involved. The church is also concerned about the time factor. There is a need to fill the pastoral vacancy as soon as possible. Therefore, before an invitation to consider a pastorate is accepted, the individual should feel strongly that it is God's will for him to do so. There may be a temptation for a pastor to accept an invitation, feeling he will be more appreciated by his present congregation if they know he is being sought by others. This is not proper motivation.

When the potential pastor has visited a church he must then decide if he will allow his name to be submitted for a vote. If he does not feel checked in his spirit after seeking God's will, he should allow the congregation to express its sentiment in voting.

After the vote has been taken, the minister will be contacted by the official board. If the vote is favorable, in accordance with the church's constitutional provision, an official call will be extended.

The minister should be sure he understands all the details of the call. If there are still unresolved issues including such areas as moving expenses, these should be clarified.

Whitesell gives sound advice concerning weighing salary and benefits in the decision to accept the call:

> If the salary and other benefits are not as much as you expected, this does not necessarily mean that you should reject the call. If your heart inclines toward the invitation, you might make some sacrifice in order to accept. The Lord will make it up to you in time.[4]

The minister should take no more time than necessary to be comfortable that he knows God's will in the matter to give the church his decision. He should call the appropriate church official to inform him of the decision and then mail a written acceptance (or rejection) to the church.

---

[4]Whitesell, "Guidelines for Candidating," p. 35.

Proper Procedures for Resignations

Once the call has been accepted, the minister should resign his present pastorate immediately. His resignation should be written out and presented to his church board in a meeting specially called for the purpose. His resignation will then be announced to the church congregation in the first Sunday service thereafter.

When a pastor of a church resigns, he should communicate immediately with the officials of his district, declaring his intention to them and briefly acquainting them with his future plans.

There should be a period of some weeks between the time of this announcement and the pastor's departure to his new field of service. Resignations followed by swift and sudden departures are neither good for the church nor for the man who has relinquished his office. The church is abruptly left without spiritual direction, and the fleet-footed servant of the Lord incurs the suspicion of indifference toward the flock he recently shepherded.

The interim between the pastor's resignation and his departure should be used by him to prepare the way for his successor and make the transition as smooth as possible. All office records should be up to date and available to the new pastor.

The departing pastor should pray with the congregation for God's will in the selection of a new pastor. However, he should not interfere in the selection of his successor. If he is asked for advice on the subject, he should not refuse to give it. But he should offer only as much assistance as is requested.

Once the pastor leaves, he should endeavor to sever his close ties with the church. This may not be easy. As Robert Palmer writes:

> If a minister has been in one church for an extended time, many people there have known no other pastor. He has undoubtedly stood with members of that congregation in times of sorrow, trouble, and joy. He has offered sound counsel and has watched the children grow into youth and adults. He has dedicated their babies, married their young couples, and buried their dead.
>
> It is difficult for members of a congregation to let the former pastor go. They sometimes will call for advice, or write asking his opinion about what is going on in the church since he left.[5]

---

[5]Robert E. Palmer, "My Brother, My Successor," *Advance Magazine*, October 1976, p. 13.

When such contacts are made, the minister should endeavor to make the members of his former congregation know their loyalty and support are to the new pastor whom God has given them. A great deal of responsibility falls on the shoulders of the church board following a pastor's resignation. If friction has caused the pastor's resignation, the board's first duty will be to heal wounds in the membership with as much grace and wisdom as possible.

During the period between the departure of the pastor who has resigned his office and the election of a new pastor, the church board may ask a minister to serve as interim pastor. While the latter assumes pastoral duties, such as preaching, visitation, and supervision of the church departments, he should not make major decisions that affect the general policies of the church. During this time the church board will be obliged to meet more frequently not only to consider a prospective pastor but also to provide the interim pastor with helpful guidelines to assist him in his ministry.

The Pastor's Length of Service

How long should a minister remain in his pastorate? Many answers could be given to this question because there are no two situations alike. There are saintly men of God who became pastors of churches as young men, and after the passing of many years they still retain the leadership of the church, together with the love and respect of their congregations. There are other ministers who believe it is God's will for them to make their spiritual contributions to several churches by pastoring for shorter periods of time. No general rule can be given to determine how long God wills that a minister remain as pastor of a congregation.

There are, however, some observations that could be made concerning the tenure of the pastoral office. The Scriptures make it very clear that various ministries are needed in the church for the development of God's people (1 Corinthians 12:28). A pastor who recognizes the needs of the congregation will try to provide for them and thus usually have a longer tenure. He will seek through diligent study to improve his own ministry, but he will be aware of the fact that other servants of God can also make a valuable contribution to the congregation. A wise pastor will arrange for special meetings to bring complementary ministries to the congregation.

Suppose a pastor is gifted in doing the work of an evangelist. Undoubtedly, the church membership will be increased. Financial conditions will be gratifying. Church groups will enlarge. Perhaps new buildings will be erected.

The preaching of salvation for the lost is an important part of Christ's Great Commission. But after sinners are saved and brought into Christian fellowship, it is necessary for them to grow in grace and in the knowledge of Christ (2 Peter 3:18). Evangelism needs to be balanced with teaching. There must be the milk of the Word for babes and strong meat for mature believers (Hebrews 5:12-14).

A good shepherd will be solicitous for the welfare of his flock. Such a minister may realize after a period of some years that a congregation might profit from the ministry of another pastor. The realization may prolong and intensify his times of prayer. In a secret place with his Lord, he may be brought to understand it is God's will for him to minister to another flock.

This is an honest and justifiable reason for resigning a pastorate, even when members of the church plead with him to remain and offers of an increase in salary are made. A real servant of God, guided by the Holy Spirit (Romans 8:14), knows in the depths of his soul there is no greater place for him in this life than the center of God's will. Therefore, after what may seem to be a brief pastorate to some, he will terminate his service in one church and begin it in another.

There are also cases where a minister's length of service is determined not by his type of ministry, but by divine guidance into other fields of service. A minister may be noted by officials of the district and recommended for a particular office. It sometimes happens a pastor's name is placed in nomination at a district council, and by the end of the session he finds himself installed in some administrative or supervisory office. In such a case, we can be assured God makes provision for the church as well as for the man. The pastor will leave, but another man of God's choice will be provided.

A pastor should recognize it is unfair and disruptive to a congregation for him to stay in a pastorate for a short time merely to accomplish his own selfish desires. When a minister accepts a pastorate, he should do so with the intention of being God's undershepherd to that congregation to the best of his ability for as long as God gives him the special pastoral burden for that congregation.

When a troublesome situation arises to which there seems to be no solution, when a certain member or members express dissatisfaction with the pastor, or when some other difficulty presents itself, it is very tempting for a pastor to look for greener pastures. However, in these times of discouragement the pastor must first seek God for a solution to the problem. Running away from the situation may not be the answer. The discouraged pastor must first seek God for a solution to the problem, and in doing so remember there are no perfect churches. Another church he may accept could have more serious problems than the one he leaves.

Sometimes the tenure of a pastorate is dictated by a growing ground swell of congregational dissatisfaction. A pastor who becomes insensitive to the needs of his people can pursue policies that displease them. At first the criticism may be minor, but if the mind of the Lord is not sought, it can grow into a problem of serious dimensions. Curiously enough, there have been times when other ministers and district officials have become aware of a pastor's problems before he actually recognized them himself. In such cases, district officials have communicated with the pastor and signified their willingness to act as arbitrators between his viewpoint and that of the congregation.

When the pastor and people are amenable to mature spiritual counseling, the problem can be solved, and impaired fellowship and confidence restored. If the breach is too great, however, or if the pastor maintains his viewpoint in a headstrong manner, the only alternative is to suggest he resign. A sensible minister will follow the advice of his district officials, who not only act in the best interests of the church, but also in the interests of his own future welfare. It is a distressing situation when a stubborn man insists on a vote of approval by the membership and is rejected by the majority of ballots.

When a Church Needs a Pastor

When a good shepherd leaves one flock for another place of service, there is always a deep realization of loss, and expressions of grief are sincerely displayed. But while the members of the church board share these experiences, they have to deal with a problem of greater magnitude—the church needs a new pastor. When this happens, it is helpful to know the common proceedings of a church board in their search for a pastor. The following includes some of the procedures a church goes through in such a situation.

During this time, there can develop a surprising recognition of certain abilities in the church membership. The Holy Spirit gives gifts for Christian service to all Spirit-filled believers. The men's Bible class may have been taught previously by the pastor, but probably there is a gifted layman who can teach the class effectively. Some men and women may assume the work of visitation. Although we are informed that God has set apostles, prophets, evangelists, pastors, and teachers in the Church, we must not forget He has also added "helps" (1 Corinthians 12:28). When a church is temporarily without a pastor, these gifted "helps" can bring great blessing to the membership.

Usually the church board becomes a pastoral search committee. First, however, the constitution and bylaws of the church are checked. Sometimes they will prescribe important procedures. In performing its duties, the board will usually communicate with persons who represent a variety of ages and interests in the congregation. For a church to remain strong, an incoming pastor must meet the needs of the entire membership.

When the pastoral search committee is selected, a chairman and secretary may be appointed, and specific responsibilities assigned to the members. Some general guidelines of operation should be agreed on. For example, the committee has to decide whether or not to invite any candidate who is willing to be considered, or whether all applicants or suggestions should be screened. Should the committee ask the congregation to make a choice after several applicants have been presented, or should the congregation vote immediately after each candidate has been presented?

Members of successful search committees agree the most workable procedure is for the committee to do extensive screening and interviewing, and then present the one they feel might be God's will for the church. As soon as possible after his appearance before the congregation, the committee usually asks the congregation to express itself by voting.

The critical task of the pastoral search committee is to match the nature and abilities of a minister to the nature and needs of a congregation. Several serious questions are usually considered: What are the strengths of the church? What are the weaknesses? What goals does the church have? What does the membership as a whole want and need in a pastor?

Most important of all, the committee will look for a man who has the scriptural qualifications for the office. These are listed in 1 Timothy 3:1-7 and in Titus 1:5-9. The committee will want to recommend a man who most fully possesses these qualifications.

A list of potential pastors is made. The congregation may be requested to offer suggestions of men they feel should be considered. The officials of the district in which the church is located are usually asked to recommend ministers the church might consider. The reasons for contacting them are obvious. They know the church and its membership, for undoubtedly they have preached before the congregation on several occasions. They also have on file the names and qualifications of men who have ministered in the area to churches with similar complexities and needs. Furthermore, they are deeply involved, personally and spiritually, in the Christ-honoring development of every church in the district.

Each person whose name is submitted to the committee will be informed by letter that his name has been offered for consideration. The letter will also contain general information about the community in which the church is located and about the size and type of congregation.

After the committee has prayerfully studied all the responses, several are selected for particular consideration. These are then regarded as prospective pastors from whom more detailed information might be sought. When these ministers know they are receiving serious consideration, they usually also request more information from the church board, such as proposed pastoral duties, the annual budget of the church, and the special interests of the membership.

Each minister is then evaluated in such areas as his experience, doctrinal beliefs, ability, character, personality, and family. In some cases the search committee may secure cassette tapes of services conducted by a minister they may be considering.

Whenever possible, committee members may try to hear the minister in his own pulpit. They would not assemble in his church like an official delegation, for this would be an announcement of their intention. They would probably enter unobtrusively and quietly take their seats. As the service progresses, they would be alert to the spiritual

tone and atmosphere of the church and to the minister's empathy with
the congregation.

After their basic work is completed the pastoral search committee
or the board reports to the church members and makes a recommendation. It is also customary that time be set aside solely for prayer
concerning the future leadership of the church. In this way, the Lord's
guidance through spiritual communion will be sensed by all concerned.

The time has now come for one of the ministers to be invited to
preach before the congregation. His traveling expenses, lodging, and
meals will, of course, be taken care of by the church. If he can come
a day or two before the time when he is scheduled to speak, he will
have more opportunity for consultation with the committee, who
could also take him on a tour of the community. This initial visit will
give the church and/or the prospective pastor an opportunity to with-
draw if some considerations are found unsuitable.

In some cases a candidate may be invited for a second weekend. In
this way he and his family can have maximum exposure to the church
members and they can better meet with the board or committee.
Searching questions and candid answers should be exchanged in all
the general discussions. Such a procedure will bring greater insight
and understanding to the visiting minister and the members of the
church.

When the prospective pastor preaches to the congregation he will
usually present his best sermon, which, though enjoyable, will be
evaluated carefully by the congregation for evidences of a truly
pastoral spirit. While someone from the church will usually be in
charge of the services, the minister would be wise to ask for information concerning the customary type of service. A member of the committee might discuss this with him, mentioning the usual worship patterns.

The prospective pastor's sermon may be evaluated by the following
questions: Is the sermon easy to follow? Does it have spiritual depth?
Is it expository or topical? Does its content reflect a commendable
degree of spiritual maturity on the part of the speaker? Does the
speaker faithfully deal with passages of Scripture, or does he use them
as a springboard for his own views? Does he expound the Scriptures
and apply their teachings to the congregation? Does he appear in

command of himself and the situation? How would his voice and manner of delivery affect a congregation over a period of years? How does the congregation respond to his preaching?

A few days after the minister's appearance before the church, the membership will probably render a decision by voting on whether or not to extend a call. The minister should be informed that the vote will be taken, and then promptly notified of the results.

When a new pastor is installed in a church, its members will realize that no minister is perfect, and that an incoming pastor will differ in some ways from his predecessor. They will recognize that no minister will excel in every pastoral function. A wise membership is one that is aware of its needs, and it will choose a pastor who is strong where it is weak.

The call to pastor a local congregation is a challenge of great responsibility. The direction of many lives, besides those of the pastor and his family, will be influenced during the term of pastoral tenure. The pastor and the church should both seek diligently to have God's choice for that particular time. When this criterion is met, the pastor and the church can expect growth and God's blessing.

Suggested Reading

Bedsole, Adolph. *The Pastor in Profile*. Grand Rapids: Baker Book House, 1958.

Evans, William. *How to Prepare Sermons and Gospel Addresses*. Chicago: Moody Press, 1913.

Gibbs, Alfred P. *The Preacher and His Preaching*. Kansas City, KS: Walterick Publishers, n.d.

Jowett, John Henry. *The Preacher, His Life and Work*. Yale Lectures. New York: George H. Doran, Co., 1912.

Oats, Wayne E. *The Christian Pastor*. Philadelphia: Westminster Press, 1964.

Phelps, Austin. *The Theory of Preaching*. Grand Rapids: William B. Eerdmans Publishing Co., 1947.

Wilder, John B. *The Young Minister*. Grand Rapids: Zondervan Publishing House, 1962.

3

The Pastor
and
His Personal Life

OWEN C. CARR

Introduction

THE BIBLICAL PATTERN

Whether it is living or giving, God speaks to the subject in His Word. Often He is specific. Sometimes He gives broad guidelines. Certainly, in a matter as important as the administration of His church, He would not be silent. Because the Church is so near to the heart of our Saviour, its supervision is frequently in focus. However, the Lord is more concerned with the *administrator* than the *administration*.

Moses. A modern philosophy emphasizes that the ministry and the laity are equal in all ways and there should be no distinction between them. Many ministers taken up in this philosophy tell their congregation, "Just call me Joe." But as you read the Old Testament, it is obvious that God made a distinction between the people and His God-called leaders.

When Aaron and Miriam tried to emphasize the equality of all the people with Moses, God made an awesome distinction that they would never forget (Numbers 12:1-16).

Moses was an outstanding leader. He chose "to suffer affliction with the people of God, than to enjoy the pleasures of sin for a season" (Hebrews 11:25). God sets a different standard for His leaders, and He expects a different performance.

Joshua. The minister often claims the promises God gave Joshua when he became leader of Israel:

Owen C. Carr is president of Valley Forge Christian College of the Assemblies of God, Phoenixville, Pennsylvania.

> There shall not any man be able to stand before thee all the days of thy life: as I was with Moses, so I will be with thee: I will not fail thee, nor forsake thee. Be strong and of a good courage: for unto this people shalt thou divide for an inheritance the land, which I sware unto their fathers to give them. . . . Have not I commanded thee? Be strong and of a good courage; be not afraid, neither be thou dismayed: for the Lord thy God is with thee whithersoever thou goest (Joshua 1:5, 6, 9).

But God would place greater emphasis on the conditions of those promises, because they concern the character of the individual:

> Only be thou strong and very courageous, *that thou mayest observe to do according to all the law,* which Moses my servant commanded thee: turn not from it to the right hand or to the left, that thou mayest prosper whithersoever thou goest. This book of the law shall not depart out of thy mouth; but thou shalt meditate therein day and night, that thou mayest observe to do according to all that is written therein: for *then* thou shalt . . . have good success (Joshua 1:7, 8).

Paul. Although God called Jeremiah before his birth, the fact remains that ministers are made, not born. Paul states this concept repeatedly (Ephesians 3:7; Colossians 1:23, 25).

Paul was called to be an apostle (Romans 1:1; 1 Corinthians 1:1). A Spirit-filled ministry demands a God-given call. Other churches may select ministers because of their ability or their social concern. But in a ministry where a man speaks as a prophet, standing between God and the people and calling them to be reconciled to God, nothing short of a divine call will enable him to fulfill his ministry.

Paul magnified his office (Romans 11:13). Never is the minister to magnify himself. But he must, if he is God's man, magnify his office. Whatever work God calls you to do must be the most important work in the world to you. If it isn't, you should not be involved in it.

Christ. "The Son of man came not to be ministered unto, but to minister" (Mark 10:45). Always, Jesus is our ultimate example. He stated, "They that are whole have no need of the physician, but they that are sick: I came not to call the righteous, but sinners to repentance" (Mark 2:17).

His love was expressed in total giving. The minister who truly loves the flock over which God has made him overseer, will express that love in total giving. "Christ . . . loved the church, and gave himself for it" (Ephesians 5:25).

HUMAN PHILOSOPHY OR DIVINE REVELATION

Man's Emphasis Is on Results. Some years ago a speaker made the national circuit speaking on success. He had a lecture titled "The 57 Rules for Success." He would speak at great length on "1—Produce the Goods." After the audience began to wonder how long this lecture might continue, he would then come to his second point and declare, "Produce the goods, and the other 56 rules make no difference."

That is a human philosophy. God does not call us to be failures. But He does not weigh success on the same scale man uses. Numbers, buildings, income, etc., are the things that impress man. God is more concerned with *how* the goods are produced. He is more concerned with motives than with success.

God's Emphasis Is on Character. In discussing a certain young minister, one person remarked, "There is no substitute for personality." Perhaps, but there is something that so far surpasses personality that the two are not even in the same league—*character.* Nowhere in God's Word do you see a premium on what we call personality. God's reward is for the "good and faithful." Not everyone can have a charming personality, but everyone can have character. Everyone can be good. Everyone can be faithful.

PRIESTHOOD OF THE BELIEVER

A modern philosophy again urges, with insistence, that because every believer is a priest, no ordained ministry is necessary. Some churches even operate without an ordained pastor.

While Scripture teaches that all believers are priests, the Bible also makes it clear that there is a need for the voice of the prophet. The great lack in the church today is the prophetic voice, anointed by the Holy Ghost, declaring, "Thus saith the Lord!"

Modern emphases would destroy the scriptural concept of a God-ordained prophet. Paul told Timothy, "Preach the word; be instant in season, out of season; reprove, rebuke, exhort with all long-suffering and doctrine" (2 Timothy 4:2).

THE WORK AND THE WORKER

God is always much more concerned with the worker than with the work. No worker is indispensable. If the minister becomes proud, arrogant, rebellious, covetous, heretical, lazy, or immoral, God may remove him, as He did King Saul. He may punish him, as He did King David. Or He may keep him from his anticipated goal, as He did Moses.

This chapter will not be so concerned with the work as with the worker, the minister more than the ministry, the preacher rather than preaching. And yet, these are inseparable. The minstry is the only profession where this is inherently true. A lawyer may be proud and still succeed in his work. A banker may be covetous and still be a good banker in the eyes of his peers and the community. A doctor may be immoral and yet maintain a successful practice.

But when the "works of the flesh" replace "the fruit of the Spirit" in the life of the minister, he is on his way out of the ministry. God, because He is both holy and just, will have to deal with that minister. And He will.

"Being" is important. "If I *am* what God wants me to *be*, He will *teach* me what He wants me to *know*, and He will *help me do* what He wants me to *do*." If you learn nothing else from this chapter, memorize this one statement—it could change your life and ministry.

This truth is vividly illustrated in the life of Joseph. He never studied administration and organization, law or military science, economics or finance. All the things man would think necessary in the life of a national leader had been withheld from Joseph. From the age of 17 to the age of 30 he spent his life as a foreigner, a slave, and a prisoner. Suddenly he was thrust into a position of power. Fully equipped for this position, he conducted himself admirably. How could this be? Because through the years he had been what God wanted him to be, and God had taught him what He wanted him to know and helped him do what He wanted him to do.

Joseph resisted the temptation to immorality, but he also resisted the temptation to be bitter, unforgiving, retaliatory, and spiteful. He returned good for evil. He refused to carry a grudge. He went beyond this, to aid his enemies and provide life for those who wanted to kill him. No wonder the Bible speaks of Joseph as being "separate from his brethren" (Genesis 49:26). He was not just separated by distance, but was separated in character, determination, devotion, and obedience to God's will.

Character

Character is defined as "a composite of good moral qualities, typically of moral excellence and firmness blended with resolution, self-discipline, high ethics, force and judgment."

Too often we are concerned with *reputation*, when God's concern is *character*. If we take care of character, reputation will take care of itself.

HEREDITY

From Parents. Some of our character is inherited from our parents. Probably each of us can see characteristics in our lives that are evident in one parent or the other. It seems evident that Jacob inherited characteristics from his mother.

Through Parents. While we inherit some things from our parents, our parents also serve as a channel through which the qualities of previous generations come to us. Just as certain physical characteristics may become evident after a few generations of being invisible, so other characteristics are also conveyed from generation to generation.

ENVIRONMENT

Family and Friends. Other members of the family may have a great influence upon our character without our being conscious of it. Brothers, sisters, uncles, aunts, and cousins all play an important part in our development. This is particularly true in families that are closely knit.

Our friends, from earliest childhood through adulthood, also influence us. This is why choosing friends never loses its importance. It has been observed that while we may have hundreds or even thousands of friends during a lifetime, there will probably not be more than half a dozen to whom we would literally bare our soul and let them know everything about us. We probably never have more than two or three close friends at a time.

School and Society. Teachers, by their lives not just their subject matter, have an influence upon us. Our schoolmates and peers also affect us.

DEVELOPMENT OF CHARACTER

While ancestry, family, friends, and society may have an effect on us, the final disposition of our character depends on us. It is possible to develop character. This is evidenced throughout Scripture, as well as in modern examples. Since character can be developed, it is important that we pay particular attention to this phase of our life.

Choice of Friends. In early life, our parents choose our friends. Later they assist us in our choices. Then we choose our own.

Everyone should choose his friends on the basis of two things: those who can be of specific benefit to us in developing our lives, and those to whom we may contribute something of benefit. However, we must also carefully avoid those who are detrimental to our own development. We should avoid those whose attitudes, motives, language, concepts, philosophies, and actions tend to degrade, deprave, and detract from our relationship to God.

Reading Material. It is not the volume of what we read, but the quality. First in the minister's diet should be God's Word—not just books about the Bible, but the Bible itself.

After 25 years of public ministry, Billy Graham was asked what changes he would make if he could live those 25 years over. Although he is not a man to live in the past, or to live with regrets, he said, "If I could live these 25 years over, I would spend more time with the Bible itself, and less time with books about the Bible." God's Word, more than any other book, develops character.

Viewing and Listening Habits. Our eyes and ears are constantly bombarded with events happening around us and around the world. Much of what we see and hear is beneficial in developing good character. However, some can be detrimental to our character. Radios and television sets are equipped with controls for selection of material. Discipline demands that we be wise in our choices, because everything we see and hear becomes a part of us.

Unfortunately, we have little control over many of the things we see and hear as we go through life. Paul's admonition in Philippians 4:8 is certainly encumbent upon the ministry: "Finally, brethren, whatsoever things are true, whatsoever things are honest, whatsoever things are just, whatsoever things are pure, whatsoever things are lovely, whatsoever things are of good report; if there be any virtue, and if there be any praise, think on these things."

Relationship to God. Nothing so changes, enhances, and beautifies human character as an intimate and proper relationship with God. This is developed and maintained through a balanced devotional life.

Devotional Life

What we are going to become is developed in those hours we spend alone with God. Both quantity and quality are to be considered here. A few minutes "caught on the run" are not sufficient for God to develop His character in us.

Jesus, the Son of God, spent long hours, at times even all night, in prayer and communion with the Father. If He, being who He was, recognized His need for these extended periods of prayer, it is very possible that we, seeing who we are, will also need these times—even more than Jesus did.

ORDINATION

To Be With Jesus (Mark 3:14). If ministers are asked the purpose for which they are ordained, the frequent answer is, "To preach the Word." Most ordination services probably include that charge to those being ordained.

However, when we look at the Scriptures, we see that there is something preceding the preaching of the Word. In Mark 3:14 we read, "He ordained twelve, that they should be with him."

That these men took this ordination seriously is evident in the result of their ministry. After the healing of the lame man, in Acts 3, the apostles were called in question. In Acts 4 we read, "Now when they saw the boldness of Peter and John, and perceived that they were unlearned and ignorant men, they marveled; and they took knowledge of them, *that they had been with Jesus*" (v. 13).

While others may strive to have such letters after their names as B.A., M.A., and Ph.D., we should have BWJ (been with Jesus) after ours.

To Do His Work. After Jesus ordained the Twelve to be with Him, then the ordination was extended to cover His work:

(a) that He might send them forth to preach,

(b) to have power to heal sicknesses,

(c) to cast out devils (Mark 3:14,15).

In John 15:16 Jesus said, "Ye have not chosen me, but I have chosen you, and ordained you, that ye should go and bring forth fruit, and that your fruit should remain." Here we see that His ordination included bringing forth fruit, the kind of fruit that remains—in time and eternity.

Paul's charge to Timothy included: (a) preach the Word; (b) be instant in season, out of season; (c) reprove, rebuke, exhort with all long-suffering and doctrine (2 Timothy 4:2).

The work is important. But more important than the work is the worker. Therefore, Jesus ordained us first to "be with Him."

WHAT IT MEANS TO "BE WITH JESUS"

Living in God's Word. The Spirit-filled minister must have a grasp of God's Word. It is pathetic to hear a minister who is supposed to speak as the oracle of God, speak the philosophy of men. There is no substitute for God's Word in preaching. The minister should read the Bible through at least once each year, just to keep his own reservoir of knowledge full and current. An average reader can read the Bible through in a year, by reading only 15 minutes per day.

After we read the Word, we should take time to study the Word. Word studies, character studies, great themes, the life of Christ, Books of the Bible, prayers, and many other approaches will be beneficial to us. We should avoid getting into a rut, so that our preaching becomes dwarfed.

Memorization of the Word should be a part of the Spirit-filled minister's life. The Holy Spirit will "bring all things to your remembrance, whatsoever I have said unto you" (John 14:26). For Him to call it to our remembrance, we must first know the Bible.

"Walking Bibles" are not always good preachers. But a vast reservoir of Biblical knowledge makes it possible to add authority to preaching, since the only real authority for our message is God's infallible Word.

Meditation. In a world that is activity mad, it is difficult to take time to think. One executive spends half of one day each week in bed, with notebook and pen, making notes of things that come to him. Dozing off, waking up, noting things that come to mind, he has discovered this is the most productive time in the week.

The formula for success as found in Psalm 1 includes the element of meditation. Before it states, "Whatsoever he doeth shall prosper," it says, "But his delight is in the law of the Lord; and in his law doth he meditate day and night" (vv. 2, 3).

Worship. The Psalmist was a great worshiper. As a king, he did not have the privilege of offering sacrifices. He had a longing, however, for the house of God and the service of the priest. Perhaps he caught a glimpse of the priesthood of the believer. He was envious of the sparrow and swallows that could make nests in the tabernacle of the Lord (Psalm 84:3). Finally he cried, "Let my prayer be set forth before thee as incense; and the lifting up of my hands as the evening sacrifice" (Psalm 141:2).

There must be times of intimately sharing with the Lord, times when we meditate on His nature and His character, times when we reflect audibly upon His grace and His love, times of praise, adoration, and worship.

Although we decry heathen practices, long pilgrimages, etc., much benefit would come to us as Bible-believing, Bible-preaching ministers, if we would spend extended periods in worship.

Prayer. Both by example and teaching Jesus emphasized the importance of prayer. It is interesting that the disciples did not say, "Lord, teach us *how* to pray." Rather, they merely said, "Lord, teach us to pray" (Luke 11:1). Many ministers know how to pray, but do not know to pray. Prayer is an important part of "being with Jesus."

Not "Service." Duty is so demanding. It is impossible to escape the constant call of service. But "being with Jesus" is not the same as "being with the flock." Although Jesus is with us when we preach, "being with Jesus" is not the same as preaching. We must shun the temptation of substituting service for the Saviour. The sheer weight of our work load demands our time. Our dedication and determination make demands on our time. Our preaching and our congregation place an urgency on our time. But our calling demands our devotion. We have been called to "be with Jesus."

Anything that can be taught can be learned. And anything that can be learned can be taught. As the disciples cried, "Lord, teach us to pray," so should we.

That they learned this lesson well is evidenced by the fact that when the pressures were on them in the Early Church, they called a congregational meeting and said, "It is not reason that we should leave the word of God, and serve tables." After they outlined the necessity of selecting men from the congregation to do this, they concluded, "But we will give ourselves continually to prayer, and to the ministry of the word" (Acts 6:1-4).

Only you will determine whether you succumb to the pressures to substitute service for the Saviour.

FELLOWSHIP WITH OTHER BELIEVERS

Fellowship Around the Word. As important as it is to read the Word, study the Word, and meditate on the Word, not all revelation will come to us individually. God also speaks to other believers. It is most beneficial to have other ministers with whom to fellowship around the Word of God.

One such group met weekly. There were four ministers. The rules for this group were simple but very stringent:

(a) The meeting was held each week.

(b) The meeting started at 9:00 and ended at 11:00 a.m.

(c) No personality outside the Scriptures could be discussed.

(d) No church, church business, or church problem could be discussed.

(e) No period of fellowship extended beyond the 2 hours.

(f) No food was served.

(g) No recreation was provided.

(h) No other member could be added to the group.

Rotating the order by the initial of the last name, one minister would open with a passage of Scripture that God had blessed to him. After a brief discussion of what the portion meant to him, the group went to prayer. Prayer was not in unison. After each individual had prayed, the men arose from prayer and began a further consideration of Scripture, starting with the passage the first minister had shared. Letting the Spirit direct them, they continued the rest of the 2 hours, closing with a dismissal prayer at 11:00 a.m.

The spiritual growth and development of those four ministers was attested to by each. After several weeks, one of the ministers told his congregation, "You may think you have the same old pastor, but there is a new man inside."

Fellowship in Prayer. In two of the intimate experiences of Jesus' life, He took three disciples with Him: when He was transfigured, and in the garden of Gethsemane.

It was Jesus who said, "If two of you shall agree on earth as touching any thing that they shall ask, it shall be done for them of my Father which is in heaven. For where two or three are gathered together in my name, there am I in the midst of them" (Matthew 18:19, 20). Often throughout the Book of Acts we see the Early Church in the fellowship of prayer.

Look what happened when Ezra prayed. "Now when Ezra had prayed, and when he had confessed, weeping and casting himself down before the house of God, there assembled unto him . . . a very great congregation of men and women and children" (Ezra 10:1).

Personal Priorities

Each person must determine what his personal priorities are. No two will have identical priorities because no two people are identical. Each minister views his work in the light of his own training, experience, and understanding of Scripture.

DETERMINING PRIORITIES

Our "list of priorities" and our "actual priorities" may differ. Things we know to be important, and place on our list, are not always the ones we adhere to in practice. But we should strive to bring the two into alignment. How do we know what we really think is important? A three-point checklist may help us here.

Amount of Time Given. Certainly God does not give points for time spent in the study of His Word and prayer. However, if we determine that the most important thing in our life is a right relationship with God, and then spend 2 hours a day watching television and 30 minutes a day in prayer, God certainly knows what our priorities are. One minister confessed, "I cannot leave the television alone. If I turn it on, I will spend an entire evening watching it." A few years later he was out of the ministry.

Some ministers can always find time for golf, but find it very difficult to take time for prayer and study. Some ministers always have time for fellowship with the people of their church and other ministers, but find it difficult to have time for fellowship with God. Their priorities are distorted. Since the most important thing in our lives is a right relationship to God, we must devote sufficient time to establishing and maintaining this relationship.

Amount of Energy and Effort Expended. Some ministers will work harder at washing, waxing, and polishing their car than they will at the ministry. Some ministers will study harder to know what fishing lures to use to catch a certain kind of fish than to learn the proper method of being "fishers of men." Some ministers go in a whirlwind making investments that may (or may not) provide some sort of security for their old age, but cannot expend the same amount of energy "laying up treasure in heaven."

Amount of Money Invested. If we really think something is important, we do not hesitate to pour our money into it. One minister said, "This church does not belong to me. It belongs to the people. Therefore, let them support it." He never contributed financially to the ministry of the church he pastored. Need it be said that his ministry was never eminently successful?

Man has inverted the statement Jesus made. Often we hear it said, "Where a person's heart is, there he will put his money." But Jesus said exactly the opposite. He said, "Where your treasure is, there will your heart be also" (Matthew 6:21).

So, by the amount of time given, the amount of energy and effort expended, and the amount of money invested, we can determine what we *really* think is important. One family made a list of the things they thought were really important. They made another list of the amount of money they were putting into the various facets of their lives. They found the two lists did not coincide at all. This would be a good exercise for ministers.

THE PRIORITIES OF THE PASTOR

The Scriptures are most helpful to us as we attempt to establish priorities. Both by the teaching and the examples we find in Scripture, we determine what God thinks is important for us. Following is a list of priorities which, if adhered to, makes it possible to fulfill our commitment to God, our family, and all other obligations.

Relationship to God. How does one establish this top priority in the life of the minister? It begins, of course, at conversion. However, it does not end there. It may be enhanced by subsequent experiences such as the baptism in the Holy Spirit, crisis times in our lives, and our call to the ministry. Basically, however, a right relationship to God is established through an understanding of His Word, obedience to it, and time spent in communion and fellowship with God.

How does one maintain a proper relationship to God? The minister cannot forsake the searching of the Scriptures and maintain a right relationship with God. Again and again God's Word hammers home to the heart the truths God wants us to know. Therefore, the minister must daily search the Scriptures. The Bible speaks of "the washing of water by the word" (Ephesians 5:26). The Psalmist said, "Thy word have I hid in mine heart, that I might not sin against thee" (Psalm 119:11); and, "Wherewithal shall a young man cleanse his way? By taking heed thereto according to thy word" (Psalm 119:9).

The minister's prayer should not just be a "reading of a shopping list to God." The minister's prayer life must contain large segments of devotional prayer—time spent in becoming acquainted with God, personally and intimately; time spent in fellowship with God, letting the Holy Spirit impress upon the human heart the attributes of the Divine.

There is a real danger in always searching the Scriptures and praying to find sermons. Rather, we should search the Scriptures and pray to become more like Jesus. Sermons will become a by-product of this kind of experience with God.

Pulpit Ministry. There are many today who would tell us that the minister's family must be the first priority. However, in studying Scripture, we discover that a God-called prophet must give precedence to his mission and message.

This is supported by the examples of the prophets of the Old Testament and by the teaching of Jesus Christ. If a minister must choose between God and his family, obviously he should choose God. Jesus said, "If any man come to me, and hate not his father, and mother, and wife, and children, and brethren, and sisters, yea, and his own life also, he cannot be my disciple" (Luke 14:26). This reinforces the concept that a man's personal life and his mission and message must have precedence over his family.

This Biblical priority, though, cannot be used as an excuse to neglect the family. If a minister must choose between his ministry (used here in the broad sense) and his family, obviously he should choose the ministry. If he must choose between a specific type of ministry and his family, he should choose his family.

To illustrate, if a minister is doing the work of an evangelist, but sees that this is having a seriously adverse effect on his family, he should ask the Lord to open doors of pastoral ministry for him. In this instance, his family must be first. If a minister's wife cannot bear up under the rigors of a pastoral ministry, he should seek other types of ministry. It is not uncommon for missionaries to remain at home during a certain period of the development of their children. They have neither forsaken God nor the ministry.

Pulpit ministry is important. When a housewife invites company for dinner, she makes careful preparation. She may prepare the menu a week in advance. She carefully does her shopping. Actual meal preparation may begin a day ahead. When the guests arrive, the table is set. China, silver, and crystal are in place, and the meal is ready to be served. It would be unthinkable to invite guests for dinner and then treat them in an inconsiderate manner.

Those who attend your church have a right to expect nourishment from God's Word each time. Some ministers treat the midweek service lightly. They prepare haphazardly and serve the meal accordingly. Little thought, little preparation, and little prayer go into a most important meeting of the week. Then they wonder why prayer meeting attendance is always low!

Some pastors get a small podium and move it down in front, as though they expect a small crowd. Usually their faith is rewarded. Some conduct the service in a side room, which limits the possibility of a larger attendance. Jesus said, "According to your faith be it unto you" (Matthew 9:29).

Make your services an oasis in the desert. Your people have been out in the desert. The sun has been beating on their heads. The winds have buffeted them. The sand has blown in their eyes and teeth. They have heard God's name taken in vain and blasphemed. They have been ridiculed and criticized. They turn aside to the house of God as a, weary traveler would sit beneath the palm of an oasis and drink water from the well. They need to be refreshed for the next leg of their journey. If you make your services an oasis, the people will come regularly and faithfully.

Never come into the pulpit without personal victory. Never air your troubles to the people. Greet them with a smile, a hearty handshake, an exclamation of victory, and let them know that Jesus is alive. People have troubles enough, without being burdened with more. Then preach a positive, faith-building, Christ-centered, God-honoring, Bible-oriented message and the people will look forward to the next service.

Strengthen your pulpit ministry through saturation in God's Word and prayer. We do not minister to people when we are bringing them the dregs of an empty life. Actual ministry only occurs from the overflow of a full life. Until our own vessel is overflowing, we are not yet ministering to others. We are just trying to fill up our own supply. When our life is full and begins to overflow, only then do we minister to others.

Pulpit ministry may also be strengthened by listening to other men of God. Secure the tapes of ministers who are excelling in their ministry. Exposure to weak ministries does little to strengthen our own. One minister reads the sermons of great preachers, both past and present, and finds personal enrichment in the activity.

Family. The family is vitally important. Paul emphasized it very strongly in 1 Timothy 5:8, "But if any provide not for his own, and specially for those of his own house, he hath denied the faith, and is worse than an infidel." This certainly covers more than just material provision.

In the family relationship, the minister's first priority must be *the companion.* It is unthinkable that a minister should maintain a first loyalty to parents. The Bible teaches that we should leave our parents and cleave to our companion. Someone has suggested that the "leaving" directly affects the "cleaving." Children come into a home that is already established, and they will leave to create a home of their own. Therefore, in the family relationship the wife (or husband) must have top priority.

The responsibility of parenthood continues throughout life. No one has a right to bring *children* into the world, without accepting the full responsibility of that action. This includes first the influence of a godly life, and then the scriptural and spiritual teaching that will help them develop and mature as Christians. After this will be those things society considers important—food, clothing, housing, education, etc.

Incumbent upon believers is the responsibility to "honor thy father and thy mother" (Exodus 20:12; Deuteronomy 5:16; Matthew 15:4; Luke 18:20; Ephesians 6:2). This is a lifelong obligation. One man said he used his tithe to support his aged parents. It is despicable when a man cares so little for his own parents that he would take the money that rightly belongs to the church to pay a family obligation.

Obviously, there comes a time when God's call takes precedence over the wishes of our *parents*. But they still are entitled to honor and respect.

For many of our *relatives*, we will be the only gospel they will ever read. Although we may be separated from them by the call of God that places us in the ministry, we can never separate ourselves from them as a godly influence on their lives.

Obviously, our relationship to God and our pulpit ministry have a direct bearing on our relationship with the local congregation. Therefore, *the church* is not actually fourth in this list of priorities, although for our consideration it is so numbered. As it relates to the family, the church should come just after the companion and children of the minister.

The pastor who shepherds the flock of God has a tremendous responsibility to the *congregation*. It is not easy to be a shepherd. Jesus said, "The good shepherd giveth his life for the sheep" (John 10:11). Jesus also said, "The Son of man came not to be ministered unto, but to minister" (Mark 10:45). Again He said, "As my Father hath sent me, even so send I you" (John 20:21).

Being a pastor is probably the most demanding work in all the world. It demands 24 hours a day, 7 days a week, 52 weeks a year. Even on your day of rest or your vacation you are never free from the burden of the pastorate. Many pastors have suggested that it takes a week of vacation before they can actually lay down the burden of the church. After that they begin to relax and rest.

Hebrews 13:17 describes the attitude with which the pastor must regard his responsibility: "They watch for your souls, as they that must give account, that they may do it with joy, and not with grief." Watching for the souls of the people is a full-time job with eternal implications.

No one has a right to join an organization without being willing to make a vital contribution to that work. Although the local congregation must take precedence, we also owe an allegiance and loyalty to the parent organization.

1. The *sectional* officers and the sectional program are worthy of our financial support, moral backing, and faithful attendance at scheduled functions.

2. This loyalty extends to the *district* level. A good rule to follow is

this: Be the kind of member of the district that you would like the members of your church to be. Support the district officers as you expect the church to support you. Back the district financially as you expect the church members to back your program.

This basically fulfills the scriptural premise: "Therefore all things whatsoever ye would that men should do to you, do ye even so to them" (Matthew 7:12). And, "Whatsoever a man soweth, that shall he also reap" (Galatians 6:7). As we join hands at the district level, the home missions outreach of our church can be more effective. This is a part of the Great Commission.

3. Although we may feel far removed from the *national office*, we are still part of the total denomination. We do not exist because of the national office, the national office exists because of us. When we, as a body, elect men to serve us on the national level, we owe them our allegiance and support. By cooperating with the national (international) office, we extend our witness around the world. A great missionary program would not be possible were it not for the support of local pastors and congregations. He is nearsighted indeed, who cannot see the need to extend beyond the doors of his own church to reach a lost and dying world.

The district and national offices are responsible for the screening of ministers and missionaries. The local congregation and pastor are hardly qualified for this. There are many benefits that accrue to the local pastor and congregation by cooperating with the denomination.

In addition, we do have certain responsibilities in our own *neighborhood*. Keeping our house and lawn in good order is one of them. Some churches and parsonages are a disgrace to the neighborhood. This is a reflection upon the minister, the congregation, and the gospel of Jesus Christ.

Not only do we have a responsibility to the aesthetics of our neighborhood, but to *the neighbors* themselves. A newspaper editor suggested, "If a man is not a good neighbor, he is not a good Christian, regardless of whether he was immersed, sprinkled, or dry cleaned." It is difficult to witness to our neighbors if we are not a good neighbor.

We also have a *civic responsibility* to our city, county, state, and national governments. There will always be pressures to make the pulpit a soapbox for some political cause. This must be diligently resisted. The pulpit is for the proclamation of the gospel. People come to hear, "Thus saith the Lord," not current events. However, we do owe a certain amount of our time to help make the city, the county, the state, and the nation a better place in which to live. This may be done through participation in various organizations.

Self-discipline

Of all the professions, the ministry has the greatest freedom in establishing its own priorities, its own work schedule, and its own pace. Therefore, it is essential that the minister be a person of self-discipline.

DISCIPLINE OR DISCIPLINARY ACTION

Discipline. The definition of discipline is "training that develops self-control, character, or orderliness and efficiency." Discipline is that inner quality that makes us do what we ought, not what we want. The discipline of the minister's life is not imposed upon him by an organization, denomination, or congregation. It comes from a right relationship to God, a proper sense of mission, and a proper set of values and priorities.

Few things are so intolerable as a lazy minister or one who is not a "self-starter." Any minister, at times, may find it difficult to "get in gear." But the normal pattern of the ministry should be that the minister disciplines himself to establish proper priorities, pay diligent attention to his spiritual life, and set a pace of labor that will guarantee success in the ministry.

Disciplinary Action. An Air Force officer aptly described the difference between discipline and disciplinary action. He said, "We expect the men in the military to be disciplined. This means they will do what they are supposed to do. If they do not, then disciplinary action is initiated."

The same may be said of the ministry. Occasionally disciplinary action is necessary. It is with sorrow and regret that a district initiates disciplinary action. It is never necessary where the minister has disciplined himself.

USE OF TIME

This is the stuff of which life is made. When you are "out of time" you are finished. Some ministers never seem to have time to do anything, while other ministers have time to accomplish many things. Yet, God has given to each of us exactly the same amount of time. Kings and queens, presidents and prime ministers, and business tycoons and paupers have the same amount of time. It is not how much time you have, but what you do with it that matters.

Priority Determines Use of Time. When you have a proper understanding of your own priorities, it will be easy to say "yes" and "no" to the demands placed upon you. We do not have to explain each decision to others, so long as we have a proper understanding of what we are doing, where we are going, and what we are about. Someone has suggested, "Never explain. Your friends do not need it, and your enemies will not believe it." Find out what God wants you to do, and then budget your time accordingly.

Annual Planning Calendar. Although your denomination may provide an annual calendar, this will not be sufficient for you personally. Your own calendar must include those events of the national, district, and sectional levels and the local congregation, as well as personal obligations. It would be worth the time to develop a calendar in five columns, so you could always see what is going on from the national level to the personal level. The time spent in developing this calendar could save hundreds of hours a year. It will help you see where you must go to accomplish your God-given goals.

This approach greatly aids in planning. If you have a missions convention coming up in November, you could write a note on your calendar for the month of May to finalize all the missionaries who would be in attendance at your convention. By June you should have all of their publicity in hand. By August you should have housing arrangements made for them and be putting together the essentials of the convention. By September your own printing should be laid out and regular promotion started in the local congregation. By the time November comes, only the last minute preparation needs to be done. The advantage of an annual planning calendar is that it helps you plan, prepare, and promote effectively, and makes execution of your plans possible.

Weekly Schedule. Certain things come up each week—pulpit ministry, visitation, correspondence, etc. When we establish a weekly schedule, it will eliminate last minute pressures. Nothing takes a toll on our physical and emotional well-being like undue pressure. Regular periods of study, prayer, sermon preparation, visitation, etc., will help us fulfill our ministry without concern or alarm.

Daily Schedule. It is good to commit as many things as possible to habit and routine. However, we must not be a slave to our daily schedule. This is the one thing that can be shifted easily without doing detriment to our overall objectives.

We live in a busy age. There are tremendous pressures on us to accomplish many things. Observation makes us aware that church administrators, pastors, evangelists, missionaries, and professors become too occupied. When we are too busy for extended periods of devotion, we are too busy. When we are too busy to spend extended time with God's Word, we are too busy. There are always demands on us to "do" rather than "be."

Self-discipline demands we establish proper priorities and adhere to them strictly. Martin Luther has been quoted as saying, "If I fail to spend two hours in prayer each morning, the devil gets the victory through the day. I have so much business I cannot get on without spending three hours daily in prayer." Many ministers have discovered that the more time they spend in prayer, the more of their work is accomplished by the Holy Spirit.

PHILOSOPHICAL PRESSURE

There is a pressure to make the ministry a "profession." Although in the broad sense of the word the ministry is a profession and a minister is a professional man, the truth is that for the Spirit-filled ministry, the minister is a God-called man and the ministry is a calling.

There is a bit of modern philosophy that says, "If the businessman can be in his office at 8:00 a.m., so can the pastor." Again, priority. Are we going to be businessmen or able ministers of the gospel? The businessman may be in his office by 8:00 a.m. but he does not find it necessary to feed the flock of God two, three or four times per week. To the businessman, the most important thing may be to have the doors of his office open for customers at 8 a.m. To the minister, the most important thing is that right relationship to God.

It is more important that the minister spend the first 2, 3, or 4 hours of the day in the Word of God and prayer than that he be available at an office. The people will soon discover that his time spent with God pays bigger dividends than having an open office. A secretary that simply says, "I am sorry, the pastor is in prayer and cannot be disturbed," easily solves the problem.

Many a fine congregation would gladly trade their businessman and executive for a prophet of God who would declare with power and authority, "Thus saith the Lord," and be able to pray the prayer of faith. This is really what a Spirit-filled, Pentecostal ministry is about.

Self-motivation

There are numerous driving forces known to mankind. The world capitalizes on these in business. We are only going to consider a few in our discussion on self-motivation.

LOVE

Love Is the Greatest. It was God's love that prompted Him to send Jesus Christ to be our Saviour. It was love that caused Jesus to give His life. It was love that sent the apostles out to evangelize the world.

It is love that causes a parent to rush into a burning building in an attempt to rescue a child. No amount of money could persuade people to do what they have done for love. No person has a right to be in the ministry who is not a person of love. It is love that causes men to leave security and well-paying jobs to pioneer a church. It is love that causes families to leave home and country to do missionary work.

"But now abide faith, hope, love, these three; but the greatest of these is love" (1 Corinthians 13:13, *NASB*).

Love for God. To answer the call to the ministry is an expression of love for God. When we stand at Calvary and experience the magnitude of God's love for us, we are made aware that we ought to love as He loves. Love for God in the human heart is a tremendous driving force as the Bible and Church history will attest. Jesus said, "Thou shalt love the Lord thy God with all thy heart, and with all thy soul, and with all thy mind, and with all thy strength" (Mark 12:30). Often we hear this quoted with the emphasis on the heart, soul, mind, and strength. Perhaps the emphasis should be on the word *thy.* We are not free to measure our love against the love of another. God demands all. Not more than someone else or less than someone else, but the total capacity we possess to love. Only this will suffice.

Love for People. A person has no right to be in the ministry without a genuine love for God; it is equally true that no one should be in the ministry without a genuine love for people—all kinds of people. We must love the unlovable, the unlovely, and the unloving. Some people are easier to love than others, but this does not make it right for us to show partiality in our love. Jesus said, "As my Father hath sent me, even so send I you" (John 20:21).

Some people seem unlovable. But God loves them. As His representative, we must love them too. Some people are unlovely. Physically or socially they are unattractive. But our responsibility before God is to love them as much as we do those who are lovely. Some people are unloving. We lavish love upon them, but they do not reciprocate. Yet, we must go on loving, since that is how God loves us.

To be able to love the socialite and the gutter bum; the college graduate and the illiterate; adults, youth, and children; people of every nationality; those who like us and those who do not—this ability is not only a measure of our love, but a test of whether or not the love of God really dwells in us. To be motivated by love makes the work of the ministry a most rewarding vocation.

DESIRE

Desires Born of Appetite. Some have taught that desire is the greatest driving force known to man. Obviously, for the minister, this must not be true. However, desire does have its place in motivating an individual. There are many things in the natural that will prod a minister to success. Size of church, acclaim by his fellowman, position, possessions, sense of accomplishment, security—these are just a few.

Often we hear people quote Mark 11:24, "What things soever ye desire, when ye pray, believe that ye receive them, and ye shall have them." They indicate that regardless of how this desire is born, it can be achieved in the time of prayer. Many desires are born while window-shopping or looking through the catalog, while observing a neighbor's possessions, or while hearing of the success of a friend. These are desires born of appetite.

Desires Born in Prayer. What Mark 11:24 probably means is, "When you are in prayer, what things soever you desire, believe that you receive them, and you shall have them." Not desire born of appetite, but desire born in prayer. Many missionaries, pastors, evangelists, and other Christians have sought God earnestly. During this time of seeking the Lord, a desire has been born in their heart. Realizing that this desire is sanctified, they dare to believe God for it, and it becomes reality.

Psalm 37:4 says, "Delight thyself also in the Lord; and he shall give thee the desires of thine heart." We need to examine our desires to be sure they are God-honoring and pleasing to our Master. Desires born in prayer will be. Those born of appetite will not be. Pursuing desires born of appetite will end in frustration or even destruction. Pursuing desires born in prayer can lead to tremendous spiritual victory and success for the kingdom of God. Desire born in prayer can be a great factor in self-motivation.

SERVICE

No person has a right to be in the ministry who does not have a desire to serve. Jesus said, "I am among you as he that serveth" (Luke 22:27). Luke 2:37 indicates that Anna "served God with fastings and prayers night and day." Obviously this is one beautiful way to serve the Lord. Since we deal with the matter of devotion elsewhere in the chapter, we will consider here the other aspect of service.

To Others. "Whatsoever thy hand findeth to do, do it with thy might" (Ecclesiastes 9:10). Romans 12:11 states, "not slothful in business; fervent in spirit; serving the Lord." Essentially we serve the Lord by serving others. Jesus taught this: "For I was ahungered, and ye gave me meat: I was thirsty, and ye gave me drink: I was a stranger, and ye took me in: naked, and ye clothed me: I was sick, and ye visited me: I was in prison, and ye came unto me. . . . Inasmuch as ye have done it unto one of the least of these my brethren, ye have done it unto me" (Matthew 25:35, 36, 40).

As Unto the Lord. As our love for God is measured by our love for man, so our service to God is determined by our service to man (1 John 4:20, 21; Colossians 3:17, 23, 24; Matthew 10:40-42; Proverbs 19:17).

The person who detests people should leave the ministry. Because there was something terribly wrong with the human race, God sent His Son. Because those same needs continue to exist, God sends His ministers. If we are unwilling to come to grips with the needs, sorrows, burdens, sins, failures, sicknesses, and heartaches of people, we should find some other occupation.

Ruling as a Servant. One of the ministry gifts mentioned in Romans 12:8 is "ruling." The minister must not rule as a despot or dictator, but as a servant. Jesus did. Paul did. Peter did. And so must we.

The wise old men of Israel counseled King Rehoboam saying, "If thou wilt be a servant unto this people this day, and wilt serve them, and answer them, and speak good words to them, then they will be thy servants for ever" (1 Kings 12:7). Here is a mutual servitude. If the king would serve the people, the people would serve him. This is certainly true in the ministry. We are to rule as a shepherd rules, willing to give his life for the sheep.

MOTIVES

We often think of being careful about our actions, words, and thoughts. However, the Lord looks beyond this. He is concerned about why we think what we think, say what we say, and do what we do.

Doing the Right Thing. It is not possible to always do the right thing. We act on the basis of the information we have available at the moment. Sometimes action can be delayed, but not always. At times we must make a decision and move immediately.

There are mistakes of the head and mistakes of the heart. A congregation will be tolerant of mistakes of the head. They will not be so quick to forgive mistakes of the heart. It is important that we keep our heart right. As a man "thinketh in his heart, so is he" (Proverbs 23:7). "Keep thy heart with all diligence; for out of it are the issues of life" (Proverbs 4:23). Jesus said, "Out of the abundance of the heart the mouth speaketh" (Matthew 12:34).

Doing the Right Thing With a Wrong Motive. It seems paradoxical that we can do the right thing, but with the wrong motive. A minister was praying for souls. God suddenly stopped him with, "Son, you are not really interested in souls." He began to argue with the Lord. Then the Lord let him see what was really in his heart. The Lord reminded him: "You have been successful as an evangelist. You have a reputation among your brethren. Now you are pastoring. You are afraid that if souls are not saved in your pastorate, you will be held in low esteem by your brethren. You are more concerned with your reputation than you are with souls."

As important as it is to see souls saved, it is more important that we have a right motive in wanting to see them saved. This rule applies to everything we do, say, or think.

Doing the Right Thing With the Proper Motive. God made it clear to Samuel that He does not judge as man judges, "Man looketh on the outward appearance, but the Lord looketh on the heart" (1 Samuel 16:7). Jesus said, "Blessed are the pure in heart: for they shall see God" (Matthew 5:8). This does not just mean that sometime, somewhere, out in the future, we shall see God. But if our heart is pure, if our motives are right before God, we shall see God work in our lives even now.

Since God doesn't see as man sees, but looks on the heart and judges not only what we do but also why we do it, it is important that we maintain a right relationship to God and to our fellowman. Only then can our work be what God wants it to be. Again we see the importance of God's Word. Hebrews 4:12 tells us, "The word of God is quick, and powerful, and sharper than any two-edged sword, . . . and is a discerner of the thoughts and intents of the heart."

Continuing Education

A minister was elected to a large and well-known congregation. Within a short time, the congregation was dissatisfied. It was not long before they asked him to resign. The reason was given by a member of the congregation, who said, "Somewhere along the line he stopped studying." His material was stale. He was stale. The pitiful thing is that a minister may become stale without knowing it. However, the congregation always knows it. A continuing education is a necessity for the minister. There are a number of ways in which this can be accomplished.

FORMAL EDUCATION

Nearby College or University. Many churches are located near a college or university. By spending a few hours each week on classroom work and diligent study, many ministers have extended their formal education far beyond their college days, often going on to advanced degrees.

Obviously, this is not for everyone. A formal education does not really make the difference between success and failure in the life of a minister. Some ministers who are eminently successful do not have a great deal of formal education. If you can be highly educated, as the apostle Paul was, and then forget "those things which are behind"

and "count them but dung," you will have a proper attitude toward
the degree you have earned.

Correspondence. For those who cannot enroll in a college or university, there are many correspondence schools available. Almost any
subject you desire to study can be pursued through correspondence.

INFORMAL EDUCATION

Consistent Reading. It has been wisely observed, "He who will not
read is not better off than he who cannot read." The minister who
continues to be a diligent reader, will greatly enhance his education.
His audience will never know whether he learned his material in the
classroom or in his own study. And they won't really care.

Personal Library. Many ministers yield to the temptation of adding
books to their library to impress people. Many of the volumes on the
shelf have never been opened. A personal library should be chosen
with care, and the books that remain in the library should be those
that have a lasting and continuing benefit. The minister needs books
that help him understand God's Word.

PRACTICAL EDUCATION

Another part of a minister's education is that which we can call
"practical." Some people receive a great deal of book learning, but
never learn to put it into practice. Such education is worthless. Many
things are going on about us that we can share. These real-life experiences become a permanent part of our education.

Observation. One of the most important things a minister can do to
increase and enhance his education is to be observant. We have the
opportunity to be in services conducted by other men and to listen to
messages preached by others. Without being critical for the sake of
criticizing, we can still learn from our peers.

Many ministers do things better than we do. When we observe this,
we should be quick to change. We should search for the right way to
receive an offering, conduct a song service, pray in public, make announcements, begin a message, give an altar call, etc. Many could
greatly improve their ministry by observing how others approach
these parts of a service. When ministers go to district or national
meetings, they can learn how to conduct efficient church business
meetings.

Just as we may learn from others how to improve what we are doing, we may also improve by observing their blunders and mistakes. Since we are not going to live long enough to make all the mistakes ourselves, wouldn't it be wise to learn from the mistakes of others?

Application. No matter how much we have learned, it does no good—either for us or our congregation—unless we are willing to apply it. More ministries have died from getting into a rut than from any other cause. When you see something that works, try it. You may discover it will need to be adapted not just adopted. Feel free to do either. There are no patents or copyrights on the methods ministers use in conducting services, making announcements, performing marriages and funerals, or conducting business sessions. Adopt, adapt, experiment, and change, but do not die of stagnation.

Trial and Error. How does a person learn to drive a car? How does a person learn to bake a pie? These things may be studied in books, but the real learning process comes from trial and error. Do not be afraid to fail; you can learn from your failures.

It is said that when Thomas Edison was looking for a filament for the light bulb, he tried hundreds of experiments without finding something that would work. A friend remarked, "Why don't you quit? You have tried a thousand things and have not learned anything yet." To which Edison replied, "Oh, but I have. I have learned a thousand things that will not work. I am only looking for one that will."

He is foolish indeed who will not learn from his mistakes. Many people quit when they make a mistake, for fear of failing again. But failure can be as important as success in the learning process. Use failures as stepping-stones, not roadblocks. Most successful ministers have so many failures on their record that they refuse to think about them. Most of those whose ministries have failed have very few failures to their credit. Only a few—and they quit trying. That is the biggest error of all.

Health

We often think of food as the great necessity. In fact, we often hear "food, clothing, and shelter." But these are not the great necessities. In order of importance there are five God-ordained necessities: air, rest, water, food, and exercise.

AIR

We may live for days without food, but we live only moments without air. This is the highest priority. Not only do we need air, but we should be careful of the kind of air we breathe. Many of us are subjected to stale, stagnant, or even polluted air.

REST

Some of us are inclined to ignore the fact that we must rest. We consider it a waste of time to go to bed. We try to run on insufficient sleep. To do so is an insult to God's intelligence. He is the One who has designed the human body to require rest.

Sleep. Each person has his own basic requirement for sleep. Studies have shown that a few individuals can actually operate on 4 hours of sleep daily. A few more can get by on 5 hours. Many can operate effectively with 6 hours. However, the bulk of humanity needs 7, 8, or 9 hours sleep, with the great majority requiring 8 hours per day. Find out what your daily requirement is and get it faithfully.

Relaxation. Rest is more than sleeping. It is also relaxing. One woman, whose husband worked hard every day, could not understand when he would come home in the afternoon and say, "My, but I'm tired. I think I'll go play a round of golf." Then, when he returned he was refreshed. This did not make sense to her.

However, when she became weary, she might take one of her daughters and go shopping. Although this would probably have exhausted her husband, to her it was relaxing. Rest and relaxation are a part of the recreative process of life. Our bodies and minds are refreshed in this manner. Although we think of food as being so essential, we can go many days without food, but in a matter of hours the body begins to break up unless it gets rest.

DIET

Drink. Without a sufficient intake of water, the body will dehydrate. We can go much longer without food than we can without liquid.

Sufficient Food. Many ministers are overweight. At one time it was observed that the pastors of the 10 largest Sunday schools in America were not overweight. This probably speaks of their self-discipline. An obese minister can be a reproach to the gospel. The Bible teaches us to be temperate in all things. Since the body is the temple of the Holy Ghost, we should take care that our bodies do not get too much food and thereby impair our ministry. Sufficient food, yes. Excessive food, no!

Proper Food. In America we have the privilege of selecting our diet. Some countries do not have that opportunity. Their basic diet is the same year after year.

The pastor must not only be an example in the kind of life he lives, but also in his diet. Our consumption of food should be sufficient to keep us looking well and feeling strong, and aid us in being mentally alert.

RECREATION

Physical Exercise. In a society where we live a life of ease, it is easy to neglect the physical exercise that is essential to our well-being. We sit in our car, home, church, and office. When we visit our people we sit.

Some ministers find it to their advantage to join a local YMCA or health club. Others regularly play golf, handball, or tennis. Some prefer hunting or fishing. However, for just the investment of a good pair of tennis shoes and gym socks, we may get exercise by jogging, walking, or hiking.

Whatever our personal taste may be, the important thing is that we do take care of our bodies. As one older minister observed, "My work is so important that I must take time for recreation. If I do not, my body breaks down. When that happens, my work is finished. So, because of the importance of my work, I must take time for recreation."

As some ministers are intemperate in eating, others are intemperate in recreation. Some neglect this area altogether, while others are excessive. There are ministers who play golf every day. Regardless of who suggests it or when, they are ready to play golf. However, they may not be as eager to spend time in God's Word or in prayer. Their people know where to find them, by placing a call to the local clubhouse. This is a reproach to the ministry. Others are intemperate in hunting or fishing, and it becomes almost an obsession. The Bible tells us to be temperate in *all things.*

Mental Health. A laboring man may return home at night bone tired. His muscles ache. He is exhausted. A businessman, who may not lift anything heavier than a pencil or a book throughout the day, returns home just as weary. But he is brain weary. One is as real an exhaustion as the other.

Because the ministry is both physical and mental, the minister must beware of a weary mind. When we become brain weary, our work is definitely affected. It becomes difficult to study, to pray, to counsel, and to preach. We need those activities that will help rejuvenate the mind.

Every minister with a few years of experience knows what it is like to have sermons leaping off the pages of the Bible. At other times, nothing seems to come. Or he may have gone on vacation and in the midst of relaxing, suddenly messages begin to come, ideas and plans for his work begin to formulate, and he becomes eager to get back on the job. What has happened? His mind has been revived by rest. In the ministry, an alert mind is one of our greatest assets.

Avoiding Frustration

In almost any ministers' seminar, the question will be asked, "How can I avoid frustration?" Frustration seems to be the plague of the ministry. It need not be so. There are a few simple rules that help us avoid frustration in the ministry.

One of the things that causes frustration is not being able, at the end of the day, to see what has been accomplished. The bricklayer can look back on his day and see what he has done in 8 hours. The carpenter can see what he has done. The farmer can see how much of the field he has plowed. But, alas, the minister looks back at the end of the day and often cannot see any visible accomplishment. Because of this, he often thinks nothing has been done. In this lies the seed of frustration.

The following simple suggestions can keep you from frustration.

DISTINGUISH BETWEEN GOALS AND WORK SHEET

Goals are always long-range. Never say, "My goal for today is . . . ." Set goals soon after arriving at a pastorate. Reevaluate them periodically. In establishing goals, set some for 3 months, some for 6 months, some for 1 year, some for 2 or 3 years, some for 5 years, and some even farther into the future. Goals are those major things toward which you strive.

Every pastor should pastor two churches at once. Not the one he is now pastoring and the one he is going to get as soon as he can, but the one he is now pastoring and the one it is going to become.

The best way to *establish goals* is in the prayer closet. God knows what He wants each church to become. As God unveiled to Joseph His plan for Egypt, God can reveal to the pastor His plan for the church. Boards, committees, and consultation have little benefit in establishing goals. Most of the people have no idea what God wants for the church.

God has placed the pastor as leader of the congregation, to set the pace in leadership, not to follow the whims of the people. How long would it have been before Israel would have gotten out of Egypt if Moses had begun with boards, committees, and consultation?

As goals are born in prayer, so the *method of execution* can be born in prayer. Many projects are lost by launching them prematurely or improperly. Many goals are not attained because they are never launched at all. There is a proper time for attempting any project.

Not only is timing important, but the method of presentation is also important. If a project has been born in your heart in prayer, and if it is important to share it with your congregation, then its importance requires that you find how God wants it presented. If the method of presentation is the difference between failure and success, and if you value what God has given you, you cannot afford to approach it in a haphazard manner.

God did not bring Israel out of Egypt in one single action. It was a deliberate, step-by-step plan. We can learn from this that it is important that we approach projects of magnitude with deliberation, prayer, and planning.

When the people are not aware of what the pastor is trying to launch, he cannot expect immediate enthusiasm and response. Hints and suggestions carefully placed in board-meeting agendas and in sermons can help pave the way for what God is wanting to do. So when the project is made public, the groundwork has been laid and the people have been conditioned.

Check up on your goals periodically, but not daily—perhaps every quarter or every 6 months. See if you are gaining on your goals. If so, rejoice and forge ahead. If not, find out what is detaining you and correct the situation.

While goals are long-range, *a work sheet* is used on a daily basis. In the evening before retiring or in the morning after arising, make a list for the day. This may include correspondence, hospital calls, counseling, planning, boards and committees, church services, etc.

Some suggest the work sheet should be drawn up with top-priority things first. Others suggest the first items should be those that will not take long to complete, so as to get them out of the way. Still others recommend the first items should be those we dislike doing, so we are forced to do them first. The best plan is the one that works best for you, since you are the one who is going to have to give account for the stewardship of your time and talent.

Almost invariably the work sheet for any given day will have more on it than can be accomplished. The work sheet is your servant. Never become a slave to it. At the end of the day you will probably have a few items to place on the next day's work sheet. If you find the same item being carried over from day to day, it probably means you are neglecting an unpleasant task. Or, possibly, you have something on your work sheet that does not really need to be done.

The top priority of the minister must be the spiritual aspect of his work and the congregation he serves. There are times when the work sheet for the entire day must be ignored in order to minister to the spiritual needs of the flock. When this happens, the minister must not feel guilty. His goals, which are most important, are still intact. Only the work sheet has suffered.

It is inevitable that interruptions will come. Remember that in many instances "interruptions" *are* our work. God has called us because His people have needs. Their needs cannot always be worked into our time frame. Therefore, when they call, it may seem like an interruption. However, it is only an interruption to our work sheet, not to our ministry or our goals.

Necessary interruptions are those that concern the life of the congregation, the spiritual or physical well-being of members of the flock, or those crises that can arise in the life of any individual without warning. The sensitive minister, being led of the Spirit, will gladly give himself, rearrange his schedule, and minister to God's people. Many ministers have learned that what they thought was an interruption turned out to be the opportune time to lead a soul to Christ.

You will not serve long in the ministry before you discover there are *unnecessary interruptions*. It takes time and experience to learn how to sift these out. Someone once said, "He who has an hour to waste, usually spends it with someone who doesn't." There are people who chronically call on the telephone. They feel it is their privilege to preempt the pastor's time and that their problems are more important than anyone else's. They may try to speak to the pastor (or his wife) for an hour or so each day.

There are those who feel it is their privilege to drop by the office, unannounced and without an appointment, and that the pastor must drop everything to take as much time with them as they desire. There are those who wish to share trivia with the pastor (or his wife) and take time away from the essentials for that which is peripheral. The wise pastor will soon distinguish between necessary and unnecessary interruptions. The one can be God-ordained. The other can be a thief of time. Usually unnecessary interruptions can be handled tactfully. If not, they must be dealt with anyway, since no one has a right to rob the minister of his God-appointed responsibilities.

SUCCESSES AND FAILURES

Almost every minister is haunted by the specter of failure. Almost every minister desires to be successful. Perhaps this is true because we have grown up in a success-oriented society. Businessmen, professional men, and salesmen drive themselves to be successful. Failures are spoken of with disdain and contempt.

Whose Servant Are You? Paul teaches us in Romans 14:4, "Who art thou that judgest another man's servant? To his own master he standeth or falleth." The minister is first, last, and always a servant of the Lord. To hear Him say in that day, "Well done, thou good and faithful servant," is success.

At the outset of your ministry you should determine who your Master is. Your peers? your congregation? or the Lord? If it is the Lord, then you must serve your congregation as is pleasing to the Lord. If it is the Lord, then you must cooperate and fellowship with your peers in a manner that is pleasing to the Lord.

Being fully aware of who your Master is certainly avoids frustration in the life of the minister. People may not be satisfied with your work, even when God is. God never expects more than your best, but people sometimes do.

The Measure of Success. In God's work, faithfulness, not accomplishment, is the measure of success. Not everyone can be a great orator, but everyone can be faithful. Not everyone can be a great organizer, but everyone can be faithful. Not everyone can be a great administrator, but everyone can be faithful.

The end does not justify the means. Some ministers build a great congregation by stealing sheep from a neighboring church. It makes their own record look good in the eyes of their denomination, but God is keeping a different set of books. Some ministers build a church around their own personality. It looks good for the time being, but when they leave—as someday they must through transfer or death— what remains of their work will be the proof of their building.

The Last Chapter. The last chapter of your work will not be written this side of eternity. First Corinthians 3:5-15 paints the picture of the last chapter. "Every man's work shall be made manifest . . . it shall be revealed by fire; and the fire shall try every man's work of what sort it is" (v. 13). Here God speaks to us of building with "gold, silver, precious stones, wood, hay, stubble" (v. 12). That will be an interesting day. What our peers, our denomination, or our congregation thinks will be of no importance at all. Our record in that day will not stand by comparison to any other person's work, whether great or small. It will be measured by the talents, abilities, and opportunities God gave us.

POSITIVE ATTITUDES

One of the greatest assets a minister can have is a positive attitude.

How to Acquire a Positive Mental Attitude. We come again to God's Word, prayer, and our personal relationship with God. There is no book in all the world as positive as the Bible. When you see what God did with shepherds, slaves, prisoners, emigrants, and displaced persons, you are made to realize that "God is no respecter of persons: but in every nation he that feareth him, and worketh righteousness, is accepted with him" (Acts 10:34, 35).

Have you ever spent time with an individual that lifted your spirit? Have you ever spent time with an individual who left you depressed? It is obvious that the company we keep does affect our attitude. Therefore, the more time we spend in the presence of God, the more positive our attitude will become.

How to Maintain a Positive Mental Attitude. Positive mental attitudes are maintained the same way they are achieved. People sometimes wonder what happened to their marriage. Their love was developed by careful attention and lost by neglect. Some ministers have started out with the call of God on their life, diligent application of themselves in prayer and study, and then have fallen by the wayside. The reason is probably that they have left their first love (Revelation 2:4).

A daily diet of God's Word, coupled with an extended period in prayer, can create a positive attitude that nothing can destroy.

Pastoral Pitfalls

This chapter concerning the personal life of the pastor would not be complete if we did not consider the pitfalls that can destroy him and his ministry. Although many more could be listed, only four of the most treacherous will be considered.

PRIDE

Pride has nothing to do with externals. It is an attitude of the heart. The poorest, most illiterate, and most untalented can be proud.

Self-exaltation. When the Bible tells us that "pride goeth before destruction" (Proverbs 16:18) and "only by pride cometh contention" (Proverbs 13:10), we are made to see the adverse effects pride has on a man and his ministry. We may not be inclined to believe every quarrel is caused by pride, but the Bible states that. If the devil cannot succeed in getting us to be proud about material or physical things, he will infect us with pride about our spirituality. It is just as damaging as any other kind of pride.

Meekness is Not Weakness. Some people are afraid to be humble for fear they will be weak. But God says of Moses that he was the meekest man on earth (Numbers 12:3). There is nothing to indicate he was ever weak. Humility provides a strength of character that comes from no other source.

DISCOURAGEMENT

One minister said, "When I pray for the sick, and they are healed, I must guard against pride. When I pray for the sick, and they are not healed, I must fight discouragement."

The Devil's Tool. If the devil cannot get us to be proud, he can defeat us if he can get us discouraged. There is probably no one so hard to help as a discouraged minister. To become discouraged is to act as though God has died. To become discouraged is to doubt His faithfulness, His power, and His promise. Many a minister who has withstood every other onslaught of Satan has fallen prey to discouragement.

David in his distress "encouraged himself in the Lord" (1 Samuel 30:6). If you do not tell your troubles to your congregation, and there is no reason to do so, they will never know the troubles through which you pass. You will not find it convenient to go to members of your congregation or members of your board and express your discouragement, but you can bare your heart before God, as the Psalmist did when he talked to himself, saying, "Why art thou cast down, O my soul? And why art thou disquieted within me? Hope thou in God: for I shall yet praise him, who is the health of my countenance, and my God" (Psalm 42:11). Obviously, the Psalmist was talking to himself, bolstering his faith, and encouraging himself in the Lord.

Pride in Reverse. What is discouragement, but pride in reverse? If we were not proud, we would probably not become discouraged. It is concern about what others think or about what we think that causes discouragement. We set certain standards for ourselves, and when we do not attain them, we become discouraged. Or we imagine that others have set standards for us that are impossible to attain, and we become discouraged. Our pride suffers a terrible blow.

MONEY

The Bible does not teach that money is the root of all evil. Rather, it teaches that "the love of money is the root of all evil" (1 Timothy 6:10).

Attitude Toward Money. Money is a servant. Man teaches, "You can't take it with you." But Jesus taught that you can send it on ahead. Jesus said, "Lay up for yourselves treasures in heaven, where neither moth nor rust doth corrupt, and where thieves do not break through nor steal" (Matthew 6:20). When this world is enveloped in flames, our treasure can be safe on the other side.

The minister must be an example in the manner in which he manages his money. The good pastor will be able to say, "Do as I do," or as Paul said, "Be ye followers of me, even as I also am of Christ"

(1 Corinthians 11:1). It really is "more blessed to give than to receive" (Acts 20:35). The person who does not think so, has never really tried it.

Money must not be a master. It is a pity to see a person who has been mastered by his money. He becomes a slave, constantly driven. The desire for money is never satisfied. Many persons—some of them in the ministry—have driven themselves beyond measure in a desire for money. One minister fell by the wayside and later became an alcoholic. When a friend was asked the cause, he said, "He was always reaching for another dollar."

Personal Finances. Most ministers, looking back on the early days of their ministry, speak disparagingly about their early *salaries.* However, in retrospect, most of us will have to admit that although it was not all we needed, it was probably more than we were worth.

Some of us may find it necessary, as did Paul, to work with our hands at some point in our ministry. If so, there is nothing wrong with honorable labor. Many pioneer pastors have supported themselves until the church could suppport them. Few ministers will make too much money in the ministry.

The Bible teaches that "all the tithe . . . is the Lord's" (Leviticus 27:30). We have not given anything to the Lord until we exceed the tithe. The minister must be an example to his congregation in *tithing.* Though the tithe is the minimum, there is no ceiling placed on how much we can give. Some ministers have found the joy of giving 25 percent and even 50 percent of their income to the Lord.

Probably the best way to keep from becoming covetous is to constantly increase our level of *giving.* Since it is impossible to outgive God, and since Jesus himself promised a rich return, there is no way to hurt yourself by giving. "Give, and it shall be given unto you; good measure, pressed down, and shaken together, and running over, shall men give into your bosom. For with the same measure that ye mete withal it shall be measured to you again" (Luke 6:38).

Someone said, "You can't outgive God." To which a friend replied, "No, but it is fun to try." A good way to develop the grace of giving is to do so by percentages. Beginning with the 10 percent that already belongs to the Lord, add 5 or 10 percent as an offering. Then add another 5 percent, then another, and another, and another, and experience the joy and blessing of unselfishly sharing what God has given.

Most denominations have a rule for the tithe of the minister. By all means, you should comply willingly and faithfully to those requirements. No man has a right to be a part of an organization he is not willing to support. There are so many needs (missions, building programs, evangelists and guest speakers, colleges, scholarships, etc.) that it seems unthinkable that a minister who lives on the generosity of God's people would not himself be generous.

As you read the Bible through, make special note concerning the Lord's teaching on giving. Share these truths with your congregation. The key to the windows of heaven is held in the pocketbook, as we discover in Malachi 3.

Not only is God interested in how we earn our money and the portion we give, but He is also concerned with how we *spend* the balance. Being bereft of the necessities of life is not necessarily a proof of humility. On the other hand, being surrounded with all the lavish provisions of a modern society is not necessarily proof of God's prosperity. It may be a sign of poor stewardship.

It has been wisely observed, "If our outgo exceeds our income, our upkeep will become our downfall." Occasionally a minister brings reproach upon himself and God's work by not being able to pay his bills.

As God prospers the minister, he may desire to invest for future income. There is nothing wrong with this. The error comes in becoming so involved in *investments* that it detracts from the work of the Lord. Most of us are not wise enough to play the stock market. Nor do we have the time for it. There is always a temptation to put our money where we can make a fast increase. This is probably one of the most dangerous things we can do. The tried and proven methods are safer and usually require less of our time.

Credit is—or can be—a good thing. On the other hand, credit can be an enemy. If you use credit, use it wisely. Never abuse it.

A rule of thumb is that, except for the purchase of a house, you should never be in debt for more than a total of 5 months' income. Another rule of thumb indicates we should not owe more for a house than two-and-one-half times our annual income. Thus, our total indebtedness should never exceed three times our annual income. Remember, this is the upper limit and it will place a considerable strain on your budget. Monthly payments for all debts, mortgages, etc., should not exceed 33 percent of our monthly income.

Some church boards make a credit investigation on prospective pastors and staff members. This is not an invasion of privacy and is well within the prerogative of a church board. The sad truth is that one church board, having three names before them, found that two of them were bad credit risks. If we keep our finances in proper order, we will not be afraid of anybody making a credit investigation on us.

Handling Church Money. Often ministers in smaller churches or home missions works find it necessary to handle the church finances. However, as soon as possible, this should be given to the care of members of the congregation. Some ministers of large congregations do not even have their names on the church checking accounts. The church finances should be set up in such a way that an honest and accurate accounting can be given to the members of the congregation.

WOMEN

Samson, David, and Solomon were not the only men to fall because of the opposite sex. Although not many ministers fail in this way, even one is too many. Beware of the woman who is always passing compliments, giving personal attention, or bestowing small favors.

Personal Morality. Only two sins in the Old Testament were not covered by sacrifice: murder and adultery. This should help us see the importance God places on personal morality. Although the Gentile Christians were excluded from some of the requirements the Jewish believers felt incumbent upon them, there was still a strong prohibition on sexual sins (Acts 15:20, 28, 29). They were included in the list of things that keep a person out of heaven (1 Corinthians 6:9, 10). Nothing so thoroughly and completely destroys a minister and his minstry as immorality.

The Appearance of Evil. The Bible teaches, "Abstain from all appearance of evil" (1 Thessalonians 5:22). This is the area of the minister's life in which this admonition most appropriately applies. Paying too much attention to a person of the opposite sex can lead to questions in the minds of others. Although it is true that "man looketh on the outward appearance, but the Lord looketh on the heart," it must be emphasized that man can only inspect the fruit by looking on the outward appearance. And Jesus said, "By their fruits ye shall know them" (Matthew 7:20).

Blameless. The first requirement listed in 1 Timothy 3 for a bishop is that he "must be blameless." Obviously, this does not demand perfection, but it does require that a minister so live that his personal life is without blame before the congregation or the community.

Conclusion

The emphasis in this chapter on two things—God's Word and prayer—is significant. The personal life of the pastor cannot be separated from these two important, dynamic elements.

THE FINAL AUTHORITY

God's Word Still Stands. Since the Bible is God's Word, we must accept it, not just theoretically but practically. It is universal. If it is not, then God needs to write a new book, or books—one for primitive people and one for educated people; one for urban people and one for rural people.

Should God update His message and write a book for this modern day and consult our modern philosophers? We totally reject that concept. But hasn't the church done exactly that?

No, God does not need to reevaluate the situation and provide a new book. We must reevaluate our approach to the ministry and come back to the Book.

The Bible's Teachings and Illustrations. If we diligently search the pages of God's Word, we will find all the instructions we need for every phase and facet of our ministry. Its authority is final. Its doctrine is pure. It must be applied to our life again and again: "But the word of the Lord was unto them precept upon precept, precept upon precept; line upon line, line upon line; here a little, and there a little" (Isaiah 28:13). God's Word must be laid on our lives like a pattern is laid on material, and our lives must be cut to the pattern.

The Example of Jesus. Every minister should make a careful and conscientious study of the life and teachings of Christ. We may never attain His quality, but we can certainly strive toward it. To have a lesser goal only increases our possibility of failure.

A THREE—STEP FORMULA FOR SUCCESS IN THE MINISTRY

The veteran missionary-evangelist Stanley P. MacPherson shared this formula for success in the ministry. It would be difficult, if not impossible, to improve upon it.

1. *A Godly Life.* Without a godly life, it makes little difference what we say. A godly life is the first requirement of the minister, and the final benediction on his ministry.

2. *Generous Amounts of God's Word and Prayer.* Every day the life of the minister should be saturated with God's Word and prayer. Not little snatches here and there, but large, daily diligent applications of both.

3. *Persistence.* In every area of life where man wishes to excel, persistence is important. This is true of the athlete, the scientist, the inventor, the businessman, and the minister. Stick-to-it-iveness is a characteristic every minister needs to develop. Often the only difference between success and failure is that one minister held on longer than the other.

If we live a godly life, if we daily spend generous time in God's Word and in prayer, and if we diligently stay on the job, success in the ministry will be our portion, and we will one day hear, "Well done, thou good and faithful servant."

Suggested Reading

Brandt, R. L. *Praying With Paul.* Grand Rapids: Baker Book House, 1966.

Clark, Wayne C. *The Minister Looks at Himself.* Chicago: Judson Press, 1957.

Olford, Stephen F. *Heart-cry for Revival.* Old Tappan, NJ: Fleming H. Revell Company, 1962.

Ravenhill, Leonard. *Why Revival Tarries.* Minneapolis: Bethany Fellowship, Inc., 5th ed., 1962.

Riggs, Ralph M. *The Spirit-filled Pastor's Guide.* Springfield, MO: Gospel Publishing House, 1948.

4

The Pastor
and
His Family

DELMER R. GUYNES

The Divine Ideal

Idealism in the establishment of a model is a concept well understood by the American community. Practically every industry wishing to sell its goods seeks out an ideal and projects a model use of its product. This technique is very effective in sales growth.

These ideals are only rarely attained, as we often learn after a hasty purchase. A new suit just never seems to fit quite as well as it is modeled in the clothing store. The ideal vacation, home, or position never seems to materialize quite as we anticipated. This is not to say, however, that the ideal represented in the model is not of great worth. It is always important to see the ultimate possibilities of our lives so, we may constantly keep our projections right and our aims high.

Models in the Scriptures are of great consequence to us, especially if they represent the divine ideal. They are important for two reasons: (1) They keep our eyes focused on high-level goals toward which we can constantly work; otherwise we are satisfied with far less than we can attain. (2) They represent that which in God through His resources is attainable. Therefore, as we focus on the divine ideal we are not confronted with a hopeless task. Divine resources are made available to us by which the ideals set forth in the Word of God are attainable.

The man of God and his family are set forth, especially in New Testament teaching, in rather idealistic terms. Since God has provided

Delmer R. Guynes, Ed.D., is the China representative, Division of Foreign Missions, Assemblies of God.

these ideals for His children, they are important and by His grace attainable. A very significant model for the minister's family is described in the following extended passage from Ephesians:

> Wherefore be ye not unwise, but understanding what the will of the Lord is. And be not drunk with wine, wherein is excess; but be filled with the Spirit; speaking to yourselves in psalms and hymns and spiritual songs, singing and making melody in your heart to the Lord; giving thanks always for all things unto God and the Father in the name of our Lord Jesus Christ; submitting yourselves one to another in the fear of God. Wives, submit yourselves unto your own husbands, as unto the Lord. For the husband is the head of the wife, even as Christ is the head of the church: and he is the saviour of the body. Therefore as the church is subject unto Christ, so let the wives be to their own husbands in every thing. Husbands, love your wives, even as Christ also loved the church, and gave himself for it; that he might sanctify and cleanse it with the washing of water by the word, that he might present it to himself a glorious church, not having spot, or wrinkle, or any such thing; but that it should be holy and without blemish. So ought men to love their wives as their own bodies. He that loveth his wife loveth himself. For no man ever yet hated his own flesh; but nourisheth and cherisheth it, even as the Lord the church: for we are members of his body, of his flesh, and of his bones. For this cause shall a man leave his father and mother, and shall be joined unto his wife, and they two shall be one flesh. This is a great mystery: but I speak concerning Christ and the church. Nevertheless, let every one of you in particular so love his wife even as himself; and the wife see that she reverence her husband.
>
> Children, obey your parents in the Lord: for this is right. Honor thy father and mother; which is the first commandment with promise; that it may be well with thee, and thou mayest live long on the earth. And, ye fathers, provoke not your children to wrath: but bring them up in the nurture and admonition of the Lord.
>
> Servants, be obedient to them that are your masters according to the flesh, with fear and trembling, in singleness of your heart, as unto Christ; not with eyeservice, as menpleasers; but as the servants of Christ, doing the will of God from the heart; with good will doing service, as to the Lord, and not to men: knowing that whatsoever good thing any man doeth, the same shall he receive of the Lord, whether he be bond or free.
>
> And, ye masters, do the same things unto them, forbearing threatening: knowing that your Master also is in heaven; neither is there respect of persons with him (Ephesians 5:17 through 6:9).

Although this passage cannot be limited to a minister's home only, it is helpful to think of the entire passage as reflecting various dimensions of the minister's home.

The ideal minister's home is a home established by the will of God.

There is open communication between family members, and the nature of that communication is highly spiritual, Biblical, and positive. Spiritual fullness is the primary motivation within the family relationships. An attitude of thankfulness for all things is very evident, and the relationship between members is characterized by submission one to another within and without the lines of authority.

In the vertical relationships that develop up and down the authority levels of the home, there are overriding demonstrations of sacrificial love, especially in the use of authority. Reverence and honor are the proper, respectful attitudes of those who recognize the divinely established authority for the home. Fathers are to assume teaching, nurturing roles that do not anger children, and children are to obey parents as a matter of conscience and faith toward God. Workers in the home are to serve respectfully as unto the Lord, and they are to be treated kindly without threatenings.

The apostle Peter emphasizes that each individual stands independently before God both in access to the resources of grace and in the bearing of responsibility for behavior.

> Likewise, ye wives, be in subjection to your own husbands; that, if any obey not the word, they also may without the word be won by the conversation of the wives; while they behold your chaste conversation coupled with fear. Whose adorning, let it not be that outward adorning of plaiting the hair, and of wearing of gold, or of putting on of apparel; but let it be the hidden man of the heart, in that which is not corruptible, even the ornament of a meek and quiet spirit, which is in the sight of God of great price. For after this manner in the old time the holy women also, who trusted in God, adorned themselves, being in subjection unto their own husbands: even as Sarah obeyed Abraham, calling him lord: whose daughters ye are, as long as ye do well, and are not afraid with any amazement.
>
> Likewise, ye husbands, dwell with them according to knowledge, giving honor unto the wife, as unto the weaker vessel, and as being heirs together of the grace of life; that your prayers be not hindered (1 Peter 3:1-7).

It is important to note from this passage that God is no respecter of persons and will bring each into account for his behavior in the family relationship. Few, if any of us can feel we have attained the divine ideal. However, we learn from our mistakes and shortcomings and press on toward the high purposes for which we are created in Christ Jesus (Philippians 3:12-14; Ephesians 2:10).

If the minister and his family are to be representative of that which is ideal for the Christian community, then these Biblical sketches of the ideal family are of serious import to him for his home. This is underscored heavily in Paul's writings to Timothy in which he states that the qualifications for ministry as an overseer (bishop) of the house of God include assuming the proper Biblical responsibilities toward his family:

> A bishop then must be blameless, the husband of one wife, vigilant, sober, of good behavior, given to hospitality, apt to teach; not given to wine, no striker, not greedy of filthy lucre; but patient, not a brawler, not covetous; one that ruleth well his own house, having his children in subjection with all gravity; (for if a man know not how to rule his own house, how shall he take care of the church of God?) (1 Timothy 3:2-5).

The Dynamics of the Pastor's Home

A DESCRIPTION OF HOME DYNAMICS

A pastor's home seldom contains a static or unchanging atmosphere. Most homes are anything but motionless; they are generally very dynamic. There is continuous activity or change. The activity can be both *overt* and *covert*, for there is generally a great amount of external and internal action taking place.

Covert dynamics (the internal, often unnoticed behavior and activity of individuals) are sometimes the most constructive or destructive elements in the pastor's home. Overt behavior produces its own kind of dynamics and often becomes the trigger for many kinds of interaction. A home in these stressful days must be a place that can stand a great deal of tension and pressure and also provide the opportunity for these to be expressed in positive, meaningful ways.

THE INTERNAL DYNAMICS OF A HOME

Personalities. The internal dynamics of a home are affected by the personalities within the home, the atmosphere of the home, the material and cultural dimensions of the home, and, above all, its spiritual dimensions. Primarily, it is people that make a home. There is the husband and father, wife and mother, the son(s) and/or daughter(s), and there may be others who become a part of the family structure in the minister's home.

It is very important to note that in the economy of God, people are different. We have observed an identical set of twins, and yet discovered that while there are very close physiological similarities, there are usually very significant psychological differences. One person is forthright, outspoken, and deductive in his approach to life; the other is shy, quiet, and inductive in his orientation to life.

The background and early home experience of husband and wife will largely determine the basic approach to family living in their own home. Their particular perceptions of individual behavior in the home, in the church, or in other relational involvements of which each is a part will largely be determined by distinct temperament factors.

The pastor must recognize the distinctiveness of the people in his home; and upon recognizing individual distinctives he must make it his business to understand the needs of each unique person. The head of each household must apply himself diligently to understanding the varying dispositions, temperaments, and personality characteristics of those within his house. The exhortation of Proverbs 4:7, "With all thy getting get understanding," is a definite imperative. It is not only the spiritual dimension that will be of serious consequence to the well-being of his home, but the human dimension as well. The personality differences of each individual in the home will produce dynamics that are of great significance.

A most helpful study in this area of personality differences is the study of human temperaments. The late Dr. O. Hallesby has written a simple yet meaningful explanation of the four basic human temperaments in his book *Temperament and the Christian Faith.*[1] Others have taken his work and amplified it to almost an unrecognizable degree; nevertheless, it and the amplifications offer helpful material in understanding individual differences within the family unit.

Atmosphere. The atmosphere of the home is of great consequence. It is in this area that the pastor's own temperament as well as that of his wife are most likely to strongly influence the home. This can be good and bad, positive and negative. If the man of the house is more buoyant and lively and joy is his natural expression towards life, it is not unlikely that the home will reflect the same attitude. If, on the other hand, the head of the house is introverted and somewhat nega-

---

[1] See Suggested Reading.

tive in his approach to life, this too is likely to be reflected in the atmosphere of the home. It is here that the wife's temperament and sense of family responsibility come clearly into focus. The wife, generally speaking, is more closely integrated into the home scene and is therefore a greater determiner of the internal atmosphere of the home. It is very important that husband and wife understand their individual temperaments and the effect these have on their home's atmosphere.

The atmosphere of the home should reflect cleanliness and orderliness. Perhaps the meticulous order that some feel to be essential is not necessary since there should also be a comfortable and relaxed atmosphere. Certainly there should be the pervading atmosphere of prayer, praise, and reverence for the Word of God. It should not seem unnatural for open expressions of prayer and praise to be made frequently by all members inside the home.

The Scriptures are rather careful in emphasizing that the minister's home should reflect an atmosphere of hospitality to those who come within its gates ("given to hospitality," 1 Timothy 3:2). What tremendous blessing there is in finding a home setting with all the members of the family hospitably disposed toward each guest. All of those things that are helpful in reflecting a wholesome, spiritual, healthy, positive, clean, comfortable, buoyant atmosphere are important to a home and should be given attention by the husband, wife, and other family members.

The intrusions of the outside world into the home atmosphere through modern communication media are very consequential. The pastor must be sensitive to the influence of the various media. Television is likely to play a role in determining the atmosphere and should be controlled with discretion. It is by far the most pervasive medium for communicating a total idea; often times it projects something so vividly that little remains for the imagination. If care is not taken, it can absorb all the meaningful interaction within a home, leaving very little time and opportunity for wholesome family relationships.

Music should be, and is likely to be, a significant contributor to the home atmosphere. The music interests of the mother and father are likely to be in rather serious conflict with those of the children. Parents should be sensitive to the difference between what the children feel is interesting and easy to listen to, and their own tastes;

however, it should be understood that the atmosphere within the home must be maintained in a positive, wholesome, spiritual way. No one person's tastes should be allowed to dominate the entire atmosphere of the home, especially in a negative and unspiritual sense.

Material Dimensions. Several factors regarding the material dimensions of a pastor's home need to be kept in careful focus. It is important that the physical aspects of the pastor's home or house reflect a true sense of value. The pastor stands before his congregation and before the community as a spiritual leader whose primary concerns are for the spiritual well-being of his congregation and his family. Some pastors have placed such unbalanced emphasis on the material aspects of the home that the true sense of eternal perspective which Christians should have has been destroyed. It is important, however, that a pastor's family not be required to exemplify a vow of poverty and that being a part of the pastor's family does not deny the privileges and responsibilities of normal human living. Consequently, the pastor should take a reasonable amount of concern regarding the material factors in his home.

Preferably, the home should be located away from the church so it does not become the center of congregational traffic at service times. The church should provide its pastor with adequate living facilities. However, it is in the interest of both the pastor and church if the pastor may own his own home in a location of his choosing. In this way he will assume personal responsibility to maintain it and make sure it is in keeping with the needs of his family.

It is important to the internal dynamics of the pastor's home that the family feel they live in a reasonably comfortable and secure situation. The psychological and spiritual well-being of the pastor's family requires that each member be made to feel important to the church, important to the pastor himself, and consequently not relegated to an insignificant or obscure role. The pastor's wife should feel reasonably at ease with the facilities she has for entertaining guests, especially members of the congregation. It is essential that the pastor's children do not feel themselves to be second-rate citizens because of the kind of home in which they must live as the preacher's kids.

It may not be possible or feasible for the pastor to provide the very finest of material benefits in his home. However, he can certainly maintain and improve that which he has so it will be adequate for the needs of his family, exemplary to the members of his congregation, and an asset to the community in which he lives.

Cultural Dimensions. A minister is to be heavenly minded, but that does not necessitate total neglect of present cultural values. The internal dynamics of the home are greatly affected by cultural factors, and some pastors' homes are culturally deprived. There is much in the world that God has made that can and should be experienced, read about, seen, heard, and explored.

The quality of life in the home is often determined by the breadth of cultural opportunities available to the family. Those having grown up in a pastor's home have spoken of the positive influence that many guests and visitors exerted on their lives. They gained a broadened understanding of human nature and conduct. The most treasured memories of home sometimes are the occasions when guests have come and shared the rich background of their experiences. While the pastor's home should be maintained in such a way that Jesus always has preeminence, it is also important that there be enough cultural exposure that the children learn to function in a world of great variety. They must be able to relate to constantly changing cultural patterns for the sake of a viable Christian witness, if nothing more.

There should be good books to read and wisely selected television programs to watch, so that each may exert a positive and broadening cultural influence. The pastor's home should be a place where that which is positive, good, and culturally meaningful can be explored and entered into in a very meaningful way. This of itself will create a very positive dimension to the internal dynamics of the pastor's home and will help eliminate the cultural isolation that sometimes characterizes the children of ministers.

Spiritual Dimensions. The spiritual dimension of the home is of such consequence that it must have priority over all else. The pastor is a spiritual leader. He projects this image in his church; he projects this image in his community; and, it is important that he project himself as the spiritual leader of his home. It is not likely that his wife and children recognize in him the dynamics of spiritual ministry as readily as the church congregation does. They tend to know him too well. Familiarity in this instance does not necessarily bring contempt, but it does eliminate the possibility of a cover-up. One of the pastor's greatest challenges is to recognize the spiritual needs within his own home and to minister to them with the same deliberation and concern as he demonstrates toward the church congregation.

The pastor must make a determined effort to make sure his house is a house of prayer, a place where the Bible is read, and a home in which the Spirit of God is present and honored. The pastor's home is a most significant place for the display of the fruit of the Spirit by family members. This becomes vital to the positive internal dynamics of the home. The pastor, with his many responsibilities and pressures, needs special assistance in this area. With the intensity of his involvement in the church and the constant pressure to maintain a spiritual attitude toward the members of his congregation, he finds it psychologically easy to relax from this demand in the home. It is there he can "kick off his shoes" and "let his hair down," so to speak, and the resulting "sagging psyche" can produce unbelievably negative and unspiritual attitudes.

Family members should see in their father a spiritual leadership different from that which the church sees. Children will certainly resent a straight carry-over of that relationship to the home. They need to see spirituality lived out in everyday life. They need to see parents who know how to be a Christian witness in public and in private. They need to know that Christianity works at the very grass roots of human living and relationships. The pastor who can only project a spiritual attitude in the pulpit or in the church is creating for his family some very great conflicts in the development of their spiritual and emotional lives.

THE EXTERNAL DYNAMICS OF THE PASTOR'S HOME

The external dynamics of a home may be thought of as those factors affecting the home from the outside. In the case of a pastor, this involves the church and the church community. The pastor cannot be insensitive to this influence and, in turn, he must be aware of the influence his home will have or should have upon that church community.

There is also the community in which he resides. This may be a large city, a subdivision, a small rural community, or a combination of all. Each kind of community that touches the pastor's home will exert a distinct influence and must be taken into consideration.

The school life within the community is of great consequence. It is necessary for the pastor to be aware of this dynamic external dimension that will very largely determine a sizable percentage of the out-of-church activities and involvement of his family.

The Church. The pastor has been chosen by the church to provide spiritual leadership, and he owes a primary responsibility to the congregation of people who form his church. It must be understood and accepted that this congregation will have a rather direct influence on the quality of life in his home.

The pastor must decide how close he should bring his family group into that of the church. How much distance must his family have in order to retain their integrity as a family unit? There is no fixed principle here; however, the pastor must try to understand the needs of his family and seek to meet those needs without creating a contradiction between his family life and his church life.

Some congregations make a great demand upon the pastor's home. This must be understood and dealt with. On the other hand, there are churches where the pastor relates to the church and they to him without putting the entire family into the pastoral setting. This situation, while allowing the family some degree of freedom and liberty to maintain their own identities, may cause a sense of alienation from the spiritual life of the church. Whatever the circumstances may be, the pastor must realize his home environment will be greatly affected by the congregation to whom he ministers. The degree to which his family's ideals, convictions, opinions, and needs will be determined by those of the congregation will have to be evaluated deliberately, with full input from every person concerned. It is a healthy thing for the pastor to be able to talk openly of these things with his church board as well as with his family, so that some form of *modus operandi* may be agreed upon by all concerned.

The Community. The community in which the church exists and where the pastor's home is located cannot be ignored. Communities differ according to ethnic groupings and vocational or professional involvements. There are communities that are known for their intellectual atmosphere, others for their social atmosphere, many for their recreational activities, and an increasing number for their particular type of social problems. Larger communities are often stratified in varying degrees of social and intellectual levels, each having unique problems.

Political movements and the influences of other churches and religious bodies in a community are all significant as a pastor considers how his family relationships will be affected by these external factors. *The School.* There is nothing more singularly influential in determining the behavioral characteristics of children, and consequently of the entire family, than the educational institutions in a given community. The pastor's children will have to attend public or private schools. These will be highly structured educational and social entities that are often unyielding in religious matters. The pastor will find that the educational and sociological implications of these institutions have an increasingly direct bearing on his home and its well-being. A pastor must seek to bring these influences into proper perspective, relate them to the needs of his family, and then with great determination control, as far as possible, their influence on his family.

It is highly probable that the minister's home will be greatly influenced by what happens in the elementary, junior high, or high school in the neighborhood or community. The minister must attempt to evaluate these influences. It is very dangerous for a pastor to put his head in the sand, like the proverbial ostrich, and hide himself from the social and intellectual influences of the school systems.

Of such importance is the influence of the schools that the pastor-father should pay careful attention to what goes on in the local school system and to how this directly affects his own family as well as others in the church. He should provide as much input as he possibly can into the public education program. This is not only so he can exercise some control over the influences that are exerted by the educational institutions; it will also show his children that their father is concerned about these things and that he does indeed take a very aggressive and serious attitude toward the powerful influence these institutions impose on the Christian family.

In thesis research for a graduate degree at Southern Methodist University, the writer studied the attitudes of high school principals toward the religious beliefs of Assemblies of God children. The most significant findings had to do with the concern expressed by the principals about the lack of positive input from the Assemblies of God church community. Surely the pastor should take a leadership role in this area.

The Pastor and His Wife

Scripture is emphatic: Eve in God's divine purpose was created as a helpmate for Adam (Genesis 2:18). Solomon wisely said, "Whoso findeth a wife findeth a good thing, and obtaineth favor of the Lord" (Proverbs 18:22). The pastor who wants his ministry and his home to be successful in the right sense of the word will find there is no more dynamic factor than the role his wife will play. Consequently, it is of the utmost importance that the future pastor pay careful attention to the selection of a wife; then, having chosen and been chosen, he should pay careful attention to her needs.

THE MATTER OF CHOICE

It is true that there are many in the ministry today whose companions were already chosen when they entered or answered the call to the ministry. In such cases any reflections that relate to the choosing of a companion are superfluous. God takes the man where he is and, while the husband-wife team may not be the ideal one, the same grace of God that converts the soul and equips the man of God for ministry, works in these human relationships just as wonderfully.

God very often uses the natural selection processes for bringing man and woman together. Consequently, it should not be thought that a marriage determined before one's call and involvement in the ministry is in any wise inappropriate. If God calls a married man into the ministry, He does so with the full realization that this man is obligated to a wife. At that point it is up to the two individuals concerned to search out the grace of God that will enable them to fulfill in the most adequate manner the purpose God intends them to realize and accomplish. As a matter of fact, God is mindful of the man He calls long before the call comes. (See Psalm 139:13-17; Jeremiah 1:5; Ephesians 1:4.)

On the other hand, there are numerous occasions when young people feel the call of God prior to marriage and then can match the choice of a life's partner with their consciousness of divine direction. It is then incumbent upon the person to select a companion carefully in the light of divine guidance.

The story of the search for Isaac's bride, while not exactly typical of western cultural methods, contains some very meaningful indicators for those at this stage of life. The element of divine guidance in the bringing of Isaac and Rebekah together stands as a model procedure for the man of God who seeks to bring unto himself that one person who is to share all of his life's secrets and the most intimate of his inner feelings and concern for the work of God.

It is of primary consequence that one, in deference to Proverbs 3:5, 6, look to the Lord in confidence in this vital area of human relationship, leaning not upon human understanding alone but acknowledging his need for divine assistance. The Lord will surely direct the steps of one who so trusts Him in these matters.

The ministry is not an easy road, and it requires singleness of heart and purpose. Contradiction between the minister and his wife in the work of the Lord brings problems that sometimes are beyond human capacity to handle. More often than not the results are either a very ineffective ministry or the abandonment of the ministry entirely.

What should a prospective minister look for in choosing a companion? Aside from natural factors that seem to take care of themselves, one should seek a companion whose life is as open to the things of God as is his own, one whose desire is to do the will of God and to work in God's harvestfield, one who can take a secondary role in the public relationships in which the pastor is involved but who also can take individual initiative in those areas where the home and ministry require it.

It is impossible to give exact directions as to what one must do in the selection of a wife when the ministry is in focus. However, it should be apparent that each individual who feels a call from God on his life should give consideration to matrimony only in the light of that divine call. It is too much to ask his companion or himself to be unequally yoked together in this, the most significant of all involvements.

RELATIONSHIPS IN THE HOME

According to 1 Peter 3:7, the husband's responsibility is to relate to his wife according to knowledge so his prayers will not be hindered. It is fundamental to this relationship that the husband understand that a woman has needs that are as authentic and genuine as those of his own male nature. It is important in the home that the minister love his wife and make that love apparent to all concerned. The children must know he loves her; the church must know he loves her; and, above all, she must know he loves her.

It is true that the work of the Lord always comes first. However, it is not true that the minister is to be so involved with the work of the Lord that his wife goes unattended and uncared for (1 Corinthians 7:5). In this entire passage (1 Corinthians 7:1-40) the apostle Paul so recognizes the binding effects of marriage that he advises extreme caution in committing one's life in holy matrimony. The ministry brings great pressures on the marriage relationship.

In Luke 14:26,27, Jesus puts family and personal relationships in their proper perspective for those who would be His disciples. He states that a man must "hate" his wife. The word *hate* is used in a comparative sense, meaning to "love less than." In reality, the best meaning is that Jesus must be put in proper relationship to all earthly affections. The passage does not imply that the wife should be despised or forsaken, or that the children should be forsaken; rather, it means that devotion to Jesus and His work should be given the place of priority. In reality, the verses imply that Jesus must be placed between each human relationship. If Jesus has the primary consideration, even in this most human of relationships, He will enhance it and make it everything it needs to be to each party concerned.

RELATIONSHIPS IN THE CHURCH

It is always discouraging to see a wife who preempts her pastor-husband in the church activities. This kind of behavior is largely due to the husband's passive attitude and to the quality of the relationship between them. The husband is the head of the wife as Christ is the Head of the Church (Ephesians 5:23). It is important to the church's relationship to Christ that it is the husband who leads the way in the husband-wife relationship. This does not preclude the possibility that the wife may very well be strong in her own right and in the role she fulfills in the Lord's work.

It is important to the church and to the wife that the pastor reflects his love for his wife in the congregation, even as Christ loved the Church and gave himself for it (Ephesians 5:25). It is contradictory to the purpose of Christ for His church when a pastor neglects his wife in the work and fellowship of the local church. The congregation needs to look upon them as a team, as a single entity in the work of God, though they will often not fulfill the same function.

It is a serious matter for the husband to embarrass his wife in the congregation or to cause her in any way to feel herself to be the object of ridicule or contempt. Great care should be taken that she not be made the brunt of jokes or illustrations from the pulpit.

Mrs. Pastor should not be forced by her husband or the church into a prescribed role. She should be allowed to fit normally into the wife's place within the congregation. As far as leadership opportunities for her are concerned, she should have the privilege of responding to these in whatever way she feels best.

It is important in a church where there may be a dominant female personality in the congregation that the pastor not allow such female dominance to take precedence over the role his wife plays in her relationship to him in the church. While there is room in the church for women in leadership roles, this should very carefully be administered by the pastor so his wife is not projected into a secondary relationship with him.

RELATIONSHIPS IN THE WORLD

The eyes of a community are very often focused, in the ethical and moral sense, on a minister and his family. The manner in which a pastor relates to his wife, in the context of the worldly society in which he lives, is of great consequence. While we follow the scriptural injunction that we are in the world but not of it (John 17:11,14), yet we "provide things honest in the sight of all men" (Romans 12:17). The husband-wife relationship becomes one of the finest opportunities for the reflection of spiritual integrity together with moral and ethical wholeness.

A serious problem develops from the philosophy that the home and the church are the contexts for the projection of spiritual attitudes and patterns of behavior, while in the worldly context there should be a secular or worldly projection in order to touch the world at its own level. This produces a conflict between the behavior of the husband and wife in the home and that which relates to the world. This temptation to behave within the worldly context in a worldly way carries its own kind of hazards, as many "shipwrecked" minister's homes can verify.

The pastor and his wife should not allow pressures to meet the worldly standards of dress, entertainment, and unspiritual behavior to control their activities in the world. An effort to satisfy the critical appraisal of a worldly society by either the husband or wife can be disastrous. It is not necessary or healthy for the pastor and his wife to find their relaxation and recreation in the context of worldly associations which preclude the exercise of spiritual attitudes.

It is important to the wife and the husband, and certainly to the church, that the relationship of the pastor and his wife demonstrates Christ-honoring characteristics in every circumstance. The pastor manifests good Christian grace when he makes his wife to feel secure, cared for, and important in the home, in the church, and in those necessary worldly associations into which a pastor in almost any community must enter.

The pastor must not be seen by the community as a "man about town," while his wife is the "keeper at home." This image always gives a negative dimension to the pastor's character. The more he is identifiable in the community with his wife, the better for himself and for his church.

Serious marital difficulties arose for one minister and his wife because of the social pressure she felt to buy beautiful and expensive clothing beyond the extent of their limited budget. The husband was unable to control this urge and became financially obligated to the point that he had to supplement his income by outside activity. The distance between the two became so great that periodically a real temptation arose to separate and go their individual ways. Thankfully, they were able to come to grips with the real problem, deal with it, and are today happily married and performing well in the ministry.

A young minister and his wife, on another occasion, found that a sense of irresponsibility and poor management on the part of the husband forced the wife to find outside employment. This in turn exposed her to the overtures of worldly people. It was necessary to her employment, or at least she felt it so, that she should dress and behave in a manner requested by her employer. Over a period of time she lost her identity with the church community entirely and with it her identity with the ministry of her husband.

One young minister's wife, a very attractive young lady, was naively unaware that, as she moved about through the community and surroundings of their pastorate, she was the object of flirtation from a number of sources. Misunderstanding the intent of some communications from men in the community, she responded flippantly and became a source of many problems to her home, to the ministry of her husband, and to his relationships with the church. It is very necessary for the wife of a pastor to understand the limits of friendly interchange with members of the opposite sex and the degree to which this can be misunderstood. The same cautions that are noted for the wife in her relationships with persons of the opposite sex also hold true for the pastor himself.

THE NEEDS OF A MINISTER'S WIFE

The emphasis put on so-called "women's liberation" is prominent in today's world. He focus on equal rights in the marital relationship and equal function in every circumstance are certainly appropriate goals. However, it is of great importance that the Biblical perspective of the marriage relationship—the minister's role and that of his wife—be clearly understood. There is no suitable alternative offered by sociological evolution or psychological theory to the Biblical precept for a meaningful and satisfying relationship between husband and wife.

According to the divinely revealed truth of Scripture, the husband is the responsible head of the wife and the family. He needs to love his wife even as he loves himself and as Christ loved the Church, giving himself for it. The wife must honor her husband and obey him in the truest sense of the term. This is obedience that is not purely servile to the master's voice, but rather a humble recognition of the line of authority that extends from God to the husband, to the wife, and to the children—in that order.

Both husband and wife should recognize that they have equal access to the grace of God and that each may draw upon that resource without concern for a divine preference toward male dominance. The availability of the divine resource is greatly affected by a mutual willingness to assume responsibility for one another. The husband must make room for his wife's spiritual growth. He should be concerned for her emotional, psychological, and intellectual growth as well. Ministers' wives have great capacities for growth in these areas and should be encouraged to pursue those goals that will give meaning and a sense of accomplishment.

The needs of a pastor's wife differ only in degree from the needs of wives in other circumstances. Such needs are nonetheless both real and significant to the persons involved. Her need for a true identity is important and her husband, the pastor, should make sure he gives her this identity without thrusting her into a place of undue prominence that would be resented by other persons in the congregation. Her needs for basic physical and emotional security are important and, while she is spiritually motivated and trusting in the Lord, it is important to her that her pastor-husband make every effort to maintain her in such a way that she need not fear physical, psychological, or spiritual loss.

The Pastor and His Children

THE NEEDS OF CHILDREN

It is interesting to observe a family with several children and to discover, as we all have, that no two are alike. In families where there are identical twins, it may be very difficult from a physiological viewpoint to tell which is which, yet psychologically each has his own distinct personality and temperament. Once the real personalities are clearly projected in the minds of those who know them, only rarely are physiological similarities mistaken. Psychological distinctives tend to make an even stronger impression than physiological ones. Every child brings his own unique contribution to the dynamics of the home. Each has his own general needs much like others, but each also has some that are unique and special.

The wise pastor does not overlook the needs of his children because of his concern for his congregation. Children go through developmental stages, whether they are a pastor's children or otherwise, and there are peculiar needs that relate to each of these stages.

Children generally need security. They need a great deal of understanding and love. They need friendship. They need opportunity for physical involvement. As they are developing, they need a certain amount of privacy, especially with respect to the congregation and the community. A "fishbowl" experience has caused some ministers' children to react negatively to the ministry because they were constantly under observation by the people to whom their father ministered. The pastor should look on his children as normal human beings whose needs require attention as much as those of the children of his parishioners.

It is not uncommon for church folk to feel the pastor's children ought to be somewhat special and behave themselves better than other children. The pastor should project an attitude toward his children and his congregation that will reduce this kind of emphasis. Certainly the pastor's home, including his children, is to be exemplary, but to allow this to be overemphasized can produce such negative reactions that the minister's children will have little interest or concern about spiritual things and the role of the church.

THE POTENTIAL IN CHILDREN

A minister ought to keep in focus the fact that his children, under normal circumstances, hold a greater potential for ministry involvement than he himself does. This is true, if for no other reason, than that they build on the foundation of their parents' ministerial experience and do not have to start at the zero level like those who have not had such an advantage. This potential for ministry is not automatic, nor does it in any way replace the need for a divine call and those spiritual qualifications that must come uniquely to each individual.

It is well for the pastor and his wife to maintain their home in such a way as to enhance the ministerial potential of their children if God should choose to use them in this way. The son or daughter of a good minister can be far advanced in the work of God if the home is conducive to their preparation for future ministerial involvement.

Aside from ministerial potential, it will usually be true that the children of ministers hold high levels of potential for many other kinds of meaningful involvement. This has been apparent in that throughout the years, children from ministers' homes have gone into worthy professions in which they have served with distinction. This may largely be due to the fact that the minister's orientation is to intellectual study and to good human relationships in the church and in the home. Therefore, whatever field of endeavor a minister's child may enter, he will very likely have an advantage over those who have not had the privilege of being reared in such circumstances.

It is very important that the minister, without doting on his children, do whatever he can to enhance the potential of each. A minister will have ministered well to his congregation and to his home if he has established such a dimension of family living that his children will exceed him in their effectiveness, whether in the ministry or in whatever profession or vocation they may choose.

CHILDREN AND THE KINGDOM OF GOD

God has no grandchildren. The children of Christian ministers do not automatically become saints. We understand the necessity of the "new birth." However, the right kind of pastoral home should be very influential in bringing children to the experience of personal salvation.

Pastors and their wives should recognize that as their children come to know the Lord Jesus Christ and are children of the Kingdom, they are as important to the kingdom of God as are the mother and father. Parents need to understand that they have only temporary stewardship responsibilities for their children, and when these children are indeed born again they belong to their Heavenly Father who has a divine purpose for their lives. This purpose is just as genuine and real as that which He has for each parent's life. It is therefore important that parents give place to the divine purpose in their children's lives. Their children need supportive assistance that will enable them to move into the will and purpose of God with liberty and freedom. It is God who seeks to accomplish His good will in their lives and to give them the guidance and grace they need (Philippians 2:13).

Children of the Kingdom become the raw material for His workmanship, and God begins the work of grace in their lives as distinctly and emphatically as in the lives of parents (Ephesians 2:10). It is not uncommon for parents to ignore this fact and to feel they are solely responsible for the total product of what their children may become. It is important that children learn early in life that God's projections for their lives are of a higher nature than their own or those of their parents.

OTHERS IN THE HOME

It is not uncommon for ministers to feel they must make their homes accessible to ministers, relatives, friends, needy persons, or employees. This is the hospitality that is spoken of as one of the requirements for ministerial leadership. The effect this has on the family and the relationships in the home is of genuine consequence.

There are pastors who feel it a serious obligation to make room for needy persons and to provide for them at least a temporary facility.

This is certainly exemplary as it relates to the hospitable attitudes of a minister. It may, however, be disastrous to his family if he doesn't do it with great caution as well as with his family's consent. The pressure of having guests in the home normally does not fall on the pastor but on his wife and children. While they may have learned not to complain or grumble, they may feel themselves constantly relegated to makeshift arrangements that give them a sense of impermanency within their own home. This is difficult for children over a long period of time and especially as they reach adolescence.

However, bringing guests into the home can often add a great dimension to its atmosphere. Guests should be carefully selected with a reasonable level of assurance in the mind of the pastor that he is not exposing his family to unpleasant circumstances. In such cases, before extending hospitality to guests the husband should defer to his wife for her concurrence.

Sometimes there are others, such as members of the extended family, who will be invited to live in the pastor's home for a period of time. The mother or father of either husband or wife, foster children, dependent relatives, and even married children and grandchildren may reside within the home. The pastor and his wife need to understand the dynamics of this situation so that it will not be allowed to hinder the ministry or the atmosphere of the family situation. When such circumstances exist for which there is no desirable alternative, the grace of God is a sufficient resource for resolving difficulties that may develop. A person in the home on a long-term basis who does not understand the complications of ministerial involvement, can at times cause real conflict to develop and affect the ministry or the home atmosphere. It is equally true, however, that many of the guests in the minister's home will add their own meaningful dimension to a happy home if given opportunity to do so.

There are occasions when employees will be serving in the home. In American culture, it is unlikely that a pastor will have servants, as is common in many foreign cultures. However, there will be occasions when special help will be hired. This is more likely to be domestic help but may include office assistance, nursing, and child care. The arrangement may be an extended one and on some occasions it may be advisable to have the person live permanently in the home. If this can be properly and meaningfully done within financial limitations, it need not be thought of as an extravagance.

The concern, however, has to do with the presence of this person in the home and how he/she may influence its atmosphere. The choice of an employee in the home, even for child care, should be of serious consequence to a minister and his family. It should be recognized that such a person will have access to the entire home. He or she will come to understand all that happens through many kinds of observations. The home will be exposed to such a person and to his/her influence both inside and outside the household.

It is important that the pastor adequately pay for the services rendered. He does not need a reputation as a profiteer who uses members of his congregation for personal advantage. It is also of consequence that a pastor behave circumspectly with regard to domestic or child-care employees in the home. No opportunity for reproach upon the home, the pastor, his ministry, or the congregation should be provided because of an unwise situation that could develop.

The extended presence in the home of an attractive or capable woman can sometimes provide a serious threat to the wife. She may be reluctant to admit this but she might develop extreme insecurities in her relationships. Rather serious emotional problems have developed out of some such arrangements. If such a person is to be brought into the home on any basis other than a casual one, it should be the wife's prerogative to establish the long-term basis of the relationship.

The Pastor's Calling

The broader aspects of the ministerial calling are dealt with in another chapter in this book. It is important, however, that the call of the minister be brought into an adequate perspective with regard to his family.

PERSONAL COMMITMENT

The focal point of the activities of the pastor, his wife, and his family, should be the fulfillment of the call God has put upon his life. It then becomes necessary that the minister himself establish the dimensions of that call and what his individual commitment must be. Such commitments should be clearly communicated to the family so there will never be any questions about where priorities lie.

The call of God does not exclude one's wife and children. The relationships of a family are so divinely instituted as to include the family in any call to ministry. While it may be true that the wife and family will often perform a secondary function, it should always be recognized as supportive to the divine purpose for the head of the household.

Luke 14:26 sets forth the commitment to discipleship in rather awesome terms. Jesus says: "If any man come to me, and hate not his father, and mother, and wife, and children, and brethren, and sisters, yea, and his own life also, he cannot be my disciple."

As has been noted, the word *hate* is used in the sense of "loving less." Obviously, Jesus is saying that discipleship means giving priority in relationships to Jesus Christ. However, in the light of texts such as 1 Timothy 5:8, where Paul lays family responsibility heavily upon the Christian community, one cannot interpret Jesus' statements to suggest improper discharge of family responsibilities.

What is really intended is that a man called of God must put Christ first, before every human relationship including himself. This implies that Jesus and His calling have priority over human relationships and that the disciple relates to every member of his family through Jesus. This in reality does not diminish human relationships but always enhances them. The pastor who understands this can relate more significantly to the members of his family and to himself by having his priorities clearly in focus. He can then go about his ministerial calling without a sense of having neglected his family.

FAMILY COMMITMENT

Some ministers feel themselves so destined by God to accomplish a certain kind of ministry that they project themselves singularly into it with little regard for the members of their family. Thankfully, there are those who have that unique ability to bring their family with them into the realization of divine purpose. This latter position is the better of the two possibilities and constitutes a worthy ideal. It is a blessed thing when the pastor who feels the burden of ministry can bring his family with him. Wives and children who, without great compulsion, can feel themselves vital to the ministry and commitment of their husband and father rarely are embittered by the sacrifices they have to make. It is wonderful to see a pastor and his entire family committed to the call God has placed upon the family.

In all probability, the happiest families in the ministry are those who are able to come to a high level of family commitment to the call of God. This tends to eliminate those contradictory elements that seem to put a pastor into conflict between the demands of his ministry and those of his home and family.

Family commitment is largely accomplished by a positive approach to the ministry within the home context. The pastor who is constantly complaining about the hardships and vicissitudes of his calling can rarely bring his family into it. On the other hand, the pastor who sees the glory of God's call and faces it with eternal optimism, hope, faith, and love for the work and who sees the ultimate victory in difficult situations and becomes excited over the possibilities of what is happening in his ministry and in his church, will provide the dynamics that will move his family with him into God's will.

A great tragedy in some pastors' homes is the open negative conversation between husband and wife during a difficult period in the ministry. After a long period of hearing negative views the children take up the same attitude and generalize it to all of the ministry. The residual effect of this is to produce antipathy and mistrust toward the call of God. A minister ought to spare himself and his family the concomitants of this negative attitude, especially if he wishes to take them with him in his commitment.

Accessible Resources

DIVINE PURPOSE

The pastor and his family are of great importance in the overall program of God. It is important to the kingdom of God that not only the minister succeed, but that his family succeed and that each member of the family have a unique kind of success within the great plan and purpose of God. This divine purpose is always moving positively toward eternal goals and is a dynamic resource for the minister and his family. God has a powerful purpose for each life. It is not merely that which must be done for God but rather it is that supernatural power that sweeps one along with a mighty current. Wherever a family is caught up in the purpose of God, all the spiritual resources of God necessary to the fulfillment of that purpose are made accessible to them.

It should be understood that the divine purpose of God for a husband and father includes every member of the family until such time as the unique purpose for each member of the family comes into clear focus. It should also be recognized that no unique individual expression of divine purpose contradicts that which pertains to another life or to the collective entity of the family even though it may entail a separate kind of activity.

The pastor should think and pray in these terms, understanding that as he pursues the purpose of God for his ministry, he is bringing with him in this divine purpose his wife, his children, and those of his household. In so doing, he exposes them to the blessings of divine purpose as well as to some minor, temporal restrictions. He is making accessible to them, as well as to himself, possibilities in divine purpose that extend far beyond this life and on into eternity. Children often do not sense this, wives do not always sense it, and sometimes the pastor and his wife do not sense it for their family. God's purpose is so encompassing, yet so unique, that all those who are part of the household unit are swept along by its tide.

THE GRACE OF GOD

We have often limited the grace of God to that moment in spiritual experience when one comes as a sinner, confesses, and is forgiven. While this is the beginning of the work of grace, it is by no means its conclusion. The grace of God extends far beyond that initial moment of conversion.

There is no place where the grace of God is more desperately needed and more significantly accessible than in the family relationships of the minister. There is a measure of divine grace for each area of stress in the minister's home. He will do well to search the Scriptures to find those measures of grace and to learn how they are obtainable.

An outstanding minister, when asked what he would do differently if he had his family to rear again, said, "I believe I would give greater emphasis to the grace of God." In the minister's home, it is easy to stress regulations, requirements, control, and legality, so as to be in conformity with divine requirements and the requirements of the church and the community. However, it is extremely important that grace as a divine resource be a vital force in every minister's home, and that this wonderful expression of divine love and power in the full

breadth and depth of its meaning be the central theme around which
all the activities of the home revolve.

THE WORD OF GOD

The Word of God is the seed of faith, and faith brings divine resources into the human dimension. The Word of God should have
prominence in the home and should be spoken, sung, listened to, read
daily, honored, revered, and carefully obeyed. It is important that the
minister not only give attention to the Word of God in his ministerial
activities but also that he recognize the dynamics of the faith-building
Word in family relationships.

It is a blessing to the members of a minister's family if he can, with
spiritual insight, bring the truth of God's Word into their hearts in a
practical way. Often the children and wife of a minister feel his ministry is for the church and what they get from him must be received
in the church. They are never really able to draw from him, within
the context of the home, the kind of spiritual nurture they need. The
attitude they develop is that the pastoral role is very different from
the father's role. Perhaps this distinction is necessary to a degree, but
what a great blessing it is when a minister-father has the capacity to
break the Bread of Life to his congregation and his wife and children
as well.

It is also important that the minister learn to receive the ministry of
the Word from his family and to appreciate the truth of God as it is
spoken by his wife or children. What a dynamic dimension of spiritual well-being is established in a home where the Word of God is
honored, treasured, spoken, and heard in a reciprocal manner.

THE POWER OF INTERCESSION

These are days of multiplied theories and approaches to family life.
There are scores, perhaps hundreds, of books that deal with successful
family living and what it takes to develop the right kind of family atmosphere. Many of these are good and need to be studied carefully;
however, we need to also seriously consider those spiritual dynamics
that may not be mentioned or emphasized in these books. Fundamental to these is intercessory prayer.

At the human level we do not understand the factors of cause and
effect that are totally spiritual. Jesus did understand these and taught
by vivid precepts and exemplified by practice that cause-and-effect

formula which, in the kingdom of God, we know to be intercessory prayer.

More than any other single thing, Jesus taught His disciples to pray, to intercede, and to importunately ask. He gave amazing promises to those who would ask properly in His name. Consequently, there is no other resource of such significant relevance as that of intercessory prayer. How important it is to the well-being of the minister, his wife, and the members of his family when an atmosphere of intercession prevails in the home. It should be understood that it is right and proper for family needs to be taken to God in prayer and answers should be anticipated.

THE DIVINE HELPER

The Holy Spirit as the Comforter (the Paraclete or "One alongside to help") has been sent from the eternal Father to effect the eternal purpose of God in human experience. He is vitally interested in every facet of our lives as they relate to God's plan.

The family, the pastor's family, is a divine institution, as clearly set forth in Scripture as is the Church. It is through the family unit that God seeks to reveal His full-orbed love and wisdom. Consequently, the Holy Spirit is present to help bring about every desirable objective in the home. This is especially true in light of the fact that the pastor-husband-father is divinely called, the members of the family share this divine purpose, and they have individual potential in the great plan of God. What a fertile field for the Holy Spirit's help!

The family ideal set forth in the beginning of this chapter was essentially a spiritual one. Undoubtedly, the key to reaching the ideal is to recognize the work and ministry of that one single Person who can make it happen. The emphasis in Ephesians 5:17 through 6:9 is on understanding the will of God and allowing the fullness of the Holy Spirit to overflow into the family setting. This produces open communication, spiritual singing, a joyous and thankful attitude, submission one to another in family relationships, respect for authority, and deep sacrificial love in the administering of authority. It produces conscientious obedience, tender care for one another, and an attitude of humble servitude to others as unto Christ.

Spiritual fullness, the Pentecostal outpouring, great spiritual experiences, and the fruit and gifts of the Spirit are not only for the sanctuary of the church but also for the pastor's home and every member in it.

Suggested Reading

Adams, Jay E. "Shepherding God's Flock," *Pastoral Leadership*, Vol. 3. Presbyterian and Reformed Publishing Co., 1975.

Blackwood, Andrew Watterson. *Doctrinal Preaching for Today; Case Studies of Bible Teachings.* New York: Abingdon Press, 1956.

Colton, C. E. *The Minister's Mission: A Survey of Ministerial Responsibilities and Relationships.* Grand Rapids: Zondervan Publishing House, rev. 1961.

Douglas, William G. T. *Ministers' Wives.* New York: Harper & Row, 1965.

Hallesby, O. *Temperament and the Christian Faith.* Minneapolis: Augsburg Publishing House, 1962.

Maslow, Abraham H. *Motivation and Personality.* New York: Harper & Row, 1954. Second edition, © 1970 by Abraham H. Maslow.

Perry, Lloyd Merle. *A Manual for Biblical Preaching.* Grand Rapids: Baker Book House, 1965.

Riggs, R. M., A. G. Ward, E. S. Williams, and Charles E. Jefferson. *Pastoral Theology.* Springfield, MO: Gospel Publishing House, 1952.

Riggs, R. M. *The Spirit-filled Pastor's Guide.* Springfield, MO: Gospel Publishing House, 1948.

————. *A Successful Pastor.* Springfield, MO: Gospel Publishing House, 1931.

Thiessen, John Caldwell. *Pastoring the Smaller Church.* Grand Rapids: Zondervan Publishing House, 1962.

Truman, Ruth. *Underground Manual for Ministers' Wives.* New York: Abingdon Press, 1974.

5

The Pastor
and
His Denomination

LOWELL C. ASHBROOK

The Rise of Denominationalism

The Early Church began without the benefit or need of organization. As men sought to carry out the purpose of God in the church, however, they soon realized their limitations and the need of coming together for fellowship, counsel, and the strength that the unity of believers could bring.

The formation of church government began rather early in ecclesiastical history as the church had to deal with problems that arose from growth and expansion. The need to recognize or approve the ministries of an expanding church and to assure conformity to a doctrinal and ethical standard made it necessary for the church to select leaders who were called elders (Acts 15:4,6), or the presbytery (1 Timothy 4:14).[1]

These elders or presbyters met from time to time in conference with other leaders of the church to work out the problems that a growing church encounters. An outstanding example is seen when Peter preached the gospel at the house of Cornelius, a Gentile. Upon returning to Jerusalem, Peter was called before the leaders of the church to account for his unorthodox conduct. Peter gave an account of his ministry in the household of Cornelius, relating how the Holy Spirit fell upon them. "When they heard these things, they held their peace,

Lowell C. Ashbrook, D.D., is pastor of First Assembly of God, West Monroe, Louisiana.

---

[1]The words *elder* and *presbytery* are used to translate the same Greek word which is one term used to describe the office of the pastor. (See Acts 20:17, 28.)

and glorified God, saying, Then hath God also to the Gentiles granted
repentance unto life" (Acts 11:18). So a whole new area of outreach
was granted the gospel because of a meeting of the brethren who were
in positions of leadership.

From all accounts, both scriptural and secular, the first-century
church accepted, practiced, and earnestly taught the ethical requirements of the Christian faith. Even those Gentiles who prior to their
conversion lived very wicked and vile lives embraced the Christian
message with every assurance that, through Jesus Christ, God had
blotted out their past sins. In the case of those who failed to maintain
the Christian ethic and behavior, quick action was usually taken to
separate them from the body of believers.[2] An extreme example where
God's immediate judgment was manifested is that of Ananias and
Sapphira, as recorded in Acts 5:1-11.

The development of organization and the election of leaders was
quite rapid and paralleled the growth and spread of the Christian
church. Wherever Paul established churches, he left behind appointed
leaders. F. F. Bruce states:

> From the first, leaders were appointed in the Christian community
> whose functions were largely comparable to those of "elders" in Jewish
> communities of Palestine and other lands. When Paul and Barnabas
> planted churches in Asia Minor during their first missionary journey,
> for example, they appointed elders (Acts 14:23) in them all. Paul,
> writing to the Christians at Philippi, salutes the church in that city,
> together with its "bishops and deacons"—or to render the Greek terms
> by words of a different flavor, its "superintendents and ministers"
> (Philippians 1:1).[3]

The early writers of the first-century church mention a twofold
order of local government—the bishops and deacons of the Philippian
church and the Pastoral Epistles. In time, however, the local church
was ruled by a leading bishop. The church, of necessity, went through
various stages of development in the first and second centuries. By the
second century larger cities had one central church with its leading
figure, the bishop. The apostle James was an outstanding example; he

---

[2]Quoted from *The Spreading Flame*, by F. F. Bruce. Copyright © 1953, American
edition published by William B. Eerdmans Publishing Company. Used by permission.

[3]*Ibid.*, p. 65.

very clearly acted as the leading figure, or bishop, of the church in Jerusalem.

One of the great churches of that era was the church of Rome. In the latter part of the third century the various bishops of different churches began coming together for consultation and common action —often meeting in the city of Rome. The emergence of the strong central church of Rome, the Roman Catholic Church, brought the church ultimately under the direct influence of the emperor. Eventual abuses of power and dictatorial edicts that affected the church and the life of its adherents, led to the rise of reformers within the church. The best known of these was Martin Luther.

Latourette summed up in a brief statement the primary causes of the Reformation when he said:

> In a sense the emergence of Protestantism was the reaction of Teutonic peoples against religious control from the Latin South. It was revolt against the attempt of Rome to dominate those who had been won to the Christian faith in Northwestern Europe after the seventh century. These folks had accepted uncritically what had come to them. Now they were becoming self-conscious and were restive under the efforts of a corrupt papacy to exploit them to selfish advantage.[4]

One of the most striking features of the 200 years between 1500 and 1700 was the resumption of the worldwide spread of Christianity. By the middle of the 18th century, Christian communities were on all five continents and on many of the islands that fringed these continents. During the years of the great migration to the New World, adherents of the many new religious beliefs which came out of the Reformation came to America. These became the basis of the many denominations now found in the United States.

It was out of these various denominations that the leaders of the Pentecostal Movement came. A revival at the turn of the 20th century, in which spiritually hungry believers were filled with the Holy Spirit, eventually culminated in the formation of several Pentecostal denominations, one of which was known as The General Council of the Assemblies of God. This new group had its organizing convention in Hot Springs, Arkansas, in 1914.

---

[4]Kenneth Scott Latourette, A *History of Christianity* (New York: Harper & Row, Publishers, Inc., 1953), p. 700. Used by permission.

The Pastor's Identification With His Denomination

VALUE OF THE ASSOCIATION

The Answer to a Common Need. Every denomination has had its beginning as a few men of common persuasion came together for fellowship and the strength of unity to accomplish their particular goals.

> The denomination arose in answer to a need felt by the local churches. The churches voluntarily united for the purpose of undertaking larger endeavors in world redemption. The denomination is a fellowship of churches working together on a voluntary basis for the accomplishment of kingdom objectives mutually acceptable to the churches involved.[5]

There are several ways by which a pastor may have become a member of his denomination: (1) He may have been born into a family that had certain denominational ties and then simply grew to maturity in that particular church. (2) Without church or denominational background, perhaps he was "born again" into the family of God in a revival or regular church service and was thereby introduced to the denomination. (3) He may have, after reaching maturity, come to his denomination because its doctrine or church government appealed to him personally.

There are few people belonging to recognized church groups who do not feel the need for fellowship, mutual understanding, and help in accomplishing their spiritual goals.

> The spontaneous Holy Ghost outpouring which swept the world around the turn of the 19th century resulted in the establishment of a number of Pentecostal fellowships. Most of these did not come from the organizational efforts of any one man, but evolved as individuals, moved by the Holy Ghost, joined together in cooperative effort to do what they had not been able to do separately. This was true in the beginning of the Assemblies of God. Those who met in Hot Springs, Arkansas, April 2-12, 1914, to worship and to discuss their kindred zeal did not think in terms of forming another denomination. Spiritual interests and a desire to reach the world with the gospel stood far and above any wish for organization. It was out of this meeting, however, that the Assemblies of God was formed and has developed.[6]

---

[5]Franklin M. Segler, *A Theology of Church and Ministry* (Nashville: Broadman Press, 1960), p. 230. Used by permission.

[6]Thomas F. Zimmerman, *et al.*, *Modern Pioneer Manual for the Pioneer Pastor* (Springfield, MO: Assemblies of God Division of Home Missions, out of print), p. 10.

> We need a strong denomination of churches, closely knit together in
> (1) love, (2) sympathy, (3) understanding, and (4) in purposes and ef-
> forts.[7]

Those Who Remain Independent. It must be said, however, that
there are some individuals who cannot work under the seeming re-
straints of a denomination. Some of them are sincere and very fine
ministers, while others simply do not want to be bound by regulations, obligations, or personal commitments. Someone has said that
this so-called rugged individualism is sometimes only a screen to hide
a desire to rule or ruin. In his book *Partnership in Missions*, Morris
Williams underscores this attitude emphatically:

> Conceivably the work of the Great Commission could be carried out
> by individual believers, each working independently of the other. Some
> people prefer to work this way, but invariably they have to call on
> others to assist them in their vision. When this happens, you have an
> organization of sorts, but it is always an organization with the "inde-
> pendents" at the top of the pile calling the shots! You see,
> "independents" are not against organization. They are only against
> organization they cannot control.[8]

Every pastor must be fully persuaded that his doctrine and his goals
are right. If he can better proclaim that doctrine and fulfill his objectives within the structure of a denomination, he should align himself
with those who share similar goals of ministry and commit himself to
those objectives.

The Pastor's Obligation to His Denomination

It is impossible to belong to any kind of an organization without
assuming certain obligations to that organization. The minister who is
the pastor of a denominational church has automatically taken on responsibility to that denomination as well as to the church he pastors.

Loyalty. One collegiate dictionary defines loyalty as "the state or
quality of being faithful; faithfulness to engagements or obligations."
Each pastor accepts certain obligations to which he must be faithful
when he becomes a part of a denomination. His loyalty is primarily to

---

[7]L. H. Raney, *The Pastor's Place* (No publisher given, 1954), p. 38.

[8]Morris Williams, *Partnership in Missions* (Springfield, MO: Assemblies of God Division of Foreign Missions, n.d.), p. 35.

the principles and goals of the organization; he must become a part of that stated purpose and devote himself to the fulfillment of those goals within the boundaries of his own call and ministry.

> If the organization is to succeed in fulfilling its aims, special individual or group points of view and interests have to be subordinated to or harmonized with those of the whole body as such. Individuals have to find satisfaction and fulfillment in making the organized aim their own aim. They have to feel a genuine stake in the outcome, as affecting them. Such unity, such harmonizing, are not impossible, but neither are they spontaneous. They have to be striven for.[9]

This bond of loyalty does not mean that one must become a "parrot" or a mechanical man who only mimics edicts from the church's national or district headquarters. By no means does loyalty deny a pastor the right to individual direction given to him by God for the conduct of his ministry, as long as he does not violate either the doctrine of his denomination or its principles of life and conduct.

> I have never understood that a minister's loyalty to his denomination should blind him to the imperfections of the same, nor prevent him from doing his utmost to correct them. There is not a perfect religious organization on earth, and it is useless to look for such, but each minister should aim to make his church the very best. He should be loyal to those who are in authority over him.[10]

The loyalty of its pastors brings a unity and strength "to the denomination, which is, in reality, a fellowship of other churches of like faith and order."[11]

It is important to the denomination's well-being that its churches be loyal, and by this, of course, we mean the individual members of each local church. The pastor has the opportunity to build loyalty toward the denomination or to sow the seeds of disloyalty among the membership of his church. It would be better, if the pastor were in disagreement with the denomination, for him to leave his pastorate and seek ministry elsewhere than to bring about a break between the church and the denomination's leaders.

---

[9]Ordway Tead, *Democratic Administration* (New York: Association Press, 1945), pp. 12,13. Used by permission.

[10]A G. Ward, *The Minister and His Work* (Springfield, MO: Gospel Publishing House, 1945), p. 56.

[11]Segler, *A Theology of Church and Ministry*, p. 232.

Should a minister find himself out of harmony with his denomination, with its doctrines or its practices, it is ethical that he sever his relations and seek a field elsewhere. It is unethical for him to remain to bring disharmony among the brethren.[12]

The allegiance of a denomination's churches, then, is dependent in a large measure upon its pastors. If a pastor is loyal, the church will be loyal. If the pastor is not a strong organizational man, neither will his church lend its support to the denomination. Segler observed, "If a meaningful dialogue is to be kept up between the local churches and the denomination, the responsibility rests primarily upon the pastor."[13]

The pastor owes much to his denomination, for it has provided him opportunities for education, a place of ministry, and many tools and materials for his work. It also affords him the fellowship and encouragement of fellow ministers. Every minister should be loyal to the denomination that supplies him with such rich resources. Segler says this loyalty can be expressed in four ways:

(1) He should know the doctrines of his faith and uphold them faithfully, withstanding and exposing false teachings which arise. (2) He can show a fraternal spirit toward his fellow workers in positions of denominational leadership, seeking always for understanding and offering his encouragement. (3) He should familiarize himself with programs of various agencies of the denomination and lead his church to cooperate in them as far as it seems best to do so. (4) The pastor should unselfishly offer his service to the denomination as he is needed. He should not be ambitious for recognition nor use his position as a means of personal advancement.[14]

It must be kept in mind, however, that the denomination is a means to an end and not an end in itself. We do not mean to imply that by their loyalty every church and every pastor would become identical to every other church and pastor. Pastors and churches are unique. Each is distinct from all others, and any attempt to standardize them would in fact work against the denomination. "What is best for the local church is best for the denomination in the long run."[15]

---

[12]Ernest S. Williams, *A Faithful Minister* (Springfield, MO: Gospel Publishing House, 1941), p. 80.

[13]Segler, *A Theology of Church and Ministry*, p. 232.

[14]*Ibid.*, p. 233.

[15]*Ibid.*, p. 232.

Loyalty to one's denomination will also be expressed in financial support. One of the primary programs of a denomination is its missionary enterprise. Through organizational effort a worldwide thrust of evangelism and teaching ministries can be realized. No pastor has the moral right to stand between his church and his denomination in such a way as to keep his church from financial participation in these ministries. There are many other ministries and services rendered to its constituency by the denomination which must have the financial aid of its churches.

Upon receiving credentials from his organization, a minister at that moment is saying, "This is my church. I am now a part of it. I will give my life's energies and talents to do the work of God within the organization of which I have become a member." The fact that he has accepted ministerial recognition immediately obligates him to that fellowship. He does owe it something. He owes it the finest kind of life and ministry of which he is capable.

Positive Representation. The pastor has many rights, privileges, and a liberty of ministry, but he must always remember his obligation to his denomination. He is obligated to every other minister of that denomination to uphold its standards and doctrines. Every minister, in a sense, shares the ministry of every other minister of his fellowship. They have the right to expect the very best from each other.

Ernest S. Williams said, "Each minister who accepts ministerial credentials, by so doing pledges himself to represent his society in such a way 'that we all speak the same thing, that there be no division among us.' "[16]

Those who granted the minister his credentials did so in faith that he would properly represent both them and the denomination. This is a moral obligation that he assumed willingly and should faithfully fulfill. No man lives unto himself. Each is responsible to someone for his life, conduct, and message. No minister should resent having to give an account of his ministry. Paul said of himself, "Ye know what manner of men we were among you for your sake" (1 Thessalonians 1:5).

Paul knew that those to whom he ministered were watching his life and he had a responsibility to them. But he was also aware that he

[16]Williams, *A Faithful Minister*, p. 80.

was even more accountable to God, for he said: "As we were allowed of God to be put in trust with the gospel, even so we speak; not as pleasing men, but God, which trieth our hearts. For neither at any time used we flattering words, as ye know, nor a cloak of covetousness; God is witness" (1 Thessalonians 2:4, 5).

Certainly it is not asking too much of a pastor to live and minister in an upright, commendable, and acceptable manner among his peers. Paul said, "Ye are witnesses, and God also, how holily and justly and unblamably we behaved ourselves among you that believe" (1 Thessalonians 2:10). Someone once said that "responsibility without accountability could only lead to irresponsibility."

Every denomination has through its lifetime developed a certain image which is that total picture the public has of the organization. This image will include the scope of its humanity, the doctrines of the church, the kind of ministers it produces, the effectiveness of its total outreach, and the manner of life lived by its adherents.

The pastor is recognized first as a representative of his church. However, his first duty is to God, next to his family, then to his church, and after that to his denomination. Last in his list of obligations is his responsibility to his community.

As he lives and ministers before his congregation, a pastor certainly ought to convey the proper "image" of his denomination. Yet every man of God must also portray to the community outside the congregation a proper image. Those outside the church will receive a favorable impression of the denomination as the pastor faithfully lives and moves among the community.

Many things in a person's life contribute to the total image he projects. Not only is his manner of conducting worship and delivering a sermon essential, but the pastor's general attitude toward the faith of those "other sheep" outside his own domain is of utmost importance.

A pastor must be very careful of his public life—his conduct around the opposite sex, and the way he handles his business, pays his debts, and keeps his word. The minister and his family must have a good report from those outside the church, so it is important that he live within his income. The influence of some pastors has been greatly marred by a failure in this area and the subsequent problems that arise when unpaid debts accumulate. When the pastor fails in this way, the church's image suffers tremendous damage. It would be better for the minister to reduce his living standard than to bring the cause of Christ into disrepute.[17]

A pastor's manner of dress will convey some concept of the man, his church, and his denomination to the public. He should always be freshly shaven, well-groomed, and fully clothed when appearing before the public. He may not be able to wear expensive clothes, but there is little excuse for an untidy appearance.

THE RESOURCES OF THE NATIONAL ORGANIZATION

The Need for Additional Resources. The local congregation, with its limitations of size and community orientation, cannot always have sufficient knowledge and insight to carry out its ministry effectively. If the pastor is to be a faithful steward and adequately fulfill the ministry of the church, he will need other sources of materials and ideas as well as personnel. The most logical place to secure resources is the denomination's national headquarters. Unfortunately, the local church often fails to utilize the total potential of its own congregation by not seeking the aid available through its denomination's various boards and commissions.

The pastor who wants his church to achieve its full capability will also seek to learn from the experience of other pastors and churches. Alvin Lindgren said, "A wise pastor will expose himself and his people to the experience of other churches."[18] The successful pastor will be one who continually seeks more effective ways of serving his congregation and leading them in the fulfillment of their goals. He ought to keep abreast of the developments in his denomination and in the church world in general. If he has a teachable spirit, he will learn from many sources and become a skilled leader of his own congregation.

A Variety of Resources. Most denominations own and operate their own publishing house and produce large selections of periodicals, church school materials, books, and pamphlets. They also handle various other items and tools necessary for the smooth operation of the local church program. Every church should make its personnel

---

[17]Homer Kent, Sr., *The Pastor and His Work* (Chicago: Moody Press, 1963), p. 64.

[18]Alvin J. Lindgren, *Foundations for Purposeful Church Administration* (Nashville: Abingdon Press, 1965), p. 256. Used by permission.

aware of these materials and tools and encourage them to use these many aids to successful church work.

Every department and specialized program of the local church is usually represented by specialists at the national headquarters whose primary function is to provide promotional ideas to be used by the local church. These specialists are often available for consultation and can travel to district or local workshops and training sessions to bring help to the workers and leaders of local churches. Pastors should be alert to such opportunities for themselves, for members of the church staff, and for key personnel of the congregation.

It is not always possible for the local church to adopt the special programs prepared and promoted by the national departments of the denomination, but the pastor will be wise to review each program carefully and then determine which can be of benefit to his local church. The denominational programs play a prominent part in the life of the church. Much time, talent, and money are represented in any program developed and fostered by the denomination.

Sometimes the pastor may not find a great personal interest in a particular national program but members of his church staff or congregation may find it to be just the spark or help they need. A wise pastor should make certain, before he rejects a program, that he is not missing an opportunity to enlist his congregation in a worthy program of evangelism or spiritual growth.

WHAT THE PASTOR CAN EXPECT FROM HIS DENOMINATION

Since the pastor has an ethical responsibility toward his denomination, it is only right to believe that his denomination has certain responsibilities and obligations toward him. There ought to be a two-way flow of communication, respect, and love in every fellowship. The total group can be no stronger than the many individual units that make up the whole. It actually owes its existence to its churches and ministers and, therefore, must be cognizant of needs and seek means to provide those helps and guidance that will help to fulfill its stated purposes. "The denomination is a means to an end and not an end in itself."[19]

Leadership. One of the best methods of producing loyalty is to in-

---

[19]Segler, *A Theology of Church and Ministry,* p. 232.

spire it by leadership that is able to identify and communicate mutual beliefs and goals for the followers.[20]

Leaders may come to positions of leadership in a denomination either by appointment or by election. We recognize that God has set those in the church in positions of leadership by divine appointment, and we must learn to accept elections within an organization as the will and purpose of God. Romans 12:6-8 and 1 Corinthians 12:28 both speak of divinely appointed positions of leadership: "Having then gifts differing according to the grace that is given to us . . ." (Romans 12:6); "He that ruleth . . ." (Romans 12:8); "And God hath set some in the church, first apostles, secondarily prophets, thirdly teachers, after that miracles, then gifts of healings, helps, *governments*, diversities of tongues" (1 Corinthians 12:28, *italics added*).

Pastors may rightfully look to their denominational leaders for spiritual excellence. The leaders should convey a bold, aggressive, and spiritual image and the sense of well-being and confidence that under God we can and will fulfill our stated goals and mission.

Guidance. There is a need today for that spiritually dynamic leadership that inspires the young and less experienced minister. This is especially true in the area of personal morality, as our generation is bombarded with all sorts of immorality which affects every segment of life. W. Curry Mavis speaks directly of the problem:

> Moral idealism is low in all aspects of life. The whole situation is made even more crucial by the fact that thousands of pulpits are quiescent on basic issues of morality because of the fear of offending contributors.[21]

The young pastor feels strengthened when he can look to the leadership of his denomination and see men of faith and action who provide a sense of direction to the organization.

Assistance. Most young people need both encouragement and assistance to prepare for and fulfill the call God has placed on their lives. The denomination may offer training programs through the local church which often form the foundation for later training in one of

---

[20]Jesse K. Moon, *The Five "W's" and "H's" of Organizational Loyalty* (Waxahachie, TX: Southwestern Assemblies of God College, 1976), pp. 2,5.

[21]W. Curry Mavis, *Beyond Conformity* (Winona Lake, IN: Light and Life Press, 1958), p. 78. Used by permission.

the denominational colleges. Home study courses are offered to help train the young minister who is denied the opportunity of formal training. A constant stream of ideas, suggestions, helps, and tools will assist the pastor in the promotion of all phases of his ministry.

Perhaps the greatest need for assistance in the life of the minister is in the first few years of his ministry. Getting started is not always an easy path. For some it is extremely difficult. As talents and gifts are developed and his ministry is more in demand, he will find a place to minister more readily; but before his gifts have made a place for him, the young minister needs help from his denomination. The various boards, committees, and older ministers will do well to remember those early trying years of their own ministry.

Association at the National Level

As an Ordained Minister

In the Assemblies of God, a minister becomes a member of The General Council of the Assemblies of God at the time of his ordination. This gives him equal status with all other Assemblies of God ministers. His ordination opens opportunities of ministry in the Assemblies of God, far beyond what could be otherwise attained. This may or may not be true in other denominations. "It [ordination] is an essential key for acceptance in pastoral, evangelistic, administrative, teaching, chaplaincy, and other ministries."[22]

Qualifications for Ordination in the Assemblies of God. Before applying for ordination a pastor must have served a minimum of 2 years as a licensed minister, either as a pastor or an evangelist. The district councils will have varying requirements for ordination with regard to the candidate's education. Perhaps a review of the Constitution and Bylaws of the General Council would more clearly define the qualifications.

In terms of maturity of ministry, three classifications of ministry are recognized, viz., the ordained minister, the licensed minister, and the Christian worker. An applicant for ministerial recognition must give testimony to having experienced the new birth (John 3:5) and to having

---

[22]*Theological and Functional Dimensions of Ordination,* With an Official Position Paper on the Assemblies of God View (Springfield, MO: Gospel Publishing House, 1977), p. 50.

received the baptism in the Holy Spirit according to Acts 2:4. The Spirit-filled life will enable him to fulfill the threefold mission of the Church (Article V, par. 10 of the Constitution).[23]

It will be noted that of the three levels of ministerial recognition, we deal here only with ordination. Later we will deal specifically with the licensed minister and the Christian worker.

We read further from the Constitution and Bylaws concerning qualifications, "Qualifications for ordination are outlined in the New Testament Scriptures. 1 Timothy 3:1-7; Titus 1:7-9."[24] And in the same Article VII additional qualifications are spelled out:

> All ordinations shall take place under the auspices of the district councils. Applicants twenty-three years of age or over who shall have met the necessary requirements shall appear before the credentials committee of the district where they reside. No person may be ordained to the ministry until he shall have held a license to preach and shall have been engaged in active work as a pastor or evangelist for at least two full consecutive years.[25]

Ordination is performed only after a careful examination of the candidate as to qualifications on six essential points:

1. The genuineness of his Christian experience.
2. The reality of his divine call to the ministry.
3. The sufficiency of his spiritual, moral, emotional, and social maturity.
4. The sufficiency and correctness of his understanding of Bible content and doctrine.
5. The adequacy of his preparation and practical abilities.
6. The acceptability of his knowledge of and allegiance to the Movement's policies and programs.[26]

Place of Ordination. The actual ordination of a ministerial candidate is held at the district council by the district superintendent, with the laying on of hands and the prayer of the district presbytery. His ordination is recognized by a certificate of ordination from the

---

[23]General Council of the Assemblies of God, *Constitution and Bylaws*, Revised 1975 (Article VII, Section 1, Springfield, MO).

[24]*Constitution*, Article VII, Section 2.

[25]*Constitution*, Article VII, Section 4.

[26]*Dimensions of Ordination*, p. 55.

General Council. "This credential is renewed annually when the minister fills out a questionnaire which is filed with his district and the General Council."[27]

BENEFITS OF ORDINATION

To the Minister. Many benefits accrue to the minister and to his church as a result of his ordination and association with a national church organization.

1. Ordination serves as a goal which represents a high level of spiritual, moral, emotional, social, intellectual, and ministerial maturity.
2. Ordination provides the minister the opportunity of corporate judgment as to the genuineness of his Christian experience; the sufficiency of his spiritual, moral, emotional, and social maturity; the reality of his divine call; the correctness of his doctrine; the adequacy of his preparation and practical abilities; and the acceptability of his allegiance to the Movement's policies and programs.
3. Ordination gives evidence of a mature level of personal and professional accomplishment and effectiveness.
4. Ordination opens opportunities of ministry in the denomination. It also provides reasonable assurance that the fruit of one's ministry will be preserved.
5. Ordination qualifies the minister to meet civil requirements for certain functions of ministry such as funerals, weddings, serving on certain community, state, and federal boards or agencies, etc.
6. Ordination allows a minister to participate fully in the life of the Movement; supporting, contributing to the formulation of policies and programs, refining doctrine, holding office, and many other general or specific benefits.[28]

One other benefit of ordination in a denomination is that it enables a minister to move from one part of the country to another, and because his ordination is recognized, he is accepted and welcomed as a minister in his new location.

The ordained minister, though he belongs to the national organization, also retains a membership in the district or local organization, and consequently he is amenable to the district officers for his ministry, his doctrinal stability, and the appropriateness of his conduct.

---

[27] *Ibid.*, p. 54.

[28] *Ibid.*, pp. 50,51.

Right of Appeal. If an ordained minister is called in question by the district for any reason, or if disciplinary action is taken against him, that minister has the right, if he so desires, to appeal the decision of the district to the Credentials Committee of The General Council of the Assemblies of God. Full provisions for protecting the rights of a minister are outlined in the Constitution and Bylaws of the General Council of the Assemblies of God (Article IXB, Sections 1-15).

Responsibilities of the National Office. The Movement should recognize that it has certain obligations to maintain in the matter of ordination. Adherence by the national office to these responsibilities is a distinct benefit to the ordained minister.

1. The Movement should ordain only those who meet the Biblical qualifications as represented in the six points of examination.
2. The Movement should solicit the highest levels of personal life and ministerial proficiency among its ordained ministers.
3. The Movement should provide the means of spiritual, moral, emotional, social, intellectual, and professional growth among its ordained ministers.
4. The Movement should provide opportunities for fruitful ministry.[29]

BENEFITS FOR THE LOCAL CHURCH FROM NATIONAL COOPERATION

The pastor has relationships with his church and with his denomination. His roles as pastor and as a member of an international denomination need never be in conflict; rather, they should bring benefit to the pastor personally, to the church as a body, and to the denomination as a whole.

There are many ways a local congregation is benefited by its association with a denomination. It has the opportunity to share in the gigantic mission of world evangelism through the combined efforts of a much larger group. A church can thus participate in ministries that would be utterly impossible if attempted by itself. The pastor who leads his church into such participation of worldwide ministry has the personal satisfaction of being an integral part of a tremendously successful enterprise.

The pastor and his church are further benefited by the continuing opportunities for learning and improvement through the various agencies that furnish literature and information regarding the life and

[29]*Ibid.,* p.56.

work of the church. The churches support the denomination's many service functions with their combined financial resources. The prayer of Jesus, ". . . that they may be one, as we are" (John 17:11), should characterize the attitude of every pastor toward his denomination. "The denomination draws its life from the churches. They create it and sustain it."[30]

CORPORATE DENOMINATIONAL EFFORTS

There are some aspects of the denominational goals that must have the unified support of the churches to assure success. It is true that a church may fulfill its local goals without help from those outside its membership, but to accomplish those greater goals will require the joint efforts of many congregations.

Missions. For instance, a church may send one missionary to a remote part of the world, but unless many missionaries are sent to all parts of the world simultaneously, the Church's mission (Mark 16:15) will never be fulfilled.

Only through the channels of its missions division, or missions board, can a denomination systematically and effectively launch a program that will reach the world with the gospel. The only possible way to reach this kind of goal is through the united efforts of many local churches.

The Printed Page. The assurance that one will always be able to secure doctrinally correct literature and church school material would be practically impossible unless the denomination owned and controlled its own publishing house. Such a venture would be beyond the ability of a local church. Publication of printed material, therefore, becomes one of the denomination's major projects. Its headquarters has the advantage of being in contact with the broad spectrum of its constituency from which to draw specialists, authors, and writers to carry on the editorial work of a publishing business. This is a highly specialized field requiring a unique talent. Most local churches would be at a complete loss to produce their own material even if they had the financial resources for publication.

Colleges. Many of the great colleges and universities of America were started by the church in the early days of our country's history.

---

[30]Segler, *A Theology of Church and Ministry*, p. 231.

It is still true today, as almost every denomination operates its own colleges and institutes to train youth and ministers. Here too, with such large expenditures necessary for the formation and operation of a college, it usually takes the combined resources of the denomination to keep the doors of a college open. The tuition a student pays covers only part of a college's operating costs. If capital improvements—new buildings, equipment, expansion, and renovation of old buildings—are to be realized, additional funds must be forthcoming to the college.

The logical source of such funds for a church-related college is the constituency of its denomination. To provide the funds needed to train its own youth and produce trained ministers is not expecting too much of a denomination's churches.

Radio and Television. Many local churches produce and sponsor their own radio and television programs. These are usually limited in both production and coverage. Occasionally local talent does produce high quality programming. However, it is quite reasonable to assume that the denomination would be able to acquire the talent to air the very finest type of program, thus representing the denomination and at the same time having a far greater coverage and ministry. A good example of this is *Revivaltime*, the worldwide radio ministry of the Assemblies of God.

Other Corporate Efforts. There may be other such ministries undertaken by the denomination that would be beyond the ability of the local church. These are orphanages, child placement centers, institutional chaplaincy, prison ministry, and ministry to the handicapped. The corporate effort of the denomination's churches actually extends the ministry of the pastor and the local church far beyond the boundaries of the local parish.

THE PASTOR, THE KEY TO COOPERATION

Often the pastor becomes involved in his own efforts and fails to see the larger picture of denominational vision. There are also times when the church members themselves resist the appeals for giving to support denominational projects.

The pastor must remember that his is a dual role. He is first a representative of his own church and then a member of his denomination. As pastor he will be involved personally in the promotion of those projects that are usually the result of his own vision and burden, but he must not shirk the responsibility of sharing the burden of the greater denominational vision. He has the dual role of interpreting the denomination's vision and need to the congregation and of representing the church to the denomination. The measure by which a local church supports the various projects of the denomination will more often than not reflect the pastor's own attitude toward those denominational objectives.

The Pastor and His District

THE STRUCTURE OF THE DISTRICT

The national organization of most denominations is made up of many state or provincial councils of churches, usually called districts or conferences. The local church will be a member of the state council as well as of the national organization. The pastor usually is better acquainted with the state organization than he is with the national organization, for it is on the state or local level that he begins his ministry.

In the Assemblies of God, for instance, the young minister will usually gain his first ministerial recognition through the local church of which he is a member, and then begin his ministry in one of the several sections of the district. Each district will have its own constitution and bylaws by which the purpose and function of the district programs are set forth. Provision is made for the officers of the district and for the main departments that serve the constituency.

Sectional Divisions. Most districts are divided into as many sections as is necessary to adequately delegate and promote the work of the state organization. In the Assemblies of God, an elected official, called a presbyter, is over each section. The District Council, as it is called, is made up of ministers and churches meeting annually in convention, with each minister and a delegate from each church comprising the voting constituency.

Officers. The district has an executive board comprised of a superintendent, assistant superintendent, secretary-treasurer, other such officers as may be needed, and the presbyters, who are the ministers elected to oversee the work in their respective sections.

Superintendent. The district superintendent will have close contact with both the churches and pastors of his state or district. He is available for ministry and assistance in the local churches. Pastors should look to their superintendent for advice and counsel. He is always available and has a God-given burden to assist in every situation. The pastor will draw his church into a close relationship with the other churches and with the denominational leaders by his own attitude and desire for fellowship.

PROMOTION OF DISTRICT WORK

Supervision of Promotion. The entire work of the district will come under the supervision of the district superintendent. With his executive board, planning meetings are held to determine both the emphasis and timing of the various departmental programs. The leaders of such departments as youth, Sunday school, women's ministries, and missions will serve under the direction of the district board and be accountable to the superintendent for the fulfillment of their duties and the realization of their objectives.

The constitution and bylaws will give direction as to the qualifications of the various leaders and will also indicate whether they are to devote their full time to the office or whether the office is to be filled on a part-time basis by a local pastor.

Cooperation of Pastors. The various programs of the district are twofold: (1) to serve its constituency, the churches, and ministers, in the promotion of their corporate worship and training of the people for Christian service; and (2) to fulfill the church's mission by planting new churches and encouraging the support of both home and foreign missions.

The only way the district can be successful in fulfilling its purpose is by the cooperation of its ministers. The district will provide many opportunities for its pastors to increase the effectiveness of their ministry. Conventions, conferences, seminars, training sessions, and rallies are promoted on both the district and sectional levels and are designed to assist the pastor and his congregation. The alert pastor who is looking for ways to increase his own effectiveness will take advantage of these various meetings. Most districts provide camps during the summer for preteens and teenagers, as well as adults, and are excellent opportunities for the members of the local church to broaden their religious experience.

Finances. The financial burden of maintaining an executive office and staff has to be carried by members of the district. Certainly it is not asking too much of a pastor to support the organization that has given him the opportunity to minister. In fact, he very likely agreed to give a certain amount of his income to the district when he received his credentials. To do less than he agreed is a violation of his own integrity. The members of the church he pastors should also be given opportunity to support the work of the organization. Some men seem to feel little or no responsibility to their denomination. By their attitude they are saying, "Let someone else pay the bills," thus appearing ungrateful toward their denomination.

Avoiding Politics. Occasionally pastors become extremely critical of those who hold office in the denomination. They may form or become members of a clique whose only objective seems to be to find fault with those who are in positions of leadership. Usually these are men whose own personal ambitions for high office have never been realized. Adolph Bedsole said, "Denominational loyalty does not require blind conformity nor does it rule out constructive criticism."[31] There is a vast difference, however, between constructive criticism and that which is motivated by selfish ambition.

Young pastors should avoid church politics. As much as we would like to deny the existence of such profane activity, we cannot if we are to be realistic. There are those selfishly motivated persons who seem to thrive on the waves caused by political activity within the denomination. They can be as "busy as bees" and as "sticky as syrup" as they push their favorite candidate or promote their particular project. Their actions can only bring havoc to the church and the disfavor of God. They should be avoided like the plague.

The district council officials, and particularly the superintendent, are in a strategic position to assist the pastor who has encountered some problem in his ministry. It may be a conflict with his church board, difficulty in a building program, a lagging congregation, or a problem of a more personal nature; but whatever the problem, the pastor should not hesitate to call the superintendent and ask for his guidance and prayers. It may well be at one of those times, which every pastor will face, that he feels his ministry has come to a halt. He may be overcome with discouragement. His superintendent can encourage him in these times.

---

[31]From *The Pastor's Profile* by Adolph Bedsole. Copyright 1958 by Baker Book House and used by permission.

When it is time to move to a new field of labor, the superintendent can be of assistance to the pastor. One should never hesitate to call on the officials for their help in any matter. They stand ready to assist the ministers and are always gratified when one calls on them for their counsel or guidance or whatever other help they may offer.

RELATIONSHIP WITH FELLOW PASTORS

Proper Attitude. As our Lord faced the cross and His own agony and death, He prayed with deep concern for His followers and all who should later come to know Him. His prayer was for their mutual love and continuing unity. He knew how important it was to their testimony that there be no division among them. He prayed, "That they all may be one; as thou, Father, art in me, and I in thee, that they also may be one in us: that the world may believe that thou hast sent me" (John 17:21).

The apostle Paul had this same burden on his heart when he wrote the following words to the church at Philippi: "Only let the lives you live be worthy of the gospel of Christ, in order that, whether I come and see you or, being absent, only hear of you, I may know that you are standing fast in one spirit and with one mind, fighting shoulder to shoulder for the faith of the gospel" (Philippians 1:27, *Weymouth).*

There is nothing that will nullify preaching as quickly as division among God's ministers. Paul said he wanted them to stand shoulder to shoulder, not as antagonists, but as fellow soldiers fighting the good fight of faith. How sad it is to see neighboring pastors acting as though they were enemies instead of brothers. Division, whether caused by differences in politics, ethics, or doctrine can only disrupt the unity of the Spirit and degrade the ministry of the Word of God. Pastors should strive to bring about a more perfect bond of fellowship among fellow ministers. Paul's words, ". . . with one mind striving together for the faith of the gospel" (Philippians 1:27), should characterize the relationship of fellow pastors.

There is strength in unity. How much more can be accomplished when pastors strive together to achieve common goals instead of striving with each other. The personal peace of mind that comes when one is at peace with his brethren vanishes immediately at the entrance of strife. The story is told that Leonardo da Vinci became angry with a certain man during the time he was working on his famous painting

"The Last Supper." He so completely lost his temper that he lashed the man with bitter words and threats. When he returned to his canvas and attempted to work on the face of Jesus, he found he was so upset he could not paint. Finally, he sought the man and asked his forgiveness. The man accepted his apology and da Vinci was able then to finish painting the face of Jesus.

In one sense of the word every pastor is painting the face of Jesus. Could some of the feeble attempts to portray Him result from disrupted fellowship with a brother minister?

Love. Paul, in speaking of the inseparable relationship existing between the Church and Christ, indicated that the basis of this unity is love (Romans 8:38, 39). When love is present, nothing can break the bond of unity. Love is the one quality of life that enables us to overcome the tendency to be critical and find fault with our brother. If we truly love, we will be long-suffering and kind toward our neighbor (1 Corinthians 13:4).

Pastors who love their fellow workers are mature men of God and will by their attitude invoke the blessing of God on their ministry. To be jealous and contentious or suspicious and self-seeking is to be immature and devoid of the true spirit of Christian charity. Such unchristian attitudes should never be found among God's ministers.

Respect. Because a brother's ministry is different and perhaps not as polished, talented, or gifted as ours is no reason for us to look down on him. If he is one whom God has chosen and upon whom rests the blessing of the Holy Spirit, we must respect him. God has chosen him. We must accept him as a member of the Body. The apostle Paul said it this way: "The eye cannot say unto the hand, I have no need of thee: nor again the head to the feet, I have no need of you. Nay, much more those members of the body, which seem to be more feeble, are necessary" (1 Corinthians 12:21, 22).

The Christian attitude should be one of respect for the gifts and calling of God upon the life of a brother in the Lord. Paul said, "The body is not one member, but many" (1 Corinthians 12:14), and every minister is needed and has a God-given purpose in the body of the Church. His ministry may be, and very likely will be, different from ours; and he may or may not enjoy the same measure of success that has been ours, but he is still a vital and important part of the Church. Consequently, he is due the respect of his brethren.

A RIGHT STANDARD OF ETHICS

What Are Ethics? The Greeks set a code of ethics for those practicing the art of healing in 400 B.C. called the Oath of Hippocrates. In
that document is set forth the ideal that the physician's one business is
to heal. What is distinctive about the oath is its noble simplicity of
aim and its exacting code of honor. This code sought to cover all the
possible situations in which a physician might find himself.

There is no such code or oath by which a minister swears, but he is
nonetheless bound by a greater code of right and wrong which covers
all eventualities of his life—the Word of God.

The word *ethics* is used often in the ministry. Its meaning is quite
simple. It is defined as "the science of human duty, or the principles
of right action." Using that definition, we can set a standard or code
of right conduct among pastors, remembering always Paul's words:
"But as we were allowed of God to be put in trust with the gospel,
even so we speak; not as pleasing men, but God, which trieth our
hearts" (1 Thessalonians 2:4). Paul said further: "Ye are witnesses,
and God also, how holily and justly and unblamably we behaved ourselves among you that believe" (v.10).

We will give account to God who tries our hearts, for our attitudes,
our words, and our deeds with regard to our fellow ministers. Our
ethics, or the sum of those principles that govern our actions, will rise
up against us in judgment. We must be certain that the ethical code
by which we conduct our ministry is in accord with God's Word.

Ethics in Action. In every area of our relationships with our fellow
ministers we should be conscious of our ethical code, which will
govern our words and actions. In dealing with church members, especially those of another man's church, we must be especially careful.
A proper code of ethics will not allow us to say anything against that
pastor or anything to encourage his members to attend our church.

In such matters as visiting the members of another church, casting
reflections on another's ministry, raising money among businessmen
who belong to another congregation, and in many other ways, a minister may violate courtesy and a proper ethical standard. In so doing,
he will alienate himself from his brethren and will be judged by God.

A partial list of some other areas of ministry where an ethical standard should be followed contains the following:

1. Showing excessive attention toward members visiting from another assembly.
2. Enticing members of another church by giving them a Sunday school class or other position after they have visited your services.
3. Accepting members of a neighboring church without contacting the pastor.
4. Entering into conversation that is critical of a fellow minister.
5. Taking advantage of a fellow minister's pulpit to preach things controversial or to promote oneself.
6. Working against a host pastor's best interests either among the members or from the pulpit, while serving as an evangelist.
7. Failing to work in complete harmony with the elected pastor while holding membership in a local church as a minister.

"And as ye would that men should do to you, do ye also to them likewise" (Luke 6:31). This Biblical command sums up the guidelines for practicing good ministerial ethics.

CONCLUSION

There is no sadder sight in life than that of a minister who has come to the last lap of the Christian race and has allowed bitterness to invade his spirit. Someone has said, "What you are now you will be when you grow old, only more so."

If one is a chronic griper and faultfinder in his younger days, it is very unlikely that he will be a gentle, sweet-natured older person. A pastor should enjoy the fellowship of his denomination and profit by his association, and although he may not always agree with everything that is done, he can continue in fellowship without alienating himself from his brethren. As the minister comes to the winter of life, there should be a richness and mellowness of character. He should be surrounded by friends who love and appreciate him for his faithful years of service to the Master.

Ralph Turnbull said, "No man's work need end in a long drift of gloom. If there has been apparent lack of success throughout life, let the closing period be rededicated to the happy acceptance of the will of God, so that all bitterness is cast out."[32] How sad to see some who have been disillusioned by their own lack of success or a failure in their own spirit and have become bitter toward their denomination! "Wise is the man who does not repine or become bitter in spirit but

---

[32]Ralph G. Turnbull, *A Minister's Obstacles* (Old Tappan, NJ: Fleming H. Revell Co., 1959), p. 141.

exultantly goes forward expecting the autumn and latter rain to come
in a new splendor unknown in youth."[33]
Would that the prayer of Ignatius Loyola be ours:

> Teach us, Good Lord, to serve Thee as Thou deservest: to give and
> not to count the cost: to fight and not to heed the wounds: to toil and
> not to seek for rest: to labor and not to ask for any reward save that of
> knowing that we do Thy will.[34]

Suggested Reading

Bedsole, Adolph. *The Pastor's Profile.* Grand Rapids, MI: Baker Book
House, 1958.

Bruce, F. F. *The Spreading Flame.* Grand Rapids, MI: William B.
Eerdmans Publishing Company, 1953.

Kent, Homer, Sr. *The Pastor and His Work.* Chicago: Moody Press,
1963.

Latourette, Kenneth Scott. *A History of Christianity.* New York:
Harper and Brothers Publishers, 1953.

Lindgren, Alvin J. *Foundation for Purposeful Church Administration.*
Nashville: Abingdon Press, 1965.

Mavis, W. Curry. *Beyond Conformity.* Winona Lake, IN: Light and
Life Press, 1958.

Segler, Franklin M. *A Theology of Church and Ministry.* Nashville:
Broadman Press, 1960.

Tead, Ordway. *Democratic Administration.* New York: Association
Press, 1945.

Turnbull, Ralph G. *The Minister's Obstacles.* Westwood, NJ: Fleming
H. Revell, 1959.

Ward, A. G. *The Minister and His Work.* Springfield, MO: Gospel
Publishing House, 1945.

Williams, Ernest S. *A Faithful Minister.* Springfield, MO: Gospel
Publishing House, 1941.

Williams, Morris. *Partnership in Missions.* Springfield, MO: Division
of Foreign Missions.

Zimmerman, Thomas, et al. *Modern Pioneer Manual for the Pioneer
Pastor.* Springfield, MO: Division of Home Missions.

[33]*Ibid.*, p. 142.

[34]*Ibid.*, p. 142.

6

The Pastor
and
His Preaching-Teaching

RICHARD E. ORCHARD

The Pastor in His Study

No greater mandate was ever given to men than that given by God to the pastors of His church: "Feed the flock of God which is among you, taking the oversight thereof, not by constraint, but willingly; not for filthy lucre, but of a ready mind; neither as being lords over God's heritage, but being ensamples to the flock" (1 Peter 5:2, 3). If this mandate is carried out faithfully, the pastor is assured, "When the chief Shepherd shall appear, ye shall receive a crown of glory that fadeth not away" (v. 4).

To feed God's flock is a high and holy calling toward which a minister must give unstintingly of his time and energy. The task of preparing spiritual food for the congregation is far more exacting than the preparation of food for one's body, in that the consequences are eternal and the servant must ultimately give an account of his labors to his Master.

A wise pastor will not feed the same thing to his flock every Lord's Day. Their rounded-out spiritual growth requires as much variety in spiritual food as the Word of God has to offer, and the preacher must be versatile in preparing that food lest his people weary of the same general diet.

THE PASTOR'S UNIQUE POSITION

While all of God's gifts to the Church are important (apostles,

Richard E. Orchard is pastor of First Assembly of God, Rapid City, South Dakota.

157

prophets, evangelists, pastors, and teachers), the pastor has a unique responsibility to fill, in that he stays with the flock to feed them regularly and to comfort them in their various life-experiences. Other ministry gifts may be seasonal or short-lived before a congregation; the ministry of the pastor-teacher is continuous. Therefore, he must forever fight against mediocrity and strive always to attain greater proficiency in his life's work—that of perfecting the saints and edifying the body of Christ. While a pastor has an outreach ministry to sinners, his primary ministry is to feed the flock of God.

THE NECESSITY OF PREPARATION

If the call of God to the work of the ministry has come upon a man's heart, he should earnestly enter into preparation for his life's work. Our Lord himself exercised the office of the ministry in both preaching and teaching, and by extending His divine grace in every way possible to those in need (Matthew 4:23, 24). Therefore the ministry of Christ should be the ideal. The task of following in His footsteps takes deliberate preparation. Without diligent preparation, there is the danger of beginning in the Spirit and ending in the flesh. Then the pastor becomes a mere hireling.

The nature of the pastor's calling demands that he be a lifelong student. Those who refuse this discipline never become eminent in their profession. At best they are mediocre, leaving no lasting impression or permanent influence on the Church. A pastor, of necessity, must be pious, but piousness alone is no substitute for being studious.

THE PASTOR'S STUDY

Its Privacy. As with men in all professions, it is important that the pastor have a study or workshop. Some prefer a separate room in the parsonage, while others prefer one in the church building. It should be kept as private as possible even though its uses may be many. The study (or office) of some pastors is used for board meetings, counseling, committee meetings, study, prayer, or simply a place of escape to quietness.

Keep the study locked, or keep a "Private" sign on the door. Just as the pastoral office requires due respect and honor, so the minister's study should have due honor. It is a place where the man of God wrestles with God for power and victory, where he gains renewed strength, and where he forms his dreams and plans for the advancement of God's kingdom. If it is not kept a quiet and holy place, it may soon become a place for perpetual visits from idle people, and those incessant knocks at the door can rob the pastor of his time and efficiency.

Its Furnishings. The furnishings of a pastor's office will often reflect the financial condition of the pastor or the congregation, but in any case there are some necessities essential to a proper pastor's study. Study habits are greatly aided if the room is airy and well lighted. If the study is used for counseling there should be appropriate seating for those who come. A large desk and good lighting at the desk are necessary. A layout table or desk beside the main desk is of great value for setting out several open books or papers during a time of intense study and research. If the church owns a lot of secretarial equipment and business machines, they should be kept in a separate room to preserve the atmosphere of the study.

Decorations in the office may include plaques, suitable pictures, souvenirs of travels, gifts from missionaries, and other memorabilia accumulated during past years of ministry. Ministers, like other professional men, tend to gather around them tokens of past events and their offices may contain things that recall pleasant memories. But the main items of such a room should be conducive to the work at hand— the study and research materials necessary to perform the pastor's work.

Its Basic Function. For 6 years the center of Jonathan Edwards' ministry was a tiny 4-by-8-foot nook he called the "study," yet from such confined quarters came the writings that made him known among the philosophers and theologians of the world.[1]

Whether the office is starkly simple, small or large, or arranged to resemble a museum, its primary function is to provide a place for reading, writing, prayer, and the general preparation of the heart and mind of the minister. From it he must go forth to feed the people under his care. Whatever other functions it may serve, it should be the place where God and His servant work together on the promotion of the work of God in that community.

Our way of life has made us familiar with the purpose of a lawyer's

[1]Ola Elizabeth Winslow, *Jonathan Edwards: Basic Writings* (New York: The New American Library, Inc., 1966), p. 25.

office, a doctor's office, a dentist's office, and that of some other professional men. We go there for expert advice. We go to see a person schooled in a particular field of learning in which we need help. So with the office of a pastor. It is his place of study and the place where people with problems come to speak with a man who is schooled in the Bible and well-read in the problems of human living.

THE PASTOR'S STUDY HABITS

Dr. G. H. Gerberding, when commenting on the study habits of ministers, asked some pointed questions:

> Why should it be necessary to show the need and importance of study? Does not the divine Word demand it? (Acts 7:22; Hosea 4:6; Philippians 1:17; 1 Timothy 3:2) Are not ministers rightly supposed to be leaders of religious thought? Should they not be in advance of the people to whom they minister?[2]

While study habits have nearly as much variety as men themselves, it would appear the best time for study is in the morning when the mind is fresh, and when there is less probability of interruptions. Most pastors like to make their hospital calls during the prescribed visiting hours except for emergencies, and most house calls are more convenient in the afternoon or evening hours. Therefore, the morning hours are usually the most suitable for quiet reading and sermon preparation. It must be said, however, that some ministers like the late hours of the day for quiet study—the time when the demands of the day are usually past. Few people will disturb a minister late at night unless the call is extremely important.

There are many circumstances that can alter a pastor's study habits, such as the demands of his family, the size of his church, extracurricular activities. At any rate, he must plan his day to give sufficient time to study for his public presentation of the Word of God. The anointing and influence of the Holy Spirit cannot be expected without due preparation. David once said he would not offer unto the Lord that which did not cost him something (see 2 Samuel 24:24). And that rule is an excellent one for all pastors to follow.

The Discipline of Study. Solomon was a preacher, and out of his

---

[2]G. H. Gerberding, *The Lutheran Pastor* (Minneapolis: Augsburg Publishing House, 1903), p. 17.

own experience he observed, "Much study [reading] is a weariness of the flesh" (Ecclesiastes 12:12). Every minister will acknowledge the tiredness he has experienced after long hours with his books, sorting information, correlating, outlining, and putting his material in order for presentation; but the discipline is necessary in the preparation of food for the flock of God. It is a joy to listen to a well-prepared sermon delivered with thoughtfulness and grace, and well-ordered from start to finish.

A preacher may not always be seated at his desk, but he should always be preparing—finding sermon material in fragments of conversation, in worthy news events, in exciting experiences of life. Such material will be woven into the fabric of his sermons. Experiences gleaned in extensive travel are usually listened to with great interest. Stories to illustrate scriptural truth are always legitimate in a sermon. Simple truths can become fascinating when illustrated. Such was the method of Jesus, and the gospel record is replete with parables that made eternal truths alive to His audiences.

Preparation of the Heart Through Prayer. The ministry that comes solely from the mind of the preacher will carry little life with it. The heart of the man must be warmed by the subject matter he presents.

Heart preparation cannot be accomplished by the perfunctory prayer of a few minutes duration. In one of Smith Wigglesworth's anecdotes he declared, "I bathed myself in prayer." Luther claimed to have prayed at least 2 hours each day. Rees Howells, the Welsh Intercessor, said he spent 3 hours each evening with his Bible on his knees after working 9 hours in the mines. These and many others testify to the value of long seasons alone with God.

A minister may not always be in the act of prayer, but he must live in the spirit of it. If his heart is really in his work, there will always be a sense of dependency on God. The Christian minister above all men should carry out the New Testament command to "pray without ceasing." He has to deal with God in relationships that touch others as well as himself. Men like Andrew Murray, E. M. Bounds, and C. H. Spurgeon wrote much about prayer because they found it to be the source of power for their own far-reaching ministries.

It is interesting to note that Jesus did not say, "If you pray . . . ," but, "When you pray . . ." (Matthew 6:5, *NASB).* Prayer is a normal exercise for every child of God, and especially for the shepherd of the

flock. Our Lord set the pattern by praying before every major inci-
dent in His life. His plaintive question to the disciples in the Garden,
"Could ye not watch with me one hour?" (Matthew 26:40), indicated
His desire that they pray even though their bodies were weary. It indicated also that prayer may be an exercise of the soul requiring
laborious effort that would not always be pleasurable. When the heart
is warmed and filled with the subject matter, the lips will speak with
authority; it is of first importance that a preacher prepare himself
before he prepares his sermon.

D. Martyn Lloyd-Jones likened a minister's praying to starting a
cold car. One needs at times to use a "spiritual choke" by first reading of someone else's deep prayer life. This has a tendency to warm
and stimulate the heart toward prayer.[3] If the minister in his pulpit is
confident that he has done his best to prepare his own heart through
prayer, he may rest securely on the promise, "Thy Father which seeth
in secret shall reward thee openly" (Matthew 6:6).

We cannot wonder at David Brainerd's success when we read in his
diary such notes as this: "Lord's Day, April 25—This morning spent
about two hours in sacred duties, and was enabled, more than ordinarily, to agonize for immortal souls; though it was early in the
morning, and the sun scarcely shone at all, yet my body was quite
wet with sweat."

A man may not have many talents. His delivery may not be as polished as people may like. He may not have the natural charisma of
some eminent public figures. But if he comes from the prayer closet
with a fresh anointing on his heart, he will find people listening.

Preparation of the Heart Through Bible Reading. Preparation for
the pulpit requires regular Bible reading. It should be done systematically, not at random. The minister who reads the Bible only to find
texts has fallen into a fatal error. The Word of God is first and foremost the Bread of Life, the Manna provided for the nourishment of
the soul; and the minister must be nourished himself before he can expect to nourish others. If the Book is a remedy for the sorrows of life,
it must first be such to the leader of the flock. If it unveils a Saviour
and Friend to be with us in our daily walk, it must first unveil such a
Person to the minister's heart.

---

[3]D. Martyn Lloyd-Jones, *Preaching and Preachers* (Grand Rapids: Zondervan
Publishing House, 1971), p. 170.

It is interesting to note the wealth of Biblical knowledge Stephen used when witnessing before the council. Without the use of notes, he was able to extemporize in detail on the history of the nation from the call of Abraham to the rejection of Christ. (See Acts 7.)

Jesus also, when speaking to the disciples on the Emmaus Road, brought forth treasures from the Word of God: "Beginning at Moses and all the prophets, he expounded unto them in all the scriptures the things concerning himself" (Luke 24:27). To these men the Word of God had been their soul-food; when the occasion required, they were able to give forth of that fullness.

Preparation of the Mind. While it is possible to know a little about everything and not much about anything, the minister should be conversant in a wide range of subjects. His first love, of course, should be to acquire a knowledge of the Word of God so he feels at home in the Book.

He must, however, be knowledgeable in current events; this will require the reading of periodicals, both religious and secular. His daily conversation is not always with members of his congregation about spiritual matters. He is thrust into community affairs, with doctors, lawyers, and educators, and he should be able to speak with them on a professional level.

Jesus once said, "The poor have the gospel preached to them" (Matthew 11:5), but His ministry extended to the rich young ruler, the scribes and Pharisees, and the community leaders—and He had a message for them all.

It is appropriate that a minister be one of the best educated men in the community. He is in God's business, and he should be able to match wits with the devil's best representatives.

Some ministers are uneducated because they never had the opportunity of formal ministerial training. Some were poor and had few books. But young preachers must not hide behind those isolated examples if the opportunity for a good education is afforded them. God puts no premium on ignorance. Moses was educated in all the wisdom of the Egyptians, Daniel in the wisdom of the Chaldeans, Paul at the feet of Gamaliel, and Solomon sought to know the wisdom of his day. One of the great themes of the Scriptures is a continuing encouragement to study and prepare for greater things.

It takes time to read. The pastor must be a student his whole life. If he is too busy to read—he is too busy. As the mind is used carefully, it becomes more adept at remembering and recalling. The mind of a diligent student will become a treasure house for bits of poetry, pungent quips, quotes from famous men, and innumerable fragments of information gleaned from histories and biographies that will aid in conversation and preaching.

Preachers, like all students, recognize the need to give the mind a rest. To relieve the mind does not mean one must stop reading; rather, the need quite often is a change of pace. Read something different—a biography, a bit of poetry, a history, the memoirs of some interesting person. For complete diversion, it is well to develop a hobby completely apart from study such as a sport, a game, gardening, making music, painting, or anything that is a welcome diversion from the tedium of the office. Indulge in these things with moderation, enough to give the mind respite from its normal toil.

Preparation for Divine Approval. "Study to show thyself approved unto God, a workman that needeth not to be ashamed, rightly dividing the word of truth" (2 Timothy 2:15). The pastor-student does not make a studied effort to be approved merely to please a congregation. He must ultimately give an account unto God. To stand approved of God will be the soul's delight. Acts 2:22 tells us Jesus was "a man approved of God." The Heavenly Father spoke that approval twice in the early life of Jesus—at His baptism and at the Mount of Transfiguration —"This is my beloved Son, in whom I am well pleased" (Matthew 17:5).

To follow in the footsteps of Christ must be the pathway and goal of the pastor's life. God will never expect of us more than we are able to produce, but He does expect us to live up to our potential. To be approved of God means our study has brought us to the place where we are "rightly dividing the word of truth" (2 Timothy 2:15). Because man is what he is, he will never be in total agreement with everyone else on everything, but there are basic lines of truth in the Scriptures which are vital to the work and to which we must subscribe.

The priests and scribes had one interpretation of the Scriptures while Jesus had another, though they both had the same writings of the Law and the Prophets. Jesus and His followers read the promises of God in the light of present needs, and the priests and scribes read them in the light of bygone days. The same struggle goes on today in the battle to "rightly divide the word of truth." Differences among good scholars concerning minor points often cause one to ask, "Wherein is the truth?" The diligent student will search, pray, and ask for the guidance of the Holy Spirit, *and he will be loving and tolerant with those who differ.*

In one of his teaching sessions, a noted teacher said, "No man has a corner on truth. No church has a corner on truth. Truth is too big for any man or any one group to have it all." When we stand before the Throne and see things in a better light, all of us will change our views about some things; but none will ever be sorry that he has been diligent, studious, prayerful, and wanting above all to please his Lord.

The Pastor's Preparation of Sermon Notes

The question often comes, "What shall I preach about next Sunday?" The problem becomes serious for the long-term pastor.

The Selection of an Appropriate Topic. Of all the thousands of possible subjects to speak about, how is it that one certain subject will suddenly captivate the pastor's heart and cause him to work on it for the next service? The fact is that *a sermon must be born.*

A message is often born in a time of prayer when the heart is earnestly seeking God. Or a topic may be suggested by reading the Word of God. A text that may have been read many times before suddenly comes alive and unfolds into an outline. Sermons are sometimes born while listening to another sermon. They may be suggested by a rich spiritual experience. At such times it is well if the pastor will jot down a few notes as a reminder and later work the material into a full message.

Some excellent topics may be suggested by sermons and incidents in the Bible. To the woman at the well Jesus preached on "Living Water." To the rich young ruler He spoke on "The Cost of Discipleship." When washing the disciples' feet, He taught a lesson on "Humility." Paul, on Mars' hill, spoke on "The Unknown God." To King Agrippa his message was "The Glory of Christianity." In the Sermon on the Mount, Jesus preached on "The Fundamentals of Christian Living." The Olivet Discourse could be titled "Signs of the Endtime."

Topics are important, and the right title to a message can alert the listener to that which follows. While a minister may have a great deal of latitude in choosing his titles, he should never be light and frivolous in handling sacred themes. The minister must be reverent himself if he is to build reverence into his audience.

Organizing Appropriate Material. The material for religious instruction is almost infinite, and it must be wisely chosen. In addition to material from the Bible, which always must be the center and foundation of the religious curriculum, there is an inexhaustible source of material from nature, biography, history, and life itself. It can be welded together and permeated with religious application to reach people's thoughts and hearts.

> Besides the deathless accounts of the heroism of such men as Elijah, Daniel, and Paul, we have the immortal deeds of Livingstone, Taylor, and Luther. Besides the womanly courage and strength of Esther and Ruth, we have the matchless devotion of Florence Nightingale, Frances Willard, Alice Freeman Palmer, and Jane Addams. Besides the stirring poetry of the Bible, and its appealing stories, we have the marvelous treasure house of religious literary wealth found in the writings of Tennyson, Whittier, Bryant, Phillips Brooks, and many other writers.[4]

Many illustrations can also be drawn from the lives and works of contemporary persons.

The preparation of the sermon is basically centered in the gathering of material. If the pastor is well acquainted with his library, he will be able to go to a number of volumes and find pertinent material for his topic. He may wish to attach a clipping from a periodical to his sermon notes. He may wish to read his text from a number of other translations, and these renderings will have to be placed in good order in his notes.

All available material on a chosen subject should be brought together. This may mean several parallel passages in the Bible, excerpts from a commentary, and gleanings from other books in his library. Something from history, science, biography, the daily paper, or a magazine will help in building the body of the message.

Think! And write as you think. Concentrate on the sermon. Bring illustrative material from the files of the mind. A sermon becomes boring when one deals strictly with generalities. Put down the major points you wish to emphasize and get illustrations to portray them.

---

[4]George Herbert Betts, *How to Teach Religion* (New York: Abingdon Press, 1910), p. 111.

Selecting an Appropriate Text. There are occasions when the pastor may want a special text to fit the topic he wishes to expound. Some texts are well-worn. The experienced preacher will sometimes search for a text that is little known but gives shape to his theme. The text may fall into an outline by itself, but it should always be an integral part of the message. It is the height of folly to take a text and utterly depart from it.

The difficulty in choosing a text is not that there are not enough, but that there are so many. A minister will do well to search his Bible for a text that will arrest the attention of his audience at the very beginning.

A minister once preached on the topic "Harps and Javelins," using for his text 1 Samuel 18:10, 11, which tells how David played his harp before Saul and then had to run from Saul's javelin. People wondered as the text was read what truth could be brought from that reading. The preacher wished to present a contrast in the nature of the old life and the new life in Christ. After reading the text, he said, "It is the Saul-like nature to throw javelins, but it is the David-like nature to play a harp." Instantly the audience manifested an appreciation for the text. The obscure story had provided a magnificent springboard to a great truth.

Another master pulpiteer once preached on the text, "They journeyed from Oboth, and pitched at Ijeabarim, in the wilderness which is before Moab, toward the sunrising" (Numbers 21:11). Most preachers would not look twice at such a text, but he made it come alive by showing Israel's moving toward the sunrise of a better day after a number of miserable wilderness experiences. It was a lesson in a faith and hope that ever moves onward.

The choice of a proper text awakens interest and gives the preacher an authority and boldness in the proclamation of truth. It will help keep his mind from wandering. With a "Thus saith the Lord" as the basis of the sermon, he may speak with the authority of heaven, for it is God and not man who speaks from the text. With such authority no preacher need be timid about proclaiming the will of God.

Our Lord selected a text before preaching His first sermon. The ministering priests of the synagogue handed Him the Book of Isaiah, and "he found the place where it was written . . ." (Luke 4:17). After reading from Isaiah 61, He closed the Book and sat down (according to the custom) and began to minister to the people. The text and the subject matter of His discourse fitted together so marvelously that "all bare him witness, and wondered at the gracious words which proceeded out of his mouth" (Luke 4:22).

Making an Appropriate Outline. One minister feels his need for a long outline carefully divided into many subdivisions. Another feels his need to have simply a text and to extemporize, relying solely on the inspiration of the moment. Another may have a minimum of notes, just enough to give a sense of direction and to recall a few pertinent facts and illustrations to his mind.

In the study of homiletics, one is encouraged to arrange his address with an introduction, the body of the message, and a conclusion. These three appear mandatory in any address, whether long or short.

The *introduction* should include appropriate remarks to the audience upon first entering the pulpit, the reading of the text, and an introduction to the body of the message.

The *body of the message* contains those major points of exposition or argument with their appropriate illustrations. These should be set forth in the best logical order, and all extraneous material should be carefully selected to fit these main points.

The *conclusion* should be short. A brief summary of the major points of the sermon is in order, then the message should be concluded. One teacher suggested the pastor should stand up, speak up, stop, and sit down. To go from one conclusion to another only destroys the effectiveness of the message.

One expositor suggested that in a 30-minute address, 5 minutes would be sufficient for introductory remarks, 20 minutes for the body of the message, and 3 to 5 minutes to draw a conclusion. No hard-and-fast rules can be made. A pastor, when preparing his outline, must ask, "Will the sermon be a simple exposition of a passage or verse of Scripture? Will it be a character-building message? enlargement on a Biblical doctrine? or a direct appeal to sinners?" The answer will often lie partially in the speaker's own strengths and weaknesses.

In any case, a proper outline is valuable. Jonathan Edwards wrote most of his sermons in longhand and read them to his audience with few gestures. Finney, on the other hand, confessed to planning no text or sermon at all when going on some preaching missions, preferring to rely strictly on sudden inspiration for that hour. He acknowledged, however, that he had read himself full and prayed himself hot.

The use of notes has been criticized in some circles, but many preachers need an outline in front of them to keep from wandering. If poetry or quotes are used in a message, a minister will be wise to have them written down, even though he may have memorized them. A lapse of memory in front of an audience can be overcome if the material is on the pulpit. Whether notes are long or short, they must be used with discretion lest the speaker become bound to them.

Following One Major Theme. Volumes can be written on sermon preparation. It is a very technical art that the minister should study well. A homiletical presentation of an interesting subject is a thing of beauty, but to listen to a disjointed and disconnected accumulation of material is trying indeed. Stay with one basic theme in a sermon. Introducing too many subjects into a discourse will only lead someone to ask, "What was he driving at?" Every point in the message should complement every other point.

Outlines that are simple and clear are easily remembered. For that reason some pastors use alliteration, or headings with the same word or sound. Other outlines may be filled with opposites and contrasts. If variety is considered the spice of life, it is preeminently so in the offerings of a minister to his congregation.

Aiming at the Main Objective. Let it forever be settled in the preacher's heart and mind that he has one main objective in his ministry—that of setting forth the Lord Jesus Christ in all the facts of His lovely life and ministry before the people. That, and that alone, is the fulfillment of the call God has placed on his heart. He is not an entertainer. He must not let himself become just "a pleasant sound." Before ever trying to please men, he must seek to please God. All of his life, whether public or private, must be focused toward that end.

The Pastor and His Library

Books are the juices squeezed from the cluster of the ages. They represent earth's wisdom and delight and are the footpath across the hills along which the generations have trod.

— W. A. Quayle

A minister once stated he could tell if another minister's preaching was dead or alive by the number of new books in his library. There is some validity to this observation. Books of theology as well as books of science can become period pieces and obsolete. They may voice the research and accepted thought of their day, but new truth continually comes forth from the inexhaustible riches of God's Word. Therefore, new books are needed as a repository to capture and hold that truth.

THE IMPORTANCE OF BOOKS

The apostle Paul had a high regard for books. He testified to having been taught at the feet of Gamaliel, one of the most eminent teachers of his time. To Timothy he wrote: "The cloak that I left at Troas with Carpus, when thou comest, bring with thee, *and the books*, but especially the parchments" (2 Timothy 4:13, *italics added*).

By the time Paul wrote these words he had been preaching approximately 30 years and had had unusual spiritual experiences, even to being caught up into the third heaven—yet he wanted books. In his admonitions to Timothy and concern for his ministry, he further counseled his young friend to "give attendance to reading" (1 Timothy 4:13).

Books are one of the indispensable pleasures of life, and the best time to acquire the taste for them is when one is young. Lord Macaulay said, "I would rather be a poor man in a garret with a love for books, than a king on a throne without that love." Edward Gibbon, historian of the Roman Empire, declared that a taste for books was the pleasure and glory of his life and he would not part with it for the riches of the Indies.

A book is a permanent embodiment of thought and a channel through which the thoughts of one man may become mental enrichment to another. If we could not read, we would be closed up in our own narrow world. Reading opens windows to that which others have seen and heard and experienced.

A pastor's library is one of his best friends, so he should be an enthusiast after good books. There is no boundary to his fellowship with his library. Jonathan Edwards collected all the knowledge of divinity he could find to aid him in the pursuit of knowledge. The more he read, the more he wrote. He was an excellent example of the pastor-preacher coming to an enlarged ministry through his passion for books and the habits of study acquired in his library.

THE SELECTION OF BOOKS

The choice of books is a serious duty for the preacher, and a good rule is to buy only those books you wish to keep as permanent possessions. The indiscriminate purchase of books is folly. Books are to be read or to be used for reference. If a minister does not know what is in his books and is not able to go to the proper book for the material he wants, his library is worthless to him.

The Christian student will want books that exalt the Lord Jesus Christ. If he is "determined not to know any thing . . . save Jesus Christ, and him crucified" (1 Corinthians 2:2), then his reading material must be focused to that end.

Many build their libraries by joining book clubs, thus adding a book or two each month. This practice is not always wise, for often a book is added that the minister would not purchase if he had browsed through it first. This is not to say, however, that there are no good books from these sources.

THE MINISTER'S BASIC LIBRARY

The Pastor's Sword. A preacher's tools are his Bible and his books. When starting to build his library, he should be concerned with those basic books to which he will often refer for help. Most important is a good Bible, preferably one with a leather cover that will wear well for several years. Today the choice is almost unlimited. Some Bibles give the simple text while others have sufficient notes and helps to be a library in themselves.[5]

The preacher's Bible is his sword. The use of it day by day builds a familiarity with its pages which makes it easy to find a passage quickly. Another person's Bible may seem somewhat strange. The personal Bible will acquire marginal notes, underlined words, and markings that make it uniquely personal as a daily companion.

Over 500 translations of the English Bible, in whole or in part, have been made since the King James translation of 1611. In view of these many translations, one is apt to be confused and ask which is the best for daily study and pulpit ministry.

It is interesting to note that while 9 to 11 percent of the world speaks the English language, 90 percent of the work of modern mis-

---

[5]Reference Bibles such as *The Dickson Analytical Bible* and *Thompson's Chain Reference Bible* have literally thousands of excellent helps.

sions has been done with the Authorized King James Version. It came
into being when the English language was at its best, and is unsur-
passed in the reverent expression of divine truth.

More recent translations are available in clearing up ambiguities
and obsolescence in the Authorized Version brought about by language changes in the passing of time. The sermon builder will find
many of these of great worth in preparing for pulpit ministry, and he
should endeavor to add several translations to his library as foundational material.

Other Research Books. Foundational books for a pastor's library
should include an unabridged Bible concordance, a Bible dictionary, a
book on Biblical manners and customs, a dictionary of the English
language, and a Bible atlas. Assistance can be obtained in selecting a
sermon topic by using *Torrey's Topical Textbook* or *Nave's Topical
Bible.*

For one who has not studied Greek, much help can be received
from *W. E. Vine's Greek-English Dictionary. Strong's Exhaustive Concordance* gives all the Hebrew words with their English translations
plus all the Greek words of the Bible with their English equivalents.
There are many more that could be classified as basic research books.
The shelves of most Bible bookstores will have books with reservoirs
of knowledge along the line of those mentioned above.

Devotional and Expository Commentaries. Good commentaries are
vital to the theological student. We are indebted to those men who
gave many years to prepare expositions of the whole Bible for future
generations. Among them, the works of Adam Clarke and Matthew
Henry have been the mainstay for thousands of ministers in their
search for seed-thoughts, helps, and sermon nuggets. The scholar who
is versed in Hebrew and Greek will find much delight in the work of
Adam Clarke. Those looking for more devotional content may turn to
Matthew Henry.

Other well-known foundational commentaries include *The Preach-
er's Homiletic Commentary, The Pulpit Commentary,* and *The Ex-
positor's Bible.* There are also many commentaries on individual
Books of the Bible. Examples include *Romans Verse by Verse* by
William Newell; *The Holiest of All,* a devotional commentary on
Hebrews by Andrew Murray; *Genesis* by Griffith Thomas; and *The
Visions and Prophecies of Zechariah* by David Barron. Such single-

volume commentaries are of immense value to the student who may find it impossible to acquire a set of commentaries.

The commentary that appeals to one may not appeal to another. Today's great flood of printing gives the student a choice in selecting those works that will undergird all his studies and satisfy his personal inclinations.

THE MINISTER'S GROWING LIBRARY

Without a doubt, more books have been written on theology than on any other field of learning. The Bible, because it is the Word of God and stands without equal among all the world's literature, has been the object of study and research far beyond that of any other book. Its verses, words, and letters have been counted. Its teachings have occupied the minds of earth's greatest scholars. The limits of its height and depth have never been discovered, and the work of finding out its secrets goes on in each generation.

When the disciple John was closing his account of the life of Christ, he said, "And many other signs truly did Jesus in the presence of his disciples, which are not written in this book" (John 20:30). And his final statement is significant: "There are also many other things which Jesus did, the which, if they should be written every one, I suppose that even the world itself could not contain the books that should be written" (21:25).

The Confusion of Books. While standing in a Bible bookstore with a friend, a noted minister was asked, "If you were to select some of these books for your own library and spiritual food and ministry, which would you choose?"

Quickly the minister reached for *Milestone Papers* by Daniel Steele, *The Way to Pentecost* by Samuel Chadwick, *The King of the Earth* by Eric Sauer, *In the Day of Thy Power* by Arthur Wallis, and a few more.

He was then asked, "Why have you selected these particular volumes in preference to all the other books on the shelves?"

"These books," he replied, "are not for fast reading. The reader must go slow, and intersperse his reading with meditation and prayer. Many ministers nowadays are required to prepare radio and television messages, two or more sermons on Sunday, and midweek talks. Too often under the pressure of meeting deadlines they look for something short, to the point, condensed sermonettes—some quickies to get new nuggets of thought without too much reading and concentration. The net result is a ministry without depth and sermons that are skin and bones with little meat on them."

The Selection of Devotional Books. In his selection of books, the minister will be wise to look for a positive approach to the major doctrines of the Bible—the sonship of Jesus, the finished work of Christ at Calvary, His physical resurrection, and kindred doctrines of evangelical Christianity. In the work of God, workers can differ on many things such as organization, disciplines, forms, methods, and conduct of services. Because of the prevalence of differences we have a great number of denominations. But we cannot afford to differ on the basic fundamentals of the Christian faith that have to do with the redemption of lost souls.

For that reason, the preacher must be selective in the devotional books he reads for his personal welfare and from which he gets many of his ideas and illustrations in sermon building. He will do well to obtain books by authors who have been Christ-centered and who have for long years of ministry been consistently in the foreground of bringing blessings to the Church with their literary offerings. In this regard we could name F. B. Meyer, James Stalker, John Owen, F. W. Krummacher, and G. Campbell Morgan; and there are many other names of equal stature whose writings are readable, devotional, and consistently true to the basic teachings of the gospel of Christ. Congregations throughout the world have never ceased to thrill at the eloquence, the insight, the poetry, and the exposition of the Scriptures from those pens.

Some excellent volumes are strictly expository with little or no true devotional material in them. Other volumes are expository with an emphasis on devotional aspects, such as *Studies in the Prophecy of Jeremiah* by G. Campbell Morgan, in which he says: "In these meditations it is not our purpose to consider the whole prophecy by way of analysis or full exposition, but to listen for the accents of the voice divine" (Old Tappan, NJ: Fleming H. Revell Company, 1955; p. 10).

F. B. Meyer, author of *A Devotional Commentary on Exodus*, described his work as "a treatise which is primarily intended for purposes of personal devotion" (Grand Rapids: Zondervan Publishing House, reprinted 1952).

It is well for the evangelical minister to have a major segment of his library composed of such devotional material, for these are the kinds of books that aid in the development of piety, faithfulness, prayer, and the qualities of a true spiritual life.

The Selection of Biographical Books. Every man can profit from the experiences of other men, and the pastor who expects to do a work for God can be especially helped by examining the lives of great men in the Christian world. God uses men. He reaches down and picks men up and uses them as tools, weapons, and vessels to destroy Satan's kingdom and to establish the kingdom of God.

Biographies and autobiographies are an indispensable part of a minister's library. It is only natural that a minister will be drawn to his own choice of reading material, but there is profit for every reader in looking at the work of God in the lives of His choice saints. While the libraries of laymen may be filled with volumes about politics, war, economics, and various histories, the preacher's library must reflect his life's work. He is an integral part of the same ongoing program as the men in his books. He must consider himself a part of the continuing plan of God, and thus learn from the experiences of previous laborers in the vineyard.

What minister has not been blessed in reading the life of C. T. Studd who went as a missionary to Inland China, and later to India and Africa? Who has not been thrilled with the life of David Livingstone, who preached Christ in Africa while surveying for the British Empire? The lives of William Carey, Adoniram Judson, and Jonathan Goforth will help one see the moves of the Holy Spirit in opening up new territories where Christ could be made known. Biographical material for one's library need not be limited to the lives of those in the Christian world. Often the life of a great military or political leader will give the pastor valuable illustrations with which to enhance his preaching.

It must be emphasized that the finest biographies that make for the richest sermons are right in the pages of God's Word. The detailed life of Joseph forever enshrines those virtues that made him a type of our Lord Jesus Christ. The life of Daniel, statesman to both the Babylonian and Medo-Persian empires, stands like a mountain peak of character among all humanity. The life of Abraham, father of the faithful, who "looked for a city . . . whose builder and maker is God"

(Hebrews 11:10), has blessed the Arab, Jewish, and Christian world with its drama. Every pastor should endeavor to portray these lives to his congregation.

"And what shall I more say? for the time would fail me to tell of Gideon, and of Barak, and of Samson, and of Jephthah; of David also, and Samuel, and of the prophets" (Hebrews 11:32). Any minister wishing to find sermon material can have many months of preaching by simply using the biographies of the Bible.

The Selection of Prophetical Books. "We have also a more sure word of prophecy; whereunto ye do well that ye take heed, as unto a light that shineth in a dark place, until the day dawn, and the daystar arise in your hearts: knowing this first, that no prophecy of the Scripture is of any private interpretation. For the prophecy came not in old time by the will of man: but holy men of God spake as they were moved by the Holy Ghost" (2 Peter 1:19-21).

It is a generally accepted rule in Bible interpretation that the amount of space given to the exposition of any theme is a criterion of its importance. By that standard the subject of prophecy is one of the most important in the Word of God.

The Old and New Testaments combined contain many predictions. It stands to reason that all Biblical interpretation that omits the study of prophecy is necessarily incomplete. Furthermore, the continuity of the Biblical revelation is more clearly demonstrated by fulfilled prophecy than by anything else.

This "light that shineth in a dark place" must have our attention. Our Bibles would be strange indeed if we eliminated the major and minor prophets, the Olivet Discourse, the predictions spoken by Christ and the apostolic writers, and most of the Book of Revelation. When one considers this vast amount of prophecy and adds those predictions from the writings of Moses and David, it is difficult to understand why congregations are so little conversant with the subject. Perhaps too many ministers are like the veteran pastor who said, "I never speak on prophecy because I don't know anything about the subject."

On occasion, prophetic preaching has fallen into disrepute because of poor exposition, date setting, and foolish speculation. Things seen "through a glass darkly" have been dogmatically declared. Nevertheless, in all the years of the Christian Church, the subject has been pursued as part of our heritage and hope. Modern research and study of the Books of Daniel and Revelation, and a fresh look at Israel in the light of ancient covenants, have brought a resurgence of prophetic teaching and preaching, and a hunger has been born in people's hearts to learn more on the subject.

The student and gospel worker who wishes to keep up with the fast-moving events—the rise of Russia, the activities of Israel, the Middle East in the news, the changing international situation—will do well to see that his library contains some of these prophetical works. The Bible is a living Book for all time and all ages, and a knowledge of current events in the light of the Holy Scriptures is necessary for a well-rounded ministry in our world today.

The Selection of Miscellaneous Books. As the years go by, the preacher's library will naturally accumulate books that are other than devotional, biographical, or prophetical. He will wish to have some books on administration, missions, and methods, and sermon books by noted ministers. He will want some minister's manuals to give guidelines in conducting weddings, funerals, baptisms, and other ministerial functions.

It is recommended that the pastor learn to read and enjoy portions of classical poetry and extracts from the masters of prose—Cowper, Milton, Bunyan, Ruskin, Shakespeare, and others. Those men quoted much from God's Word, and it has been said that a miniature Bible could be put together with their accumulated quotations.

A pastor's reading will also include periodicals from his own and other denominations to keep him abreast of the activities over a wide spectrum of God's work. It is to his advantage (and that of his audience) that he keep informed concerning the affairs of his time and the world around him. One or two good secular magazines can be a source of information on world affairs.

In the area of miscellaneous books it is well if a pastor can obtain those volumes that will acquaint him with other religions. To speak sensibly to those of other faiths, religions, or cults, one has to read and have a working knowledge of their beliefs. He may not wish to spend much time with them, but selected volumes will be helpful as resource material.

A PASTOR'S READING RULES

William Quayle stated that when books master a preacher they are his foes; but when the preacher masters books, they are his good friends.[6] This being true, it is well to have some rules for the use of books. The following guidelines may be helpful.

1. *Read Many Books.* Read several at one time to keep from going solely in one direction. A mixed diet of fiction, poetry, prose, history, science, music, and biography, will keep the mind filled with fresh inspiration and illustrations.

2. *Read Books That Challenge the Intellect.* The mind can be stimulated to deeper thinking by being challenged. Avoid reading too many books that are far beneath one's education and ability to comprehend.

3. *Read Fiction.* The world of fantasy helps the imagination to grow and become fruitful. Eastern conversation is interesting because it is filled with imagery, similes, metaphors, and types. The Bible is replete with these language structures. Jesus used them freely to communicate truths to his listeners. When the words of a speaker are generated from the fertile and sanctified imagination of a diligent student, they capture the attention of his audience.

4. *Read Theological Material Based on Your Denominational Beliefs.* Most preachers work within the framework of their organization and must be especially knowledgeable in their doctrinal emphasis. To be a guide, one must know the road.

5. *Avoid Parroting a Book After It Is Read.* A sermon or conversation should let the personality of the speaker come through, rather than being a carbon copy of what he has read. There is nothing wrong in quoting or in paraphrasing, but a book should be only a stimulus to more effective preaching.

THE COMPANIONSHIP OF BOOKS

The authors of most books are dead, yet the reader feels an affinity with them through reading. The opening of a new volume is a doorway to a new horizon, a step toward a new adventure. The author Charles Lamb felt that grace should be said before reading as well as before eating, because books are our mental food.

The Bible will ever stand supreme and should be read every day. When speaking of the pastor and his library, we must understand that

---

[6]William A. Quayle, *The Pastor-Preacher* (New York: Methodist Book Concern, 1910), p. 36.

no other book, or combination of books, can ever supplant the necessity of reading the Word of God. The pastor who concentrates on preparing continually for his work will find three companions—the companionship of God, the companionship of friends, and the companionship of books.

The Pastor and His Preaching

THE CALL TO PREACH

"The Lord said unto me, Go, prophesy unto my people . . ." (Amos 7:15). What better or simpler way is there to define the call to preach? "The Lord said, 'Go'!" It is always that way, for no one should ever get into the preaching ministry unless the Lord calls him to the task.

If the order of words has any meaning in the Scriptures, it is interesting to note that Paul placed precedence on his call to preach. In 1 Timothy 2:7 he stated, "Whereunto I am ordained a preacher, and an apostle, . . . a teacher of the Gentiles. . . ." He used the same order in his second letter to Timothy, "Whereunto I am appointed a preacher, and an apostle, and a teacher . . ." (1:11).

There are many places where a layman's ministry is effective. He may testify and enthusiastically give an account of his religious experiences, or even exhort as the occasion requires. But it is something else to be called to a lifetime of pulpit ministry. It is evident by the number of fruitless ministries and decaying churches that many pulpits are occupied by men without a specific call to the work. They may have made good lecturers in some other field, but not in gospel ministry.

To stand before a congregation each Lord's Day for several years and meet the needs of the people is no easy task. The minister must have some real abilities, a call, and a desire to please God, and he must never stop working diligently to improve himself in his labors.

THE NATURE OF PREACHING

Expounding the Word of God. Preaching is the spoken communication of divine truth with a view toward a decision or commitment. This work is the highest and greatest and the most glorious calling to which anyone can ever be called.

The nature of preaching is to know the will and Word of God and to proclaim them in relation to the options and situations of our time. If it is true that God seeks self-disclosure and self-giving, then preaching is designed to show that truth. It is through the written Word and through preaching that God takes the initiative in making himself known.

The tides of history in many countries have found direction according to the preachings of dedicated ministers. Following the French Revolution, the preaching of Wesley in England helped keep the British Isles from a similar revolution and changed the course of the British Empire. The preaching of John Knox (whose cry, "Give me Scotland or I die," brought reformation to that land) helped stem the tide of Catholicism in the wave of a heaven-born revival. The ministries of Finney, Whitefield, and Edwards in the early American Colonies set the religious and moral tone that affected the constitutional foundations of our land.

God's Voice in Human Affairs. Preachers have been God's voice in all phases of human living. They have been given one major task—to preach the Word. Strange as it seems, preaching is a major tool in God's hand in the overall work of redemption, for from the beginning of the gospel record to the present time preaching has occupied a prominent place in the Church.

The nature of preaching is to declare something. In the Biblical sense of the term it means to declare the God who is unknown to the world (Acts 17:23), to declare Jesus Christ as the Son of God with power (Romans 1:4), and to declare the gospel (1 Corinthians 15:1). Paul summed it up when he wrote, "Preach the word" (2 Timothy 4:2).

Noah was known as "a preacher of righteousness," (2 Peter 2:5). Most of the Old Testament prophets were known to plead, urge, rebuke, and thunder forth God's Word. It was their mission in their generation to call people to righteousness and true holiness.

In the New Testament the first thing we are told about John the Baptist is that he came "preaching in the wilderness of Judea" (Matthew 3:1). The first thing we are told about Jesus after His wilderness temptation is, "From that time Jesus began to preach . . ." (Matthew 4:17). The continuity of this fact is seen in the ministry of the disciples. After Jesus ascended into heaven, "They went forth, and preached every where" (Mark 16:20).

THE OBJECTIVE OF PREACHING

God had a definite objective in mind in giving apostles, prophets, evangelists, pastors, and teachers to the Church. The combined ministries of these workers was "for the perfecting of the saints, for the work of the ministry, for the edifying of the body of Christ: till we all come in the unity of the faith, and of the knowledge of the Son of God, unto a perfect man, unto the measure of the stature of the fulness of Christ: that we henceforth be no more children, tossed to and fro, and carried about with every wind of doctrine, by the sleight of men, and cunning craftiness, whereby they lie in wait to deceive; but speaking the truth in love, may grow up into him in all things, which is the head, even Christ" (Ephesians 4:12-15).

This is perhaps the most comprehensive statement in the Word concerning the objective of all the ministries, including preaching, teaching, and other work carried on in the name of Christ.

To Show That All Are Lost. Our object in preaching is not merely to get decisions; it is to bring people to a knowledge of the Truth. It is to get people to change their thinking, their behavior, and their way of life. It is to get them to seek first "the kingdom of God, and his righteousness" (Matthew 6:33). Our message is that every man must be born again, and whatever may happen to him short of that is of no value whatsoever from the standpoint of his relationship to God.

Our object in preaching is to show that all have come short of the glory of God. None is righteous in himself, and the whole world lies guilty before God. When the emphasis of a message is aimed at the conversion of sinners, the preacher will wish to bring convicted ones to a decision for Christ.

To Set Forth the One Remedy. Another objective is to show the world there is one gospel—only one. If all men are fallen, then the same ladder of redemption must be used for all. The religionist or worldly person will claim that all roads lead home and all religions are headed in the same direction. This is a lie from Satan. A visit to some foreign countries where millions are bound by ideologies that do not include Christ will show to what poverty and degradation of mind and spirit their religion has reduced them.

The objective in preaching is to show that Christ meets the need of the whole man—body, soul, and spirit. Dr. Donald G. Barnhouse once likened man's fall into sin to being struck by a bomb. The destruction caused the spirit of man to become dead in trespasses and sin, the soul of man to be depraved in all its parts, and the body of man to be so affected as to daily tend toward the grave. The objective of the gospel is to relight the candle of man's spirit so he can have communion with God again. Once the spirit of man is functioning properly toward God, the process of teaching and disciplining the soul of man goes on to perfect and mold the character of man into the likeness of Christ. Provision has been made for the body of man in divine healing through faith, and for the ultimate resurrection of the body to glory and immortality when the body shall be fashioned "like unto his glorious body" (Philippians 3:21).

To Bring Many Sons Unto Glory. A preacher once said, "God loves the Lord Jesus Christ so much that He has purposed to populate the entire universe with an innumerable company of people just like Him—and we are the raw material of that plan."

God is engaged in the work of redemption. Ministers, especially preachers who know in which direction God is going, are in the vanguard of God's program. The souls won to God through the preaching of the gospel are known as "heirs of God, joint-heirs with Christ," and are slated for positions of rulership in worlds and ages to come. For this reason, whether in season or out of season, they are glad to preach God's Word. They know the Word is God's power unto salvation to everyone who will believe.

To Carry on God's Program. From generation to generation in the Christian Church, the objective of preaching has been to carry forth the truth of God. Many who are illiterate can understand preaching. Poor readers can understand preaching. Young and old can be ministered to through preaching. The act of preaching can reach the rich and poor, the bond and free, all nationalities, all creeds, and is the act selected by God for reaching the hearts of men.

Paul amplified this truth in his letter to the Romans:

> For whosoever shall call upon the name of the Lord shall be saved. How then shall they call on him in whom they have not believed? and how shall they believe in him of whom they have not heard? and how

shall they hear without a preacher? and how shall they preach, except they be sent? as it is written, How beautiful are the feet of them that preach the gospel of peace, and bring glad tidings of good things! (Romans 10:13-15).

To Counter the World's Foolishness. The world is steeped in the foolishness of its own vaunted wisdom, a so-called wisdom that leaves God out. Therefore, "after that in the wisdom of God the world by wisdom knew not God, it pleased God *by the foolishness of preaching* to save them that believe" (1 Corinthians 1:21, *italics added*). The preaching about a crucified Saviour has always been a stumbling-block to the Jews and foolishness to the Gentiles. But God has declared that "the foolishness of God is wiser than men" (v. 25), and in the "foolish" act of preaching He sends His glorious gospel around the world and saves them that believe.

There are those who claim science and religion offer different answers to life's problems. The Bible speaks of the "oppositions of science" (1 Timothy 6:20). There are many unproven theories of science, suppositions, speculations, and so-called scientific "facts" that have no real foundation of truth. There is nothing in any field of true science that contradicts the Bible. Truth is truth, whether in Scripture or in a science textbook. Many science textbooks have become obsolete in the light of further research, but the Word of God has endured unchanged throughout the centuries. The preaching of the Word of God helps to counter the foolishness of pseudoscience with its attendant errors.

THE MAIN THEME OF PREACHING

> I have sought out acceptable words, that if possible I might prevail upon you to forsake sin and turn to God and accept Christ as your Saviour and Lord.
>
> —*Jonathan Edwards*

The Three-part Gospel. The main theme of preaching was put in capsule form by Paul in 1 Corinthians 15. He declared he had preached it to them and they had been saved by believing it. He said: "I delivered unto you first of all that which I also received, how that [1] Christ died for our sins according to the Scriptures; [2] and that he was buried, [3] and that he rose again the third day according to the Scriptures" (1 Corinthians 15:3, 4). Jesus used the same theme on the road to Emmaus when He spoke to two bewildered disciples about the sufferings of Christ and the glory that was to follow (Luke 24:26).

The gospel story is the story of reconciliation. It sets forth a lost world on one hand, a grieving God on the other, and the ministry of Christ standing between the two with a hand on each saying, "Be ye reconciled to God" (2 Corinthians 5:20). Paul developed this theme in 2 Corinthians 5:18, 19: "And all things are of God, who hath reconciled us to himself by Jesus Christ, and hath given to us the ministry of reconciliation; to wit, that God was in Christ, reconciling the world unto himself."

Such is the basic theme around which all other themes must revolve. The work of Christ on our behalf must be preeminent. Preaching that is otherwise is not scriptural preaching. It is interesting to note that when the Ethiopian eunuch in the chariot was reading Isaiah 53, Philip started at the same place and "preached unto him Jesus" (Acts 8:35). No doubt if the Ethiopian had been reading in any other part of the Scriptures, Philip would have started at that place and preached Jesus, because Christ is the main theme of the entire Bible, and Philip was following God's pattern for preaching.

Whatever topic or line of discourse the preacher chooses to pursue, true preaching demands that the message be tied to the basic theme— Christ, His death, His burial, His resurrection, and His reconciling of the world unto God.

THE ACT OF PREACHING

The Element of Personality. The preparation for the sermon has been completed, the time for proclamation has arrived, and the minister moves toward the pulpit to preach his message. It is an important moment. All the parts of the meeting such as the singing, praying, and giving have been leading up to the preaching of the Word.

One veteran pastor of 40 years said, "I have never felt completely at home on the platform." Another said, "I die a thousand deaths every time I climb the steps to the pulpit." Is this the way it should be? Yes!! Woe to the preacher who treats the act of preaching in a light manner, as though it were easy and he could handle the situation any time by himself. He must remember to be dependent on God all the time. He may feel confident in that his homework has been well done, but he must not lose that sense of dependence on God.

Preaching has as much variety as there are preachers. Some prefer to stand quietly at the pulpit and speak in a conversational voice. Some use gestures sparingly, while others use them generously. Some enjoy preaching on open platforms where there is liberty to move from one side to another. Still others leave the platform on occasion while delivering their message.

None of these methods is wrong and none can be called right in itself. The whole personality of the preacher must be involved. All his faculties—body, soul, and spirit—must be engaged in the dynamic act of preaching. Effective speaking involves action, and the entire personality must be involved.

In the delivery of the sermon there must be a sense of authority. While some preachers lose their audience easily, others seem to hold them in the palm of their hand from the beginning to the end of the sermon. After all, the minister in the act of preaching is a man under commission. He should be aware of his authority. He is before the people as a special messenger.

The Element of Spiritual Freedom. True preaching is an activity under the influence and power of the Holy Spirit. An interesting feature about true gospel preaching is that some of the best things that are said were not thought of before the message, nor were they in the preacher's notes. Sudden inspirations, illustrations, and side remarks may come during the message to enhance its value. The inspiration of the audience will have its effect on the sermon. Godly people in the congregation may be praying for the preacher and the immediate effects of that praying will be manifest. The response, eagerness, and intense listening of the people—will help inspire and give life to the preacher and his message.

The same Spirit that helped the minister in his study and preparation of sermon material, will also help in the delivery. The preacher will be buoyed up by divine inspiration. He must, however, be open to the Spirit. If he is bound to his notes, in fear of the audience, or ill-prepared, he may find himself struggling through the message and faced with an uncomfortable audience.

Preaching is designed by God to do something to people. It is one of the marvels of preaching that the Holy Spirit can take an address by a preacher and break it, as Jesus broke the loaves and fishes, and feed everyone in the audience spiritual food that will satisfy them.

The Spirit has worked in some services to the point where the minister himself was astonished at what he said in his message. A higher function than his mind took over while he was preaching. From such services the people go away saying, "We heard from God today."

The Element of Seriousness. A sermon can be very entertaining, but the minister must not mount the pulpit with the idea of entertaining. The ministry of the Word of God is serious business. The minister must not be a joker or buffoon. If he feels frivolous and allows that frivolity to spill over to his people, the worth of the gospel message will be marred. It was said that when the saintly Robert Murray McCheyne of Scotland went into the pulpit, many in the audience would be seen weeping before he even preached. His presence reminded them of the presence of God, and they were anticipating a divine word to their hearts.

The great themes a preacher deals with tend toward seriousness. He must deal with building character, with life's priorities, with reconciling hearts to God, and with giving people a new horizon. He must speak of death and resurrection, of sin and its forgiveness, and of the power of God and the power of Satan. It is impossible to be anything but serious in view of some of these truths if they are properly dealt with. He may be an extremely lively preacher in his delivery, but serious in his demeanor. The audience will sense his attitude and respond accordingly.

The Element of Passion. Whitefield often preached with tears streaming down his face. The heart of Paul was moved with compassion as he saw the idols of Athens. The heart of Jesus was stirred when He considered Jerusalem steeped in religion, but far from God.

Compassion for people will creep into the voice of the preacher if it is in his heart. It will show in his eyes, in his delivery, and in his choice of words. The urgency of getting people back to God is an urgency that must consume the preacher's soul. He stands between God and man. He may love to preach, but he must also love those to whom he preaches. Perhaps the reason for so many churches and so few revivals is the lack of passion in preaching. Sermon delivery can become a perfunctory thing, a task, a chore, a Sunday exercise, and people can salve their consciences by attending the sermon, and then feel they have done God a service. Great preaching has that element of love that reaches the hearts of the congregation.

The Element of Emotion. The idea that there should be no emotion in religion is wrong. It is easy to become intellectual in religious matters as though they were divorced from feelings. Of course, the promotion of emotionalism in a religious service should be censured and deplored. Ministers and people who think the production of noise and pandemonium in a meeting is spiritual do the work of God a great disservice.

True emotion has to do with heartfelt response to the Word of God. Think of the emotion that gripped doubting Thomas when he felt the wounds in the hands and side of Jesus. Dropping to his knees, he cried out, "My Lord and my God." That's emotion. Think of the woman at the well of Samaria after Christ had forgiven her sins. She rushed back into the city and said to the people, "Come, see a man, which told me all things that ever I did: is not this the Christ?" (John 4:29). That's emotion. Imagine the emotion shown by the deaf, blind, lame, and withered when perfect healing was given them.

How can a man suddenly realize the damnation of his lost condition without emotion? Israel trembled under the giving of the Law. The Philippian jailer cried out with conviction, and Agrippa was greatly moved at the preaching of Paul. To promote and obtain a proper and true emotional response from an audience, the preacher himself must feel the truths he is holding forth. Preaching is really logic that is on fire, reasoning that convinces and convicts, and theology that burns in the soul.

THINGS TO AVOID IN PREACHING

The art of preaching is the greatest art in the world. It is a pity the art hasn't been developed more. It suffers often by the introduction of things into the sermon that take away from its luster. It is well to look at a few of those obstacles.

Avoid Scolding the Audience. Pastors often scold people for not attending Bible study or the midweek prayer service, but the ones who should be listening are not there. The listening audience is probably the faithful ones.

Don't Worry About the Size of the Crowd. Jesus ministered to many or few with equal fervor. He was pleasing God, not looking for the applause of man. It is too easy for the sermon to rise or fall according to the number present.

Never Bring Your Personal Troubles to the Pulpit. Everyone in the audience has all the troubles of life he can carry without being burdened with someone else's problem. Stand in the pulpit as God's man and endeavor to lift the people closer to God.

Avoid Trying to Expound on Subjects With Which You Are Totally Unfamiliar. Scientists and schoolteachers in the audience will listen carefully if you feed them truth with which they are unfamiliar, but they will laugh to scorn the preacher who speaks erringly in areas of science of which he knows nothing.

Never Be Afraid of Truth. The Bible has survived all forms of persecution and criticism, and it needs to be expounded with an air of certainty. Truth will not die. No amount of scientific advancement will ever make the Word of God obsolete.

Avoid the Editorial "We" in Preaching. Speak directly, as man to man. Much of the glory and power of preaching is in its directness. Conviction comes upon hearts when the Word is preached with power from an anointed and vibrant personality. Responsibility is on the speaker. "We" implies someone else's responsibility.

Avoid Preaching to One Person or to a Small Group in the Audience. The message is meant to feed all in attendance. Bearing down on someone's personal sin in the presence of other people is folly.

Let all ministry exalt the Lord Jesus Christ and aim at building up the work of God in the hearts of men and women.

The Pastor and His Teaching

The pastor or preacher is also a teacher. While a sermon may have the elements of inspiration and exhortation, it is also meant to instruct.

Through an educational committee composed of a representative from every educational department of the church, the pastor can provide activities that will educate the membership of the church in the essentials of Christian doctrine and personal devotion. Jesus was the great Teacher, and the minister, His representative, must be a teacher also.

In the list of gifts to the Church (Ephesians 4:11), we find the office of a teacher to be a separate office from that of the evangelist or pastor. The distinction is made in the ministry of Jesus in Matthew

4:23, "Jesus went about all Galilee, *teaching* in their synagogues, and *preaching* the gospel of the kingdom" *(italics added)*.

Preaching is defined as urging, expounding, or declaring, while teaching carries the thought of instruction. There may be a fine line between the two at times, yet there is a ministry of teaching that is separate from preaching. In the office of the pastor, preaching carries with it the elements of teaching. A Sunday school teacher, on the other hand, may do an excellent job of teaching and yet not be qualified to preach or assume the pastoral office. Volumes have been written on teaching methods for all ages, but our concern is primarily the pastor and his teaching.

PASTORAL GOALS IN TEACHING

Newborn converts are "saints" in the language of the Bible, but they need to be perfected, and the aim of teaching is "the perfecting of the saints." To see a new convert rejoice and manifest childlike faith and happiness in his newfound experience in Christ is a wonderful thing; but just as a child grows in the home, so a convert should grow spiritually in the church.

Paul wrote: "When I was a child, I spake as a child, I understood as a child, I thought [reasoned] as a child: but when I became a man, I put away childish things" (1 Corinthians 13:11).

In Hebrews 6:1 we are told to leave the principles (beginning words) of the doctrine of Christ and "go on unto perfection." It is the pastor's duty to help bring the saints to maturity.

Teaching to Impart Fruitful Knowledge. Life demands knowledge. To be without knowledge is to be as a ship without a rudder, left to drift on the rocks and shoals. The pastor's aim should be to acquire a vast knowledge of the Bible himself and then seek to get as much of it as possible into the minds and hearts of his people. Biblical knowledge is wonderful. It builds character and brightens the personality. The diligent student will thrill at the discovery of truths that suddenly come to light. As the pastor opens wonderful things from the Book of God, God's people will respond in praise, thanksgiving, and wonderment. Children should be taught the Word at an early age. The catechisms given in many churches have made children lifelong adherents to those churches. So the child who is indoctrinated in God's Word at an early age will find it easier to find the Lord in an experiential manner.

Teaching to Instill Right Attitudes. The character of a true saint of God who has walked close to the Lord for many years is a thing of beauty. It is the product of responsiveness to the teaching of the Word. It is the development of interests, ideals, loyalties, and enthusiasm becoming to the kingdom of God.

Conversion to Christ is an "about-face" from the former life. It is becoming "a new creature in Christ Jesus." However, at conversion the convert is a baby spiritually. Much teaching and guidance are necessary before that new babe can mature into the likeness of Christ. The new babe in Christ is a saint, but there is no backlog of spiritual experience as yet, no prayer life, no church loyalties, no understanding of the ways of God. He has just been born again and he needs much teaching.

This is the material the pastor must work with in his teaching. The foundation of the Christian life must be laid for the new convert so he can grow properly and quickly. But while teaching the new ones, the pastor must also provide food for the older saints who are moving toward ever greater maturity.

The Bible contains all the regulations for a well-ordered life in the church, the home, society, and wherever a Christian may find himself. To develop the right attitude and know what to do in any situation requires much training. The pastor can help people know what Jesus would do if He were in the same situation as His people.

Teaching for Higher Living. God does not put all Christians into the pulpit or on the mission field, but there is a place for all. He wants Christian shopkeepers, nurses, professional men, musicians, and administrators. If Christians are to be the salt of the earth (as Jesus taught), they must be scattered around to savor and season living conditions in all places. To be lights in the world, they must go where the darkness needs to be dispelled. Tact, diplomacy, and adaptability are all skills needed for the best of Christian living in our complex world.

There are many things unbecoming to Christians. They must watch their language, dress, deportment, and attitudes. No sweeter fellowship exists on earth than that between true Christians who are deeply in love with Christ. All too often that fellowship becomes marred by a Christian who lets down and becomes careless in speech or action.

Paul's letter to Philemon sets forth the courtesy, mannerisms, and tender heart of the great apostle. By word and by action Jesus taught His disciples to be kind, humble, and compassionate, and He demonstrated the highest of Christian virtues at all times.

All these things are areas of teaching the pastor must present "for the perfecting of the saints, for the work of the ministry, for the edifying of the body of Christ" (Ephesians 4:12). When John said the Bride "hath made herself ready" (Revelation 19:7), he was referring to the Church—those people who had responded to the love of Christ and the teachings received from those placed over them in the churches to help them.

TEACHING AND THE GREAT COMMISSION

All teaching has two elements—the subject taught and the person taught. The teaching pastor is not only teaching the Bible, he is also teaching people. He is perfecting the saints by informing them of the truths in God's Word. He is edifying the body of Christ.

It is relatively easy to master a given amount of subject matter and present it to a class. Professional teachers in the public schools do this all the time. It is a far more difficult thing to understand the child and to master the inner secrets of the mind, the heart, and the springs of action of the learner.[7]

The Great Commission makes these two points clear. There is *something* to be taught and *someone* to be taught. Note it very carefully: "Go ye therefore, and teach all nations [someone to be taught] . . . teaching them to observe all things whatsoever I have commanded you" [something to be taught] (Matthew 28:19, 20).

Teaching the Word of God. "All things commanded" is the subject matter to be taught. One who teaches the Bible need never run out of material. It is an inexhaustible mine of information. Think of its types and shadows; its visions, dreams, and covenants; its biographies and histories; its precepts and doctrines; and its poetry and philosophy. There is really no need to belabor one point and make a teaching session tedious.

A teacher suggested, "Don't be afraid to give people the Word of God in big chunks. They will eat what they want and leave the rest."

---

[7] G. H. Betts, *How to Teach Religion*, p. 30.

Another said, "Be not forever hammering on the same nail. Yours is a large Bible."

After 2,000 years, people are still struggling to plumb the depths of the parables of Jesus. Whole books have been written on the death, burial, resurrection, and priestly ministry of Christ. The pastor-teacher should be well-versed through diligent study in all of these areas of Biblical knowledge.

Teaching All Nations. The message of the Bible is for everyone. The human heart is capable of taking the divine impressions, and knowledge has a transforming ability when applied by the Holy Spirit to the inner man. Religious attitudes can be cultivated. Enthusiasms can be kindled. Ideals can be shaped, interests take root, and loyalties become grounded.

The Great Commission is the root command to our missionary programs. It is the mandate of the Church—go and teach all nations. The task of the Church is not to Americanize or Christianize, but to evangelize and teach. God is unalterably opposed to heathenism in any form. He is not willing that any should perish. The religions of the heathen have no ability to save the soul and prepare people for eternity; therefore, it is necessary to go and teach. It is the missionary's task—and the pastor's task. In fact, God's program cannot really be divided between home and foreign. The field is the world, and the command is to go into all the world to teach men and women to observe the precepts of Christ.

The Spirit of the Message. Among all the artifacts found by archaeologists in their research into antiquity, nothing has ever been found that was penned by Jesus—no papyrus, tablet, shred of parchment, or clay shard. In view of the veneration paid in the Christian Church to the relics of saints, imagine what would have happened if an autograph by Christ had been preserved.

It is easy to become extremely literal in all Bible interpretation. It is also easy to get into the rut of spiritualizing whatever the Bible has to say. We do know that precepts and commands spoken in one generation have application to succeeding generations and must be accepted as relevant to all humanity. That is why Jesus said, "It is the Spirit that quickeneth; the flesh profiteth nothing: the words that I speak unto you, they are spirit, and they are life" (John 6:63). Therefore, we are assured that as teachers go forth with the Word of God under the anointing of the Holy Spirit, the work of God will be accomplished in the hearts of men in all countries, whatever their background, culture, race, education, or religion.

TEACHING WITH AUTHORITY

The Example of Jesus. Matthew 5 through 7 constitutes a teaching session where great multitudes were in the audience (4:24 to 5:1). The disciples were present, and Jesus was the Teacher. "He opened his mouth, and taught them. . . ." In this message He set forth the foundational precepts for Christian living. It is divided into 20 paragraphs. It includes the Beatitudes, the Lord's model prayer, and instructions in giving, marriage and divorce, forgiveness, fasting, faith, judging and praying, bearing fruit, and other subjects. Thirteen times in this message He used the phrase, "I say unto you." When the message was ended, "the people were astonished at his doctrine: for *he taught them as one having authority,* and not as the scribes" (Matthew 7:28, 29, *italics added).*

How did the scribes teach? With uncertainty. They quoted from someone else continually or used such fluid terms as perhaps, maybe, it could be, we think, they think, we guess so!

How did Jesus teach? With authority! One searches the Gospels in vain for such words as perhaps, maybe, we think, and we guess, for Jesus spoke with certainty. At the first service following His wilderness temptation, "All bare him witness, and wondered at the gracious words which proceeded out of his mouth" (Luke 4:22).

The Example of the Apostles. In Acts 5 the apostles were imprisoned after healing the sick and casting out unclean spirits. An angel of the Lord opened the prison and said, "Go, stand and speak in the temple to the people all the words of this life. And when they heard that, they entered into the temple early in the morning, *and taught*" (vv. 20, 21, *italics added).* When the high priest inquired the whereabouts of the apostles, it was told him, "Behold, the men whom ye put in prison are standing in the temple, *and teaching the people*" (v. 25, *italics added).*

We see, then, that the ministry of teaching was a main factor in the spread of the Christian faith after Jesus ascended into heaven. His disciples and apostles were diligent to get the message to as many hearers as possible. They taught in homes, synagogues, the temple, the marketplace, and wherever a forum was provided for them.

The Example of Paul. Few men have reached the teaching ability of Paul. He wrote at least 13 Books of the New Testament. He believed in the baptism in the Holy Spirit and had experienced it, and was happy to say, "I thank my God, I speak with tongues more than ye all" (1 Corinthians 14:18). But he knew that to teach people he must use a language they understood. "In the church," he said, "I had rather speak five words with my understanding, *that by my voice I might teach others also,* than ten thousand words in an unknown tongue" (v. 19, *italics added*). This in no way minimizes the value of speaking in other tongues, but it places the emphasis on the need for people to receive teaching they can understand.

In his first letter to Timothy, Paul said a bishop must be "apt to teach" (3:2), and in 2 Timothy 2:24 he stated that the servant of the Lord must be "apt to teach." He also urged Timothy to commit the testimony concerning Paul and his ministry and doctrines "to faithful men, who *shall be able to teach others also*" (2 Timothy 2:2, *italics added*).

THE PASTOR'S TEACHING METHODS

Teaching by Observation. Preachers need to have eyes and ears that are wide open. The little things that occur daily can become a wealth of information during a teaching session. Rocks, grass, cattle, homes, fields, etc., make excellent illustrative material and constituted the material that so enhanced the ministry of Jesus.

It was said of Henry Ward Beecher that one day he looked at some jewelry through a window in Brooklyn. Going into the store he asked the proprietor if he could take a few jewels home for a day or two, and he was granted permission. The following Sunday he announced his text: "And they shall be mine, saith the Lord of hosts, in that day when I make up my jewels." A less observant preacher would have seen and admired them, and gone his way.

How observant Christ was. He saw and heard, and used His observations in the fabric of His teaching. For example: "Behold a sower," "Consider the lilies of the field," "Have ye not heard?" Great truths were illustrated all around Him because He was observant of things from which He could make a spiritual application.

Teaching by Exposition. A pastor's expository message is essentially a teaching message. The text is explained. Its relationship to the context is set forth. The writer, the background, the time, place, audience, and occasion—all these make points of teaching in the expository sermon.

The pastor who uses the expository method of preaching will invariably develop into a good Bible teacher. As he goes through a Book chapter by chapter, or verse by verse, he is forced to grapple with various themes as they are reached. This form of preaching-teaching is considered one of the finest ways to minister to a congregation. It builds a wealth of Biblical knowledge in the pastor's mind through his hours of study, and it indoctrinates the people with a variety of spiritual food.

The wise pastor will encourage his people to keep their Bible always with them during his preaching. When he is feeding the flock on a Sunday morning, they will feel more a part of the service if they can look up a few parallel references at his prompting. When he says, "Friends, please turn with me to Jeremiah, chapter 20," they will feel called on to cooperate while he is preaching, and they will be participating in the learning process.

Teaching With Duplicated Notes. Some pastors have found it profitable to outline a good book in a series of lessons, then mimeograph those lessons so each member of the class may have a copy to follow while the pastor is teaching. A good outline in the hands of a listener will help him see the lesson as well as hear it. In case a question is asked later in the teaching session, the outline will give a point of reference. An outline, or the lesson in digest form, gives the student something to take home for later review. In some Bible classes, students make notebooks of the series of lessons taught by the pastor. An outline also gives an air of informality to the class—something to hold, to read, and to make further notes on. Better attention is often assured by this approach.

This method is especially effective for the midweek Bible study. Putting a series of lessons together often takes many hours of work, but good books that have blessed the pastor's heart will also bless his people.

The advantages of this method are many. The pastor has a sense of direction each week, rather than teaching in a hit-and-miss fashion. If the series is especially interesting, those who miss a night will often ask for a copy of the missed lesson so they can catch up on the information. In a series of lessons, a doctrine can be more fully expounded than in a one-night exposition.[8]

Miscellaneous Helps in Teaching. Helps or props that catch the listeners' attention and reinforce the message are always legitimate and useful. The use of an object lesson or a chalkboard will help make the teaching session more interesting. Maps of the Mediterranean and the Middle East are useful in teaching the missionary journeys of Paul. Wooden figures of the beasts in Daniel's visions aid greatly in explaining those visions to a class.

Above all, teaching must get the truth to the hearts and minds of the listeners, or it is not true teaching. To that end, all helps may be considered proper and worthwhile. May God help us to *go and teach* that the work of God may be advanced and edified.

Suggested Reading

Bartlett, Gene E. *The Audacity of Preaching.* New York: Harper and Brothers, 1961.

Betts, George Herbert. *How to Teach Religion.* New York: Abingdon Press, 1910.

Bounds, E. M. *Preacher and Prayer.* Grand Rapids: Zondervan Publishing House, 1952.

Evans, William. *How to Prepare Sermons and Gospel Addresses.* Chicago: Moody Press, 1913.

Fuller, David Otis. *Spurgeon's Lectures to His Students.* Grand Rapids: Zondervan Publishing House, 1945.

Henderson, George. *Lectures to Young Preachers.* Edinburgh, Scotland: B. McCall Barbour, 1961.

Lloyd-Jones, D. Martyn. *Preaching and Preachers.* Grand Rapids: Zondervan Publishing House, 1971.

Meyer, F. B. *Expository Preaching, Plans & Methods.* Grand Rapids: Zondervan Publishing House, 1954.

Pattison, T. Harwood. *The Making of the Sermon.* Philadelphia: The American Baptist Publication Society, 1898.

Quayle, Wm. A. *The Pastor-Preacher.* New York: The Methodist Book Concern, 1910.

---

[8]For an excellent treatise on tools, methods, and types of study, see G. Raymond Carlson's *Preparing to Teach God's Word* (Springfield, MO: Gospel Publishing House, 1975).

7

The Pastor
and
Personal Counseling

RICHARD D. DOBBINS

Since the days of the apostles, the historical functions of the clergy have involved the healing, sustaining, guiding, and reconciling of God's people.[1] These have all been included in the comprehensive term *pastoral care.* Once again, within this tradition of intense concern for persons, today's pastors are finding an increasing number of people turning to them for counseling. Broadly defined, counseling is a helping relationship extended to persons with various needs by persons with various professional backgrounds. C. H. Patterson has suggested that counseling includes a great variety of helps:

> The process of helping individuals may be conceived as varying on a continuum. At one end help may be given in the form of simple information. An information center with its specialists is an example. Further along the continuum more technical information may be given— faculty "advising" with regard to the choice of an educational program is an example. Then counseling towards an educational-vocational or occupational choice may be further along the continuum, followed by premarital or marital counseling. Therapeutic counseling, or counseling in the area of general personal adjustment problems would follow; and at the extreme end would be intensive psychotherapy or psychoanalysis.[2]

Richard D. Dobbins, Ph.D., is founder and director of Emerge Ministries, Akron, Ohio.

[1]William A. Clebesch and Charles R. Jackle, *Pastoral Care in Historical Perspective* (New York: Jason Aronson, 1964), pp. 8, 9.

[2]C. H. Patterson, *Counseling and Psychotherapy: Theory and Practice* (New York: Harper & Row, Publishers, Inc., 1959), p. 8.

Falling between the work of the guidance expert and that of the clinical psychologist or psychiatrist on this continuum is the work of the pastoral counselor. In larger communities, a variety of sources offer the help of a counseling relationship. School counselors, student personnel workers, social caseworkers, doctors, lawyers, ministers, and counselors in numerous agencies are available to those seeking help. In smaller communities, however, ministers, physicians, and lawyers are often the only professional people available as counselors. The pastor then becomes an important person in helping people deal with crises, make decisions, or adjust to people and circumstances.

Gurin, Veroff, and Feld report significant findings concerning distraught counselees:

> The most frequently consulted source of help or advice was a clergyman—42 percent—followed by a doctor—29 percent (physicians who were not specifically designated as psychiatrists are referred to here as doctors).[3]

Some of the obvious factors involved in this preference are the following:

1. A relationship already exists between the minister and the troubled in many cases.

2. Less social stigma is attached to seeing a minister than to seeing a psychologist or psychiatrist.

3. There is less fear of the pastor's ability to see through a person's defensive behavior into hidden areas of his life.

4. No fee is involved.

5. Usually, there is no waiting list to delay some hope of immediate relief.

How deeply troubled are the people seen by today's pastor? Some have believed the minister sees only the discouraged and occasionally depressed. However, evidence exists to suggest that "people seeking pastoral counseling might not differ greatly from those seen in clinical practice by psychologists or psychiatrists."[4]

Confronted with this degree of human suffering, clergymen have begun to realize their need for additional training in this area of

---

[3]From *Americans View Their Mental Health*, by Gerald Gurin, Joseph Veroff, and Sheila Feld, p. 307, © 1960 by Basic Books, Inc., Publishers, New York.

[4]E. E. Wagner and R. D. Dobbins, "MMPI Profiles of Parishioners Seeking Pastoral Counseling," *Journal of Consulting Psychology*, XXXI, No. 1 (1967), pp. 83, 84.

ministry. A brief look at the rapid growth of the modern pastoral counseling movement will confirm this observation.

The Pastoral Counseling Movement

Shortly after the turn of the century, both the ministry and the medical professions began to see benefits to an interdisciplinary approach to people's problems. In 1903 William James employed the science of psychology in the study of religion in *The Varieties of Religious Experience*.[5] About this same time, a few isolated courses in psychology appeared in the offerings of seminaries. However, the first practical breakthrough in clinical pastoral experience came in 1922 when William S. Keller, M.D. of Cincinnati offered to accept responsibility for a few seminarians to do clinical training under his supervision during the summer. This proved to be so successful that in 1923 the Cincinnati Summer School in Pastoral Clinical Training was launched.[6]

Meanwhile, Anton T. Boisen, like his contemporary, Clifford Beers, was learning the great human need of the emotionally ill during his own stay as a patient in a state mental hospital. Following a tour of military duty during World War I, Boisen experienced a severe emotional disturbance which resulted in his confinement in the Westborough State Hospital in Massachusetts. During a 2-year convalescent period, he studied the meaning of his illness and those of other patients around him. Boisen concluded that the experiences of many of the patients suffering from functional mental illnesses were similar to those in religious conversion, as described by William James in *The Varieties of Religious Experience*. The only difference was the outcome. James talked of the successful reconstruction of the person through conversion while Boisen observed the deterioration of the person through functional mental illness. Because of this similarity between the experiences, Boisen reasoned that the church had something unique to offer the emotionally disturbed.[7]

---

[5]William James, *The Varieties of Religious Experience* (New York: Longmans, Green, and Co., 1902).

[6]R. J. Fairbanks, "The Origins of Clinical Pastoral Training," *Journal of Pastoral Care*, IV, No. 37 (1943), pp. 13-16.

[7]A. T. Boisen, "Theological Education via the Clinic," *Religious Education*, XXV (1930), pp. 235-239.

From those recent and humble beginnings, the pastoral counseling movement has grown to the place where today there is no lack of opportunity for students wishing to pursue training in pastoral psychology and counseling at the graduate level in existing seminaries and schools of theology.

The Place of Counseling in Pastoring

As people struggle to maintain a sense of identity and control over the direction of their own lives in a dehumanizing society that is becoming increasingly impersonal and complex, the demands on pastors for counseling can be expected to increase. More and more laymen are expecting their pastors to seek additional training in the academics and practice of counseling. The conscientious pastor will want to evaluate prayerfully this pressure to become increasingly involved in counseling. As J. E. Dittes has said: "Perhaps the most annoying, persistent, and handicapping resistance which a minister can face is the difference between his and his laymen's expectations of what his role should be. . . . The issue may be whether . . . he should give main attention to preaching or counseling."[8]

Although crisis counseling needs will have to be met, the pastor has some choice as to how much additional time he wishes to make available for the troubled. Each minister should carefully assess the extent of his response to this increasingly urgent issue. Such an assessment should include:

1. *An honest appraisal of his own ministerial gifts and talents.* If the pastor feels he is not personally suited to this particular ministerial task, he may want to limit his commitment to counseling.

2. *A careful look at the other demands on his time.* Counseling is an important ministry, but there are also other urgent pastoral roles to be considered. Besides being a spiritual leader, a pastor may be expected to be a teacher and scholar, an administrator and fund raiser, a home visitor, an arbitrator in disagreements, a marriage and family-relations expert, and a wise counselor.

3. *An inventory of local referral sources available to the pastor,* especially those that offer counseling services consistent with the believer's faith. When there are such professional persons in the area,

[8]J. E. Dittes, *The Church in the Way* (New York: Charles Scribner's Sons, 1967), p. 276. Permission granted.

utilizing them whenever possible will release more of the pastor's time for other tasks.

If a minister chooses to devote a major share of his time to counseling, he may need to acquire additional training. Depending on the unique needs of the minister, he may pursue one or a combination of the following: self-study, workshops and seminars, or formal graduate training. Those pursuing pastoral counseling skills at the graduate level usually are interested in one of three areas of applied ministry.

GENERAL PARISH COUNSELING

More and more ministerial students are seeking some training beyond the undergraduate level to prepare them for the counseling demands of a general parish ministry. Such training can also benefit the pastor in other functions of the ministry. For example:

> If the preacher has acquired a thorough understanding of personality development and habitually sees people as individuals with distinctly personal histories, if he accepts their present habits and characteristics in the light of their earlier conditioning experience, he can develop a manner and method in preaching that gives people the feeling they are understood.[9]

A SPECIALIZED MINISTRY IN PASTORAL COUNSELING

Some seminarians are more attracted to counseling than to other areas of pastoral ministry, so they prepare themselves as pastoral counselors. As current trends in ministry continue, an increasing number of such persons will be needed to staff pastoral counseling centers proliferating around the country and pastoral counselor positions being created on multiple-staff ministries of larger metropolitan churches. The pastor's work in administration, Christian education, community relations, and other areas will be helped also by his deeper understanding of people.

If this rise of a specialty in pastoral counseling is to be healthy and constructive, pastoral counselors and pastoral counseling centers must remain responsive to the needs of local congregations and communicative with their pastors. Where such ethical relationships are care-

---

[9]Thomas Alexander, Cumming Rennie, and Luther Ellis Woodward, *Mental Health in Modern Society* (New York: The Commonwealth Fund, 1948), pp. 262, 263.

fully fostered, there is real potential for service. Specialized professional counselors with advanced academic training offer valuable assistance to the pastor in the form of service and in continuing educational opportunities. These specialists can also assist the church by speaking for them to mental health professionals.

INSTITUTIONAL CHAPLAINCY

As medical and behavioral scientists are beginning to see more clearly the advantages of an interdisciplinary approach to human behavior which includes a person's religious ideation, a larger place is being made for the pastoral counselor on the staffs of hospitals, prisons, and industrial clinics.

Those interested in pursuing graduate-level training in pastoral counseling should become familiar with the philosophy and requirements for membership of the two professional organizations for pastoral counselors:

1. American Association of Pastoral Counselors, Three West 29th Street, New York, NY 10001.

2. Association for Clinical Pastoral Education, 475 Riverside Drive, New York, NY 10027.

The Pastor as a Counselor

THE PERSON OF THE COUNSELOR

Not everyone is personally suited to the counselor's task. However, there are some basic characteristics that seem to be common among those who are effective in helping troubled people.

1. *Empathy.* The counselor should be able to enter sufficiently into the counselee's thoughts and feelings and to reflect accurately both verbally and nonverbally that he is sensitive to the feelings and thoughts the counselee is experiencing.

2. *Respect.* Helping another person requires one to reflect a genuine regard for the worth of that person and confidence in his ability to benefit from the counseling relationship.

3. *Genuineness.* Counseling requires one to stay in touch with his own feelings, both positive and negative, and to express them in helpful ways to the counselee during the exploration of his problem. There needs to be an openness on the part of the counselor which allows the

counselee to get to know him as a human being while maintaining the counselee's concerns as the main focus of their relationship.

To a great extent, these ideal-counselor characteristics can be summed up in three desirable pastoral abilities:

1. *Demonstrate compassion.* Compassion is the ability to imagine oneself to be in another's place so accurately that he feels, to some degree, what the other feels. This is what motivated Jesus. He was "moved" with compassion (Matthew 9:36; 14:14; Mark 6:34). Being compassionate helps one to a clearer understanding of what life looks like to another. Great pastors are men of compassion, like their Lord.

2. *Keep confidences.* Confidences entrusted to the pastor should be shared with no one who is not professionally involved with a person's care. As a rule, even the minister's spouse should not have access to them. A pastor's reputation for keeping or breaking confidences is readily available among his members. The pastor who fails to keep people's confidences will seldom be sought as a counselor.

3. *Take a constructive approach to people's problems.* A judgmental or moralizing approach seldom helps. Enabling people to discover the best possible options for their circumstances, consistent with Scripture, can be very rewarding. However, care should be taken to insist that they determine the option to be pursued and exercise the responsibility for pursuing it. Effective counselors do not make people's decisions for them.

The presence or absence of these personal qualities is frequently projected from the pastor's sermon. As the pastor delivers his sermon, some persons in the congregation may be deciding whether or not to seek his help with a problem. They may be struggling in their own minds with the possible reaction of the pastor to their dilemma. "Will he treat me with respect and confidentiality? Does he really care about me?" In fact, research has confirmed that the way a pastor chooses to express himself through his sermons is related to the time he spends in counseling each week. In one study, a Sermon Content Preference Scale was devised to measure the way pastors chose to express their sermon thoughts in relation to three bipolar dimensions:

1. *Nurturant vs. Threatening.* Content consistent with good mental health habits would be considered "nurturant." References alluding to fear, shame, and guilt would be considered "threatening."

2. *"This Worldly" vs. "Other Worldly."* References to events or

conditions perceivable in the space-time world would be considered "this worldly." References to events or conditions not perceivable in the space-time world would be considered "other worldly."

3. *Person-centered vs. Dogma-centered.* Content referring to events or conditions involving people would indicate "person-centeredness." References to some religious belief held to be authoritatively true would constitute "dogma-centered" content. Pastors choosing to present their sermons through words reflecting a this-worldly, nurturant, person-centered approach to preaching spent more time in counseling than did those who chose other-worldly, threatening, and dogma-centered approaches to preaching.[10]

THE PHILOSOPHY OF THE COUNSELOR

The demand on pastors for counseling has risen faster than has the number of available training programs where faith and science are well integrated. As a result, an increasing number of pastors are seeking to develop their counseling skills by taking courses at nearby colleges and universities or pursuing independent-study programs. When utilizing a secular resource, a pastor needs to give special care to integrating his developing philosophy of counseling with Scripture.

Theological vs. Psychological. Although it is beneficial for a pastor to be aware of psychological processes in behavior, the more important insights he brings to the counseling process are theological. An interdisciplinary approach broadens his understanding of a person's behavior, but his focus of treatment is theological, not psychological. This is a primary difference between pastoral counseling and psychological counseling.

The psychologist primarily focuses on the psychological dynamics of a person's behavior. The pastoral counselor primarily directs his attention to the theological processes involved. Only when counseling embraces man in relation to God is it truly pastoral. It is the acknowledgment of an added divine dimension in reality that differentiates pastoral from nonpastoral counseling. In fact, the wise pastor confines his counseling to theologically related concerns and resists any temptations to play psychologist or psychiatrist with other areas of his members' lives.

[10]Richard D. Dobbins, *The Function of the Sermon in the Pastor's Role as Counselor* (unpublished dissertation, University of Akron, Ohio, 1970), pp. 46-63.

It is a mistake for the minister to assume he must become a psychologist to be effective in counseling. However, he will find a growing awareness of the psychological implications of Scripture extremely helpful in counseling as well as in other aspects of his pastoral work. For example, such an awareness will add to the practicality of his preaching. It will enable him to minister the gospel in ways to help people form healthy attitudes toward God, themselves, and others. It will increase the wisdom and effectiveness of his use of Scripture in counseling. The believer's respect for the authority of God's Word makes its skillful use a powerful therapeutic resource. This is an area of mental-health ministry that is foreign to most psychologists or psychiatrists.

Biblical vs. Humanistic. Academic psychology builds its postulates on the presuppositions of natural humanism, either rational or existential. Rational humanism infers that man's discovery of the "good life" is to be found in an intelligent and disciplined application of his reason to the challenging issues confronting him. On the other hand, existential humanism holds that meaning for man is to be found primarily in the development of his human ability to experience life in the present. In neither form does natural humanism recognize the existence of God or of a supernatural world view.

However, both the existence of God and a supernatural world view are essential to the evangelical pastoral counselor's position. In fact, he builds his views of man and his understanding of human behavior on a Biblical base that presents (1) man in need of salvation as a result of the sin problem; (2) God as responding in love to provide salvation for man in Jesus Christ; and (3) man as being a responsible participant in the process. The "good life" is perceived as one lived in a network of healthy relationships with God, self, and others, both now and in eternity. This life begins with man's personal acknowledgment of his sin problem by his acceptance of Christ as Saviour and Lord. It continues to develop as man willingly discovers and applies the principles of Scripture to his daily life. These principles are to be interpreted and applied in ways that are compatible with the believer's temporal and eternal health and well-being.

There are theories of personality and psychotherapy defined by eminent humanistic scholars which, in some ways, are compatible with Biblical views of man and his behavior. As the church has benefited from accepting, modifying, and applying discoveries from the natural sciences to the work of the ministry, so there is much for the pastor to gain from a careful look at discoveries in the area of the behavioral sciences. However, whatever insights are borrowed from academic psychology should be integrated with the Biblical view of man and consistently validated by an exegetically sound interpretation of the Word of God. An adequate job of integration is evidenced when those approaching the pastor for help see him as offering them a Biblically based counseling ministry.

A Program of Pastoral Counseling

Jesus' Great Commission involved both preaching and teaching (Mark 16:15, 16; Matthew 28:19, 20). Preaching is a primary tool of evangelism. Its goal is saving people. On the other hand, teaching is a primary pastoral ministry designed to bring continued healing to the lives and relationships of the saved. Expanded God-awareness and added inner strength for the stresses of life are direct results from learning and doing the teachings of Jesus. In the final analysis, regardless of the theories and techniques involved, counseling is teaching on a one-to-one or group basis.

Historically, the focus of evangelical Christianity has tended to center on saving the lost. Without distracting from this essential emphasis on evangelism, additional attention needs to be directed toward healing the saved. This is the primary focus of pastoral counseling. Gordon Allport has observed that religion has a responsibility to the whole man:

> All religions teach compassion for sufferers here and now, whatever their conception of ultimate salvation may be. Christ himself healed the sick and cast out demons. Religion does have a duty to foster wholeness of personality. When it does not do so, it may be justly criticized.[11]

Therefore, the conscientious pastor will want to provide for the counseling needs of his parish. Some of the areas to be considered are premarital counseling, marriage counseling, family counseling, crisis counseling, and personal counseling.

[11]Gordon W. Allport, "Behavioral Science, Religion, and Mental Health," *Religion and Medicine: Essays on Meaning, Values, and Health,* ed. David Belgum (Ames, Iowa: Iowa University Press, © 1967), p. 86. Reprinted by permission of Iowa State University Press, Ames, Iowa 50010.

PREMARITAL COUNSELING

Very few couples go to another professional for premarital counseling. Therefore, the pastor should be careful to plan well this excellent opportunity for preventive ministry. For that reason, a more thorough treatment of premarital counseling is given here than will be applied to the subsequent areas covered.

When a couple approaches a pastor for his assistance in marrying them, some far-reaching theological concerns are raised. Among them should be the following:

Divorce and Remarriage. The pastor will need to know if either spouse has a living partner from a previous marriage. If so, he will need to determine as best he can the circumstances involved in the failure of the former marriage. This information is necessary in helping him decide whether he can morally or ethically officiate at their wedding.

The Couple's State of Faith. Paul was focusing on this theological issue when he forbade believers to be "unequally yoked together with unbelievers" (2 Corinthians 6:14). When couples are not united in faith, some pastors do not feel morally free to perform the ceremony. In such cases, the pastor should communicate his position to the couple as soon as possible to minimize any resulting awkwardness.

Structure of the Marriage Relationship. The New Testament teaches that in Christian marriage, the relationship between a man and his wife is to be modeled after the relationship between Christ and the Church (Ephesians 5:22-33; Colossians 3:18, 19; 1 Peter 3:1-7). Couples entering into Christian marriage need to understand the difference between their relationship and that of a couple entering secular marriage. Although unbelieving couples may be married by a pastor, he does not launch them into Christian marriage. Their marriage relationship is recognized by God, but it is defined by law and custom plus whatever modifications the couple's unique ideas about marriage may contribute. Although there is room for creative expression in Christian marriage, the basic relationship is defined by Scripture.

These concerns alone establish the importance of premarital counseling. However, when one understands that the only professional preparation for marriage given most couples comes from the minister, the importance of this phase of pastoral counseling becomes even more obvious.

By far, the most important training for marriage a couple receives is that of observing the example set before them by their parents. However, even when both sets of parents have established healthy marriages, there is still a body of information about the differences between single life-styles and a married life-style which can help a new couple make the transition with much less awkwardness and fewer misunderstandings. If either or both sets of parents have suffered divorce, the need for premarital counseling is all the more urgent.

How many sessions should be spent with a couple in premarital counseling? This will vary with couples. When either or both of the spouses live outside the local area, it may be impossible to have more than one session with them. With other couples, special situations may suggest the wisdom of meeting together four to six times before the wedding. However, in most cases, three well-structured sessions will be sufficient. These sessions should cover:

The Adjustment Period. The Clinebells have observed that all marriages go through a period of adjustment:

> No matter how adequate a couple's engagement experiences were, there are many problems to be met in the early post-wedding years. Most of the problems of marriage aren't really problems until after marriage actually begins. They have little reality for the couple until an existential collision with the problems occurs in the actual business of living together.[12]

This period usually lasts from 1 to 3 years. When a pastor alerts a couple to it and offers some practical suggestions for coping with it, he performs a valuable service.

Trouble Spots. Early in the marriage, trouble may develop in any of the following areas: (1) money management, (2) anger management, (3) sexual maladjustment, (4) in-laws, (5) religious differences, and (6) unrealistic expectations. The pastor can render a valuable service by organizing a helpful body of suggestions to offer couples for resolving conflicts stemming from these potential trouble spots.

---

[12]H. J. and Charlotte Clinebell, *The Intimate Marriage* (New York: Harper & Row, Publishers, Inc., 1970), p. 111.

Communication. Couples attempting to build compatible marriages often complain of difficulty in communicating with each other. An entire session could be spent helping engaged couples learn some important communication skills. This might be done by introducing them to an effective model of communication such as the one found in Virginia Satir's chapter in *Peoplemaking.*[13] Healthy marriage communications require an accurate exchange of information and feeling. Satir calls this *integrative* communication. She also lists and describes four unhealthy styles of communication: blaming, placating, superreasoning, and irrelevant.

Of even greater concern than a couple's ability to talk to each other is the ease with which they can pray together. Believing couples should be encouraged to overcome any spiritual timidity early in their marriage so they can talk comfortably to God together. The inability to pray together deprives a couple of a major source of strength in their marriage relationship (1 Peter 3:7; 1 Corinthians 7:5).

Sexual Information. Many deep and painful sexual problems in marriages could have been avoided by adequate and accurate information communicated in premarital counseling. The pastor's first concern is to be sure the couple's religious attitudes toward sex are healthy. By sharing key passages of Scripture with them, he can give them Biblical permission to enter freely into the joys of married love (1 Corinthians 7:3-5; Hebrews 13:4). A helpful source book to recommend for this purpose is *Intended for Pleasure.*[14] The authors, a Christian physician and his wife, have done an excellent job in providing believing couples with a marriage manual that is consistently correlated with Scripture.

Wedding Ceremony. At some point in the premarital counseling program, the pastor will need to talk over the details of the rehearsal and ceremony with the bride and groom. At this time, the spiritual and traditional significance of the marriage ceremony may be shared with them.

A wise pastor will organize the material to be covered in premarital counseling according to his own assessment of the couple's needs.

---

[13]Virginia Satir, "Patterns of Communication," *Peoplemaking* (Palo Alto, CA: Science and Behavior Books, 1972).

[14]E. and Gaye Wheat, *Intended for Pleasure* (Old Tappan, NJ: Fleming H. Revell Co., 1977).

Content and emphasis will vary from couple to couple. However, what is suggested here may serve as a basis from which to proceed.

MARRIAGE COUNSELING

When approaching marriage counseling, the pastor should remember that in each couple he sees there are at least three sets of behavioral dynamics operating: one motivating the behavior of the husband, another functioning within the wife, and a third created by their interaction with each other. This raises the possibility that disturbances within either or both of the mates may be affecting the relationship. On the other hand, both husband and wife may be reasonably healthy emotionally and their discomfort attributed to a particularly painful but predictable stage of development through which their marriage relationship is passing.

In assessing the degree of disturbance and attempting to define its sources, it is helpful to see each partner separately for at least part of a session. However, since it is their relationship that is of primary concern, unless one partner or the other appears to be seriously disturbed, the trust and openness essential to successfully negotiating their differences can most easily be built by seeing the couple together. This is called conjoint marriage counseling.

Knowing certain nonthreatening facts about the couple's relationship can help the pastor postulate where some of the stresses may be. Simply knowing the ages of the mates and how long they have been married to each other raises some possible explanations for existing difficulties. For example, Erik Erikson has devised a model of eight developmental stages through which a person passes in his growth and development. These are correlated with age. He assumes a person to be healthy to the extent that he exhibits the positive rather than the negative characteristics associated with each stage.[15] Berman and Lief, insisting that individual and marital development are interrelated, have applied this model of psychosocial development to marriage. They divide the marital cycle into seven stages according to ages:

Stage 1 (18-21 years). The marital task is to shift from family of origin to new commitment; the marital conflict results when original family ties conflict with adaptation.

[15]E. Erikson, Childhood and Society, 2nd ed. (New York: W. W. Norton and Company, Inc., 1963).

Stage 2 (22-28 years). The task is provisional marital commitment; the conflict is uncertainty about choice of marital partner and stress over parenthood.

Stage 3 (29-31 years). The task is commitment crisis and dealing with restlessness. The conflict: doubts about choice come into sharp focus. Rates of growth may diverge if spouse has not successfully negotiated Stage 2 because of obligations as a parent.

Stage 4 (32-39 years). Marital task is productivity: children, work, friends, and marriages. Conflict is that husband and wife have different and conflicting ways of achieving productivity.

Stage 5 (40-42 years). Task is summing up; success and failure are evaluated and future goals sought. Conflict is that husband and wife perceive "success" differently, with conflict between individual success and remaining in the marriage.

Stage 6 (43-59 years). Task is resolving conflicts and stabilizing the marriage for the long haul. Conflict is conflicting rates and directions of emotional growth; concerns about losing youthfulness may lead to depression and/or acting out.

Stage 7 (60 years and over). Task is supporting and enhancing each other's struggle for productivity and fulfillment in the face of the threats of aging.[16]

Viewing a marriage from this broader perspective enables the pastor to be more objective in his efforts to understand what is happening in the relationship. Over the years, the demand for marriage counseling can be reduced considerably by an effective, Bible-based, educational course for those anticipating marriage and for young marrieds. The big problem areas of marriage such as communications, money management, anger management, sexual maladjustment, in-law relationships, approaches to discipline, and division of household tasks can be approached from a preventive point of view. Excellent teaching materials are available on these subjects. If the pastor does not teach this class, it is extremely important that the couple chosen to teach exemplifies what the pastor sees as a wholesome marriage and family.

Pastors wanting to develop greater insight into the dynamics and mechanics of marriage counseling will find competently taught in-service training programs helpful. A growing body of literature on the subject challenges one's self-study habits. Here is a list of journals and books that represent some of the better references.

---

[16]Ellen M. Berman and H. I. Lief, "Marital Therapy From a Psychiatry Perspective: An Overview," *American Journal of Psychiatry* CXXXII, No. 6 (1975), 583-592. Copyright 1975, the American Psychiatric Association. Reprinted by permission.

Journals

The Family Coordinator: Journal of Education, Counseling, and Services (The National Council on Family Relations, Minneapolis, MN).

Journal of Marriage and the Family (The National Council on Family Relations, Minneapolis, MN).

Journal of Marriage and Family Counseling (American Association of Marriage and Family Counselors, Claremont, CA).

Books

H. J. and Charlotte H. Clinebell, *The Intimate Marriage* (New York: Harper & Row, Publishers, Inc., 1970).

Handbook of Marriage Counseling, eds. Ben N. Ard, Jr., and Constance C. Ard (Palo Alto, CA: Science and Behavior Books, 1969).

H. G. Hendricks, *Heaven Help the Home* (Wheaton, IL: Victor Books, 1973).

O. Q. Hyder, *The People You Live With* (Old Tappan, NJ: Fleming H. Revell Co., 1975).

D. Mace, and Vera Mace, *We Can Have Better Marriages* (Nashville: Abingdon Press, 1974).

Marriage and Family Enrichment: New Perspectives and Programs, ed. Herbert A. Otto (Nashville: Abingdon Press, 1976).

C. McDonald, *Creating a Successful Christian Marriage* (Grand Rapids: Baker Book House, 1975).

E. Wheat, and Gaye Wheat, *Intended for Pleasure* (Old Tappan, NJ: Fleming H. Revell Co., 1977).

FAMILY COUNSELING

Often pastors are consulted by parents who are experiencing difficulty in their relationships with their children. Being able to put parents in touch with appropriate information about normal child development and the resulting changes expected in healthy parent-child relations is frequently all that is necessary to bring relief to the situation.

An annual parenthood class offered through the adult department of the church's Christian education program can make this kind of information available on a group basis. Such a class should be taught by a competent, spiritually mature person. Care should be taken to enlist as many fathers as possible.

Until recently, even the behavioral sciences assumed the mother to be the all-important figure in the life of the preverbal and preschool child. However, without detracting from the importance of the mother's influence, current research is confirming the wisdom of Scripture in placing the primary responsibility for the care of children on the father (Ephesians 6:4; Colossians 3:21). In *The Role of the Father in Child Development*, the author pleads for joint responsibility in parenthood.

> Society and its institutions must appreciate the importance of the father's role and encourage paternal participation in childrearing. All the evidence we have suggests that childrearing is most enjoyable, most enriching, and most successful when it is performed jointly by two parents, in the context of a secure marital relationship. This is a simple fact that we would be well advised not to ignore.[17]

Perhaps the most difficult distance for parents to bridge is that which frequently develops between them and their adolescents. The story of the prodigal in Luke 15 suggests that this painful situation is not new. Happily, it also teaches both parent and adolescent that their estrangement from each other is temporary. Much relief can be brought to parents by simply observing that the unpleasant chapter a child may presently be writing in the story of his life is not the end of the book.

In addition to this kind of supportive help, a pastor may find he is able to offer more practical help if his own understanding of family relationships is deepened. The Scriptures should be his first resource in such a study. They contain valuable, time-tested insights into human behavior. Discovering the daily practicality of Biblical truth and learning to apply it to ongoing situations will enhance the pastor's effectiveness as a family counselor.

Other references that can help the pastor gain a clearer understanding of the dynamics involved in family situations include the following books: E. Erikson, *Childhood and Society* (New York: W. W. Nor-

---

[17]*The Role of the Father in Child Development*, ed. Michael E. Lamb (New York: John Wiley and Sons, Inc., 1976), p. 33.

ton and Company, 1950). Virginia Satir, *Helping Families Change* (New York: Jason Aronson, 1976). Burton White, *The First Three Years of Life* (Englewood Cliffs, NJ: Prentice-Hall, 1975).

Family counseling frequently involves similar dynamics and processes to those found in crisis counseling. Rather than discuss them separately here, the focus will proceed next to crisis counseling.

CRISIS COUNSELING

The English word *crisis* comes from the Greek word *krisis*, which is related to the Latin *cernere*, both of which mean "to separate." A crisis situation is one that disturbs homeostasis. It marks a turning point from which a situation moves with marked deterioration or improvement. The situation involved may vary in complexity from one of personal health to that of organizational well-being. The single identifying characteristic of any crisis is the presence of a precipitating event. Pastors often are required to lead people and organizations through crises. The risks of this sensitive ministry are often frightening, but the challenge is rewarding. People are never more open to change than when they are in crisis. The Scriptures repeatedly illustrate that God is creatively active in crises. Developing skills as an effective crisis counselor equips the pastor to be a co-worker with God in this redemptive process.

A pastor has definite advantage over other professionals as a crisis counselor. First, he is God's personal representative. This in itself introduces an intangible but important resource from which those in crisis can draw. Second, the pastor can make a contact with people in crisis before they come to him for help. Every other professional must wait to be called, but the minister may go where the crisis is without first being invited. Third, unlike other professionals who may be meeting people in crisis for the first time, the pastor usually has an ongoing relationship with the troubled of his congregation; this understanding encourages immediate rapport. Finally, pastors have access to communities of faith from whom support for people in crisis can be enlisted.

Since the mid 1960's, a rapidly growing body of research has given birth to the area of crisis theory and crisis-intervention techniques. Many useful insights for pastors can be gained by reviewing this work. Much can be learned from M. Bard, who trained teams of policemen as family crisis-intervention workers.[18] Certainly, those interested in any kind of "help-line" telephone counseling would want to discover what E. S. Schneidman learned in pioneering the use of telephone interview at the Los Angeles Suicide Prevention Center.[19] Gerald Caplan, the major figure from psychiatry in crisis theory, also has much to share with ministers. He defines four phases through which a crisis passes:

1. *Impact.* During this time, people involved in crisis may exhibit dazed shock. One moment they may be wanting to run away from the situation; another moment, they may reflect hostility and a desire to fight. This emergency fight-flight response is often accompanied by considerable disorientation and destructibility.

2. *Emotional Turbulence.* Even after impact, a person's attempts to express himself reveal his thoughts to be very ambiguous and uncertain. Feelings of rage, guilt, anxiety, and depression often surface. A person's ability to cope is immobilized. Previous ways of responding to threat are temporarily unavailable or ineffective.

3. *Mobilization of Internal and External Resources.* During this phase, a person explores his physical and social environment for new opportunities. He begins the task of reconstructing a new world of activities and relationships. Sometimes during this process, certain previous goals are relinquished as unobtainable.

4. *Long-term Reconstruction and Reequilibrium.* Although this is the goal, the outcome may still go in either of two directions. Physical, psychological, or social disorders may become chronic or the person may discover a new dimension of growth and an improved level of functioning.[20]

Understanding this process through which people in crisis pass should be especially helpful to pastors since most of the people experiencing conversion are in a crisis process. Hopefully through pastoral care and the support of loving relationships in the body of Christ, the efforts of these people toward reconstruction and reequili-

---

[18]M. Bard, *Training Police as Specialists in Family Crisis Intervention* (Washington, DC: United States Government Printing Office, 1970).

[19]E. S. Schneidman, "The National Suicide Prevention Program," *Organizing the Community to Prevent Suicide,* eds. J. Zusman and D. L. Davidson (Springfield, IL: Charles C. Thomas, 1971), p. 19.

[20]Adapted from *Principles of Preventive Psychiatry,* by Gerald Caplan, pp. 40,41, *passim,* © 1964 by Basic Books, Inc., Publishers, New York.

brium will result in their growth and the development of their potential for the kingdom of God.

PERSONAL COUNSELING

In trying to be of as much help as possible to troubled people, it is beneficial for the pastor to have in mind a series of critical questions he is endeavoring to answer for himself as he talks with a person.

What is troubling this person? Skillful listening will reveal this. Jesus taught, "For out of the abundance of the heart the mouth speaketh" (Matthew 12:34). It is from the feelings and thoughts within a person that his communication comes. His conversation will reveal: (1) the clarity or confusion of his ideas, (2) the accuracy or inaccuracy of his information, (3) the maturity or immaturity with which he is organizing his information and expressing his ideas, (4) the appropriateness or inappropriateness of his feelings, (5) the intense or shallow nature of his feelings, and (6) the maturity or immaturity with which he expresses them.

In attempting to discern the nature of the difficulty, seek simpler explanations first before assuming more complicated ones are necessary. In other words, attempt to understand the problem in the simplest possible terms. This will permit treatment to begin with the simplest possible approach. If that is sufficient, nothing more complicated will be necessary. If that is not adequate, more complicated measures still can be taken. For example, if a man goes to a doctor complaining of a headache, the wise doctor will try aspirin before recommending brain surgery.

What can I do to help the person? The skillful pastor will be listening for the troubled person's images of God, himself, and others to surface as his thoughts and feelings are shared. Pastoral counseling is identified with an effort to bring relief and healing to persons by intervening in their religious ideation. In other words, pastoral counselors assume that a successful attempt to help a person form and maintain healthy ideas about God, himself, and others will have positive generalized effects on other aspects of his personality.

A believer's respect for the authority of God's Word makes it possible for the pastor to use Scripture effectively in helping the believer understand some important concepts:

1. *God loved His enemies enough to send His Son to die for them, but He loves His children even more* (Romans 5:8, 9). Many people seen in counseling see God as more angry than loving. Therefore, their relationship with God is one of fear rather than of love. They see Him as One who punishes His children more than He rewards them.

2. *Although man is unworthy, he is not worthless.* The fact that man was redeemed at such a great cost to God establishes the worth of man at a price far in excess of silver and gold (1 Peter 1:18-20). Troubled people often feel worthless. Discovering their worth to God helps restore hope and a healthy self-esteem.

3. *Others can be accepted even though what they do is not approved.* Friction between and among people is often due to their lack of acceptance of each other. Jesus demonstrated the possibility of extending acceptance to people without approving their deeds (John 4:5-30; 8:1-11). A person is more likely to turn away from the disapproved and embrace the approved in a climate of acceptance than in an atmosphere of attack and rejection. Simply altering a person's ideas about God, himself, and others in ways like this can bring about substantial changes in his life.

Does this person need help I cannot give? A wise pastor knows the limits of his competency in helping people. When a person is responding to his counseling ministry, he will evidence a greater inner comfort and relate to others in more loving ways. Healthy spiritual experiences will similarly affect people (Luke 2:52; Acts 2:46, 47; Matthew 5:16). When a person is growing worse or showing no improvement, in spite of all that is being done for him, other sources of help should be considered if they hold any realistic hope. Even though a person indicates an unwillingness to listen to anyone else, his pastor may be able to persuade him to accept additional help. It is wise to build a list of competent people in other helping professions for use in referral of such cases.

The Practice of Pastoral Counseling

Unlike other professional counselors, pastors may do their counseling in a variety of places such as at the altar, at the back of the church, in homes, on the street, and in hospitals. However, it will save the pastor time and provide greater privacy if people are trained to come to the pastor's study for counseling whenever it is possible. A notice in the bulletin each week posting the hours set aside in the pastor's schedule for this ministry will help. Appointments can be scheduled for those to be seen. Usually, 1-hour sessions are adequate. In longer sessions, the material covered tends to be repetitive.

Correlating counseling time with hours when others will also be in the building can safeguard the pastor from unwarranted suspicion which could be raised if he were alone with a woman counselee. If no one else is in the building or there is no one in an outer office, it is a good practice for the pastor to leave his office door ajar when counseling a woman alone. Although the number of ministers who commit adultery is extremely low, when that tragedy does occur, it often involves a woman the minister has seen or is seeing for counseling.

A pastor needs to be aware of transference feelings being directed toward him by those he sees in counseling. These are feelings a person has had toward others in the past which become activated by the counseling process and directed toward the counselor. They can be negative or positive in nature. Under the influence of such feelings, a counselee may see the pastor at various times in the counseling process as father, son, brother, friend, or lover. Even the trained counselor may not always be aware as to how these transference feelings are prompting the person being seen to view him.

One of the best indicators of the nature and direction of transference feelings is the countertransference being experienced by the pastor. Countertransference feelings are those feelings generated in the counselor by the counselee. To identify them, the pastor needs to ask himself after each counseling session, "How did spending an hour with this person leave me feeling?" An honest appraisal of these feelings is a pastor's best defense against their defeating his purpose in helping the counselee. Sexual feelings disguised by the counseling relationship can be most treacherous and tragic in their consequences. For this reason, it is usually best, in those cases where sexual matters are a prominent part of the problem, for sexual counseling to be done by another professional person to whom the pastor can make a referral.

At the first or second session, the pastor should gain from the person or persons being seen an understanding of their goals in seeking counseling. The goals should be defined as clearly and realistically as possible. Making notes of the material covered in each session and the counselor's impressions of the session will be beneficial in keeping the counseling relationship goal-directed. To preserve confidentiality, it is advisable to number the case files. Delete all family names or other obviously identifying data from the case notes. Under lock in a place separate from the case files, a ledger identifying the case number and name of the counselee can be kept. Pastoral counseling cases seldom extend longer than 10 or 12 sessions spread over 3 to 6 months. By this time the presented needs usually have been met or the people have been referred to someone else. If the same person or family needs help again, carefully kept case records will be of valuable assistance. However, in the event a pastor leaves a parish, it is advisable for him either to take his records with him or to destroy them.

A pastor is never more like his Master than when he is compassionately listening to troubled people and ministering to them. Hopefully, in the process, both he and they are being helped; he is learning how to preach and teach the gospel in ways more practically related to people's daily lives, and they are discovering the daily benefits of practicing what they hear him preach and teach.

Suggested Reading

Bane, J. D., A. H. Kutscher, R. E. Neale, and R. B. Reeves, eds. *Death and Ministry: Pastoral Care of the Dying and the Bereaved.* New York: The Seabury Press, 1975.

Clinebell, H. J. *The Mental Health Ministry of the Local Church.* Nashville: Abingdon Press, 1972.

Hyder, O. Q. *The People You Live With.* Old Tappan, NJ: Fleming H. Revell Co., 1975.

Jackson, E. N. *Parish Counseling.* New York: Jason Aronson, 1975.

Kelsey, M. T. *Healing and Christianity.* New York: Harper & Row, Publishers, Inc., 1973.

Lamb, M. E., ed. *The Role of the Father in Child Development.* New York: John Wiley & Sons, 1976.

Oates, W. E. *Pastoral Counseling.* Philadelphia: The Westminster Press, 1974.

Sall, J. J. *Faith, Psychology, and Christian Maturity.* Grand Rapids: Zondervan Publishing House, 1975.

Switzer, D. K. *The Minister as Crisis Counselor*. Nashville: Abingdon Press, 1974.

Wheat, E., and Gaye Wheat. *Intended for Pleasure*. Old Tappan, NJ: Fleming H. Revell Co., 1977.

8

The Pastor
and
Evangelism-Missions

ROBERT M. GRABER

I have been in the Christian ministry for 20 years. I love my calling. I have a glowing delight in all its services. I am conscious of no distractions in the shape of any competitors for my strength and allegiance. I have but one passion, and I have lived for it—the absorbing, arduous, yet glorious work of proclaiming the grace and love of our Lord and Saviour Jesus Christ.[1]

So spoke J. H. Jowett in his introductory remarks at the 1911 Yale Lectures. What he said epitomizes the high calling of every pastor. The dimensions of this pastoral responsibility are awesome and breathtaking, and they can only be understood as they are experienced. But there must be only one passion—and that is to proclaim the Lord Jesus Christ.

Since there are so many tasks that demand the pastor's attention, it is important for him to determine his priorities. Two of the most important areas of ministry are evangelism and missions—outreach at home and abroad. Every conscientious pastor should have a clear understanding of these two vital ministries.

In recent years there have been many national and international conferences on missions and evangelism, dealing with every facet of these important subjects. However, while the speakers have amplified their importance, few have sought to define their relationships and

Robert M. Graber is pastor of Bethel Temple Assembly of God, Canton, Ohio.

---

[1]From *The Preacher: His Life and Work* by J. H. Jowett. Reprinted by Baker Book House, pp. 9, 10, and used by permission.

differences. Evangelism is one of those subjects that has suffered equally from being oversimplified and overcomplicated. After years of looking at evangelism, assessing it, and being stimulated by it, the writer has concluded that one of the best definitions of evangelism— its nature, content, and goal—is the one produced by the World Missionary Convention in Edinburgh in 1910:

> To evangelize is to so present Christ Jesus in the power of the Holy Spirit that men shall come to put their trust in God through Him, to accept Him as their Saviour, and serve Him as their King in the fellowship of the Church.

When this report was adopted for publication in a book that was given wide circulation, the words "in the fellowship of the Church" were supplemented by the phrase "and in the vocations of the common life." It was a good addition!

More than half a century later, the Lausanne Congress on Evangelism, held in Lausanne, Switzerland in 1976, offered this definition of evangelism:

> To evangelize is to spread the good news that Jesus Christ died for our sins and was raised from the dead according to the Scriptures, and that as the reigning Lord, He now offers the forgiveness of sins and the liberating gift of the Spirit to all who repent and believe.

Here we have more attention given to evangelism's content and less to its aim and purpose. Both statements are good. Neither presumes to be comprehensive or final.

The Lausanne statement of faith continues with this word:

> Missions is the church's activity of evangelism on a worldwide scale. It is the church transcending itself and breaking through the chains of provincialism and involving itself in the needs of peoples of the whole world so that they may communicate the gospel to them.

It is readily seen, then, that evangelism is the heart of missions and missions is the supreme task of the Church. Since there is such a wide range of material to cover in each of these subjects, let us look at them separately, define their meanings, and then relate how the pastor is to implement them in the church.

Evangelism

Evangelism is one of the noblest words in the Christian vocabulary. It is the proclamation of the Christian gospel; the sharing of the glad tidings that salvation through Christ is available on terms that anyone can meet. The word *gospel* means good news, and evangelism is the telling of that good news. The apostle Paul asks in Romans 10:14,15 *(NIV)*:

> How, then, can they call on the one they have not believed in? And how can they believe in the one of whom they have not heard? And how can they hear without someone preaching to them? And how can they preach unless they are sent? As it is written, "How beautiful are the feet of those who bring good news!"

The force of Paul's words is that you cannot get to know about Jesus unless someone comes to tell you. There has to be a journey and a going forth. That simple piece of logic underlies the whole exciting ministry of Paul as we see it described in the Book of Acts and interpreted in his Epistles. It underlies some of the most moving chapters of Christian history—the missions of William Carey to India, Hudson Taylor to China, Robert Raikes to the streets of London, and D. L. Moody to Chicago and the world. The haunting phrase of Isaiah quoted by Paul, "How beautiful are the feet of those who bring good news," has been remembered from generation to generation because it is truly what men feel.

So every pastor must have a clear understanding of what could rightly be called Biblical evangelism. Old Testament evangelism consisted largely of revivals, and there were generally no personal efforts to win converts. Old Testament revivals had no resemblance to the special meetings of our day. They were not protracted meetings or evangelistic crusades, but periods of returning to God marked by spiritual fervor and repentance.

In the New Testament we find a full-orbed evangelism. Jesus used both mass and personal evangelism, and the disciples followed His example. Paul also used writing to extend the work of the Lord. To get a clear understanding of the New Testament concept of evangelism, we need to clear up some false impressions.

PSEUDO EVANGELISM

First, everything we do in the work of the church is not evangelism. Too often we do everything but evangelize. A pastor can reason that he is so busy in the work of the church, and the church is so busy in its many activities, that the commission given by Jesus Christ is neglected. It is tragically possible to spend much time doing good yet never evangelize.

Second, leading people to unite with the church is not evangelism. Those who are converted should be led to join the church, but church membership comes after conversion. Gaines Dobbins once remarked at a conference, "Conversion is the end of all evangelism—but it is the front end!" The pastor's goal in evangelism is the conversion of the individual, and not an ever-increasing church roll, as important as that may be.

Third, evangelism is not the proselyting of members of other churches. Paul was resolute in his determination not to build on another man's work. Proselyting may produce quick growth, but evangelism is not involved. It is easy to discern this spirit in others, but very difficult to see it in our own lives. How easy for any pastor to take the path of expediency for immediate growth, and neglect the road of evangelism.

True Evangelism

Evangelism is the proclaiming of Jesus Christ as God and Saviour and persuading men to become His disciples and responsible members of His church. This distinguishes evangelism from philanthropy, from church work *per se*, and from bringing about desirable changes in the structure of society. Those are good things to do, but they are not evangelism.

The glad tidings also has assurance for those who have repented and believed. It reminds them that Christ can keep those who have come to Him. The gospel for the believer is as prominent in the words of Jesus and His disciples as the gospel for the unbeliever. Consistently we find such statements as these: "My sheep hear my voice, and I know them, and they follow me: and I give unto them eternal life; and they shall never perish, neither shall any man pluck them out of my hand" (John 10:27,28). "I know whom I have believed, and am persuaded that he is able to keep that which I have committed unto him against that day" (2 Timothy 1:12).

Always there are these two aspects of the gospel—the good news that Christ saves and the good news that He keeps whom He saves.

THE HISTORY OF EVANGELISM

The history of evangelism follows the pattern of an up-and-down graph. More than once the conclusion might have been reached that evangelism was dying or dead. During Christianity's first three centuries, evangelism was at a high level. Then during the next 1,000 years, the general direction was downward. The Reformation brought the graph line upward, and in the last five centuries there has been a steady increase. The time lapse between evangelistic deadness and evangelistic life has grown encouragingly shorter. Each era of evangelistic fruitfulness has had its own characteristics and leaders.

It remains to be seen what distinctive pattern the evangelism of our day will take, since it is obvious the Holy Spirit works differently in each period of history. It remains the responsibility of every pastor to be challenged by the need of his own day and to develop an appropriate philosophy of evangelism. Then he must keep it before his people, so they are equally challenged. The vision Christ has given the pastor of a lost world must become the vision of the congregation.

POWER OF EVANGELISM

The power Source for all evangelism is the Holy Spirit. Fortunate indeed is the pastor who learns the inviolable truth that the work of the Lord can progress only if it is done in the power of the Holy Spirit. The great truths of the gospel are ineffective without that power. Power is released when truth is operating. The gospel of Jesus Christ is the power of God unto salvation, but men become recipients of grace through the work of the Holy Spirit. There can be no world evangelization apart from the Holy Spirit. This great truth is seen in the Lord's instructions to His disciples just before He ascended into glory: "Tarry ye in the city of Jerusalem, until ye be endued with power from on high" (Luke 24:49).

Jesus knew the enthusiasm His ministry, miracles, resurrection, and ascension had generated in His followers could soon be suppressed by

226 AND HE GAVE PASTORS

the cold, cynical world around them. He knew they would meet with determined opposition, bitter criticism, and entrenched wickedness; and against these, by themselves, they would be no match. They would need more than knowledge, vision, and zeal. They must have the power of God. Jesus, therefore, linked His program of evangelization with the power of the Holy Spirit. In one sentence He gave the scope, nature, and equipment of His evangelistic program (see Acts 1:8). The scope was the world, the nature was witnessing, and the equipment was the enabling power of the Holy Spirit.

To read the Book of Acts is to see the Holy Spirit played the prominent part. Jesus continued His ministry on earth through the Holy Spirit, so the Book of Acts could rightly be called "The Acts of the Holy Spirit." The outpouring of the Spirit on the Day of Pentecost occasioned an evangelistic thrust more intensive and longer lasting than any in the history of the Church. The Holy Spirit led them step-by-step in an ever-increasing advance in world conquest. He led Philip to go to Samaria where his ministry resulted not only in signs, wonders, and miracles, but in many conversions. The Holy Spirit fell on the Gentiles in the house of Cornelius as Peter preached Christ to them. Paul and Barnabas, the first two commissioned missionaries, were sent forth by the church at Antioch.

In each case, the Church was taking another step in global evangelism. All through the pages of Acts, the followers of Christ are aware of the presence of the Holy Spirit and give an account of their ministry in terms of His power.

The Pentecostal Movement has picked up Zechariah's time-honored words: "Not by might, nor by power, but by my Spirit, saith the Lord of hosts" (Zechariah 4:6). They have become the watchword of the Church and the personally claimed promise of each pastor for his ministry. Who is sufficient in these days when the souls of men are jaded and worn by affluence? How can the pastor awaken men who have been made impervious to the claims of the gospel by the permissiveness of this age? What can awaken men from complacency and indifference but the gospel of salvation preached and taught in the power of the Holy Spirit?

The gospel is dynamic only to the degree that the Holy Spirit attests and confirms its proclamation. Men cannot come to Christ of their own volition, for no man can come to the Father except he be drawn

(John 6:44). Men are led of the Holy Spirit to have an experience with Christ. Christ is revealed by the Holy Spirit as the answer to all moral and spiritual needs. In this respect, the Holy Spirit accomplishes a number of very important works of grace.

First, He convicts of sin, righteousness, and judgment! How does He reprove the world? He does not do it alone! If He did, He would supplant the Church. No, His work is one of partnership with all believers who give testimony to Christ. Then, as the truth is proclaimed, written, or lived by the witness, the Holy Spirit empowers truth to convict men of their lostness without Christ. New Testament clarity is unmistakable—the Holy Spirit convicts through the truth of the gospel. Paul corroborated this teaching when he said to the Corinthians: "The natural man receiveth not the things of the Spirit of God: for they are foolishness unto him: neither can he know them, because they are spiritually discerned" (1 Corinthians 2:14).

When Jesus gave His disciples the program for world evangelization, He declared: "Repentance and remission of sins should be preached in his name among all nations . . . but tarry ye . . . until ye be endued with power from on high" (Luke 24:47, 49). The disciples were to be instruments and the Word of God was the message, but the Holy Spirit was the power. All the sermons in the world could not convict even one sinner of his sin. It is the Holy Spirit who through the Word of God convicts men of sin.

Second, it is the Spirit who regenerates the believer. The great work of regeneration is what Christ referred to in John 3:5, and what Paul explained in his Epistle to Titus: "Not by works of righteousness which we have done, but according to his mercy he saved us, by the washing of regeneration, and renewing of the Holy Ghost" (Titus 3:5). The sinner becomes a son of God by the Spirit's direct action.

Third, the Spirit empowers the believer for service. Jesus' words, "Ye shall receive power, after that the Holy Ghost is come upon you" (Acts 1:8), were given to encourage His disciples in the work of evangelism. They were not going forth in their own strength, but in His. He had emphasized this truth initially when He commissioned them: "All power is given unto me in heaven and in earth. Go ye therefore, and teach . . . and, lo, I am with you alway" (Matthew 28:18-20). Every believer is clothed with the power of God and invested with His authority.

EVANGELISM IN THE CHURCH

The work of evangelism is the task of the Church. It is the imperative of the Church. When the Church ceases to evangelize, it fails to fulfill its reason for being.

In 1968, the Assemblies of God held a Council on Evangelism in St. Louis, Missouri that may well be recorded as one of the most significant meetings in its history. The council was called as part of the Movement's intensive self-study program. The reason for the council and the self-study was the deep sense of concern among the leaders for the spiritual life and evangelistic effort of the Assemblies of God. The sense of concern was crystallized and articulated by the Executive Presbytery in May 1967. Contained in the extensive statement are two important observations concerning evangelism and the role of the believer in the activity:

> The Assemblies of God recognizes that its mission is to be an agency of God for evangelizing the world, [and it] exists expressly to give continuing emphasis to this mission in the New Testament apostolic pattern by encouraging believers to be baptized in the Holy Spirit, which enables them to evangelize in the power of the Holy Spirit with accompanying supernatural signs.[2]

It was to this purpose the Assemblies of God dedicated itself, and it is for this purpose every church must aim. Our mission is His commission, and His commission is world evangelization. The task of the Church is many-faceted, but its first thrust is evangelism. As this is given first priority, all other tasks can be realized as well.

Evangelism is essential to growth. God has no other plan for the growth of His church and the expansion of Christianity. The church at Jerusalem was an evangelistic church. The reasons for its rapid growth are found in the record of Luke: "And the Lord added to the church daily such as should be saved" (Acts 2:47). Growth came daily and continually as their witness was empowered by the Holy Spirit. Rest assured it is the will of God for the Church to grow—it is the desire of the Holy Spirit to assist in it and it is the promise of Jesus to accomplish it: "I will build my church" (Matthew 16:18).

The church must have a vision of her mission in the community,

---

[2]*Our Mission in Today's World* (Springfield, MO: Gospel Publishing House, 1968), p. 212.

and it becomes the duty and privilege of the pastor to impart to the church that vision. No church will become an evangelistic and growing church without this pastoral concern. "Like pastor—like people" is an old cliche, but it nevertheless drives home this important truth: If the pastor has a passion for evangelism and an overwhelming desire to see his church grow, then his people will catch his vision, and together they can become a dynamic force in the community.

PASTORAL EVANGELISM

Dr. C. E. Autrey, in his practical and readable book *Basic Evangelism*, makes an insightful statement: "The greatest single need in evangelism today is pastoral evangelism."[3]

He is not implying that every-member evangelism and revival efforts are not vital. What he is suggesting is that without pastoral evangelism, there will be no evangelism, at any level. The pastor is strategically placed at the forefront in evangelism, and his leadership there will be reflected in the church.

In a recent survey conducted by an organization seeking to discover reasons for church growth, one conclusion more significant than others was that there are very few conversions when a church is without a pastor. This situation is all the more serious because so many churches have a frequent turnover in pastors. Pastors are leaders in evangelism and church growth. Without that leadership, the church will flounder like a ship in a storm.

The Pastor With a Heart for Evangelism Will Have a Love for Lost Souls. This love, begotten in him by the Holy Spirit, issues forth in an urgent desire to warn and win the lost. Like their Master, pastors are called ". . . to seek and to save that which was lost" (Luke 19:10), and they must do it at all costs.

For more than 40 years in London, C. H. Spurgeon took time to win at least one person a day outside his pulpit ministry. It was said of D. L. Moody that he could hardly wait to finish a sermon so he could go to the inquiry room to talk with people individually. There was a consuming love in his heart and a burning desire to see sinners receive eternal life.

A notable example of pastoral evangelism is Richard Baxter of Kid-

[3]From *Basic Evangelism* by C. E. Autrey. Copyright © 1959 by Zondervan Publishing House, pp. 40,63. Used by permission.

derminster, England. When Baxter was called to the pastorate in Kidderminster, the church was in deep spiritual darkness because of the lack of spiritual leadership. Richard Baxter employed three creative techniques that proved to be very effective. He was a passionate and earnest preacher of the gospel. He preached every time "as a dying man to dying men." At first the people did not receive him well, but soon he became very popular. His church was filled to capacity and it became necessary to build balconies to care for the ever-increasing congregation.

Baxter employed a unique type of personal evangelism. He arranged for every family in his parish to come to his house, one by one. There he would spend at least 1 hour speaking to that family about spiritual matters and salvation. Then he would take each member of the family apart from the others and tenderly urge him to make a decision to receive Christ. Most of the families were won. Every family was greatly affected.

The third technique employed by this brilliant and intellectual pastor was to lead the families to set up family worship in their homes. As a result, the city of Kidderminster became a veritable colony of heaven in a time of spiritual darkness and wickedness.

Richard Baxter was a man of great intellectual ability. He had one of the sharpest minds of his generation. He was a master of mathematics, physics, and medicine. Being a man of great ability and many talents, he was able to meet the challenge of a crucial hour in the history of his nation and his community. He wrote 168 books, became an encouragement and an example to the clergy of his day, and through his personal ministry won thousands to Christ.

This was one man's way of being a leader in evangelism. We could say the same of many of the great pastors of our own day and our own Movement—men with burning hearts seeking only to lead their people in their quest for lost souls.

A Pastor With a Heart for Evangelism Will Be a Man of Prayer. It has been stated and restated by saints of all ages: "Men who do not have power with God will not have power with man." Bounds, Finney, Moody, Torrey, and Graham all declared it. They may have shifted the adjectives and adverbs around, but the emphasis was emphatic: No man can have the power of God on him and within him unless he spends time in God's presence. The writings of Leonard

Ravenhill may be especially helpful, for he reached into the devotional lives of many of God's great saints and passed on secrets of prayer and praise and heavenly power. Mark it well, Pastor, you may succeed superficially without prayer, but your power with men is commensurate with your power with God.

John Tauler, of 14th-century Europe, was the most powerful preacher of his generation. People came many miles to hear him. One day he became aware that he was preaching more to excel than to bless the hearts of men and glorify God. He closed the door of his study and spent long hours before God in prayer. When Sunday came and the hour to preach was approaching and the crowds had gathered in the church, his assistants urged him to come and preach. He replied, "Go back and tell the audience I will not preach today. Neither shall I ever preach again unless God comes with me into the pulpit."

For long days Tauler prayed. Finally he came to his pulpit with such power that many people were convicted and fell prostrate along the benches, in the aisles, and upon the floor. Tauler's prayers brought a great turning to God in his day. It is the pastor's intensely personal devotions and consecration to God that determine his power with men in evangelism.

The Pastor With a Heart for Evangelism Will Creatively Seek Ways to Perpetuate the Burden of His Heart. It may be through an active series of evangelistic crusades that could be long or short. These meetings must be planned well in advance, with the evangelist's schedule in mind. Promotion can never begin too soon, but don't oversell a good thing. Set measurable goals and a plan to attain them; implement all plans with tangible work assignments. Evangelists need a great deal of consideration both in their accommodations and in love offerings. Since most evangelists only receive an average of 35 paychecks in a year, the pastor and church need to be as generous as is financially possible. Some great evangelists have left the field because churches were miserly in their consideration of their needs.

The pastor is the key in training the important levels of leadership in the congregation to understand these things. Good pastoral theology embraces these mundane issues, and ministers ought never to hold back part of a large love offering for an evangelist. This has happened at times and, as a result, the evangelist, the pastor, and the church have suffered. Do your best for your evangelist, and God will reward you in similar fashion.

The pastor with a heart for evangelism may seek to extend his ministry by training others (a method we shall discuss later). Through his counseling ministry with the sick, the bereaved, or those experiencing domestic problems, he may lead people to look to God for help and eventually lead them to a decision for Christ. He may use film ministries, coffee house ministries, street meetings, telephone ministries, ministry in institutions, tape ministries, or family education and seminars to fulfill the desire of his heart for evangelistic outreach.

One of the greatest joys of the Spirit-filled experience is that God leads our steps unerringly. Every day we may be led to people (churched or unchurched) and given a word in season to help them in their need. Truly, "The steps of a (good) man are directed and established of the Lord" (Psalm 37:23, *Amplified Bible*).

The pastor can teach classes in any part of his weekly service schedule for new converts, for inquirers, for new members, for the unenlisted in Christian service, and especially for soul winning. The strength of his own desire to share the passion of his heart will cause him to communicate it creatively and relevantly to his people.

LAY EVANGELISM

It used to be that when the subject of evangelism was discussed or treated in a book, church leaders spoke of only two or three types of visitation work. An intensive visitation program, put on once or twice a year, sought to win and enlist members in the church. Then there were the weekly visitation programs that sent out workers two-by-two, 52 weeks out of the year. In some churches, the visitation was handled entirely by the Christian education staff.

About the year 1960, a number of different groups and movements arose spontaneously in different parts of the country. They all had the same vision: mobilizing and equipping a vast lay army of the church to do the work of the ministry. After centuries of clergy-oriented ministry, the Holy Spirit was finally breaking through man-made molds to create the type of church He intended should exist from the beginning, and which did exist for the first three centuries of this era. That this lay emphasis is the movement of the Spirit of God in our time has been evidenced by the tremendous eagerness with which thousands of ministers are responding to the opportunities and potentiality of lay multiplication evangelism.

Laymen cannot only be trained to witness, they can also be trained to train others to witness, and thus multiply their labors. The results of such a lay evangelism program have been astonishing and would be unbelievable to those who do not understand the spiritual power engendered by such a ministry.

James Kennedy, senior minister of Coral Ridge Presbyterian Church of Ft. Lauderdale, Florida, has written a stimulating and thought-provoking book *Evangelism Explosion*. In it he shares how God in His grace led him into lay evangelism and how he led his church into this program, "until in nine years their church grew from none to more than two thousand people."[4]

Dr. Kennedy outlines how a whole congregation can be motivated and mobilized to perform this task. He chooses trainees and in 4 months of one-evening-a-week sessions, he trains them in the science and art of house-to-house evangelism. He teaches them, goes with them, and demonstrates how it is done. Then the trainees graduate into trainers and, in turn, train others.

Kennedy builds much of his one-to-one soul winning on two very important questions:

1. Have you come to a place in your spiritual life where you know for certain that if you were to die today, you would go to heaven?

2. Suppose you were to die tonight and stand before God and He were to say to you, "Why should I let you into My heaven?" What would you say?

Armed with great scriptural indoctrination and warnings to avoid cliches, generalities, arguments, and frivolities, the lay witnesses are to identify with the person and amiably be themselves.

The same is true of the Campus Crusade Movement, which has been used so signally of God in the evangelization not only of thousands of young men and women on the campuses of America, but also in the "evangelism explosions" of our major cities. Bill Bright's four spiritual laws may not suit everyone, but they are an effective tool in

[4]D. James Kennedy, *Evangelism Explosion* (Wheaton, IL: Tyndale House Publishers, © 1971), p. iii. Permission granted.

234 AND HE GAVE PASTORS

the hand of any earnest Christian who desires to win someone for Christ.[5]

Many more tools are now available to the pastor. He must discover and use the program with which he is comfortable and that he feels is the most effective.

YOUTH EVANGELISM

Where could there be a more fertile field for evangelism than among children? Yet our greatest losses in the church come among the teens. Here is where a strong youth program is necessary, and undergirding that program must be an evangelistic thrust that will win and retain the youth through these crucial years, so their whole lives may be lived in service for Jesus Christ. Among the major problems youth face are: (1) the need for self-esteem, (2) the lack of family unity, (3) achieving acceptance and favor, (4) developing a personal faith, and (5) protecting the welfare of other people.

How often teens take in everything we seek to share, hear all the great Christian speakers, listen to hundreds of testimonies, know their responsibility to Christ, and yet remain inwardly bitter and rebellious toward God! Some have serious doubts about their salvation, never set goals for their lives, are primary causes of strife in their homes, follow loose dating practices, and keep company with questionable friends. This description would not be too unusual for some teens today, but when this same teen can give you his testimony of salvation and see no discrepancy between his life and his testimony, there is something very wrong. Jesus Christ is given verbal recognition, but He is not Lord of that teen's life. To induce such a person to witness will drive him from Christ, producing increasing internal conflict and torment.

The solution to such problems is to use the Word of God. All areas of life must be scrutinized by the strong light of God's Word. The moment teens see that God is living life with them and they become honest with themselves, appropriate adjustments in living will follow.

The program of youth evangelism in the local church can be structured in many ways, depending on the size of the group. It can be graded according to the school system, or simply as the junior high and senior high programs. Whichever program is chosen, publicize it

---

[5]Bill Bright, *Four Spiritual Laws* (Arrowhead Springs, CA: Campus Crusade), © 1965.

well. Notify all the teens and ask for volunteers to participate in the evangelism-outreach program. Inform them of the requirements for being a part of the effort. Select a catchy phrase or alphabetical letters to identify the program. Young people love to make commitments, so it is easy to motivate them with such disciplines as these:

1. Have a quiet time each day.
2. Memorize one verse each week.
3. Attend the meeting each week.
4. Attend the services of the church.
5. Talk to one person about Christ each week.
6. Give a testimony at a youth service, social, or church gathering.
7. Learn to present the gospel.

Adult sponsors must be deeply involved in the lives of the young people and follow up on their spiritual growth. Failure to fulfill requirements or the continued missing of assignments, should disqualify the teen from membership in the evangelism outreach. These programs can extend for a month or longer, on weekends or at any specified time. The object is to get young people talking to others about Jesus Christ. It is far better to keep youth and adult visitation separate; teens usually aren't as impressed with adult conversions as they are with those among their own peer group. Young people need to see their friends receive Christ—friends who seem to have no spiritual need and might laugh at their witness, but who are looking for Christ and will respond.

The results of youth evangelism and visitation are often surprising. Teenagers find that other teens do not always reject invitations, that friends and not just strangers are interested, that the youth group is a great fellowship, that it is fun to share the gospel, that the Holy Spirit really did anoint them, and that witnessing for Christ can become a very real and natural part of life.

Never assume programs will automatically work. The leadership demonstrated by the youth minister and/or the sponsors is the secret of success. Time and energy are needed by the carloads; it takes time to win the confidence of teens and to know them personally. If you are not constantly with them, you will fail to be effective. Young people for some reason prefer not to share their youth minister with others.

CHILD EVANGELISM

The most effective method in evangelism in the 20th century is the Sunday school. Churches that are building large memberships have live, growing Sunday schools. It is the place where enlistment begins, for a majority of all converts come through the Sunday school. Every Sunday school seeks to accomplish (1) the salvation of the soul, and (2) Bible teaching that results in strong, mature Christians.

The church that gives no attention to children is not fulfilling God's type of evangelism. Child evangelism is the utilization of every method, avenue, and means to win the lost child to Christ and retain him for the Kingdom. It is not a once-a-year effort, but a regular week-by-week and day-by-day ministry designed to meet the continuing spiritual needs of boys and girls.

F. B. Meyer is reported to have said at a great convention, "If the world is ever to be saved, it must be saved through childhood." Many reports have been circulated concerning the possibilities of salvation before and after certain ages, but one conclusion sums up the importance of child evangelism: "Only one person in 1000 is converted following the age of 20." Furthermore, a majority of all ministers, evangelists, and missionaries are won to Christ through the Sunday school before the age of 12. But millions of children are not being reached by any church. With juvenile and parental delinquency terrorizing our nation and the devastating effects of television on young impressionable minds, America stands as one of the most fertile fields for child evangelism.

To hold the children it has, and to reach out and win "other lost sheep," the church must have a well-planned and well-balanced year-round program. There are many church activities that can be carried on within the educational facilities of the church.

1. *Vacation Bible school* is an invaluable and specialized period of instruction provided as an educational and evangelistic ministry to children. It adds an additional 15 to 30 hours of Christian education and results in great spiritual growth. Vacation Bible school requires long-range planning, promotion, and staff and curriculum development, but the far-reaching results of this ministry more than justify the effort.

2. *Children's church* (extended Sunday school sessions that continue

through the worship hour) is a tremendous opportunity to win children to the Lord. It demands competent and dedicated leadership, but when every up-to-date method of communication is employed, children will remember what they have learned.

3. *Children's revivals, released-time programs, weekday activities, family nights, Missionettes,* and *Royal Rangers* are other useful ways to evangelize children. At the present time, hundreds of churches are utilizing their facilities throughout the week for preschools, day-care centers, and Christian elementary and secondary schools. What an exciting way to reach children for the Lord!

There are many out-of-church activities that can be used to strengthen the program for the evangelism of children.

1. *Home Bible clubs* are designed to reach the unchurched children of a neighborhood who may not be allowed to attend the church. Home Bible clubs are conducted on a weekly basis. They should be packed full of fun and inspiration, and not more than 1 hour long.

2. *Boys' and girls' camps* are a "must" in this day. All their lives, these youngsters will remember the spiritual experiences as well as the fun, food, and fellowship of other young people.

The joy and privilege of winning children to the Lord is immeasurable, and only those who are involved can share its blessings. The pastor is uniquely a part of child evangelism and he too enters into that joy!

MASS EVANGELISM

When churches join together cooperatively for city-wide meetings, there must be a unified desire, a harmonious spirit, and an unselfish determination to work for the whole and not just the part. How often churches have been fragmented and relationships broken because one man or one church dominated the mass meeting and selfishly garnered the results. Whether a community can benefit by this type of evangelism is for the local churches to decide.

Ministerial and Christian ethics must prevail in leadership, finances, results, and follow-up. Here is where the motives of hearts are revealed, as well as the ability to keep a right spirit even if we do not reap as many converts as others. Are we concerned only about our church, or are we concerned about the community as well? Can I rejoice in my brother minister's success, or will I become bitter and cynical and vow never to associate in such an effort again? These are not easy questions to answer, but they must be squarely faced if we are going to join in the city-wide efforts of mass evangelism.

Ministerial ethics have far-reaching effects. What a pastor sows in his ministerial conduct, he will reap in return from some other direction. He ought to treat visiting friends from other churches as he would want other ministers to treat his people. To take unfair advantage of some other pastor's members will only come back upon himself. The same principle holds true for the treatment of the evangelist in the mass meeting or in the local church. Treat him as you would want to be treated.

The pastor and the church must determine what positive results can come from mass evangelism and cooperative city-wide crusades. How marvelous when churches in one denomination and churches of all faiths can join forces in a community witness.

Missions

The International Congress on World Evangelization, held in Lausanne, Switzerland in 1974, chose as its theme "Let the Earth Hear His Voice." Billy Graham in his opening message to the congress said:

> We have heard the voices of the psychologists and psychiatrists with their commendable attempts to unravel the mysteries of human behavior and the human mind. . . . We have heard the men of war, the military, the defense ministers advising us as to the path of peace. . . . We have heard the voice of the diplomat shouting peace one day and war the next day. . . . We have heard uncertain voices in theologies that speak of a dead God and point us to . . . those who shred the Biblical faith. . . . We have heard the voice of the economists with their predictions of inflation, depression, and world famine. We have heard the anguished voice of history crying out from the crucible of pain, telling us lessons we never seem to be able to learn. We have heard the voice of Satan himself lying, flattering, oppressing, afflicting, influencing, destroying, sowing discord, spreading false doctrine, and gathering his forces for another massive attack against the kingdom of God. . . . We have heard all these voices, now "let us hear the voice of God."[6]

---

[6]International Congress on World Evangelization, *Let the Earth Hear His Voice* (Minneapolis, MN: World Wide Publications, 1975), pp. 16,17. Used by permission.

THE MEANING OF MISSIONS

The Great Commission of Christ directs all disciples to "let the earth hear His voice" by taking the gospel worldwide. We have already seen that missions is the church's activity of evangelism on a worldwide scale, that evangelism is the heart of missions, and that missions is the supreme task of the church. The church is God's agent in missions. To speak of this task without relating it to the church is to lose the Biblical perspective and develop an incomplete evangelism. Melvin Hodges has written: "The church is God's agent in the earth—the medium through which He expresses Himself to the world. God has no other redeeming agency in the earth."[7]

Missions makes little sense divorced from the Christian community. A missionary call is a call to something, and that something is more than a doctrine, an experience, or the exercise of faith. The missionary call beckons men to Jesus Christ and to the body of Christ.

Christianity is Christ, and the grand theme of the Bible across the centuries is the person and work of Jesus Christ. In Jesus Christ men find God. In the deepest sense possible, missions is the good news that the great God of heaven, out of a heart of infinite love for wayward man, came down to this world to become one of us that He might redeem us from our sins and bring us back into fellowship with himself. Christianity is Jesus Christ, and missions is the declaration of who He is, what He has done, and how men can receive Him and know Him.

Dr. John R. W. Stott makes a careful distinction between mission and missions. He points out that God is the source of "mission" and that "mission" primarily arises out of the nature, not of the church, but of God himself. The living God is a sending God; which is another way of saying that God is love, always reaching out after others in self-giving service.[8]

The idea of a sending God is seen throughout the Bible. He sent forth Abraham, commanding him to go into the great unknown and promising blessings to him and all the world if he obeyed. He sent Joseph into Egypt, overruling his brothers' cruelty, to preserve a godly

---

[7]From A Guide to Church Planting by Melvin Hodges. Copyright 1973. Moody Press, Moody Bible Institute of Chicago, p. 15. Used by permission.

[8]Taken from Christian Mission in the Modern World by John R. W. Stott. © 1975 by John R. W. Stott and used by permission of InterVarsity Press.

remnant. Then He sent Moses to the oppressed Israelites in Egypt with good news of liberation. From that time on, He sent a continuous procession of prophets with words of warning and promise to His people. Even after the Babylonian captivity, He graciously sent the Israelites back to their land and sent more messengers with them, and to them, to help rebuild the temple, the city, the walls, and the national life. Then at last, "When the time had fully come, God sent forth his Son" (Galatians 4:4, *RSV*). And after that the Father and the Son sent forth the Spirit on the Day of Pentecost (John 14:26; Acts 2:33).

This truth is essential if one is to understand the Biblical background of missions. The primary mission is God's, for it is He who sent the prophets, His Son, and His Spirit. Of all these missions, the mission of the Son is central, for it was the culmination of the ministry of the prophets and it embraced as its climax the sending of the Spirit. And now the Son sends as He himself was sent. During His public ministry, Jesus sent out first His own disciples and then the Seventy as an extension of His own preaching, teaching, healing, and ministry. After His death and resurrection, He widened the scope of the mission to all who call Him Lord and call themselves His disciples. Thus, we see that *missions*, as we understand the term today, began with *mission* and *mission* began with God.

THE MANDATE OF MISSIONS

The missionary mandate is usually restricted to the last words of Christ as recorded in Matthew. This familiar passage is known as the Great Commission, and not without reason: it contains the marching orders given by the risen Christ to His disciples just before His departure from the world. These words surely form part of the mandate, but they should not be regarded as the whole mandate. When speaking of the Great Commission, it is easy to be guilty of either oversimplification or overcomplication.

Dr. Harold Fickett, while speaking at the great "Founder's Week" in Moody Church, recalled a story related to him by William Mueller, who at that time was the distinguished professor of church history at the New Orleans Baptist Theological Seminary. Dr. Mueller told about a monastery in his native Germany that trained Christian brothers for lay work in the church. There was one Christian brother in the monastery who lived in mortal fear of getting the assignment of conducting chapel and preaching a sermon. He decided to head off that assignment. He went to the monitor and said, "Sir, I'm willing to do any amount of servile work that you assign me. I would be happy to go out into the garden and weed it. I'd be happy to get down on my knees and scrub the floors. I would be thrilled to be your personal dishwasher, but please don't ask me to conduct chapel and preach the sermon."

The monitor, recognizing that this was what he needed more than anything else, said to him, "You have that assignment for tomorrow morning. You are to be in chapel, you conduct the chapel service, and you preach the sermon."

The next morning this intimidated brother stood behind the pulpit, his knees knocking together, so frightened he did not know what to do. He began his sermon by saying, "Brothers, do you know what I am going to say?" They all shook their heads in the negative. He said, "Neither do I. Let's stand for the benediction. *Pax vobiscum* (peace be with you)."

This performance infuriated the monitor and he said, "Young man, I'm going to give you another chance tomorrow morning. I don't want you to do what you've done today!"

The following day arrived and the intimidated brother began as he had done the day before. "Brothers, do you know what I am going to say?" They all nodded their heads in the affirmative. He went on, "Since you already know, there's no point in my saying it. Let's rise for the benediction. *Pax vobiscum.*"

Livid with anger, the monitor came to him and said, "Look, I am going to give you one more chance, and if you don't make good, I am going to put you on bread and water in solitary confinement and let you think it over."

The third morning the scene was the same. This brother stood before his peers and said, "Brothers, do you know what I am going to say?" Some shook their heads in the affirmative; some shook their heads in the negative. He smiled at them and said, "Let those who know tell those who don't know!"[9]

That story is an excellent definition of *mission* and evangelism. It

[9]Harold L. Fickett, Jr., *The Priority of Evangelism* (Chicago: Moody Bible Institute, 1974), pp. 54,55. Used by permission.

succinctly compacts Jesus' words of the Great Commission: "Let those who know the gospel tell those who don't know the gospel."

GOD'S CHARACTER

To understand the sending of the Son into the world and the sending of all men to herald the gospel, one must grasp something of the heart and mind of God for mankind. This great Christian mission originated in the heart of God—it is His work and not man's—and it grows out of His essential character. If God were any other kind of God, there would be no Christian mission. The Scriptures were not written to prove the existence of God; that is taken for granted. What the Bible does reveal is the character of God, and His person can never be divorced from His character. Robert Speer wrote many years ago on this truth:

> The supreme arguments for missions are not found in any specific words. It is in the very being and character of God that the deepest ground of the missionary enterprise is to be found. We cannot think of God except in terms which necessitate the missionary idea. Though words may reveal eternal missionary duties, the grounds are in the very being and thought of God, in the character of Christianity, in the aim and purpose of the Christian church, and in the nature of humanity, its unity and its need.[10]

The Scriptures say much about the attributes and nature of God. Two verses are closely linked with the underlying concept of the mission of the church. The apostle John, in his first Epistle, makes two great declarations concerning the character of God: "God is light" (1:5); and, "God is love" (4:16). These two attributes have always been an integral part of the character of God, but they were never fully manifested until the coming of Christ. They constitute an important dimension of the missionary mandate: (1) Man was made by God and for God; (2) It was God's intentions for man to glorify God and fellowship with Him; and, (3) Man was made in God's image so He could have an object worthy of His everlasting love.

Through Christ, John shows us that God is love; slow to anger; plenteous in mercy; full of compassion, grace, and truth; and always ready to forgive. God's love is like himself—eternal, inscrutable, and

---

[10]Robert E. Speer, *Christianity and the Nations* (Old Tappan, NJ: Fleming H. Revell, Co., © 1910), pp. 17,18. Used by permission.

immutable. He loves mankind with an everlasting love (Jeremiah 31:3). This indestructible, all-inclusive love of God prompted Him to send Jesus to be the Saviour of the world (1 John 4:9, 10). This glorious fact is the foundation of all missionary endeavor. Without it, there would be no missionary mandate.

But there is more to the character of God than just His love. God is light as well as love, and light in Scripture stands for holiness and truth (Romans 13:11-14; Psalm 43:3). The difference between the love of God and man's love is like comparing light and darkness. The love of man is tainted with pride, but the love of God is pure and holy. Because of his tainted love, man has great difficulty in understanding the true nature of love. The beauty of God as light is His holiness and truth. His throne is a throne of holiness (Psalm 47:8). His kingdom is a kingdom of righteousness (Matthew 6:33). His law is perfect (Psalm 19:7), and His scepter is a righteous one (Psalm 45:6).

We must always remember the righteous, loving, holy character of God. To keep it in balance, however, we must also see that the Scriptures reveal His wrath. Rejected love reveals wrath from heaven (Romans 1:18). To reject God's love in Christ makes a man subject to God's wrath (John 3:36). The character of God, then, is not broken up into separate entities in themselves—wrath reserved for the ungodly, and love reserved for His children. All men are creatures of His hand and objects of His love. His anger is kindled against sin, for He cannot tolerate sin no matter where it is found. He loves the sinner at the same time that He hates the sin. The one is the corollary of the other—to love righteousness is to hate iniquity.

If God were only a God of love and not light, there would be no need of mission. He could save all men by a word. But because God is also a God of light and holiness, repentance of sin is required. God's love makes it possible for the repentant sinner to be saved; God's holiness makes it necessary for the sinner to repent. God's character demands "mission" in the world, for the missionary mandate is rooted in God's character.

THE GREAT COMMISSION

The wording of the Great Commission appears in different forms, for Jesus seems to have repeated it on several occasions. "Go into all the world and preach the gospel to the whole creation" is the familiar command in Mark's Gospel (Mark 16:15, *RSV*). "Go . . . and make disciples of all nations, baptizing them . . . and . . . teaching them" is from Matthew (Matthew 28:19,20, *RSV*). Luke records Christ said that "repentance and forgiveness of sins will be preached in his name to all nations" (24:47, *NIV*). In Acts 1:8 it is declared that His people would receive power to become His witnesses to the ends of the earth.

The cumulative effect of these Scriptures is clear. It is in terms of preaching, witnessing, and making disciples that we define the nature of the mission of the Church. Some people feel evangelism is the exclusive meaning of the Great Commission. But there is more to it than that. The hunger of families, the poverty of the jobless, the helplessness of the sick, the weakness of the aged, the loneliness of the shut-in—these realities upset the narrow application of the Great Commission and force one to look again at the social implications of the gospel.

We must read again the commission as stated in John 20:21: "As my Father hath sent me, even so send I you." Christ's mission is the model for ours. That means our life should be a life of service (Mark 10:45). Jesus emptied himself and took on himself the form of a servant (Philippians 2:5-8); supplying us with a perfect model of mission and service. In our day, we need a discerning eye to maintain the right priority between a person's eternal destiny and his material needs, while ministering to both.

Sometimes we give the Great Commission too exclusive a place in our Christian thinking. John R. W. Stott reminds us: "We've emphasized the Great Commission and forgotten the Great Commandment."[11]

The Great Commission does not supersede the Great Commandment, but it adds to God-love and neighbor-service a new and urgent dimension. If we love our neighbor, we shall no doubt share with him the good news of the gospel. But if we truly love him, we will not stop with evangelism; we will go beyond his soul's need to his material needs and total welfare.

We are sent like Jesus to serve; we go—we witness—we love! The gospel lacks visibility if we merely preach it. And it lacks credibility if in our preaching we are interested only in the souls of men and not their total welfare. Mission does not describe everything God does in

---

[11]Stott, *Christian Mission in the Modern World,* pp. 22, 29.

the world, but it does describe what the Church has been sent to do—
to be the "salt of the earth" and "the light of the world" (Matthew
5:13-16).

THE LOSTNESS OF MAN

If the condition of man were other than it is, there would be no
need for the Christian mission. The needs of the world are deep and
long-standing. The Church cannot be true to its own gospel if it turns
a deaf ear to the world's needs. No Christian can deny that man's
deepest need is spiritual. If man is made in the image of God and
possesses an immortal soul that will live as long as God lives (either in
fellowship with God or alienated from Him), it stands to reason that
his greatest need is to be saved.

This was undoubtedly the teaching of our Lord when He said:
"What shall it profit a man, if he shall gain the whole world, and
lose his own soul? Or what shall a man give in exchange for his
soul?" (Mark 8:36, 37). Paul makes us realize the most profound question any man can ask during his life is, "What must I do to be
saved?" (Acts 16:30). On the answer to that question hangs man's
happiness and fulfillment here, and in the hereafter as well.

The Scriptures clearly teach that mankind is alienated from God
(Ephesians 4:18), hostile to God (Romans 5:10), and under the wrath
of God. The sinner's only hope is to turn from his wicked way, repent,
and believe the gospel. There is no other hope held out to him; he has
no options! It is imperative for him to hear and understand the gospel.

How often we hear the words, "Is man really lost?" For that answer
I can only turn to the Bible and see that all have sinned and come
short of the glory of God (Romans 3:23). All are children of wrath
(Ephesians 2:3). All are under condemnation (Romans 3:19). "As by
one man sin entered into the world, and death by sin; and so death
passed upon all men, for that all have sinned" (Romans 5:12).

Man is alienated from the life of God (Ephesians 4:18), ignorant of
the truth of God (Romans 1:25), disobedient to the will of God (Titus
3:3), and under God's wrath (John 3:36). The virus of sin has pene-
trated every fiber of his being, darkening his mind (Ephesians 4:18),
and enslaving his will (John 8:34). He is what theologians term
"totally depraved." All the writers of the Scriptures declare this sober-
ing truth, from Moses to St. John in the Revelation: man is hopelessly

lost, incorrigibly rebellious, and willfully wayward. He is not a sinner because he sins, he sins because he is a sinner.

Nowhere is the lostness of man more vividly portrayed than in the three parables spoken by Christ in Luke 15. There we have the lost coin, the lost sheep, and the lost son. One great preacher said, "The coin was helplessly lost; the sheep was heedlessly lost; the son was willfully lost." Man has gone astray not like a bird, but like a sheep (Isaiah 53:6). He has no homing instinct. Left to himself, he will always travel the downward road further and further into the wilderness of sin (Luke 15:13).

Another question that arises is this: "Are the heathen lost?" And what will God do about those who have never heard the gospel? Is it fair to punish them for rejecting a Christ of whom they are completely ignorant? Many of them are searching and doubtless would believe if they had an opportunity. Are all these people going to be forever lost through no fault of their own? To these questions we can offer a few comments.

1. If one is worried about the fairness of God's judgment, he should remember God is more concerned about His fairness than man will ever be. "Shall not the Judge of all the earth do right?" (Genesis 18:25).

2. Men are always judged on the basis of their knowledge and not on their ignorance (Romans 2).

3. All those who seek after God sincerely will find Him (Jeremiah 29:13).

4. If you are deeply concerned about the lost and those who have never heard the gospel, this may be a sign that God is wanting you to go tell them.

THE MISSIONS CONVENTION

To know and understand the meaning and work of missions yet never communicate it to your people is worse than not knowing it at all. The most successful promotion of missionary evangelism is found in missions conventions. The church that has missions built solidly into its calendar every year is the church that is able to be of significant help to world outreach. A missions convention is for this purpose.

Creating a Mood. Mobilize every force in your church as you prepare. This means the youth group, the Men's Ministries, the Women's

Ministries, the Sunday school classes, the choir, and all other church groups should have a part. One group can make a world map with the names and locations of the missionaries supported by the church, and then post it in some conspicuous location. Another group can prepare bulletin-board displays of mission-field pictures. Another group can prepare a literature table featuring promotional materials provided by the Division of Foreign Missions. The Women's Ministries group may wish to display some of the articles it is currently preparing to send to missionaries overseas.

These activities help to create a "missions mood" before the missions convention actually takes place. Not only do the displays themselves call attention to missions, but there is an educational value to those preparing such displays. The effort to create a missions atmosphere in the church is well worth the time and trouble it takes. Flags, maps, posters, banners, curio displays, literature stands—all will contribute to the success of your missions convention.

Providing a Program. Avoid the common mistake of making your convention too long. It is better to have a few fast-moving services containing several interesting features than to spread your program thin over many days. Use a varied format for services, including short missions films. Your own circumstances must dictate whether you have services on Friday, Saturday, and Sunday, or according to some other plan.

It is not necessary to have a large number of missionaries present to have a good convention. Too many missionaries can sometimes turn out to be a discouraging drag on your program because of the greater financial load involved in providing reasonable offerings for each of them.

Plan far enough ahead so you may obtain the missionary speakers you prefer. If possible, include speakers who are already part of your program. Balance the team with representatives from various parts of the world and from different kinds of missions ministries.

You may wish to plan your missions convention simultaneously with two or three other nearby churches. A cooperative effort of this kind sometimes makes it possible for each church to enjoy the ministries of a greater number of different speakers than it could afford if it had to bear the travel expenses alone for all of them. If the number of speakers matches the number of participating churches and the number of services planned, it will be possible for each church to have a different speaker in each successive service. Of course there are advantages to having the same missionary speaker for more than one service. Your people will come to know him better, and he will have a better opportunity to share his vision more completely with them.

Consult with the leaders of the church. If your church does not have a missions committee, you may find it helpful to establish one. Delegate as much responsibility as possible. Try to select dates that can be repeated year after year with minor adjustments. Treat the missions convention as a time of great importance, and make numerous announcements well in advance so your people will look forward eagerly to the occasion.

Planning the Finances. Think through carefully the costs of the kind of convention you want. Remember that most missionaries need much more than their expenses if they are to meet their necessary budget and return to their fields. Take one or more advance offerings for convention expenses during the weeks or months of preparation.

Give your people opportunity to commit themselves to missions by estimating their missions giving for the following year. No "pull" is necessary. The simple opportunity to make "faith promises" will enlist many people in missions participation on a regular basis, which is by far the best way. Use faith-promise envelopes provided by the Division of Foreign Missions or some of your own design.

Explain your missions budget clearly—and, if necessary, repeatedly —to your congregation. In the long run, the thoughtful acceptance of missions is better than an emotional appeal that is independent of a continuing plan. Keep your fund-raising time short. Three to five minutes, prayerfully planned, is plenty in any one service. And be sure to keep the church informed of the amount of cash received and faith promises made.

Write the Divisions of Foreign and Home Missions for help in planning your missions convention. It can prove to be a time of rich spiritual experience and blessing.

THE FAITH-PROMISE PLAN

A faith promise differs from a pledge in two distinct ways. First, a faith promise is a commitment to God. Usually the church does not consider this a pledge and does not send a statement of an unpaid balance. A faith promise is paid as the Lord enables the individual to do so. Second, a faith promise is made on the basis of the anticipated blessing of God. It is not a pledge of money in possession, but an exercising of faith in God—faith that God will provide money which can be given for missions. Numerous individuals testify that in response to their faith, unexpected funds came to them which they channeled to missions.

It is important that every pastor start a faith-promise plan for missions in his church. The great churches of our Movement, both small and large, are churches with vision who challenged their people. They lifted their eyes and looked at the harvest. Here are some words of counsel for establishing a faith-promise plan in the local church:

1. A complete financial report of the missions activity of the church is an important background from which to communicate a new missions vision. Often it takes years to develop the full missions potential of a church. It is the result of long-range planning with clearly defined objectives. The secret of an effective missions program is that the church members understand clearly its objectives. Throughout a missions emphasis or convention the people should know what to expect. They should look forward to a faith-promise offering as a time of blessing and victory. Everyone should know an offering will be taken and pray that new goals will be reached.

2. Recruit all the leaders of the church—the Sunday school, the youth, the Men's Ministries, and the Women's Ministries. The Sunday school is perhaps the most organized function of the church. Therefore, the Sunday school can often be used as a means through which total participation is realized. Most churches experience a great increase in missions giving as they make family participation their aim.

3. Explain the faith-promise plan and the entire church missions program to your leaders. Do this well in advance of the missions convention or annual emphasis. Unite in prayer for the coming convention. Explain how the faith promises are to be taken. Outline the missions budget—which missionaries are supported, the amount of support, special projects, and goals. The financial goals of the missions program should involve everyone in the church.

4. Important to the success of the missions offering are the ushers. They should not appear embarrassed or apologetic while receiving the faith-commitment cards. To avoid this and instill an attitude of faith

and a knowledge of their duties, meet with them in advance for a time of prayer and instruction.

5. Totaling the faith promises (whether in one, two, or three services, or at the conclusion of the convention) should be carefully and prayerfully planned. It should not be done haphazardly or tacked on the end of a long service.

The pastor is the key to the missions-power potential of the church. A missions vision begins with his Christlike, unselfish spirit. The pastor who leads his people in this manner fulfills the will of God. This was expressed when God gave His Son, and is now expressed through us as we give the gospel to the lost. Developing a missions church takes conscious effort, carefully planned and wholly dedicated to reaching the lost. The Promotions Department of the Division of Foreign Missions stands ready to help any pastor who wishes to unlock the missions potential of his church.

THE CONVENTION BUDGET

There is no one answer to meeting the missions-convention budget. Local conditions vary; churches vary. Nevertheless, there are basic principles that can be followed in developing a missions program.

The faith-promise plan is one. Used effectively, this plan can realize the potential missions power of a church. As individuals make the faith promise a part of their commitment to the church, strong regular offerings will result. Although this means the church will have a strong, well-supported missions program, it may also mean the actual cash raised during the missions convention may be less.

The missionary must make his furlough time as productive as possible. Therefore, it is necessary that he receive more than just enough to meet his expenses. Doubtless he will have commitments to the national church or the field fellowship to raise extra funds for urgent needs on the field. This, however, need not cause a financial bind if careful plans are made. With a planned yearly program, the pastor and missions-convention committee can meet the convention budget and the needs of the missionary through any of four possible approaches.

1. Receive missions-convention expense offerings in advance. Place them in reserve until needed. From this fund, cover advertising, accommodations, and travel expenses. This will free actual cash received during the convention for on-the-field needs.

2. Cover the expenses of the convention—advertising, accommodations, travel—from offerings received during the convention. Then, commit a regular monthly amount to the missionary's needs and field projects, etc. This can be repeated each year with new participants.

3. Cover convention expenses from general or other departmental funds. This will release the convention offerings for the missionary's needs or projects. This is especially helpful when developing a missions program where none or little has previously existed.

4. Set aside a portion of each month's missions giving to cover the expenses of the annual convention or emphasis. This will relieve the strain produced by trying to raise convention expenses and adequate offerings for the missionaries in three or four services of the convention.

Any one of the preceding plans, or a combination, may be suitable for your church. Whichever plan you use, be sure to communicate with your people. Make certain they know and understand the goals of their missions program!

FAITH-PROMISE PLAN FOLLOW-UP

Following through on the program is just as important as its proper launching. The following suggestions are for your consideration in making the program work for the entire year.

1. *Keep the program before your people.* Keep a record of the progress of receipts of faith promises. The week following your convention, divide your faith-promise total by 12 and set this amount as your monthly goal. For example, if your total of faith promises for 1 year was $2,400, your monthly goal is $200. Announce your progress each month. This may be done on Missionary Day or at any other time. Make these announcements as often as you feel it will be profitable.

2. *Compile a list of those who make a faith promise.* From the faith-promise envelopes that were filled out during your convention, prepare a list of the names, addresses, and amounts of those making faith promises. This should be kept in *confidence* since it is not a pledge, but a *faith promise.* Instruct the people to use the church envelopes for giving and to mark faith-promise offerings "FP." By keeping a record you can tell when someone needs encouragement to

continue monthly giving. Any encouragement should be discreetly given, for this must be kept in confidence.

3. *Encourage your people to report to you faith-promise blessings and answers to prayer.* Ask for such testimonies occasionally, possibly once a month. These testimonies will encourage others to continue their faith promises.

4. *Encourage your people to give all missionary money through the church, even though it may be designated to an independent missionary.* This should be done for their own protection if they desire to deduct it on their income tax return.

5. *Bring in missionary speakers periodically.* This should be done monthly, or at least bimonthly. These speakers will keep your people in touch with the field.

6. *Preach a missionary message to your people occasionally.* They enjoy the messages of the missionaries, but nothing can take the place of a sermon on world evangelism by the pastor. The church will often be receptive to your message when they will not hear an outsider.

7. *Administer the missionary program.* World evangelism is the church's main job. Therefore, the pastor and church board should be responsible for the missionary program. If a man is not interested in missions, he should not be on the board. How can he help the pastor lead the church if he does not believe in the main purpose for which the church exists?

When the church makes a monthly pledge toward the support of a missionary, have this approved by the board and recorded in the minutes. This will assure better cooperation from the church in keeping the commitment. In the event of a change in pastors, the incoming pastor will know whom the church supports, and the missionary's income will not be interrupted while he is on the field.

When a pledge is made toward the monthly support of a missionary, keep the commitment. Much hardship has been suffered by missionaries when churches discontinued their pledges while the missionaries were on the field.

8. *Plan world-evangelism prayer meetings.* Plan these meetings for the evenings to enlist the men. If too many of your missionary activities are carried on by the Women's Ministries, the church may be inclined to leave missionary work to the women. God bless the ladies for their willingness to carry the load, but world evangelism is the

duty of the *whole church* and demands the work of everyone. At these prayer meetings bring the requests of all missionaries before the Lord. Pray for each one individually. Report answers to prayers.

9. *Carry on regular correspondence with your missionaries.* Regular letters from the church will show the missionary you are interested in him. This will improve his morale and result in better work on his part.

Read the missionary's newsletters. Watch for reports of achievements, prayer requests, and special needs. Some excerpts from these letters can be used in your church bulletin, or they can be read when you are taking your monthly missionary offering or mentioning your faith-promise progress.

The missionary correspondence should be done by the pastor if he has a secretary. If the pastor desires, however, he may appoint a corresponding secretary who can handle all correspondence with the missionaries. The corresponding secretary can carefully read all newsletters and give the pastor excerpts of special achievements, prayer requests, and special needs that he may use in his announcements, bulletins, etc.

Extreme care should be exercised in choosing a corresponding secretary who will work in complete cooperation with the pastor. The corresponding secretary *should never report to the church.* This is the pastor's prerogative.

10. *Request taped messages from the missionary.* If you have a tape recorder or can borrow one occasionally, ask the missionary to send short taped messages to the congregation. These can be played before the missionary offering or during a prayer meeting. And why not tape a service and send it to the missionary? He will enjoy it.

World evangelism is a job to be worked at full time. Keep the vision of the need ever before your eyes. Read about missions, pray about missions, and talk about missions until you are absorbed with the Great Commission and can pass it along to your people.

Never forget the charge to the Church, and never let your people forget their responsibility to reach the lost of all lands. As this is done, you will see sacrificial giving by your people that you never thought possible. Don't fear for your general income. God will take care of that, and without fail you will see an increase in it too.

"There is that scattereth, and yet increaseth; and there is that withholdeth more than is meet, but it tendeth to poverty. The liberal soul shall be made fat: and he that watereth shall be watered also himself" (Proverbs 11:24, 25).

"And this gospel of the kingdom shall be preached in all the world for a witness unto all nations; and then shall the end come" (Matthew 24:14).

"After this I beheld, and, lo, a great multitude, which no man could number, of all nations, and kindreds, and people, and tongues, stood before the throne, and before the Lamb, clothed with white robes, and palms in their hands" (Revelation 7:9).

Suggested Reading

Autrey, C. E. *Basic Evangelism*. Grand Rapids: Zondervan Publishing House, 1959.

Douglas, J. D. *Let the Earth Hear His Voice*. Minneapolis: Worldwide Publications, 1975.

Stott, John R. W. *Christian Mission in the Modern World*. Downers Grove, IL: InterVarsity Press, 1975.

Horne, Charles S. *The Romance of Preaching*. Old Tappan, NJ: Fleming H. Revell Co., 1914.

Lindsell, Harold. *An Evangelical Theology of Missions*. Grand Rapids: Zondervan Publishing House, 1970.

Neill, Stephen. *Salvation Tomorrow*. Nashville: Abingdon Press, 1976.

_____. *The Unfinished Task*. London: Lutterworth Press, 1962.

Newbigin, Lesslie. *The Good Shepherd*. Grand Rapids: Wm. B. Eerdmans Publishing Co., 1977.

Schuller, Robert H. *Your Church Has Real Possibilities*. Glendale, CA: Gospel Light/Regal Publications, 1974.

_____. *Christ the Liberator*. Downers Grove, IL: InterVarsity Press, 1971.

Wagner, C. Peter. *Your Church Can Grow*. Glendale, CA: Gospel Light/Regal Publications, 1976.

9

The Pastor
and
Special Ministries

EDWARD B. BERKEY

The special ministries of the busy pastor permit him at times to scale the heights of joy and happiness; but at other times he must descend into the valley of sufferings and there like his Master be "touched with the feelings of [their] infirmities" (Hebrews 4:15). He must realize with Solomon that there is "a time to weep, and a time to laugh" (Ecclesiastes 3:4). Also among his duties are occasions when he is called to perform some formal ministries that require his demeanor and preparation to be appropriate for the occasion.

The late Myer Pearlman gave some wise words of counsel for the pastor as he ministers in some areas that warrant reverence, dignity, preparedness, and structure graced with the Spirit's anointing:

> It hardly needs to be said that set forms of devotion are uncongenial to those who practice a simple mode of worship and who stress spiritual liberty in prayer and preaching.
>
> Yet, while recognizing this fact it still remains true that there are special occasions where an appointed order is necessary for a well-conducted service. And if this is so, why be content with forms that are crude or badly prepared?. . . Jesus prescribed the form known as the Lord's Prayer: "When ye pray, say . . . ." The prophet Hosea once said to his countrymen: "Take with you words, and turn to the Lord: say unto him . . ." (Hosea 14:2).
>
> There need be no morbid fear of lifeless ritual. As long as the spiritual vitality of the church is maintained the use of necessary forms will never become merely formal.[1]

Edward B. Berkey is pastor of Bethany Assembly of God, Springfield, Massachusetts.

[1]Myer Pearlman, *The Minister's Service Book* (Springfield, MO: Gospel Publishing House, n.d.) p. 3.

That we might consider the diversities of the special ministries the pastor is called on to fulfill, let us first look at "Joyous Ministries," next "Ministries of Comfort," and then briefly at some "Formal Ministries."

Joyous Ministries

THE WEDDING

We will ever be grateful that the Holy Spirit recorded the beautiful picture of Jesus and His disciples sharing the joy of the unnamed bride and groom (John 2:1). It speaks to us of the importance Jesus placed on the public recognition of the holy union of a man and a woman in marriage.

Marriage Counseling. As soon as an engaged couple has determined a desired date for the wedding and shared it with the pastor, he should set up an initial conference that will then lead to a counseling session or sessions—if the pastor determines he is able to marry the couple. There are several questions the pastor should ask in the initial conference.

1. Are both saved?
2. Has either one of them been married before?
3. How long has the couple been engaged?
4. How do the parents feel about this marriage?
5. Is either of the couple a member of another church?
6. When and what type of wedding is being planned?

The answers to these questions will give important information to the pastor, permitting him to pursue certain areas in greater depth. Every pastor must determine, between himself and God, whether or not he will participate and perform a wedding ceremony between two unsaved individuals, or one saved and one unsaved person. Various arguments can be advanced in either direction. Whatever the resolution for an individual pastor, this decision should always be communicated in a spirit of love rather than in judgment.

Even though the pastor is clear throughout his ministry and his counseling regarding the teaching of God's Word relative to premarital sex, there may be times when he will be requested to perform wedding ceremonies where pregnancy occurred prior to marriage. However, if it is deemed advisable, it is certainly proper for the minister to conduct such a ceremony although the circumstances may dictate that it be private or semiprivate. This ministry need not suggest acceptance of sin, but it can show God's forgiveness and love which Jesus demonstrated to those who were condemned by this world.

The pastor should manifest a genuine desire to help such couples. It is also his responsibility to show the couple that marriage is not mandatory. Sometimes marriage under these circumstances is not advisable. If the pastor determines the couple is not in love or does not really desire to get married, he certainly should counsel accordingly. If, on the other hand, the pastor determines through counseling that the couple is in love and they do desire to be married, he should do his best to assist them in making it a significant and meaningful experience.

The pastor should remember that marriage counseling begins long before his first conference with a couple. His pulpit ministry should include practical and scriptural teaching on relationships between the sexes, marriage, the home, child rearing, and the importance of the family in God's plan. A couple reared in the church should come to a marriage counseling session with an insight into Christian marriage because of the teaching ministry of the pastor. It is suggested the pastor refuse to perform a ceremony unless a couple will participate in marriage counseling. At least four major areas should be covered by a pastor in these sessions.

The prophet of old uttered these words of wisdom: "Can two walk together, except they be agreed?" (Amos 3:3). Therefore, give attention to *compatibility in the area of finance.* Since this is considered the number one cause of marital problems, it is important to give some practical direction concerning living within a budget, honoring the Lord with the tithe (Leviticus 27:30), and preventing the marriage from undergoing unnecessary strain because of unwise stewardship of what God has entrusted to them.

The second area for consideration is *compatibility as two social beings.* Here the counselor can lead a couple into a discussion and better understanding of each other. Particular attention can be given to the small things of life, for Scripture indicates it is the little foxes that spoil the vines (Song of Solomon 2:15). The pastor has an obligation to help the dreamy-eyed couple to understand some of the small frustrations that take place in a relationship. He does the couple a disservice if he suggests in the counseling session that they will have a "perfect marriage." Each couple needs to understand there will be problems, but a husband and a wife can have a good marriage as they appropriate the resources of divine grace and follow practical as well as scriptural principles.

The third area that must be considered is *compatibility as two spiritual beings*. The pastor should emphasize each partner's individual relationship with the Lord and their joint relationship with Jesus Christ as the Head of their new home (2 Corinthians 6:14). This affords the pastor an excellent opportunity to encourage personal as well as family devotions and to recommend appropriate material. The pastor also has opportunity to emphasize to the prospective husband his responsibilities before God as the head of the home.

The fourth area that definitely must be considered is *compatibility as two physical beings*. As the pastor deals with the couple's physical and emotional relationship, he should place great stress on the importance of the individual within a marriage and on the necessity of caring for and understanding the needs of one's mate. The pastor does the couple a disservice if he does not give adequate discussion concerning sex and possible problems in this area. In avoiding discussion of this subject, the pastor may be understood as suggesting that the sexual relationship in marriage stands apart from God's ideal for a marriage union. It is important to point out that sex, within the bonds of marriage, is a God-given gift (Hebrews 13:4).

It is fitting for the minister to consider with the couple 1 Corinthians 7:3-5, and 1 Peter 3:7. Some or all of the following books might be made available to the couple: *The Art of Understanding Your Mate* by Cecil G. Osborn (Grand Rapids: Zondervan, 1974); *How to Be Happy Though Married* by Tim LaHaye (Wheaton, IL: Tyndale House); and *The Act of Marriage* by Tim and Beverly LaHaye (Grand Rapids: Zondervan, 1976). At the conclusion of the counseling session, the pastor might present them with a gift copy of *Sexual Happiness in Marriage* by Herbert J. Miles (Grand Rapids: Zondervan Publishing House, 1967).

Caring for Wedding Details. The pastor should be acquainted with the laws of his state regarding marriage and with his particular obligations. This information is available at the county courthouse or the office of the city or town clerk. A great deal of responsibility is placed on the pastor in regard to details surrounding a wedding ceremony. At the initial conference or when the pastor determines he will be able to perform the wedding, he would do well to set some objectives for the couple to achieve in their wedding.

1. It should be beautiful. Thus there should be a rehearsal with each person participating in the wedding being present. A prior rehearsal will help to avoid embarrassing and unexpected situations arising at the time of the wedding ceremony.

2. It should be sacred. This can be achieved as a couple discreetly chooses the music to testify of their faith in Christ. The attitude and dedication of their attendants will help achieve this objective.

3. It should be very personal. The couple must be made to realize that this is their wedding, and within the proper decorum and recognition of marriage as a divine institution, they should certainly express their individuality.

4. It should be marked by the presence of the Lord. They too can have His miraculous presence at their wedding just as the couple did so many years ago. *The Living Bible* tells it this way: "Jesus and His disciples were invited" (John 2:2). Encourage the couple to begin to pray that their wedding will be a lovely witness of their faith by the beautiful presence of Christ made real to every guest by the power of the Holy Spirit.

It is beneficial for the pastor to have a brochure to give to each couple outlining responsibilities such as age requirements, health demands, and the number of days notice for the marriage certificate. As it relates to the church, the brochure or information sheet should inform the couple of any expenses that would be incurred if they use the church, such as the custodian, candles, candelabra rental (if the church does not have one), cleaning of the aisle runner (if the church furnishes one). Also it should include any guidelines concerning flash pictures during the ceremony, the possibility of having the wedding recorded, delivering the marriage license so the pastor will have time to make out a certificate, the regulations for use of the church fellowship hall, along with the telephone numbers of the music director, custodian, and organist. It would be advisable, too, if the brochure proposed some suggested honorariums for participants (other than the pastor) whom the couple may ask to assist them in the wedding. Often someone (possibly the pastor's wife) serves as a coordinator of the events at the church, and this can be of great assistance to a couple.

On the night of the rehearsal, things will move more smoothly if the pastor has a typed list of detailed instructions for the wedding party. Such attention to details not only gives the participants a clear understanding of their responsibility at the rehearsal, but also allows them to take the instructions home with them to peruse so they can approach the wedding more confidently.

A Celebration of Joy. On this festive day when the focus is turned on the bride and groom, the pastor should be dressed in a manner appropriate to his official position in the ceremony as God's representative. He should not be dressed in a way that would draw attention to him as an individual. His poise, spiritual strength, and calmness will be a silent means of ministering to the couple and helping to make their day one filled with the happiest of memories.

To be consistent, the phraseology used in weddings should be as follows: the minister "performs" the ceremony, "solemnizes" the marriage, "officiates" at a wedding, "marries" a couple, "gives" the vows, and pronounces "the union."[2] An appropriate form for a ceremony may be found in *The Minister's Service Book* and *Minister's Manual II.*[3] The minister may wish to write his own ceremony, or a couple may wish to write their vows.

It is always expected that the pastor and his wife will be invited to the ceremony, and whether the couple be Christians or not, the wedding affords a beautiful occasion to represent the Man who graced the wedding in Cana, ate with sinners, and went about doing good. Above all, the minister has a unique opportunity of ministering and entering into a relationship with a couple that will be cherished by them as long as God gives them memory.

THE LORD'S TABLE

Emphasizing Scripture Teaching. There are many names used for the Lord's Supper, some with a scriptural foundation and others with-

---

[2]Cleland McAfee, *Ministerial Practice* (New York: Harper and Row Publishers, Inc., 1928), p. 138.

[3]Both are available from the Gospel Publishing House.

out. The term the *Lord's Supper* is probably the most common and is especially appropriate because Jesus instituted the memorial. It commemorates the death of Jesus (Luke 22:19, 20) and anticipates His return (1 Corinthians 11:26). It is the Lord's Supper because everything in it centers on Him.

Some Christian fellowships use the term *Eucharist*. Although this term is not in our English Bible, it is based on a Biblical concept. It is taken from the Greek word *Eucharistea* which means "The Thanksgiving." Jesus gave thanks when He instituted the Lord's Supper.

Frequently we speak of this blessed service as the *Communion*. This too is a Biblical term (1 Corinthians 10:16). The Greek word translated *communion* really means "fellowship." Thus, it is appropriate to call the service *Communion* because we have fellowship with Christ and with our fellow believers.

Other names given this ordinance of the Church are the *Lord's Table* (1 Corinthians 10:21) and the *Breaking of Bread* (Acts 2:42). Another term, although without Biblical foundation, does suggest the sacredness of the occasion: the *Sacrament*. The Latin *sacramentum* refers to the oath by which the Roman soldiers swore their allegiance to Caesar, to obey him in whatever he wished, even if it meant death. Certainly no less surrender is demanded of Christian soldiers.

Then there is the Roman Catholic term the *Mass*. Many years ago the Roman Catholic Church dismissed all non-Christians before the serving of the Lord's Supper. The term is taken from the Latin *Missaest* meaning "you are dismissed."

Charles Erdman states the following concerning the actual service:

> It must be conducted with dignity and solemnity and the feeling of tender emotion; yet there must be a spirit of confidence, cheerfulness and hope. All haste and confusion must be avoided and every effort must be made to fix our thought upon the presence, grace and redemptive power of the living Christ.[4]

The minister who is called on to preside at the Lord's Table should encourage all friends and visitors to participate according to their faith. It is fitting to point out that ours is not a "closed communion" and one need not be a member of our church to share in this ordinance. Welcome every follower of Christ to the Lord's Table, and give

[4]Charles Erdman, *The Work of the Pastor* (Philadelphia: Westminster Press, 1928), p. 109.

instructions to hold the emblems until everyone is served. Appropriate music or worshipful and meaningful choruses can be most helpful as the congregation looks back to Calvary, looks inward in self-examination, and looks forward to the hour when Christ shall come again.

Need for Careful Planning. G.C.S. Wallace observes the importance of planning and preparation before the pastor administers the Lord's Supper:

> Let the minister study how in administering the supper he may give due place to reverence, simplicity, quietness and deliberateness. Then, there will be no bustle or no hurry, no appearance of casualness or empty informalism, and no indication that at His own supper, the Lord is forgotten. At the Lord's table the disciples should ever be able to say with full conviction, "His presence we have."[5]

A minister needs to be prepared physically, mentally, and spiritually. To contribute to the dignity, reverence, and meaningfulness of this service, the pastor, as well as the men who assist him in administering the ordinance, should be dressed in their most conservative and appropriate attire. All who take part in preparing the Communion, serving the emblems, and in caring for the "communion ware" should be thoroughly instructed as to their responsibilities. A printed diagram, along with instructions and schedule, should be distributed to the leaders who will be assisting in serving Communion. Each should be well aware of the significance of the Lord's Supper and have his heart fully prepared as to the importance of this ordinance.

As children come to the age when they leave junior church and join the adult services, it is important they receive training from a worker, pastor, assistant pastor, or deacon as to the full significance of the Communion service. It is helpful if, prior to their graduation into the adult service, they can sit in the balcony or as a group observe a Communion service and be informed of the meaning of this ordinance.

Ministering Healing and Blessing. As Pentecostal believers reverently and thankfully remember the efficacious death of our Lord Jesus Christ, they should fully appreciate the blessings of Christ's atonement which are so appropriately set forth by the bread and the fruit of the

---

[5]G. C. S. Wallace, *Pastor and People* (Nashville: Broadman Press, 1936), p. 109.

vine. The sick should be regularly reminded how His body was broken that ours might be healed. Although there is no virtue in the broken bread itself, there is healing as we appropriate the glorious truth, ". . . by whose stripes ye were healed" (1 Peter 2:24). As the Israelites received healing when they looked to the brazen serpent in the wilderness, so the children of the Lord today can look to Him "who forgiveth all thine iniquities; who healeth all thy diseases" (Psalm 103:3).

Many Christians come to the Communion service suffering from guilt and condemnation because of failure. How important it is that in their unworthiness they see anew the worthiness of Christ's sacrifice and appropriate cleansing and justification through the death of Jesus Christ. Oh the joy that comes to the heart that is contritely exposed to Calvary! The believer is able to say with the Psalmist: "Blessed is he whose transgression is forgiven, whose sin is covered" (Psalm 32:1).

Often men and women receive healing, forgiveness, and grace during the Communion service; this should be expected at a time when the suffering of our Saviour is recalled and appropriated into the life of the worshiping Christian. It is proper to give people an opportunity at the close of such a service to go to an altar to be prayed for by the elders and to further partake of the provisions of grace.

WATER BAPTISM

Bible Baptism. There are few services that bring more joy to the pastor and congregation than the occasions when believers publicly confess Jesus Christ to be their Saviour and Lord in the ordinance of water baptism. The wise pastor should stress in his pulpit ministry, personal counseling, and teaching situations the scriptural position regarding this act of obedience. The new convert can immediately be introduced to this truth by including a tract on water baptism in the literature he is given at the altar. There should be frequent opportunities for obedience in this ordinance of the church.

The Bible teaches us that believers were baptized almost immediately after their conversion (Acts 2:41; 8:12; 9:18; 10:48; 22:16). Our teaching should clearly set forth that the divine order is, "Repent, and be baptized" (Acts 2:38), and that Jesus taught "saving faith" as a prerequisite when He said, "He that believeth and is baptized shall be saved" (Mark 16:16). Matthew's Gospel makes it clear that part of our commission is to preach water baptism. The formula Jesus gave is found in Matthew 28:19—"in the name of the Father, and of the Son, and of the Holy Ghost."

From the Word of God, the faithful minister must proclaim that water baptism is an outward testimony of what has happened inwardly with the experience of salvation. It is not an addition to or the completion of one's salvation which has been fully provided by Christ. It is an act of obedience and love through which the believer publicly identifies himself with Jesus Christ as Saviour and Lord.

The pastor will encounter those who were baptized as infants, and they may wonder whether they should be baptized again. It is helpful to show them that in Acts 19:3 the Ephesian believers had been baptized previously but as they came into fuller knowledge of the truth, they gladly obeyed the scriptural pattern. There will also be those who received and unfortunately were taught "baptismal regeneration." We must trust the Holy Spirit to help them see that salvation is only through faith in Christ and His work at Calvary (Ephesians 2:8, 9).

Public Witness. Harry S. Garrett in *Minister's Manual I* gives these helpful guidelines:

> The baptismal service may be held in a baptistry, an outdoor pool, or in running water. The minister should be certain the candidates understand thoroughly the ceremony through which they will pass and that they have experienced a change of heart. The candidates should understand that baptism is a declaration of dedication and a symbol of one's faith.[6]

Happy is the pastor who is able to have a baptismal service every Sunday. Not all may have that joy, but many more should have a baptismal service every month. If this is not feasible, these opportunities should be as frequent as possible. Experience has proven the more frequently such services are held, the more likely believers are to take this important step. "Intention Cards" could be made available in an accessible place. As the pastor preaches on water baptism and appropriately promotes the service, each one who returns an "Intention Card" should receive a letter with instructions on what to bring,

---

[6]Harry S. Garrett, "A Baptismal Service," *Minister's Manual I* (Springfield, MO: Gospel Publishing House, 1965), p. 80.

the time of the prebaptismal class, and perhaps some words of encouragement to invite friends to this meaningful service.

The prebaptismal class is very important in teaching every candidate the beautiful meaning and symbolism of this ordinance (Romans 6:3-11). Each believer should receive a clear understanding of the Word so this service becomes a moment of declaration, appropriation, and exultation. Candidates should be informed that the minister will baptize them "upon the confession of their faith." Clear instructions, augmented with some wise guidelines, can make this a very inspiring time as the congregation hears each candidate tell briefly, but clearly, of God's saving grace through Christ Jesus in his life.

If the baptismal class is conducted prior to the evening service, each candidate could be fitted by the deacons and deaconesses with a black robe; special baptismal gowns are usually weighted at the hems. The deacons and deaconesses can also be most helpful in providing for an orderly flow of candidates into the baptismal tank. Proper dressing rooms, suitable containers in which to place the wet robes, and someone to hang up the robes should also be arranged for. Certificates of baptism may be prepared prior to the service and presented to the candidates by a deacon following the service, or they may be mailed from the church office. The pastor should take care that he is dressed appropriately for the service. A white shirt with a black tie and a black baptismal robe add dignity that helps make this service an effective witness to the power of the gospel of Jesus Christ.

If a church does not have a baptismal service each week, the pastor might preach a sermon on water baptism prior to the ordinance itself. Or, if such a service promises to be quite long and there are guests and visitors in attendance, the pastor might bring a brief message from the baptismal tank, following the immersions. Such planning gives a beautiful opportunity to encourage men and women to commit their lives to the crucified and risen Redeemer.

Ministry of the Spirit. The baptism of Jesus, with the Spirit of God descending on Him in the form of a dove (Matthew 3:16), is closely paralleled in the Book of Acts with water baptism and the coming of the gift of the Holy Spirit. Candidates should realize there should be this close correlation in their lives also. The promise of Acts 2:37-39 clearly associates obedience in this ordinance with the promise of receiving the gift of the Holy Ghost. Note the obedience of the believers at Samaria (Acts 8:17) as well as the disciples at Ephesus (19:6) prior to their baptism in the Spirit.

Pastors do a disservice to candidates if they do not encourage them to believe that God will fulfill the promise of Acts 2:39 as they meet the conditions of the preceding verse, namely repentance and water baptism. Many have found the heavens to open upon their soul as they came out of the waters of baptism. It is an opportune moment to provide a place for the newly baptized believers to appropriate the promised gift of the Holy Spirit.

RECEPTION OF NEW MEMBERS

The Membership Class. Although we are not here considering the merits of church membership, it is well that all who indicate a desire to become members of the church should be aware of these practical reasons for church membership:

1. Membership is important for efficient organization. God is a God of order. The creation of the celestial heavens attests to God's precision and perfect timing. When we observe that the "Church" in the wilderness was organized as to the exact location of the tribes in relation to the tabernacle, the order of the march, and the echelons of leadership, we can appreciate God's emphasis on all things being done decently and in order (1 Corinthians 14:40).

2. Membership is practical for handling church business. It has often been said, "That which is everybody's business is nobody's business." Property should be owned by the corporation, and those who are of like-precious faith and support that local church should be a part of the business as well as the spiritual affairs of the church.

3. Membership helps develop both loyalty and responsibility. Only through faithful attendance at a solid Bible-preaching church will maturity be realized in the life of the believer. As trained believers are progressively given opportunity for greater responsibility, they immeasurably contribute to a strong local church.

4. A growing membership contributes a greater united effort for the spread of the gospel (Acts 2:47). With the spiritual, physical, social, and financial influence of a growing body of believers, the work of the Master can be more readily advanced.

Even if the church is large, there are many advantages to the pastor accepting the joy of teaching the membership class. It affords him an excellent opportunity to become acquainted with the candidates, and they will be able to relate to him in a more personal way. This is an ideal time for them to learn and understand his role of leadership in the local church (Ephesians 4:11; Hebrews 13:17), to be given insight into the pastor's "heartbeat" and vision for the assembly, and to receive sound doctrinal teaching regarding the tenets of faith.

In some churches it will be convenient to have a membership class during the Sunday school hour. Others will find it necessary to schedule one at a different time. Churches often have a "New Life Class" or "New Converts' Class" in which the basic doctrines of the church are taught. The pastor should be sure each candidate knows what he can expect of the church and what the church expects of him. After all the aforementioned areas are covered, the pastor might distribute to each candidate a copy of the constitution and bylaws and conclude by giving instructions about the installation service.

The Public Reception. New members should be received during a public service, preferably the Sunday morning worship service. However, because of the press of time and the desire to emphasize the importance of the Sunday evening service, pastors may choose to make this joyous ceremony a part of the evening service. The reception is best placed early in the service, so its details and anxieties may be off the minds of both the prospective members and the pastor. The reception ceremony should be marked by both warmth and dignity. The organist may softly play "Blest Be the Tie That Binds" or "A Glorious Church" while the pastor slowly calls the names of the new members. By deliberately announcing the name and giving each new member time to reach the altar before the next name is called, the congregation is able to associate the name with the person; such consideration conveys a sense of each individual's worth to the body.

The pastor should distinguish between those who are coming to be received on the profession of their faith and those who are being transferred from a sister church. This distinction can be easily made by calling first those who have recently made a confession of their faith, then those who are coming into membership by way of transfer.

It is generally preferable to allow the new members to be seated at random in the congregation, with their families and friends, until their names are called. There may be occasions, however, when for the sake of time, it might be better to have all the new members seated in the front of the church.

After a suitable affirmation of their faith and promises of faithfulness, the pastor should offer a prayer for the new members and for their service in the congregation. This prayer might include a mention of the churches from which the new members have come, asking that their places may be filled by new workers and that those churches might receive blessings in accord with the blessings that have accrued to the present church.

At the end of the prayer, it is proper for the pastor, pastoral staff, and the church leaders to extend "the right hands of fellowship" (Galatians 2:9) to the members who have been received. The secretary of the board could be the last one in line in order to give each member a church identification membership card as well as a certificate of membership.[7] All of this activity is time consuming, but it emphasizes the importance of personal relationship with the church. The rest of the congregation should be encouraged to seek out the new members following the service and welcome them to the local body of believers.

The Ongoing Relationship. It certainly would be appropriate and encouraging for the pastor to send a personal letter of welcome to each of the new members and to officially welcome them by means of the church bulletin or newspaper. This could include a brief biographical sketch of each new member as an introduction to the congregation.

One of the responsibilities of the pastor is to give leadership and direction in successfully integrating the new members into the life of the local church. Usually, the membership card provides opportunity to list areas of interest and possible service; it would be beneficial if this information were forwarded to the respective department head. A yearly Christian service survey of the entire congregation can assist the pastor in securing help in needed areas, in learning of talents and interests he was not aware of, and in giving the individual member opportunity to make himself available for ministry within the body.

Periodically (possibly quarterly, semiannually, or annually), the pastor and leaders of the church could invite those who have come into the church within a given period of time to a fellowship dinner.

---

[7]Both are available from the Gospel Publishing House.

Board members and their wives could be seated at different tables, as hosts and hostesses, so they may become better acquainted with the new members and also assist them in making new friends. The fellowship dinner should provide opportunity for the recent members to meet and fellowship with those who are seated at the other tables.

DEDICATION OF CHILDREN

Biblical Examples. We have ample basis in God's Word for the dedication of children. The Old Testament contains the record of Hannah bringing Samuel to the house of the Lord so she might dedicate him to His service (1 Samuel 1:24-28). On several occasions in the New Testament we read of mothers bringing their little children, small enough to be held in the arms of Jesus, for His blessing (Mark 10:13-16), while others received a touch by the compassionate and loving Master from Galilee (Luke 18:15-17). In Luke 2:22, we read of Joseph and Mary bringing the infant Jesus to Jerusalem to present Him to the Lord for dedication shortly after His birth.

Encouraging High Family Ideals. The wise pastor recognizes that the spiritual health of his congregation is closely related to the spiritual life of each family. He takes advantage of the many excellent opportunities to focus the congregation's attention on God's high standards for marriage and the home—such as Mother's Day, Father's Day, the Christmas emphasis on the home in which Jesus was reared, and the month of June which is traditionally considered "wedding month." Certainly, the pastor need not wait for a holiday to respond to the direction of the Spirit in speaking to the needs he senses among the flock on this vital matter. Through premarital counseling, marriage seminars, practical and sound Biblical preaching, and the good example of the parsonage family, the pastor can create an appreciation for the Christian home that will be a beautiful testimony in the community.

The dedication service should always be preceded by a conference with the parents to insure that they clearly understand the purpose of the service. It is important that there be no misconceptions; there is no mystical spiritual experience or blessing for the infant in this service. The parents may come from different theological backgrounds from that of the pastor, and this conference is a good opportunity for additional teaching. It should be clearly pointed out that infant dedication is in no way linked with the rite of baptism, as practiced in some churches. It is important for parents to realize the dedication service is designed to make them aware of their great responsibility in the upbringing and spiritual training of their child, and that in the dedication service they are publicly accepting that responsibility. To be sure the parents have a clear understanding of such a service, the pastor could give them a copy of C. M. Ward's booklet *This Child Shall Be Lent Unto the Lord* at his first contact with them following the child's birth.

The Public Service. When parents make known to a pastor their desire for a service of dedication, the event should be scheduled at the earliest convenient time. This important step should be taken by parents while the spell of the child's advent is still upon them. The service is of great significance to the parents, and the minister is responsible for making it as beautiful as possible. It should be designed to remain in the memory of the parents as a future reminder of a past commitment. The Sunday morning worship service is usually the most convenient time for such a dedication, but many pastors appreciate having the service on a Sunday night when the schedule is less crowded.

Each pastor must decide for himself whether or not he will participate in a dedication service for an infant whose parents do not profess a personal relationship with Jesus Christ. Whatever his decision, it is recommended that great care be taken to manifest the love and compassion of the Master who said, "Forbid them not" to come unto Me (Luke 18:16).

When parents express a desire to have their child dedicated, the pastor has an excellent opportunity to emphasize the obligations one undertakes in dedication and the necessity of a personal relationship with Jesus Christ if the obligations are to be discharged properly. If only one parent desires to dedicate a child, that parent should certainly be permitted to do so. This is not the ideal situation, but it is important the parent have that privilege. The pastor may suggest that a believing friend or relative stand with the parent to support him or her.

Some excellent dedication services are found in *The Minister's Service Book* and *Minister's Manual I.* One of the most meaningful dedication services is one in which the pastor leads the parents in commitment and delivers a charge to them; then the father, as the priest of their home, prays a prayer of dedication for himself, his wife, and their child. Such a service is likely to be of greater significance to the parents.

To help contribute to the beauty of the service and to assist the pastor in having the full name of the parents and the child, it is recommended the certificate of dedication be prepared prior to the service. On the envelope should be typed, for example: "David Mark Doe, son of Mr. and Mrs. John Doe." As the pastor extends congratulations and expresses some warm words of encouragement after the dedication, he should present the certificate to the parents. In addition, the pastor should see that the child is included on the cradle roll. An event of such importance should also be on file in the church office.

Ministries of Comfort

THE FUNERAL

The Christian View of Death. There is no time when the pastor, the church, and the individual believer have greater opportunity to manifest their faith in the God of all hope than at the death of a believer. Confidently we declare with the apostle Paul, "Absent from the body, . . . present with the Lord" (2 Corinthians 5:8). Assuredly we rest on the immutable words of our Saviour, "Because I live, ye shall live also" (John 14:19).

Paul sets forth clearly in 1 Corinthians 15 how ". . . in Christ shall all be made alive" (v. 22). The man who was persecuted and imprisoned because of his hope in the resurrection of the dead (Acts 23:6) distinctly states the divine plan to the Thessalonians when he writes: "The dead in Christ shall rise first: then we which are alive and remain shall be caught up together . . . to meet the Lord in the air" (1 Thessalonians 4:16, 17). The pastor, through his pulpit ministry, personal counseling, and his ministry at the time of death, must show how "the righteous hath hope in his death" (Proverbs 14:32).

The Christian has the hope of resurrection, a new body, heaven, seeing loved ones, eternal life, and seeing his Saviour. How fortunate is the pastor who can comfort his congregation with the knowledge that we ". . . sorrow not, even as others which have no hope" (1 Thessalonians 4:13). Ours is "the God of all comfort; who comforteth us in all our tribulation, that we may be able to comfort them which are in any trouble, by the comfort wherewith we ourselves are comforted of God" (2 Corinthians 1:3, 4).

It is good for a pastor, under the direction and timing of the Holy Spirit, to bring a message to his congregation on the subject, "When Death Comes to Your Home." Such a sermon will afford him an excellent opportunity to teach people (1) how to demonstrate their faith, (2) to have a good relationship with their pastor and the church family, (3) to use wisdom in planning a funeral service and burial that is in keeping with their way of life and standard of living, and (4) to exercise their faith if they are ever called on to face the challenge of an uncharted future.[8]

As the pastor teaches his people to demonstrate their faith, he will have opportunity to make some observations concerning cremation. It should be observed that cremation is a heathen custom and certainly not fitting as the last testimony of a child of God who was made in the image of God. In Scripture, cremation is associated with the judgment and wrath of God. (See Joshua 7:25; 2 Samuel 23:7; and Jeremiah 49:2.) Although the pastor may share these views, this may not necessarily be reason for him to refuse to officiate at a funeral where the body will be cremated. It would be hoped, though, that he might be allowed some opportunity to discuss with the family the general nature of the funeral service.

Time for Tenderness. Homer A. Kent outlines the responsibilities and opportunities that confront the pastor when a death occurs in a family:

> When the pastor is notified of a death of one in his congregation, his immediate response should be: 1) to make a visit without delay to the home of the deceased and this visit should demonstrate immediate concern; 2) this first visit should present Christian truths concerning the sufficiency of God's grace, the comfort of God's Holy Spirit, rather than involve any discussion of funeral arrangements; 3) the pastor should be prepared to deal with various problem situations that arise, sometimes characterized by a rebellious spirit, or the knowledge that the loved one was not prepared to die. This can often be a time of teaching the

---

[8]See also *The Effective Pastor* (Springfield, MO: Gospel Publishing House, 1973), pp. 116, 117, for helpful suggestions.

careless some important spiritual principles. The pastor may find them in great shock, not knowing what steps to take and the pastor can give aid in practical matters.[9]

In a conference concerning the funeral, the pastor should attempt to ascertain answers to the following: (1) When and where is the funeral to be held? (2) What are the hours for viewing at the funeral home and when will the family be viewing for the first time and the last time; especially if the casket is to be closed for the funeral service? (3) If the service is to be held at the church, would there be viewing prior to the service and, if so, for how long? (4) Is anyone to assist the pastor, and in what capacity? (5) Is anyone to sing? what hymns? Who will provide the accompaniment? (6) Who will act as pallbearers, and who will contact them?

Ministry to the bereaved is one of the most delicate tasks a pastor is called on to provide. His sensitivity, compassion, guidance, and strength are a source of inestimable blessing to those passing through the valley of death or bereavement. During the time of bereavement the pastor is afforded the wisdom of God, the comfort of the Scriptures, and the outflowing of the Holy Spirit to draw the sorrowing closer to God.

Various Aspects of the Service. Sometimes the pastor is asked to conduct the funeral of someone who is in no way associated with the church. The minister should endeavor to pay his respects at the funeral home if it is not convenient to visit the home of the deceased. He should obtain from some close relative the necessary and accurate information concerning the deceased.

Concerning ministry when the deceased and bereaved are not Christians, Jeff P. Brown says: "This makes the task much harder for the pastor. He must avoid any statements that would tend to hurt the already broken hearted. At the same time he will present God's Word relative to salvation and the resurrection."[10]

The pastor must always remember funeral services are not really for the deceased, but for the living. He does not know the inner secrets of

---

[9]Based on information by Homer A. Kent, Sr., *The Pastor and His Work* (Chicago: Moody Press, 1963), pp. 162, 163. Used by permission.

[10]Jeff P. Brown, *A Handbook for the Preacher at Work* (Grand Rapids: Baker Book House, copyright 1958), p. 49. Used by permission.

any man's heart or the secret communion he may have had with God. Therefore, he should graciously leave that soul in the hands of a wise and loving God, knowing that "the Judge of all the earth [shall] do right" (Genesis 18:25).

The funeral service should be conducted with dignity and beauty so it will be a fitting testimony to the believer's faith and a continuing source of comfort and grace to bereaved hearts. The service should go on uninterrupted. Each participant should have a typed copy of the order of service. Suitable services are found in *Minister's Manual II.*

Funeral sermons should be short. A well-prepared minister should be able to say what needs to be said in 15 to 20 minutes at the most. The sermon should be thoroughly and appropriately scriptural and include the way of salvation through Him who said: "I am the way, the truth, and the life: no man cometh unto the Father, but by me" (John 14:6). In this regard, Homer A. Kent states:

> This is no time to present the uncertainties of men. A "thus saith the Lord" is what folk need to hear. Good chapters from which to develop funeral messages are: Psalm 23, 46, 91, and 103 with their assuring note; John 11 and 14 with their stories of resurrection power and matchless comfort; First Corinthians 15 the classic chapter of the resurrection; 2 Corinthians 5:1-10 with its urgent argument to be ready to "appear before the judgment seat of Christ"; 1 Thessalonians 4:13-18 with its graphic description of what takes place in the experience of the believer when Christ comes for His saints; 2 Timothy 4:5-8 with its account of the apostle Paul's readiness to depart this life; and Revelation 21 and 22 in which blessed truths concerning the "better country" are presented.[11]

At the graveside or committal service, the minister usually stands at the foot of the casket, although he should cooperate if arrangements provide for him to stand at the head of the casket. The committal service begins as soon as relatives and friends are properly situated. Various committal readings can be used, but Scripture is the most appropriate for a Christian burial. Good choices include the raising of Lazarus (John 11), portions of Revelation 21, or portions of 1 Corinthians 15. After the Scripture reading and any additional remarks the minister may feel are appropriate, prayer and a fitting benediction (such as Hebrews 13:20, 21 or Numbers 6:24-26) can conclude the

---

[11]Kent, *The Pastor and His Work*, p. 168. Used by permission.

committal service. A brief personal word with bereaved friends should assure them of continued interest and prayers and promise a visit in the immediate future.

If a lodge or fraternal order has a service at the grave, it is preferably concluded prior to the committal service by the pastor. If there are military rites, these are customarily performed after the committal.

MINISTRY TO THE SICK

Establishing a Scriptural Relationship. The servant of the Lord Jesus Christ has a divine directive to minister to the sick. In Mark 16:18 Jesus said, "They shall lay hands on the sick, and they shall recover." Jesus sent His disciples out with the commission to "heal all manner of sickness and all manner of disease" (Matthew 10:1). The New Testament minister fulfilled a ministry of bringing to needy lives the blessings of the atonement (Acts 3:6; 28:8, 9). Peter emphasized this divine provision (1 Peter 2:24) as he looked back to Isaiah's prophecy, "With his stripes we are healed" (Isaiah 53:5).

Every congregation should learn the obedience of faith as set forth in James 5:14-16. Because a pastor is not omniscient, he must train his people to call him or notify the church office when they are ill. Visiting the sick is one of the most precious privileges, as well as one of the most necessary tasks, of any pastor. Neglecting the sick will cause great criticism of a pastor. However, no one sick person should be allowed to monopolize the time and strength of a pastor who must also give care to an entire congregation. If the pastor fails in this part of his ministry, he will soon lose the confidence and love of his people. If a sick person cannot depend on the pastor at such a time of crisis, he will wonder if he can depend on him at any time. The pastor's faithfulness and compassion are absolutely essential. The pastor must be available for emergency calls at all hours of the night, although a congregation should be taught to avoid nonemergency calls late at night or early in the morning.

When the Pastor Calls. The pastor's demeanor during the sick call should always be calm, cheerful, and helpful. The call should be brief, but free from the inference of haste; avoiding the impression of a professional or job-oriented activity. If the sick person is confined to his

276 AND HE GAVE PASTORS

home, it is proper to telephone before making the visit. When making hospital calls, it is sometimes advantageous to avoid public visiting hours. The pastor can thus minister to the ill at a time when their attention is not divided and the purpose of the visit can be accomplished. He must always honor the authority of the doctors and nurses in the hospital. His gracious consideration of their responsibility and guidelines can create an excellent rapport that will provide future privileges. The pastor should give the sick some appropriate literature, such as an edifying book from the church library, the *Pentecostal Evangel*, and possibly a devotional book in lieu of flowers.

Using Our Spiritual Resources. The Spirit-filled pastor must always remember what Jesus said in Luke 4:18—"The Spirit of the Lord is upon me, because he hath anointed me to preach the gospel to the poor; he hath sent me to heal the brokenhearted, to preach deliverance to the captives, and recovering of sight to the blind, to set at liberty them that are bruised." He also said to His disciples, "As my Father hath sent me, even so send I you" (John 20:21). How necessary it is to be mindful of the enabling of His Spirit as we enter each sick room, spiritually prepared to minister of His wisdom, power, and faith.

Knowing that "the weapons of our warfare are not carnal, but mighty through God to the pulling down of strongholds" (2 Corinthians 10:4), we need to appreciate anew "the sword of the Spirit, which is the word of God" (Ephesians 6:17). The pastor must allow the Holy Spirit to give through him "a word from the Lord" to build faith, scatter doubts, and cheer the hearts of the ill. The visiting pastor will encounter many cases where he will feel quite helpless, but "our sufficiency is of God" (2 Corinthians 3:5), and in our weakness His strength shall be manifest. We must ever remember it is "not by might, nor by power, but by my Spirit, saith the Lord" (Zechariah 4:6). As we keep filled with the Spirit, living waters will flow from our lives to bring grace and healing to man.

A wise and godly minister who had experienced some miraculous healings in his life and ministry gave this wise counsel to a younger minister: "In the ministry of praying for the sick and trusting God, if you do not make room for the sovereignty of God, you are going to encounter some cases for which you will not have an answer."

Formal Ministries

INSTALLATION OF OFFICERS

Basic Objectives. An installation service is of great benefit to the officers, the congregation, and the orderly operation of the church. At this time the pastor has opportunity to set forth the scriptural guidelines and requirements for such leaders, to make known their responsibility to the pastor and to Christ, to challenge and charge them in the fulfillment of their responsibilities, and to urge them to fulfill their office through the enabling power of the Holy Spirit.

If it is not feasible to include all of these guidelines in the installation service, the pastor should, nevertheless, acquaint each officer with his responsibilities, preferably in the form of a job description. Church leaders should also be informed of the pastor's philosophy of leadership, his vision and goals, and his confidence in the particular role each officer will play in the ministry of the church.

Suggested Formats. The installation service should take place as soon after an election as possible. The Sunday following the election might be appropriate. To establish the unique and separate calling of each ministry, the installation of board members should be separate from the installation of the Sunday school staff. Usually, youth officers would be installed in a youth service. By having separate installations, the pastor has an opportunity to set forth some helpful distinctives for each area of ministry. Appropriate Scripture passages and services can be found in *Minister's Manual III* as well as *The Minister's Service Book.*

The pastor may wish to use the suggested service as a guideline from which he can develop his own installation service placing stress on distinctive objectives and philosophies of the pastor and the church. The minister should strive to achieve a sense of dignity in the service, a consciousness of responsibility, and a spirit of dedication to the lordship of Jesus Christ. A recognition of our dependence on the ministry of the Holy Spirit should pervade the ceremony.

DEDICATIONS OF PROPERTIES / GIFTS

Purpose of Dedication. Zenas J. Bicket, in *The Effective Pastor,* emphasizes the importance of dedicating church facilities:

Every venture of the church, whether spiritual or business, should be initiated and carried out with a prayer for God's blessing and use. Nowhere is this more important than in the dedication of buildings and other facilities which will be used over a number of years for the glory of God. . . . As members see that inanimate buildings and facilities are dedicated to God, they will be challenged to dedicate and rededicate their lives to God's service. Further, the dedication of public church facilities should suggest that the individual Christian dedicate his possessions—his home, his car, his vocation, and all his resources—to the service of Jesus Christ.[12]

Dedication of an Organ or Piano. It is likely a pastor and a congregation will have occasion to dedicate instruments of worship, such as an organ or a piano, even more frequently than a new edifice. These dedications generally take one of two forms. The dedication of an instrument could be included in a general service, or a special program of music could be scheduled using the new instrument.

A separate dedication service would usually have either a printed order of service or a printed special announcement, including a description of the organ or piano as furnished by the manufacturer. It would also be appropriate for the printed order of service to give proper recognition to those exercising musical leadership in the church, and particularly those whose ministry in the church focuses on the instrument being dedicated. The hymns and music used should demonstrate the range and effect of the instrument. One or more of the numbers could give opportunity for congregational worship, thus demonstrating the importance of the instrument in worship. A master or artist of the instrument could present a special sacred, dedicatory concert.

The dedicatory address or sermon should stress the importance of praise and instruments of praise in our worship. Obviously, nothing exactly like our church organs or pianos existed in Biblical times, but Scripture indicates the worshipers used any instrument available. (This is suggested in Psalms 92, 98, and 150, and 1 Chronicles 25:6-8.)

It should be easy to remind the worshipers of the threefold ministry of the organ [or piano]—in sustaining the congregation in its praise, in sus-

[12]Zenas J. Bicket, *The Effective Pastor* (Springfield, MO: Gospel Publishing House, 1973), pp. 150-152.

taining the special voices (the choir) which lead from time to time, uttering for us thoughts which we are not ourselves prepared to utter, and in making direct appeal to our spirit of worship in nonverbal music.[13]

The prayer of dedication should set apart the organ or piano for its future ministries of joy, sorrow, worship, communion, praise, or exaltation. Finally, the dedication of an organ or a piano should also include a dedication and setting apart of the organists and pianists involved in this special ministry.

Dedication of Buildings. David considered building and dedicating a house of worship to the Lord as one of the greatest privileges afforded a spiritual leader. It is evident from the Scriptures that Solomon addressed the triumphant moment of dedication with care, thoroughness, humility, and faith. The manner in which the glory of the Lord filled the tabernacle in the wilderness when "Moses finished the work" (Exodus 40:33, 34) and the way in which "the priests could not stand to minister" at the dedication of Solomon's Temple (2 Chronicles 5:14) should cause every pastor to yearn to see the Lord do it again. Such a momentous occasion should be planned with the cooperation of a committee or church board and given the prominence and preparation it deserves. Some may find a week of dedication services appropriate, with the act of dedication at the beginning of the week. Others may wish to place their emphasis on one service of dedication.

The pastor and those working with him should carefully consider those whom they wish to invite to participate in the service. The architect, general contractor, civic leaders (mayor, town manager, congressman, etc.), district officials, a guest speaker, musicians, former pastors, and members of the building committee are some possibilities. Such friends of the church as fellow clergymen, businessmen, subcontractors, former members, and workmen involved in the erection of the church should receive a formal invitation to the dedication service. Every pastor can gain much assistance as he consults with other ministers and gleans ideas from their experiences, observes copies of their dedication programs, and seeks to make the occasion truly glorifying to God and a fitting tribute to the church.

Minister's Manual III contains appropriate services for "Ground

---

[13]McAfee, *Ministerial Practice*, p. 150.

Breaking," "Cornerstone Laying," and the "Dedication of Buildings."
Also, *The Minister's Service Book* has services of dedication.

* * * * *

The opportunities presented to the pastor for effective outreach
through special ministries are manifold. Whether those ministries are
joyous ones, comforting ones, or the more formal ceremonies of installation or dedication, the pastor should be at his best as God's
representative to the people he has been called to serve.

Suggested Reading

Bicket, Zenas J. *The Effective Pastor.* Springfield, MO: Gospel
Publishing House, 1973.

Brown, Jeff P. *A Handbook for the Preacher at Work.* Grand Rapids:
Baker Book House, 1958.

Erdman, Charles R. *The Work of the Pastor.* Philadelphia:
Westminster Press, 1928.

Kent, Homer A. *The Pastor and His Work.* Chicago: Moody Press,
1976.

McAfee, Cleland B. *Ministerial Practice.* New York: Harper & Row
Publishers, Inc., 1928.

Pickthorn, William E., ed. *Minister's Manual,* Vols. 1, 2, & 3. Springfield, MO: Gospel Publishing House, 1965.

Wagner, Charles U. *The Pastor: His Life and Work.* Schaumberg, IL:
Regular Baptist Press, 1976.

Wallace, G. C. S. *Pastor and People.* Nashville: Broadman Press,
1936.

10

The Pastor
and
Congregational Services

THOMAS E. TRASK

Planning the Service

At one time or another, probably everyone has left a church service wondering what its purpose was supposed to have been. With proper planning, prayer, and firmly established goals, the service need never receive this kind of reaction.

It is the pastor's responsibility to see that each service has been properly planned and then to communicate to those participating in the service what he desires to accomplish. And it is well to do an evaluation following the service to see whether the desired goal was accomplished. The Scriptures state: "Let all things be done decently and in order" (1 Corinthians 14:40). The greatest safeguard against things happening in a service that would cause embarrassment to the pastor and congregation and displeasure to our Lord, is to have the service well planned.

Some people feel a structured or planned service does not permit the Holy Spirit to work in the manner He chooses. But one has only to consider this great universe to see the order established by our Creator and to appreciate the fact that we serve a God of orderliness. He will not be uncomfortable in a service that is carefully planned, especially when He has had a part in the planning.

Certainly, there are times when God wishes to break in upon the planned order of a service. As the pastor is sensitive to the leading of the Holy Spirit, his spirit will bear witness with the divine Spirit that

Thomas E. Trask is pastor of Brightmoor Tabernacle, Detroit, Michigan.

the departure from the plan is of God. We need to be open and flexible or we can miss what God wants to accomplish in a service. A service can be structured without being rigid.

It is wise to plan each Sunday well in advance. One should plan at least a year in advance so that guests who are to participate in the services can be secured. (Some pastors plan as much as 2 years in advance.) A common criticism of the church is that every service is the same. When this attitude prevails, attendance is seldom consistent. By long-range planning, however, emphasis can be given for special days and special occasions, thus providing a varied program.

When a service is properly planned, the personnel taking part can be prepared. The choir, for example, can plan its music to complement the theme of the service. If there are several ministers on the staff, the planning can be done at a regular staff meeting. This provides an excellent means by which to gain input from individuals in various departments of the church. Prayer should be the foundation for all planning. As one seeks the Lord, the Holy Spirit will direct, guide, inspire, and enable.

THE WORSHIP SERVICE

Before we can plan a true worship service, we must first understand *what worship is.* Worship is the act of giving honor, respect, and reverence to a Being who is worthy of the same. So real worship ought to mean a continual conversion of thoughts, standards, and aims from a self-centered to a God-centered focus. In direct proportion to the vitality, richness, and sincerity of our worship, the world will come to acknowledge the Saviour whom we worship.

Jesus taught about worship and its importance in John 4. Its practice was not left optional. "God is a Spirit: and they that worship him must worship him in spirit and in truth" (v. 24). Paul taught the Colossians that part of our worship is "teaching and admonishing one another in psalms and hymns and spiritual songs, singing with grace in your hearts to the Lord, . . . giving thanks to God" (Colossians 3:16, 17).

The word *worship* comes from the Anglo-Saxon noun *worthship.* As we recognize the "worth" of God, the normal response is praise to Him, love expressed to Him, thanksgiving, singing, and confession of our unworthiness. We often sing the words of Revelation 4:11: "Thou art worthy, O Lord, to receive glory and honor and power: for thou hast created all things, and for thy pleasure they are and were created."

All true worship must be Christ-centered! Through worship we acknowledge our unworthiness, recognize His worthiness, and glorify His name and His works. For worship to happen, all thoughts must be brought into captivity and focused on Christ. One of the most attractive aspects of our Assemblies of God services is Pentecostal worship. When believers enter into true worship, God is given opportunity to minister to them by His Spirit; and the lives of men and women are affected as a result. In worship, the Christian offers up his whole personality, and the fire descends on the offering. As a result of worship, God imparts faith, vision, sensitivity to spiritual things, power, and divine love. In the act of worship, man becomes God-conscious.

The pastor has a vital role in leading the congregation in worship. He must demonstrate an attitude of reverence and humility. He must make certain the worshipers' attention is God-directed rather than man-directed. He must be more concerned about bringing glory and praise to the Lord than to himself. He needs spiritual perception to be aware of what God wants to accomplish in people's lives. He must have confidence in his God-given leadership ability. He must know beyond doubt that God is, "and that he is a rewarder of them that diligently seek him" (Hebrews 11:6).

A gentleman once visited a Quaker meeting. After waiting awhile, he leaned over to a man beside him and asked, "When will the service begin?" The man replied, "The service will begin when the worship is concluded." And our service to the Lord Jesus Christ can begin only after we through worship have discovered His loveliness, His passion, and His power. True worship will provide the dynamics for Christian living as well as service.

As with every other aspect of Christian devotion, the worship service must have a goal. Help toward this end is found in the acrostic on the next page.

THE EVANGELISTIC SERVICE

The churches that are experiencing the greatest growth are those churches that have maintained a strong emphasis on the evangelistic service usually held on Sunday evening. What does the term

---

THE ELEMENTS OF WORSHIP

A Adoration   The Ability to Show Love

C Confession   Realizing Who God Is . . . and Who We Are Not

T Thanksgiving Appreciation, Gratitude

S Supplication   Calling on God for Ourselves and for Our World

---

evangelistic mean? It describes the strong emphasis of the Pentecostal Movement on reaching the unsaved. When the congregation knows an altar call will be given in the Sunday evening evangelistic service (the term *evening* is used only because that schedule has been traditional), they can invite their unsaved neighbors and friends, knowing that the plan of salvation and a new life in Christ will be presented. Opportunity should be given in every evangelistic service for men and women to accept Jesus Christ as Saviour.

One pastor remarked to his district superintendent, "By the time I finish with Sunday morning, I'm too tired to have much of a service on Sunday evening!" This is a mistake! A pastor should be rested and refreshed when he comes to the evangelistic service.

The structure of the evangelistic service is somewhat different from that of the worship service. Songs selected are of a different type and tempo from those sung in the morning service. Testimonies from Christians in the congregation are helpful and encouraging too in the evangelistic service. The Psalmist David said, "Let the redeemed of the Lord say so" (Psalm 107:2). The pastor can lead the congregation in fulfilling this command of Scripture by calling on someone to give a personal testimony that will glorify the Lord.

An added feature in a Sunday evening service that has been used effectively is called "People to People." A family from the congregation comes to the platform for a 3-minute interview. This gives the congregation an opportunity to become acquainted with fellow members and hear a testimony that is directed toward bringing glory to God.

The evangelistic service is usually not as limited in time as the Sunday morning service, and it lends itself to more special music (choirs, instrumentals, ensembles, etc.) and congregational singing. This encourages individuals to be more open before the Lord and to allow Him to have His way in their lives. But the pastor must guard against getting into a rut.

The sermon topic for the evangelistic emphasis should be announced prior to the service to create interest. The message should be of sufficient length to accomplish its desired goal, but not so long as to keep people from responding to the invitation. One of the most cherished times in Pentecostal services is the altar service, when men and women are invited to come to the altar for a time of prayer. It is also the time when an invitation is given to those with spiritual needs. The various parts of the worship and evangelistic service will be discussed in greater detail under "Service Structure."

SPECIAL SERVICES

In addition to special holiday services, emphases should be planned throughout the year for the various age-groups, needs, and interests of the congregation. A great deal of variety can be incorporated into the church program through a water baptismal service, the Communion service, a missions convention, baby dedications, youth emphases, installation of board members, membership recognition, special musicals, senior citizens emphases, recognition of graduates, a "Kouples Klinic," prophetic emphases, soul-winning emphasis, and illustrated sermons. Those participating in special services should be made aware of the purpose of the service and what is desired as a result.

Of particular importance are services geared to the youth of the church. Young people are one of the church's greatest assets. Young people who are saved and committed to Christ have an opportunity in the church to meet a future spouse with a similar dedication and join their lives to rear their children in the church. It is God's desire that the cycle of Christian families should be repeated in each generation within the full-orbed ministry of the local church. This fact, in itself, shows what a profitable investment the church can make for the kingdom of God through its young people.

It is important for the congregation to believe that young people can and should be reached for Christ. Without this kind of a vision, young people will perish. Youth today are not so much rejecting the gospel as they are rejecting the church; so the church needs a new and strong emphasis on ministry to this important age-group. It must be made as vital as any other area of church ministry with regard to financial support, scheduling, and adult interest. The pastor must make certain the youth ministry does more than just entertain. Lives can and will be affected for Christ if there is a right philosophy concerning this very important segment of the congregation.

Ministry to youth must be planned to meet the needs of young people in today's culture. We cannot reach contemporary youth with methods of 40 years ago. The message never changes, but the methods do! The message of the gospel must be presented in a positive manner so young people can see that life in Christ is relevant to them on a very personal level.

Effective youth ministries are those that reach young people at their respective age-levels—junior high, senior high, college, career, and young married. While it is not always possible in a newly formed group to segregate ages and interests in this way, the breakdown should be accomplished as soon as possible. As the youth group grows, senior high, college, and career groups could be combined for a weekly service, with separate meetings for junior high and young married persons. Each of these age-groups should have a leader, along with a council made up of young people of that age.

There should also be fellowship groups within each of these divisions so the young people can have a much-needed personal contact with their peers and their leaders. In these fellowship units, more prayer and openness can be expressed and a greater degree of discipleship encouraged.

The youth pastor who heads the total youth ministry of the church should meet regularly with the divisional youth leaders to keep abreast of everything happening within the various groups. Young people need and want to get involved. The pastor must make provision for them in the church and the congregational services.

Service Structure

CALL TO WORSHIP

Creating a Proper Atmosphere. The purpose of the call to worship is to bring the congregation to a consciousness of the presence of the

God whom they have come to worship. They are reminded that their purpose in attending the house of God is to participate in divine worship. The call to worship brings a reverence and quietude upon the congregation and prepares their hearts for what God desires to accomplish. In some churches the organist plays for a brief time just prior to the call to worship. Then as individuals enter the sanctuary, they are immediately brought into an atmosphere of reverence.

Reverence is a feeling of deep respect, love, or awe. No one on earth should have a greater consciousness of respect and love for God than men and women who have been touched by the power of God. As a church, we must keep the wonder and awe of an almighty God ever before us as we see His lovely work in His dealings with mankind. We should stand in awe as we witness people being saved, healed, delivered, filled with the Holy Spirit, and touched by His mighty power! This is reverence, and our Lord deserves all our love, respect, and awe.

The need for reverence in our churches cannot be stressed too strongly. Some people feel that our Pentecostal worship, especially the active participation of the congregation in our worship services, encourages carelessness. But this very mode of worship should make us ever *more* conscious of God and of the need for reverence, as we sense His Spirit at work in our midst.

People must be taught that the church is God's house and, as such, is different from any other building. It is a place that has been dedicated to worship. Those who attend are guests in God's house. Children must be taught from the earliest possible age that it is not a place to run, play, talk loudly, or behave improperly. And just as one would respect the furnishings and the people in a home he visits, so we should esteem the church furnishings and the other people who are visiting with us in God's house. If a guest were visiting in someone's home and in the middle of the conversation got up rudely and walked out, in all probability the host would be offended—and rightly so. Yet, how often do people get up in a service, even during the message, and walk out of the sanctuary without justification!

People should be attired in their very best when worshiping in the house of God. We must keep in mind that we are coming into the presence of divine Royalty. That should command the finest we have. When a service begins, the doors leading to the sanctuary should be closed, thus eliminating the noise and confusion in the vestibule and hallways. If it should become necessary for a person in the congregation to speak to someone nearby, it should be in a low voice or whisper.

People should be taught that when the gifts of the Spirit are being manifested in the congregation, the utmost reverence should prevail; God is talking to His people. No one should be talking or looking around. Everyone should give attention to what is being said, for God has chosen to manifest himself in a special way. We should honor Him by being reverent in His presence.

Another area sometimes overlooked in our churches is reverence at the altar when people are praying. Loud talking can be very distracting; and it is tragic indeed when people who are praying at the altar are hindered and leave without receiving what they needed to receive from God.

Young people need to be taught, and constantly reminded, that they should be reverent before God during every part of a service. They can show reverence by participating in the singing, the prayer, the giving, and by being attentive during the ministry of the Word. Every part of the service gives God an opportunity to minister to them, and for them to give reverence and honor to Him.

Reverence prepares the heart for the Holy Spirit to do His office work. In one church, a young lady plays the piano and sings worship choruses just prior to the worship service. The congregation is invited to sing with her or just sit quietly for 7 or 8 minutes until the call to worship is given by the pastor. This direction of thoughts and minds toward God usually concludes with a reading from God's Word.

Reading of the Scriptures. It is well for the congregation to know the Scriptures will be read in unison every Sunday morning. How important is Scripture reading? The Word of God must be the central theme of all that transpires in a service. It is a beautiful sight to see entire families read together from the Holy Bible.

> *The Bible? That's the Book, the Book indeed,*
> *On which who looks as he should do aright,*
> *Need never wish for a better light*
> *To guide him in the night.*
> *   —George Herbert*

John Quincy Adams said it so well:

> I speak as a man of the world to men of the world, and I say to you, "Search the Scriptures!" The Bible is the Book of all others to be read at all ages and in all conditions of human life; not to be read once or twice through, and then laid aside, but to be read in small portions of one or two chapters a day, and never to be omitted unless by overwhelming necessity!

Jesus said, "Heaven and earth shall pass away, but my words shall not pass away" (Matthew 24:35). God's Word is eternal. Invite the congregation to join the reading of Scripture by using one of the following approaches: (1) "Take your Bibles and turn with me to *(reference)* for the reading of the Word." (2) "I invite you to open your Bible to *(reference)*, and let us read in unison." (3) "Let us hear what the Lord has to say to us through His Word, as found in *(reference)*."

Time should be allowed for the congregation to locate the Scripture passage. During this time, the organist can softly play some worshipful background music. The moderator or pastor should read slowly and clearly enough so the congregation can read with him or follow him, whichever method is used. The Scripture selection may be the text or portion from which the message is to be delivered. At the conclusion of the Scripture reading, one of many closing statements might be used: (1) "May the Lord add His blessing to the reading of the Word." (2) "May the Word of God find lodging within our hearts." (3) "May the Spirit of God impart the truth of His Word to our hearts."

Prayer. It is through prayer that worship to our Heavenly Father blesses the souls of men and women. It is in this part of the service that a sincere effort must be made to avoid mere repetition, perfunctory use of words, or deadness of expression. There must be a freshness of spirit in public prayer.

Jesus' disciples said, "Lord, teach us to pray," thus expressing their desire to know more about prayer. The person praying aloud in the service should desire that the congregation join him in spirit when he prays. We can all recall those whom we love to hear pray, particularly those who have learned that prayer is conversation with the Lord.

Many pastors like to have soft background music during the time of prayer; it tends to maintain a reverent attitude within the body of worshipers. Also, singing a worshipful chorus a couple of times prepares the hearts of the congregation. Worship choruses such as "Come, Holy Spirit, I Need Thee," "I Will Praise Him," or "Have Thine Own Way, Lord" can help bring the congregation into an attitude of prayer. Choruses such as "Only Believe," "God Answers Prayer in the Morning," and "Reach Out and Touch the Lord" can be helpful in encouraging believers to reach out in faith as they pray.

The prayer need not be lengthy, and the theme of the prayer should recognize the presence of the Lord. It should be an expression of thanksgiving for the privilege of gathering together and for God's goodness to His people.

1. *Prayer Requests.* Time should be given in the service for bringing prayer requests to the attention of the congregation. An effective way of handling requests is to have individuals write each one on a Prayer Request Card made available by the church. These can be provided in the pew racks or on a literature table in the lobby. The card should be filled out and handed to an usher who, in turn, will take it to the pulpit or hand it to the person who will be praying.

Prayer requests submitted in this manner should always be mentioned; however, it is not always necessary, or wise, to read the request in detail. The person reading the requests aloud should acquaint himself with each request before sharing it with the congregation.

In medium-sized and smaller churches, the pastor may find it appropriate on occasion to use different persons to lead in prayer. If the person being used is not seated on the platform, it is advisable to call him to the platform so the public address system can be utilized and the entire congregation can hear. Usually, men who serve on a church board or other leading people of the congregation are qualified to lead a congregation in prayer. The pastor must be careful that only those who are loved and respected by the congregation are used in this capacity.

2. *Benediction.* The purpose of this prayer is to ask that the Lord's blessing rest upon the people of the congregation as they are dismissed. It should not be lengthy, but it can still leave the congregation with the feeling that it has been good to be in the house of the Lord.

MUSIC

The choice of appropriate music is vital to the overall impact of the congregational services. It should never be treated as an afterthought. Planning is needed in all the various musical ministries of the service, including congregational singing, special numbers, and the offertory.

Hymns (Praise Psalms). The Old Testament contains numerous references to the place of music in worship. David, of course, gives us the prime example as he praised the Lord through both song and instrument. First Chronicles 15:16-24 describes in detail David's organization of the Levitical choir and orchestra.

The apostle Paul, writing to the Colossians, said, "Let the word of Christ dwell in you richly in all wisdom; teaching and admonishing one another in psalms and hymns and spiritual songs, singing with grace in your hearts to the Lord" (Colossians 3:16). Many congregations have discovered anew the value of instruction in doctrine and in the principles of Christian conduct day by day through the ministry of singing.

Music has always held an important place in the life of the Christian. In the Colossians passage, note the encouragement to "minister" to one another. They were to build up the body of Christ. The church today is more frequently singing praises, psalms, and Scripture choruses. The practice is revitalizing worship in the church. No other singing can surpass the very Word of God as a basis for edification.

The value gained from the use of good hymns depends not only on a wise selection but on thoughtful, prayerful singing. John Wesley established some rules that are as timely now as they were when he made such effective use of hymn singing in his great crusades.

1. Learn the tune.

2. Sing the words as they are printed.

3. Sing lustily and with a good courage.

4. All sing. If it is a cross to you, take it up, and you will find it a blessing!

5. Sing in time. Do not run ahead or stay behind.

6. Above all, sing spiritually. Have an eye to God in every word you sing. Aim at pleasing Him more than yourself or any other creature. Attend strictly to the sense of what you sing and see that your heart is not carried away with the sound, but offered to God continually.

Hymns are to be used in worship. When corporate singing is skillfully led, the presence of God is sensed and His will is wrought in the hearts of His people. The person leading the congregation in singing should be careful to select hymns and choruses that are in the same tempo or directed toward the same spiritual objective. When a spirit of worship prevails and the tempo is suddenly changed, the entire atmosphere of the service can be altered.

Songs. Christian music is for edification. A person leading a congregation in singing should be sensitive to the spirit of the service and open to the gentle leading of the Holy Spirit. If a service is progressing in an evangelistic vein, then the choruses and songs used should lend themselves to sustaining or intensifying this mood. If, however, a service takes on a more worshipful, reflective tone, the song leader should seek to continue this obvious direction of the Holy Spirit. Songs in the hymnal are usually identified as to the message conveyed in the song or the type of service to which it will best lend itself. In the selection of choruses, the song leader must use his own judgment and be sensitive to impressions prompted by the Spirit.

Again, the aspect of planning needs to be emphasized. The song leader will never be a success if he is picking out the songs while the opening prayer is given. Songs need to be chosen prayerfully, then followed by or interspersed with choruses that flow easily and logically. If the choruses chosen are in the same key as a preceding song, there need be no break or interruption in the worship continuity. It is very helpful if the song leader has a notebook with songs and choruses commonly used, grouped according to the two or three keys in which each can be sung. He can use this tool in helping to plan for a meaningful song service. Often the song leader can have several choruses ready and, as the tone of the service is sensed, he can choose from them. The song service needs forethought and planning just as a sermon does.

Special Music. The responsibility for special music is often delegated by the pastor to another person. This might be the staff minister in charge of music or a volunteer layman. Regardless of who ultimately handles the area, the pastor needs to give his support and direction.

A key part of the special music for most services and for the music department of the church in general should be the choir (or choirs).

Whenever possible, vocal soloists should be members of the choir. There may be exceptions in this area, but the musical ministry will usually be more meaningful when soloists participate in the choir program. The choir should be well rehearsed and prepared. It should prepare as faithfully as the pastor prepares for his part in the service. Depending on the format of the service, the choir might sing a short number in opening, a number following prayer, and/or a regular number or two scheduled elsewhere in the service.

Soloists and vocal ensembles will naturally develop from the choir. The person in charge of music should carefully watch for people who are musically qualified and have a desire to minister beyond the choir presentations. The quality of their ministry is always important, but we should not overlook the fact that individuals have an inherent need to minister and to learn how to minister. Oftentimes inexperienced talent can be given opportunity at first in less demanding services such as youth or midweek services. Never overlook the need for allowing "new" talent to develop.

Those who are asked to share their talent in a service should be asked far enough in advance so they can make proper preparation. They should be expected to prepare adequately so their music ministry in the service is composed, confident, and anointed through prior communion with the Holy Spirit. They should also be told that it is not necessary to speak or give a testimony unless requested to do so by the person in charge of special music. They can be reminded that their ministry is one of song, and others in the body are to have the ministry of testifying in the service. Also, those who provide the special music must be aware that they are not performing or entertaining; they are ministering unto the Lord, not merely displaying their special musical ability. The persons providing special music should be dressed appropriately (as described under "Platform Manners").

Offertories. In dealing with the topic of offertories, we need to be reminded of the purpose of the offering: We worship our Creator through the giving of the firstfruits of that with which He has blessed us. The offertory need not always be done by the pianist or organist. It can take the form of an instrumental number on the flute, cello, trumpet, etc. Sometimes even a vocal solo might be appropriate.

The important thing to remember is that the offertory is never just a "time filler"; if it becomes that, the person singing or playing the offertory feels his ministry is of little worth. But if the pastor sees the value of the offertory and demonstrates his personal appreciation for it, the congregation will too, and this part of the service can take on a whole new meaning. The offertory should continue until the offering has been received. Then, it is appropriate for the service moderator to wait until the piece is completed by the musician before going to the pulpit to move into another phase of the service.

Relationship of the Pastor With the Music Director. A good relationship between the pastor and the music director is of great importance to the church program. The music director should be directly responsible to the pastor for his programming and for seeing that the pastor is advised of his plans for the music of the church. He will, of course, plan nothing that does not have the full approval of the pastor. A job description should be given to the new music director so he will know exactly what is expected of him.

The following information covering areas of responsibility may be helpful in preparing a job description:[1]

1. Select, in consultation with the pastor, the congregational songs for the regular worship services. Keep a record of the songs and the dates on which they are used so as to check what kind of musical diet the congregation is receiving and to include specific songs or themes which have been overlooked.

2. Schedule appropriate special music for the regular worship services. Seek a balance between vocal and instrumental music. Provide opportunity for as many as possible to minister in music, not just a few of the best musicians, as long as the participants contribute to the worship or Christian teaching functions of music. Musicians with less experience might be used in departmental and some outreach activities.

3. Develop and maintain a sanctuary (adult) choir. (The minister of music normally is the director of this group.)

4. Develop and maintain a church orchestra.

5. Supervise the general conduct of the graded and youth choirs. Work closely with any directors who are assigned to the individual choirs.

6. Maintain a team relationship with organist and pianist.

7. Integrate the total music program of the church so there is variety, acceptable quality of music, and a spiritual tone pervading the whole. Be familiar with the musical talents of individuals in the congregation, either by a music survey or by close personal observation.

---

[1]Zenas J. Bicket, *The Effective Pastor* (Springfield, MO: Gospel Publishing House, 1973), pp. 158, 159.

8. As part of the annual church calendar and in consultation with the pastor, select, prepare, and present special musical programs such as Easter or Christmas cantatas.

9. Be familiar with denominational and other resources such as hymnbooks, sheet music, orchestral arrangements.

10. See that sufficient songbooks are provided for the church auditorium and the Sunday school departments.

11. Catalog and safeguard the music books and sheet music not currently being used.

12. Be familiar with copyright restrictions and set an example for musicians by honoring the rights and property of others.

13. Supervise maintenance of church organ, piano(s), and other instruments.

14. Present needs for music, instruments, and related items to be included in the annual budget.

15. Be a service ministry to other departments of the church. Cooperate with the youth minister and the minister of Christian education to provide musical talents for their services as needed.

16. Coordinate the musical ministry of any radio and television programs which the church may include in its outreach.

The music director should have sufficient latitude to allow him to develop a musical program that will serve the best interests of the congregation and the various age-groups who participate in the ministry of music in the church. The pastor and the music director should together coordinate the activities of the music department with the special events and special services on the church calendar. Scheduling outside musical groups should always be cleared with the pastor, and there should always be an understanding with the pastor as to the agreements made with such groups concerning honorariums, accommodations, travel expenses, and the selling of records or other materials.

TESTIMONIES

The Psalmist said, "Let the redeemed of the Lord say so" (Psalm 107:2). There is still a place for testimonies in a service. However, this part of the service needs to have special direction. In middle-sized and large congregations, it is sometimes best to select one or more individuals to give a word of testimony, rather than opening the testimony service to the entire assembly. When a testimony time is opened to the entire assembly, one person can dominate that part of the service and take more time than he should. The persons being asked to give a testimony might be told what the pastor wants them to share. Testimonies given by persons for whom the Lord has recently done something specific are a blessing and an encouragement to others. The testimony can be in an area such as healing, salvation, baptism in the Holy Spirit, or God's provision for material needs.

Another way to handle a testimony service is to call a person to the platform for a brief interview. The pastor's intention to do this should be conveyed to the participant prior to the service. By this means, the moderator is able to guide the testimony by asking questions or suggesting points of emphasis. Testimonies need not be lengthy.

Personal testimonies are a blessing to the body of Christ. They strengthen the faith of both speaker and listener as Christ is shared in the public service by personal witness to God's faithfulness.

ANNOUNCEMENTS

Welcoming Guests. The people most in need of personal attention in any given church service are the first-time visitors. Yet we often hear of visitors in our churches who are never acknowledged or noticed. This is inexcusable!

One of the surest ways of acknowledging guests is for the pastor to take time within the service structure to welcome them. It is a good idea to have a packet prepared to be given to each first-time guest. The contents of this packet may vary, but here are a few suggestions: The *Pentecostal Evangel* (International Edition), a brochure of the local assembly, a small gift (such as a calendar for the wallet, a pocket secretary, a pen, or a pencil), and a visitor's registration card. The church brochure should include the schedule of regular services, the departments of the church and their activities, a brief word from the pastor, and a picture of the pastor and the staff.

As the pastor welcomes the guests, ushers should be prepared with a supply of these packets and distribute them to the people who signify by their raised hands that they are first-time visitors. The pastor should ask the guests to fill out the visitor's card and drop it in the offering plate when the offering is received. Ample time should be allowed between welcoming guests and receiving the offering so the visitors can complete these cards. When guests are acknowledged in this way, members of the congregation find it easier to welcome the visitors personally at the close of the service.

Some churches have found success in having a church family "adopt" a new family. The host family invites the guest for dinner and/or fellowship and an opportunity to become better acquainted.

General Announcements. The announcements made within the service structure are most important, for it is at this time that the pastor or moderator communicates with the congregation concerning matters of importance and general interest. A handout bulletin places printed announcements in the hands of the congregation so they can refer to the church calendar later in the week.

Care should be taken in making vocal announcements so that the listeners do not think of the upcoming meeting as "just another service" on the church calendar. There should be something special for each person in each service, and everyone should be encouraged to attend. All activities should be clearly stated with times and places designated. The tone of voice used to make the announcements tells the congregation how important the particular events are to the pastor. It has been said that "an informed congregation is a happy congregation!" General announcements can be informal, yet helpful and informative.

When a handout bulletin is used, it is not necessary to read the entire contents from the pulpit. To do so would negate the purpose of the bulletin. A reminder by the pastor to the congregation to check the bulletin for the schedule of events on the church calendar can conserve a great deal of time. The larger the church, the more necessary it becomes to conserve announcement time.

Special Announcements. Special announcements call attention to an event or events that do not usually occur. If these "special" announcements are made along with the usual mention of the regular schedule of events, they will not be noted by the congregation. Like regular announcements, these should be concise and as informative as necessary to convey the message to the congregation.

Information concerning special events should be written down so the person making the announcement does not have to rely on his memory. A pastor usually has many details on his mind just before and during the service. The information submitted to him for a special announcement should be accurate as to such factors as time, place, and date. All special announcements submitted should be typed or legibly written and given to the head usher or the pastor *before* the start of the service. This allows the pastor or person making the announcement to acquaint himself with the details. It also helps avoid the simultaneous scheduling of conflicting events.

The pastor should see to it that the church office is apprised of special announcements. It is very likely that calls will be received during the week for further information relating to the announced events.

RECEIVING THE OFFERING

Cheerful participation in giving should be another way a congregation enters into worship. The apostle Paul believed and taught that giving is an essential experience for all believers: ". . . enriched in every thing to all bountifulness" (2 Corinthians 9:11). He then went on to emphasize that giving brings edification: "For the administration of this service not only supplieth the want of the saints, but is abundant also by many thanksgivings unto God" (v. 12).

The person receiving the offering should never apologize for doing so. People are being given an opportunity to obey the Lord. We are instructed to bring "all the tithes into the storehouse [local church] . . . upon the first day of the week" (Malachi 3:10; 1 Corinthians 16:2). It is well to thank the congregation for their faithfulness in standing by the work of the Lord with their giving. The use of a sentence that aptly describes the true nature of the offering is appropriate: "We will now wait upon you for the Lord's tithe and your offering."

When a special offering is taken, the pastor should state clearly what the money is to be used for. When an offering has been designated for a specific person or project, that offering in its entirety should be given for the purpose stated, unless specifically designated otherwise by the individual contributor on his contribution envelope. All contributors should be encouraged to use contribution envelopes for the sake of accurate accounting at the end of the year.

Giving is one of the highest expressions of love!

Ushers and Their Ministry

The desire to feel wanted is universal, and the church usher can make this a reality for every person he welcomes to the service. He

says by his gracious manner, kindness, and warmth, "We want you
here! We are glad you have come! We want you to feel welcome! We
desire to help you in any possible way!"

The impression the usher makes on those he meets and greets is an
important and lasting one. He represents the Lord, the pastor, the
church officers, the congregation, and the denomination as he welcomes visitors and regular members of the congregation.

THE IMPORTANCE OF USHERING TO THE CHURCH SERVICE

In most public places, ushering seeks only to serve and please people. The ushers direct people to their seats in the most rapid and efficient manner possible. Ushering in the church, however, is a service
rendered to God and an important contribution to the overall effect of
the church service. The church usher is himself part of the worshiping
congregation, and his efforts to maintain an atmosphere of reverence
and order before, during, and after the service are made to please
God, not man (Colossians 3:23). The church usher has his particular
duties to perform just as the minister, the organist, and the choir have
their duties and ministries. His role in freely offering himself and his
services contributes greatly to the atmosphere of worship.

THE USHER AS AN AID TO WORSHIP

Since ushering itself is an act of worship, the church usher can encourage and promote the worship of God in a number of ways.

He Helps to Prepare the Congregation for Worship. The worshipers
have to be seated, hymnals and literature need to be supplied, and an
atmosphere of worship must be created. The usher sees to it that the
congregation assembles in an orderly way. The New Testament admonishes, "Let all things be done decently and in order" (1 Corinthians 14:40), and the church usher is in a position to carry out this
admonition by his quiet command of the manner in which people
conduct themselves in the church.

He Acts as "Host" for God. Our Lord said, "Come unto me" (Matthew 11:28), and the invitation is still valid today. The church usher,
in many ways, is God's hand of invitation extended. As such, he looks
after the comforts and needs of all the congregation. Some of those he
serves will be visitors who need to be made welcome. Some will be

members who should be made to feel their membership and presence is valued by this servant and representative of God.

He Promotes a Positive Image of the Church. The usher is representative of the general character of the church he serves. The first impression most visitors have of the church at worship is received from the usher who welcomes them. The usher's attitude will quickly indicate whether the church is interested in welcoming strangers, whether the members are kind and friendly, and whether the things the church stands for demand respect and support. The usher can be the means of encouraging a visitor to return and worship regularly, and of attracting a person to Christ or repelling him. The church usher should promote favorable public relations.

He Helps Win Souls for Christ. The important aspect of evangelism consists of attracting outsiders to the church services where they can hear the gospel preached and where the invitation for salvation is given. When they come it is imperative that the church usher help secure visitor's names and addresses. This makes it possible for the pastor and members of the congregation to visit the guests and become better acquainted with them. Ushers can be of great help in the church's work of evangelism.

THE MAKING OF A GOOD USHER

Attitude. Because church ushering is such an important phase of the Lord's work, the man chosen to serve as an usher should be enthusiastic about his assignment. He should consider his task a sacred duty and a great privilege. He should feel honored that he is considered to be a man of fine Christian character, ability, and judgment.

The usher should look on his work as a position of great responsibility. He is not merely a crowd handler. He is a servant of Christ with an opportunity to "do good unto all men, especially unto them who are of the household of faith" (Galatians 6:10). Although he should feel the importance of his office, he should not feel important in himself. If he has the right attitude, he will never make himself conspicuous or become domineering. He is in the office to *serve!*

Conduct. Courtesy, quietness, reverence—these are the primary qualities required in the conduct of an usher. He should be pleasant, kind, and hospitable, and always ready to lend assistance to those in need of help or direction. He should never slouch or lean against the walls or pews, and he should never, never chew gum while on duty! There should be no loud talking or idle conversation among the ushers. Discussion of any business other than that of ushering can be a hindrance to the work God wants to do in the service.

Personal Appearance. Ushers should dress appropriately in keeping with the best local customs. They should be neat, clean, and properly attired in a suit with a shirt and tie. Trousers should be pressed and shoes shined. This will speak well of the man and his church. Some churches provide blazers or uniform jackets for their staff of ushers. It is desirable to identify ushers in some way so people can tell who is an usher. Identification badges are most commonly used and can be purchased at any Christian supply store.

Training. No one should be allowed to usher without some training. Ushers must be told what to do and when and how to do it. Only the best is good enough in the service of our Lord!

The head usher should be capable of delegating assignments to the ushering staff and of organizing the group into an enthusiastic, willing, dedicated team. He should be a Christian gentleman who is faithful to the church services and very dependable. He should be chosen because of qualities that command respect. He must know the wishes of the pastor with regard to the administration of the ushering staff. This requires a continuing and close working relationship.

The ushering staff should be called together for regular ushers' meetings in which they can enjoy an interchange of ideas and suggestions for improving their personal involvement in the ministry of ushering. Each should be provided with a good usher's manual (available at most Christian supply stores) they can read and put into practice.

TECHNIQUES OF USHERING

People seem to do their best and most efficient work when they are organized. This is as true with church ushers as with any other group in the church. The regular ushers' meeting is also an ideal opportunity for words of commendation from the pastor and the head usher and for reaffirming the importance of the usher's responsibility to serve people. A regular meeting can also create among the staff a "team spirit" which is so necessary to the morale of any organization.

Meeting People. A basic requirement in meeting people is a genuine friendliness. An usher should convey friendliness by every look, word, and deed. It is important for an usher to call people by name and shake hands with them as they are greeted. This is why ushers should make it a point to remember names. A notebook and pencil should be available for writing down new names and those that are hard to remember. Actually, a friendly handshake *after* the service, using the person's name, is often a more effective welcome than a greeting upon arrival. Ushers should never show partiality to their personal friends in greeting people at the church.

Ushers must always be tactful and courteous. They should be able to handle difficult situations without hurting anyone's feelings. They should have the capacity to be "all things to all men" (1 Corinthians 9:22). If an usher makes a mistake in handling a situation, he should apologize and, if possible, correct the matter. In every case of hurt feelings, he should make an effort to straighten out the matter as soon as possible. "A soft answer turneth away wrath" (Proverbs 15:1).

Controlling Crowds. Most people have the habit of coming to church just on time, and this sometimes causes a noticeable congestion at the beginning of a service. But disorder and confusion can be avoided in handling large numbers of people entering the sanctuary at the same time if the ushers are prepared with a carefully laid out plan of action. In larger churches it may be necessary to have ushers stationed down the aisles. It is better to direct worshipers from one usher to another than to have ushers walk the full length of a long aisle.

It is always advisable to have extra ushers on hand for special services where additional seating must be brought in for an overflow crowd. Arrangements for these special needs are the responsibility of the head usher.

Ushers must always remain calm, self-confident, and poised. If they become excited, the people waiting to be seated will become restless. If the usher goes about his duties quietly and calmly, the people will be quiet and patient, thus making the atmosphere of reverence a reality.

Seating the Worshipers. In seating worshipers, ushers must take into consideration the seating capacity of the church and the probable attendance at a given service. They should know where to seat people to obtain the best possible atmosphere of worship. Ushers can and should learn people's preferences as to seating. However, one of the most frustrating problems an usher faces is the contest between the early arrivals and the latecomers for the aisle seats. Some churches have their ushering staff request that people move toward the center as they are seated. Some people sitting next to the aisle are more willing to stand and allow the latecomer to slip by and move toward the center of the row than to move to the center themselves. These are the occasions when an usher must exhibit great patience.

As a general rule, the church should be filled from the front to the rear. Most pastors prefer this as it puts the people in front immediately into a spirit of worship without the distraction of watching others being seated. In fact, filling the front pews first is the secret of getting people to sit in the front. If the rear and center seats are filled first, the impression is created that the front pews are undesirable since others have avoided them. Also, people are self-conscious about going down the aisle past a church full of people. They would not have this fear when the front of the church is filled first.

Special Needs. Special consideration is always needed for the hard-of-hearing, the nearsighted, mothers with babies, those in wheelchairs or physically handicapped, those who are habitually late, children and young people, and visitors. An alert usher can see to it that all of these "special" people are seated in a section of the sanctuary that is best for them. The nursery facilities can be shown to the visitor with children. Physically handicapped people can be assisted to a section of the sanctuary where they can see and hear easily. Parents with young children can be seated near the rear; latecomers should also be seated near the rear. Many churches find it helpful to reserve a section of rear pews for parents with small children, persons who are ill, and for latecomers. It is always inadvisable to seat children or young people in the balcony or in other secluded sections of the sanctuary where giggling, whispering, and inattention are more likely to occur.

It is desirable to seat visitors well to the front if they do not indicate a preference for a position further back. This encourages their mingling with the rest of the congregation after the service and facilitates their meeting as many people as possible.

Other Special Duties. Other special duties of ushers include receiving offerings, serving Communion, and other such tasks outlined by the pastor and the official board of the church. Every usher who performs his work faithfully and in the right spirit will have the satisfaction of rendering an important service to the Lord Jesus Christ himself.

The Pastor's Role in the Service

PLATFORM MANNERS

"First impressions are lasting impressions!" This age-old cliche is especially true of the proprieties (or lack of them) that occur on the platform during the church service. The manner in which the personnel who participate in the service conduct themselves is of prime importance.

First, platform personnel should enter the sanctuary at the same time, after first gathering in a side room for prayer and briefing by the pastor. An order of service should be established, preferably in written form, with a copy provided for each participant.

The attire of those participating in the service should not distract from worship or the message to be delivered. Cleanliness, neatness, and overall good grooming should be of utmost concern. It should be kept in mind that the pastor and his staff are not *performing for* the congregation, but are *ministering to* them. Attire that attracts undue attention to platform personnel, detracts attention from the worship of the Lord.

The manner in which a person sits while before an audience says much to that audience. If his manner is one of reverence and dignity, the congregation will recognize it and be influenced to display the same attitude. If his manner is one of carelessness or frivolity, that spirit will be conveyed. Conversation between persons on the platform should be limited to that which is absolutely essential to the service.

The pastor should always be the central figure among the platform personnel. The service should be under his direction, and those responsible for establishing the order of the service should always consult him in advance to determine his wishes concerning the service and what he anticipates as a result of each of the parts of the service. Every aspect of the first part of the service should point toward the message and what should be accomplished in the hearts of the listeners.

THE SERMON

Style. Every minister should learn to be himself and to be natural with his own sermon style. In endeavoring to copy some noted preacher and his style, many good men have lost the effectiveness of their own unique message and mode of expression. One should be observant and open to areas of improvement in sermon presentation. Manner, voice, and gestures all combine to make the message effective; never should they detract from the One whom we seek to exalt. Jesus declared, "He that speaketh of himself seeketh his own glory" (John 7:18).

R. M. Riggs in *The Spirit-filled Pastor's Guide* gives a strong caution: "We must never use the pulpit as a place for self-display, or to win self-praise, but seek in all conscientiousness and earnestness to bring praise and glory to our Lord and Master."[2] The apostle Paul writes in 2 Corinthians 1:12: "In simplicity and godly sincerity, not with fleshly wisdom, but by the grace of God, we have had our conversation in the world, and more abundantly to you-ward."

Content. The Assemblies of God is known worldwide for being a Bible-teaching, Bible-preaching Movement. We continue to enjoy phenomenal growth because we preach the Word! It is the Word that is "quick and powerful" (Hebrews 4:12). Jeremiah stated it beautifully: "Is not my word like as a fire? saith the Lord; and like a hammer that breaketh the rock in pieces?" (Jeremiah 23:29).

Stories and illustrations should be used to illustrate, not to entertain; and they should never comprise the major part of the message. The minister should be careful to use proper grammar and to utilize the English language to the best of his ability. However, care should be taken to insure that the vocabulary does not incorporate such unfamiliar words that the congregation cannot easily follow the train of thought. The same care should be taken to delete all language that is in any way questionable, such as crude expressions or slang. James states it this way: "Who is a wise man and endued with knowledge among you? let him show out of a good conversation his works with meekness of wisdom" (James 3:13).

Length. The motto of a famous public speaker was: "Stand up to be

---

[2]Ralph M. Riggs, *The Spirit-filled Pastor's Guide* (Springfield, MO: Gospel Publishing House, 1948), p. 236.

seen! Talk up to be heard! Shut up to be appreciated!" It is better to leave the listener wanting to hear more than to overfeed him. It is a decided lack of wisdom for a man to continue to speak when the Holy Spirit has brought the message to a close. It is quite possible to bring men and women to a point of decision and then, by continuing on, to have them lose the desire to make a decision.

How does one know when the time has come to bring the message to a close? When the anointing has lifted! One man, endeavoring to explain the anointing, put it this way, "I can't tell you what it is, but I can tell you when it isn't!" Allow the Holy Spirit to grant you the fruit of your message!

THE ALTAR CALL

Many men have preached a masterful sermon and have brought people to a place of wanting to accept the Lord Jesus Christ but have failed to see the need of a strong altar call. Consequently, they have not had the joy of seeing people saved as a result of their ministry. In some cases this has left the preachers disappointed, sad, and frustrated.

One hurdle that must be overcome is the fear, "What if no one responds?" Many times this is an ungrounded fear. In most cases, people who have been touched by the Holy Spirit will respond if given the opportunity. Matthew 10:32, 33 is the scriptural basis for public profession: "Whosoever therefore shall confess me before men, him will I confess also before my Father which is in heaven. But whosoever shall deny me before men, him will I also deny before my Father which is in heaven."

Public Confession. A public invitation is still one of the greatest soul-winning means of evangelism for the church today. C. M. Ward says he has learned over his many years of preaching that "it is better to preach shorter sermons and give longer altar calls." Evangelist Billy Graham has used, and continues to use very effectively, a public-commitment approach in his crusades.

The Invitation. Tell the people exactly what you want them to do. Be very specific so they understand what is expected of them. Ask for heads to be bowed, with Christians praying. Ask those who wish to accept Christ to raise a hand. Assure them you are not asking them to join the church. Then, ask the congregation to stand reverently, and have the congregation or choir begin singing an invitational song. It should be the same song during the entire invitation. Ask those who raised their hands to come forward so you may pray with them. Trained Christian workers should be ready to pray with those who respond to the invitation. It is well to have these altar workers walk the aisle with those who are coming forward to accept Christ as Saviour.

The Sinner's Prayer. The pastor or person praying with the one who has come forward should lead him in the "Sinner's Prayer." Scripture passages should be given to the convert assuring him of Christ's forgiveness. Altar workers who do not yet have a grasp of significant Scripture verses to help converts should use marked Bibles or Christian Workers' Testaments.

The new convert should be instructed as to the four ways he or she can keep what was received. The following four steps are recommended:

1. Read the Bible daily.
2. Begin every day with prayer.
3. Attend every service possible.
4. Witness to someone else of the joy of salvation.

Packets should be given to new converts containing a tract such as *Now That I'm a Christian* and a copy of the booklet *Now What?*[3] by Ralph Harris.

Welcome the New Converts. It is important that those who respond to the invitation during the altar call receive a welcome and congratulations on the decision they have made. If the person is from the local community, follow-up contact should be made immediately. Such follow-up has been proven to be most effective when someone is assigned to fellowship with the new convert and to help him become grounded in the faith.

Selection and Training of Altar Workers. One of the best opportunities for a beautiful ministry in the local church is in the area of altar work. A pastor should not try, all by himself, to minister to those who respond to the invitation. Instead, he should have qualified personnel assisting him at the altar. This allows him to be free to direct the congregation or to pray with various people as they come forward.

[3] Available from Gospel Publishing House, 1445 Boonville, Springfield, MO 65802.

Selection of these workers should not be left to chance—to just anyone who offers to work in this area. These key persons should be carefully chosen by the pastor. They should be selected on the basis of the
following characteristics:

1. Living a consistent Christian life
2. Faithful to the house and work of the Lord
3. Acquainted with the Bible, particularly those passages dealing
   with the plan of salvation
4. Of a gentle spirit (not argumentative)
5. Sensitive to the direction of the Holy Spirit

As in every area of person-to-person ministry in the church, the
altar worker should take every precaution against displaying offensive
breath by the use of breath mints. But he should *never* use chewing
gum.

Workers should be aware of the various reasons why people respond
to an altar call. Some come for salvation, some for dedication to
Christian service, others to be drawn closer to the Lord. Some just
want someone to pray with them. Still others don't know why they
have come forward; these persons need to be assured that they have
responded to the beckoning of the Holy Spirit.

The Christian counselor (altar worker) should feel free to inquire
why the person has come forward and what he desires from the Lord.
He should always have his Bible with him, clearly marked with key
verses that can be used to take the inquirer through the Word as a
basis for his faith.

The altar worker should be instructed to avoid the use of the word
feel or *feeling* in speaking about salvation. The new convert should be
instructed that salvation is not based on *feeling* but on fact, as stated
in God's Word. Furthermore, the counselor should never in any way
demean the church with which the seeker has been affiliated previously.

If at all possible, the altar worker should step out into the aisle at
the same time the inquirer steps into the aisle and walk to the altar
with him—men with men and women with women. The altar worker
should counsel and pray with the person until he is assured the seeker
has found what he was seeking to receive from God. Many churches
ask the counselor who prays with a person to be responsible for fol-

low-up on him, to help and encourage him until he becomes established in his Christian walk.

It is important that an altar card be filled out by the altar worker and given to the pastor or person in charge of the altar workers so follow-up can be made on the new convert. Follow-up would include such things as assignment of a visit to his home, adding his name to the mailing list, and advising Sunday school personnel of his new-found faith.

The outreach ministry of the church is not the sole responsibility of the pastor. In fact, churches that leave the whole task of winning souls to the pastor are stagnant churches. But when all in a congregation recognize and accept their responsibility to be fishers of men, there will be many willing hands to draw in the net and introduce men and women to a new life in Jesus Christ. The pastor who leads his congregation to play an active role in the worship and evangelistic services is a wise pastor indeed. God will use and richly bless his ministry.

Suggested Reading

Bicket, Zenas J. *The Effective Pastor.* Springfield, MO: Gospel Publishing House, 1973.

Garrett, Willis Otis. *Church Ushers Manual.* New York: Fleming H. Revell Co., 1924.

Kent, Homer A. *The Pastor and His Work.* Chicago: Moody Press, 1963.

Pearlman, Myer. *The Pentecostal Pulpit.* Springfield, MO: Gospel Publishing House, n.d.

Perry, Lloyd M. *A Manual of Pastoral Problems and Procedures.* Grand Rapids: Baker Book House, 1962.

Swarm, Paul. *Guideposts for the Church Musician.* Decatur, IL: Church Music Foundation, 1949.

Williams, Ernest S. *A Faithful Minister.* Springfield, MO: Gospel Publishing House, 1941.

11

The Pastor
and
Christian Education

ROBERT H. SPENCE

The Christian education program of a local church provides the pastor with an excellent opportunity to extend himself and his teaching ministry beyond the limitations of personal contact and presentation. As the man of God becomes involved in the ministry of Christian education, he will find it emerging in importance among his many and varied responsibilities. The burden and passion of a man's life can be communicated to others through Christian education.

Defining Christian Education

Christian education is accepted and recognized as a vital arm of the church for building up the body of Christ. The various components of this important ministry find greatest fulfillment when they are seen as an obedient response to the Great Commission. To His disciples of every generation, Jesus declared: "Go ye therefore, and teach all nations, baptizing them in the name of the Father, and of the Son, and of the Holy Ghost: teaching them to observe all things whatsoever I have commanded you" (Matthew 28:19,20).

No ambiguity exists in the wording of this divine mandate. As surely as the church is "to go," it is impelled "to teach," or as marginal readings explain, "to make disciples." Emphasizing and reinforcing the responsibility given to the followers of Jesus is this additional statement: "Teaching them [the new converts] to observe all things whatsoever I have commanded you."

Robert H. Spence, D.D., is president of Evangel College, Springfield, Missouri.

As one traces educational developments throughout history, it is obvious that various and diverse groups have attempted to accomplish their respective goals through the means of education. At times the immediate purposes of formal education programs have been uncertain and obscure. As a science dealing with the principles and practices of teaching and learning, education is intended to develop mental capabilities and to cultivate moral capacities. Through study or instruction, with discipline of mind and character, education is a means of preparing a person in a systematic manner for a calling or vocation. Over the span of centuries, however, the long-range objective of education has been expressed in terms of the formation of character.

Christian education, in a very real sense, is the spiritual work of developing attributes of Christlike behavior and life-style. Intricately tied to the objective of helping people *become*, Christian education is intended to teach people to observe the things Jesus commanded and to build lives that demonstrate a likeness to Jesus Christ.

Scriptural Basis for Christian Education

The effective pastor is very much aware of the fact that the education program of the church is reaching and involving people in the midst of unparalleled turmoil in this world. The social and political conditions described by Paul in his second letter to Timothy will always have a contemporary note:

> This know also, that in the last days perilous times shall come. For men shall be lovers of their own selves, covetous, boasters, proud, blasphemers, disobedient to parents, unthankful, unholy, without natural affection, trucebreakers, false accusers, incontinent, fierce, despisers of those that are good, traitors, heady, high-minded, lovers of pleasures more than lovers of God; having a form of godliness, but denying the power thereof: from such turn away (2 Timothy 3:1-5).

As he accepts the challenge of leading people in turbulent times, the pastor must give preeminence to the Word of God. First, he must be sure of his own faith in the inspiration of the Scriptures. Second, he must believe that in the Word of God there are answers for the needs of others. Not only will the Bible provide direct encouragement, but the examples the pastor finds in the Word of others coping with similar problems will also aid him in teaching God's Word in a practical and pertinent manner.

As the individual's concept of Christian education is formulated, it is helpful to gain the perspective of the Old Testament emphasis on teaching spiritual truths. When the destruction of Sodom was being contemplated, the sharing of that knowledge with Abraham was considered by God himself. The awesomeness of human involvement in divine counsel defies explanation. The justification is found in these words: "Seeing that Abraham shall surely become a great and mighty nation, and all the nations of the earth shall be blessed in him" (Genesis 18:18). As the Holy Spirit inspired the writing of that verse, a further reason was given for providing Abraham with a preview of the divine plan: "For I know him, that he will command his children and his household after him, and they shall keep the way of the Lord, to do justice and judgment" (v.19).

Predating what we know as Christian education by millennia, this passage in Genesis stresses the importance God himself attached to teaching divine commands from one generation to the next. Recognizing the principles involved enables us to understand the priority the education program of the church should occupy during this dispensation. Right living cannot be assured without a clear communication of divine truth. For Abraham and his direct descendants, the teaching of divine commandments depended entirely on verbal transmission. With Moses, however, we see the introduction of written law. Unchanging rules that were clearly stated had implications for the teacher and students alike. Consistency could be maintained even though new generations and fresh leadership were facing new challenges.

As Joshua was called to succeed Moses, the importance of teaching and spiritual training was once more noted. The new leader was encouraged by the assurance, "As I was with Moses, so I will be with thee: I will not fail thee, nor forsake thee" (Joshua 1:5). The Word of the Lord to Joshua was not limited to assurances of divine accompaniment. In addition to the promised blessings, the message emphasized the responsibility of undeviating adherence to the Law. The Lord spoke strong encouragement to Joshua:

> Only be thou strong and very courageous, that thou mayest observe to do according to all the law, which Moses my servant commanded thee:

turn not from it to the right hand or to the left, that thou mayest prosper withersoever thou goest. This book of the law shall not depart out of
thy mouth; but thou shalt meditate therein day and night, that thou
mayest observe to do according to all that is written therein: for then
thou shalt make thy way prosperous, and then thou shalt have good success. Have not I commanded thee? Be strong and of a good courage; be
not afraid, neither be thou dismayed: for the Lord thy God is with thee
whithersoever thou goest (Joshua 1:7-9).

In 2 Chronicles 17, the establishment of Jehoshaphat's kingdom is
described. Very clearly he is presented as a man who walked in the
ways of his forefather David and sought after the Lord. The abundant
riches and honor he enjoyed did not satisfy a continuing spiritual
hunger. Even though he was personally involved in worship and in
positive acts of righteousness, he realized the people of the nation had
great spiritual needs. Moving in what he felt was the will of God,
Jehoshaphat sent his princes to teach in the cities of Judah; and along
with them, Jehoshaphat sent Levites. Significantly, we have this as the
record:

> And they taught in Judah, having the book of the law of the Lord
> with them; they went about through all the cities of Judah and taught
> among the people. And the fear of the Lord fell upon all the kingdoms
> of the lands that were round about Judah, and they made no war
> against Jehoshaphat (2 Chronicles 17:9,10, RSV).

The teaching of God's Word produced revival. As the populace
turned to God with repentance and confession, the fear of the Lord
became prevalent throughout the land.

A similar occurrence is recorded in the Book of Nehemiah. Chaotic
and desolate conditions stood as mute testimony of God's judgment on
sin. The prosperity the nation of Judah had enjoyed no longer existed.
The glory of God was but a memory as the nation existed only in exile. In the providence of God, a work of restoration was begun.
Nehemiah led a group who shared his vision for repairing the walls of
the city of Jerusalem. The need for the reconstruction of the walls was
obvious, but of greater importance was the spiritual restoration that
was needed. Recorded in Nehemiah 1, the story unfolds:

> The words of Nehemiah the son of Hachaliah. And it came to pass in
> the month Chisleu, in the twentieth year, as I was in Shushan the
> palace, that Hanani, one of my brethren, came, he and certain men of

Judah; and I asked them concerning the Jews that had escaped, which were left of the captivity, and concerning Jerusalem. And they said unto me, The remnant that are left of the captivity there in the province are in great affliction and reproach: the wall of Jerusalem also is broken down, and the gates thereof are burned with fire. And it came to pass, when I heard these words, that I sat down and wèpt, and mourned certain days, and fasted, and prayed before the God of heaven, and said, I beseech thee, O Lord God of heaven, the great and terrible [awe-inspiring] God, that keepeth covenant and mercy for them that love him and observe his commandments: let thine ear now be attentive, and thine eyes open, that thou mayest hear the prayer of thy servant, which I pray before thee now, day and night, for the children of Israel thy servants, and confess the sins of the children of Israel, which we have sinned against thee: both I and my father's house have sinned. We have dealt very corruptly against thee, and have not kept the commandments, nor the statutes, nor the judgments, which thou commandedst thy servant Moses. Remember, I beseech thee, the word that thou commandedst thy servant Moses, saying, If ye transgress, I will scatter you abroad among the nations (Nehemiah 1:1-8).

Again, the teaching of the Word of God provided the means of bringing people to a place of awareness of their need to get right with God and live according to His Word.

The New Testament writers placed heavy emphasis on the responsibility the Church has to see people grow toward Christian maturity. The writer to the Hebrews expressed it this way: "Therefore leaving the principles of the doctrine of Christ, let us go on unto perfection; not laying again the foundation of repentance from dead works, and of faith toward God" (Hebrews 6:1).

The Holy Spirit, when revealing to the apostle Paul the ministry gifts for the Church, made the purpose of these gifts very clear. Paul shared this revelation when he wrote to the Ephesians: "And he gave some, apostles; and some, prophets; and some, evangelists; and some, pastors and teachers; for the perfecting of the saints, for the work of the ministry, for the edifying of the body of Christ" (Ephesians 4:11, 12).

With very few exceptions, local congregations of believers noted for their dynamic growth are characterized by an active and vital program of Christian education. As we observe these churches, however, we note a great deal of variety and even differing points of view as to the purpose and direction of the teaching ministry and the total education program of the local assembly.

Philosophy of Christian Education

Successful Christian education programs do not occur by accident. Those teaching ministries that have resulted in changed lives did not simply evolve. At the present time or at some time in the past someone must have occupied a leadership role in the church who was capable of communicating his ideas and philosophy of Christian education to others who were willing to share his vision and help implement his plans.

There are occasions, to be sure, when outstanding Christian education programs have been conducted without the formality of written documents describing the philosophical basis of the ministry. But even where there is no formal summation of priority and purpose, the attitude of the pastor and the action of the leadership of the church have constituted a nonverbal communication of philosophy.

When asked to describe the Christian education program of the church, there are some pastors who respond with a review of their current promotional efforts or tactics for Sunday school attendance. Unfortunately, Sunday school attendance figures have too often been the sole determinant of the effectiveness of a teaching ministry. In these situations, Sunday school is the sum total of Christian education.

To develop an adequate Christian education program, the pastor, more than anyone else, must come to grips with philosophical questions. Without a clear understanding of the purpose of the educational ministry of the church, and without an articulation of the objectives of teaching and training, Christian education will function at a level beneath its full potential and, in all probability, will only be a series of activities.

The pastor need not be fearful of formulating his personal philosophy of Christian education. Theoretically, *philosophy* is an attempt to think consistently about life as a whole. Technically, the word means "love of wisdom." As a working definition, it might be said that philosophy of Christian education is an attempt to organize thoughts and concepts regarding the most effective means of accomplishing the objectives of spiritual training.

Just as a person may have difficulty stating in a single sentence his philosophy of life, so is it difficult to give a succinct summation of a philosophy of Christian education. Education itself, because of its complexity, is difficult to define with a simple statement. Innumerable books containing the writings of learned men on the subject of philosophy of education are available to pastors who desire a serious study of the subject. Comparing the various schools of thought concerning the preferable means and methods of communicating ideas will bring into focus contrasting beliefs concerning the most effective approach to accomplish the objectives of education.

The purpose of this chapter, however, is not to review secular schools of philosophical thought. Neither is the purpose to offer a treatment of historical trends in the area of educational philosophy. Rather, it is the intention of the writer to identify two basic ideas a pastor will encounter as he seeks to determine the place and purpose of Christian education within the framework of the local church. Closely related to that purpose is the intention to encourage the pastor to develop a ministry of Christian education that will meet the prevailing needs of the body of believers for whom God has directed him to serve as the spiritual leader.

There have been men throughout the history of the church whose philosophy of Christian education has led them to substitute education for evangelism. Where religious education is offered in the place of evangelism, there is a danger of it simply becoming "humanism" dressed in academic robes. Education in and of itself is not a redemptive process.

The pastor will encounter some in the church world who have been influenced by humanistic and behavioristic schools of philosophy and as a result have designed programs of Christian education on the premise that man is supreme rather than God; and inasmuch as he is inherently good, man needs only the right kind of environment to grow into a beautiful creature. Those who adopt this position usually abhor any definite standards of behavior and rebel against specific definitions of right and wrong. In this context, issues are seen only with relative values and human failures are blamed on society.

In formulating his personal philosophy of Christian education, the pastor with a desire to see this ministry fulfill its scriptural purpose of edifying the body of Christ, will base his beliefs and concepts squarely on the Bible. For that reason, top priority must be given to prayerful study of the Word of God to develop a clear understanding and teaching approach regarding the great truths of: God and His Son, Jesus

Christ; man and his need for a Saviour; repentance and salvation producing a new birth; and Christian growth that leads to maturity. The crucial point in determining a pastor's direction will be his concept of balance between education and evangelism.

Some pastors see Christian education as a ministry to those already committed to Christ. They see the teaching ministry as one that introduces the convert to the truth and leads him through a series of studies acquainting him with God's Word, to become a more effective member of the church. On the other hand, there are pastors who conceive of the Christian education program of the local church as a means of enlisting the unreached and the uncommitted. These men see the organizations that make up a total Christian education system as lending themselves to community contacts and having appeal to individuals of various groups that might not be attracted to regular worship services or the usual evangelistic endeavors conducted in the sanctuary.

With statistical studies indicating a consistent ratio between active participants in the local church program and the number of people enrolled in Christian education activities, some pastors have placed a priority on increasing the enrollment in the various Christian education endeavors such as Sunday school, children's activities, Bible clubs, and camping programs. Interestingly enough, in a movement that has had firm convictions about standards of church membership and where prevailing practice has consistently limited church membership to those who meet a definite criteria, there has been a very accommodating attitude toward enrollment and enlistment in Christian education activities.

The individual pastor must come to the place where he has definite convictions and well-formulated concepts as to where his Christian education program will accept people. If he sees his education ministry as primarily a teaching and training vehicle for those who are already in the church, this will be reflected in his organization, curriculum, and choice of personnel to implement the program. If the pastor believes the various elements of his Christian education program should be utilized to enlist the unreached and unsaved, then his resources will be channeled in a way that will provide contact with the unconverted and assure a presentation of the gospel message to them. Strong busing programs are a direct result of this concept.

Very successful and attractive Christian education ministries can be cited that have embraced seemingly contrasting concepts. It is not a matter of saying one is right and the other is wrong. Rather, it is a demonstration of the diversity that often characterizes a move of God's Spirit.

To work successfully, a philosophy of Christian education must be formulated within a man's heart as he remains open to the direction of the Holy Spirit. Although his concepts may differ from those of his neighbor, a pastor can lead with a sense of purpose and an assurance of faith if he has a clear vision and an understanding of the program of Christian education needed for the body of believers he has been called to serve. If a pastor attempts to adopt all the ideas and innovations of those around him, he will live a life of utter frustration. A particular emphasis or technique may be well received and effective in one congregation, but a total failure with another group even within the same city.

Without question, the philosophy of Christian education held by the pastor will determine the focus of attention and the methods employed to attract and hold people in the program.

Organizational Structure for Christian Education Programs

MINISTERIAL LEADERSHIP

As with other ministries of the local church, the direction taken by the Christian education program will depend on the leadership of the pastor or the designated member of the ministerial staff. The full responsibility of Christian education need not rest on the minister, but his attitude and concern will influence others, particularly those whose abilities and talents can be dedicated to fruitful teaching ministries.

The ministerial leadership role will not be the same in every church. The key factors in determining the extent of the pastor's direct involvement will be the length of time since the congregation was formed, the present size and composition of the church, its location, and the available personnel and equipment.

Serving under divine appointment, the pastor is expected to provide leadership in discerning the will of God for the Christian education program as much as for any other endeavor of the church. Through a continued application of spiritual principles, the pastor should identify goals that are unique to his church and avoid the adoption of stereotyped methods and programs. A wise leader will not only share his vision but also his specific objectives so others will be aware of them and can support them.

The importance of the leader being able to inspire and involve others cannot be overemphasized. Recognizing the work that needs to be done, and even knowing procedures and techniques that will accomplish the goal, will not necessarily assure success. Perhaps as much as any other program of the church, Christian education depends on cooperation and working together to accomplish agreed-upon objectives.

BOARD OF CHRISTIAN EDUCATION

In a church of limited size, the pastor and Sunday school superintendent will formulate plans and determine the direction of the Christian education program. However, as the church grows, the pastor may well utilize a Board of Christian Education. In its initial stages, it need not be large. Even a committee of three can be a distinct asset in establishing priorities and giving oversight to teaching ministries. In a larger church, the size of this board can increase to seven, nine, or eleven. With a larger group, it should include persons with professional and academic training that could add further dimension to the responsibility and effectiveness of this board.

Even in its primary stages, there should be a definite and stated purpose for the Board of Christian Education. A written description of its function and purpose should be produced so the members of the board will understand their responsibilities and those who work with the Christian education program will have an appreciation of the board's role and function.

RELATIONSHIPS

The extent of responsibility assigned to the Board of Christian Education will be determined by the desires and practices of the congregation and the pastor. Some of the decisions the board will be called on to make are: adoption of Sunday school curriculum, approval of textbooks and materials, appointments of teaching personnel, initiation of additional auxiliary organizations (such as those that will serve various age-groups in a family night program), and acquisition of audiovisual equipment. Under no circumstances should a Board of Christian Education usurp the authority and responsibility of the official church board. Careful attention must be given to relationships with the deacons of the church or the official church board. A policy statement should identify and describe the respective roles of the church board and the Board of Christian Education.

By virtue of its name and understood assignment, the Board of Christian Education will be concerned with all activities in which the church is engaging in Christian education. With few exceptions, the Sunday school will be the largest and most extensive of these. Weekday Bible clubs, family night training programs, and possibly children's church activities will be the concern of the Board of Christian Education as well. With all of these endeavors reviewed by one board, harmonious relationships can be maintained among the various groups so that complementary and cooperative attitudes prevail rather than competition.

INTERNAL ORGANIZATION

The various components of the Christian education program will require organizational structure within each group. It must be remembered that organizational procedures are a means to an end and not an end in themselves. If administrative procedures are too cumbersome and personnel too numerous, the purpose of administration will be defeated. Each assignment should have a specific and justifiable reason for being. Jobs with impressive titles should not be created just to make people feel they have an assignment even if there is no real work to be done.

Organizational patterns will change with growth. For example, in a beginning Sunday school a superintendent can oversee the entire program. As the school increases in enrollment, departmental superintendents may be utilized. Continued growth may lead to further division of departments. Some schools reach a point in their development where a full-time minister of education offers administrative supervision in place of a Sunday school superintendent. The organizational structure of any Christian education program should fit the need that exists rather than superimposing an administrative chart found in a set of suggested guidelines.

Developing a Christian Education Program

OBJECTIVES

When assuming responsibility for the establishment of a new assembly or accepting the responsibility of a new church, a pastor will devote much of his time in the beginning to formulating objectives and establishing goals. The Christian education program, because it will involve so many of his people and because it has the potential for touching the maximum number of people, should be one of his first concerns. Objectives, carefully and prayerfully selected, will reflect the vision of the pastor and the direction in which his ministry will develop.

The goals of a Christian education program may appear obvious. For example, a pastor might state as an objective for the Sunday school, "To enlist the unchurched and uncommitted," or, "To provide a means whereby committed Christians can engage in a serious program of Bible study." On the other hand, the objectives may be more specific. Recognizing a weakness in doctrinal knowledge on the part of teenagers could prompt a pastor to select as an objective, "The teaching of Christian doctrine," or, "Introducing the doctrines and beliefs of the Assemblies of God."

As worthy and as ambitious as objectives may be, they do not stand alone. There must be a sublisting of immediate steps that will lead to the realization of the goals. The difference between growth and stagnation in a Christian education program is not the lack of long-range goals, but rather the failure to have an awareness of the steps necessary to reach the final objectives. Intermediate steps must be obtainable, and they should provide for a sense of accomplishment as progress is made toward the long-range objectives.

The pastor should remember that a congregation, whether large or small, will readily recognize the existence of a definite plan of operation. Furthermore, if intermediate steps are well identified, the congregation will sustain an attitude of faith and confidence as it moves in harmony with his vision.

STAFF RECRUITMENT

Wise and visionary leadership functioning with an adequate organizational structure cannot alone accomplish the objectives of Christian education. A prepared staff of workers is absolutely essential to carry out agreed-upon plans. Identifying and enlisting well-qualified staff members may present the leader his greatest challenge. The most obvious step in staff recruitment is to announce the need and call for volunteers. Careful attention must be given to assigning volunteers to areas in which they have expertise and can serve effectively. With few exceptions, however, Christian education leaders will not have enough volunteers. Some means must be devised to find those persons with potential and ability who may be hesitant to volunteer because of timidity or lack of self-confidence.

The pastor with longer tenure has an advantage in staff recruitment if he has closely observed his congregation. Knowing members' educational experiences and vocational involvements would enable him to uncover hidden talents. People whose employment requires teaching and training should be looked on as prospective workers.

The pastor and leaders of the Christian education program should not overlook one method of enlisting staff members that has proven to be a very fertile area of recruitment in many churches. For a person who has never assumed sole responsibility for a Sunday school class or a group of youngsters in an auxiliary organization, the thought of standing before a group and leading a discussion or teaching for an extended period seems impossible. However, that same individual, because of a desire to be involved and an interest in teaching, may happily agree to be an assistant or helper. Encouraging such a person to take this first step often leads to a very effective and satisfying role as a teacher or leader once he has gained some experience under the guidance of a qualified instructor.

In recruiting staff members, the expectations of the person should be clearly articulated. Teachers and leaders in the Christian education program become models for those who are enrolled in their classes. In many cases, they will be the first and sometimes the only contact youngsters have with a leader in the church.

Physical attractiveness and formal education are not the only considerations in enlistment. Of greater importance are qualities such as loyalty to Christ, demonstrated love for Christ's church, devotion to the work of God, a New Testament Christian life-style, regular attendance at church services, and faithfulness to previously given assignments.

TRAINING ACTIVITIES

Reluctance to accept assignments in the Christian education program often stems from a lack of preparation and training. Prospective workers often say, "I do not know how to be a teacher." Those responsible for the overall direction of the Christian education program must accept responsibility for training workers—all workers, not just those who have not had previous training.

In a small church, or with a beginning congregation, the pastor may have little choice but to use immediately those volunteers whose previous training and experience he has little knowledge of. Even in these circumstances, however, he can conduct regular workers conferences to deal with procedures and topics that will increase the effectiveness of his staff members. Priority should be given to such topics as subject matter to be taught, methods and procedures for more effective teaching, improved recordkeeping, and more effective follow-up of visitors and absentees.

In a small church, the pastor will have a more active role in workers conferences. He should look on this as an opportunity to communicate directly with those who provide leadership in the various components of the Christian education program. By all means, detailed plans should be made for every workers meeting to insure that those attending can view the meeting as beneficial and the time well spent.

Larger churches will be able to offer continuing training activities either during the Bible study hour on Sunday morning or at some other time during the week, such as Wednesday evening as a part of family night activities. If this type of program is feasible, it is well to have either the pastor or a well-qualified teacher lead these training activities. The training should consist not only of studies that will increase Biblical understanding, but also methods of classroom leadership that will improve communication and group participation.

CURRICULUM SELECTION

The curriculum adopted for a Christian education program will determine not only what is taught but also to a certain degree how it is taught. This vital area cannot be taken for granted. Curricular materials reflect spiritual concepts and definite philosophical positions. Publishing houses operated by church groups and denominations are expected to reflect through their writings and religious materials the beliefs and convictions of the denomination. Curricular materials should be chosen first on the basis of compatibility and harmony with the church's doctrinal beliefs. Second, they should be selected on their ability to provide the local church with a balanced program of study that will assure continuity to the total program.

METHODS AND MATERIALS

The Christian education program of the church can be exciting, interesting, and attractive—and it should be! A reference to Christian education need not bring to mind a mental image of a dull setting with an instructor lecturing for an entire class period to a group of disinterested, absentminded students. The employment of different methods and a variety of materials can make Bible study enticing. Showing films, displaying models, organizing panel discussions, and playing records and tapes can add to student involvement.

Living in a different time and culture makes it difficult for students to fully grasp or appreciate the meaning of many customs and habits of Biblical times. With films, either movies or slides, it is possible for living conditions, clothing styles, and even geographical features of Bible lands to be presented in an understandable manner. A model of the tabernacle or Solomon's Temple, for example, will offer a perspective that would be impossible with verbal communications alone. Meaningful discussions can precipitate personal decisions regarding truths that otherwise would be left as purely abstract ideas.

The pastor and designated leaders of the Christian education program should take the initiative in introducing staff members to improved methods and materials. This may be done on an individual basis or in workers conferences. Sectional or district Christian education leaders could be invited to share their experiences and introduce new concepts. Occasionally, the leader of an outstanding Christian education program from another church or city might be invited to share practices and ideas that have proven to be successful.

Modern technology and communication make it imperative that the church take advantage of the innovative methods available for teaching the Word of God. Youngsters have grown accustomed to having facts presented to them in school through the most modern devices and are accustomed to being entertained by cartoons that use the latest in technology. The church should teach, even in its manner of presenting the Truth, that the spiritual message is more important than any other message the child may hear.

Teaching Aids

Because a particular Christian education activity may last for only 1 hour, there is a tendency on the part of leaders and workers to function with the minimum equipment and facilities—a room, some chairs, and a speaker's stand. But the Christian education program deserves the best. The quality of the program may be measured in terms of the interest developed among students or participants by the teacher or leader. A desire for excellence is also demonstrated by classroom appearance. Especially for younger students, bulletin boards, book displays, and interest centers are important. They are more than decorations; they are teaching aids.

The pastor should periodically request an inventory of the teaching aids available to the various staff members involved in the Christian education program. He should encourage those responsible for securing equipment to make sure that maps, charts, and globes are available to those who will be teaching courses that relate to the travels of Biblical characters. Chalkboards, with an adequate supply of chalk and erasers, or overhead projectors with the necessary writing materials, should be accessible to those classes that normally use the lecture method. An assignment should be given to someone to see that these materials and aids are ready for use at the appointed hour. It is too late when the session starts to send a member in search of equipment.

Facilities

Rarely will a pastor find himself working with a congregation that has perfect facilities. Whether the church is large or small, there are always inadequacies. Facilities are simply instruments to accomplish a mission. And the pastor must assert his leadership in helping a congregation use fully all available space and work diligently for improvement. He must guard against the development of an attitude that accepts mediocrity because the program lacks ideal facilities. Daily or weekly usage of a building creates maintenance problems. Those who constantly use the facilities become accustomed to dull paint, broken windows, a missing baseboard, or other examples of disrepair that a visitor would immediately see. Out-of-date literature, broken furniture, and unused equipment should be properly disposed of or stored.

Should the opportunity present itself for planning new facilities, not only the pastor but also the entire staff should visit other church buildings and educational centers, such as kindergartens and day-care centers. Preference should be given in planning and construction to children, who are very impressionable. Unfortunately, many churches make the mistake of providing attractive and comfortable classrooms for the adults, while allowing the children to be fitted into what is left.

SPECIALIZED NEEDS

The development of the Christian education program in a local church must be planned in light of the unique needs and requirements of the various groups it will serve. The pastor should list not only the obvious groups (such as children, youth, and adults), but also those that may not have been considered, such as handicapped or retarded people.

Those who share the vision of this ministry with the pastor may join him in asking such questions as these: "Why do we need to serve this group? What specialized problems or challenges do they present? What are their needs? How can we minister to these people? What special requirements would there be in terms of staff, materials, or facilities?"

Many communities have no spiritual ministry to youngsters with birth defects or mental retardation. Those churches that have responded to this need have been amazed at the reaction of not only those they were seeking to assist but also their families. The same is true for ministry directed to those with physical handicaps. In most cases, renovations in buildings to make them accessible to wheelchairs and to people with physical impairments have led to an appreciative response by those who were previously unable to attend.

Because some people have work schedules that extend around the clock and throughout the week, the church has an opportunity to offer an extension ministry to those who cannot attend regular services or activities. Bible study groups may be formed at fire stations, nursing homes, convalescent hospitals, and other locations where people are available and interested. The pastor and church that truly desire to minister to spiritual needs through Christian education activities will not overlook such opportunities to take the message to these special groups.

Christian Education Activities

SUNDAY SCHOOL

As has been noted, Christian education is a multifaceted ministry of the church. By virtue of its organization and its recognized availability to provide Bible training to every age-group, the Sunday school will carry the major portion of the Christian education program. It is not the only activity in which the church can be involved in Christian education, but it must be given first consideration because of the large number of people it involves, the number of staff members who serve, and the amount of space it requires.

There is no limit to the potential of a Sunday school program that remains relevant and alert to people's needs. One of the largest Sunday schools in the nation for many years maintained a stable average weekly attendance of approximately 4,000. The personnel in the program were convinced their maximum potential had been reached. A new minister of Christian education joined the staff, and in assuming his responsibilities he refused to believe the school had grown as large as it could grow. Through study and investigation, he became convinced that some reorganization within the school would provide potential for continued growth. The Board of Christian Education accepted his proposals and the church responded favorably. With the reorganization and the institution of new methods, attendance figures began once more to show an increase.

The pastor should occasionally observe the Sunday school program, as much as possible, through the eyes of a visitor. If he approaches it in this manner, he will ask himself, "Where shall I park? What door should I use to enter the building? How will I know what direction to take? Will there be someone to greet me and make me feel welcome?

Will there be someone to assist in getting my children to their respective classes? How will I be welcomed?" The handling of visitors is a key to Sunday school growth. The pastor need not conduct a routine program under the assumption that no further growth is possible—no matter where he is serving. In recent years, many of the more outstanding churches in terms of Sunday school growth have been in small towns and even in rural areas where people had assumed that a strong Sunday school program was impossible to establish.

Of all the Christian education programs the church can be involved with, there is more help available for the Sunday school than for any other. This help is in the form of books, seminars, conventions, consultants, and printed materials.

RELEASED TIME

In many metropolitan areas of the United States, students in public schools are allowed to leave the school premises and go to the church of their choice for religious training. This "released time" practice evolved as a compromise in the church-versus-state controversy regarding religious training. With court decisions placing restrictions on activities such as prayer and Bible reading in public classrooms, alternative plans were devised whereby students could receive moral and spiritual training in their own churches from their own church leaders.

In localities where released time programs are in effect, the church can develop an added dimension for Christian education. This opportunity for a time of religious training should not be ignored.

VACATION BIBLE SCHOOL

The vacation Bible school comes under the heading of Christian education activities and should be under the general oversight of the Board of Christian Education. If a vacation Bible school has been conducted for a period of years without variation, it may lose some of its appeal and impact. However, this activity also will lend itself to innovation and new ideas.

Some churches have found that scheduling the vacation Bible school for an evening hour and including sessions for teens and adults has given new impetus to the program. Not only has this variation pro-

vided an occasion for teaching and training classes previously unavailable for adults, but also, because of adult involvement, it has led
to a larger enrollment of children. As with other Christian education
activities, the keys to a successful vacation Bible school are planning
and adequate staffing.

Religious publishing houses have made available courses with
themes that are current and imaginative. Interesting and useful hand-
craft materials and projects can be used. An increasing number of
churches have facilities or adjacent playgrounds to make activity
periods more enjoyable. Transportation equipment makes it possible
for children to attend who in the past were unable to because of the
distance.

FAMILY NIGHT ACTIVITIES

Family night programs have become the rule rather than the exception as church leaders have looked for times in which various organizations can meet without overtaxing families' schedules and over-
loading the church calendar. The usual practice is to have a training
program for preschool children and then offer specialized activities
through groups such as Missionettes and Royal Rangers. Youth and
adults may meet in a chapel or in the main auditorium.

Adopting this arrangement has appeared to be the most practical
and feasible approach to involving a maximum number of church
families in the most convenient manner. The various organizations are
excellent vehicles for teaching and training. The schedule is not
without some concern, however. The additional staffing required is
immediately apparent if meetings are held concurrently. Without an
adequate staff and proper orientation the activities can proceed with a
lack of spiritual content. Organizations that could be marvelous
means of Christian education can become activity-oriented to the extent that the participants are never aware of any spiritual purpose.

A successful family night program must have close coordination
and supervision. There should be an agreed-upon time limit so all
leaders know how long they are responsible for their respective
groups. Few things can conclude a beautiful worship time in the sanctuary more quickly than a group of youngsters entering noisily to look
for their parents because their activity has already concluded.

SUMMER CAMP

Throughout the nation, summer camping programs are available under the auspices of the church. Districts have led the way in providing camps for boys and girls. While youth camps have been supervised by youth departments, the boys' and girls' camps have frequently been conducted by the Sunday school department.

Some churches have sufficient strength and available personnel to run individual camping programs. Having a child or a teenager for 5 days without interruption in a controlled environment provides an opportunity for Christian education at its best. The careful choice of curricular materials for teaching sessions will determine the effectiveness of the endeavor. Most campers look forward to recreation and physical activity, so the program must be appealing if it is to hold their attention. Study topics and subjects must be interesting as well as meaningful.

Some churches offer variations of the camping program with shorter retreat periods. Two or three days can be effectively used with proper planning. Other churches offer another variation of the camping program with 1 day per week devoted to special activities and outings.

DAY-CARE CENTERS

An increasing number of churches have found opportunities of Christian education by opening day-care centers. Suited to serve the needs of working mothers, the day-care center allows an alert staff to not only teach youngsters the Word of God at a very impressionable age, but also reach families that may have no church affiliation and no commitment to Christ.

As an activity, the day-care center is extremely confining and demanding. Unlike volunteer programs (such as the Sunday school and vacation Bible school), the day-care center requires a paid staff and regular hours every working day.

The key factor in the decision to become involved in such a program may be the availability of facilities and an adequate staff. State regulatory agencies establish the criteria not only of the type of facility and the number of children it can serve, but also of the qualifications and number of staff members required. While this venture should not be entered into as a profit-making enterprise, the church can expect a day-care center to cover its expenses and make a contribution toward the improvement of the facilities being used.

Christian Education Through a Day-school Program

Education has been a concern of the church from the earliest days of formal education. Predating the formation of the United States, churches maintained schools and established colleges. A vast majority of the colleges founded in our nation prior to 1850 were Christian colleges or church-related colleges to prepare and train ministers.

Along with this has been the long-standing practice of churches maintaining parochial schools. Some groups, such as the Roman Catholics and the Lutherans, have been prominent in the operation of parochial school systems. Recently, there has been a new emphasis on church involvement in primary and secondary education. This may be seen as the most notable development in the field of Christian education in recent years. All over the nation there are churches organizing Christian day schools as alternatives to the secular program of the public system. From both an educational standpoint and a Christian perspective, the Christian day school is of inestimable value.

In cities where Christian day schools are the most successful, there was a recognition on the part of parents and church leaders that conditions prevalent in the secular school system were unacceptable and gave little promise of improvement. The widespread use of drugs and the teaching of inappropriate subject matter most frequently served as the motivation for organizing a Christian day school.

There is no standard pattern for the formation of a Christian day school. The common element found in the establishment of all such schools is that one or more persons became convinced a Christian day school could provide an effective ministry. If a church and its leadership recognize the advantage of including a Christian day school in its Christian education program, the resources can be developed to accomplish the objective.

ADMINISTRATION

The Christian day school must have a governing board of responsible individuals interested in the development of the program and capable of setting policies for an administrative team to follow. Ideally, the school board should include individuals who have had experience and training in the field of education. While they need not be cognizant of all current trends, they should have an understanding of changing methods. The school board must have a good working relationship with the official church board. Close liaison can be maintained by having at least one representative on the school board who is also on the church board. Under no circumstances should the two boards drift into a competitive position. While the school board will have immediate oversight of the program, it must always function in a supporting capacity to the official church board.

Small or developing schools may utilize church personnel for day-to-day administrative oversight. However, as a school grows, it deserves and will demand full-time administrative supervision. As the school concerns itself with raising its academic standards, it will require personnel who are conversant in the field of education and can keep the entire institution abreast of new developments.

FACULTY

While the board and the administrators are important, the choice of faculty members will determine the maintenance of a Christian testimony in a school. The integration of faith and practice on the part of the faculty will be demonstrated by their teaching procedures and concepts. Inasmuch as the Christian school is dedicated to offering students a quality education in a spiritual atmosphere, the selection of faculty must include consideration of the academic preparation of the various faculty members.

The colleges maintained by the Assemblies of God have given special attention to training teachers for Christian day schools. Teachers who receive their postsecondary education in these institutions gain a theistic world view and the kind of philosophical base that enables them to engage in an effective day-school ministry.

CURRICULUM

Regulations differ among the various states regarding curricular requirements for a school. Consequently, those organizing a day-school program should consult with their state's department of education. It is important that the Christian day school meet the state's requirements. It can do so without impairing its Christian purpose and testimony.

The curriculum in a Christian school will cover the same subject areas found in the secular system. The difference will be in interpretation, perspective, and understanding. It is possible for the Christian school to deal with basic subjects such as history, science, and social studies in a way that offers the student an understanding that he would not have in a secular setting. For example, a secular presentation of science gives the impression it is only nature at work. The Christian perspective helps the student understand that science is the story of the outworking of God's laws.

The curriculum of a Christian school consists of more than just the addition of Bible study or a chapel period. In compliance with scriptural exhortations such as, ". . . bringing into captivity every thought to the obedience of Christ" (2 Corinthians 10:5), and, ". . . that in all things he [Christ] might have the preeminence" (Colossians 1:18), the Christian school curriculum becomes a vehicle for acquainting the student with the One who made this world and placed man in it.

FINANCES

Undertaking a Christian day school program will present a financial challenge that may exceed any previously experienced by the pastor or the church. There must be a clear understanding on the part of the church board and the congregation that a day-school ministry may require subsidizing for a period of years. When the full impact of this ministry is considered, such a subsidy can be appreciated. In making financial arrangements for the school, those assigned the study task must keep in focus all facets of the school program: faculty salaries, equipment, materials, office expenses, and such things as dues to school associations.

A Christian day school is not a profit-making venture. Tuition charges should be set with an attempt to maintain fiscal responsibility of the institution while at the same time keeping the program within reach of a maximum number of students. In cities where there are other schools of a similar nature, tuition charges should be comparable. Tuition discounts for more than one member of a family enrolled or for other special cases should be determined by the school board.

FACILITIES

In many cases Christian day schools operate in church buildings that were built with the idea in mind of conducting a day-school program. In other cases, a school functions successfully over a period of years, convincing the church of the wisdom of adding facilities to an existing plant that was specifically designed to accommodate a Sunday school program. Joint usage by church and school groups will require patience and understanding by all involved.

Utilizing facilities for both church and school purposes is a demonstration of good stewardship. School personnel should be careful to require proper maintenance of the facilities. It is advisable that the major share of the cost of maintenance be borne by the school.

Attractive facilities can be an important factor in a parent's decision to enroll his children in a Christian day school. Adequate accommodations that are properly furnished and maintained say to parents and students the school is in business to stay.

CONCLUSION

Undertaking a Christian day school ministry involves heavy responsibility. It should not be entered into lightly. Parents may be inclined to enroll their children in a Christian day school because of problems in a secular school. With the passing of time, the crisis will be forgotten. Sustained enrollment will depend on the Christian day school's success in upholding superior academic standards and giving the quality of education that the parents will feel justifies the cost. The spiritual rewards of this ministry are quickly attested to by those involved.

Christian education programs in the local church are not developed and conducted simply because the church should be doing something. The "something" a church should be doing is obeying the Great Commission left to all Christians by Jesus. When Christian education programs are seen as ways of fulfilling that commission—bringing people to know Christ as their Saviour or to know Him better as their Lord and Master—they will become important parts of the outreach of the church.

Suggested Reading

Gangel, Kenneth O. *Leadership for Church Education.* Chicago:
Moody Press, 1970.

Getz, Gene A., and Roy B. Zuck, eds. *Adult Education in the Church.*
Chicago: Moody Press, 1970.

Irving, Roy G., and Roy B. Zuck, eds. *Youth and the Church.*
Chicago: Moody Press, 1968.

Kienel, A. Paul. *The Christian School: Why Is It Right for Your
Child.* Wheaton: Victor Books, 1974.

LeBar, Lois E. *Focus on People in Church Education.* Old Tappan,
NJ: Fleming H. Revell Company, 1968.

Person, Peter P. *An Introduction to Christian Education.* Grand
Rapids: Baker Book House, 1958.

Richards, Lawrence O. *A Theology of Christian Education.* Grand
Rapids: Zondervan Publishing House, 1975.

12

The Pastor and Total Church Leadership

RICHARD L. DRESSELHAUS

It is a fact that the growth, progress, and development of any church will be in equal measure to the quality of leadership given to it by the pastor. For this reason, it is appropriate that we turn now to a discussion of the pastor as the leader of the total church program. The emphasis will be on Biblical patterns and practical principles of leadership.

A Definition of Spiritual Leadership

J. Oswald Sanders has defined spiritual leadership as "a thing of the Spirit . . . conferred by God alone. When His searching eye alights on a man who has qualified, He anoints him with His Spirit and separates him to his distinctive ministry (Acts 9:17; 22:21)."[1]

This definition is reminiscent of the testimony of St. Francis of Assisi who, when confronted with the question, "How is it that the world desires to follow you?" replied:

> Thou wishest to know? It is because the eyes of the Most High have willed it so. He continually watches the good and the wicked, and as His most holy eyes have not found among sinners any smaller man, nor any more insufficient and sinful, therefore He has chosen me to accomplish the marvelous work which God hath undertaken; He chose me because He could find none more worthless, and He wished to confound

---

Richard L. Dresselhaus is pastor of First Assembly of God, San Diego, California.

---

[1]From *Spiritual Leadership* by J. Oswald Sanders. Copyright 1967. Moody Press, Moody Bible Institute of Chicago. Used by permission.

the nobility and grandeur, the strength, the beauty and the learning of
this world.[2]

There is a striking truth here. True leadership has to do with the
burden of the Lord. It is the fulfillment of a divinely given commission. No man can explain his being chosen. He merely accepts the
mission in the power of the Spirit. Such was the case of Jeremiah, the
weeping prophet, who stood in awe of God's call: "Alas, Lord God!
Behold, I do not know how to speak, because I am a youth" (Jeremiah
1:6, NASB). Or Isaiah, who in like manner found the call of God
unutterably mysterious, yet glorious: "Woe is me, for I am ruined!
Because I am a man of unclean lips, and I live among a people of
unclean lips; for my eyes have seen the King, the Lord of hosts"
(Isaiah 6:5, NASB).

Leslie Parrott adds dimension to our definition of spiritual leadership by observing that there are three kinds of leadership:

> First is the authoritarian. . . . This person tries to manipulate and
> force people to his own will, assuming his judgment is best for every-
> one. Manipulation, bending people to one's own will against their
> wishes, has been thoroughly tried at many times and places in man's
> history, and it does not work—at least not for long . . . . Other pastors
> and lay leaders try the *laissez-faire* approach. . . . This kind of pastor
> becomes the executive secretary of the board. . . . [He] simply tries to
> find out what the church board wants and then does it . . . . The really
> productive and useful pastor or lay leader is the man with the democra-
> tic way of working with people. This leader tries to show the people
> what they can do, and by various ways releases the potential ability of
> the church board to outline and execute a forward-looking set of
> policies and plans.[3]

How can the prophetic style of spiritual leadership, observable in
both Testaments, be reconciled with what Parrott calls "the democratic way of working with people"? This is a hard question. And the answer each man gives will largely determine the type of ministry he
will have and the quality of leadership he will give.

Or, another pertinent question: Are Biblical patterns of leadership

---

[2]*Ibid.*, p. 23. Used by permission.

[3]From *Building Today's Church: How Pastors and Laymen Work Together* by Leslie
Parrott. Reprinted 1973 by Baker Book House and used by permission.

incumbent on the church today? Lawrence O. Richards comments on what Dr. Gene Getz calls "functional equivalence:"

> The issue which we should be concerned with is not, "Have we reproduced the New Testament Church and its offices," but, "Does our church leadership today function in the same way as did the leadership of the New Testament Church?" Call a man what you will—pastor, teaching elder, preaching elder, brother, deacon, president, etc. Equivalence of function is the issue, and nothing else.[4]

In other words, our concern ought not to be the production of the exact style and structure, but rather the duplication of the burden and mission. Is it not possible that even today a man of God may feel the hurt and cry of the Lord for our world, much as did Isaiah and Jeremiah for the world of their day, and yet express that mission and burden in a slightly different way? The argument, then, is for a prophetic ministry within the context of today's church. A prophetic ministry does not necessarily demand an autonomous approach to leadership.

God's voice is not silent in our day. He is still calling men with vision and commitment. And they are going out to change the world and build the kingdom of God. Nothing less than the dynamic of this kind of call will compel the world to repentance and give the church the quality of leadership that will make it a viable influence for positive change in our day.

Biblical Patterns of Leadership

The Bible is a textbook on leadership. Men and women of different ethnic backgrounds and varying political and cultural persuasions are seen in their respective places of leadership. Noah led his family to join him in building the ark. Abraham was an explorer, priest, and founding father of the nation of Israel. David was Israel's greatest king and spokesman. Peter was able to argue convincingly at the Council of Jerusalem, as recorded in Acts 15. Each of these men was a leader in his day. And a careful study of their lives will highlight qualities of leadership men and women of God must possess in our day. Now we will single out three great men—Moses, Jesus, and

---

[4]Lawrence O. Richards quotes Dr. Gene Getz in *A New Face for the Church* by Lawrence O. Richards. Copyright © 1970 by Zondervan Publishing House. Used by permission.

Paul—and deal in more detail with the patterns of leadership that emerge through a study of their lives.

MOSES: LEADERSHIP THROUGH DELEGATION

The godless ways of the Egyptians could not snuff out the flame that burned in the hearts of Amram and Jochebed. The birth of Moses amidst adverse circumstances did not hinder them from seeing the potential greatness resident in the child. Through God's providence, Moses became one of the most brilliant military and political strategists the courts of Pharaoh had ever produced.

When confronted with the choice of ethnic and religious identity or retaining his position in Pharaoh's palace, Moses determined in his heart to be an Israelite. The heavy burden of his people had made its mark. The bondage of his people had become oppressive to him. Unfortunately, he acted out of anger and indignation. Now tagged a murderer, broken in spirit, and bewildered by the rapid turn of events in his life, Moses fled for refuge to the land of Midian.

During those years the Lord dealt mightily with Moses. Finally, through a dramatic visitation of God, the angel of the Lord spoke from the burning bush and gave Moses the call to liberate the people of God. It is significant that the call came at a time when Moses felt the full weight of human inadequacy. He was a rejected man.

Is it any wonder he asked: "Who am I, that I should go to Pharaoh, and that I should bring the sons of Israel out of Egypt?" (Exodus 3:11, NASB)? Is it any wonder this well-educated statesman, a product of Pharaoh's court, had to admit: "I am slow of speech and slow of tongue" (Exodus 4:10, NASB)? It must have been a moment of truth for Moses when he had to face the fact he would now be a nobody back in Egypt. His authority would be challenged. Moses' awareness of this is indicated in the question he asked God: "Now they may say to me, 'What is His name?' What shall I say to them?" (Exodus 3:13, NASB).

It is interesting to observe that it was not until the fourth plague that Moses finally began to speak on his own behalf. Did this mark a renewed confidence in himself? Had the years of rejection finally given way to a new self-assurance? It seems so. From that time on Moses led Israel with courage, conviction, and determination.

Measuring the Task. Considerable time had now passed. Jethro studied the marks of fatigue that were apparent on the countenance of Moses. The load had gotten too heavy. And interestingly enough, it was not Moses who diagnosed the problem; it was Jethro, his father-in-law: "The thing that you are doing is not good. You will surely wear out, both yourself and these people who are with you, for the task is too heavy for you; you cannot do it alone" (Exodus 18:17,18, NASB).

The pastor's task is demanding. He is called on to accomplish a wide variety of tasks—he is a counselor, administrator, educator, builder, orator, teacher, and an almost endless number of other things as well. Or is he? Maybe that is the problem. Has the average pastor carefully assessed the dimensions of the assignment? Has he really stopped to consider the priorities for his own ministry? Perhaps, much like Moses, he has plunged on without measuring the task.

A Divine Plan. Jethro was unique. He not only exposed the problem, he also offered a viable solution: "You be the people's representative before God, and you bring the disputes to God, then teach them the statutes and the laws, and make known to them the way in which they are to walk, and the work they are to do" (Exodus 18:19,20, NASB). This was the first part of the plan. The people were to be taught. God's plan is that people be instructed to care for themselves and to bless others. Self-dependence, in this sense, is the by-product of good leadership.

But Jethro was more specific: "You shall select out of all the people able men who fear God, men of truth, those who hate dishonest gain; and you shall place these over them, as leaders of thousands, of hundreds, of fifties and of tens. And let them judge the people" (Exodus 18:21, 22, NASB).

Moses was then left only with those disputes that Jethro judged to be "major disputes." And then came the promise: "If you do this thing and God so commands you, then you will be able to endure, and all these people also will go to their place in peace" (v. 23). This was the second part of the plan. Moses knew it in his heart. No time was wasted.

Controversy rages over the question of structure and organization within the church. Some argue for a very loose, flexible approach to leadership, while others press for boundaries and guidelines. The story of Moses is helpful at this point. The divine plan spoken through

Jethro was simple, yet adequate. The plan was such that it could be easily understood by everyone, yet comprehensive enough to be workable for 2 million people living under adverse circumstances. Such are always the plans that originate with God. They are designed to meet a need, to achieve the maximum value from human effort, and to spread the work load over a broad base.

In our day the plan of God for Moses may be termed "planning by objective" or "goal-oriented planning." At any rate, the emphasis is on the end more than the means, on achievement more than on methodology.

Implementation. In a very practical way, Lawrence O. Richards addresses this matter as it relates to the leadership of the total church. He speaks of the contrast between "the church that is" and "the church that must come." The difference he sees is one of emphasis. In "the church that must be," it is people who count—their interrelationships, their ministry to one another and to the Lord, and their commitment to be the people of God together. This, in his view, is in marked contrast to the more historical emphasis on structure, organization, and what he calls "churchmanship."[5]

Our day demands an approach to church leadership that places form after function and methodology after goal. People must feel they are the church and the organization called the church is there to serve and not be served. Paul clearly states: "Now you are Christ's body, and individually members of it" (1 Corinthians 12:27, *NASB*). And we must keep the accent in the same place—we are His church.

JESUS: LEADERSHIP THROUGH EXAMPLE

Jesus is the pastor's Subject, his Source of power and inspiration, his Counselor and Guide, and his supreme Example for effective spiritual leadership. We turn now to a study of Jesus as a model for the pastor in discharging his responsibilities as the undershepherd of the flock of God.

Perhaps the matter of criteria needs to be faced at the outset. By what standards do we measure the success of Jesus as a spiritual leader? His ministry was brief in duration. He attracted multitudes, but they followed Him only briefly and often for the wrong reasons.

---

[5]Richards, *A New Face for the Church*, pp. 51, 52.

Jesus was not an author. The only writing He did was quickly erased from the sand. His travels were limited to the small areas of Galilee and Jerusalem. And when He died, He was alone, except for a handful of faithfuls who had hidden out of fear. Can it be said, then, that Jesus is a pastor's model for spiritual leadership?

Let us look at it from another side. Consider the Lord's insight into man. John records that Jesus "knew what was in man" (John 2:25). Recall the way Jesus ruled His spirit in the face of unjust criticism and railing accusations. Or, think of the depth of His teaching—so simple the children gladly heard, yet so profound it startled the brilliant and highly educated of the day. Then stand back and weigh the impact of His life after the passage of 2,000 years. He stands in the 20th century as the King of kings and Lord of lords whose kingdom shall last forever and ever.

The Method. Robert E. Coleman has summarized the method of leadership used by Jesus:

1. Selection. Jesus called twelve men to follow Him. He chose a small, intimate group with whom He could personally work.
2. Association. Jesus not only called these men, but He lived with them and poured forth His life and teaching into their hearts and lives.
3. Consecration. Jesus expected absolute obedience from His disciples. They were committed to their Master and willing to obey His teaching.
4. Impartation. Jesus gave His very Spirit to the disciples. There was a flow of divine power from the Master to the disciple.
5. Demonstration. Jesus did not teach by precept alone but by example as well. He was a model of that which He taught. The disciples knew because they saw.
6. Delegation. Jesus, knowing that His time was short, gradually shifted the responsibility of the Kingdom to the disciples. Jesus was not afraid to delegate both responsibility and authority. He taught that their work would be a continuation of His, and that the authority of the Father would be theirs as it had been His.
7. Supervision. Jesus assigned a task to the disciples and then assisted them to be sure the assignment was completed successfully. When the disciples returned saying, "Why couldn't we?" Jesus was there to answer their question and help them to be ready to continue on in the work.
8. Reproduction. Jesus expected that His life would be reproduced through the ministry of the disciples. In this way Jesus has had a continuing ministry right up to our day.[6]

---

[6]Robert E. Coleman, *The Master Plan of Evangelism* (Old Tappan, NJ: Fleming H. Revell Company, 1963), *passim.*

The pastor who adopts the leadership plan employed by Jesus will be a great asset to the kingdom of God. In principle, it embodies the necessary ingredients for effective leadership. The plan is simple, personal, dynamic, motivational, perpetual, and manageable, and it can be duplicated. Is it any wonder Jesus changed both His world and ours?

Implementation. The pattern of leadership that comes to us from the example of Jesus has powerful ramifications for the church today.

1. An overworked pastor should look for a few faithful workers into whose lives he may pour himself.

2. A growing church should seek ways of becoming small as it becomes large. Some churches have set up "care groups" comprised of eight to twelve people who meet monthly for fellowship, study, prayer, and counsel.

3. A church board should be more concerned with quality of ministry and depth of community penetration than with "artificial" means of measuring church success, such as random statistics of attendance and finance.

4. A church member should view himself as a vital link in the total outreach of the church. He should feel a commitment that transcends personalities and petty misunderstandings.

5. The church as a whole should view itself as an alive and vital organism, reproducing itself as a consequence of its inner life.

PAUL: LEADERSHIP THROUGH RIGHT PRINCIPLES

Any study of great spiritual leaders must include the apostle Paul. Through his ministry, the young fledgling church, with its sectarian and local character, became international in mission and character. From the isolated streets of Jerusalem, the gospel spread to the most influential centers of commerce and culture known to the ancient world. Emperors and governors found themselves face to face with a doctrine of truth that was changing their world. And it was Saul of Tarsus, the apostle Paul, whom the Spirit used as the driving force behind this movement. We will now study the fundamental principles of leadership that were clearly demonstrated in the life and ministry of Paul.

Spiritual Leaders Are Called. The serious student of the writings of

Paul is struck immediately with the fact that Paul knew he had been sent of God to proclaim the gospel to the Gentiles. He described that call in a variety of ways, yet always with the same depth of unquestionable conviction: "I was made a minister, according to the gift of God's grace which was given to me according to the working of His power" (Ephesians 3:7, *NASB*). Notice his expression of gratitude: "I thank Christ Jesus our Lord, who has strengthened me, because He considered me faithful, putting me into service" (1 Timothy 1:12, *NASB*).

The apostle knew his ministry was by divine appointment. Whether in a defense before magistrates, under the scourge of a prison beating, or wandering over hot desert sands—it did not matter—he was a man of God under appointment. His message had authority. He was fearless in confronting intellectuals with the claims of the risen Christ. And there is only one explanation: Paul knew he was called! This is a fundamental principle of spiritual leadership.

Spiritual Leaders Are Servants. The apostle Paul had a servant's heart. He called himself a love-slave *(doulos)* of Jesus Christ. His spirit was one of humility and self-abasement. He gladly gave of himself to bless the lives of those to whom he had been sent to serve. How appropriate are the words from 1 Corinthians 9:19: "For though I am free from all men, I have made myself a slave to all, that I might win the more" *(NASB)*. An effective pastor never loses sight of this fundamental principle of leadership.

Spiritual Leaders Are Dependent. The apostle Paul lived as a demonstration of the gospel of grace he preached. By his own testimony he stated: "My message and my preaching were not in persuasive words of wisdom, but in demonstration of the Spirit and of power, that your faith should not rest on the wisdom of men, but on the power of God" (1 Corinthians 2:4, 5, *NASB*). It was Paul's conviction that the message he proclaimed was its own defense. It was neither his responsibility nor his right to seek an authentication of the gospel through his own abilities and persuasiveness.

Paul believed that through his weakness and brokenness the gospel could shine forth ever more brilliantly: "God has chosen the foolish things of the world to shame the wise, and God has chosen the weak things of the world to shame the things which are strong" (1 Corinthians 1:27, *NASB*). His repeated testimony was that he ministered in weakness: "When I am weak, then I am strong" (2 Corinthians 12:10, NASB).

Spiritual Leaders Are Examples. Paul went so far as to exhort his followers: "Be imitators of me" (1 Corinthians 4:16, NASB). A few chapters later, he extends the truth by naming the model that had been the guide for his own life: "Be imitators of me, just as I also am of Christ" (1 Corinthians 11:1, NASB). In Philippians 3:17 he says: "Join in following my example, and observe those who walk according to the pattern you have in us" (NASB).

Some may argue that Paul was headstrong, proud, and arrogant. But, in truth, it takes great humility of spirit and a resolute faith in God's power to be willing to ask someone to follow the example of your life. It also brings into clear focus the necessity for good "models" of leadership. Every pastor is called to "model" the message he preaches. Not that he, by his virtues, is the authentication of his proclamation, but that he strives to be an "example to the flock" of a life lived in the power of the gospel.

Spiritual Leaders Are Visionary. It is easy for us to sit in comfort and marvel over the spiritual accomplishments of the apostle Paul. but I wonder if we realize the loneliness of the man as he followed a vision God had placed in his heart. Paul was compelled by an urging in his spirit: "I am under compulsion; for woe is me if I do not preach the gospel" (1 Corinthians 9:16, NASB).

The pattern of the visionary is clearly demonstrated in Acts 16:9, 10. Paul had a vision of a man from Macedonia who was pleading with him: "Come over to Macedonia and help us." Without this vision Christianity could have remained an Eastern religion and the West would have been left without the gospel. A pastor is a visionary. He is appointed by God to see the possibilities and opportunities long before others. The man of God who allows the Spirit to develop this quality of leadership will lead a full and adventurous life. Where would the church of today be in its outreach without the availability of men with this quality of leadership?

Spiritual Leaders Are Delegators. Paul knew how to leave the work of God to others. His pattern was to establish a preaching point, win men to Christ, teach them basic spiritual truths, ordain elders among the converts, and then move on to a new place of ministry. This method was the key to the forward thrust of the Early Church. Interestingly, whenever the same approach is used today, the church enjoys great revival and blessing. But the key is delegation. It would have been much easier for Paul to have stayed in one city, built a great church, and settled into a comfortable routine. Fortunately, such was not his choice.

Spiritual Leaders Are Joyous. The Epistle of Philippians was penned while Paul was in prison. He had lived to be an old man. But now great uncertainty hung over his life. He expected his life would soon be offered. Yet, in this Epistle the apostle expressed his great joy in Christ: "Always offering prayer with joy . . . that your love may abound still more and more in real knowledge and all discernment" (Philippians 1:4, 9, *NASB*).

Any man who is trying to do the work of the Lord without the joy of the Lord will indeed be miserable and an unprofitable servant. Pastors carrying heavy responsibilities and duties must bear them in the joy of Christ. It is a key to personal survival and to an effective and fruitful ministry.

Spiritual Leaders Are Priority-conscious. The apostle, though a tentmaker by trade, was not confused in his scale of values or his priorities. By his own confession he was a single-minded servant of the Lord: "May it never be that I should boast, except in the cross of our Lord Jesus Christ, through which the world has been crucified to me, and I to the world" (Galatians 6:14, *NASB*).

It was a grasp of the Cross and its compelling power that pointed all of life in one direction for the apostle. And in our day, too, pastors who live by priorities will be fruitful and prosperous in the Lord's work. The limitations of time and human energy preclude a life of great diversity and optional efforts. Only men with singleness of heart will fulfill the call of the Lord in their lives. This is not to suggest an attitude of narrowness and isolationism, but rather a focus on the necessity of living and serving on a priority basis. Paul did—and so will every successful worker in Christ's kingdom. This is one of the most difficult lessons for busy pastors to learn and practice.

Principles for Effective Leadership

A brief summary of the leadership qualities of Moses, Jesus, and Paul has been instructive in helping us grasp a perspective on the Biblical view of spiritual leadership. It is now time to turn to a concise statement of practical principles that will guide a pastor in giving effective leadership to the entire church program.

The local pastor has a wide range of responsibilities and duties. He has appropriately been compared to an island hopper. He settles in to give assistance to one department in the church that needs his attention. Having "gotten things rolling" there, he is then called to assess the needs of another department. He continues his circuit, only to find it is time to start all over again! Such are the variety and demands of the local pastorate.

The ministry of the pastor is unique. His assignment is characterized by a wide diversity of responsibilities. He must work with a mixture of contrasting personality types. And he is confronted daily with criticisms that range from the constructive to the absurd. Some pastors, after a time, have found the cost too high and the pressure too great, and they have chosen another vocation.

This need not happen. There is a way to assure that the pastor may fulfill his calling and rejoice in his achievements. There are basic principles for spiritual leadership that, when followed, bring a man of God into fruitfulness and blessing.

KNOWING THE MIND OF GOD

Frustration will always persist for a man who has never learned to know the mind of God. That man, while appearing to do the work of the Lord, is more at work building his own kingdom than the kingdom of God. He goes from task to task with little sense of priority. He lives with the deep suspicion that he is making choices that are bringing to himself and his people something less than God's best. His is a life of sorrow and it ends in regret.

The Scriptures give us clear insight into the ministry of the Lord as it relates to the will of God. Jeremiah could speak to the disintegrating political and spiritual condition of Judah because he knew the Lord had placed His very words in his mouth. Isaiah and the other prophets spoke with the same assurance. "Thus saith the Lord" was persistently on their lips. These great men of God had an ear to the heart of God; they knew the mind of God.

Nothing is more needed in the church of Jesus Christ today than men of God who know the mind of God, take time to seek divine wisdom, and then have the courage to live by what God says. Misdirected zeal has turned good men away from God's best and made them temporarily satisfied with a quality of church life that is artificial and shallow. The appeal here is for pastors who will make it their first priority to learn the ways of God and then proceed to fulfill God's call the way He prescribes.

Prayer and Leadership. J. Oswald Sanders points out the necessity of a prepared heart as it relates to leadership:

> The spiritual leader . . . influences others not by the power of his own personality alone but by the personality eradicated and interpenetrated and empowered by the Holy Spirit. Because he permits the Holy Spirit undisputed control of his life, the Spirit's power can flow through him to others unhindered.[7]

If this response is to be achieved, the pastor must give himself to prayer. It is the means by which strength and guidance come.

Jesus, facing the demands of the multitudes, often withdrew to the hills for prayer and spiritual enrichment.

Moses, with whom God spoke face to face, lived in an atmosphere of continual communion and prayer.

Paul, whose ministry touched so many thousands, was a man who understood well what it meant to dwell in the heavenlies with Christ.

In our day, pastors are caught in a whirl of activity and sometimes find it difficult to take time to pray. Could this be the reason some churches seem to lack clear direction? Is this the cause behind the many frustrations that pour into the lives of some pastors? May it not be true that in the hurry of doing God's work, sincere men have failed to become true men of God, men who through prayer have entered into the ways of God in building His kingdom?

John Wesley said: "God will do nothing but in answer to prayer."

S. D. Gordon emphasized the necessity of prayer: "The greatest thing anyone can do for God and for man is to pray."

E. M. Bounds put it another way: "God shapes the world by prayer. The more praying there is in the world the better the world will be, the mightier the forces against evil."

Paul E. Billheimer concludes: "Prayer should be the main business of our day."[8]

---

[7]Sanders, *Spiritual Leadership*, p. 20. Used by permission.

[8]Paul E. Billheimer, *Destined for the Throne* (Fort Washington, PA: Christian Literature Crusade, 1976), p. 51.

And if prayer holds this high place in the ministry of the church, the pastor, as he gives direction to its program, must himself be a man who prays.

The Courage to Obey. It is one thing to gain a hold on the mind of God for His work, but it is another matter to have the courage to obey. The pastor is often caught between what he senses to be the will of the people and what he knows to be the will of God. Expedience calls from one side and the voice of God calls from the other. This is the area where the true man of God gains victory or suffers defeat. He may know what is on God's heart—but what shall he do? It is his right answer to this question that will build his character and chart the course of his ministry.

True spiritual perception must be foremost in every pastor's consideration of his ministry. God is not silent, nor has He left His servants without direction in doing His work. It is time that those who lead the most important work in the world be tuned to the heartbeat of Him whose work it is.

UNDERSTANDING PEOPLE

With the call to lead comes also the God-given ability to understand people. The pastor who possesses this insight and goes on to build strong relationships with those to whom he is sent to serve will enjoy an anointed and effective ministry. Paul E. Johnson has spoken well to this matter:

> Relationship is the Key to the vocation of the pastor. With this key doors of opportunity open to him; without, the key doors remain closed and shut him out with an unmistakable sense of futility and failure. The pastor who is unrelated to people may be an eloquent pulpit orator, a brilliant scholar, a stern ascetic who sacrifices personal pleasure and gains for a cause, or a tireless administrator of church business. But his labors as a pastor of souls will be futile, and he will somehow fall short of healing their conflicts or inspiring spiritual growth to fulfill the deepest hungers of his people.[9]

A wise pastor will be a student of people. He will understand their distinguishing qualities, their predictability or unpredictability, and their vast potential to be the true people of God.

---

[9]From *Psychology of Pastoral Care* by Paul E. Johnson. Copyright © 1953 by Pierce and Washabaugh. Used by permission of Abingdon.

The Potential of Variety. In the apostle Paul's teaching on the inner qualities of the Church, he uses an apt and descriptive metaphor. The Church, in Paul's teachings, is typified by the physical body. That is, just as a physical body has many different members, yet all function together to form the whole, so also is the Church.

Think for a moment on the wide variety within the Church. In the typical local church you will find believers representative of many different ethnic, educational, and geographic backgrounds, to say nothing of the wide diversity in personality types or in spiritual growth and development. Could it be that variety is part of the genius that makes the Church a vibrant influence in the world?

It has been suggested, and rightfully so, that unity does not demand uniformity. The unity of the Body transcends personality types and all forms of individuality; it has as its focus the person of Christ. A pastor who resists the temptation to insist that each member of his church be a copy of himself, and instead fosters variety and creativity in the body, will see the boundaries of his church expanding beyond his most optimistic hopes. God has made every man uniquely after himself, and each must be given the opportunity to be the fullest expression of that creative act. A true pastor will see the potential of variety in his church!

Assessing Personality Types. Following is a list of phrases describing some of the personality types encountered in the local church:

1. The Isolationist. This individual is a hider. He hides from himself, from others, and even from God. He is so insecure that exposure of almost any kind appears to him as a threat. The pastor wonders what he can do to get through to this person who hides behind a wall of aloneness.

2. The Overachiever. This individual is an activist. He wants to be on the front line of all that is happening in the church. He is first to volunteer for every new program suggested by the pastor. The problem, however, is only cloaked by these good deeds. He will eventually become weary in well-doing and a casualty to the church.

3. The Zealot. He is the kind who gets on every bandwagon that rolls by the church. He picks up on issues that can be the rallying point for change. He is vocal on all controversial issues and feels compelled to be both heard and regarded. When his causes die for lack of support, he seeks reasons outside himself for his failure to be suffi-

ciently convincing to provoke action and reform. The pastor always
wonders what Brother Zealot will bring up next.

4. The Loco. This is the individual who is viewed by the community as odd or peculiar. He may carry a bag at all times, wear buttons
on his lapel, say the same thing each time he is met, or in some other
way set himself aside socially. The pastor will need special grace and
wisdom in ministering to this brother. But peculiar as he may be, his
love for Christ is beyond dispute.

5. The Dogmatist. He is the individual who is convinced that on
every issue there is but one opinion—his. Long before all the details
are known, he has already made up his mind. In fact, with each challenge comes a further resolve that his position is correct. He is a kind
of law unto himself. The dogmatist is one of the most difficult for the
pastor to work with. Repeated attempts at reason are usually unfruitful.

6. The Offendable. This is the individual whose feelings are very
tender. If a comment is made that he feels may be directed toward
him, he is immediately thrown into a condition of self-pity. He has
such a low esteem of himself that he sometimes seeks comfort in his
own sulking. The pastor finds it hard to avoid his disfavor.

The foregoing is limited in its scope and description. Hopefully, the
vast majority of church members are in love with Christ, enjoy the
fellowship of the entire body, are cooperative with church leadership,
and can be counted on year after year to be faithful in their service to
the Lord.

The fact remains, an effective pastor, as he directs the total church
program, must be prepared to work with a variety of personality
types. And he must believe that with the call to serve has come a
special gift from the Lord to accept and work with a wide assortment
of personalities. Both the challenge and the rewards are great!

Living in Truth. First John 1:7 says: "If we walk in the light as He
Himself is in the light, we have fellowship with one another, and the
blood of Jesus His Son cleanses us from all sin" *(NASB).* The text here
suggests that "living in truth" is a prerequisite to true fellowship with
God and man. Out of honest and open hearts flow the forgiveness and
redemptive grace of Christ.

The Gift of Patience. Pastors are sometimes discouraged by either
the lack of response or the wrong response to their leadership.

Criticism, misunderstanding, gossip, and slander tie their hands with feelings of rejection and frustration. The pastor must not yield to these destructive, negative emotions. God has called him to bless His people and bring to them the living Word of God. The key is patience—the willingness to wait and watch as the Lord works. While this waiting process is not to be equated with indolence or passivity, it does mean the man of God must believe that, given time, the Word he proclaims will bear fruit in the lives of those who listen. A harvest is always the consummation of a process. The pastor must admonish, encourage, correct, and chide, but always with a patient heart.

Pastors have acted impulsively and later realized the tragic effects of their haste. The Lord calls every pastor to a life of trust and patience. He must believe Jesus Christ is the Lord of the harvest and the Head of His church. If a pastor serves in humble obedience, he may be encouraged that the Word will never return void and unfulfilled—it will do its work. But it will demand a patient spirit.

HANDLING PRAISE AND CRITICISM

Billy Graham was once asked how he handled criticism. He stated that he handled criticism just as he handled praise: he didn't give undue regard to either. This is a valuable and practical principle to follow. No pastor will escape criticism; it is a "hazard of the job." In like manner, he will also receive praise. It is well that he be encouraged and strengthened by it (praise will often accomplish that), but he must never let it affect his spirit. Jesus calls every pastor to a life of obedience, and praise and criticism must be subordinate and incidental to that call.

The Ministry of Encouragement. Leslie Parrott states, "The pastor must be a specialist in giving recognition and credit for work well done."[10] His point is well taken. People must feel their efforts are appreciated and accepted. Hopefully, that desire will be borne out of an eagerness to see others blessed and not to bolster an insecure self-image. But in any case, the Holy Spirit has chosen to give to the Church the ministry of helps and encouragement.

The pastor should see himself on both sides of this ministry. He must pray for the ability to encourage the people of God, to support

---

[10]Parrott, *Building Today's Church*, pp. 44,45.

them, to speak well of their achievements, and to motivate them to continue in service. But he must also be prepared to receive the ministry of encouragement himself from the people to whom he has been called to serve. Some pastors find it difficult to be in a place of need. They want to preserve an image of invincibility and strength. This posture is not pleasing to the Lord or uplifting to the pastor. Members of a congregation want to uphold their pastor in prayer and encourage him with kindness. The pastor should receive such gestures of encouragement with deep gratitude and thanksgiving.

Learning to Live in Peace. The Psalmist prayed: "Though I walk in the midst of trouble, Thou wilt revive me" (Psalm 138:7, *NASB).* Pastors often walk in the midst of trouble. Their lives are sometimes filled with conflict. They deal continually with disappointments and controversies. But the important thing is how conflicts are handled.

If a pastor chooses to face difficulties with an aggressive and hostile spirit, he will only contribute to the problem. However, if he faces the problem with patience, faith, and self-control, he will find a peace in God that is supportive and healing. A positive confession, a surrendered life, a confident spirit, and a praying heart will keep a pastor in proper relationship to the disquieting aspects of his work.

Handling Discouragement. The pastorate provides the occasion for great spiritual successes and victories. To see God's work go forward, to see people coming to Christ, and to see the newly converted being rapidly brought to spiritual maturity is an incomprehensible joy. But when a plateau has been reached, the people's vision has diminished, or the work has lost momentum, the pastor's temptation to discouragement is very real.

The key to victory over discouragement is for the pastor to remember continually that he is the undershepherd, that he is called to be obedient, that the work is not his but the Lord's, and that all human ways of measuring success must be repudiated. If he will keep his priorities in order, discouragement will shun him. Pastors must be Biblically grounded, spiritually oriented, and disciplined in their thinking.

MAINTAINING A CREATIVE ATTITUDE

People gravitate to creative thinkers. The pastor with vision and creativity will inspire people to follow his leadership. While newness and originality should not be goals in themselves, neither should traditionalism be guarded as the only acceptable way to further the Kingdom. People are looking for new ways, an approach that reflects fresh inspiration, and a program that has brand-new possibilities. An effective pastor will expose himself to new ideas. He will explore what other pastors are doing so it may, in turn, inspire him. He will refuse to be boxed in. He will view the kingdom of God as dynamic, moving, happening, and ever new and thrilling, and see himself as part of that thrust. The pastor is on the cutting edge of the most aggressive and exciting enterprise on the face of the earth. Why should he allow himself to retreat into a small world of little ideas and stifled dreams? He dare not—for the Kingdom's sake.

Recognizing Personal Potential. The church is filled with people who equate meekness with weakness and humility with self-abasement. Nothing could be further from the truth. True meekness and humility mean a man has come to the place where he honestly sees the great potential of his life as he lives it in obedience to the Lord and for God's honor and glory. Many pastors are too proud and afraid of being proven wrong to stand up and say: "I can do all things through Christ who strengthens me."

God seeks men who will look deep inside themselves and see the capacity for spiritual greatness just waiting for release. The kingdom of God needs men of full persuasion who can measure their potential in the context of faith and reliance. Moses felt weak and inept to journey back to Egypt and be an emancipator. It was not until he had seen God work miracles before Pharaoh that he had the courage to speak on behalf of his own convictions. Then Moses came alive. He began to understand the latent potential of his life when placed in the hands of God. The rest of the story is one of victory after victory; a man had recognized his potential in God.

The Power of the Positive. Coupled with feelings of inferiority are feelings of negativism: the emotion of predisposed failure, the feeling that things are sure to go wrong. This view on life sees the impossibilities before it sees the possibilities. It is an orientation that begins by trying to show why any good idea simply will not work.

To put this matter in clear perspective, note that Jesus Christ is the very personification of a positive attitude. He had a mission to accomplish and He allowed nothing to break His determination. All who truly follow Jesus live in the light of all that Christ can do. The devil, on the other hand, is the author of every negative notion. It is Satan who says, "Impossible!" He is the originator of every conceivable objection. Negative people are unwittingly servants of Satan. This is not to suggest a careless, indiscriminate, blind kind of attitude toward life and ministry, but instead to put the accent where it belongs—on the possibilities of spiritual greatness, by God's grace and power.

RECOGNIZING THE COST OF LEADERSHIP

J. Oswald Sanders speaks well to this matter:

> A cross stands in the way of spiritual leadership, a cross upon which the leader must consent to be impaled. Heaven's demands are absolute. "He laid down his life for us: and we ought to lay down our lives for the brethren" (1 John 3:16). The degree in which we allow the cross of Christ to work in us will be the measure in which the resurrection life of Christ can be manifested through us. "Death worketh in me, but life in you." To evade the cross is to forfeit leadership.[11]

That is a strong but true statement. The Cross rises up at every intersection of the pastor's life, and he must deal with it. Will he choose his own way or the way of obedience? Will he lay aside his personal rights for the work of God, or will he fight to the finish to establish his rightness? Will he suffer death within himself to produce life in others? It is all a question of what the pastor does with the Cross. He cannot avoid it, either in his living or his preaching.

The Example of Jesus. Jesus said, "Blessed are the gentle, for they shall inherit the earth" (Matthew 5:5, *NASB).* Dietrich Bonhoeffer, in applying this principle of the Kingdom to the disciples of Jesus, makes the following observation:

> When reproached, they hold their peace; when treated with violence they endure it patiently; when men drive them from their presence, they yield their ground. . . . They are determined to leave their rights to God alone. . . . Their right is in the will of their Lord—that and no more.[12]

It was the Lord himself who set the example for a high level of commitment. Jesus did not count the Cross a price too high to pay.

---

[11]Sanders, *Spiritual Leadership,* p. 105. Used by permission.

[12]Dietrich Bonhoeffer, *The Cost of Discipleship* (New York: The Macmillan Company, 1959), p. 99.

His 3-year ministry was aimed at Calvary. He demonstrated in His own life the cost of being a servant of God. And He calls His disciples to come and follow Him. No man so fully laid aside His own rights as did Jesus. On the cross He did not yield to angelic hosts who stood by ready to intervene on His behalf. He was the suffering Servant of the Lord, and His refusal to compromise His mission in the slightest way produced for all men a salvation full and free.

A Servant's Heart. The pastor is first a servant of Jesus Christ. But he is also a servant of those to whom he is called to minister the life of Christ. Any man who is not prepared to be a servant dare not claim obedience to a divine call. No man is so miserable as the man who has the responsibilities of a pastorate but does not care to be a servant. He will chafe under the heavy demands, the unreasonable expectations, the uncertainties of the pastorate as a vocation, and the continual burden of knowing people are depending on him. A servant counts it all joy and a privilege, but only a servant can do that.

Young men and women who are considering the ministry need to settle this matter of servitude as part of their response to the call of God on their lives. Is he or she prepared to accept a life-style that revolves around the Lord's work? Will the continual demands of people become a burden too heavy to bear once the novelty of a new pastorate has worn off? Does the will of God for His kingdom have a place of preeminence in the heart? Can criticism and rejection be borne with joy and peace? It is all a vital part of servitude!

Companionship in Loneliness. Every pastor needs someone with whom he can openly share both the joys and sorrows of his life. Usually a wife is able to fill this place; but if for some reason that relationship is not possible, a mature friend or family member should be sought to assist the minister in his times of need.

No vocation is perhaps more people-oriented than the ministry. Yet no vocation has so much potential for loneliness as the pastorate. Many pastors feel lonely and wonder to whom they can turn for true fellowship, counsel, and love. Lawrence O. Richards points out one of the reasons why the pastorate can be lonely:

> Somehow most of us insist on locating the pastor somewhere "above" us, and in viewing him as somehow different from us. Aware of this, a pastor often feels forced to maintain a facade of perfection, lest he

"destroy the confidence" of the people in him. And he is often told to
resist developing close personal friendships within his church lest he be
thought to "play favorites." And thus a real and deadly distance
develops.[13]

While the caution has merit, a pastor's need for fellowship and
identity must not shield him from real relationships with his people.
The pastor is himself part of the body to which he ministers; and, as
such, it is the whole body's opportunity and responsibility to consider
the pastor's needs as well as their own.

The fact remains, however, that the pastor often stands in a place of
loneliness. Confidences are his to keep, burdens are his to bear, and
decisions are his to make. To whom should he turn in times of need?
First, a pastor is assured of a divine presence that will strengthen and
guide him. Second, a pastor, if he is married, will find if he maintains
a strong relationship with his wife, she can be a faithful counselor and
confidante in times of crisis and need. A pastor may also gather about
him a small group of Christian brothers with whom he can meet
regularly for fellowship and prayer. In summary, the pastor who is
prayerful and obedient will find adequate help and ministry from
those who consider it a privilege to be an encouragement to him in
his work.

An Overview of Leadership Responsibilities

We must now look at the scope of leadership responsibilities in the
local church that directly or indirectly involve the pastor. Some
pastors have sought to be specialists in one area of church ministry or
another. But most pastors agree the typical pastor is more in the tradition of the general practitioner. His concern is for a wide variety of
needs and circumstances that arise among the people. A high degree
of flexibility and adaptability is imperative. The pastor's ministry
must be to all ages and all departments within the church.

MINISTERING TO ALL AGES

Some pastors are justifiably criticized for relating well to one particular age-group in the church to the exclusion of the others. Their
argument is predictable: "I've always liked young people." Or, "Now
that I'm older, I feel more at home with my age-group." This luxury

[13]Richards, A New Face for the Church, p. 114.

is not allowable for the pastor. His call includes every person who comes under his ministry. He must keep the whole span, from cradle to grave, in equal focus.

Children. A pastor who loves and notices children will be a pastor well-loved by everyone. Just a momentary glance, a pat on the head, a kind word—all these tell the child his pastor really does care. Nothing is more flattering to a child than an adult's recall and use of his name, a bent knee to get a good view of a new dress, or a little pinch on the chin. While such gestures seem trivial, they speak volumes to a child who is still searching for his own identity.

A true pastor will seek opportunities to enter a child's world. A visit to the nursery, a casual stop in a primary department during Sunday school, or taking a moment to play a game with a child while visiting in a home does so much to bring the pastor within reach of a child. The example of Jesus in this respect is instructional and challenging: "Let the children alone, and do not hinder them from coming to Me" (Matthew 19:14, *NASB*).

Youth. This group provides a golden opportunity for the pastor to be a "shaper" of lives. Youth possess the capacity for rapid spiritual growth as well as an exciting openness to new ideas and truths. The youth of any aggressive church will be on the front line of its forward thrust.

Young people do not usually make heavy demands on the pastor. They are only looking for a man who is real, who knows how to be transparent, and who can give and take with equal freedom. Most of all, they look for a man who can be followed as an example of godly living and who will faithfully teach them the Word of God.

Some pastors have carelessly adopted a negative and censorious attitude toward the youth of the church. They have stressed the letter of the law nearly to the point of death. These pastors have failed to balance prohibitions with declarations of life. Their impact has come through in a negative vein, and young people turn away in disgust and rejection. Youth must be challenged by the power of the gospel— presented in a positive, bright, and uplifting way. This is not to suggest that they should be unguided in areas of practical living. It is only an appeal for a balance between law and grace, discipline and love.

Adults. These are the individuals with whom the pastor will work in the actual operation of the church. They are usually the ones who support the church financially, serve on a variety of committees, and give the church its overall stability and strength. Obviously, this group must have the continual support, love, and guidance of the pastor.

Several specific challenges are presented by this group. People in this age-group may have: (1) an unresponsiveness to programs that involve change; (2) a suspicion of new ideas, approaches, and methods; (3) a traditionalistic mind-set that produces satisfaction with the *status quo*, whether it is good or bad; (4) a tendency to become weary in well-doing after years of service.

In balance, however, this is the group that will provide the pastor with the support he needs to build the church. A successful pastor will cultivate a close relationship of trust with the adults of his congregation. He will stay clear of presumption, dogmatism, and other egotistical manners that build walls and hurt God's work.

COORDINATING ALL DEPARTMENTS

It is impossible to speak here in more than a surface way about the pastor's responsibilities in coordinating the various departments of the church. Every church has its own unique department structure and administrative flow. The usual departments found in the local church are as follows: (1) Christian Education; (2) Men's and Women's Ministries; (3) Boys' and Girls' Ministries; (4) Youth; (5) Music; and (6) Auxiliary Groups (i.e., prison ministry, college ministry, etc.)

It may be helpful to enumerate certain principles of administration that will be useful in a variety of settings:

1. *Team Spirit.* All the departments must feel they are a vital part of the total church program and that their efforts are complementary to the efforts of the other departments.

2. *Communication.* Ways must be devised to keep the leadership of every department fully informed of the programs and plans of the other departments. A single mimeographed piece can help accomplish this task. Most of the difficulties in the local church can be reduced to a problem in communication. A good pastor will keep the need for good communications before him at each step in the administrative process.

3. *Leadership.* The key to an aggressive and successful department still rests with its leadership. There is no program or administrative

technique that will counterbalance a poor choice of leadership in any given department. Is the job accurately defined? Do we have an individual in that position who has the ability to do the job as described? The pastor should spend much time in prayer and study to be sure he has the right people in the right places doing the right things.

4. *Planning.* Does each department of the church take time to ask: "Where are we going? What are our goals? Where do we want to be a year from now?" It is imperative for the pastor to insist on departmental planning that is goal- and method-oriented. Too often departmental leaders operate in a vacuum, isolated from the other departments and unsure of exactly where they are going.

5. *Focusing.* Every church should have a statement of philosophy relative to its ministry. Each department can then set out to develop programs that will be compatible with the stated aim and goal of the whole church. One church has built its philosophy around a three-part motif: (a) upward in worship; (b) inward in commitment; and (c) outward in evangelism. All departments are asked to reflect this three-pronged thrust in their programming.

6. *Accountability.* Departmental leaders will appreciate a vehicle of expression whereby they can determine the level of success enjoyed by the department and also discover ways of being more productive and creative as a department. Accountability should never be viewed in a negative context. It is a measure of achievement and a resource for encouragement.

Motivating Lay Leadership

A nationally known football coach was asked his definition of the game of football. He replied: "Twenty-two men who desperately need rest, and 22,000 people who desperately need exercise." Such is the condition in the church. Too few are doing too much, while too many are doing too little. It is the responsibility of the pastor to be a "facilitator" and, by the power of the Holy Spirit, see the reserve of untapped spiritual potential released to bless the work of God.

EQUIPPING LAYMEN FOR MINISTRY

Howard A. Snyder sets the tone for a consideration of the rich potential latent in the laymen who frequent our churches:

The church is never a place, but always a people; never a fold but always a flock; never a sacred building but always a believing assembly. The church is you who pray, not where you pray. A structure of marble can no more be a church than your clothes of serge or satin can be you. There is in this world nothing so sacred but man, no sanctuary of man but the soul.[14]

In other words, the church is people. And how people grow, relate, serve, share, worship, and love are the issues that matter most. It is the pastor's joy to implement the process whereby men, women, boys, and girls grow up into spiritual maturity to serve God and one another.

It is not difficult to conclude even after a cursory survey of the church in our day that the Holy Spirit is producing a revival in the pews of our churches. Laymen are coming alive in the best of the Reformation tradition. They are taking their places in ministry unto the Lord, ministry to the saints, and ministry to the world. The church of Jesus Christ is rising up in our day, and laymen are leading the way.

Typical of the contemporary church scene is the helpful analysis given by Dan Baumann in *All Originality Makes a Dull Church*. He sees five distinct categories into which aggressive and successful churches fit:

1. The Soul-Winning Church. This is the church that views its mission to be primarily and fundamentally the winning of souls.
2. The Classroom Church. This is the church that sees the central mission of the church to be one of teaching the principles of God's Word and equipping the saints for ministry.
3. The Life-Situation Church. This is the church that makes it its business to speak to the average man on the street about issues of great importance to him. That man gets the message that finally someone loves him and that the great God of this universe will help him.
4. The Social-Action Church. This is the church that addresses itself to the social needs of the day and rallies support for just and right causes. The words of Jesus, "Love your neighbor as yourself," become in spirit the supportive theology for the social-action church.
5. The General-Practitioner Church. This is the church that is a combination of the other four. It seeks a balance between evangelism, discipleship, social reform, and personal development.[15]

[14]Taken from *The Problem of Wine Skins* by Howard A. Snyder. © 1975 by Inter-Varsity Christian Fellowship and used by permission of InterVarsity Press.

[15]Dan Baumann, *All Originality Makes a Dull Church* (Santa Ana: Vision House Publishers, 1976), *passim*.

Clearly, the focus is on laymen. The more traditional "preacher-driven" model is yielding to new forms and methods. Mr. Average Layman has stood up to be counted. And sincere pastors are seeing it as the answer to prayer and the sovereign and exciting work of the Holy Spirit in our day. All this is not to suggest that the pastor has abrogated his leadership or terminated his responsibilities. But it does mean there is revival in the church.

The apostle Paul describes the process:

> And He gave some as apostles, and some as prophets, and some as evangelists, and some as pastors and teachers, for the equipping of the saints for the work of service, to the building up of the body of Christ; until we all attain to the unity of the faith, and of the knowledge of the Son of God, to a mature man, to the measure of the stature which belongs to the fulness of Christ (Ephesians 4:11-13, NASB).

This translation lays stress on the specific function of the pastor: the equipping of the saints to do the work of service and to build the body of Christ.

The pastor who puts this Biblical injunction into practice within the context of the local church will find himself more and more involved in helping laymen to discover their specific ministries and in the operation of the gifts given to them. He will no longer seek to be the "prime mover" for everything that transpires in the name of the church, but will rather help to mold others to be the inspiration and motivation for the many functions of the church. In this way the pastor will multiply his own ministry many times over.

The Gifts of the Spirit. The gifts of the Spirit (1 Corinthians 12:8-10) have been given to build up and edify the body of Christ. Paul clearly teaches that all should be done decently and in order (1 Corinthians 14:40). He also teaches: "The spirits of prophets are subject to prophets; for God is not a God of confusion but of peace" (1 Corinthians 14:32,33, NASB).

The pastor who provides a good instructional basis for the operation of the gifts and is willing to exercise the necessary control will find a full and free flow of the gifts of the Spirit in his church. Conversely, if people are abusive or ignorant in the use of the gifts, many people will be discouraged from becoming involved in this area of ministry. The Holy Spirit will help the committed pastor to create an atmosphere of freedom and control in which the gifts may operate.

In many of our churches visitors are confused by the presence of the gifts in the services. It is helpful for the pastor to explain at the proper time the Biblical basis for that which has transpired. Most people need only an explanation to feel at ease. For example, the pastor may say: "That which we have just experienced is described in 1 Corinthians 14. There it teaches that the Holy Spirit may spontaneously come on a believer and prompt him to speak in a language he does not understand. That utterance is to be interpreted by the original speaker or by another believer. The end result is to build up and strengthen the church." The people in the congregation who have brought with them friends who are uninformed about the gifts will deeply appreciate the pastor's sensitivity at this point. It helps to build a strong, dynamic, and well-accepted Pentecostal church.

The Ministries of the Holy Spirit. The ministries of the Holy Spirit are outlined in Romans 12:6-8:

> And since we have gifts that differ according to the grace given to us, let each exercise them accordingly: if prophecy, according to the proportion of his faith; if service, in his serving; or he who teaches, in his teaching; or he who exhorts, in his exhortation; he who gives, with liberality; he who leads, with diligence; he who shows mercy, with cheerfulness (NASB).

Most of the activities we consider as service in the local church will fit into one of these categories.

Why is it that too few are doing too much, while too many are doing too little? What is the explanation for the shortage of qualified workers to carry on the many facets of the church's ministry? The fault lies in the church's failure to show people that they have a ministry and then to give them an opportunity for its operation. A pertinent question to ask is this: "What is the ministry the Lord has given you?" Following a positive response should come practical suggestions on how that ministry gift may be used.

The pastor who makes this principle the motivational thrust in recruiting and training workers will be rewarded with success. Believers in the church should serve in places of responsibility out of a deep sense of commission and faithfulness to God, not merely to satisfy a desperate pastor who simply "can't find anyone to do it."

A noted preacher has commented that recruitment of workers should ultimately boil down to one thing: "What does God say about it?" The only answer that is legitimate from a potential new recruit is this: "No, I don't feel God wants me to," or, "Yes, I believe God wants me to." Only on this basis can the pastor expect service of duration and quality. If, indeed, this is the Lord's work, then He is well able to direct the affairs of men in carrying out His work.

The Fruit of the Spirit. The fruit of the Spirit are given in Galatians 5:22, 23: "But the fruit of the Spirit is love, joy, peace, patience, kindness, goodness, faithfulness, gentleness, self-control; against such things there is no law" *(NASB).*

The gifts and ministries of the Spirit have their final validation when the fruit of the Spirit are also present in a life. A man who speaks prolifically in an unknown tongue, yet is not gentle, can hardly be regarded as authentic. A brother who gives large sums of money, yet is without self-control, can hardly be respected as a true disciple of Jesus Christ. A man who claims great prophetic gifts, yet is not faithful, can hardly be trusted as a true spiritual leader.

The call today is for men who will demonstrate true godliness in their daily lives. The world is watching, and it has the right to expect that the Church, His body, will be an accurate reflection of His character. The Church is without excuse, for the Spirit has been given to produce in the followers of Christ the qualities of character that will make them like their Master.

OPPORTUNITIES FOR INVOLVEMENT

The equipping of the saints is the first of a two-step process. The pastor must discover ways by which the gifts and ministries that have been given may find expression. A successful pastor will ask the Lord for the ability to recognize ministries and gifts as well as wisdom in assigning places of service. A layman who knows he has received a gift for ministry will become discouraged if he is not helped into a place of useful service in the church.

The following principles will be helpful in building the church through the involvement of laymen:

1. *Recognize Gifts and Ministries While They Are Still in the Embryo Stage.* Most pastors can recall instances when the encouragement to become involved was based largely on a deep conviction that a certain person was going to be used to fill a certain place in the body of Christ, even though that gift was hardly yet visible. The early recognition of a layman's potential is important.

2. *Allow Time to Mature.* Service should be in a "graduating" pattern. An assignment that is too demanding can be a source of discouragement. Give a layman an opportunity to move from one level of service to another, without feeling under pressure.

3. *Provide Resources for Growth.* A new recruit is sometimes told: "Do your best with what you have; you'll get along just fine." That approach is tragic and will produce casualties in the church. Compare that with this: "I know you are just beginning. But we will provide you with a variety of helps and learning opportunities. You'll never be left to shift for yourself." Laymen will be very appreciative of the pastor who not only "deputizes" but also helps "train."

4. *Require Accountability.* Laymen will respond to goal-oriented planning and progress reporting. If a task is important enough to require time and energy, it is also important enough to merit a response to leadership. Great motivation is found in successful achievement. And only with accountability can success be measured.

A church blessed with strong lay leadership and active lay involvement will be a great church. It will be filled with people who feel they belong and who take great pleasure in seeing the church move forward.

The Reward of Effective Leadership

The work of the Church is the most exciting and important work on the face of the earth. And to be called of God to be a leader in the Church is a high privilege and a joyous delight. The reward for effective leadership comes when the pastor sees lives being changed, new hope rising in broken lives, and a flood of peace flowing into a life of despair. This, if there were nothing more, would be enough to satisfy the servant of the Lord.

DEVELOPING MEASURABLE OBJECTIVES

The pastor, like the layman, is wise to set measurable objectives for his own life and for the church he pastors. A measurable objective is a statement of intent and a goal that can be measured. For example, a measurable goal would be: to reach every home in the community with a printed piece of gospel literature; to read two books per month; or, to establish a core group of men interested in becoming true disciples of Christ.

Admittedly, however, there are many objectives that are not so easily measurable. For example: to see the church committed to prayer; to see greater participation in worship and praise; or, to see greater consistency among the members of the church. Yet, the mere statement of objectives like these will have a direct impact on programming and planning in the church. It is interesting that even the objectives noted here will yield to a kind of measuring process if someone will attempt to do so.

Pastors can be as discouraged by the lack of a plan for the future as by the failures of the past. It may not be so much that the church has not grown in the past 5 years but that there seems to be no plan for a change of direction in the future—this is the most disheartening of all. The setting forth of clear objectives, coupled with a plan for action, will set a pastor on his way to a ministry of creativity, success, and personal reward.

LONG-RANGE PLANNING

"Where will this church be 10 years from now?" That is a valid and fair question. But most pastors do not bother to ask this question or they say nothing about searching for its answer. Granted, it is the Lord who will build His church; yet, He uses men, and that calls for planning. The church must understand that the Holy Spirit is active in every aspect of its growth and development; and this involves planning as well as fulfillment.

A successful pastor will seek first to know the will of God for the future of the church, and then proceed to plan for the fulfillment of that vision. Tragically, some pastors get so occupied with the daily demands of the pastorate that they fail to see the bigger picture—the long-range goals of the church.

A pastor will be highly motivated if he will look into the future and plan for great things. New churches are built when a pastor and the board look ahead and do some long-range planning. Television ministries are launched when leadership asks penetrating questions about reaching a growing population with the gospel. Schools are started because someone dares to stand back and say: "How can we change our world in the future?" All of this requires long-range planning. It is essential. And it brings with it great reward and pleasure to God and to leadership.

THE POTENTIALS OF FAITH

The pastor is called to give leadership to the total church program. He must coordinate the departments, give direction to a variety of committees, and work closely with the staff, whether paid or volunteer. His days are filled with a variety of demands. There will be times of victory and times of defeat. He will see the church rise to plateaus of spiritual greatness, and he will see the church plunged into the valley of testing and trial.

But this is where faith comes in. The pastor is not alone. He does not carry on his ministry in his own strength. He is a man both called and equipped by God. He meets the challenge of his calling with faith —a quiet reliance and sure trust in the living God. And it is his high privilege and unequaled joy to see the church march on in the power of the risen Christ to change our world and, finally, to bring in the kingdom of God on earth.

Suggested Reading

Augsburger, David W. *Communicating Good News.* Newton, KS: Faith and Life Press, 1972.

Baumann, Dan. *All Originality Makes a Dull Church.* Santa Ana, CA: Vision House Publishers, 1976.

Johnson, Paul E. *Psychology of Pastoral Care.* New York: Abingdon Press, 1953.

Parrott, Leslie. *Building Today's Church.* Grand Rapids: Baker Book House, 1973.

Richards, Lawrence O. *A New Face for the Church.* Grand Rapids: Zondervan Publishing House, 1970.

Riggs, R. M. *The Spirit-filled Pastor's Guide.* Springfield, MO: Gospel Publishing House, 1948.

Sanders, J. Oswald. *Spiritual Leadership.* Chicago: Moody Press, 1967.

Snyder, Howard A. *The Problem of Wine Skins.* Downers Grove, IL: InterVarsity Press, 1975.

Walker, Paul L. *The Ministry of Church and Pastor.* Cleveland, TN: Pathway Press, 1965.

13

The Pastor
and
His Community

JAMES K. BRIDGES

Never have the opportunities for serving Christ and fulfilling one's ministry in the church and in the community been greater. To the pastor who has a proper understanding of the relationship of the church and the community, the possibilities for developing a fruitful ministry and building a successful church are unlimited.

Defining the Church and the Community

Our purpose in defining the Church and the community is not to discuss at length ecclesiology or sociology, but to see and understand the Church in relation to its earthly setting, the community of people to whom it is called. The Lord Jesus Christ did not leave the identity or mission of His blood-bought church to be defined by those who enter its membership. These have been clearly defined in Scripture.

A good starting point for a study of the New Testament view of the Church and the community is Paul's statement to the Corinthians concerning social relationships: "I am made all things to all men, that I might by all means save some" (1 Corinthians 9:22). In writing to the Colossians, Paul explained that he was not only a minister to the body of Christ, the Church, but also minister "to every creature which is under heaven" (Colossians 1:23). John Wesley's famous declaration, "The world is my parish," ought to be each pastor's true sentiment.

The church of our Lord Jesus Christ is truly an *ecclesia*, a "called-out body." It is not called out of the world to be separated as an

James K. Bridges is assistant superintendent of the North Texas District of the Assemblies of God, Fort Worth, Texas.

island isolated from the mainland, but "separated unto the gospel of God" (Romans 1:1) that it may be returned to the world as a blessing, as salt to season and as a light to show the way (Matthew 5:13-16). The great intercessory prayer of our Lord for His followers, recorded in John 17, is a revelation of the Church's relationship to the community. Jesus besought the Father not to take the believers out of the world, but that they should be kept from the evil of this world and continue to fulfill their purpose. Jesus revealed that the Church is an extension of the eternal plan of the Godhead: "As thou hast sent me into the world, even so have I also sent them into the world" (John 17:18). He reiterated this theme during His resurrection appearance when He stated: "As my Father hath sent me, even so send I you" (John 20:21).

The minister must understand that the conciliatory role the Church has been given—"the ministry of reconciliation" (2 Corinthians 5:18)—is to be carried out in the community of which it is a part. It is to the community that we are sent as "ambassadors for Christ" with the "word of reconciliation" which has been "committed unto us" (vv. 19,20).

The principle of outreach set forth in Acts 1:8 also tells us something of how we should define the Church. It is to be an agency of God constantly reaching out and enlarging its concept of responsibility and accountability. The community concept of the local church begins with its own "Jerusalem" and continues to extend its influence as opportunity allows, enlarging its community "unto the uttermost part of the earth."

But outreach to the community must not be defined solely in terms of geographical boundaries. The in-depth penetration of the various aspects of community life is also a part of the Great Commission. In discussing attitudes toward the community and people, Franklin Segler describes this all-encompassing penetration by the Church:

> Christ has purposed to redeem the whole world, and all of it belongs to Him—its industries, pleasures, arts, social institutions—and the church is obligated to claim it all for Him. In this concept, there is no such dualism as the sacred and the secular in life. Religion has as much right out in the community life as it does within the four walls of the church.[1]

[1]Franklin M. Segler, A Theology of Church and Ministry (Nashville: Broadman Press, 1960), p. 227. Used by permission.

The pastor's attitude toward the community and his concept of the scope of his ministry does much to determine the nature and direction of the ministry of the local body of believers. Many pastors have too narrow a concept of their pastoral responsibilities. The dictionary defines *community* as "a group of people having common ties or interests, living in the same vicinity and subject to the same laws." But Christ answered the inquiry, "Who is my neighbor?" with the well-known Parable of the Good Samaritan, thus illustrating that even those of different interests or social standing should be included in the outreach of His followers.

Perhaps many of us should be included in the outreach of His followers.

Perhaps many of us should ask God, as Jabez did in 1 Chronicles 4:10, "Enlarge my border" *(Amplified)*. When a man exudes the attitude, "I belong to the whole city and the city belongs to me," he is going to draw an increasing number of people under the umbrella of his ministry. A spirit of sectarianism circumscribes greatly the ministry and influence of a pastor in his community.

MISCONCEPTIONS CONCERNING THE CHURCH AND THE COMMUNITY

The antagonism many people imagine between the church and the community makes it difficult for the church to fulfill its ministry. An atmosphere of hostility sometimes develops, and the church falls into a role of defensiveness. But the Church is intended to be an aggressive body. Jesus himself told Peter that strong confidence was to be a prominent characteristic of the Church: "Upon this rock I will build my church; and the gates of hell shall not prevail against it" (Matthew 16:18). Again, the aggressive nature of the Church is revealed to us by the Gospel writers when they record the instructions of our Lord to His disciples, directing them to go into all the world to preach, teach, and baptize. With the all-inclusive and all-sufficient power of Christ, the Church should be free from any intimidation or fear of the enemy.

The position a pastor takes toward his community, however, may be damagingly negative if it springs from personal misconceptions rather than scriptural principles. How many pastors view their communities with hostility—as an enemy to be feared? As this same attitude is reflected in the members of their congregations, the emphasis shifts to a concern for the existing group of believers to the exclusion of those yet unreached. Viewing the community with a critical, condemning spirit also causes the focus of the local church to turn inward, leading to unfruitful lives and ultimate spiritual death. "The church which lives to perpetuate its own institutional structure and self-interests is idolatrous and not Christian in its purpose."[2]

An understanding of the makeup and jurisdiction of the community in which a pastor ministers helps prevent harmful attitudes and promotes successful community relationships. There is a learning process that goes on as a minister observes the life and nature of his community. His knowledge of the community's strengths and weaknesses, its historic background, and its projections for the future aid him in interpreting the church to the community and the community to the church.

There are many exclusive organizations in our world that determine who may or may not be a part of their system. While the church has been given a criteria for membership, its doors are open for all to come in and find a welcome fellowship. When the church begins to dictate who can and cannot attend its services, it has already moved beyond scriptural authority. Any pastor who sees his congregation as an exclusive "country club" has lost sight of the church's reason-for-being. Although the church is a purchased possession, it must never take on an air of being aloof from the community in which it ministers. A servant's garb should be our clothing (John 13:4), and a willingness to serve our attitude (Mark 10:44,45).

While the church is not to be exclusive concerning fellowship, it cannot accept into its membership any but those who have truly made the spiritual transfer into the Body invisible; who can testify that "the Spirit itself beareth witness with our spirit, that we are the children of God" (Romans 8:16). The Church is to be viewed as having its origin from above. Thus, its membership must partake of divine life as well. As nearly as possible, the visible church should place into its membership only those who give testimony and witness to such a new birth. Taking into membership those who have given no evidence of "newness of life" (Romans 6:4), who give no testimony to the "joy of sins forgiven," can be disastrous to the local assembly—if not immediate-

---

[2]Segler, A *Theology of Church and Ministry*, p. 225. Used by permission.

ly, certainly in the not-too-distant-future. For the pastor to open the local church government to unsaved or carnal leadership is to move the church into jeopardy and invite certain curtailment of the Holy Spirit's activity.

MINISTRIES BEYOND CHURCH MEMBERSHIP

It is true that a minister's first concern is to the faithful membership of the local congregation to which he has been called as pastor (shepherd). But limited vision will cut a ministry short. In a sense, the pastor may say with Jesus, "Other sheep I have." To spend all one's time on the active and inactive membership list is to overlook a ready-made visitation field—those who live on the fringes of the church, whom we call adherents.

Every church has a number of people who have never joined the assembly, yet loyally attend and in many instances support and work in behalf of its programs. For various reasons, they are not a part of the church's membership. The fact that they attend meetings, support programs, and identify themselves with the church reveals an interest that should be cultivated. But perhaps a lack of dedication, petty grievances, hurts caused by insensitive church members, or even a simple lack of motivation have prevented them from taking the step into full fellowship and responsibility.

The pastor's demonstration of concern for the adherent's particular situation, his prayers and positive attitude, and his affirmation of the adherent's worth to the congregation could be the missing element needed to bring that person into a deeper spiritual experience and greater areas of service. Adherents comprise a vast area of resource for the pastor to utilize when considering personnel needs. Many loyal churchgoers will enter into a healing, mutually beneficial bond with the church when challenged with the need for service and warmed by brotherly love and kindness.

> The true work of Christ cannot be contained within the four walls of the church building. At the conclusion of morning worship, God never stops at the church door; He goes forth in the lives of his people to serve the world of persons.[3]

In the light of his worldwide commission, does the pastor move beyond the church walls, recognizing he has an obligation to the

---

[3]Segler, A Theology of Church and Ministry, p. 225. Used by permission.

whole world which lies in wickedness (1 John 5:19) and needs the grace and righteousness of God? Paul's admonition is that "supplications, prayers, intercessions, and giving of thanks, be made for all men" (1 Timothy 2:1). Only when a pastor enters into such a vision and concern will he launch an outreach beyond the confines of his own pastorate.

If the pastor is not motivated to carry the gospel outside the church, to reach people where they are, neither will the congregation move toward that end. A selfish motivation—a desire for success as interpreted by the numbers of people contacted—will not work. The goal of outreach is to win souls for the Lord. When motivated by love and concern, community outreach becomes a refreshing and inspiring avenue of blessing.

The pastor is the key to making his a community-conscious church. His fearless attitude, his vision for the lost, and his wholesome approach to community life open doors for both him and his people. He can foster a willingness to participate in the community without losing sight of ultimate goals and priorities. He can lead the church in the exaltation of God in the workaday world as well as in the house of worship.

The Pastor and Civic Relationships

The very fact that a minister lives in a certain locality and shares the benefits of the community places a degree of civic responsibility upon him. The extent of a pastor's involvement in civic activities is a highly individual matter, calling for a serious evaluation of priorities and a skillful management of time. Failure to handle such considerations wisely has brought great frustration to many ministers. Some have refused involvements altogether, while others have so overextended themselves that every area of their lives has suffered.

Yet the principle of building rapport and establishing communication within one's community cannot be easily laid aside. The Scriptures provide an interesting commentary on David's success with people: "All Israel and Judah loved David, because he went out and came in before them" (1 Samuel 18:16). The interaction of ministers with the people around them is interpreted by most persons as evidence of real concern on the part of the clergy. In their own churches, pastors who move in and out among their people are far more effective than those who appear only in the pulpit. The same principle applies in the community. Being able to see and talk to ministers in person brings people closer to them. We must avoid becoming like the proverbial preacher who was "invisible six days a week and incomprehensible on the seventh."

There is a fear on the part of some ministers that close contact with people will somehow lower them in the eyes of the people and cause a loss of respect. That fear reflects the misconception that respect can only be earned by some haloed perfection completely beyond our humanity. Interacting with people on a day-to-day basis can be a threat when the minister has become caught up in superficial role-playing.

A pastor cannot separate his spiritual ministry from his daily lifestyle. His one-to-one relations in the community play a large part in determining the effectiveness of his public ministry. This is especially true in a smaller community. The pastor must never ignore the value of informal contacts. Holding oneself aloof or looking down from an "ivory tower" will accomplish nothing. People often have wrong attitudes and strange ideas about ministers. When the pastor participates as a faithful citizen, the community has opportunity to relate to him as a neighbor. It is as a man moves among the people, taking his place among them and helping to shoulder the community load, that he becomes accepted and effective in his community witness. He also finds that mutal appreciation, respect, and compassion develop as he participates in the community life.

Paul warns Titus, "Let no man despise thee" (Titus 2:15). Influence is a most valuable asset to the ministry. How sad the minister whose personal life has been so lived that both private and public influence have been lost! The *Amplified Bible* renders this passage: "Let no one despise or disregard or think little of you—conduct yourself and your teaching so as to command respect." And *The Living Bible* adds, "Don't let anyone think that what you say is not important." The man whose personal life has lost its testimony is a man whose pulpit ministry will be ineffective. In such cases, the work of the church in the community is greatly impeded.

One of the greatest responsibilities of the minister to his community is to strengthen the godly home life. The best possible way to make the quality of life in the church and community what it ought to be is to make the homes what they ought to be. By exemplary living in the home, the pastor can strive to establish his people in their home life and thus aid their growth toward mature, fruitful Christian living. Deficiencies in the minister's home will greatly handicap his ministry. A pastor who has not established his home on Biblical principles will be unable to so direct his people. It is impossible for a minister to lead others beyond his own experience.

> The home life of the minister is his most potent instrument for good in the community, yet the one aspect of his life that is too often ignored. A godly home life will speak volumes to a spiritually needy community. Yet this is frequently the point at which the minister's testimony is weak.[4]

COMMUNITY POLITICAL INVOLVEMENTS

The pastor is *a private citizen* in his community. Along with other men, he should exercise his rights of citizenship. Of course, the minister wisely avoids partisan politics for the sake of his members who may belong to a party other than his own. However, he need not hesitate to take a stand on moral issues during a political campaign. Ministers have been champions of justice for all men throughout the centuries. A minister of Jesus Christ, motivated by His unselfish love, will be a concerned citizen of his country.

As a Movement, we do not believe our world is getting better. On the contrary—it is deteriorating morally and spiritually. A pastor must take the lead in standing against the tide of evil. We recognize the truth that all that is necessary for evil to triumph is for good men to do nothing. The minister who leads his congregation in a firm stand on moral issues will do much to make the community a decent place in which to live.

Should the pastor take part in shaping the political life of the community? To what extent should he actively engage in any political movement that would entangle him with local interests and persons? Answers to these questions vary quite widely among the brethren. While no one absolute position would fit all situations, there are times when a minister of God must take a stand for truth, no matter how difficult it may be. The following principles give guidance for political conduct:

---

[4]From *Building Town and Country Churches* by Harold L. Longenecker. Copyright 1961, 1973. Moody Press, Moody Bible Institute of Chicago. Used by permission.

1. No minister should in public speech or sermon take part in partisan politics.

2. The minister not only has the right but is obliged to speak upon moral questions, in the pulpit or out of it, be the political implications what they may.

3. When a minister speaks on burning moral questions, he must understand thoroughly every phase of the situation.[5]

Although the pastor's first responsibility is to his own church, he is *a public man* with a debt of service to his community. As a servant of the Lord, he dare not restrict his ministry to a prescribed field. The church is only one among many institutions in the community. The pastor should cooperate with all such institutions as much as he possibly can. He is a member of a community team and, as such, should take his place alongside other community leaders in working for the betterment of the community. The wise minister understands that the measure of spiritual accessibility to a community is often commensurate with the degree to which he takes his civic responsibility. Let the man of God assume his role of leadership and use it to better the community and exalt his Lord.

HUMANITARIAN ORGANIZATION INVOLVEMENTS

A serious consideration for every pastor is the extent of his involvement in community affairs. How much time can he afford to spend in such activities? How can priorities be established and maintained? The decision to join an organization or club to promote humanitarian efforts is one most pastors face from time to time. It must be carefully thought through, for it involves a great portion of the minister's time, energy, and finances. The pastor must feel the objectives of the club or group he is considering are in keeping with his primary purpose for being in the community: to advance the cause of Christ and to help people in their needs.

It would be ideal if all community organizations never violated a minister's convictions about social matters. But this is rarely the case. Clubs will include in their activities things we cannot approve of and would not participate in.

One of the errors many ministers make is to think they are expected

---

[5]Nolan B. Harmon, *Ministerial Ethics and Etiquette* (Nashville: Abingdon Press, 1928), pp. 65-67. Used by permission.

to compromise their testimony when taking part in a community service club. This need not be. A pastor's presence can influence an organization to choose a better way of doing its business and to keep its operations ethical and morally aboveboard. The minister who is respected and sought out for personal counseling will maintain his integrity and testimony in a mature and discreet manner.

The community service club provides some unique opportunities and open doors into the hearts of people in the community. Ready-made ministry is available during those occasions when programs emphasize patriotism, God and country, loyalty, and good citizenship. Ministers are the logical ones sought out to prepare and present such topics.

In determining the extent to which a minister should participate in community organizations and activities, one should use the following questions as practical guildelines:

> Is the activity essentially good or bad?
> What will be the result of involvement both to the minister and the church?
> How will the work of the Lord be affected?
> Could it be that the unchurched might get the wrong impression?
> Might people be prejudiced against the church because of this choice?
> What effect will the minister's engagement have upon his primary calling?[6]

Condensing his observations on this controversial subject, Jay Adams suggests three guidelines to follow in considering involvement in various clubs or groups:

1. Will the contemplated association in any way lead to compromise or confusion of the gospel of Christ?
2. Will the contemplated association cut into my time too deeply to justify it? Will it square with my priorities before God?
3. Will the contemplated association indicate to the community that Jesus Christ is to be identified with the program of this organization?[7]

The position of the Assemblies of God regarding secret organizations is found in the General Council Bylaws, Article VII: Doctrines

---

[6]From *Building Town and Country Churches* by Harold L. Longenecker. Copyright 1961, 1973. Moody Press, Moody Bible Institute of Chicago. Used by permission.

[7]Jay E. Adams, *The Pastoral Life* (Grand Rapids: Baker Book House, 1974), p. 55. Permission granted.

and Practices Disapproved—Membership in Secret Orders (Section 4). Along with setting forth scriptural objections to secret orders, it urges the pastor to refrain from such identification and to direct the members of the congregation away from such affiliations. Appreciation for our Movement and its Biblical position on this matter will lead the faithful pastor to act accordingly.

PUBLIC SCHOOL SYSTEM INVOLVEMENTS

The pastor must recognize the importance of the schools of his community, whether he is a parent or not, and he should demonstrate his interest. "Protestantism has a great stake in the public school system in America."[8]

There is no greater field for evangelism today than the public schools of the United States. The minister must not overlook this potential for winning souls and influencing the community. Whatever success he may have through witnessing in the public school has both an immediate value and a long-range value of touching the lives of present youth and of potential citizens.

The minister who has chidren should, along with his wife, become involved in the local Parent-Teacher Association. This benefits his own children, giving them the satisfaction of seeing their parents involved in the school program; but there are other advantages as well. Ministers who participate in the P.T.A. are often selected for leadership in the organization. What an excellent opportunity to lend wholesome influence and help in the decisionmaking policies and projects that affect his children and his community!

It would be well for a minister to attend an occasional meeting of the school board for no other reason than to indicate his interest. He needs to learn first-hand the quality of the local school system. He should become acquainted with the superintendent of schools, the administrative officials, and the school board members. If he has children in the public schools, he should assume at least a normal amount of interest in the school where his own children attend. He might visit the classroom or an occasional assembly, or offer to share impressions of a trip with the class. When asked to hold membership in or speak at P.T.A. meetings,

[8]James L. Christensen, "Public Relations in Your Community," Reaching Beyond Your Pulpit, ed. Frank S. Mead, p. 128. Copyright © 1962 by Fleming H. Revell Company. Used by permission.

he should accept graciously. The children and youth from his church
will be elated if their minister shows interest in their affairs.[9]

The pastor with an awareness of what is going on educationally and
with a sensitivity for dealing with people may profitably seek further
involvement in school affairs. The decision to run for the school board
or serve on a school committee often sounds too political for many
pastors. Also, many feel they would be committing too much time to
such endeavors. The pastor who does accept such an assignment must
do so with the intention of bringing the Christian witness to bear on
the educational scene. He can give valuable leadership to an American institution that is in dire need of godly wisdom and counsel.
Many in the community will look to a qualified pastor to fill such a
position, realizing he will be a man of honesty, integrity, and wisdom
—virtues sadly lacking in many quarters.

Some decisions that must be made will make people unhappy. However, the manner in which a decision is made is often more important
than the decision itself. When people feel their welfare is being protected and their best interests are being served honorably, they are
more tolerant of the leadership. Who is more capable than a wise
pastor to fill such an important leadership role?

The use of "released time," in which a school allows students to
receive religious instruction from a local church or pastor, is not a
widely known practice across the country. Yet many school systems
allow teaching the Bible as literature, provided a qualified pastor is
available and adequate facilities are convenient. Every pastor should
look into the possibility of such Bible training, especially where he
knows he has students interested in the program. While such teaching
is to be nonsectarian, a faithful, Spirit-led presentation insures against
a liberalism that denies the Scriptures as the inspired Word of God.

Reciprocal relationships and mutal understanding are essential in
working with a school system. School officials cannot be expected to
show interest in the churches' viewpoint when the churches make no
effort to work together with the schools. A growing problem is the en-
croachment of school activities on scheduled church services. Traditionally, Wednesdays and Sundays have been reserved for church
functions. Infringement increases as school organizations proliferate

---

[9]Mead (ed.), *Reaching Beyond Your Pulpit*, p. 129. Used by permission.

and activities escalate. What is the answer to these mounting conflicts? It is certain that no easy solution is forthcoming! Only as the leaders of schools and churches work together is there any hope of solving these problems, especially in smaller towns and communities where interdependence is essential to community harmony.

The pastor with a congenial spirit and an evident concern for youth will find an entrance into the school official's office. Without sacrificing the local church program, the pastor can show a willingness to work together with school officials. He can develop such a cordial relationship that he may even become a special confidante to the school principal, superintendent, and other personnel. Such access will often give the pastor a direct influence on major decisions affecting the school system and, ultimately, the community.

Obviously, there are programs a pastor cannot support. It is understood the church will not endorse activities that are contrary to the convictions of its members. Yet, there are many school projects and programs the pastor can support. Musical programs (band and choral), interscholastic league competition, sporting events, honor society activities, speech and debate tournaments, technological and vocational programs are examples of programs the pastor can and should support. In these, let the pastor participate, while his obvious absence at other functions will speak volumes as to his dissent.

From time to time, opportunities will come where the prepared pastor will be invited into classrooms to discuss religiously oriented topics such as current events in the light of Bible prophecy. These topics can open the door to presenting the truth as it is in Jesus. The minister who effectively presents himself and his Lord can be assured of individual follow-ups that will give him an opportunity to present the complete work of Christ to hearts that have become interested through the working of the Holy Spirit in the Scriptures. Some will also come to the church services to hear more of that which has arrested their attention, giving the pastor and the congregation a chance to open their fellowship to students and school personnel.

The Pastor and Institutional Relationships

A pastor's outreach to the community will call for interaction with various community institutions. His rapport and cooperation with the personnel of these institutions will have much to do with his effectiveness as a community leader. Along with performing his ministry to the people served in community institutions, he must cultivate the goodwill of the institutional authorities to insure a continuing openness and acceptance.

BENEVOLENT INSTITUTIONS

A pastor must give much attention to his ministry to the sick if he is to be a good steward of his calling. Whether he visits the sick at home or in the hospital, this activity will consume a great portion of his time and energy. A compassionate pastor will try to develop his skills and abilities to their fullest to reap the greatest returns for the kingdom of God. Our Lord placed a high premium on ministry to the sick when He identified with the sick and showed He considered ministry to them equivalent to ministry to himself (Matthew 25:35-40).

One of the first areas to be considered in *a hospital ministry* is that of relationships with the physicians, nurses, and other professional people who have close contact with the patient. Larger hospitals may have a full-time chaplain or a staff of chaplains. Getting acquainted with the chaplaincy program in the hospital is basic to a pastor's understanding of his place in the total ministry there. Not only is it the best policy to work in harmony with existing programs, but these programs can also be a source of valuable assistance to a visiting minister. A manual on the hospital chaplaincy has been produced by the American Hospital Association and is available to ministers. Its purpose is to bring about a better understanding among the hospital administration, the medical staff, and those engaged in carrying out an effective ministry for patients.

Many hospitals provide pastor-physician seminars through their chaplaincy program. A pastor will do well to take advantage of this opportunity to get acquainted with the chaplains and doctors. He will also learn many practical details regarding hospital protocol, procedures, and facilities.

Some pastors have felt the intimidation of hostile physicians who have acted rudely to ministers and churchmen simply because of their lack of respect for the spiritual well-being of the patient. Sadly enough, a few ministers have responded in kind, adding to the breach existing between clergymen and physicians. Fortunately, more and more doctors and hospital personnel are taking interest in the total well-being of the patient; and because of psychosomatic studies, they are seeing the interplay between the spiritual and the physical. This is giving rise to a greater degree of dialogue between ministers and doctors than ever before.

If a pastor expects to visit regularly within a particular institution, he should be especially careful to make himself known to the authorities there. They will inform him of hospital rules and regulations. Ministers are usually permitted some latitude as to visiting hours, but to take undue advantage of such a privilege would be quite improper. Identification is very beneficial to the pastor, especially in the larger hospitals. Many chaplain's offices now request each minister to identify himself and his denominational affiliation. A small badge with the minister's name and church identification will help hospital personnel and patients to know who he is at a glance.

Taking the time to introduce himself to the head nurse and to make a general preliminary inquiry about the patient he is to visit, will show the pastor's recognition of the importance of the hospital staff and will probably facilitate the visit by reducing unnecessary interruptions. A pastor will also find nurses are more hospitable when he observes all regulations and tries to avoid visiting at hours of the day when the patient is to receive care or food. After a visit, the pastor should speak once again with the head nurse, reporting on his time with the patient.

In preparing for hospital visitation, a minister should keep certain general principles in mind:

1. Check with the physician or a close relative concerning the nature of the illness.
2. Do not try to diagnose the nature of the illness to the patient or try to offer therapeutic help which may conflict with the work of the physician.
3. The pastor's task is to provide spiritual help.
4. The pastor should dress in appropriate attire for such visits.
5. The pastor should pray before each visit as well as at the time of visitation. There may be a few instances when it will not be possible to have prayer at the time of the call.
6. The pastor should report at the hospital desk and find the exact room number.
7. The pastor should carry his Bible or Testament when calling.

8. The pastor should ask for permission to see the patient. This can be obtained from the nurse on the floor.[10]

During the visitation time there are additional suggestions a minister should observe:

1. Do not sit on the bed.
2. Do not discuss your problems with the patient.
3. Do not stand at the foot of the bed.
4. Avoid loud talk or laughter which disturbs.
5. Call a nurse to help the patient in and out of bed, etc.
6. Avoid visiting during meal time.
7. Since pastors can visit anytime, you may find more privacy visiting at other than visitors' hours.
8. Never visit when you have a communicable disease.
9. Never leave food without permission.
10. Make visits brief (an average of 15 minutes).
11. Do not ask embarrassing questions or talk of unpleasant things.
12. Be cheerful, positive, and optimistic.
13. Make the visit spiritual in nature.
14. Speak kindly to others in the room.
15. Cooperate with hospital personnel.
16. Be sincere in prayer and full of faith.
17. Visit often. People discourage easily.[11]

When a pastor is willing to cooperate with hospital personnel and is careful to show the proper consideration for them and their duties, his spiritual ministry will gain a much wider acceptance. Although his visit may be intended for the benefit of a parishioner, the blessing of his ministry will overflow to other patients and to the hospital staff.

Just as a church must reach beyond social and racial barriers in proclaiming the good news, it must be careful to include all age-groups in its outreach. A most productive endeavor into which any pastor may lead his church is ministry to the increasing number of people in *retirement and senior-citizen homes.* These homes range from exclusive retirement centers for the financially well-off to government-subsidized facilities for the middle class and poor. Every community has or is seeking some program for the elderly, and the church will do well to minister Christ to people at this level of need.

---

[10]Lloyd M. Perry and Edward J. Lias, *A Manual of Pastoral Problems and Procedures* (Grand Rapids, MI: Baker Book House, 1962), p. 148. Used by permission.

[11]Perry and Lias, *A Manual of Pastoral Problems and Procedures*, p. 148. Used by permission.

Ministry to the aged in benevolent institutions needs to be carefully coordinated with the administration. People at this stage of life have plenty of time on their hands. Consistent contact with them can meet crucial needs. In the light of tendencies toward pessimism among the elderly, a minister should convey good, positive attitudes. Cards and occasional remembrances as well as short visits do much to relieve the depression and anxiety so prevalent among those who may feel forgotten and alone.

It is not impossible that when our Lord shall call to mind the sick who were visited, the naked who were clothed, the hungry who were fed, he may also add: "I was aged, and ye noticed me; old and infirm, and ye paid attention to me." Old people, too, are among "the least of these."[12]

Some progressive pastors and churches are developing facilities for the aged within the physical complex of the church. By taking this responsibility, along with day-care programs and other community services, they are accepting the role of the church as one of meaningful benevolence toward all ages.

Even in situations where a systematic outreach by the church has not been developed, a pastor would do well to encourage the older members of his congregation to participate in the functions of local senior citizens' centers to convey a Christian witness. The encouragement provided by a concerned pastor could cause senior citizens in his congregation to have a dynamic, positive influence among their peers. As in other areas of ministry, consistency, punctuality, and descretion are valuable assets for ministers and ministry groups. Let each witness keep uppermost in his mind the fact that a positive presentation of the gospel of our Lord Jesus Christ and of His claims on the lives of all men is essential for successful ministry among all ages.

CORRECTIONAL INSTITUTIONS

The pastor is a key person in initiating a prison-ministry outreach from the local church. Every city and town will have local jail units that will provide opportunity for ministry. Generally, the county seat is the location for county jails. Churches in those cities should accept the added responsibility of ministry to these institutions.

---

[12]Harmon, *Ministerial Ethics and Etiquette*, p. 109. Used by permission.

As in other types of institutional ministry, the first step to take in establishing a jail ministry is to get acquainted with the authorities in charge of the institution. The local chief of police is in charge of the city jail; the county sheriff is in charge of the county jail. These officials need to develop confidence in the local church desiring to engage in a jail ministry. They must know the ministry groups will be faithful and punctual—using only the time allotted to them for ministry.

As the doors for ministry open to the local church, the pastor needs to become acquainted with city and county jail policies regarding inmates, facilities, etc. Care should be taken not to break the rules or lose the confidence of the officers. When the ministry begins to bear fruit, additional measures will be needed to provide for the growth of the new converts. When officers see the evidence of spiritual change in the inmates, they may cooperate with additional ministries such as water baptism and Communion.

Follow-up through correspondence becomes necessary when the inmate is released or transferred. When he is sentenced to a state or federal prison, he must initiate contact with the minister. Then the minister will be able to correspond with the inmate and make personal visits.

The minister must communicate with the penal institution he wishes to visit far in advance of the actual visit. This contact should be through the official chaplain's office. Arrangements ahead of time will prevent the disappointment of making a trip in vain. Of necessity, the regulations and policies of correctional institutions are adhered to much more closely than those of other institutions. The wise minister will acquaint himself with all such rules and seek to abide by them.

Increasing opportunities are presenting themselves to qualified ministers all over the country to serve as chaplains in penal institutions. The office of the Assemblies of God National Prison Representative is open and available to ministers, providing information and assistance concerning ministry in correctional institutions.

On the local level, additional steps can be taken to strengthen relations with community law-enforcement officers. The pastor should lead his congregation in showing appreciation for the police force. If possible, the local police should be honored on Law Enforcement Sunday by being invited to attend the church services and being given special recognition. The chief of police, county sheriff, or other representatives need to be shown the church supports good government and good law enforcement. The minister should encourage his congregation to join in community programs that support the local police. Such efforts will increase the mutual respect between the law-enforcement agencies and the religious community.

OTHER COMMUNITY INSTITUTIONS

In the course of his ministry, a pastor will discover even his associations with business institutions in the community can either enhance or diminish his effectiveness. Certain pastoral functions require that a pastor develop a working relationship with various business institutions. Because of his regular dealings with them, a pastor must be sure to treat these particular institutions with deference and respect.

The funeral home business has been under public attack from many quarters, and some of the protest has been warranted. As in other rather exclusive types of business, the cost of burial services has escalated well beyond the ability of many people to pay. The pastor can be of service to his members in helping them arrange a funeral in keeping with their financial ability.

Having a good rapport with *the funeral home directors* in one's community can be of inestimable value to the pastor who must frequently officiate at the burying of the dead. Reciprocal agreements with the funeral directors will make a rather difficult experience much more tolerable. It is true that some funeral homes consider it their responsibility to oversee everything and to direct the minister in all decisions. A pastor should be fully aware of the family's wishes, informed on appropriate funeral procedures, and acquainted with the people in charge of the arrangements. If this is the case, the family will consult freely with him for his help in the time of death.

The scheduling of the funeral service may give rise to misunderstandings and difficulties. Clear communication is most important at this time. The funeral director will generally consult with the pastor before determining the time for the service. Since both the schedules of the pastor and the funeral home may produce conflicts, it is important that they work together in a spirit of cooperation. When the pastor and the funeral director can work together with a minimum of conflict, the interests of the family are best served.

Having a reliable source of flowers for sick calls, funerals, and weddings will greatly benefit the pastor. He should cultivate a friendly, working relationship with *local florists*. Too often, pastors express little care for the appearance of the sanctuary and other church facilities. The use of flowers helps to provide a beautiful atmosphere and environment for worship. Some pastors and churches have a local florist take a special interest in the church and see that arrangements are prepared weekly for the services. Most churches must rely on a faithful worker who has the ability to arrange floral designs and will assume that responsibility as a ministry to the church. Special occasions such as Mother's Day, Easter, and Independence Day are times when the florist's help is particularly important to the church.

A word should be said concerning institutional and social referral services. The pastor is constantly approached for help in areas of need the church is not equipped to handle. Persons with these specialized needs should be referred to organizations or services designed to meet those needs. The pastor is often questioned about adoption, housing, legal problems, retardation, unwed mothers, and many other personal and social needs. It is obvious he has neither the time nor the training to meet all these needs. Knowing what resources are available and how to contact the services and institutions best equipped to help in such cases is a necessity for the serving pastor.

A manual such as *The Church and Community Resources*, by Marcus D. Bryant and Charles F. Kemp, can be of assistance to a minister when a referral is necessary.[13] This manual provides information regarding the pastor's community responsibilities, and it can serve as a handbook listing local, state, and national agencies providing social services for people with various needs.

Community social services are not in competition with the church. On the contrary, their common purpose in serving humanity should create an atmosphere of complementary service. Since almost every community has such resources at its disposal, the pastor should become aware of them and use them to assist the work of the church.

---

[13]Bryant and Kemp, *The Church and Community Resources* (St. Louis: Bethany Press, 1977).

The Pastor's Relationships With the Religious Community

MINISTERS AND CHURCHES OF OTHER DENOMINATIONS

One of the greatest joys a minister can have in his pastoral experience is to have a harmonious relationship and close Christian fellowship with the other ministers and churches of his community. There is a sense of strength that comes to a pastor when he knows other pastors are truly dedicated to the Lord Jesus Christ and are striving to bring the community to an awareness of His saving grace.

Unfortunately, this is not the case in many communities. The New Testament concepts of the ministry and the church have degenerated into a "country-club" social idea with no redemptive value whatsoever. Those who embrace such a concept have lost sight of the sinful estate of man and the need for salvation through the sacrificial atonement of the blood of Christ. If this type of thinking prevails, it becomes very difficult to find a common denominator for ministry.

Whatever the situation may be in his community, the pastor needs to be acquainted with his fellow ministers. He needs to know as much as possible about them—their spiritual experiences, beliefs, depth of concern, and commitment for reaching the community. This knowledge will enable a pastor to relate to those ministers and share with them the burden of winning the city to Christ. Often, a mature minister of the gospel has opportunity to encourage his fellow ministers and lead them into deeper spiritual experiences.

The apostle Paul has been considered a "loner" by many, but his life and writings show he greatly depended on and appreciated those who were called to minister alongside him. It was Paul who constantly emphasised the joyful thought of being related together as "fellows":

> fellow soldier—Philippians 2:25
> fellow laborer—Philippians 4:3
> fellow servant—Colosians 1:7
> fellow prisoner—Colossians 4:10
> fellow worker—Colossians 4:11

This is the Biblical concept for ministerial relationships: seeing other ministers as co-laborers in the same vineyard, reaching for the same goals and objectives, and accomplishing the same ends.

Regardless of the scriptural admonition, there are pastors who re-

fuse to work as team members in the community. They find it difficult to associate with pastors of other denominations. Running their
own programs without regard for other pastors, they isolate themselves and their people from the mainstream of Christian witness. The
community views this as a breach in testimony and finds it difficult to
interpret the truth of John 13:35—"By this shall all men know that ye
are my disciples, if ye have love one to another."

Other ministers may project an image of superiority and aloofness
that does not actually reflect their real attitude. But because of carelessness, they convey the wrong image and damage their effectiveness
in relating to others.

Perhaps the most widely known organization for promoting ministerial cooperation is the local ministerial association. The ministerial
association creates a setting in which a group of ministers may work
cooperatively to advance the cause of the gospel. There are some instances where the association may have shirked its duties or abused its
privileges and, by so doing, lost stature in the eyes of the people of the
community. But for the most part, the ministerial association enjoys a
respected place of influence in the community. There are many advantages to participation in the ministerial association. "The minister
who is too busy to associate himself with his brethren in the ministerial association or to attend conferences and conventions is circumvent-
ing his influence."[14]

In many cities, major religious functions such as rest-home services,
radio ministry, hospital ministry, jail ministry, and school religious
exercises are supervised by the ministerial association. Some communities have given the ministerial association exclusive rights to these
ministries. To be involved, the minister must be an active participant
in the ministerial association. The Spirit-filled pastor has a community
responsibility that can best be fulfilled through such participation.
And further, he has a message that needs to be heard—a witness that
needs to be made. Here is an avenue for proclaiming his message and
demonstrating his faith.

Joint community services have functioned best where an active and
harmonious ministerial association exists. United services give an opportunity for the churches of the community to come together occa-

---

[14]Mead (ed.), *Reaching Beyond Your Pulpit*, p. 123. Used by permission.

sionally and project a community witness for Christ without the provincialism of the denomination. The idea, of course, is not to berate the denomination, but to emphasize the overall purpose of the Christian community. Christians of different denominations are given the chance to meet believers of other churches personally and share their Christian faith. For the community to sense a spiritual unity among its churches and pastors is a giant step toward the fulfillment of the Great Commission in that locality.

United services are traditionally held on such special days as Christmas, Thanksgiving, Easter, and Memorial Day. In smaller communities, joint meetings of churches are more common. Yet the possibility does exist even in large metropolitan areas when there is sufficient interest among the pastors and churches.

The strength of the ministerial association varies from city to city. The level of success and effectiveness of the association depends on the caliber and quality of the ministers who participate. The ministerial association can become a strong force to stand against evil in the community. Amid growing efforts to promote alcoholic beverages, morally degrading pornographic magazines, and illicit and perverted sex in television and movies, the ministerial association can speak out in protest and cause its influence to be felt. But the association need not limit itself to defensive measures. It can initiate positive steps for keeping the community clean. It can do much to promote patriotic and spiritual programs to strengthen the moral fiber of the community.

The Spirit-filled pastor may encounter problems in dealing with theologically liberal ministers in the ministerial association. Their desire to make the association a social action club with no spiritual impact will bring their experience in Christ into question. The Pentecostal pastor must take a position and stand his ground. A strong, positive, evangelical voice needs to be heard and felt in the association. When he conducts himself with wisdom and discretion, an Assemblies of God pastor will have a great influence in turning the tide on many issues and guarding the spiritual and ethical principles of the ministerial association in the community.

The Assemblies of God pastor, when relating to ministers of other denominations in the community, must determine how far he may go without compromising his convictions or destroying his unique role as a Spirit-filled minister. He must guard against leaving an impression of superspirituality. Yet, at the same time, he must never forget his calling and experience in Christ through the Holy Spirit.

The problem of coping with extremely liberal ministerial views in the ministerial association is not so acute in larger communities where there are separate groups for evangelicals and liberals. But in smaller communities it is sometimes difficult to keep a ministerial association active due to the small number of churches and the obvious differences among the ministers. The presence of liberal pastors leads some ministers to feel they should not join the association at all. Others recognize the need for a positive voice for evangelicalism and are not intimidated by the liberal element, no matter how rank.

The attitude of a pastor toward the community will be reflected in his congregation. He must lead his church into the realization of a spiritual responsibility and accountability for every class of people within their outreach. With this attitude will come the realization that just one church cannot do the job alone. With a cooperative spirit, Christians of different churches can have an appreciation for one another and, at the same time, appreciate their own particular fellowship. When members of other churches see a zealous church truly giving witness to the grace of God in their lives, they will be challenged and strengthened. Lazy Christians will be stirred up and begin to serve the Lord more effectively. What an excellent way to fulfill the admonition of Scripture: "Let us consider one another to provoke unto love and to good works" (Hebrews 10:24).

There is a standard by which the pastor can determine into which church associations he can lead his congregation. Although churches may not agree on all minor matters, there is no need for compromising basic convictions. Where there is faithful adherence to the divine inspiration of the Scriptures, the deity of Christ, His substitutionary atonement and bodily resurrection, salvation by grace through faith, and related doctrines, churches of basically similar beliefs ought to have a common interest in one another, pray for one another, and labor together in forwarding the cause of Christ in the community.

Because of the unprecedented move of the Holy Spirit among all denominations today, causing us to realize the shortness of time and the urgency of completing our mission, the Assemblies of God has made provision for its ministers to participate in and be used by the

Holy Spirit to minister in non-Assemblies of God churches. As the opportunity presents itself, and where our Fellowship is not endangered, "Ministers shall not be limited or restrained from entering open doors to preach this Pentecostal message."[15]

This openness to other churches indicates our desire to relate to them properly as fellow members of the body of Christ, fulfilling our Lord's mandate, and to share with them our message and experience in the Holy Spirit. Zenas Bicket gives wise counsel to the pastor and church who endeavor to relate to other denominations: "A Pentecostal congregation should recognize it has a special message to share with other members of the community whether in established churches or not. . . . Pastors or churches so busy with internal programs that they cannot minister to outside groups will have to answer to God."[16]

And further, the official position of the Assemblies of God concerning the charismatic movement recognizes the importance of finding a ground of fellowship with those outside our organization whenever possible. "The Church is the Body of Christ, the habitation of God through the Spirit, with divine appointments for the fulfillment of her Great Commission (Ephesians 1:22,23; 2:22; Matthew 28:19,20; Mark 16:15, 16)."[17]

Fortunate is the community that has all of its churches and pastors, no matter what their historic ecclesiastical persuasions, actively engaged in fulfilling their reason for being! The impact of a joint effort among the denominations of any community in carrying out the threefold commission of preaching, teaching, and making disciples is much needed today.

MINISTERS AND CHURCHES OF THE SAME DENOMINATION

The Bible has spoken clearly regarding the relationship ministers should have with each other. There are to be no elements of jealousy and competitiveness which bring division to the work of God and

---

[15]"Doctrines and Practices Disapproved" (Article VIII, Section 9), The Bylaws of the General Council of the Assemblies of God, rev. 1975, p. 103.

[16]Zenas J. Bicket, ed., The Effective Pastor (Springfield, MO: Gospel Publishing House, 1973), p. 31.

[17]Statement of Fundamental Truths (Article V, Section 10) of the Constitution of the General Council of the Assemblies of God, revised to August 14-19, 1975, in the General Council Minutes, 1975, p. 79.

among the workers of God. First Corinthians 3:6-9 presents a beautiful picture of harmony and cooperation between the ministries of Paul and Apollos, concluding with the exemplary statement for all preachers in all times: "For we are laborers together with God" (v.9).

Cooperation should start with members of one's own profession. Someone has observed that people are generally jealous only of persons engaged in the same kind of business. Bankers are envious of other bankers, teachers are jealous of other teachers, doctors compete with other doctors.[18]

And sadly enough, ministers may become jealous of other ministers.

A proper relationship between ministers demands three prerequisites: frankness, comradeship, and cooperation. This is definitely true of men of God who are of the same communion. Pastors working together in the same city or community need all three ingredients to make a smooth, harmonious, and successful relationship. False ideas of success and pressures of competition sometimes create undue strain on ministers of the same denomination even when such stresses are not felt toward ministers of other groups. Tendencies toward unethical conduct toward each other must be rejected.

As in all other relationships, a right spirit is necessary if there is to be continual harmony and fellowship. There are several specific hazards to be avoided to maintain Biblical attitudes toward fellow ministers.

Do not consider colleagues as competitors. A minister with a cooperative spirit and a friendly personality will go out of his way to welcome ministerial newcomers to the area. He may use the mail, the telephone, or a personal visit. This small courtesy will open the door to many new friendships. Courtesy is a virtue that will take a minister a long way in building good relationships with his fellow ministers.

Ministers should be complementary to each other. There is a friendly competition that adds enthusiasm to church and Sunday school attendance programs. The presence of this type of competition may force a preacher out of laziness and contribute to church growth. But even this form of competition should be carefully supervised lest a wrong spirit creep into the minister's heart or overtake his congregation.

[18]Mead (ed.), Reaching Beyond Your Pulpit, p. 122. Used by permission.

Pastors who minister in adjacent areas of a city or community for a long period of time and maintain a close friendship and mutual esteem are upholding the highest moral conduct and ministerial ethics. They do not stoop to the base tactics of trying to persuade members of other churches to join their congregation. Selfishness does not dictate their actions toward one another. When there are situations involving overlapping interests, these ministers are mature enough to sit down and discuss the problem. Their top priority is the overall welfare of the work of God.

Too many pastors have broken fellowship over the relocation of laymen. When members of a congregation decide to change churches, there is often a suspicious attitude on the part of their former pastor. He puts the new pastor at arm's length and makes him feel as if it were a crime to receive the members who are transferring to his church. This is displeasing to God.

A pastor ought to find out the reason for his members' leaving and assess the matter honestly. If the cause is something in the pastor or church that should be corrected, the pastor should be mature enough to face the issue and make appropriate changes. If the matter cannot be resolved, the pastor should release the people to leave and notify the receiving pastor of their intentions, keeping a good spirit throughout the entire process. A wise pastor will want to talk with the former pastor about the reasons for the relocation of members before receiving them into membership in his church. At times it is far better for some people to change churches—better for the people and better for the churches involved. It is the mutual goodwill of the two pastors in working out problems such as this that keeps a spirit of harmony throughout the years.

Do not become jealous or critical of a colleague. Where criticism is necessary, be certain it is constructive and given in a way that will be understood by all to be a demonstration of love. Unfortunately, criticism among ministers often "concerns some little, unimportant method of work or some insignificant idiosyncrasy."[19]

The ugly manifestations of jealousy show in the way we criticize our fellow ministers. Instead of looking for the best qualities in the lives of our colleagues, we exaggerate their weaknesses and run down

---

[19]From *The Minister's Mission* by C. E. Colton, Copyright © 1951 by C. E. Colton.

their achievements. The prevalence of such a practice should cause us to look at some of the leading professional organizations of our time and note their strict adherence to a code of professional ethics. No organization should have a higher standard of conduct and sense of ethics than an organization of ministers of the gospel of Jesus Christ.[20] "Nothing is more insidious than ministerial jealousy and no refined frailty more despicable and none more fatal ultimately to both happiness and usefulness."[21]

Jealousy destroyed Israel's first king. Saul allowed the spirit of jealousy to so possess him that he could not rejoice in the victory of God because the victory was being wrought through David rather than himself. How many ministers in our day have succumbed to the same spirit? Rather than thanking God for David and giving the glory to God, Saul allowed himself to be eaten within by the cancerous spirit of jealousy. Uncontrolled jealousy led him to attempt murder, robbed him of his kingdom, and eventually destroyed his right standing before God.

"He that ruleth his spirit [is better] than he that taketh a city" (Proverbs 16:32). The pastor who cannot conquer the spirit of jealousy toward his brother minister is a preacher who will eventually destroy his own ministry and severely damage the work of the kingdom of God. Proverbs 25:28 gives us a sober picture of the devastation of jealousy when it possesses the spirit of a man: "He that hath no rule over his own spirit is like a city that is broken down, and without walls." The havoc is justly likened to a city that has lost the protection of its walls and is consequently subjected to destruction.

A minister of the gospel has a responsibility to initiate faith and unity among his brethren, not just refrain from negative attitudes and actions hurtful to the fellowship. The apostle Paul urged the church at Ephesus to a spiritual activity: ". . . endeavoring to keep the unity of the Spirit" (Ephesians 4:3). The reward of such an effort is described in the same chapter: "The whole body fitly joined together and compacted by that which every joint supplieth, . . . maketh increase of the body" (v.16). And to know that the true Shepherd and Bishop of the

---

[20]Colton, *The Minister's Mission*, p. 178.

[21]Jeff D. Ray, *The Highest Office* (Old Tappan, NJ: Fleming H. Revell Co., 1923), p. 241

Church is pleased with our performance toward our brethren is in itself our greatest reward.

In relating our ministries and our churches one to another we must not forget the words of our Lord Jesus Christ recorded in Matthew 7:12: "Treat other people exactly as you would like to be treated by them—this is the essence of all true religion" *(Phillips)*. Undoubtedly, there is no greater text or Christian ethic to live by. Most of our relationship problems with ministers and churches could be solved by simply following this principle of the Master.

Suggested Reading

Adams, Jay E. *The Pastoral Life.* Grand Rapids: Baker Book House, 1974.

Bicket, Zenas J., ed. *The Effective Pastor.* Springfield, MO: Gospel Publishing House, 1973.

Colton, C. E. *The Minister's Mission.* Grand Rapids: Zondervan Publishing House, 1961.

Harmon, Nolan B. *Ministerial Ethics and Etiquette.* Nashville: Abingdon Press, 1950.

Kent, Homer A., Sr. *The Pastor and His Work.* Chicago: Moody Press, 1963.

Longenecker, Harold L. *Building Town and Country Churches.* Chicago: Moody Press, 1973.

Mead, Frank S., ed. *Reaching Beyond Your Pulpit.* Old Tappan, NJ: Fleming H. Revell Co., 1967.

Segler, Franklin M. *A Theology of Church and Ministry.* Nashville: Broadman Press, 1960.

Thiessen, John C. *Pastoring the Smaller Church.* Grand Rapids: Zondervan Publishing House, 1962.

Turnbull, Ralph G., ed. *Dictionary of Practical Theology.* Grand Rapids: Baker Book House, 1967.

14

The Church
and the
Community

EDWARD S. CALDWELL

Sirens wailed and an ominous pillar of black smoke billowed into the evening sky as tongues of flame licked at a wooden structure. Within moments a large crowd gathered to watch the battle between firefighters and flames. Soon the members of the media arrived to press through the spectators—reporters, photographers, and television cameramen.

That night a fire-gutted church received more public attention than it had accumulated in its entire 30-year history! Lifelong community residents reading accounts of the fire in the morning paper mumbled that they did not remember a church in that part of the neighborhood.

One might ask: Which was the sadder tragedy—a church burned in a few hours or a church ignored for 30 years?

There's a Community, as Well as Souls, to Win!

The primary element needed if a church wishes not to be ignored by its community is good *public relations*. Of course a church can also obtain attention through bad relations. But those ministers who sincerely desire to make an impact on their communities for the cause of Christ should never seek attention merely for the sake of notoriety, be it good or bad.

Bad public relations—outlandish promotional schemes, ministerial immoralities, devious financial procedures, news accounts of angry

---

Edward S. Caldwell is pastor of Glad Tidings Assembly of God, Springfield, Missouri.

399

church disputes, and unfair treatment of people in the community—
have helped to keep many out of church, and ultimately out of
heaven. Jesus says some severe things about individuals whose actions
cause others to stumble (Matthew 18:6, 7). And Satan is quick to
utilize the media to spread any derogatory report about ministers or
churches, and thus multiply the number who will stumble. On the
other hand, many ministers have learned to use good public relations
so effectively that scores of people are attracted to their churches
week after week, and many of these visitors are transformed by the
power of the gospel. So it can be said that good public relations are
an integral part of effective evangelism.

A church's public relations can be defined as the degree of
understanding and goodwill it has achieved. It is a combination of
publicity; promotion; and, most important of all, continual activities
and relationships that enhance the church's reputation and ability to
serve. The primary purpose of public relations is to help the church
obtain and maintain a climate in which it can prosper best.

Credibility is indispensable to the church that seeks to represent
Jesus Christ. To be considered untrustworthy is to be rendered useless
in the propagation of the gospel. So anything a church attempts in the
arena of public relations must be saturated in unadulterated truth and
honest good relations. Image-building based on falsehood or
misrepresentation cannot be condoned.

THE IMPORTANCE OF "HIGH VISIBILITY"

If people are to be attracted to your church, they must know it exists. Throughout the centuries, church officials cognizant of this fact
selected prominent hilltop locations as building sites. In some cities,
an imposing church edifice stands atop each hill. Indeed, church bell
towers and steeples serve as historic landmarks in thousands of towns
and cities across the Christian world.

In a practical sense, many hilltop locations afford disadvantages
that outweigh the single benefit of visibility. The lack of convenient
accessibility, inadequate space for future expansion, and parking areas
that are on steep slopes can nullify the visual benefits of erecting a
church on high ground. So other methods of obtaining "high visibility" must be found.

Even a church located in an out-of-the-way place can do much to create public awareness of its existence. The most obvious way to gain "high visibility" is through the media. Newsworthy articles about interesting church events create public awareness in the newspapers. Radio and television stations can be utilized to arouse public interest. And outdoor advertising affords yet another opportunity for gaining "high visibility."

Why is "high visibility" so important? Take a look at the churches with impressive growth rates and you will discover every one of them is highly visible within its community. Not every one has an ideal location but, despite that fact, the existence of each is known to the general public.

THE IMPORTANCE OF WINNING PUBLIC CONFIDENCE

Sad to say, one of the most misunderstood institutions in all the world is the local church. Some people think of churches as social clubs for a select few. Others consider the church as a "mutual admiration society" where religious people assemble to congratulate each other on their holiness. Still others believe that only when they "clean up their lives" will they be welcomed in a church. The simple fact that a church is a place where people go to receive spiritual assistance is not as commonly known to the unchurched as most churchgoers assume.

The first essential in reaching any community involves public confidence. No one will come and accept the message preached by a church unless he is convinced the church actually lives up to what it claims to be. That means people must have some idea of what the church claims. Does it believe people burdened by guilt can be forgiven? Does it believe homes wrecked by sin can be restored? Does it believe sicknesses can be miraculously healed? Does it believe ineffective people can be changed into dynamic witnesses through a baptism of divine power? Such claims will attract attention, providing people know about them. Then comes the acid test: Can the church deliver what it claims?

If the answer is a resounding yes, then the church is on the way to winning public confidence. But if the church claims more than it can deliver, it writes its own epitaph. No amount of advertising can rectify the damage of public confidence lost.

Editors and Reporters:
Relationships With Media People

One of the first places a minister needs to visit after accepting a new pastorate is the local newspaper. He should speak to the city editor who will direct him to the religion editor or the reporter assigned to religious news. Many newspapers consider the arrival of a new clergyman to be a newsworthy event. When this attitude exists, the minister's first visit with a reporter may turn out to be a full-fledged interview. At the very least, the minister will learn on his first visit something of the newspaper's policy and the deadlines for church news.

Unlike radio or television, a newspaper is not licensed by any public authority, so the news it prints and the services it renders are decided by the owners and no one else. Of course a newspaper does seek to serve its readers, but a minister should recognize that he cannot compel an editor to do his bidding.

RELIGION EDITORS WANT NEWS

News is anything that interests people; the greater the interest, the bigger the news. Don't ask a newspaper editor to "give my church some publicity." Remember his job is to give his readers news. So if you give him genuine news, he will give you coverage. You may call it publicity; he will call it news.

One rule of thumb for identifying a newsworthy event or topic is to ask yourself this question: "If this story were about another church, would I want to read it?" If so, then take your story to the religion editor.

Conventions Are News. Not every church is invited to host a regional or state conference, but many do. Such conventions provide opportunities not only to further the interests of the event itself but also to gain some good publicity for the host church. But a church need not wait for others to sponsor a convention; it can sponsor its own. For example, a series of meetings featuring two or three missionaries constitutes a "missionary convention." Another example: two or three guest ministers with some expertise in family counseling can be presented as featured speakers in a Marriage and Family Conference.

There are several ways to gain good publicity from such conferences:

1. Prepare an advance newsstory listing topics and speakers.
2. Provide the newspaper with pictures of the speakers, along with biographical information about them.
3. Give the paper a complete account of the conference just before it opens.
4. Invite the press to send reporters.
5. Provide a story that summarizes the convention and its accomplishments after the event ends.

Special Events Are News. An alert pastor can gain much worthwhile publicity by making the most of such things as significant church anniversaries, mortgage burnings, rallies, dedications of new facilities, and any other event that is truly different from routine church services. However, avoid the temptation of doing "something different" just because it will gain public attention. Ministers who preach from church rooftops or allow themselves to be targets for cream pie tossers might gain some news coverage, but they lose much more in public respect. Unfortunately, others also lose when ministers engage in cheap publicity stunts, including the sister churches of the denomination. When a minister deliberately makes a laughingstock of himself, he does a disservice to the body of Christ.

Projects Are News. When a church decides to build a new sanctuary or expand its present facilities, the newspaper will welcome information detailing the proposed expansion. When the youth of the church involve themselves in a fund-raising project to benefit some missionary, the newspaper will want to know all about it. Such stories counterbalance news of teenage crime and violence. When your church launches a program to assist displaced families, or any time your church adopts a program that flows beyond the walls of your sanctuary, the newspaper will want to know about it. But unless you contact the press it is likely the potential publicity value of such projects will be lost. A cynical world needs to know about the involvement of local churches in practical demonstrations of Christ's love. True, the local church stands to gain some good publicity. It is equally true that some previously hardhearted newspaper readers can be melted by learning about the selfless compassion exhibited by members of a church in their own community. Such publicity can serve as a first step toward winning some cynics to the church and to the gospel.

People Are News. The pastor himself is a newsworthy person—his installation, speaking engagements, denominational duties, travels, attendance at conventions, civic recognitions, interchurch participation, articles, and books written. Guest speakers are also newsworthy. One of the best ways of getting publicity for your church is by bringing in a guest speaker. Ask the speaker to provide a glossy photo and a biographical sketch of himself. Provide the newspaper with the photo and an advance story telling of his coming, quoting freely from the biographical material, and explaining the purpose of his visit.

Sometimes members of the congregation become newsworthy—a child who wins a Scripture memorization contest, a youth who attains high honors for his church-related activities, a collegian who attains special recognition on his campus, a Sunday school teacher or officer who is honored for outstanding service, an elderly saint who deserves notice for an anniversary marking many years of faithfulness. How often complaints are raised about all the bad news in the paper, but how little is done to bring news about truly good people to public attention.

Placing Your Stories

Pastors should know how to write a news item suitable for publication, but many do not. When this is the case, just put down all the facts, with special attention to the correct spelling of names, and the newspaper can do the rest. But there are advantages to being able to provide finished copy. The kind of church newswriting the paper expects can be determined by carefully examing the church pages of the paper.

Some general publicity rules to follow in church newspaper publicity are:

1. Have only one person contact the newspaper.
2. Establish contact with the person in charge of church news.
3. Double-space your neatly typed article.
4. Double-check dates, names, times, and places.
5. Meet the newspaper's deadline for church-page copy.
6. Express thanks for any coverage given, because newspaper space is valuable.

Pictures. Sometimes a good photograph with an informative cutline beneath it has greater publicity value than a lengthy article. So a pastor needs to keep in mind situations that would lend themselves to newsworthy pictures. Newspapers rarely use snapshots taken by amateurs, especially those in color. If a church is fortunate enough to have a professional photographer, his picture may be acceptable; however, some newspapers restrict themselves to photos taken by staff members only.

If a pastor has an event or well-known personality scheduled for his church, he should talk to the city editor. If the editor agrees that a photo would be newsworthy, he will assign a cameraman. Usually a newspaper photographer comes with instructions. He seldom needs or wants anyone to tell him how to take his pictures. But even the best photographers sometimes fail to be careful enough about backgrounds, and backgrounds can make or break a picture. So be watchful, and point out problems that might ruin the photograph.

Assist the photographer with accurate left-to-right identification, correctly spelled names, titles, and hometowns (of visitors). Be sure the cameraman has correct information about dates, times, and the purpose of the event.

Follow-up. Editors get daily complaints from people, but only occasional notes of thanks. A letter summarizing the success of the event not only reassures the editor it actually occurred, it also improves the likelihood of his cooperation for future requests of news coverage.

GETTING CHURCH NEWS ON THE AIR

Radio stations are more numerous now than ever before, and more local stations select one particular segment of the community as their "target." So we have sports stations, country and western stations, classical music stations, and an ever-increasing number of Christian stations, among others.

Community Bulletin Boards. Many stations seek to serve their listeners with "community bulletin boards"—announcements of upcoming events that are presented without charge. A pastor should learn which stations provide such a service and utilize it whenever he has an event that merits public attention. When placing paid spot advertisements on the station, don't forget to suggest that the information also be placed on the free announcement service.

Newswriting for Radio. Brevity is of utmost importance to radio stations, so thought needs to be given as to how to say what needs to be
said in as few words as possible. The copy needs to be typed and
double-spaced for easy reading. If there may be a pronunciation problem with the name of a person or place, a pronunciation note should
be placed on the page (e.g., *Smyth* rhymes with *scythe)*.

Telephone Contacts With Stations. For the sake of accuracy, most
radio announcements should be provided in written form, but occasionally a time factor requires using the telephone. For example, when
severe weather requires the cancelation of services a pastor may contact as many radio and television stations as possible with the cancelation notice. No charge is made for such notices at most stations.

COPING WITH UNFAVORABLE NEWS ITEMS

Headlines You Don't Want. The business of the press is to print, not
to suppress news. Sometimes a newsstory is bad news for a church.
When it is your church, the temptation is to ask the editor not to
publish the story. This approach seldom works and often causes further harm. When there is news that seems harmful to your church
and you are approached by reporters, you will be wise to cooperate.
Obvious evasion and "no comment" can make things worse. Answer
the reporters' questions and point out any extenuating circumstances
there may be. The reporters are doing their job and they will appreciate your cooperation and will be aware of what it is costing you
to be completely truthful. If you fail to cooperate, they will be forced
to contact other sources that may be less informed, and the resulting
story will lack the accuracy you expect in news coverage.

Letters to the Editor. Occasionally preachers object to the editorials
published by newspapers. It is a fact that some newspapers publish
editorials that are completely contrary to Biblical teachings. But a
preacher shows more wisdom if he attacks the moral issue instead of
the newspaper. A courteous letter to the editor may be appropriate.
Such a letter should contain thoughtful and persuasive logic instead of
wild accusations and wrath. At other times the newspaper may
publish a particularly praiseworthy editorial or article. The minister
who takes time to express his appreciation in writing will eventually
reap valuable goodwill.

Radio and Television:
Multiply the Influences of Your Church

The Great Commission must be fulfilled, and the electronic media make it possible to take the gospel to "every creature." The cost of air time varies dramatically from large city stations to stations located in small towns. Sometimes considerable cost differences exist among the stations located within the same city. A pastor who desires to reach beyond those who assemble in his church should become informed about air-time costs within his locale. Whenever financially feasible, a ministry on the airwaves should be given serious consideration.

UTILIZING A DENOMINATIONAL BROADCAST OR TELECAST

When a denomination produces a radio or television program, it does so to serve the churches of the fellowship. So the individual churches should give first consideration to using the broadcast tapes offered by the denomination. But the local church's responsibility does not end with providing the air-time cost for such a program. To obtain maximum benefit from a broadcast, the local church must take steps to identify itself with that broadcast. Such steps must be in harmony with the guidelines established by the denominational media office. Perhaps a 30-second spot announcement naming the local church can be aired immediately following the broadcast. Other suggestions might be considered: provide the newspapers with a news release about the broadcast being aired locally; include the name of the broadcast, station, time, day, and spot on the dial in church ads; stamp church literature and gospel tracts with the broadcast information; include the broadcast on billboards that advertise the church. In short, use every means possible to identify the local church with the national broadcast.

PRODUCING YOUR OWN RADIO BROADCAST

A pastor who hopes to go on the air needs to think before he signs a contract with a radio station. He must never assume that contributions from listeners will cover his air time costs; if his church cannot carry the expense, he should stay off the air. Mail response to a locally produced broadcast is usually insignificant. A radio ministry that becomes preoccupied with pleading for financial assistance is no ministry at all. Instead, it becomes a liability to the cause of Christ.

Once the question of financial capability has been resolved, the next consideration is format. *Format* is a term borrowed from printing. It means "the shape, size, and general arrangement of a publication." Applied to a radio program, *format* describes the program design into which the content is inserted and through which the content moves. It is a basic outline that provides the structure for all programs. Of course, content is more important than format, so it is well to decide on objectives and content before choosing the format.

Church Services on the Air. Some radio stations arrange for remote facilities within the church building so church services can go on the air "live." Other churches tape-record their services so selected portions can be aired. The advantage of such a broadcasting procedure seems to be the accomplishment of two goals through a single effort—one sermon suffices for both audiences.

Unlike television, which can keep the viewer in touch with what is going on, radio listeners are annoyed by the long pauses that frequently occur when singers or speakers are moving toward the microphone. Another problem is that church auditoriums rarely have the right acoustical qualities for radio broadcasting, so even an edited tape of a church service leaves much to be desired in quality of sound. Perhaps the most important consideration is that a minister addressing a crowd expresses himself quite differently from the way he talks when he is in someone's living room. And that is where radio is—right there in a living room or bedroom or automobile, with an audience of one, two, or a few.

On the other hand, the minister might sacrifice the effectiveness of the congregational service to give top priority to an effective radio broadcast. Some churches might tolerate such an arrangement, others would not.

Sermons and Sermonettes. In some communities, one or more radio stations provide a time-slot for a "minister of the week." This public service time is offered without charge, and ministers do well to accept the invitation to speak when it is offered by the station. Often it is by this means that clergymen are initiated into radio broadcasting. When a congregation has been given advance notice about their pastor being on the air, they can later be questioned about the idea of his producing his own broadcast. Also, the minister gains some idea of the preparation required, so he can decide if he wishes to invest the required time on a round-the-year broadcast. Effective radio sermons, regardless of length, require adequate preparation time; listeners quickly become bored with the cliche-ridden talks given by preachers who ramble on and on. A preacher only fools himself when he believes fluency of speech is all he needs on the air.

If a minister is dedicated to reaching people with God's Word, he can build a radio audience much larger than the crowd he sees in church each Sunday. Indeed, some in his radio audience will be attracted to become part of his sanctuary crowd.

Religious Newscasts. Some stations will provide air time without charge to a minister who is willing to prepare his own copy and be the newscaster for a weekly religion-in-the-news broadcast. The station manager may be just waiting for a clergyman to offer his services. To prepare such a newscast the minister reporter must obtain adequate sources for news. Newsworthy items can be gleaned from religious magazines and newspapers. Arrangements can be made for the station to set aside religious items that come via the wire services. There are religious news services to which a clergyman can subscribe, and he can write and ask that his name be added to the mailing lists of the public relations offices of several major religious organizations.

Of course, a newscaster must be completely objective, reporting news about all denominations. In appreciation for the minister who prepares an objective religious newscast, a station manager expects him to report his own church activities and invite listeners to visit his services.

Religious "Disc Jockey." Some stations that would not welcome a preaching program may respond favorably to a format of recorded gospel music interspersed with timely comments from a friendly-voiced minister. Indeed, some ministers have been given free time at the beginning or end of a broadcasting day for this "disc-jockey" approach. Unless a minister is at ease in changing records on the station's turntables, he should prepare his entire broadcast by tape recording, thus eliminating errors that might arise from nervousness.

Other Formats. Interviews, Bible questions and answers, dramas, telephone call-ins, live talent shows—all of these formats have proven workable for religious broadcasts. Creative thinking is welcomed by radio stations, so a minister should discuss his innovative ideas with the station's program manager. The station is vitally interested in the success of every program it airs; ever mindful of the importance of maintaining a large listening audience. A church-sponsored program that builds that audience will be welcomed on the program log.

PRODUCING YOUR OWN TELECAST

Television offers one of the quickest ways for a minister or church to achieve "high visibility" within a community. In some cities the demand for television time by religious broadcasters has produced waiting lists of churches. Many congregations are willing to pay substantial amounts for air time in order to be included in the rather crowded Sunday morning television schedule. Some stations restrict all religious telecasts to Sunday mornings; other stations open their logs for religion at other times. Even more selections of time-slots are available when cable TV is serving a community.

When a church is contemplating a television ministry, the first step is to learn what times might be available and the cost (cost varies with day and time). The next step is to select a program format that can be maintained regularly.

Televising Services. Some church buildings lend themselves to television camera coverage; some do not. When it is determined that television coverage of church services is desirable, arrangements for remote camera crews must be made with the station. The problem of "blank spaces" while persons are moving to and from microphones is less distracting than on radio, yet such wasted time must be cut to an absolute minimum or viewers will switch to another channel. In fact, the entire service must be planned to be of such a high quality that it can compete with religious programs being carried on other channels at the same hour.

Variety Formats. A church that produces its television program in a station's studio obtains the advantage of using facilities specifically designed for televising. Usually such studios are not very large, so the program must be designed to fit into the available space. Small musical groups are usually more effective than large choirs because of the space problems. Since these are usually 30-minute programs, the sermon must be brief. The church will probably have to work with the station in designing and building any special sets that are desired.

Some churches have experienced considerable success with 5-minute telecasts, and several programs can be video-taped in one session. The minister may wish to change his tie or jacket between segments so the viewer will not be conscious that the filming was all done on one day.

Interview Formats. People are interested in people. That's the reason for the ongoing popularity of television interviews. In-depth interviews with people who have interesting life stories can form the basis for very worthwhile television programming. This approach requires a constant search for people who will "come across" on camera and whose stories are captivating. The interviewer must have the ability to draw out the story from his guest, and to keep attention on the guest rather than on himself.

Panel Formats. When community issues are aired, some stations invite a panel of qualified persons to participate in an on-the-air discussion. This format is sometimes used by public television stations for controversial topics. The panel has also proven an effective format for some interchurch religious telecasts. But when such a panel is presented by one church only it is unlikely any controversy will emerge. Instead, the panel members will merely be reinforcing each other, and the viewer may suffer boredom.

Musical Formats. A church that has a variety of high-quality musical talent may want to produce a "seasonal special"; Easter, Christmas, and other holidays lend themselves to such programming. The minister or another representative of the church must contact the station management well in advance and explain their proposed special. If the station is willing to sell the air time, an all-out production can be launched by the church. Since a special does not have a regular listening audience, a strong publicity campaign is needed to ensure the maximum audience.

Other Formats. With inexpensive access to cable TV, the kinds of religious formats are multiplying. Children's programs featuring puppets, magic, and stories are becoming economically feasible. The video cassette is headed toward becoming a standard visual aid in churches; and many of the programs placed on three-quarter-inch video tape for cable TV will become available for church audiovisual libraries. Lectures, demonstrations, and home Bible study courses will also serve the dual role of cable TV and in-church visuals. We have only begun to see the impact of television in the church!

Advertising: It Doesn't Cost, It Pays!

Suppose major department stores placed ads in the media that merely announced their name and address, the hours they were open for business, and the name of the store manager. How much store traffic would such advertising generate? Almost none! Yet countless churches limit themselves to that kind of advertising—and many more never use the media at all.

Two reasons exist for churches not advertising: some consider commercial advertising out of harmony with their role as Christ's representatives on earth; others say they cannot afford to advertise. The first group is committed to a point of view that is unlikely to be altered by argument, theological or otherwise. But the second group only needs to learn the truth behind this maxim: It *pays* to advertise.

The key to successful advertising is motivation. Within the context of church advertising, this means presenting reasons why it would be beneficial for the person seeing or hearing a church advertisement to attend the church.

Sermon titles, for example, can be like baited hooks used by fishers of men. A well-phrased sermon title can attract people to visit a church. It may appeal to a reader's area of interest, it may promise to supply information on a subject about which he is curious, or it may offer a solution to a problem that has been troubling him. A sermon title has an important mission, and is well worth the time it takes to think about it. Of course, if a title is merely a tricky play on words designed to attract a crowd without being backed by a sermon of substance, then the disappointed visitors will be unlikely to return.

Other "hooks" used to attract visitors through advertising include outstanding musicians, musical groups, guest speakers, films, dramatic presentations, and other special events. But remember that people have reasons for selecting a new church beyond programming. Some are looking for a truly friendly church, a church with excellent facilities for baby care, a church with adequate off-street parking, a church with a ministry to single adults, or a church with a sanctuary that can be reached without climbing stairs. Church advertising needs to point out such benefits to the general public.

Pastors want to attract new people to their congregations. This is right. Advertising is one important means to create that attraction.

Money paid for advertising must be viewed as an investment, not an expense. The object of the investment is to attract more people to visit the church, accept the gospel, and become a part of the congregation. Whenever church advertising contributes to someone being added to the congregation, the money invested is being recovered many times over. From a spiritual point of view, it can be said that money spent in advertising to bring the unconverted to church is money invested in soul winning. The dividends from such investments are unending.

Where then should the church's advertising budget be invested? It should be invested where it proves to bring the best response. That does not mean a pastor should select only one avenue of advertising. He should try a variety of methods, carefully evaluate the response to each method, then adopt the combination of advertising media that produces the highest return for the money invested.

NEWSPAPER ADVERTISING

Size. Newspapers charge for display advertising by the column-inch. An ad that is one column wide and 5 inches deep is charged on the basis of five times the per-inch rate. If an ad is two columns wide by 5 inches deep, the charge is 10 times the per-inch rate, and so forth. Some small-circulation papers have a very low rate, while major newspapers have a substantial per-inch charge.

A pastor must learn which newspaper reaches most of the people he seeks to attract to his church. In some instances this may be a neighborhood weekly that is delivered to every home in the area without charge. After he has determined which paper he should use, the cost of advertising space will influence the size ad he will purchase. Variety is important in advertising, and that means changing ad sizes from time to time—sometimes a tall one-column ad, sometimes a square ad, and sometimes a short, wide ad. But continuity is also important in ads—that's why a brand name like *Coca Cola* is almost always printed in the same script, and *Coke* appears in but one kind of type on an unending parade of soft drink ads. Churches need identification with the public just as products do, so a church is wise to ask a commercial artist to design the church name in attractive lettering for use in advertising. A simple map should be drawn if an address alone is not adequate for newcomers to find the church.

Layout. The theme of an ad helps to determine the way that ad will be designed. If a guest speaker is to be featured, his photograph will be given prominence—a one-column ad can do it. If a group is to be featured, the ad may need to be two or three columns wide. If a dynamic sermon topic—perhaps on a controversial subject—is to be featured, then an investment in a large ad with big type might be appropriate.

The purpose of ad layout is not so much art as it is communication. Newspapers provide column-ruled sheets for use in designing ads. By using a felt-tip pen the pastor can draw his ad as close as possible to the way he wants it to appear in the paper. Copy for the ad should be typed, line for line, with careful attention to spelling. This sheet should be submitted to the paper along with the ad design.

Copy. It is doubtful there are many people who carefully read all church advertisements. People scan such ads, so the object is to catch and stop that scanning eye. That means there must be something unique about the wording of the ad. Perhaps it will be a thought-provoking sermon title, a catchy phrase about the guest singing group, or a line like "professional nursery attendants on duty at all services." The proposed copy for any ad should be examined with this question: If I were not from this church, is there something about the wording of this ad that might make me want to come?

RADIO ADVERTISING

Selecting Stations. In most areas the radio dial is filled with stations across the entire band. Each station has its listeners, so those who buy advertising spots must select the station or stations from which they expect the most likely response to their advertising. If a gospel singing group is to be featured at the church, a series of spots on a station that plays gospel music would be logical. If a country-western singer is coming to the church, spots might gain the most attention on a country-western station. Advertisements about a Bible prophecy speaker might ideally be featured following newscasts on a station that stresses news features.

Copy. Copy for radio spots is different from newscopy. It must be written to fit a specific time frame. The writer does well to read his proposed copy aloud to see if it will fit the 30-second spot he is purchasing. Reading the copy aloud also helps identify wording that may not be easy for the announcer to say or for the listener to understand.

It has been said that you write with your ear for radio. Copy for radio spot announcements needs to be typed, all in capital letters, and triple spaced.

The aim of radio advertising is to catch the casual listener's attention for a few seconds so he will hear and *remember* your message. Unlike the printed word, repetition is required in radio advertising. A church address needs to be repeated; the time and date of the event need to be repeated. This is accomplished in the wording of the spot announcement itself and by repeating the spot several times a day for four or five days, or more.

Music and Special Effects. Radio stations have a wide variety of music and usually some sound-effects records. A trumpet fanfare or the roar of a crowd can serve as an attention-getter for a spot announcement. Countless other devices can be suggested by the station personnel. Of course, gimmicks can never substitute for advertising an event that has merit in itself, but special effects can be an attention-getter. For example: If a musical guest is being advertised, a few bars of his music can open the spot, with copy that reads: "You are listening to the heartwarming voice of _____ who will be in concert this Sunday night at _____."

TELEVISION ADVERTISING

Selecting Stations and Times. The cost of television spot announcements runs so much higher than radio spots that even greater care must be exercised in selecting the station and time for a spot announcement. Advertising rates vary drastically depending on the time of the day or night when a spot is aired.

The impact of television advertising attracts more dollars from the world of merchandising than any other form of communication. And while some may not know it, the cost of spot announcements on this medium is within the grasp of most churches. Pastors owe it to themselves to find out the advertising rates available on the television stations serving their communities.

Production Assistance. Most television stations will provide production assistance to church advertisers. Color slides, words on the screen, videotaped backgrounds, and various camera techniques can be combined to make a truly professional spot announcement. Production costs should be understood by the pastor before making the spot.

Copy. One of the benefits of speaking on television comes from the fact that a script need not be memorized, because the copy can be projected right on the studio camera. This makes it appear the speaker is looking right at the person watching his television set at home. For this reason the copy prepared for use on a television spot needs to have a from-me-to-you personal quality. As is the case with radio copy, it needs to be timed so it will exactly fit the number of seconds purchased.

OUTDOOR ADVERTISING

Church Signs. Even if a church is located on a busy avenue, it can remain virtually unnoticed for lack of an adequate sign. How deflating to hear someone say, "I drive down that street on my way to work every day, but I never noticed your church."

Above all, a church sign should look professional. A pastor would do well to check with zoning officials about the maximum size sign that would be allowed on the church property. Then he should seek the services of a sign company to prepare a sketch of one or more pro- posed signs. Vandalism is a fact of life in many areas, so a sign needs to be reasonably resistant to such damage. Unfortunately, some elaborate signs have been erected only to be devastated by high winds. A simple, sturdy, professionally designed and painted church sign may be as effective as an ornate, expensive, illuminated masterpiece. The lettering needs to be larger on a street with high-speed traffic, while a church on a slow-paced residential street would find a sign with smaller letters quite adequate.

Billboards. Sometimes churches lament about their location, par- ticularly when traffic has been rerouted somewhere else. The answer for the hard-to-find church may well be signs along the well-traveled routes. These signs should not only extend an invitation to your church, they should also tell the traveler how to get there, perhaps with a simplified map. Professional sign companies can assist in ob- taining locations for such signs.

Whenever a large-scale meeting is planned, such as a city-wide evangelistic crusade, contact should be made with the billboard com- panies about the cost of renting several signs as part of the advertising effort. Some churches effectively use billboards as part of their publicity program.

Portable Signs. Illuminated signs with changeable letters are mounted on trailers and available for rent in many cities. Such signs can be attention getters during revival campaigns, vacation Bible schools, and other special events.

Moving-message Signs. Giant signs operated by computers spell out messages in lights to hundreds of passing motorists. These computerized billboards can be utilized for invitations to gospel services, and they can be used imaginatively in other ways for furthering the cause of Christ.

Bus Signs. Both the outside and the inside of public buses provide space for advertising. The rates are usually reasonable, so a pastor should investigate the possibilities of this kind of advertising. Benches at bus stops also provide an inexpensive and appreciated means for getting your church before the public.

PRINTED ADVERTISING

Do you understand such printing terms as "half tone," "duotone," "bleed," "30-percent screen," "font," "letter press," or "offset press"? If not, then it is doubtful that you are properly trained to design printed advertising without some professional help. Print shops are everywhere—some staffed by unimaginative press operators who will deliver what you order just as plain and simple as you roughed it out on a sheet of paper; others have staff members who will respond with creative enthusiasm if only the customer will ask for help. The most inexpensive type is sought out by all too many pastors, when the high-quality creative craftsman is what churches really need.

The printing craft may be somewhat mysterious to a clergyman—that's to be expected. Therefore, a clergyman needs a qualified advisor in the printing trade. A minister should discuss any item he wants in printed form with his printing advisor, allowing him to make suggestions about the type faces that might be used, how color solids and screens could be included, how a unique fold might be employed, and so forth.

Handbills. When a special event is scheduled, one of the best ways to get people involved in spreading the word is to provide them with handbills announcing the event. There is a direct relationship between the attractiveness of a printed piece and the willingness people have toward distributing it. Crudely worded copy printed in black ink on

cheap paper has very little appeal to anybody—to the one who is supposed to hand it out or to the one who is supposed to receive it. On
the other hand, a printed piece that is colorful, attractive, warm, and
inviting can help in recruiting volunteers for neighborhood distribution campaigns, as well as in motivating those who seldom get involved to pick up a few copies of the attractive invitation to share
with their close friends and relatives.

There is no rule that says a handbill must be a flat miniature
poster. All kinds of novel ideas can be employed to make a distribution piece unique. For example, a cute baby picture might be featured
on the cover, with an intriguing line of copy like: "Want to know
why I'm so happy?" Many a person will retain a picture of a darling
baby when they would not ordinarily give a second glance to regular
church publicity.

Perhaps the term *handbill* is completely outmoded. What a church
needs is creatively designed printed material that will attract people
first to itself, then to the church it represents.

Posters. In most communities merchants will cooperate with
churches by allowing them to place posters in the windows of their
business establishments. Printed posters need a rather large
photograph to attract interest, with the who, where, and when in
large readable type. Ask the printer for advice in using color borders
around the photo; a block of color can also draw attention to the
poster.

Whoever is assigned to poster distribution needs instruction before
visiting businesses. The volunteers should be told to obtain permission
from the manager or owner of a business before placing a poster in a
window. Easily removable tape should be carried by the volunteers
for use when needed. Finally, there should be a follow-up crew to take
down the posters when the advertised event is over. Proper manners in
one poster campaign will leave the doors open for future efforts.

Bumper Stickers. Signs and witty sayings seem to be on everybody's
vehicles. Reading these signs while waiting for signal lights takes some
of the boredom out of errands. The trick in creating a bumper sticker
is to make it so clever that a driver will point it out to his passenger.
"I Attend First Church—Why Don't You?" may create a negative
response. But a frowning face with "Need a Face Lift? Try First
Church!" may bring a friendly grin.

Be sure to discuss the quality of materials to be used in printing bumper stickers. Some glue backings are almost impossible to remove. Some paper deteriorates rapidly, and some inks fade quickly" A plastic-type material, with easily removed glue and nonfading inks, is preferred, even though the cost may be somewhat higher.

Other Printed Advertising. Every time some new kind of printed advertising is needed, it is wise to consult a creative person who is knowledgeable about printing. Originality is often the key to a successful advertising effort. It should go without saying that Christian principles should never be trampled on by anything that is printed for a church. Nothing trashy, garish, or in bad taste need ever be distributed in the name of "originality." Good church advertising must create goodwill toward the church it represents. Only harm results from printed materials designed to attack other churches. How sad that so much printers' ink has been spilled in hate campaigns. Such so-called advertising only serves to soil the hands of those who distribute it.

YELLOW PAGES ADVERTISING

Many churches are listed in the yellow pages of most telephone directories. There they are, stacked neatly according to denomination— listing church name, address, phone number, pastor's name, and maybe, just maybe, the schedule of services or the existence of a day-care center. Some churches have their listing in a box, at a small extra fee.

But a pastor needs to place himself in the shoes of a newcomer to his city. That newcomer wants to find a church of his denomination or at least one like the one he attended back home. So what does he do? More often than not he looks in the yellow pages. Remember, he is new in town, so street addresses mean very little to him. A church can make it easy for newcomers to visit by purchasing a one-column by 2-inch display ad in the yellow pages. That ad can include a simple map showing the location of the church in relation to main highways; it can provide additional information about the church, and it can urge newcomers to visit. The charge for such advertising is billed monthly with the church telephone. The cost of such an ad is probably higher than a newspaper ad, but the yellow pages attracts newcomers—a prime target in church advertising.

SPECIALTY ADVERTISING

Every few days a church mailbox contains offers for specialty items to be imprinted with the church name—pencils, pens, bookmarks, key chains. Such items can prove useful for gifts on Mother's Day, Father's Day, and other occasions.

Occasionally the church telephone carries the voice of a friendly salesman offering some sort of advertising opportunity that will assist some service club with a fund-raising effort. Naturally, a pastor does not want to lose the goodwill of these organizations, but the true advertising worth of some offers is doubtful.

Motel and Restaurant Directories. In smaller towns there may be some merit in listing all the churches on attractive display boards—a service offered by some firms. Such a feature would have merit in the motel lobbies and restaurant entrances of a small resort community. But in cities of a larger size, the yellow pages provides a more logical place for tourists to check when looking for a church to visit.

Ads in Programs for Community Events. Goodwill is part of the goal in publicity. And goodwill is probably the primary good gained by a church ad in the printed program of an event sponsored by one of the service clubs in a community. The church will want to evaluate carefully each opportunity to determine whether the possible good justifies the expenditure.

Publicity: Your Church Image Is on the Line!

What comes into an individual's mind when someone mentions a particular church? Does he think: "That's the run-down building on Cedar Street." Or, does he think: "That's the church over on Cedar Street that has such big crowds on Sunday nights." Whatever comes to mind when a person thinks of a specific church can be defined as that church's "image," so far as that person is concerned.

While it is true every person may have a different impression of a church, it is also true the church itself carries the responsibility for achieving a positive image in the minds of the majority of people. That means a church's image is always on the line. Everything the church is, says, or does will have an effect on the mind of someone. One massive publicity campaign cannot offset the accumulated impressions made by the church in its sundry contacts with the people.

LETTERS

The church's image travels with every letter sent. There is no such thing as an unimportant church letter. An attractively designed letterhead can help present your church in a good light. It must be remembered that church stationery should not have the appearance of a promotional folder. Not only is gaudy stationery in bad taste for a church, but a clutter of pictures and copy on the letterhead detracts from the content of a letter.

Personal Letters. Any letter sent to one address only is a personal letter. The writer of the letter is a person and the one who reads it is a person. If this simple fact is ignored, letters written to businesses can end up sounding abrupt or harsh. Never forget the reputation of the church rides in some measure with every letter sent by the church. A neatly typed, well-worded letter not only conveys the message of the writer, but it also gives the recipient a favorable impression of the church. The exact opposite occurs when a church letter is sloppy in appearance and filled with poor grammar and misspellings.

Among the most important personal letters sent by a church are those written to first-time visitors. There is a strong temptation to use a duplicated form letter in response to those who sign the church guest book or complete a visitor's card. A selection of predictated letters is practical, including one for local married couples, one for single visitors, and suitable letters for out-of-town visitors. But since visitors are prime prospects for the church, every effort should be made to impress these people favorably—and a form letter can never equal a personal letter for impact.

Some churches have experienced difficulty in motivating visitors to complete visitor's cards. This problem can be overcome by offering a gift to the visitor. "Please fill out the visitor's card you will find in the pew rack. We will send an attractive gift to you." Cloth bookmarks and inexpensive books are suitable for this purpose, and the cost is well repaid by the goodwill that can be won.

Duplicated Letters. Duplicated letters tend to sound distant and impersonal. This common fault of form letters results from the writer being too conscious of the fact that many people will be receiving the letter. Instead of carrying a tone that says, "I'm talking to you, my friend," the letter seems to say, "I'm talking to a large crowd, and you are merely a part of that crowd."

Much could be said about duplicating equipment. Office supply companies offer a wide variety of mimeographs, duplicators, multilith presses, and so forth. Each church should invest in the best equipment it can afford. However, even the best equipment can do nothing more than reproduce the wording fed into it. If the wording of a letter tends to be impersonal, that letter will have minimal impact regardless of how well it is printed.

How does a writer make a letter personal? The answer is simple: write the letter to *one person*. Forget the fact that many copies are to be mailed. Mentally picture one person and write a personal letter that you believe will motivate him to respond in the way you desire— to attend the meeting, to give to the cause, to understand the problem, to volunteer his services. That letter, written to one person, will be much more suitable for duplication than one that begins: "Dear church friends," and then continues to speak in plurals, such as "all of you" and "everyone is invited."

MAILINGS

Many churches have found it profitable to develop and use a mailing list. But poorly done publicity by mail can be worse than none at all, so a pastor needs to be well-informed and properly equipped before launching a mailing program. Perhaps the first place to visit is the local post office. Ask the postmaster to explain the costs and requirements of the mailing options open to churches. If one or more possibilities seem to fit your plans and budget, then the next step is to be certain you have the addressing, duplicating, and folding equipment to handle the job. At least one more consideration must be answered: Do you have sufficient time to invest in preparing the mailings you hope to send?

Midweek Bulletins. A weekly bulletin can keep everyone on your list informed about upcoming church events. It can be an effective publicity tool, provided it reaches your audience well in advance of the events it is announcing. Experience will prove just how well the post office services the mail handled under the class of permit your church uses. It should be noted that permit mail is set aside during the rush of Christmas (check the dates involved at your post office).

A midweek bulletin becomes a mirror reflecting your church. Two extremes should be avoided. The first is a bulletin that makes the church look bad—sloppy duplicating, inept wording, and clumsy typing. The other extreme is a bulletin so elaborate that the best part of a planned event is the flowing verbal picture carried in the mailer. Writers of midweek bulletins need to beware of overselling, and thus destroying the credibility of both the publication and the church.

Calendars. The once-a-month mailing of a church calendar can provide those on your mailing list with a covenient summary of church events. Ideally, such a mailing should be posted in each recipient's home, but it is naive to believe this will actually be the case. Another problem is that such a publication tends to make the church program seem overly repetitious.

A monthly mailing that stresses only special events for the month ahead will avoid the problem of repetition, but the events scheduled for late in the month will receive less publicity value than those coming immediately after the mailing is received.

Newsletters. When an event of outstanding interest is scheduled, a newsletter can be prepared that will build interest and participation in that event. But sometimes a newsletter designed to inform, rather than promote, should be used. Much goodwill can be built through an interesting and informative letter that reports on topics of interest such as progress in the building program, increases in missionary giving, reports from missionaries the church supports, or recent developments in the Sunday school or youth department.

IN-CHURCH PUBLICITY

Neither the exteriors nor the interiors of some churches ever change; other churches have new banners, new posters, and new displays almost every week. While a certain sense of constancy is evoked by unchanging surroundings for worship, a sense of monotony can also emerge. And the church that engages in an unending series of promotional events also courts the danger of monotony. Monotony is a deadly foe of spiritual vitality.

Posters and Banners. If any church-sponsored event succeeds, it will do so first because the people of the church get excited about it. The place where these people can best be reached is obviously *within the church.* And the time to get excitement going is before the special event starts. That means banners should be in place 2 or 3 weeks before the great rally, missionary convention, or evangelistic crusade. Where the banners should be placed depends on the design of the building. Each major entry area should have an appropriate banner. Not every sanctuary lends itself to the display of banners, but when a banner can be displayed before the entire congregation, it will have a powerful impact.

Unless the church has an exceptionally skilled volunteer sign painter, the services of a professional sign shop should be secured. The comparatively small cost of a truly well-executed banner will far outweigh the weak impact of a hard-to-read and distractingly amateurish sign.

On the other hand, volunteer help can be used for posters to be placed in assembly halls and classrooms. In fact, those assigned to work on the posters will become knowledgeable about the event their posters are promoting and will help spread the word to their acquaintances. For some events preprinted posters are available, so all the volunteers need do is add the date and time. To avoid posters being taped to walls where paint or wood finishes might be damaged, a responsible person needs to be in charge of any poster project.

Bulletin Boards. Strategically located bulletin boards, readily seen in entrances and lobby areas, can be ideal for in-church publicity notices, if they are properly used. All too often a church bulletin board becomes a catchall cluttered with everything from thank-you notes and missionary letters to posters of events both past and future.

For bulletin boards to serve as a publicity vehicle, not more than one or two events should be publicized at any one time. If missionary letters are to be posted, a special bulletin board should be reserved for that purpose. It may also be appropriate to reserve another bulletin board for "miscellaneous notices." But to imagine publicity posters will gain attention when they are mixed with everything else is wishful thinking. Some bulletin boards should be reserved for special events. That means there will be times when these boards are empty. But by using them only when an event is to be promoted, their promotional power will be increased,

Although pulpit announcements are covered in another chapter, it is appropriate here to remind the reader the most important publicity vehicle is the oral announcement to the assembled congregation.

Literature Racks and Tables. Every member of a congregation serves as a publicity agent for the church in a greater or lesser degree. One way of increasing the outreach effectiveness of regular attenders is to provide them with up-to-date gospel literature that has been stamped with the church's name and address. Carefully selected tracts and booklets should be attractively displayed in an easily accessible place. From time to time the congregation should be urged to visit the literature rack and obtain suitable tracts to share with their friends and neighbors.

Weekly denominational papers and other publications, such as daily devotional guides, should be made available to members and visitors. A church needs a cabinet or table designed for this purpose. Sometimes the same table contains the guest register. Care needs to be exercised that the table does not become a place for nonessential items, like Bibles left in the pews or other lost-and-found things.

PRINTED PUBLICITY

Church Brochures. A printed folder that describes what your church has to offer can be an excellent publicity tool. Such a folder need not be elaborate to be effective. The front cover will probably feature a recent photograph of the church; the other panels will contain copy and pictures of what the church provides in Christian education, youth activities, and other ministries. Guidance should be obtained from the printer during the design stage of such a folder. Such matters as the size and quality of paper and the shop's folding capabilities need to be discussed.

Some churches produce very elaborate full-color brochures describing their various ministries. The impact of such impressive publicity is strong, but it can also be very expensive. One consideration affecting the cost of printing anything is the quantity to be printed. If a very large number is to be printed, the cost per copy becomes rather small compared to the cost of printing only a limited number of copies. So when a wide distribution effort is planned—5,000 or more—the per-unit cost of a specially printed folder can be quite reasonable.

Pictorial Directories. One way to produce a publicity booklet with no direct cost to the church is to work with one of the several companies that produce pictorial directories for churches. Such a project has its pitfalls. The company sets up a temporary photography studio in the church. Church families are asked to schedule appointments with the photographer. Total cooperation on the part of the church-goers is expected but seldom achieved. People soon learn the photographer is going to try to sell extra pictures for home and friends—that's what finances the pictorial directory. Some families resent the implied obligation to buy additional pictures.

, So a church should exercise care in entering a contract with a pictorial directory company. The better companies try to protect the church's relationships with members. These companies also seek to produce a booklet that not only contains photographs of those attending the church, but they also cooperate in taking the photographs requested by the church to make the publication into an attractive publicity booklet for church visitors or prospective members. Of course, the church should expect the company to provide an ample supply of the books for publicity use, beyond the copies given to those who are pictured.

Telephone Directories. Churchgoers appreciate a simple booklet listing the names, addresses, and telephone numbers of the people who attend. In some cases, the business people of the congregation are willing to place ads in a church telephone directory. Although not an obvious publicity tool, such a booklet can provide much goodwill and information for newcomers. Care should be exercised in preparing a directory of any kind—no one likes being left out. Also attention should be given to the accuracy of names, addresses, and telephone numbers.

Visitor's Cards. Some churches obtain visitor's cards from almost every guest, while other churches with about the same number of guests have little success in getting those guests to turn in their cards. The difference is motivation. If visitor's cards are placed in pew racks with no attention drawn to them, it is no wonder the visitors ignore them. If the pastor·welcomes visitors and encourages them to complete the cards, so much the better. But if the visitors are told they will be sent a gift because they complete the card, then the percentage of response takes a sharp turn upward.

Ideally a church should have its own visitor's cards, preferably printed on stock of a distinctive color. It is helpful to list: Mr., Mrs., Miss, and Mr. & Mrs. The guest then circles the appropriate title followed by his name, address, and telephone number. The card should contain a brief welcome to the church and also state that a gift will be sent if the completed card is placed in the offering. Some churches ask the visitor to indicate his reason for visiting. The card can list the various kinds of advertising the church uses with a box by each. The boxes checked by the visitors will help the pastor in analyzing the effectiveness of his advertising.

DUPLICATED PUBLICITY

Expensive equipment can never substitute for creative thinking; the publicity value of a duplicating machine depends more on the originator than it does on the machine. But the fact remains that machines wear out, and worn-out equipment can seriously detract from the appearance and effectiveness of duplicated church publicity. Usually a major overhaul by a qualified repairman can restore an older machine, but sometimes the only answer is replacement.

Sunday Bulletins. Some churches prefer to use a personalized bulletin cover that features a photograph of either the sanctuary or the exterior of the church. Some elect to imprint the back cover with information covering regular church activities, then mimeograph special announcements on the inside pages. Other churches leave the back cover blank to provide additional space for mimeographed copy. Several companies offer weekly bulletin covers with a different full-color cover for each Sunday (usually they can be ordered with brief essays or poems on the back cover or with that area blank). The church name can be imprinted by the company at a minimal charge.

Great care should be exercised by the person who prepares the bulletin stencil to check the accuracy of dates, times, places, and spelling. Mistakes and misspellings harm the publicity value of a bulletin.

Special Emphasis Bulletins. An event of major importance may require its own bulletin. A special bulletin can be prepared to promote an upcoming vacation Bible school, an Easter or Christmas play, a missionary convention, or a protracted meeting. Not only does the special bulletin give added space to describe details of the planned event, it also lifts that event to something beyond routine church activities. Of course, additional copies of special bulletins should be made available to churchgoers for distribution among their neighbors.

Telephone Calls

A voice with a smile should answer a church telephone. The image of the church is on the line every time the telephone rings. The caller may be a brokenhearted person seeking spiritual help, and the tone of voice he detects can profoundly alter whether or not he will ask for counsel or turn to another source.

Telephone Manners. Good public relations requires good telephone manners. Not that an incoming call should receive top priority. A pastor interrupted by the telephone while in a counseling session should graciously offer to call back later. If he has a secretary, she should be instructed about when phone callers are to be told he is not available. It is wise for the secretary to learn the name of a caller before explaining the pastor is not available. She should then make a notation of the caller's name. In that way, the minister can return the call as soon as it is convenient. Returning such calls with as little delay as possible promotes good public relations.

Promotion via Telephone. Although it is one of the best communication devices available, the telephone is seldom thought of as a promotional tool. A church would be wise to prepare a telephone list similar to a mailing list. Just prior to a special event, a group of telephone volunteers can be instructed about what needs to be said as they contact the persons on the list.

Another use for telephone volunteers develops in connection with a church's radio or television ministry. Listeners can be urged to call in for spiritual help and trained counselors can be on hand to minister to the callers.

Automated Telephone Messages. The recorded telephone message is becoming commonplace. Individuals who call when no one is present to answer the telephone are invited by a recorded voice to leave a message. A church may wish to use such equipment. If so, the all-important thing to remember is that good public relations requires a minister call back promptly.

Dial-a-prayer and dial-a-sermon have been used with high levels of response. A pastor may wish to contact the telephone company about the possibility of such a service. The important key is to find a way to let the public know this telephone ministry is available. Newspaper ads or radio spots can point people to the special telephone number.

The recorded message should conclude with an invitation to the sponsoring church.

Church Appearance: That Building Speaks to Passersby

A congregation may be a spiritual powerhouse, but if it is housed in a shabby building, its full potential will never be realized. It is not a question of whether the building is made of marble or lumber; it's a question of upkeep. Is the paint in good condition? Do rock surfaces need to be sandblasted? Is the parking lot a weed patch? The answers to these and similar questions determine to a large extent how a church's spiritual worth is estimated by outsiders.

EXTERIOR APPEARANCE

The Church Building. However humble it may seem now, that church made its members proud when it was first erected. If there is reason to be ashamed of it now, the reason is related to lack of maintenance. Sometimes volunteer work is the solution; sometimes it is the problem.

A pastor needs to put himself in the place of an outsider while looking at the exterior appearance of his church. What is the condition of the brick, stone, lumber, or other materials? Is painting all that is needed—or do carpentry repairs need to be done first? Should a specialist be contacted for advice? Cost estimates should be obtained and a financial plan mapped out. Every day that passes without improving a church's shoddy appearance costs the congregation in public relations and in the loss of potential newcomers.

Other Buildings on Church Property. It may be a large educational unit or a small storage building, but if it is located on church property its appearance cannot be ignored. Every building belonging to a church is the responsibility of the congregation. Neighbors in the immediate vicinity rightfully expect upkeep to be maintained on all the buildings located on the church property. When this is done, the church is a credit to the neighborhood. A building need not be new to be neat.

There is something reassuring to a visitor as he stands outside a church building that has been kept in good condition. The clean walls, the sparkling windows, the polished doors—everything about the building tells the visitor this congregation loves its church. So he enters with high expectations.

Shrubs, Trees, Lawns, and Flowers. Some churches are located on a large acreage with wide expanses of grass and numerous shrubs and tress. Other churches have just a tiny lawn next to the sidewalk. Large or small, a lawn needs constant care. Well-groomed landscaping conveys the instant impression that a church is beloved of its members. Maybe the shrubs are shouting something negative about the church.

The advice of a nurseryman should be obtained if it appears that some shrubs or trees have grown so large they detract from, instead of add to, the appearance of the building. Some shrubs can be trimmed successfully; others cannot and should be replaced. Uncontrolled shrubbery detracts from the entrance of a church and sometimes even partially blocks the entryway.

Trees that once were graceful can grow into monstrosities with huge limbs that create strange noises as they rub against the church roof. Some trees can be trimmed; others should be removed. Care should be taken to explain to the congregation why it will be necessary to remove trees—sometimes a sentimental attachment exists and a pastor is wise to share the reasoning behind such decisions. Of course, a church that is concerned with good public relations will see to it that leaves are raked at least once a week during the fall. Nobody wants to rake leaves that have blown over to his yard from a neighbor's tree, especially if that neighbor is a church.

Church lawns are a quiet advertisement—either they commend the church or they condemn it. In days of water shortages and high temperatures, a church may not be allowed to water its lawn. But when water is available, there is no excuse for a burned-up church lawn. It is good public relations to have a lawn that is healthy and green. A church lawn should show evidence of loving care. It should have a "manicured" appearance—with its edges trimmed along all sidewalks and flowerbeds, with no long blades next to buildings, and with a minimum of weeds. Remember that people walk across lawns, so they should be safe, with no unexpected dips or hidden holes. Whoever mows the lawn should understand his job is not finished until excess grass clippings have been removed from the lawn and all sidewalks have been swept clean. Grass clippings should be carefully brushed out of flowerbeds so the plants will not be harmed.

In some parts of the country flowers thrive throughout most of the year. A beautiful flowerbed can brighten a church property as nothing else can. But flowers require unending care, so responsibility for perpetual care must be accepted before a flower garden is established. Better no flowers at all than a few blossoms struggling to survive in a weed-infested plot.

Parking Facilities, Driveways, and Sidewalks. There is something very inviting about a spacious parking lot to a car full of church visitors. Ample space is provided for each car in clearly marked spaces. The lot is smoothly paved and there is an attractive entrance into the church building. At night floodlights contribute to a sense of safety and security, so there is no hesitancy about attending evening services. Yes, an attractive parking lot extends a warm welcome for the church it serves.

On the other hand, consider the visitor's response to: a three-block run in the rain because no off-street parking is available; wading through muddy gravel in Sunday shoes; trembling in a dark, gloomy place for fear of muggers; or stumbling across a rock-strewn, weed-covered field where cars park helter-skelter. Can it be said a correlation exists between the condition of a church's parking lot and that church's outreach? It most certainly can! Therefore, adequate plans must be made to facilitate parking in the first place, and an ongoing program for maintaining all parking areas must be adopted after that.

Some churches provide driveways where passengers can step out at a covered entrance before the driver parks the automobile. Such driveways must be clearly marked and supervision should be provided to avoid traffic being blocked. Special consideration should be provided for assisting handicapped persons, with designated parking areas for their convenience.

Lawsuits can be filed by anyone who is injured as a result of improperly maintained sidewalks. But liability should not be the prime reason for a church keeping walks in good repair. It is a matter of maintaining the goodwill of both those who attend services and those who walk past the church during the week.

Lighting. Good exterior lighting is indispensable to safety before and after evening church services. But in addition to an adequate system of lighting during services, a church is wise to have a system of illumination throughout the night for two reasons: (1) a lighted building is much less likely to be a target for vandals or burglars; (2) a properly illuminated building is an all-night advertisement of the church. Strategically placed floodlights, operated by a light sensor or timer switches, are a wise investment.

Buses. The condition and appearance of a church bus is almost as important—in terms of public relations—as the condition and appearance of the church building itself. A bus becomes a moving billboard proclaiming a message about the church that owns it. Safety is paramount. To claim to be concerned about souls and then place people in a vehicle that imperils their lives is totally inconsistent and unforgivable for anyone who claims to be a representative of Jesus Christ. Next to safety comes the appearance of the bus, both outside and inside. A church bus should be clean. It should not be rusty. Its upholstery should be in good repair. And, above all, it should be driven in strict obedience to all traffic laws and with an extra measure of courtesy for pedestrians and vehicles because the bus represents the church.

INTERIOR APPEARANCE

Everything said about the exterior appearance of a church is also true for the inside of the building. Soiled carpets, dirty walls, scratched furnishings, musty smells—all these provide reasons why a prospective member might turn away from attending the church. A beautifully maintained interior tells the prospect the congregation loves its church, and the visitor feels he would be proud to call it his church home.

Good Housekeeping. Hard-surfaced floors should be clean and waxed (but not slippery). Carpeted floors should be vacuumed and free from stains. All furnishings and windowsills should be free from dust. Restrooms—and this is important—must be odorless and spotless! Although they may not admit it, visitors have sought out another church because of decrepit plumbing facilities in the first church they selected. The church needs to be reminded that service station chains have attracted millions of customers by their reputations for clean restrooms.

Bibles, umbrellas, sweaters, and other assorted personal belongings should never be allowed to clutter the lobby or any other place where they will detract from the neatness of the church. Such items should be gathered after each service and placed in a designated lost-and-found storage area.

Displays. Churches occasionally receive trophies in recognition for achievements in stewardship, interchurch competition in sports, Bible quiz contests, and other events. Those who participated in winning the trophy are justly proud. A church shows wisdom when it cares for such trophies by providing a case with a locking glass door. When trophies exposed on open shelves are allowed to become dusty, broken, and in disarray, those who won the events may be offended and an opportunity for making a favorable impression on visitors is lost.

Many churches seek to emphasize their worldwide vision by featuring a missions display in a selected location. These displays usually include pictures of the missionaries being supported. Sometimes a world map is posted with each missionary's location identified. While a missionary display is seldom thought of as a publicity tool, it should be. It quietly informs visitors about the church's concern for the people of other lands. Properly maintained, with nicely framed support certificates and an up-to-date map, it says: "We care about missionaries and about those they seek to reach with the gospel." If, however, such a display consists of faded snapshots, unframed certificates, a wrinkled map, and outdated letters, then the visitor receives the impression the church has almost forgotten its missionaries.

Safety. Regular inspection tours should be taken through all the church facilities by the pastor to identify any situation that might result in someone being injured. These troubled spots must be remedied without delay. Great harm can come to a church when someone is injured as a result of negligence.

THE PASTOR'S HOME

Whether a pastor lives in a parsonage or in a home he owns, he is known by his neighbors as the pastor of that church. The way his yard and home are maintained is a reflection on his church.

Someone has said the Great Commission begins at the house next door then swings clear around the world until it touches the house on the other side of where you live. That means everyone who has contact with us must be an object of our Christlike concern. No one is unimportant—that is why good public relations is an integral part of good Christianity.

Suggested Reading

Craig, Floyd A. *Christian Communicator's Handbook for Local Congregations of All Denominations.* Nashville: Broadman Press, 1969.

Fields, Wilmer C. *Religious Public Relations Handbook.* New York: The Religious Public Relations Council, Inc., 1976.

Graves, Allen W. *Using and Maintaining Church Property.* Englewood Cliffs, NJ: Prentice-Hall, Inc., 1965.

Johnson, Philip A.; Norman Temme; and Charles C. Hushaw. *Telling the Good News: A Public Relations Handbook for Churches.* St. Louis: Concordia Publishing House, 1962.

McLuhan, Marshall. *Understanding Media: The Extensions of Man.* New York: McGraw-Hill, 1964.

Mecca, Raymond G. *Your Church Is News.* Philadelphia: Judson Press, 1975.

Stoody, Ralph. *A Handbook of Church Public Relations.* New York: Abingdon Press, 1959.

Stuber, Stanley I. *Public Relations Manual for Churches.* New York: Doubleday and Company, 1951.

15

The Pastor
and
Administration

JAMES E. HAMILL

Administration is the name given to a comprehensive and essential function in any society which carries on through the instrumentality of numerous organizations. It is the function within an organization which is responsible for establishing its objects, purposes, aims or ends, for implementing the necessary organizing and operating steps, and for assuring adequate performance toward the desired end.[1]

An *organization* is a deliberate association of persons who desire to accomplish something together or to realize certain common objectives. The individual members become a part of the large organization because they cannot by themselves achieve these objectives as well, if indeed they can achieve them at all. The *administrator* is charged with the responsibility of directing and facilitating the objectives, purposes, aims, and ends of the organization.

Principles of Administration

ORGANIZATION IS ABSOLUTELY NECESSARY

The eternal purpose and mission of the church of Jesus Christ is to worship God, minister to believers, and evangelize the world. If one is to fulfill that mission, he must plan his efforts and join with others in carrying them out most effectively. Planning, programming, and uniting one's efforts with others is another definition of organization. Good organization is one of the basic factors in a successful church.

James E. Hamill, D.D., is pastor of First Assembly of God, Memphis, Tennessee.

[1]From *The Art of Administration* by Ordway Tead. Copyright © 1951. Used by permission by McGraw-Hill Book Company.

God planned and organized in the Creation. The plan of redemption, conceived before the foundation of the world, was a well organized undertaking. That organization is obvious throughout the Old Testament. In speaking of Christ's coming to the world, His death on the cross, and His resurrection from the dead, the Bible uses the phrase "in the fullness of time" again and again. Whose time? God's time—in the fullness of that time which God had planned.

Jesus planned and organized. He said often, "My hour hath not yet come," or, "My hour is come." Jesus came into the world according to an eternal and divine plan. He was born in Bethlehem, lived in Nazareth, went to Egypt, rode into Jerusalem, was sold for 30 pieces of silver; He was crucified, buried, and arose on the third day—all in the divine plan of God.

The followers of Jesus were organized into groups: the 70 witnesses, the 12 disciples, the three members of the inner circle, the treasurer. When Jesus fed the 5,000 with fish and loaves, the Scriptures tell us He had the disciples divide the people into groups of 50. That is organization.

Our Lord calls a man foolish who would try to build a structure without some real planning and counting the cost. Or what king, He asks, would fight a war without proper planning (Luke 14:28-32)?

The Holy Spirit planned and organized. He had a very definite time and day and place to come into the world and to come upon the disciples: "And when the day of Pentecost was fully come . . ." (Acts 2:1).

The Holy Spirit set in the Church apostles, prophets, evangelists, pastors, and teachers, "for the perfecting of the saints, for the work of the ministry, for the edifying of the body of Christ" (Ephesians 4:12). That is organization. The Holy Spirit placed in the Church diversities of gifts. Paul described them as diversities of gifts, differences of administration, diversities of operation (1 Corinthians 12:4-11). That is organization.

The Early Church planned and organized. One of the first problems to arise in the Early Church came about because of a lack of planning and organization. Some of the people in the New Testament church complained the widows and orphans were being neglected in the administering of such things as food and clothing (Acts 6).

ADMINISTRATION OF THE ORGANIZATION IS ESSENTIAL

A good administrator sets forth the purposes, aims, and objectives or ends of the organization he represents. He must recruit and supervise personnel as provided for in the organization. He delegates and allocates authority and responsibility. Finally, he must oversee the general implementation of the activities he has delegated. Among the chief responsibilities of the administrator then are planning, recruiting, delegating, coordinating, and supervising.

The administrator must be a leader—a leader·with vision. Men who have blessed the world, whether in science, medicine, statesmanship, economics, Christianity, or any other field, have been men with a vision. Such men are positive men. The masses will follow leaders who are positive. People are always attracted to something that is moving, dynamic, and full of life; a program or a cause that is going somewhere; or a leader who knows where he is going.

The administrator must provide information, stimulation, and inspiration to accomplish the purpose of the organization. He must be able to evaluate, analyze, plan, and project. He must make provisions for necessary committee meetings, the facilities for such meetings, and the coordination of efforts so the group can achieve the purpose for which it came into being.

The Pastor as an Administrator

It is impossible to separate the work of ministry from that of administration. Linguistically the two words are cognate and for the Christian pastor the two words are inseparable. Administration concerns the total care of the church and may be thought of as including "ministry."[2]

Inasmuch as administration concerns the total care of the church, the success of the pastor and the church will largely be measured by the pastor's success as an administrator.

The word for pastor in the New Testament is *poimen*. It means a shepherd, one who tends herds or flocks (Ephesians 4:11). Pastors guide as well as feed the flock. This ministry of shepherding was committed to the elders who were also overseers (Acts 20:17, 28). Paul says to the

[2]Ralph G. Turnbull, ed., *Baker's Dictionary of Practical Theology* (Grand Rapids: Baker Book House, 1967), p. 314.

elders of the church in Ephesus, "Take heed therefore unto yourselves, and to all the flock, over the which the Holy Ghost hath made you overseers . . ." (verse 28).[3]

The three terms *elder*, *bishop*, and *pastor* are brought together in Acts 20:17, 28. We can therefore conclude that the pastor is an elder or overseer. His work requires tender care and watchful superintendence. The Greek word for "overseer" in the New Testament is *episcopos*. It is usually translated "bishop," but the literal meaning is "overseer." The ultimate responsibility for the organization, supervision, inspiration, and success of a church must largely be accepted by the pastor. Doubtless, many pastors have failed in their total task simply because of their inability as administrators.

The pastor must be the administrator of all the work of the church. Good organization and procedure would make him an *ex officio* member of all committees, boards, and groups in the church. Of course, he is the shepherd of the flock and must not, in his administrative responsibilities, forget his spiritual obligations to those with whom he labors.

COORDINATION OF DEPARTMENTS, FACILITIES, AND PROGRAMS

The pastor should be the most knowledgeable person in the church regarding every facet of its ministry and program. He should be able (for it is his responsibility) to communicate to all individuals, committees, boards, and the total congregation the purposes and priorities of the church as well as the responsibilities of all individuals and groups within the church.

Organizations, groups, and even athletic teams must work together to succeed, accomplish, or win. Without good leadership few organizations succeed and few athletic teams win. In many cases where there is friction, a lack of cooperation, and failure, it is because of a lack of communication, coordination, and effective leadership.

Craig Thomas, a little boy who had gone to school only 2 days, announced to his grandmother, "That teacher and I are going to have trouble." His grandmother inquired, "Why, Craig, what do you mean, have trouble?" The youngster replied, "Well, I can't read, and the teacher won't let me talk." The problem was poor communication, and even the child recognized it would lead to trouble.

---

[3]*Ibid.*, p. 318.

The overlapping of responsibilities and authority by the various departments and personnel can be avoided by a strong administrator who has the total church ministry in focus and is able to coordinate plans, efforts, and facilities.

The coordination of the use of church facilities and equipment is very important to a church whose varied ministry necessitates the multiple use of its facilities and equipment. Some churches, by careful coordination, are able to use the same facilities for Sunday school, youth meetings, senior citizens' activities, men's ministries, women's ministries, and recreation, as well as a day school. The church with many activities of a varied nature will have conflicts and confusion over meeting dates and inadequately prepared facilities unless a coordinator—the pastor or someone he designates—provides direction, assistance, and firm leadership.

A church calendar is absolutely necessary. Every meeting to be held during the year, the date, the time, the room, and the anticipated attendance should be listed on the calendar. A good administrator will see that one group or department does not infringe on the prerogatives of another group. For example, the men's group should not be allowed to plan its meeting on the night that is established as choir rehearsal night; and the day school should not schedule a basketball game in the gym on a night a revival meeting is in progress in the sanctuary.

EFFICIENT DIRECTION AND INVOLVEMENT OF PERSONNEL

No church is stronger than the pastor and the people with whom he surrounds himself. This applies to both paid and volunteer personnel. Too often a pastor finds himself doing menial tasks and attending to matters in the church with which he should not have to bother, simply because he has failed to plan his work and organize his congregation. His time is taken up "majoring in minors," rather than doing the primary work God has called him to do.

The first seven deacons were appointed so the apostles could give themselves to prayer and to the studying and preaching of the Word (Acts 6). It should be noted that the pastors of the New Testament church provided for the selection of these men to administer the ordinary, but nevertheless important, affairs.

One of the tragedies of the ministry in this day is the lack of time the pastor has to devote to prayer, to studying the Word, and to feeding the flock over which God has made him overseer. The average pastor's time is taken up with so many minor tasks and secondary matters that he has little time left for his primary responsibility. Woodrow Wilson often spoke about men who were "defeated by the secondary."

A good pastor is one who understands his priorities—what is major and what is minor, what is primary and what is secondary. He then organizes his time, his efforts, and his congregation in a manner that will give him time to pursue the major tasks. This can only be done successfully when the pastor is a good administrator and is able to assign to others the secondary tasks.

One of the prerequisites for leadership is the ability to communicate vision, faith, dreams, concerns, and desires to others and to inspire and encourage them to assist the leader in reaching those goals. No one is better qualified than the pastor to direct and involve the total congregation and the individual member in the work of the Lord. As the administrator of the church, the pastor is able to coordinate all the services, facilities, personnel, and ministries to assure a smooth operation of the total church program and ministry.

Administration of the Total Church Program

There are seven basic factors in church growth; and effective administration must be concerned with all of them: spirituality, personnel, organization, facilities, promotion, follow-up, and hard work.

PLACING SPIRITUAL MATTERS FIRST

The pastor is the chief human administrator in the spiritual work of the church. The use of the term *administration* in relation to the spiritual emphasis and environment of a church may seem at first to be a conflict of ideas. But it is not. Although God himself initiates the spiritual life of any group of Christians, He uses the pastor to lead the congregation into deeper spiritual experiences and to direct the efforts of the church in fulfilling the Great Commission.

So the pastor is the God-ordained administrator of the spiritual program of the local church. He administers the ordinances of the church: water baptism and the Lord's Supper. He conducts the rites of the church: weddings, funerals, dedications, installations, and other

functions that are important in the life and ministry of the congregation. The ordinances ought to be administered in such a manner that
they will teach the lessons Jesus intended. The various ceremonies can
be conducted in such a manner that they will become instruments in
fulfilling the mission of the church.

The minister is expected to administer the worship, work, and
witness of the church. This includes the worship services. He should
lead or direct the spiritual services in such a manner that there is a
spiritual warmth and the meetings are Bible-centered, Christ-
honoring, and Spirit-filled.

Worship services, evangelistic meetings, Bible studies, and committee or board sessions should be well planned in every detail and properly announced. All participants should be confirmed. All facilities
must be prepared. All equipment should be checked and in working
order. Nothing should be left to chance in the work of God.

All meetings should begin exactly at the announced time. It is
wrong to have people come for a meeting that was announced for 7
o'clock, only to sit there waiting for the meeting to begin 15 or 20
minutes late. Most intelligent and busy people will not attend such
meetings often. In this organized world, we must move with the clock.
Services should be planned in the most minute detail, yet left flexible
so that if in the planning one misses God's plan, the program can be
changed to accommodate the will of God for that particular service.

So much depends on the minister's own spiritual condition, his attitudes, his responses, his hunger for God, and his desire to lead the
people into genuine worship, intensive study of the Word, and successful service.

Assuring a Strong Fiscal Program

The pastor is responsible for the financial welfare of the church and
the administration of its fiscal program. He is also responsible for
teaching his people both the obligation and the reward of faithfulness
in supporting God's work through tithes and offerings. God's plan for
the financial support for His work on earth was and is the tithe and
offerings of the people. The pastor and church leaders, therefore,
should not hesitate for one moment to speak often and freely about
man's stewardship obligation to God. The Bible is clear and emphatic
in its teaching regarding man and his money.

God's Word emphasizes God's ownership and man's stewardship. Much of the teaching of the Old Testament stressed this important principle. And Jesus spoke often and forcefully concerning man and his money. The majority of His sayings dealt with property and the right use of property. One out of every 60 verses in the four Gospels deals with stewardship. Money is spoken of in the Bible six times more than water baptism and 45 times more than the Lord's Supper.

The church's financial program should be a spiritual program. God's plan for financing His work on earth is a soul-growing, character-developing program. Failure to tithe is not a financial problem but a spiritual problem.

Financial matters of the church of Jesus Christ should be conducted in a precise, sound, and businesslike manner. There should be complete records of receipts, expenditures, and individual donors. There should be and must be regular reports to the board, the church, and the individual member. A church should have an annual certified audit of its financial records. If a certified audit is not feasible, there most certainly should be a professional audit.

Some churches have discovered a better way to operate the financial program and to assure meeting the fiscal obligations is to operate on a strict budget and have the congregation underwrite that budget in advance. Without exception, churches that have launched campaigns to subscribe their budget have experienced remarkable increases financially. One church that collected $142,000 in its total income for the year before going to a subscribed budget, now, after a few years, has a budget approaching $1.5 million. Any size church can and should operate on a budget. A very small or large church can have a pledged budget.

Why subscribe the budget? (1) it makes possible the projection of plans for growth and development; (2) it promises that funds for planned projects will be available; (3) it commits the people to support their church rather than other programs; (4) it provides an increase in the amount most people give to the church; (5) it reveals fiscal responsibility on the part of the church; (6) it becomes a witness of the people's concern for Christ and His church; (7) it makes numerous financial drives and appeals unnecessary; (8) it teaches giving to Christ through the church to the world.

There is a real spiritual value to the individual in making a pledge to the total church budget. Rather than giving to whatever project, program, or person that strikes his fancy, the member is taught to "bring . . . all the tithes into the storehouse," his church (Malachi 3:10).

Steps to take in underwriting the budget are the following: (1) compile and adopt the budget; (2) name a budget campaign committee; (3) persuade the congregation (using bulletins, letters, signs, brochures, newspapers, pulpit announcements, etc.); (4) set the date for Commitment Day several weeks in advance; (5) prepare pledge cards, envelopes, membership lists, etc.; (6) appoint teams to follow up those who do not pledge on Commitment Day (do not antagonize those who refuse to pledge); (7) keep a running report on campaign progress and report regularly to the congregation; and (8) seek to make budget pledging a commitment to God, a spiritual experience.

The pastor, as leader and administrator of the church, is responsible to teach the people of God to give faithfully and generously. Most pastors and congregations do not hesitate to make pledges for missions and other such projects. Why then should we hesitate to make commitments to the total budget of the church of Jesus Christ?

Selection and Supervision of Personnel

Without a proper relationship with God, there is no hope of realizing any measure of genuine success in the ministry. Next to this spiritual relationship, perhaps the most important factor in the ministry of the church is personnel. The qualifications and commitment of the personnel, both professional and volunteer, will determine what the church becomes.

It has been said the great need of the church, if it is to expand and grow, is men and money. If we get the men and lead them into the spiritual experience that is available to them, we will get the money.

VOLUNTEER WORKERS

The pastor is responsible to recruit, train, organize, involve, and direct both voluntary and paid church workers. Churches in most cases need many nonpaid workers for the scores of ministries that must be covered.

Recruiting Volunteer Workers. In these exceedingly busy days, it is not an easy task to recruit volunteer workers for the many tasks of the church. One of the chief complaints of industry and business today is their inability to recruit employees who are energetic, loyal, faithful, enthusiastic, and intelligent. Unfortunately, the same shortage of dedicated workers exists in many churches.

There are several ways a pastor can recruit volunteer workers for the various ministries of the church. First, he should give personal attention to the individual believer. This is more difficult in a church with a large membership, but one thing we must always remember as ministers: we do not deal only with the masses, however large the congregation; we also deal with people individually, one by one. We must lead and direct them as individuals. Individuals make up the masses.

A good administrator of the church will study the individual members in his congregation. He will constantly be on the lookout for those who have talent, those who can be trained and used in God's work, and those whose dedication is such that they are willing to be involved in the work of the church. He will personally solicit them for service in the Lord's army.

Second, the pastor should emphasize the spiritual privileges, opportunities, and responsibilities as he enlists workers. His people should be made to realize that whatever service is rendered, each one is doing it as unto the Lord, and therefore the ministry should be done well.

Third, the pastor can survey the membership periodically. He could provide a card or form for the people to fill out, indicating the kind of service they would like to render to the Lord through their church. New members should also be asked to indicate the service they prefer to render. This type of survey should be made annually.

Training Volunteer Workers. Christian education is indispensable to the ministering church. It should use every means available to teach and train people for places of ministry such as Bible studies, Bible classes, Sunday school, and Christian day school. The Great Commission demands the Church minister to the believer through the teaching of God's Word until that believer is grounded in the eternal Word of God and conformed to the image of Christ. No function of the church is more important than that of teaching. Jesus gathered around Him a small group of people whom He called *disciples* (learners). He taught them about the Kingdom and sent them out to make more disciples or learners.

It has been said teaching was the foundation on which Christianity became strong enough to conquer the Roman world. But a few centuries later when the church failed to teach the essentials of Christianity, it went into decay and civilization entered the Dark Ages. Christianity appeals to the intellect as well as to the heart, and to the heart as well as to the intellect. But saving faith is more than intellectual belief, volitional consent, or emotional response. It is more for the simple reason that it involves all three in a surrender; an affirmation of one's total self—the mind, the heart, and the will.

Many churches fail to grow and fulfill God's purpose and plan for them because the pastor fails to teach, train, and inspire the members to fulfill the eternal purpose of worship, work, and witness. The wise pastor, as the administrator of the church, is constantly seeking out personnel from among his congregation that he can teach and train and use in advancing the cause of Christ. He trains by doing, by finding work to assign to those who have potential.

The apostle Paul, writing to the young preacher Timothy, admonished him to teach by example:

> Let no man despise thy youth; but be thou an example of believers, in word, in conversation, in charity, in spirit, in faith, in purity. . . . Neglect not the gift that is in thee, which was given thee by prophecy, with the laying on of the hands of the presbytery (1 Timothy 4:12, 14).

Paul continued to admonish Timothy:

> Meditate upon these things; give thyself wholly to them; that thy profiting may appear to all. Take heed unto thyself, and unto the doctrine; continue in them: for in doing this thou shalt both save thyself, and them that hear thee (1 Timothy 4:15, 16).

In Paul's second letter to Timothy, he said: "My son, be strong in the grace that is in Christ Jesus. And the things that thou hast heard of me among many witnesses, the same commit thou to faithful men, who shall be able to teach others also" (2 Timothy 2:1, 2). So the minister, the church administrator, by his example is to teach the flock *to do* the work of God as well as to show them *how* to do the work of God.

The apostle Paul admonished Timothy: "Strive not about words to no profit, but to the subverting of the hearers" (2 Timothy 2:14). Then he added: "Shun profane and vain babblings: for they will increase unto more ungodliness" (v. 16). Right between these two verses that tell us not to strive about words to no profit and to shun profane and vain babblings, Paul tells us: "Study to show thyself approved unto God, a workman that needeth not to be ashamed, rightly dividing the word of truth" (v. 15).

The application is clear. If one makes a studied effort to have God's approval and rightly divide the Word of God, he will avoid profane and vain babblings and words of no profit. Then, his preaching and teaching will be with power and authority.

One cannot preach or teach with authority and power without having knowledge. Knowledge is power; knowledge makes for authority. It is true knowledge of the Word of God must be set on fire by the power of the Holy Spirit. One must inspire men to believe God, lead them to choose God, teach them to live for God, and instruct them in service to God.

Qualified and dedicated workers are an absolute essential to the success of any church. They are basic to its growth. No church will ever be larger, more efficient, or more spiritual than its leaders. Lack of adequately trained and motivated personnel is one of the great problems in churches today. The church so desperately needs consecrated, Spirit-filled, and trained lay persons to assist in accomplishing the eternal purpose.

If the church fails, it will fail because it lacks dedicated, committed members who are willing to give themselves unreservedly, energetically, and freely to the work of God. Many business enterprises fail, not because there is no market for their product or no possibility of producing that product at a profit, but because of inefficient personnel. If businessmen have real problems with the personnel they hire, and if they find it difficult to secure efficient, faithful, energetic, and enthusiastic workers for pay, how much more difficult is it to enlist faithful, energetic, efficient, enthusiastic workers for the church who will donate time and energy without financial compensation?

All this points up that the pastor, as an administrator, must be active in recruiting, training, and involving the members of his church in fulfilling the church's mission in today's world.

Leading Volunteer Workers. Inasmuch as the pastor is the chief administrator and leader of the church, it cannot be overemphasized how important it is that the congregation have confidence in him.

They must believe he is a man of God; but they must believe more. They must have confidence in his absolute integrity, his ability to lead, his sincerity of purpose, and his knowledge of God's eternal purpose for the church. When the church membership and the official board have utmost confidence in the pastor, he can do almost anything within reason in carrying out the program and ministry God has laid on his heart.

To build this confidence, the pastor must be absolutely honest with his congregation, with his board, and with others. He must never get himself in a position where the people believe he did not tell them all the truth regarding a matter or that he was endeavoring to mislead them in some matter, however important or essential it seemed to be at the time.

When a pastor's behavior is above reproach, his communication is good, his knowledge gives him command of facts and figures, his integrity is unquestioned, his ability is recognized, and his spirituality is appreciated, he can then lead with authority.

To exercise authority and leadership does not mean to dictate or to be a tyrant, but rather to guide, direct, and lead. For example, in working with a committee, the pastor needs to know how to guide them into programs that will extend the Kingdom. If one is to command respect, he must not major in minors; he must be able to evaluate conscientiously and then have the ability and courage to make proper choices. He cannot vacillate; he must make courageous decisions.

Working with the church board is tremendously important to the pastor's ministry. Many pastors have failed because they did not know just how to work with and lead the officially elected. Before going into a board meeting or a committee meeting of any kind having to do with his church, a pastor must have done his homework. He must know exactly what he is talking about. He must have all the facts and figures at hand. He must talk to such groups with authority, an authority born of knowledge, sincerity, and a desire to do God's will. A pastor exercises authority by his ability to command confidence and respect and to communicate his knowledge, wisdom, integrity, and spirituality.

There are many things that cause problems between a pastor and his congregation, board, or committees. Many times it is a lack of communication or a clash of personalities. It could be a lack of understanding the difference between policy and principle, or not understanding one's responsibility or authority.

A pastor must, at all times, communicate to the board and congregation what he is endeavoring to do, if he wants their cooperation and support. Many times the reason the board or the congregation does not go along with the pastor on some project is that it does not understand the program. The pastor has not communicated the matter fully to the people with whom he is working.

It is possible he gave serious consideration to the matter for a year or more. He may have researched and prayed about the project, and then decided to go with it; so he announced to his congregation or board that on a certain day in the immediate future the plan would be launched. Then he did not understand why the board or congregation did not enthusiastically endorse the project. The fact of the matter is, when he first began to consider the project himself, he had to give serious consideration to it before he could endorse it. Most intelligent people would certainly feel they should have some time to prayerfully consider a project before giving it their wholehearted support.

A wise administrator never discusses matters that are to come before the board with members of the board privately prior to the matter being presented to the whole board in session. He never takes issue with individual members of the board. He doesn't allow personalities to affect his relationship with board members. He is very careful not to have favorites on the board, but to treat them all alike.

A successful leader never uses his influence and position to get his way in small matters. He saves that pressure for more important matters. A wise leader never tries to drive people to do what he wants, but he endeavors to lead them, convince them, and sell them on the project.

Involving Volunteer Workers. Church leaders should make an all-out effort to involve every person in the congregation in some phase of the church program. However large the membership of the church may be, the pastor, as the chief administrator, must give personal attention to the personnel in every area of the church program. The church worker, in any capacity, is so very important that no person should be placed in any area of service, from bus driver to Sunday school superintendent, without first having the full approval of the pastor.

Organizing Volunteer Workers. The pastor should organize church workers in order to avoid duplication, to be certain that no area of ministry is neglected, and to see that all workers who desire to serve are used in some capacity.

One church is organized in a manner that involves scores of members in various facets of ministry. This church has 12 members on its board of deacons. Each board member chairs one of 12 lay committees. These are operational committees appointed by the pastor to assist and advise in expediting the work and ministry of the church. These committees are responsible to the pastor. They have no legislative power or authority to establish policy; they simply serve in an advisory capacity to the pastor and the official board of the church.

The duties and responsibilities of the committees are carefully outlined. Each committee member, when appointed, is provided with a list of his or her duties and responsibilities. For example, the Finance Committee might be charged with specific responsibilities as outlined in the illustrated listing of duties.

Duties of the Finance Committee
of _____ Church

1. Review the general finances of the church and make recommendations as to means and methods of increasing revenue.
2. Review the proposed budget each year and make recommendations to the official board.
3. Recommend means and methods of economizing wherever possible.
4. Make recommendations for the purchasing of supplies and the undertaking of needed maintenance.
5. Review salaries of staff and employees and make recommendations in keeping with the findings.
6. Give full support to the annual budget campaign.
7. Work with the various departments of the church in raising funds and keeping departments on a sound financial basis.
8. Work with the pastor on all fundraising campaigns.
9. Provide an audit of all the books annually.
10. Make reports to the official board from time to time.

Each committee should work under the general supervision of one of the pastors on the staff of the church. To assure a widespread selection of people, the proper control of all activities, and to avoid a duplication of personnel, the committees should be appointed by the senior pastor.

There should be a clearly written job description or a manual setting forth the responsibilities of the various volunteer workers in the church. (See samples at the end of this chapter.)

An example of a document of commitment that is often good to use in dealing with volunteer workers is the annual Worker's Agreement entered into by one church and its Sunday school workers:

The Worker's Agreement

In consideration of my appointment to the Sunday school staff and of the opportunity offered me to participate in the sacred work of teaching the faith of Jesus Christ our Lord, as a worker in the Sunday school of _____ Assembly, I agree on my part that:

1. I will accept and faithfully perform the duties of that office. I understand that my term of office is contingent upon my fulfilling this agreement.

2. I will make it a practice to attend Sunday school regularly, and if for any real reason I am prevented from attending, I will notify my department superintendent, or divisional director, and help to provide an acceptable substitute. If I am absent more than six (6) Sundays in the year, I understand that I may be relieved of my office.

3. I will make it a practice to come on time to Sunday school, which I interpret to mean that as a worker I am to be present *at least ten minutes early.*

4. I will prepare for each class session and will at all times manifest a real spiritual concern for the members of my class or department. My first desire will be to bring about the salvation of each pupil who does not know Jesus Christ as Saviour and Lord, and to encourage spiritual growth in those who do.

5. As a member of _____ Assembly, I will teach and live in accordance with its doctrine and set an example in life and conduct.

6. I will cooperate with the officers of the school, my department superintendent, and fellow workers. I will welcome constructive criticism and helpful suggestions, and will cooperate with all rulings and requests made for the best interest of the whole school.

7. I understand that it is my responsibility to see that all visitation assignments given me are contacted during the given week. I will report such visits to my department superintendent.

8. I will regularly attend the monthly workers conference and participate in its activities. I will attend the annual workers training

classes, and if I am unable to attend, I will study the textbook at home. I will read regularly the *Sunday School Counselor* that I might broaden my knowledge and experience in my task.

9. I will attend at least two services a week besides Sunday school, realizing the importance of worship. I will use my influence to urge those under my care to be faithful stewards of their time, talent, and money and to develop the habit of constant church attendance.

10. In case I find it impossible to continue my services for any reason, I will notify the divisional director and my department superintendent two weeks in advance.

Signed _____

Regular conferences with workers in all departments, such as Sunday school, youth, children, ushers, and all other groups, are very necessary.

PAID STAFF MEMBERS

However energetic and efficient a pastor may be, he can only do so much in the number of hours he has in each day. When the church reaches a certain size, it is necessary to add assistants, usually in some type of specialized ministry such as music, Christian education, youth, and business administration. We must recognize that God can and does call people to specialized ministry. Their calling is divine and their contribution to the advancement of the cause of Christ is exceedingly important.

Selecting Staff Members. The need for an additional paid staff member must be decided by agreement among the pastor, the board, and the congregation. Some churches require more assistants than others because of the many functions, ministries, and services the church provides for the congregation, the community, and the general public. There are several general classifications of staff personnel: associate pastor, assistant pastor, assistant to the pastor, business administrator, and director of Christian education. Full-time staff members may also be assigned such areas as youth, children, music, visitation, pastoral care, and bus ministries.

The selection of a staff member should be determined by the greatest need in the church. For example, a church might have a layman well qualified to direct the music. The pastor might be well versed in Christian education, but needing help with youth, visitation, or some other area.

The choosing of associates and staff members is of paramount importance. All staff members should be appointed by the pastor! It may be the pastor would want the advice and counsel of the church board on such matters, but the final selection on all paid personnel should be the prerogative of the pastor. This will ensure his control over those who must work under his supervision and for whom he must be responsible.

All staff members and all other personnel, including assistants, the business administrator, secretaries, and custodians, should be responsible to the pastor, who, in the final analysis, is responsible to God and the congregation for the success of the church. Such an arrangement will ensure a smoother operation of the total church program.

Directing Staff Members. The pastor must have the oversight of the total church program because he must give account to the church. As an example of this principle, the director of music should have a free hand in selecting music, musicians, choir members, etc., but the total musical program should be within the guidelines established by the pastor and church for its musical program. The pastor should feel free to make suggestions from time to time to the music director, and he has a right to expect such suggestions to be carried out. The same rule should apply to all departments and staff members.

To avoid confusion and to ensure good relationships and efficient service, all staff members should be provided a detailed job description.[4] There should be a clear understanding of the responsibilities and the authority each position carries. A church manual listing these is desirable.

Any limitations the pastor and church wish to impose on an assistant should be made clear at the beginning of his tenure. For example, some pastors do not want assistants to do such things as perform weddings or conduct funerals. The author believes personally that assistants should participate in all phases of the ministry of the church (perform weddings, conduct funerals, etc.) but these matters need to be clearly understood at the beginning.

There are qualities beyond the job description an assistant should possess. *Loyalty* to God, to the church, and to the pastor is the number one prerequisite. An absolute requirement for success on a

---

[4]See some sample job descriptions at the end of this chapter.

staff is a *genuine spiritual concern* for the people with whom the assistant works. A staff member must be *aggressive*. The church of Jesus Christ is not just to "hold the fort," but to break down the "gates of hell." A good staff member takes the *initiative* in developing plans and programs for his department within the framework of his responsibility.

It is tremendously important that a staff member be *prompt* in keeping appointments, reporting to work, and starting meetings for which he is responsible. Detailed *follow-through* on every task assigned by the job description or the pastor is vital. *Alertness* is a wonderful characteristic for a staff member to possess or develop. *Attitude* is very important in the work of God. The staff member is a member of the team. While his primary responsibility is his department, his secondary responsibility is the whole church and every member. The staff member should keep the senior pastor informed at all times as to what is transpiring in his department and in the church as a whole.

Communicating With Staff Members. Perhaps no other administrative tool is more important to good communication and successful operation of the church program than regular conferences with staff members. If a pastor has only one assistant, or if he has more than a dozen paid assistants, it is vitally important that he meet with them regularly, at a specific time on a stated day, preferably each week. Such meetings should not be just social chats over coffee, but serious, well-planned conferences where reports are received, the church's progress evaluated, and plans made for implementation.

These weekly conferences of the top-level staff should allow sufficient time to cover the total church ministry. Regular meetings with clerks, secretaries, custodians, and others are also essential. The purpose of such staff meetings is fivefold: (1) to ensure good communication among staff members; (2) to evaluate, project, and implement plans for God's work; (3) to promote teamwork; (4) to encourage and inspire each other; and (5) to receive reports from all departments.

The majority of the problems in the world are caused by failure or inability to *communicate*. This is true among nations, families, individuals, and even churches. Staff conferences make it possible to check carefully our communication. Does each assistant understand his responsibilities? Is he carrying out his assignments?

It is important that the pastor and his staff *evaluate* the church work, program, and ministry. To do this weekly is not too often. For example: What was the Sunday school attendance? Was the attendance an increase or a decrease? What contributed to this? How can we mobilize the whole church membership for an evangelistic campaign that is soon to begin? How much advertising are we going to do? How effective is the advertising? What is being done to mobilize the personal workers? What about the music? Usually some important information can be derived from such conferences.

An elementary and brief evaluation of the whole church program and ministry can be undertaken weekly. Following this evaluation, plans for the immediate future and long-range projections and programs should be made.

It is important when working with a staff to impress on them that the work of the staff is a *team effort*. If each member of the staff goes his or her separate way without proper interaction and sharing and without planning and programming together, it is very easy to become individualistic and even noncooperative in the overall ministry of the church.

One of the prerequisites for leadership is to be able to communicate one's vision, faith, dreams, concerns, and desires to others and to *inspire and encourage* them to assist in reaching those goals. A staff conference should provide a vehicle for the senior pastor to inspire his staff with the excitement of his vision. A good leader commands respect rather than demanding it. He commands it by his ability, leadership, communication, integrity, knowledge, and spiritual qualities.

When assignments are made, there should always be an accounting of those assignments. In the weekly conferences of the church staff, *detailed reports* should be given on special assignments. Reports from the minister of Christian education should cover Sunday school attendance, personnel, average attendance for the month and the year-to-date, comparisons with last year, projections for attendance in the immediate future. Attendance trends should be noted in the Royal Rangers, the Missionettes, youth meetings, choir rehearsals, choir performances, children's church, recreational activities, prayer meetings, the prayer room services, the Sunday morning worship service, the Sunday night evangelistic rally, and the day-school activities. The staff conference should be at regular times.

Some pastors arrange an annual retreat for the top-level staff. Such a retreat usually is planned for 2 to 4 days and nights, at which time there is a very frank discussion of the weaknesses and strengths of the church. In these conferences, every department and facet of the church's ministry is brought into focus. The various ministries of the church are analyzed and evaluated. Plans for the coming year are projected and means of implementing such plans are outlined. The church calendar for the whole new year is discussed. Dates are written into the church calendar for various events during the year. This eliminates the problem of departments and groups planning events on the same date, which can easily happen in a large church.

These annual retreats may be held in a resort area. While making preparations, however, the pastor must decide if this is to be just a social "getaway" for his staff or a time to devote some hard work and serious consideration, day and night, to the church and its ministry.

Reporting and Accounting by Staff Members. Good administration is being able to delegate responsibilities and require an accounting for all assignments. Both in business and in church work, the delegation should be as wide as possible. The job of the administrator is to make use of the talents, time, energy, and enthusiasm of the staff members and the volunteer workers of the church.

After delegating the different jobs and receiving the reports, the administrator has to coordinate all related activities so they are all part of the common purpose and work toward the common goal.

Staff members should give an account of their activities weekly. All of us are likely to do a better job on any task if we know we must give an account. With a detailed report from each staff member, the senior pastor is able to get an overview of the total church operation which will enable him to know where special help may be needed.

In addition to the weekly verbal evaluation reports which are recorded and become a permanent record, each staff member might be asked to turn in a weekly visitation report of the visits made (to sick members, absentees, prospects, or persons needing pastoral care) and the results of such visits. A study of these weekly reports by the senior pastor will brief him on the people being ministered to and those needing special help.

A monthly report is designed especially for departmental evaluation. It provides a total look at the department for the past month. For example, the children's director reports the attendance each Sunday during the month and the average for the month in children's church, Missionettes, the children's division of the Sunday school, the children's choir rehearsals, the nursery, Kids Klub, and other children's activities.

The monthly report form should also provide space for describing special activities during the month: the number of visits to absentees, prospects, and mothers with new babies, the number of conferences or counseling sessions, etc. (See the sample monthly report form for the education department.)

One can see what a composite overview of the church operations the senior pastor has when such reports from all staff members are filed. Of course, reports are of little value unless studied, analyzed, and used for the purpose intended.

Attitudes of Pastor and Staff. The attitude of the pastor and staff in the overall church program contributes a great deal to the success or failure of that area. The attitude we display as pastor or staff member will in most cases solicit the same attitude toward us. If our attitude is one of love, respect, admiration, cooperation, consideration, and appreciation, we will very likely reap what we sow.

The pastor should be careful to consider the desires, ambitions, position, and feelings of staff personnel. The pastor must never think of the assistant as just an employee. And the assistant should never think of the pastor as just his boss. There should be understanding, love, respect, and admiration—each for the other.

It is a good practice to refer to the assistant pastors in public and in print as "Pastor _____." The congregation should be taught that each of the clergymen on the staff is, indeed, a pastor. They should understand the chain of command, but they should also respect the assistants as pastors, not just employees of the church.

The pastor must be very careful never to embarrass his staff members before others. And the assistant should never, under any circumstances, take issue with the pastor in public or before others. In pastoral conferences, however, there should be a free expression of opinions about matters that have to do with the church. When a decision is made, though, it should become the total program of the church and all its departments.

EDUCATION DEPARTMENT   # MONTHLY REPORT

MONTH	YR

REGULAR ACTIVITIES

ACTIVITY		Week Ending Date:	Week Ending Date:	Week Ending Date:	Week Ending Date:	Week Ending Date:	Average or Total
SUNDAY SCHOOL	Adult Division						
	Youth Division						
	Children's Division						
	TOTAL						
BUS MINISTRY	SUNDAY AM Bus 1						
	Bus 2						
	Maxi 1						
	Maxi 2						
	Sun. Night*						
	Wed. Night*						
WORKER TRAINING	S.S. WORKERS CONFERENCES Adult						
	Youth						
	Children						
SPECIAL MINISTRIES							

Remarks: *co-ordinated activities

_____
Signed

The pastor should take advantage of every opportunity to express publicly, as well as privately, his appreciation for the members of his staff and for the fine work they do. If he appreciates them, it is likely the congregation will also. If the congregation appreciates the assistants, the chances are they will think a great deal more of the pastor who selected them. The assistants should also take advantage of all opportunities to express appreciation for the pastor and his leadership.

The attitude of both the pastor and the staff should be to create a "sense of belonging" on the part of all members of the staff—a team spirit. The pastoral staff ought to, and certainly can, work as a team, sharing in whatever credit there is, as well as in whatever failure there might be.

OFFICE PERSONNEL

Secretaries and other office personnel in a church are tremendously important to the smooth operation and ongoing program of the church. They should be selected with the greatest care after sincere, earnest, prayerful consideration of the many factors involved.

A high order of judgment is required in selecting top-notch applicants. The administrator, whether the pastor or someone else employed for this specific task, should give attention to getting the right person for the right job and building and maintaining good working relationships.

George Rush, for 13 years business administrator of the largest Southern Baptist church east of the Mississippi River and for many years business administrator of a large midwestern Assemblies of God church, offers the following suggestions in recruiting and developing church office workers.

Describe the Job. Every staff job should be written. The term *job description* refers to an organized summary of the duties and responsibilities involved in the position.

Establish Job Qualifications. This refers to deciding the minimum skills required for the job: the minimum educational requirements, experience requirements (if any), health, and church membership requirements. Whatever job qualification guidelines are established should be followed.

Prepare Supportive Instruments. The application form includes a variety of questions designed to get factual information about an applicant. Other supportive instruments are the character reference follow-up, the business reference follow-up, and the telephone reference.

Recruit Prospects. First, restudy the job. Review any suggested changes that may have been made. These changes may or may not be incorporated in a revised job description. Second, see if the vacancy is a promotion possibility for some present employee. If a promotion is made, then seek a replacement for the new vacancy. Third, check the application file for prospects. If none qualifies, look for names on the church roll. A placement bureau may provide leads. The local business college is another recruiting source. Businessmen in the church membership sometimes can give helpful information. A pastor or staff member of another church may be able to suggest the name of a prospective applicant.

Screen Applicants. The applicant should be interviewed. Some suggestions for the interview are as follows: (1) plan for the interview, (2) keep the appointment, (3) make the applicant feel welcome, (4) talk face to face, (5) do little of the talking, (6) give the applicant undivided attention, (7) answer his questions, (8) conclude the interview courteously.

Select and Place the Most Acceptable Applicant. Mr. Rush also makes some valuable suggestions in building and maintaining good working relationships: (1) Know organizational principles, such as identifying the levels of supervision. (2) Know organizational relationships and follow lines of authority. (3) Know managerial responsibilities; the staff supervisor has three main jobs to perform: he manages or controls, he teaches, and he handles human relations. (4) Know supervisory skills: directing, motivating, teaching, coordinating, and evaluating the work and workers. (5) Know human relations skills. The ability to get along with other people is a valuable skill: show a genuine interest in people, observe rules of courtesy, communicate clearly, criticize in the right way, keep all promises, resolve complaints promptly and fairly, treat employees impartially, give credit where credit is due, and apply what you know. The test of leadership is the accomplishment of the job.

Compensation and Working Conditions. There should always be a clear understanding with staff members of what the working condi-

tions are to be. The hours they are to work, the time of day they are
to report for work, time off, vacations, sick leave, salary, and fringe
benefits ought to be discussed and agreed on before one becomes a
member of the staff.

There should also be an agreement as to how much time, if any, a
staff member can be away from his job to minister elsewhere. There
should be a thorough understanding of the scope of the staff member's
responsibilities and the limits, if any, to be imposed on his ministry.
There will be much better relationships and working conditions between the pastor and the staff or the employees of the church if such
matters as working conditions, compensation, responsibilities, requirements, and limits are clearly understood before rather than after
one is situated in a new job.

In Conclusion

Administration is a comprehensive effort to direct, guide, and integrate associated human strivings that are focused toward some
specific ends or aims. An administrator has the responsibility of directing and facilitating the concerted efforts of a group of persons
brought together to realize some defined purpose of the organization.

The pastor must be an administrator to be really effective as a
pastor. He is the administrator of the worship, work, and witness of
the total church. Organization is an absolute necessity for the success
of the church. Administration of that organization is the pastor's
responsibility. It is essential to his success, and it is absolutely
necessary to fulfill the eternal purpose of the church!

Suggested Reading

Adams, Jay E. *Shepherding God's Flock.* Nutley, NJ: Presbyterian and
    Reformed Publishing Company, 1975.
Dobbins, Gaines S. *A Ministering Church.* Nashville: Broadman Press,
    1960.
Engstrom, Ted W. *The Making of a Christian Leader.* Grand Rapids:
    Zondervan Publishing House, 1976.
Hinson, E. Glenn. *The Church: Design for Survival.* Nashville: Broad-
    man Press, 1967.
Leach, William H. *Toward a More Efficient Church.* New York:
    Fleming H. Revell Co., 1948.

Riggs, Ralph M. *The Spirit-filled Pastor's Guide.* Springfield, MO: Gospel Publishing House, 1948.

Tead, Ordway. *The Art of Administration.* New York: McGraw-Hill, 1951.

Turnbull, Ralph G. *Baker's Dictionary of Practical Theology.* Grand Rapids: Baker Book House, 1967.

Wedel, Leonard E. *Building & Maintaining a Church Staff.* Nashville: Broadman Press, 1966.

ASSOCIATE PASTOR

Job Description

Committee Assignment: Adult Ministries Committee
Responsibilities:
1. Direct pastoral and administrative staff in absence of pastor.
2. Direct adult ministries.
3. Direct adult Sunday school division.
4. Direct adult follow-up program.
5. Direct overall visitation program.
6. Visit families where there has been a death; see that such families receive flowers, food, visits, etc.
7. Visit and counsel with members who need special spiritual help.
8. Motivate and train members of church for soul winning and visitation.
9. Develop other types of evangelism.
10. Direct counseling service; counsel with those requesting such service.
11. Direct distribution of books, periodicals, tracts, and other literature for purpose of evangelism.
12. Serve as liaison between Men's Fellowship, Women's Ministries, and other adult groups, and pastoral staff.
13. Supervise budget preparation and expenditures for adult ministries.
14. Supervise news releases, brochures, and advertising.
15. Assist pastor in any other field of ministry where requested.
16. Keep the pastor informed of all phases of the work of the church.

MINISTER OF EDUCATION

Job Description

Committee Assignments: Sunday School Committee;
                         Christian Day School
Responsibilities:
1. Direct overall Christian education program of the church.
2. Coordinate Sunday school work of all departments.
3. Supervise all activities of the Sunday school.

4. Supervise all Sunday school personnel.
5. Supervise all Sunday school records.
6. Direct all Sunday school visitation and follow-up.
7. Promote Sunday school attendance.
8. Direct all special Sunday school campaigns.
9. Direct Sunday school workers training programs.
10. Select all Sunday school personnel in cooperation with the chief pastor, staff, and department superintendents.
11. Supervise Sunday school budget expenditures.
12. Be responsible for all Sunday school literature, materials, equipment.
13. Set the example for Sunday school staff in visitation of absentees and prospects.
14. Work with the children's director in educational program for all children.
15. Work with minister of youth in educational program for all youth.
16. Develop and direct Sunday school bus ministry.
17. Direct visitation of bus workers.
18. Recruit and assign Sunday school bus drivers.
19. Perform any other duty assigned by the chief pastor.
20. Keep the pastor informed of all the work of the church for which he is responsible.

MINISTER OF YOUTH

Job Description

Committee Assignment: Youth Activities Committee
Responsibilities:

1. Direct spiritual life and Christian training of youth.
2. Direct Christ's Ambassadors (or youth group).
3. Direct Wednesday night youth meetings.
4. Direct youth division in Sunday school.
5. Direct Royal Rangers program.
6. Direct youth and junior camps.
7. Be responsible for youth choirs (in cooperation with director of music).
8. Direct youth outreach program (literature, visitation, hospital, personal witnessing, etc.).
9. Work with director of recreation in developing the whole youth recreation program.
10. Visit absentees and prospects in the youth division.
11. Assist pastor in other visitation.
12. Supervise youth-activities budget expenditures.
13. Perform any other duties assigned by the chief pastor.
14. Keep the pastor informed of all the work of the church for which he is responsible.

MINISTER OF VISITATION

Job Description

Committee Assignment: Prayer Room and Personal Work Committee
Responsibilities:
1. Visit those who make a decision for Christ.
2. Visit first-time visitors to church who request a visit.
3. Visit church absentees.
4. Visit Sunday school prospects and absentees in cooperation with minister of Christian education.
5. Visit all hospitalized members and others who request a visit.
6. Visit shut-ins confined to their homes, nursing homes, etc.
7. Direct prayer room ministry.
8. Select and train personal prayer-room workers.
9. Supervise bus service for Wednesday and Sunday night services.
10. Direct extension ministry in nursing homes, prisons, hospitals, etc.

MUSIC DIRECTOR

Job Description

Committee Assignment: Music-communication Committee
Responsibilities:
1. Direct all music for church services, radio, and television.
2. Have general supervision of all choirs and other musical groups.
3. Be responsible for upkeep of all musical instruments, such as pianos, organs, etc.
4. Supervise music-department budget expenditures.
5. Be responsible for TV and radio music, props, etc.
6. Be responsible for upkeep and utilization of all sound equipment.
7. Supervise all aspects of tape ministry for individuals and radio-TV ministry.
8. Perform any other duties assigned by the chief pastor.
9. Keep the pastor informed of all phases of the work of the church for which he is responsible.

CHILDREN'S DIRECTOR

Job Description

Committee Assignment: Children's Division Committee
Responsibilities:
1. Direct spiritual life and training of all children.
2. Direct children's division in Sunday school.
3. Supervise children's church.
4. Supervise cradle roll department.
5. Supervise nursery and nursery workers.
6. Direct Missionettes and other children's groups.

7. Supervise all recreation of those ages not covered by teen recreation.
8. Cooperate with minister of youth and director of recreation in teen recreation.
9. Cooperate with minister of youth and director of recreation in junior camps.
10. Direct primary day camps.
11. Cooperate with minister of education in Sunday school workers conferences.
12. Be responsible for children's choirs (in cooperation with music director).
13. Be an example to teachers and workers in visitation of absentees and prospects.
14. Visit mothers of newborn babies.
15. Plan, promote, and direct vacation Bible school.
16. Supervise children's division budget expenditures.
17. Perform any other duty assigned by the chief pastor.
18. Keep the pastor informed at all times of the work of the church for which he or she is responsible.

BUSINESS ADMINISTRATOR

Job Description

Committee Assignments: Maintenance Committee;
Ushers and Traffic Committee

Responsibilities:
1. Supervise all buildings, equipment, and grounds.
2. Supervise all custodial personnel.
3. Manage office personnel.
4. Manage food services and direct all food-service personnel.
5. Supervise all buses, their maintenance, use, schedules, and drivers.
6. Schedule buildings for all events except regular services and the gym and handball court. Keep a record of all events, facilities to be used, and dates to occur. Only he shall issue keys to the buildings.
7. Purchase all building and office equipment, supplies, materials, and insurance.
8. Supervise preparation of budget and work with budget committee in subscribing the annual budget.
9. Advise on budget expenditures.
10. Supervise financial reports.
11. Supervise local benevolences.
12. Serve as liaison with church and parking lot ushers.
13. Schedule all printing.
14. Perform any other duties requested by the pastor.
15. Be responsible only to the pastor, and be at the pastor's disposal at all times.
16. Shall keep the pastor informed of all phases of the work of the church for which he is responsible.

DIRECTOR OF RECREATION

Job Description

Committee Assignment: Recreation Committee
Responsibilities:
1. Supervise and direct all church recreation.
2. Organize and direct all recreation for all ages. Work in cooperation with recreation committee, children's director, youth pastor, and pastor of adult ministries to provide a total recreation program for all segments of the church.
3. Book all events in gym and handball court. Keep records of same.
4. Be responsible to see that activities building is serviceable at all times.
5. Be responsible for and maintain in good repair all equipment for recreation program.
6. Purchase and inventory all uniforms, equipment, and supplies. See that all uniforms and equipment are kept in proper order and repair at all times. Supervise the checking out and in of uniforms, equipment, and supplies.
7. Select coaches, assign players, and supervise all league athletic events.
8. Enlist, train, and supervise adequate numbers of voluntary personnel to maintain a high level of supervision and programming.
9. Establish, maintain, and enforce a code of Christian conduct for all recreational athletic functions.
10. Plan and supervise athletic and recreational budgeted and unbudgeted expenditures and income.
11. Direct recreation for children's and youth camps when requested.
12. Meet weekly with other members of church staff.
13. Keep the pastor informed of all phases of the work of the church for which he is responsible.

16

The Pastor
and
Official Church Relationships

G. RAYMOND CARLSON

Images may reflect what once was, or what is considered ideal, rather than what is. Our self-image often is not the way others see us. The image we hope to project is one of victory and growth, but at times this may be far from reality.

Churches can be riddled by power blocks. Laymen may chafe under clergy dominance and pastors may gall over what they think is infringement by selfish or ill-informed members. Impatience or distrust can only lead to bickering disuinty. When such exists, the witness of the church is greatly hindered, if not destroyed.

A positive Christian witness is dependent on the willingness of the church to face the realities of congregational life. Among these realities are the relationships of the pastor and the congregation, including various boards and committees, in conducting the business of the church. There is little reason to tolerate countless disorganized, drawn-out, and unproductive business meetings. Definite procedures for conducting business and making decisions will eliminate many of the immature squabbles that center in personalities. Issues and priorities should be the focal point.

When procedures reflect manipulation or autocratic control, problems will arise. Leadership can enhance or stifle the dynamics of the life of the church. Free debate, when voiced in the Christian spirit of kindness and understanding, is important. People resent leadership when they find they have been manipulated.

G. *Raymond Carlson, D.D., is assistant general superintendent of The General Council of the Assemblies of God, Springfield, Missouri.*

This chapter will deal with three areas of pastoral relationships in the congregation—the church business meeting, the church board, and church committees.

Church Business Meetings

The local church is in reality the body of Christ. Through the local church, God's hidden presence is made tangible and evident, both audibly and visibly in the community. The local body, to be scriptural, must assume responsibility for its government and support as well as for its propagation. Each cell in the body of Christ must develop its ability in self-government, including both administration and discipline.

Government is scriptural: "God hath set some in the church . . . governments" (1 Corinthians 12:28). The Church was born at the conclusion of a 10-day prayer meeting (Acts 2). In the middle of that prayer meeting, the 120 conducted a business meeting for the purpose of selecting a man to fill the bishopric (Acts 1:21-26).

Business procedures relate to every function of the church and the pastor. The church is admonished to do its business with diligence. The phrase "not slothful in business" (Romans 12:11) applies to all business activities of Christians and surely includes the church. Evaluation of the nature of the business functions of the church will convince one of their importance to the success of the whole program. An understanding of the mission of the church only accentuates the need for an effective basic organization to conduct the necessary business.

Across the country on any given Sunday, many sermons are preached on the duties of church members. These sermons usually stress faithfulness in attendance and financial responsibility with tithes and offerings. Other matters relating to conduct are included. How much emphasis is placed on the necessity of the member participating in the business of the church? Very little.

Capable people who really desire to do something for God remain uninvolved because they have never been properly challenged with this important facet of congregational life. Some pastors announce a business meeting as if it were an unimportant matter. One can get the idea that it is like an invitation to the funeral of someone totally unknown in the church or community.

The importance of the business aspects of church life should be stressed from the pulpit. Unless interest is shown by the pastor, very little will be found in the pew. Church business is the business of every member. But it is the specific business of the pastor and the officers to make church business every member's business. The annual meeting should be a time for the members to learn of progress and achievements—a time to be anticipated.

PREPARATION FOR THE MEETING

A successful business meeting will require prayerful, wise planning. Planning should focus on three vital areas: the member, the decision-making, and the mission of the church.

The Member. In churches with a congregational form of government, the involvement of the individual member is very important. Each member must be made to realize his place on the decisionmaking process. The member was redeemed as an individual; Christ died for him. He will maintain his individual and distinctive personhood for all eternity. First Corinthians 12 clearly defines the "many members—one body" concept.

As a redeemed person, the church member is responsible to participate with other members of the body. He must be prepared to accept his position of responsibility. Through the guidance of the Holy Spirit, members in a local church have every right to believe the will of God for them may be found in the decisions of the group. To this end, they need to be prepared for their place in the church's business decisions through faithful teaching from the Scriptures. Pastors could well devote a good portion of at least one sermon a year to the responsibilities of every member in the business affairs of the church.

The Decisionmaking. Business meetings are held for the purpose of making decisions. Any matter that affects the church is vital. If items are to be presented that will require action, the time and efforts of the individual members will be respected if leaders will make proper preparation.

There are many ways of preparing for decisionmaking (most of which will be dealt with later). There must be established procedures. The provisions of the church's constitution and bylaws must be followed. The democratic process must be respected. Communication must be established. Certain reports and proposals can be submitted prior to the meeting. Above all, the membership can be prepared for decisionmaking by prayer preparation. The aid of the Holy Spirit is imperative.

The Mission of the Church. The church's mission must always be kept in focus. What is God's purpose for the particular local congregation? What do the Scriptures teach? What are the stated objectives in the historical documents of the church? How do the individual members perceive the mission of the church?

When church members are prepared, they can come to grips more effectively with the mission and priorities of the church. They will be more attuned to the leading of the Holy Spirit and more mature in their decisions. Their stewardship of time, possessions, and opportunities will be much more effective. And the unity of the local body will be strengthened and solidified.

PROPER ANNOUNCEMENT

The chairman must acquaint himself with the provisions stated in the bylaws regarding meetings. In some states the law is very specific on matters relating to annual meetings of corporations.

What does the charter of the church provide? How about the requirements for proper announcement? For example, the documents may require that the meeting be announced 2 weeks in advance. Should the pastor and/or officers fail to comply, the meeting can be declared illegal and any action null and void.

What are the provisions for giving notice? Is an announcement from the pulpit sufficient? Must it be posted? placed in the bulletin? mailed to the members?

A general statement of the *purpose* of regular meetings is sufficient; such as elections, the receiving of reports, and specific items that are to be considered. The announced purpose for special meetings must be clearly delineated. Normally the notice would include the time, place, and purpose of the meeting. While other matters may be discussed, action is limited to the items announced in the notice of a special meeting.

TIME OF THE MEETING

Regular meetings must be held at the time the charter and/or the bylaws indicate. If both documents set the time and they are in conflict, the charter has precedence. If meetings are not held as prescribed in the legal documents, any action will be void.

Business meetings should be held when it will be most convenient for the membership to attend. The annual meeting in January was time-honored. In areas of the nation subject to severe winter weather, it was found to be more conducive to better attendance to set the time later in the year. In farming areas, good sense indicates the busy harvest season is not the best time for an annual meeting.

AGENDA

The pastor and the board should prepare an agenda that can either be distributed prior to or at the beginning of the meeting. Advance planning is necessary. No chairman can afford to come to a meeting without knowing what needs to be done. He must know the provisions of the bylaws as to the order of business, the elections to be conducted, the qualifications for office, and the length of the terms of office.

Arrangements should be made in advance regarding reports from departments and committees. Basically, an agenda includes items relating to matters of policy, organizational structure, officers, budget and expenditures, facilities and equipment, and church activities.

ORDER OF BUSINESS

As a rule, the bylaws provide for the order of business. A suggested order is as follows:

Registration. All members qualified to vote can sign the roll. In some churches the secretary/clerk reads the roll. If the bylaws provide for a quorum, which they should, the number present will determine whether or not business can be legally transacted.

Devotional. This may consist of a song, Scripture reading, and prayer.

Call to Order. When the time of a meeting has arrived, the chairman will open it (after he has ascertained that a quorum is present) by calling the meeting to order. He will state, "The meeting will come to order," or "The meeting will be in order."

In the event a quorum is not present, business is illegal but the meeting is not. The only legal business would be to fix the time of adjournment and adjourn, to recess, or to discuss the process to be followed to have a quorum. The latter could be done by a motion requesting that contact be made with absent members during a recess, urging them to attend. Even by a unanimous vote, the body present cannot waive quorum requirements to transact business. If important actions are needed, action should be taken to fix the time for an adjourned meeting and then adjourn. If action is imperative at an under-quorum meeting, the members present can act with the hope that their action will be ratified at a later meeting. However, they take such action at their own risk.

Reading of the Minutes. The minutes of the previous meeting should be read and approved. Only then do they become official. If the minutes have been distributed to the members, they may be approved without being read. By a majority vote the reading of the minutes may be postponed until a future date. If a considerable interval is to take place before the next meeting, the minutes might well be read and approved before the motion to adjourn is made. Even after the minutes have been approved, they may be corrected upon motion any time an error is discovered.

Reports. Officers and chairmen of boards and standing committees should make their reports in the order these offices and organizations appear in the bylaws. Reports from special committees follow the others. Written reports that are complete and informative promote good communication. If they are distributed to the membership prior to the meeting, a brief summary at the meeting is sufficient. Reports cover past operations, present conditions, and projections for the future. Proper reporting does much to develop confidence and create goodwill. Reports should either be accepted, rejected, received, or referred to an appropriate group for whatever further action is needed.

Basically, reports relate either to finances or activity. Guard against long and meaningless financial reporting. Present a detailed financial statement in printed or duplicated form, but summarize the report orally or in writing in significant, nontechnical language the average person can comprehend.

Unfinished Business. This refers to items that remain from a previous meeting. The chairman does not ask, "Is there any unfinished business?" but states, "Unfinished business is in order." He then states the matters in order as they are acted upon. These matters may be reflected in the minutes and may include any that have been postponed or deferred. Items that were on the agenda of a previous meeting but were not discussed, do not classify as "unfinished business."

Elections. Normally the first item following unfinished business is elections. The election of the pastor and of all officers should be by secret ballot. This assures an accurate expression of the will of the members. The bylaws determine what constitutes an election. In the event there is no stated policy, a majority vote constitutes an election.

Before a ballot is cast, the voters should be instructed on the qualifications required of the candidate, the length of the term of office, and the number of votes needed for election. Tellers should have been appointed and should fulfill their task as instructed by the presiding officer. Courtesy and good sense indicate that when a presiding officer is being voted on, he should relinquish the chair. The results of the ballot should always be announced by the person in the chair and not by the reporting teller. The teller's report becomes a part of the minutes of the meeting. The use of nominating committees will be covered in the latter part of the chapter.

For further information on voting procedures and other matters concerning parliamentary procedures, a chairman should obtain a copy of *Robert's Rules of Order, Newly Revised,* or a similar authority (see Suggested Reading).

New Business. After unfinished business has been cared for and while elections are proceeding, new business can be handled. New business may be introduced from recommendations by the official board, the church council, departments, committees, or a motion made by a member.

Proposals receive far better consideration when they have been carefully evaluated by the board. Good homework will go far to assure the success of any measure on which action is to be taken. The recommendation of a responsible group, made after a detailed evaluation, is meaningful to the membership.

Adjournment. If not already prescribed, the time of the next meeting should be set before a motion for adjournment is taken. When the motion to adjourn has been carried and announced by the chairman, the meeting is considered adjourned.

OTHER VITAL MATTERS

Essential to the success of a business meeting is good communication. Noncommunication is communication—but the wrong kind. Lack of communication indicates that nothing important is happening. People get the message they are not needed and should not be interested. They arrive at the conclusion that their insights and opinions are of little consequence.

For this reason effort must be put forth to involve people and to break down the barriers of lack of interest and discontent. One of the best ways is to foster a spirit of openness. People are quick to sense when they are being manipulated. If they suspect a hidden agenda, they may outwardly remain friendly but react inwardly. By these statements we do not mean to imply that people are being consciously deceived, but every appearance of such must be avoided.

To "tell it like it is" is generally a good policy. No one wants to "lose face." Data and facts should be correct. If the financial situation is not good, don't cover it up. People will know the facts sooner or later. Share the problem and solicit their help. Feedback can be valuable to leaders. When permitted, feedback helps cut down irresponsible talk, gossip, and backbiting. Other simple rules to follow are outlined by John E. Baird:

> First, the majority should rule.
> Second, minority rights should be protected.
> Third, the group must accomplish its business.
> Fourth, feelings must be protected.[1]

To ignore the will of the majority is to invite disaster. On the other hand, free speech and the ballot must be permitted to protect minorities. There comes a time when debate must conclude and action must be taken. "The time comes when the talk must cease, when

---

[1] As quoted by Robert N. Gray, *Managing the Church, Business Methods*, Vol. 2 (Enid, OK: The Haymaker Press, Inc., 1970), pp. 189, 190. Prepared by Dr. John E. Baird. Used by permission.

viewpoints must become votes, and when expression must change to decision."[2]

The feelings of people are important. The Bible instructs us with regard to the operation of spiritual gifts, "Let all things be done decently and in order" (1 Corinthians 14:40). The Bible also exhorts us again and again to "consider one another" (Hebrews 10:24) and to "be kindly affectioned one to another with brotherly love; in honor preferring one another" (Romans 12:10). Despite strong disagreements on vital decisions, members must treat one another with Christian love, common courtesy, and due consideration. Free debate does not involve shouting and rash accusations. Unless church members conduct themselves as Christians, they have no right to debate.

THE CHAIRMAN

Every chairman should seek to improve his leadership. His role is important. He is not in the chair to dominate; he is there to guide. Fairness and impartiality should prevail. People, not physical resources, are the real assets of the church. Every member deserves Christian courtesy and respect. Members should be motivated and trained, but not ordered. All members will at times be subordinate, but none is to be subservient. Human problems involve emotions and attitudes more often than logic and reason. Since this is so, communication begins not with words but with the spirit, emotion, and attitude. If we accept these premises, we will understand how fairness in the chair will go far to elicit cooperation. Autocratic leadership will turn people off.

A study of the New Testament reveals that the church of the first century was a democratic body where everybody was somebody and the opinion of the humblest member was heard and respected. Aggressive people with strong convictions and opinions are welcome, but there is no place for a religious tyrant in the church, just as there is no room for a political demagogue in American life. Frequently pressure is brought to bear on a chairman before and during a meeting. A person of wealth or one with carnal, self-seeking interests may try to use his influence to railroad his ideas through. The chairman who remains unswerving and maintains the principle of the Golden Rule will eventually be appreciated for his square dealing.

---

[2]*Ibid.*

The chairman should always remember he is in the chair as a servant of the people. His personal likes and dislikes must not influence him. If he abuses the privilege of the chair, he violates the very rules of the democratic process. All should have the privilege of expressing their views to the end that the wishes of the majority may crystallize into decision.

If the chairman feels he must enter into the debate, he should relinquish the chair to the vice-chairman and not return to the chair until the matter has been decided. When matters concerning the chairman are being considered by the body, he should vacate the chair.

While it is the duty of the chairman to see that every point of view finds expression, he must move matters to conclusion as rapidly as possible. The affirmative side should be permitted to speak first in support of a motion and also to make the final speech at the close of debate. Alternating positions should be presented—the affirmative, followed by the negative, then the affirmative, and so—until the issue has been fairly heard. No one person should dominate the debate.

The chairman must maintain his poise at all times. He is dutybound to check unchristian speeches and comments and must never become ruffled himself. At times he can ease situations by the use of discriminate humor that carries neither a barb nor an inappropriate reference to any member.

Speakers must be restricted to the matter under consideration. Extraneous matters divert attention and delay decisions. Time is wasted and people become irritated. Unless violations are checked at the beginning, they can result in confusion and even strife. The chairman must always remain in control of the situation.

The chairman should bear in mind that the business meeting must move along with deliberate haste. He is to manage the meeting, and he must see to it that it neither romps recklessly along or rambles idly to an aimless end. Serving in an impersonal manner, the chairman does not refer to himself as "I," but rather speaks of himself in the third person using the expression "the chair."

The Secretary

The secretary is the recording officer of the church and the custodian of its records. An efficient secretary contributes greatly to the success of a meeting. He is responsible to record the minutes, keep on file all committee reports, maintain the membership roll, and furnish committees with documents they may need to fulfill their assignments. Among other duties usually assigned to the secretary in relation to business meetings is notifying the membership of each meeting, notifying officers and committee members of their election or appointment, and preparing the order of business for the chairman. The secretary is responsible to prepare the ballots for elections. In the event the chairman and the vice-chairman are absent, the secretary will call the meeting to order and preside until a chairman *pro tem* is elected.

Members have a right to examine the minutes, providing they do not abuse the privilege to the "annoyance of the secretary." Minutes of boards and committees are accessible only to members of the respective boards and committees unless other provision is made in the bylaws or the corporate structure of the church.

The official minutes of a meeting should include: (1) the name of the organization; (2) the nature of the meeting (regular or special); (3) the time and place; (4) the name of the chairman; (5) the devotional; (6) approval of the minutes including any corrections if needed; (7) a record of the business transacted; (8) adjournment; (9) the signature of the secretary; and (10) the word *approved* with the date, one line below the signature of the secretary.

Minutes are not as a rule recorded verbatim with the exception of motions and resolutions which are to be recorded exactly as given. If a motion fails to receive a second, it is not recorded, but motions both lost and approved must be. At times the manner of voting should be indicated, such as: voice vote, show of hands, standing, secret ballot.

> Records are tremendously important. They should be maintained meticulously. They should be concise, yet comprehensive; succinct, never verbose. They should afford an over-all, accurate picture of actions taken, free from bias and the personal opinions or observations of the officer who prepares them. In no case are individuals named in the reports to be complimented or censured. Praise or blame must never be considered a part of this reporting. The records must be as free from personalities as a court clerk's records. The requirement is for factual, historical, chronological data—nothing less or more.[3]

The importance of the minutes cannot be emphasized too strongly. Their accuracy is vital. In the event of litigation, the court may

---

[3]Eugene Dinsmore Dolloff, *The Efficient Church Officer* (New York: Fleming H. Revell, Co., Copyright © 1959), p. 37. Used by permission.

render its decision on the basis of the records as maintained in the minutes. Possession of property has at times hinged on these written records. Minutes must accurately reflect actions taken that alienate title to property, such as selling, mortgaging, or conveying title in any manner. Unless minutes properly reflect authority, officers can be held personally responsible for many legal matters. Lending institutions require a record of actions taken to authorize the borrowing of funds.

All of the above only serve to indicate the importance of the task of the secretary. His compilation and maintenance of the records is vital. And yet, he must remember the records do not belong to him; he is only the custodian of the records on behalf of the church.

PARLIAMENTARY PROCEDURES

There is a proper way for a member to bring a matter before a business meeting. If the wishes to present the matter personally, he should rise and address the chair by stating, "Mr. Chairman," Upon recognition by the chair, the member has the floor and has the right to speak to the entire body. They, in turn, have the obligation to give him their attention. He should place his proposal in the form of a motion. For his proposal to survive, it must have a "second." It is then before the body for debate and action.

Only one motion can be before the body at a time. To place another motion before the house while a prior one is under discussion is to be out of order, and the motion should be so ruled by the chair. A main motion, however, is subject to a motion to amend. If amended, action must be taken on the amendment. Then debate will return to the main motion as amended. If the amendment fails, discussion will ensue on the original motion.

Motions fall into the following classifications: (1) main motions, (2) subsidiary motions, (3) privileged motions, and (4) incidental motions. Some motions are debatable, others are not; some can be reconsidered, others cannot; some are in order when another has the floor.

A *main motion* is the proposition under consideration. A *subsidiary motion* relates to the main motion and attempts to affect the main motion by amendment, substitution, committing, referring, or delaying. A *privileged motion* takes precedence over all others and seeks to aid the house. Examples are a motion to adjourn, to fix the time to adjourn, to appeal an action, or to call for a division of the house. An *incidental motion* relates to such matters as limiting debate, closing debate, raising a point of order, calling for the question, and certain procedures to facilitate action.

Conduct of Business Meetings

TABLE OF PRECEDENCE OF MOTIONS[4]

Order of Precedence of Motions (Types of motions listed in order of precedence from highest to lowest)	Requires a Second	May be Discussed	May be Amended	Vote Needed
Privileged				
To fix the time of the next meeting (made when other business is before the meeting)	Yes	No	Yes	Maj.
To adjourn (when it doesn't adjourn the assembly forever)	Yes	No	No	Maj.
Incidental				
To close nominations	Yes	No	Yes	⅔
An appeal from the chair's decision	Yes	Yes*	No	Maj.
A point of order	No	No	No	Maj.
A point of information	No	No	No	Maj.
Subsidiary				
To table	Yes	No	No	Maj.
To end discussion	Yes	No	No	⅔
To postpone definitely	Yes	Yes	Yes	Maj.
To refer to a committee	Yes	Yes	Yes	Maj.
To amend an amendment	Yes	Yes	No	Maj.
To amend a motion	Yes	Yes	Yes	Maj.
Main				
An ordinary main motion	Yes	Yes	Yes	Maj.
To take from the table	Yes	No	No	Maj.
To reconsider	Yes	Yes**	No	Maj.
To repeal (rescind)	Yes	Yes**	Yes	Maj.***

*May be discussed, but each member may speak only once.
**Opens the main question to discussion as well.
***Majority vote if notice has been given. Otherwise, ⅔ vote.

---

[4]Gray, *Managing the Church*, Vol. 2, p. 203. Prepared by Dr. John E. Baird. Used by permission.

Church Boards

A frequent cause of unrest in the life of a church is the lack of a proper understanding of the relationship of the official board to the pastor and the congregation. For this reason, serious consideration should be given to this matter.

As in other matters pertaining to faith and practice, evangelicals look to Scripture to find the pattern for church government. The Bible, at first glance, seems indefinite, for no specific government is legislated for the church. The general principles are clear, but not the details. No doubt, God in His wisdom has allowed for a measure of flexibility.

From the beginning God has provided spiritual leadership for His people. In the early economy of God, He made the oldest son in every household responsible as a family priest to give religious instruction in the home. In the days of Moses, God took the priesthood from the oldest sons and placed it in the family of Aaron, making Aaron and his sons the priests of Israel. With the founding of the Church, God replaced the Aaronic priesthood with a new type of leadership. This was through ministry gifts given for the Church Age as recorded in Ephesians 4:11: "And he gave some, apostles; and some, prophets; and some, evangelists; and some, pastors and teachers." Beginning in the Old Testament, God supplied assistance for Aaron and his sons by assigning the tribe of Levi to the task. In the New Testament, the Lord provided for deacons to assist the apostles.

A PRIORITY

The necessity of government is clear, but ministry of the Word has priority in the life of the church. If that ministry is to have its rightful place, it needs to be unhampered by distractions from secondary duties. Since government is needed to keep the affairs of the church in an orderly manner, and since the ministry of the Word is to have a high priority, the Lord has made provision for government.

God has ordained auxiliary ministries in the church, among them the ministry of serving. Have you noticed that the Lord never provided the answer until the need arose in the Apostolic Church? But when a problem came, He directed the apostles to say: "It is not reason that we should leave the word of God, and serve tables . . . .

Look ye out among you seven men of honest report, full of the Holy Ghost and wisdom, whom we may appoint over this business. But we will give ourselves continually to prayer, and to the ministry of the word" (Acts 6:2-4).

There are similarities between the assignments of the Levites in the Old Testament and the deacons of the New Testament. Instructions regarding the duties of the Levites are given in Numbers 1:50, 51; 3:5-9, 25, 26, 31, 36, 37; and 1 Chronicles 23:28-32. While the Levites were given by the congregation to the Lord, and He in turn gave them to the priesthood to assist in the service of the tabernacle, there were restrictions on their service. They could not intrude into the office of the priesthood. Violation would bring the penalty of death (Numbers 18:3).

The deacons in the New Testament were also to assist in the service of the church. Deacons are God's gift to ministers so the latter may give themselves more fully to the ministry; they are God's gift to the congregation, for their service will help the church to benefit from the ministry of an unencumbered minister. Many see the Acts 6 passage as the New Testament pattern for what we now call the office of deacon. These appointed servants are not referred to as "deacons." And it should be noted that two of them, Philip and Stephen, soon became gospel preachers.

The decision to select these men in the Apostolic Church met with the evident blessing of God: "And the word of God increased; and the number of the disciples multiplied in Jerusalem greatly; and a great company of the priests were obedient to the faith" (Acts 6:7). There is clear indication that the office of deacon continued in the church. In writing to Timothy, Paul declares: "They that have used the office of a deacon well purchase to themselves a good degree, and great boldness in the faith which is in Christ Jesus" (1 Timothy 3:13). Writing to the church at Philippi, Paul includes greetings to the deacons (Philippians 1:1).

We note that Paul's reference is to the "deacons." There was not just one, but several. In Jerusalem there were seven. Therefore, the diaconate, which consists of a plurality of scripturally qualified and duly chosen men called "deacons," is a scriptural institution. As such, deacons are a necessary part of an otherwise sufficiently developed local church.

CHOSEN TO SERVE

The word *deacon* is derived from the Greek *diakonos*. The reference in the New Testament is to one who serves. *Diakonos* is translated as servant, minister, and deacon. The word is translated *servants* in John 2:5 and *minister* (servant) in Matthew 20:26. In the Acts 6 passage the word *deacon* does not appear, but the function of the office does: "It is not reason that we should leave the word of God, and *serve* [diakoneo] tables." The word appears in Martha's complaint in Luke 10:40, "My sister hath left me to *serve* alone." All forms and uses of *diakonos* are limited to the thought of serving, helping, and assisting.

Among the ministries God has set in the church is that of *helps*. "And God hath set some in the church, first apostles, secondarily prophets, thirdly teachers, after that miracles, then gifts of healings, *helps*, governments, diversities of tongues" (1 Corinthians 12:28). Judging from the scriptural descriptions of the office of deacon, the *helps* of the Corinthian passage most likely define the office. *Helps* is derived from *antilepsis* which means to help, to relieve, to assist.

A servant is *under* authority; never *in* authority. To keep this principle in focus is to avoid misunderstanding and friction. As there was a separation between the Levites and the Aaronic priesthood (Numbers 18), there is a separation between the ministries of Ephesians 4:11, 12 and the ministry of deacons. This is not to say deacons cannot enter the ministry of preaching. Philip (Acts 8:26-40; 21:8) is a prime example. A proper understanding of the offices as given in Scripture will alleviate much of the difficulties that may arise.

The dictionary defines a servant as an "official helper." This definition clearly illustrates the office of deacon. Deacons are official helpers. While all Christians are to be helpers in the church, the "helps" of 1 Corinthians 12:28 are set in the church by the Lord; they are specifically designated to serve. The *deaconship* is the office (1 Timothy 3:13); *helps* is the function of the office; and *deacon* is the title designating the man who fills the office.

First, last, and always, the deacon is a servant. He is to be a servant in his office to his church and his Lord. Scripture never indicates that deacons are to serve as an authoritative board for the church; neither does Scripture indicate that ministers are to be subject and subservient to deacons.

A THREEFOLD DIVISION

We must focus on the Biblical ideas and ideals to safeguard the development and progress of the church. The New Testament concept presents the Church as a spiritual organism composed of many members, all having a designated function, governed by one head, subject to one will, presided over by one Person (the Holy Spirit), and in the world for one purpose—to carry out the Great Commission. This concept provides a place for all. None is shut out; work is given to all, and every member is useful. Everyone is necessary; everyone is helpful. Everyone receives power, so none may presume.

The local church has a natural threefold division—bishops (elders), deacons, and saints. "Paul and Timothy, the servants of Jesus Christ, To all the saints in Christ Jesus which are at Philippi, with the bishops and deacons" (Philippians 1:1). The minister, addressed here as bishop, is variously given other titles in the English New Testament— elder, presbyter, overseer, pastor. The titles are synonymous in that they speak of the same office, but they describe different aspects of the minister's work.

The ministry of the pastor (Ephesians 4:8, 11) is vertical in origin. He is called of God, given by the risen, ascended, glorified Head of the Church, and gifted with his ministries by the Holy Spirit. He is not and should never become a hireling of the local body of saints. He is to be maintained from the Lord's portion—the tithe is the Lord's.

The office of deacon is horizontal in origin (Acts 6:1-6). The office came into existence to care for temporal matters. The deacons were authorized by the ministry gifts; their qualifications were stipulated by the ministry. They were chosen by the saints and approved by the ministry gifts. Deacons were not and are not owners or bosses of the local assembly. Christ owns the Church by virtue of His purchasing blood. The pastor is God's man serving the church as overseer and shepherd for Christ's sake (Acts 20:28). The deacons are his helpers, caring for temporal affairs, releasing him to devote the bulk of his time to spiritual activities. Whereas ministers are ordained for life, deacons are elected by local bodies of saints.

HARMONIOUS RELATIONSHIPS

The pastor and the deacons should always have mutual counsel and respect. The responsibility of "ruling" is delegated to the pastor

(1 Timothy 3:1-7; 5:17-19; Titus 1:5-10). The Scriptures teach obedience to those who have the rule over the church (Hebrews 13:7, 17). A divided authority produces an impossible situation. Where either the deacons or another board or group assume or are considered a superior or rival authority, the potential for conflict and serious trouble is very real. The office of the pastor takes precedence according to the Scriptures, and that honor is due him because of his office.

On the other hand, there is no scriptural basis for pastors to serve with self-seeking motives. Pastors are neither bosses nor dictators. They need the counsel of responsible men in the church. Such men are there to "help" the pastor. This balance is evidenced by the word rendered *rule* in Hebrews 13:7, 17. The marginal rendering is *guide*, suggesting the idea of a shepherd guiding and leading his sheep. Respect and cooperation are earned and deserved, not demanded.

There are four realms of relationships in the Scriptures that have major similarities—that of God the Father and God the Son, of Christ and the Church, of the pastor and the local church, and of a husband and wife.

Christ himself indicated the headship of the Father by declaring, "My Father is greater than I" (John 14:28). Yet He also stated, "I and my Father are one" (John 10:30). They are bound together by mutual trust and love. In like manner, Christ is the Head of the Church (Ephesians 5:23), yet they are one Body. Christ loved the Church and gave himself for her. The same figure illustrates the relationship of a husband and wife in the Ephesians passage. These relationships picture the relationship of a pastor and the local church. He is the divinely chosen head, but he must serve with the same spirit and understanding that exist in the other three relationships. The same spirit of harmony should exist between the pastor and the deacons.

Differences of opinion will occur. Wise leaders welcome other viewpoints. Strong convictions are worthwhile. Good leaders don't want rubber-stamp persons working with them. When differences arise, neither should assume the "I am right, you are wrong" attitude. All parties involved must bear in mind that internal dissension is far more serious for the church than any attack from without. The Bible teaches that "in the multitude of counselors there is safety" (Proverbs 11:14; 24:6).

The harmony and spirit of fellowship between the pastor and the church board is contagious. It will spill over on the entire church family. On the other hand, a faultfinding, contentious, censorious spirit will contaminate the church family.

MEETING NEEDS

Let us look once again at the Acts 6 passage which instituted the office of deacon. The record states, "In those days, when the number of the disciples was multiplied, there arose a murmuring of the Grecians against the Hebrews, because their widows were neglected in the daily ministration" (v. 1). A need existed in the assembly which brought about murmuring and complaining among the members. The word *murmuring* implies not only openly expressed displeasure, but also the silent protest of an inner and perhaps greater dissatisfaction. Murmuring is always dangerous; and, unless dealt with, it becomes a threat to the unity of the assembly.

The lines were being drawn as some Early Church members sensed what they felt was discrimination. The situation was delicate. The apostles were charged to preach the Word, and to do so effectively they had to protect their position and maintain the confidence of all the people. The decision they made would affect the fellowship of the members and, in turn, the continued growth of the church.

In a stroke of genius—born without doubt of divine wisdom through the supernatural gift of the Spirit—the apostles solved the delicate problem. "The seven"—the office later came to be known as that of deacons—competently met the situation and the apostles were able to devote the major portion of their time to the ministry of the Word and prayer.

Those early deacons became the first of multiplied thousands who have served as bridge builders. They were men who filled the requirements stipulated by the apostles. As such, they were men who were big in God and able to reconcile both factions. According to the Bible, their actions brought continued growth and blessing: "The word of God increased; and the number of the disciples multiplied in Jerusalem greatly" (Acts 6:7).

BRIDGE BUILDERS

"The seven" were bridge builders. *They bridged the gap in church fellowship.* No deacon should ever become a party to promoting disunity. He should always exhibit the highest principles morally and spiritually. There is no place for unchristian prejudice. *Time* magazine carried a significant cover some time back picturing a world figure, short of stature, extending a long shadow from the setting sun. The caption in effect stated, "When small men cast long shadows." The further thought was expressed that when such takes place, the world is in trouble. How true this also is in the church. The job of being a deacon is not for a person of narrow outlook and little spirit.

They bridged the gap between the preacher and the pew. The deacon board is not a legislative body. Deacons are chosen to carry out the will of the people. The job does not imply that they are to perform their functions in an arbitrary manner without regard for the church as a whole. Neither are they to direct the activities of the pastor. Godly deacons who are instructed in the Word will uphold the hands of the pastor in every way possible. A good Biblical picture of their task is found in Exodus 17. As long as Aaron and Hur held up the hands of a weary Moses, the Children of Israel prevailed in the battle against Amalek (17:11-13). On the other hand, the deacons are properly to represent the congregation that has elected them, rather than to reflect their own personal opinions.

"The seven" bridged the gap between the sacred and the secular. Quickly someone will say, "There is no difference between the sacred and secular; we do wrong to make such a distinction." The apostolic deacons made the secular sacred. They seemingly sensed their ministry to people, however secularistic it may have seemed, was basically a spiritual ministry. The very standards of both the preacher and the deacon, as outlined in 1 Timothy 3, indicate the high caliber of people required for both offices. The transitional word between the qualifications for elders and deacons is *likewise,* indicating that both offices have much the same standard.

Teamwork is a key word for the relationships of a pastor and his deacons. Isaiah pictures it beautifully: "They helped every one his neighbor; and every one said to his brother, Be of good courage. So the carpenter encouraged the goldsmith, and he that smootheth with the hammer him that smote the anvil, saying, It is ready for the

soldering: and he fastened it with nails, that it should not be moved"
(Isaiah 41:6, 7).

Or as Kipling made the old soldier say:

> It ain't the individual nor the army as a whole,
> But the everlastin' teamwork of every bloomin' soul.

F. A. Agar forcefully states the truth:

A board of deacons should never be allowed to control the church as
if they were its bosses. They are the servants of the church for Christ's
sake, and their main objective should be to develop a body of people
capable of handling to the best possible advantage all the concerns of
the church. Instead of assembling power in their own hands, the
deacons should constantly be producing other individuals to whom
should be committed the duties and power of the church. In some
churches one finds the board of deacons in absolute and final control of
the affairs of the church, and this without any constitutional right. This
is unwise both for the officials concerned and also for the church
because it virtually destroys the democracy of the body and fails to produce a developed and participating people.

Strong wise men in Christian churches do not become bosses but are
real leaders producing a constituency with a sense of divine responsibility and human opportunity. The boss is a curse in the political realm,
but in the church he is one of the most destructive forces to be found
fighting against the purposes for which the local church was constituted.[5]

No group of people is as close to the spiritual pulse of the church
as the board of deacons. The job requires the business sense of an executive and the humility of a servant. Deacons must be persons of
good sense who know how to use the knowledge imparted to them by
God. They must think straight, speak straight, and deal straight before
everyone in every situation at all times. The task is great; the responsibility seems beyond human ability.

QUALIFICATIONS FOR DEACONS

Before considering the qualifications and disqualifications for this office as given in the Bible, let us comment upon certain factors which we
may call non-qualifications. Among these are money, education, and
political influence. These things should not influence pro or con in the
choice of deacons. The world is influenced by these considerations
because the natural, human earthly standard is then followed. The

---

[5]Frederick A. Agar, *The Deacon at Work* (Philadelphia: Judson Press, 1923), pp. 91,
92. Used by permission.

Christian and the church must be oblivious to these considerations in making the choice of a deacon. It is neither to a man's credit or his discredit that he is a man of money, education, or political influence. He should not be chosen on account of these things; neither should he be rejected because of them.[6]

This does not mean deacons should not possess high qualifications. Membership in a church ought never to be considered the only qualifying factor for eligibility to hold office.

Spirituality. This is the most important qualification. A deacon should be able not only to think God's thoughts *after* Him, but also *with* Him, as the result of a personal and abiding experience.

Capability. This qualification can either be actual or potential, but a measure of ability for the task is important. One person may be very successful in a given area, but like a square peg in a round hole in another assignment. Some men may be spiritual, but not particularly qualified for the office. But never should one who is capable be chosen if he is not spiritual.

Loyalty. The deacon must be loyal to the Lord, to his pastor, to his fellow officers, to the church, and to the denomination to which the church belongs. This loyalty will include attendance at the services, financial support, and the maintenance of his Christian testimony in word and deed.

The Bible has more to say about what kind of a person the deacon is to *be* than what jobs he ought to *do*. The primary emphasis is on the deacon's character rather than his work. This stresses the fact that what he *is*, *is* as important as what he *does*. Specific qualifications are stated in Acts 6:3 and 1 Timothy 3:8-13. In Acts, three qualifications are explicit and an additional two are implicit.

Of Honest Report. Deacons are not simply to be honest, but "of honest report." Their reputation should be without blemish. Their lives should be able to bear the closest scrutiny, and honesty and integrity should be evident in every area. "A good name is rather to be chosen than great riches" (Proverbs 22:1). Persons of good reputation *walk* in the light of the Lord Jesus Christ and, consequently, *reflect* the light of Christ. Persons of good reputation are transparent and, as a result, others look through them and see the Lord.

---

[6]Ralph M. Riggs, *The Spirit-filled Pastor's Guide* (Springfield, MO: Gospel Publishing House, 1948), p. 177.

Full of the Holy Ghost. This is a present-tense matter—not full 5 or 10 years ago, but full of the Spirit today. The enabling power of the Holy Spirit, through His gifts and graces, is a prerequisite to filling the assignment.

Full of Wisdom. This wisdom is more than intellectual prowess, educational attainment, or natural cleverness. There is a wisdom that comes only from God through Christ (1 Corinthians 1:24, 30), ". . . in whom are hid all the treasures of wisdom and knowledge" (Colossians 2:3). There is a natural wisdom which is commendable and can be recognized. It should be used. But how wonderful to receive "wisdom that is from above." It is "first pure, then peaceable, gentle, and easy to be entreated, full of mercy and good fruits, without partiality, and without hypocrisy" (James 3:17). "If any of you lack wisdom, let him ask of God . . . and it shall be given him" (James 1:5).

Full of Faith and Power. These qualifications are not in the list stated by the Twelve in Acts 6:3, but they are indicated as being exhibited in the life and ministry of deacon Stephen (Acts 6:8).

The other significant passage on deaconship is in 1 Timothy 3:8-13. Here Paul goes into greater detail than the Twelve did in Acts 6. Four broad categories of criteria are outlined: (1) Christian character; (2) understanding and commitment to the Christian faith; (3) a life of proven faith and maturity; and (4) an exemplary Christian home life. Now look at them in a little more detail.

Grave. The word has been translated as "honorable," "venerable," and "respectable." By no means does this suggest that a deacon is to be a pessimist, totally lacking in cheerfulness. But he realizes the seriousness of God's demands on his life. Responsibility rests well on his shoulders.

The next three qualities are negatives.

Not Double-tongued. In expressing himself on a matter, he will not say one thing to one person and something quite different to another. His word is his bond; it can always be taken at face value. He stands for the same thing in any crowd; he is not a shifty double-talker.

Not Given to Much Wine. When a person gives himself to intoxicants, the first thing that goes is moral restraint. The deacon—and all Christians—are to be exemplary, temperate, and not dependent on physical stimulants.

Not Greedy of Filthy Lucre. The deacon must always remember that "the love of money is the root of all evil" (1 Timothy 6:10). He will not be "chasing a fast buck," but will be aboveboard in all his financial dealings. Generosity and faithfulness in financial stewardship will be his mark.

Holding the Mystery of the Faith in a Pure Conscience. The deacon must be a firm and sincere believer in the "faith which was once delivered unto the saints" (Jude 3). He is to subscribe to the tenets of the faith as agreed on by his church. He will faithfully live up to every bit of light that falls on his pathway.

Proved . . . Found Blameless. The Bible warns against choosing men for the office of deacon too hastily. A man must prove himself, develop maturity, and give evidence of the qualities the Scriptures delineate before he is considered for the office. Age is not the principal point; time, experience, and training are involved. If a man fails in the tests listed in this passage, he is not blameless. The word *blameless* seems to indicate "above reproach."

Even So Must Their Wives. The deacon's wife is to be an example. She is to be temperate, trustworthy, and discreet while exercising self-control, and particularly so in matters of the tongue. A good man can be disqualified by a wife who is given to gossip, meddling, or feuding. A faithful wife is a helpmeet to her husband. She makes him a better man.

Husband of One Wife. Matrimonial mix-ups disqualify a person from two ministries in the church—minister and deacon. God has set the standard. We are to conform.

Ruling Their Children and . . . Houses Well. Here is the acid test of a man's ability. The word *rule* can well be translated "manage." The deacon, as well as the pastor (1 Timothy 3:4, 5), is to be able to manage his family. He should be an exemplary family man.

The qualifications for the office are rigid, but the rewards are worthwhile: "For they that have used the office of a deacon well purchase to themselves a good degree, and great boldness in the faith which is in Christ Jesus" (1 Timothy 3:13).

CHOOSING DEACONS

Without any doubt, the qualifications laid down by the apostles for the first deacons are binding on the church today. Many details are flexible, such as the number of board members and the exact method of election. But the basic qualifications outlined in Scripture are mandatory. To ignore the standard of God's Word is to invite disaster. Church functions cannot be divided into the secular and sacred, with the secular done by unspiritual members and the sacred by spiritual members. If it is church work, it is God's work. But spiritual leaders are an absolute must for the board of deacons.

The procedure used in selecting deacons for the Jerusalem church sets the pattern for us today. "Brethren, *look ye* out among you seven men" (Acts 6:3). The reaction of the congregation was gratifying: "And the saying pleased the whole multitude: *and they chose . . .*" (v. 5). By action of the entire congregation seven men were chosen.

Several points can be gleaned from the Jerusalem situation. First, a need existed and the method introduced to cure the problem was divinely given. Second, while there was no premature action, there was no unnecessary delay as soon as order and efficiency demanded that something be done. Third, the deacons were chosen by the church from among their number. Fourth, they based their choice on stated qualifications. Finally, the results were pleasing to all, and the church "multiplied . . . greatly" (v. 7).

As Christ shares with His church the privilege of ordination to the ministry, so the pastor should share with the members the privilege of the choice of deacons. The democratic process squares with the spirit of Christianity.

There are several ways to elect deacons. Some churches do so through nominations from the floor; others nominate by secret ballot which, in the opinion of some, is far wiser. Other churches request that nominations be given by the members, with the full slate being posted before the annual business meeting. Perhaps the most widely used plan, particularly in larger churches, is to employ a nominating committee. More will be said about the function of a nominating committee later. It seems best to select deacons either through the use of a nominating committee or through nomination by secret ballot.

TERM OF OFFICE

Most church bylaws provide for 3-year terms for deacons. The fact that a man has been elected once should not necessarily indicate he is a deacon for life. Churches with a sufficient number of qualified men often limit service to two or three terms with a rotation tenet—he cannot be reelected until a year has elapsed. There are pros and cons to this method, but it serves to use the talents of a wider group of people and can bring freshness and vigor to the board.

DEDICATION SERVICE

The Jerusalem church had a dedication following the selection of their deacons: "They set [the newly selected deacons] before the apostles: and when they had prayed, they laid their hands on them" (Acts 6:6). A simple service of dedication, including an appropriate Scripture reading, a charge, and prayer, on the first Sunday morning following the annual business meeting can be very meaningful to the entire church.

TRUSTEES

All incorporated organizations—and a church should incorporate—must have trustees. With a corporation, the board of directors are the trustees. Trustees serve the congregation only in legal matters relating to the financial and business affairs. They do not have spiritual functions and powers as church officers. Trustees act on behalf of the church in selling and acquiring property. Normally the president (pastor) and the secretary of the board of trustees sign legal documents, particularly when property and financial contracts are involved. Serving as custodians of the property, trustees are responsible for its proper maintenance, insurance coverage, and such related matters.

Some churches have a board of deacons and a separate board of trustees; others combine both in one official board. For most churches the latter arrangement is preferred. With two or more boards making decisions, unnecessary conflicts and confusion may result. All church interests are overlapping, and when two boards pass upon the same subject in separate meetings and are not agreed in their decision, there is every opportunity for a church squabble. If deacons are to serve as trustees, the bylaws should so state.

Many churches bring leaders of various departments into meetings with the official board in what they call the church council. Matters of vital concern are brought to this body for recommendation to the entire church.

THE WORK OF THE OFFICIAL BOARD

The pastor should be chairman of the board. He has no arbitrary authority, but is simply given a place in which he may exercise his leadership and influence. He should not be bypassed. The pastor, however, can forfeit his place of leadership by failing to accept his responsibility or by abusing his privilege. In the operation of the church, the board meeting is the guiding force for the pastor. From this center his program operates. An aggressive but cooperative board is the pastor's greatest source of encouragement. Such a board will give the pastor his most effective aid to further the work of the church.

Board meetings don't have to be marathons of confusion. They can be a joyful experience and should never be unpleasant. Consider some guidelines:

Meaningful Purpose. The church should project goals for at least 5 or 10 years ahead. With this in mind, every decision in the interim is made in the light of the long-range objectives. Board meetings should take the form of progress reports to specific shorter-range goals.

Prepared Agenda. Follow a carefully devised agenda to void wasted time. This will not preclude considering other matters, but it will insure consideration of essentials and make it possible to begin and close the meeting on time. Plan ahead. Don't spring things on other members. Leadership must never contrive and connive; it will backfire.

The same order of business suggested for the annual business meeting obtains for board meetings. The keeping of proper minutes is important. Begin on time and close on time. Sixty to ninety minutes should be the normal maximum. Avoid arranging meetings after the regular church service except in emergencies. Plan regular meetings.

Reports. Churches with even a limited staff can arrange for the agenda, minutes, and reports to be available in binders for the individual members of the board. Sections can be identified with tabs and color-coded mimeographed reports. The pastor's report, whether verbal or printed, will give a concise resume of the month's work, reviewing and projecting from a spiritual standpoint. All reports should be concise and to-the-point. At times, the longest reports conclude with the least accomplished.

Discussing Issues. Boards should avoid discussing people and confine their discussions to the issues. Lack of agreement on a particular item is not all bad. Once an issue has been defined and the facts identified, alternatives can be weighed, and the best plan of action should emerge.

There will be differences among the members in their responses. Some members may be all business. They will endeavor to do the board's business in the same manner as their own. They will demand a quick "yes" or "no." Others may hesitate to take a definite stand. There may be men who are so rushed in their own business that they relax and pass over serious matters lightly. Some fellow may believe he is entitled to make all the decisions, and everyone should fall in line with his ideas. And what about the brother who insists on expressing his opinions in minute detail?

The chairman has the task of keeping the entire group working toward the same goal. Occasionally a chairman senses that some minds are in third gear, while others are still in first, and one or two may be in reverse. The old idea of "sleeping on" a new idea is not the worst thing in the world. As a rule, it does not pay to railroad a program through. And never make your chief preparation the stockpiling of sandpaper with which to smooth "splinters." Splinters never hurt us unless we rub the board the wrong way!

Matters to Be Considered by the Board. Other chapters of the text will deal with administrative and financial matters. Suffice it here to identify some of the areas for which the official board is responsible. The board has general spiritual and business oversight.

In the area of spiritual matters, the board will work with the pastor in screening and acting on all applicants for church membership. They will assist the pastor in matters of discipline. An understanding of the pastor's prerogative in engaging evangelists and guest speakers is needed.

With regard to business matters, the board is to manage secular interests: care of the property, the comforts of the congregation in the facilities, preparation of the budget, the handling of funds, payment of bills (the treasurer is only the custodian of the funds), and execution of legal instruments such as deeds, mortgages, and insurance policies (the secretary is only the custodian of the church records). The board is responsible to see that proper announcements are made for business meetings, and especially so when legal matters are under consideration.

The official board has two other important areas of responsibility—pastoral support and leadership at the time of pastoral transition.

Pastoral Support. Pastoral candidates should have a complete understanding of the financial program of the church with particular attention to pastoral support. Areas would include: (1) salary; (2) housing; (3) utility payments; (4) car expense; (5) moving expense; (6) expense allowance for attendance at district and national meetings; (7) retirement benefits.

The pastor's remuneration should be reviewed annually, bearing in mind cost-of-living increases, the needs of the pastor, the prosperity of the church, and the length and value of his service. Boards of more progressive churches recognize these matters and make provisions accordingly. No doubt the growth of these churches comes, at least in part, as a result of their liberality to God's servant. God's blessing rests on the generous spirit.

The official board has special responsibilities during the time of a change of pastors. These matters are covered in another chapter.

Organizing the Board. Opinions are as strong one way as another with regard to giving portfolio assignments to the deacons of the church. Should a pastor and his board desire to follow such a plan, the individual members would be assigned to areas where they might have special expertise. They could be advisors to members of the pastoral staff who have direct responsibility in a given area. Any assignments given in a portfolio arrangement normally would not indicate a complete delegation of responsibility, but rather an assignment of general oversight with reports to be made to the pastor and board. If portfolio assignments are made, the pastor will need to tool out an arrangement best suited to the personnel available.

Without doubt the effective delegation of work is one of the marks of a capable leader. The capacity for the delegation of authority and responsibility, with just the right touch, is a rather rare quality. One of the greatest keys to effective leadership is not only to know the importance of delegation, but also to be able to choose the proper persons to accept responsibility. Care must be exercised to avoid "yo-yo" leadership—assigning responsibility and then pulling it back again and again. Know what people can do and assign them the task. Be explicit in the assignment. Stand by to help, but avoid interference. With the delegation of responsibility must go commensurate authority to discharge that responsibility.

The practice of selectivity and delegation is a sound Biblical principle. Jethro wisely made the recommendation to his son-in-law Moses. Jethro's suggested standards of selection of helpers for Moses are worthy of emulation. They were to be men of *ability*; their task would be exacting. They were to be men of deep spiritual *devotion*; they were to fear God and respect men. They were to be men of *honor*; covetousness and bribery must never be countenanced (Exodus 18:17-26).

Church Committees

A scientist in Winnipeg took 600 parts—from watch parts to auto parts—and built a machine. When asked what purpose it served, he answered, "None." The man built a great machine, but it had no purpose. Some organizations are like that. A church can be caught up with an organizational structure that is formulated without purpose or is never implemented to accomplish its purpose.

Committees are a case in point. Committees properly structured and staffed are responsible for work that needs to be done if the church is to fulfill its purpose. A local church body without organization can't perform all functions effectively. On the other hand, too many churches have complex machinery but lack power. They have "wheels within wheels," but the wheels aren't turning.

Organization, it has been said, links "thinking about" with "doing." Unless organization is efficient, duplication of work will occur and the effectiveness of capable people will be hampered by the aimless efforts of others. Study the accomplishments recorded in Scripture and you will find efficient organization accompanied by the anointing of the Holy Spirit. And the touch of the Spirit must never be minimized (Zechariah 4:6).

Through organization, individuals can specialize in areas where they will be most helpful. Objectives are more readily attained as efforts come under directed authority. The human body illustrates the matter aptly. Each member has a function to perform. As the members of our bodies are directed, they cooperate together to accomplish the many marvelous things we ask them to do. The picture is graphic in 1 Corinthians 12:14-27. As the members in your body cooperate to fulfill the functions of the "you," the organization in the church works to accomplish its total purpose. The organizational structure of the church is not the church, nor is it the people; it is instead designed *for* people so they may effectively serve the body.

The purpose of committees is to provide the necessary organization to handle matters that otherwise would be unattended. Some committees are a convenience; some are a necessity. Leadership must determine what committees are needed and what ones aren't.

SELECTING MEMBERS

The selection of persons to serve on a committee is very important. Some people are misfits. They may be overbearing, or they may take the "adversary" position and be ready to oppose anything and everything. On the other hand, it is well to select people with some varying points of view. "Yes" men do not make for breadth of thinking.

Appointing people to committees is a challenging responsibility for the pastor and church leaders. Wisely chosen, these persons effect well-ordered organization, harmony, and achievement. Wrong choices can result in chaotic committees. How to assure the former and avoid the latter can tax a leader's ability. The aid of the Holy Spirit is needed.

Leadership Is the Key. The choice of leaders for assignments as committee chairmen depends on factors such as these: (1) knowledge and experience, (2) accountability, (3) ability to get along with people, (4) responsibility for planning, (5) ability to stand by a decision, and (6) responsibility to train and develop people. The leader offers direction and influences members to cooperate in working toward an objective they find desirable.

A report comes from Toronto that a man called the police department to report someone had stolen his steering wheel, brake pedal, gearshift; in fact, the whole dashboard was also taken from his car. Shortly the police had another call from him relating that all was okay. He had by mistake gotten into the backseat. A committee, or any group for that matter, is in a bad way when the driver is in the wrong seat; there is no power to get going, no meshing of gears, no steering or guidance.

Perhaps it was experiences like this that caused Spurgeon to say the most effective committee possible was a committee of three: one out of town, the other sick in bed.

Involvement Is a Sound Principle. By involving others, the work gets common interest and support. The abilities of all—the strengths of some and the weaknesses of others—focus on the assignment. If the program is "mine" and he doesn't feel it is "his," he will not put his best into it. Let the committee member feel he has input and he will support the decision. When he is free to participate and his abilities are respected, he will contribute much more effectively. In fact, and strangely so, he'll then be glad for the leader to receive credit.

Don't ask people for their ideas, comments, or advice if you don't really want them. Most people won't dislike you for turning down their ideas if you can give them a good reason. But people generally are very aware of ulterior motives. Participative responses that are productive will be earned by the leader whose sincerity is sensed as he deftly moves the group to decision.

THE WORK OF A COMMITTEE

A committee that has been given the task of studying a matter and making a recommendation has a serious assignment. The research must be thorough, the facts correct, the review objective, and the conclusions logical.

Preparing the Report. When the committee has arrived at a decision, it must prepare its report in such a manner that the body to which the report is made will not only comprehend what is said, but will also be able to take proper action in a spirit of harmony. The secret is in the format of presentation. The report must be concise and yet clear. Of necessity it will be written by one or two members, but it should have the approval of the entire committee.

Anticipation and prior preparation regarding the response to the report can be helpful. Anticipate opposition. In major committees such as a building committee, visual aids will greatly enhance the presentation. Models, pictures, graphs, data, and summaries are examples. All reports should be written in the "third person." Recommendations should be placed at the end of the report. There are two ways of signing reports. The word *chairman* is placed after the signature when the chairman signs the report alone. If the report is signed by all members of the committee, the word *chairman* is not needed.

Tips to the Chairman. Begin on time. State your intention and stick to it. Be concise. Keep well organized. Dismiss at a reasonable time. Busy people will be far more willing to serve if they know their time and effort is respected.

Failure. One of the most vivid pictures of committee failure in all of Scripture is related in Numbers 13 and 14. A committee of 12 men was appointed to spy out Canaan. The overwhelming majority, 10 out of the 12, brought back a negative report and a great congregation of people was swept into unbelief. A handful of men halted a host from entering the Promised Land and gave them many years of wandering in the wilderness. How important to choose people who possess not only natural abilities, but also deep and abiding spiritual qualities.

Committees properly constituted can be of great blessing to a pastor and church. When committees are needed, keep them small for the most part, and see that they have whatever supervision is needed to complete their assignment.

The pastor should be an *ex officio* member of all committees. He will do well, however, to exercise his influence with spiritual dignity and good counsel and never by autocratic authority. Wise is the pastor who can use committees effectively. The reward of seeing previously uninvolved people become active in the tasks of the church is a rich reward.

Guidelines. Zenas J. Bicket has listed the following guidelines for administration through committee organization:

1. Do not have committees just to have committees. Recognize and use their work.
2. Rotate committee personnel to develop new leaders and involve new people in the inner workings of the church.
3. Require that committees keep minutes and records of their activities.
4. Be sure that the work of each committee results in a final report which is given proper attention by the pastor or the church board.
5. Never ignore the opinion of a committee chairman. If he has been appointed to this position of responsibility, he should be allowed to fulfill his role properly.
6. Assist and encourage a chairman who is learning to be a leader. A timid chairman who fails in his first leadership responsibility may never accept a similar task again.
7. Check regularly to see that the chairmen of the various committees

are calling their committees together and dealing with the matters appropriate to the assignment.

8. An appropriate member of the pastoral staff should serve as an *ex officio* member of each committee, with the privilege of attending all meetings.[7]

KINDS OF COMMITTEES

There are two basic kinds of committees—standing committees and special committees. Standing committees are permanent for a year and are higher in rank than special committees which are appointed for a special task. When a special committee's report has been accepted, its work is done and the committee ceases to exist.

When a board operates through working committees, items of business are referred to the proper committee. Of necessity these committees will have at least one meeting between board meetings and each will report at the regular monthly session. In many churches where this system functions, each committee, between board sessions, implements previous board actions that refer to its area of responsibility.

The committee system of board work has advantages and disadvantages. The system necessitates good communication. Care must be exercised to devise means to keep matters alive; vital matters can die in committee.

Some of the more common kinds of committees that serve a church are a building committee, finance committee, evangelism committee, visitation committee, Christian education committee, music committee, other departmental committees, nominating committee, and pulpit committee. Each pastor and church will have to make decisions as to the number and kinds of committees that can effectively serve the church's needs. Since the work that normally falls to most of these committees relates to matters covered in other chapters, attention will be given here to the nominating committee only. Let it be said, however, that qualifications and duties for all standing committees should be clearly defined in job descriptions.

THE NOMINATING COMMITTEE

Many churches, particularly large ones, use a nominating committee to select the persons who are to be voted on. Such a committee is

---

[7]Zenas J. Bicket, *The Effective Pastor* (Springfield, MO: Gospel Publishing House, 1973), p. 47.

chosen for one and only one purpose—to place before the membership a slate of nominees for the positions up for balloting.

Selecting the Committee. Great care should be exercised when choosing a nominating committee. There is some truth to the statement that nomination is almost an assurance of election. For this reason, the democratic process is affected by the work of the committee. The committee, however, only nominates; the church does the electing. Nominations from the floor may be accepted after the nominating committee has made its report. But it is recommended the church vote only on the persons nominated by the committee.

Persons on the nominating committee should have a deep spiritual commitment. They will need to have a thorough understanding of the requirements and qualifications for each of the offices. A wide acquaintance with the membership is a requisite. The committee needs representation from the various segments on church life. The members of the committee should serve for only 1 year, with the possibility of a carry-over of one member. It is good for a new committee to face this serious business each year.

This is one committee where personalities are discussed. For the good of all concerned, such discussions should be limited to the committee room and the lips of the committee members must be "sealed" when they leave the room.

Selecting Nominees. Nominees selected by the committee should possess the qualifications stated in the bylaws. They should be persons who faithfully support the church with their attendance and finances. Nominees should understand the government of the church and share the basic philosophy and vision of the pastor. Willingness to serve, whether cordially or grudgingly, is not the primary requisite. Committee members need to do their work carefully. The choices they make for nominees are exceedingly important. They must remember it is easier to get people into office than to get them out.

After the committee has prayerfully considered the qualifications needed for the office and prayerfully discussed the names of prospects, they should ask at least two members to contact the prospects. In some instances, if the prospect is willing to allow his name to be considered, it is well for him to meet with the entire committee. It is appropriate for the pastor to interview the prospects.

When the slate of nominees has been agreed on by the committee, their names are presented in nomination at the annual meeting, announced by letter, or posted for the information of the members.

SCREENING COMMITTEE

As a spin-off of the nominating committee, a screening committee is effectively employed by some churches. Nominations are submitted by the members. Arrangements are made for these names to be deposited in a box. These nominations are evaluated by the screening committee, with the procedures then being much the same as those used by the nominating committee.

* * * * *

The pastor's working relationship with the *church board* and *church committees*, as well as with the entire congregation in the *church business meeting*, is of crucial importance to an effective ministry. God can and will anoint the pastor as he labors faithfully in these situations, just as certainly as He will anoint the preaching of the Word from the pulpit.

Suggested Reading

Agar, F. A., *The Deacon at Work.* Philadelphia: Judson Press, 1923.

Bicket, Zenas J. *The Effective Pastor.* Springfield, MO: Gospel Publishing House, 1973.

Constitution and Bylaws for Local Assemblies. Springfield, MO: The General Council of the Assemblies of God, rev. 8/15/77.

Dresselhaus, Richard L. *The Deacon and His Ministry.* Springfield, MO: Gospel Publishing House, 1977.

Gray, Robert N. *Managing The Church*, Vols. 1 and 2. Enid, OK: Haymaker Press, 1970.

Riggs, R. M. *The Spirit-filled Pastor's Guide.* Springfield, MO: Gospel Publishing House, 1948.

Robert, Henry M. *Robert's Rules of Order, Newly Revised.* Glenview, IL: Scott, Foresman and Co., 1970.

17

The Pastor
and
Church Finances

R. D. E. SMITH

In the very beginning it was ordained that man should live by and administer the value the Creator had stored for him in the pristine earth (Genesis 1:28). The riches of the earth and man's relationship to his Creator were bound together in one spiritual law, the first ever given (Genesis 2:17). In the maladministration of that law man fell, and in falling, he condemned the race to all the ills inherent in the exploitation of wealth. From that day two opposing philosophies have contended for the allegiance of mankind.

THE PAGAN PHILOSOPHY

The dictionary definition of a pagan is "an irreligious person."[1] But this is not necessarily so. Pagans may be intensely religious. Witness the elaborate pageantry and the fabulous temples of heathenism. As religious persons, these pagans have given, and do give, extravagant gifts. But this is just the point. They *give* of what is their *own* to gain a sponsor for their ends. If, as they believe, God is not a Person, it follows automatically that He cannot *own* anything, and the field is open for whoever can appropriate, control, and exploit wealth.

Thus, it is not surprising that an Aryan notion—that the best title to property is conquest—was codified into law by the Emperor Justinian

R. D. E. Smith is pastor emeritus of First Assembly of God, Binghamton, New York.

---

[1]Paganism is the denial of the personality of God. This is so whether it is embraced in the Stoic doctrine of Universal Reason, the Hindu doctrine of the Divine Essence, or such modern expressions as Creative Force. Romans 1:20-32 traces the development, and eventual degradation, of paganism. The word is used in this sense throughout the chapter.

in the year A.D. 530. This pagan philosophy, which ignores the absolute dominion of the Creator and exalts human covetousness into human ownership, passed eventually into the English common law and thence down to us.

THE CHRISTIAN PHILOSOPHY

Stewardship is the Christian way of life as opposed to the pagan way of life. The Christian recognizes the divine ownership of all value (Exodus 19:5). To him, all property is a trust and money is a token of it. He is a steward[2] and, as such, he administers that which belongs to another (Genesis 39:6). "Intelligence recognizes an obligation, honor acknowledges it and fidelity maintains it."[3]

It cannot be said that the church has consistently honored the concept of stewardship, for from earliest times, its economic life has been seriously tainted with the vestiges of paganism. Even the church sometimes measures success in terms of money and its equivalents of prestige and power. How often the value of a preacher, or a college president, is equated with his ability to raise money. There is even the philosophy held by some that godliness can be measured by monetary worth (1 Timothy 6:5). It is not surprising, therefore, that a multitude of money-raising expedients have appeared in the church.

These money-raising expedients range all the way from the *optional*, where each man determines for himself how much (or how little) he may contribute, to the *coercive*. Coercive methods have ranged from outright extortion to immense psychological pressures. *Impulse* giving, sanctified by a pseudospiritual "leading," enjoys a suspect popularity in the early days of some revival movements. None of these meets the exacting standards of the Scriptures.[4]

So-called *proportional* giving, wherein a person chooses for himself what percentage of his income will be contributed, is an abnegation

---

[2]There is no exact western equivalent for the Biblical word *steward*. Possibly the closest equivalent is *trustee*.

[3]Harvey Reeves Calkins, *A Man and His Money* (4th ed., New York: The Methodist Book Concern, 1916).

[4]Two passages (Matthew 6:1-4 and 2 Corinthians 9:7) are commonly used to justify random and secret giving. Neither passage applies to the tithing standard because both have to do with charitable contributions. They do, however, apply to the broad stewardship of life which includes relief of the poor.

of the tithing principle. The proper proportion is revealed, the word *tithe* literally means "tenth," but the reason for it is hidden in the mysteries of God.

Biblically Based Stewardship

STEWARDSHIP AS A BASIC THEME OF SCRIPTURE

Stewardship is a basic theme of Scripture (Genesis 1:28; 1 Corinthians 4:1). Ownership of all things is vested in God alone by virtue of His creative and sustaining activity. This includes all material value and such intangible factors as time, energy, and talent. Man is a unique creation; he has been given dominion over the earth and all its creatures, and charged with the administration of the whole. To this end he was made in the image of God (Genesis 1:27).[5] This is not an anthropomorphism. It refers to the sum total of personality and must be understood in terms of Christ, the perfect Steward, who himself is the image of God (cf. 2 Corinthians 4:4; Colossians 1:15). It includes all those powers that qualify man to exercise dominion over the earth and its creatures, to understand and apply the laws of nature, and to modify and develop the treasures left in his keeping.

Those powers were unquestionably derivations of the attributes of God and, in his unfallen state, man's potential was unlimited. Even in his fallen state he exercises a spark of the creative attribute of God and calls it "inventiveness." The gifts of the Spirit may well be the recovery of powers lost by rebellion. Whatever powers the Christian steward may or may not have, he need not be limited in those qualities of honor and fidelity which, in the providence of God, "open . . . the windows of heaven" (Malachi 3:10).

Man is responsible. To say man is a steward is the same thing as saying he is accountable (Romans 14:12). This accountability applies to all mankind, for the responsibility is there whether or not it is acknowledged. Man's first responsibility is to God, but he is also responsible to society and to the earth itself in an ecological sense. The law of Moses abounds with instructions for the alleviation of poverty, and the writings of the prophets are full of exhortations for

---

[5]For a full treatment of this concept see G. C. Berkouwer, *Man: The Image of God* (2nd ed., Grand Rapids: William B. Eerdmans Publishing Company, 1968).

equal justice. God's first instruction contained an ecological principle, "replenish" the earth (Genesis 1:28). And the sabbatical year (Leviticus 25:lff.) was then, and is now, an ecological necessity. The Hebrews were not only guardians of spiritual truth, but also guardians over the good earth.

Man has suddenly come to the realization that the resources of this planet are not inexhaustible. The forests are ravaged, oceans of oil sucked dry, minerals depleted, and the 4 inches of topsoil that stand between man and starvation, exhausted. In his senseless wars man has paved the ocean bottoms with the wealth of nations. Every grain and fruit is bloodstained. In so many ways, man has shown his contempt for God's bounty.

In the midst of this prodigal waste there walks a people who have in their religious writings the secret of an earth whose treasures never fail. They did not devise it. Most of them do not even recognize it. It was not created, for it co-exists with God. It is the law of right, the moral law, the law by which God governs.[6] It was inherent in the mind of God, declared in primeval law, codified in the Mosaic law, reiterated throughout the history of the Hebrews, ratified by the Lord Jesus, and embodied in the theology of the New Testament. It is *stewardship*, the administration of all material value to the glory of God and the well-being of the universe.

From the very inception of the Church, early Christians found themselves in conflict with their world. It was not just that they were preaching a new religion. New religions and new gods appeared on the scene every day. Much of it was that whatever these people believed and practiced affected the economic structure. There was no riot in Ephesus until property was threatened (Acts 19:24ff.). One must remember the gods were patrons of the crafts and, indeed, of every indulgence of the people. The Judeo-Christian heritage came into conflict with Greco-Roman paganism. The battle was severe—and it was lost. Pagan attitudes respecting property persisted among the Gentile churches and do so until this day.

---

[6]C. G. Finney, *Systematic Theology* (Grand Rapids: William B. Eerdmans Publishing Company, 1951 reprint), p. 3.

The pagan doctrine of ownership or its companion evil, asceticism, soon pervaded the church. Scattered references from the Church Fathers of the third and fourth centuries indicate some attempt to keep the practice of tithing alive, but it was far from universal.[7] Prior to the Reformation the trail of scriptural stewardship is faint, with only the Waldenses and the followers of John Huss as exceptions. The Reformation did not emphasize stewardship, probably because it found itself embroiled with other particular problems that consumed the energies of its leaders. Following the Reformation, the state became the responsible head of organized religion and, having inherited Roman jurisprudence, imposed pagan concepts of property on the churches.

Not until the rise of the great missionary movements in the 18th century, notably among the Moravians and Methodists, did the claims of scriptural stewardship receive more than passing attention. Even then stewardship was confused with philanthropy and altruism. The nobility and sacrifices displayed by the early practitioners of stewardship in that age have never been excelled. They well understood that property is a trust to be administered for God; but they did not understand as well that tithing is an act of worship rendered unto God as an acknowledgment of His sovereignty.

There are certainly many reasons for the early decline and stumbling renewal of responsible stewardship. Man's innate selfishness could take two directions. It could espouse the pagan philosophy of ownership or it could take the more religiously satisfying route of asceticism. Under the latter concept, all wealth is evil *per se* and must be renounced. Early Methodism saw the loss of many of its potentially greatest men under Francis Asbury's inflexible demands that they live and support a family on the merest pittance.

Another factor that delayed the restoration of Scriptural stewardship was the practice, not by any means obsolescent, of allegorizing or spiritualizing Scripture. This procedure tends to compartmentalize man and make an artificial distinction between the spiritual and the material. To this day there are those who deplore any talk about

---

[7]"Though we have a kind of money chest, it is not for the collection of official fees, as if ours was a religion of fixed prices. Each of us puts in a small donation on the appointed day in each month, or when he chooses, and only if he chooses, and only if he can; for no one is compelled and the offering is voluntary" (Tertullian, *Apologeticus*, 39).

money in the church as being unspiritual. Yet, Christ lived in the real world. He worked with His hands, walked in the marketplace, paid taxes, and came to grips with the same problems that confront the rest of mankind. Of the some 30 parables He told, at least 11 dealt unmistakably with wasted resources. Loyalty and fidelity to man are directly related with loyalty to God.

When these very practical matters are removed from reality by some homiletical sleight of hand, the conscience is not bound. The preacher who would establish a tithing program in his church must accept and proclaim the clear and simple words of Jesus.

How is a Christian to reconcile his faith before a world absorbed in paganism? He cannot go out of the world (1 Corinthians 5:10) and yet he must find some way of existing. Charles W. Colson describes his dilemma:

> Here again was the dilemma I had encountered so many times since my conversion—of trying to live in two worlds. As a Christian I yearned to tell all, to testify in the impeachment hearings, but my lawyers—representing the world's wisdom—told me I had to keep quiet . . . . To make it worse, my courtroom defense when it came would concern my life *before* Jesus Christ entered it. The old Colson was on trial and there was a lot in this life I did not feel like defending. But how to separate the new and the old? How to live in two worlds?[8]

The problem is not solved by separating life into the "Sunday" life and the "weekday" life. Exhortations to "live above the world" do not obviate the necessity to punch the time clock.

"When I was a monk," said Martin Luther, "I allegorized everything; but now I have given up allegorizing, and my first and best art is to explain the Scriptures according to the proper sense; for it is in the literal sense that power, doctrine, and art reside."

STEWARDSHIP AS RECOGNIZING THE SOVEREIGNTY OF GOD

Tithing Recognizes the Sovereignty of God. When Adam was given custody of the Garden of Eden, it was necessary that he be taught the difference between possession and ownership. To that end, one tree was set apart (Genesis 2:17). The tree was no different from other trees. It bore edible fruit, possibly the same variety as other trees. It

---

[8]From *Born Again*. Copyright © 1976 by Charles W. Colson. Published by Chosen Books, Inc., p. 217. Used by permission.

required cultivation. When Eve said, ". . . neither shall ye touch it" (Genesis 3:3), she added to the word of God—a fault by no means singular to her. The tree's difference and significance lay in the prohibition. By that prohibition Adam was continually reminded of his dependence on Another. So long, and only so long, as he honored the tree, he declared the sovereignty of God and made the distinction between ownership and possession.

The consequence of blurring that distinction by disobedience was death (Genesis 2:17). The meaning of the Hebrew, as in the alternate marginal reference, is "dying thou shalt die"—a process would begin at a sharply defined moment. It is spiritual death, but it is also more than that. The terms of the curse (Genesis 3:17-19) required man to tear from the soil that which it had previously so bounteously offered. Since that day man has been just one jump ahead of starvation.

The tree, therefore, is a symbol of the tithe. The tenth is acquired in the same manner as is all income—that is, it requires cultivation. It is of the same substance (money), but it belongs to God in a special sense and may not be consumed for oneself (Leviticus 27:32).

Tithing Denies the Dominance of the World. Money is the dominant force in this world. Solomon recognized this fact when he said, "Money answereth all things" (Ecclesiastes 10:19). He who possesses great wealth in this world commands reverence and respect, which are forms of worship. He becomes a god to whom men must "pray" if they wish to benefit by his largess.

The tither escapes the stranglehold thus imposed by the love of money, for he has elected to live by another principle and serve another Sovereign. He has voluntarily relinquished that for which other men would, and do, sell their souls.

Tithing Becomes a Therapeutic Agent. It cleanses the life of selfishness. When on the first day of the week, a Christian separates that portion that belongs in a very sacred sense to God, he performs an act of purification. Furthermore, he forces on himself habits of careful accounting and economy, for at least in the beginning he must make do with less. Finally, he is forced into a life of faith. Like his peers he must maintain a home, provide for a family, and educate his children. He cannot think of tithing as an automatic, coin-operated vending machine. The teaching of tithing must be mixed with faith (Hebrews 4:2).

Tithing Sanctifies the "Unrighteous Mammon." Money is not evil *per se*, but it does seem endowed with an evil genius that exerts a powerful fascination on the unwary. "Gold fever" is not confined to the prospector. It is not money, as such, that Paul condemns (1 Timothy 6:10); the love of money, he contends, is the root of all evil. Jesus said, "Ye cannot serve God and mammon" (Matthew 6:24).

God has provided a way for the sanctification of money through the paying of the tithe. It is "holy unto the Lord" (Leviticus 27:32). The dual aspect of money, whether holy or unholy, is indicated in the translation of Joshua 6:17. Here the word translated "accursed" might equally well have been translated "devoted." That is, the wealth of Jericho properly "devoted" to God is a blessing; but diverted to personal use, it becomes a curse, as was seen in the sin of Achan. The application is plain: the tithe diverted from God, or the tithe reserved and not paid, is as dangerous as a ticking time bomb. Tithed money is sanctified money.

Tithing Is a Transmutation of Value. Following the Parable of the Unjust Steward (Luke 16:1-8), the Lord makes a comment bearing on the proper use of money. He says: "Now my advice to you is to use 'money,' tainted as it is, to make yourself friends, so that when it comes to an end they may welcome you into eternal habitations" (v.9, *Phillips*). When this is equated with Matthew 6:20, "Lay up for yourselves treasures in heaven," it becomes apparent that earthly treasure is capable of being transmuted into heavenly values. Stewardship, as epitomized in the tithe and the responsible administration of the remainder, is the Christian way of life by which this transmutation is accomplished.

The Parable of the Wicked Servant (Matthew 18:23-35) seems to suggest that just as the faithful steward may transmute earthly treasure into heavenly values, so the unfaithful carry into eternity an incalculable debt (vv. 30,34).

AS AN ACT OF WORSHIP

Tithing Is an Act of Worship. Worship is an act or an attitude by which the relative positions of God and man are established. It rests on truth (John 4:24). Truth is the basis by which fellowship is established and maintained.

Honesty in money matters is an absolute essential in any fellowship between men. If one man robs another, whether by force or deceit, fellowship is broken. Indeed, force is preferable to deceit because the use of force reveals self, while the use of deceit conceals the true self. In force the person is assaulted, while deceit assaults dignity and makes a fool of the victim. When we hear Jesus say, "If therefore ye have not been faithful in the unrighteous mammon, who will commit to your trust the true riches?" (Luke 16:11), we are forced to consider Malachi's pointed question, "Will a man rob God?" (Malachi 3:8). Thus, the payment of the tithe is a simple act of honesty by which the position of the Lord as Sovereign and the position of man as subordinate is established.

The payment of the tithe is an act of worship because it consists of money or its equivalent. Money is not an unfortunate materialistic appendage to spiritual things but is itself spiritual. It is essentially a measure of time given, imagination employed, nervous energy expended, or talent exercised. It represents a portion of life contributed. To place the tithe on the offering plate is the laying down of that much of life and the testimony that life entirely belongs to God.

Tithing Is a Valid Testimony. To say of a man, "He pays his bills," is not only a compliment but also a testimony to his integrity. No man hesitates to accept such an appraisal of his character. Indeed, if such a declaration were withheld when it was due, a man would be justifiably aggrieved.

The right of privacy may be justified so far as the intrusion of unauthorized persons is concerned, but not so among brethren. We are told to come to the light (John 3:21) and the injunction goes so far as to include confession of fault (James 5:16).

It is as much a valid testimony to say, "I am a tithing Christian," as it is to say, "I am a praying or a born-again Christian."

THE TITHE: GOD'S WAY OF FINANCING THE KINGDOM

It might be argued that it was improper to carry the tithing program of the Hebrews over into the church, as though the two economies were identical, if Paul had not said, "Upon the first day of the week let every one of you lay by him in store, as God hath prospered him" (1 Corinthians 16:2). Within those few words there is recognition of (1) the Lord's Day, (2) the universal obligation, (3) the divine proportion, and (4) the church as the authorized storehouse.

It is proper to use the law of the tithe, as it is expressed in the precepts of the Old Testament, to enforce the obligation on all people of all times. It is proper because that law is based on everlasting principles that would exist whether or not they had been codified into law. The code, as given by Moses for instance, is the expression of the moral law as prepared for a particular people at a particular time. The culture, the environment, and the intellectual and emotional maturity of a people might change and require a change in the expression of that law, but the basic principle of it never changes.[9] Thus, Jesus was able to say He had not come to destroy, but rather to fulfill the Law (Matthew 5:17,18). He agreed to a compression of the entire Law into two precepts (Luke 10:27,28) because the spirit of the Law was not violated.

The law of God is not arbitrary so that it changes with a mood as do the laws of men. With man, a stroke of the pen may make something legal today that was illegal yesterday. Such capriciousness is unthinkable with God (Malachi 3:6; Hebrews 13:8).

The Church Is an Authorized Clearinghouse. "Ye looked for much, and, lo, it came to little; and when ye brought it home, I did blow upon it. Why? saith the Lord of hosts. Because of mine house that is waste, and ye run every man unto his own house" (Haggai 1:9). That incriminatory verse may be paraphrased thus: "Every man has his own private program."

It is true the work of God throughout the Christian era has been largely advanced by the noble and sacrificial gifts of dedicated individuals. Nothing can withhold from them the honor due their fidelity. But the task has not been accomplished. The population of the world increases in geometrical progression while the witness of the Church lags far behind. The truth is no one person can so much as dent the magnitude of the task. This is why the church is pivotal to the entire concept of stewardship. Quibbling over "Jewish statutes" will not invalidate the Great Commission.

Is there an institution, absolutely vital to the Christian faith, even as

---

[9]An example is the prohibition against eating unclean creatures. The law of God embraces the well-being of the whole man—body as well as spirit. Thus, a good proportion of Levitical law has to do with such things as health, sanitation, etc. Man is able to adapt his practice in these things to remove a high proportion of risk, as in the inspection and preparation of pork, but the risk is still there and the consequence of violating the Law is real.

"the service of the tabernacle of the congregation" was vital to the faith of ancient Israel, an institution whose principal business is to maintain the intelligent worship of God, and to extend among men the knowledge of Jesus Christ? If such an institution can be found upon the earth, we have found the divinely ordained successor of the tribe of Levi, which in ancient days was appointed to receive "all the tenth in Israel for an inheritance, for their service which they served." If the Jew was not permitted to "dedicate" his tithe, but was required faithfully to devote it to the purpose for which God had already dedicated it, the obligation rested upon fundamental reason; it was neither local nor arbitrary. Surely, Christian intelligence will recognize the same holy obligation. If honor is required to set apart a tenth in acknowledgment of God's ownership, then honor is certainly required to administer that tenth in accordance with God's revealed purpose.

Is there, then, such an institution among men, an institution without which Christianity would perish from the earth? One answer awaits us, and reasonable men will pause not a moment to accept the word. It is the church.[10]

We are not talking about the *designation* of the tithe, for it is already designated or "dedicated" (Leviticus 27:32). The very genius of the tithe is that it must be administered by another. What we are talking about is the *delegation* of the tithe. Neither are we robbing a man of his individuality. Rather, we are asking that man to permit the church to join him in his holy vocation and thereby to enlarge not only his offering, but also his joy. The exaltation of the affluent and the diminution of the less fortunate is avoided while the ministry of the church, as a church, is rediscovered and manifested. The choice is between irresponsible entrepreneurism and responsible ministry.

A church board, or other executive body, may often be slow to act or seem to extend investigatory inquiries beyond what appears reasonable. Far better is such an approach than the impatient yielding to an impulse that later proves to have wasted God's money. Religious racketeering is prevalent, even though we would wish it otherwise. Programs that have passed the scrutiny of intelligent, experienced men will usually bear the test of scriptural stewardship.

The Tithe Alone Is Inadequate Stewardship. It is often supposed that if all Christians would pay their tithes, the world would soon be evangelized and the kingdom of God established on the earth. Not so! The task is too great and the time too short. Indeed, the task is unlimited and requires unlimited resources.

---

[10]Calkins, *A Man and His Money*, p. 297.

It must be remembered that the tithe is the recognition, not the payment, of an obligation. The obligation of a steward is to manage the total value in his possession to the glory of God. The total obligation varies from person to person as the individual circumstances vary. Jesus said of the poor widow that she had given more than all others because it constituted "all her living" (Mark 12:44).

Man and God use different accounting systems. We are accustomed to counting our money, personality, talents, education, and position in life as assets. God counts them as liabilities. These things are the investment of God in us and He expects a return. Consider how many of the Lord's parables have this theme: the Barren Fig Tree, the Good Samaritan, the Prodigal Son, the Rich Fool, the Pounds, the Talents. Indeed, the word *talent* has passed into our language in its present meaning because of the parable. Consider also a portion of the parable that is often overlooked. Of the man who was afraid and hid his talent in the earth, the master said: "Thou oughtest therefore to have put my money to the exchangers, and then at my coming I should have received mine own with usury" (Matthew 25:27). He seems to say that *any* investment is better than none. He says, "It was given you to be administered."

Thus it is that beyond the tithe there is a partnership to be considered. After the tithe is rendered, and after the family obligations are computed, then comes the opportunity to enter the real business of the universe. This is where tithes and offerings are distinguished. Not until the tithe is paid do the offerings begin.

ESTABLISHING A TITHING PROGRAM

Must Be Biblically Sound. It may sound trite, or at least superfluous, to say a tithing program must rest on a sound Biblical basis. But a study of literature on the subject will make one wonder whether more energy is expended on rationalizations and negations than on an honest examination of the subject. Literature is available, but much of it is tainted with socialism and confusion with the broad stewardship of life.[11]

---

[11]"The broad stewardship of life" refers to the obligations every man has to his family, to the poor, and to society. To charge every expenditure of missionary entertainment, charitable contributions, neighborly donations, and community benefaction to the tithe is, at best, unworthy nit-picking and, at worst, an insult to God.

Only when the Bible is employed to search out the principles governing man's use of all value and the relation of these things to a sovereign God and His plan for eternity; only when the rationalization and quibbling have given place to understanding and acceptance; and only when faith lays hold of the promise; will the soul be ready for complete committal.

Most Christians tithe by instinct (if they tithe at all), rather than because they are well taught. Pastors have testified that it took 2 to 3 years of education before their congregations were prepared to undertake a truly scriptural stewardship program. Christians will accept the authority of the Scriptures when they understand the meaning of God's Word. It is the pastor's task to see that they do.

The Bible is substantive truth. It has inherent power to validate itself. When taken as a whole, in relation to the whole, it commends itself to man's critical faculty. It is not only the context of Scripture that is in view, but also the context of life and the relation of the two to each other. The Bible is truth, and truth has self-authenticating power and power to bind the healthy conscience.

Unfortunately, the truly healthy conscience is a rare phenomenon. An innate selfishness, cultivated by a pagan culture, conditioned by a liberal theology, trained by indulgent or indifferent parents, and sparked by ambition, is not good soil for a healthy conscience. It must be healed by saturation in the Word of God.

There is a harmony of truth throughout God's creation. All things were made to do His will. From microparticles in atomic orbit to wheeling galaxies in space, all move with ordained precision. Within the circle of this divine purpose all things *work together* for good (Romans 8:28). All that is truth is supported on every hand by parallel forces converging on an ultimate destiny chosen of God. The portal of entrance to this harmony of energy is at the point where God's sovereignty is acknowledged and man once again assumes his proper place in the scheme of things.

The above being true, it can be seen that any falsehood must defy irresistible forces. Little wonder so many of man's self-determined projects come to nothing. They are not in the stream of God's purpose. Businesses fail, or succeeding they plant the seeds of moral bankruptcy. There is frustration, defeat, conflict, and despair wherever the will of man crosses the will of God. Indeed, what is the Cross but a

picture of the crossed wills of God and man? At the juncture, even the
Lord Jesus, as the Representative of man, was crushed.

The task of the preacher, therefore, is to bring man into harmony
with the eternal purpose of God by presenting the truth. A basic element of that truth is what we know by the name of stewardship: God
as Sovereign, man as subordinate; God as Owner, man as possessor;
God as Principal, man as executive.

For man, that truth begins with the payment of the tithe. By such
acknowledgment he places himself as a voyager in the stream of purpose and is carried forward in harmony with all else that moves in
the will of God. Little wonder the prophet Malachi said: "I
will . . . open you the windows of heaven, and pour you out a blessing, that there shall not be room enough to receive it" (Malachi 3:10).

Must Be Consistent. Vocabulary plays no insignificant part in the
establishment of a tithing program. The words we use reflect the
philosophy we hold. Tithes are paid, not given. The offering can be
introduced with timeworn cliches, or it can be a fresh experience each
Sunday as we "worship God in tithes and offerings." It is profitable to
preface the offering with a stewardship vignette.[12]

There is another phase of public address that can be conveniently
called "propaganda." By this is meant all those insertions of church
policy, incidental promotion, and "asides" that find their way into
sermons, announcements, bulletins, and commentary. They are not
sermons or exhortations but exactly what is indicated—propaganda.
These are a useful tool when consistent with purpose.

The pastor who determines to build a church financed entirely by
scriptural methods will find himself besieged by expedients of every
nature. These will range all the way from candy selling in the youth
department to elaborate professional fundraising campaigns. There
are at least two dangers in such expedients: (1) they become a
substitute for tithing as people learn to get money for the church
without using their own, and (2) the utilization of pagan methods will
eventually result in pagan philosophies.

Some of these battles may be lost, at least until the truth sets the
people free and fires someone's imagination. It will help to remember
these things. First, tithing is not a scheme to raise money. That is the

---

[12]See Roy L. Smith's *Stewardship Studies* in the "Suggested Reading" for an excellent
source of material.

problem with all the expedients—they are blatantly designed to raise money. Tithing is designed to get the man, and the money is a by-product. Second, tithing is an act of worship. It is designed to establish the relative positions of God and man. Third, the payment of the tithe, because it is the acknowledgment and not the payment of an obligation, sets free an immense store of value and makes expedients unnecessary.

The tithing program is not a straitjacket that laces the church into a rigid mold. It rather insures the church a sound basis for its operational expenses so it is set free to undertake a host of worthy enterprises without considering how they will affect the basic structure.

Requires Persistent Education. Because tithing is a lifelong commitment, it requires persistent education. There is no handy list of answers that can precondition the tither against every possible contingency. Life is so complex, and problems so subtle in their variations, that hardly a week will pass without an inquirer.

There is a place in the church for a counseling service where the improvident debtor can be helped to liquidate his debts and the "credit-card maniac" can be delivered. If the church has no lending library, the pastor should have a private library of books on family budgeting and debt clearance.

There is, of course, a legitimate use of borrowing power, but the man who is head-over-heels in debt might as well be in jail. He has no freedom to live, let alone freedom to move into a meaningful partnership with God. For him there is no way out except the tithing way, for if he ceases to tithe he only adds the guilt of dishonesty to the bondage of poverty.

Persistence is required because tithing is under perpetual attack. The enemy within—plain, unvarnished selfishness—will be the most obdurate. The relatively small collegiate edition of one dictionary has seven columns of words compounded from *self*. Little wonder, then, that the human race is continually plagued by the reappearance of the "old man" in this form.

Our stewardship is under attack from a pagan society. "Wherein they think it strange that ye run not with them to the same excess of riot, speaking evil of you" (1 Peter 4:4). The economic structure of our society is foreign to the Christian concept of stewardship. Government, the courts, and industry (everything having to do with property) are founded on ancient pagan principles, and only the tithe can sanctify it and stewardship redeem it.

Requires Saturation Techniques. The life of the church needs to be saturated with the stewardship principle. If stewardship is indeed the Christian way of life, as opposed to the pagan way of life, if all property is a trust and money the token of it, then all of life should be governed by that basic philosophy.

It likewise follows that there is hardly a topic the preaching pastor might undertake that would not in some context bear on stewardship. Such incidental and supporting mention does not, however, substitute satisfactorily for *intensive and direct preaching* on the subject. Occasional sermons, valuable as they may be, fail in that they miss the floating portion of the congregation and may soon be forgotten.

Series preaching is recommended for several reasons: (1) It permits a continuity of thought impossible in the single sermon. (2) Repetition of theme insures better retention, for the continued attention permits the Holy Spirit to enforce the truth on the heart of the hearer. (3) The very fact that a large proportion of the preaching schedule is devoted to the topic will point to its value. (4) Experience tends to show that congregations will grow in number as a series progresses.

Such a series can be reinforced by several methods. Tithing laymen can be recruited to give a 5-minute testimony in each service. Literature handouts that may be carried home and studied can be provided.[13]

Brochures outlining the series can be distributed in advance. If the series is properly timed, it can conclude with a budget-approval meeting or banquet. Provocative titles draw attention. The pastor who is to preach on "A Man and His Money" is assured of a hearing.

The educational departments of the church should fulfill their function in teaching stewardship and tithing. It is never too soon to begin teaching children about the employment of talent for the Lord, the choice of a profession, and the practice of tithing. Some churches provide offering envelopes for the Sunday school on the premise that it is the most broadly based department in the church. Teachers should develop a stewardship vocabulary.

---

[13]Such literature should be studied to make sure it conforms to Scripture and the stewardship policy of the church. Several sources of such literature will be found in the "Suggested Reading" list.

The financial programs of the church should be structured to distinguish between tithes and offerings. It should be made plain that tithes are undesignated and administered by whatever board is responsible. That board may find itself able, or instructed, to employ certain proportions of the general fund for ministries outside the actual operation of the church, but the undesignated principle should always apply. Control should not be so rigid that there is no room for impromptu offerings for emergencies or under the leading of the Spirit.

Literature, such as tracts and circulating library books, should always be on hand. An important adjunct would be a brochure setting forth the church's philosophy of stewardship and method of handling finance. Men whose business life depends on a responsible accounting of money may be attracted to a church whose stewardship commends itself.

Probably the most important single factor in the success of a tithing program, besides the instruction of the Word of God, is *atmosphere*. Atmosphere is that indefinable aura that permeates the "feeling" of a service. It comes about through a recognition of the truth, the approval of the Holy Spirit, a unity of understanding, a sense of fellowship and communion, and a satisfaction with the "rightness" of things. When offering time is obviously a time of worship rather than a time when a mendicant and poverty-stricken church begs for alms, then such an atmosphere results.

Characterized by Strict Honesty. Tithing is an honorable base for doing business with and for God. It is the evidence that one proposes to show himself faithful and honest in the unrighteous mammon, that he might have committed to him the true riches (Luke 16:10,11). It ill behooves such a church to fail in its corporate practice of that which it requires of its individual members.

In the church, we dare not receive offerings whose true purpose is concealed from contributors. The pastor must always be on guard against the careless or unintentional misappropriation of funds. Other questions should be asked: "Have there been unreasonable administrative costs? Are there luxuries that bear no relation to comfort or ministry? Is there a use of unworthy 'gimmicks' such as those that characterize certain 'junk-mail' appeals?" These hidden dishonesties should be avoided like the plague they are.

In the community, the church should have a reputation of honesty.

One thing is certain: every member of the business community knows whether or not a church or its pastor pays its bills. There have been times when the financial community wanted no church paper or promises. Little wonder Paul said, "Provide things honest in the sight of all men" (Romans 12:17). Honesty is the very genius of stewardship. It certainly applies to money, but it goes deeper than that. If one can face God without flinching in business matters, he ought, as well, to be able to face God in his failures and shortcomings and give honest report. If God reads the balance sheet, He probably also reads the newsletter.

Nullifying Factors in a Tithing Program. Careful application of the principles outlined here is almost certain to result in a stewardship revival. There are, however, certain factors that can nullify the positive impact of a stewardship program.

The first is *an improper goal.* The acquisition of money is not a proper goal for a tithing program. True, tithing is the revealed method of financing the work of the Kingdom (Malachi 3:10; 1 Corinthians 16:2). But the Lord our God is a jealous God (Exodus 20:5) and He, not His kingdom, must come first. Tithing is first an act of worship. Furthermore, the man must come before his money. The value of the individual in the sight of God cannot be overstated.[14]

Legalism is a foe of stewardship. It is true there is a statute of Moses that declares the Law, but it is not for honorable men. Should an honorable man receive a monthly statement, accompanied by a marked copy of the penal code, he would be justly indignant. Such a man obeys not because the statute requires obedience, but because the statute represents something of great value to God. The righteous man sees law as a rule of reason coercing the heart (Psalm 19:8).

Within this framework one must think of the deeper meaning of the Biblical word *steward.* It cannot be wholly defined in the cold and heartless western word *trustee.* Only as it is defined in the warm, almost family relationship that existed, for instance, between Abraham and Eliezer (Genesis 24) or Joseph and Potiphar (Genesis 39:6), can it be understood. Think also of the benediction of Jesus: "Blessed is that servant, whom his lord when he cometh shall find so doing" (Matthew 24:46).

---

[14]The purpose behind the secrecy enjoined in Matthew 6:1-4 is to insure the privacy and dignity of the recipient of the charity.

Quid pro quo motivation is another potential pitfall. How often is tithing urged on men as the pathway to riches! *Quid pro quo* means something for something. Jacob was the first such bargainer (Genesis 28:20-22). He then had to help God out by shuffling his father-in-law's cattle (Genesis 30:37-43).

Some men ought not to be rich. Ironically, they are often the most covetous of riches. They fall prey to the traps set for their feet by unworthy fundraising. Men ought not to be led into something they are not constituted to handle. "But they that will be rich fall into temptation and a snare, and into many foolish and hurtful lusts, which drown men in destruction and perdition" (1 Timothy 6:9). Perhaps when their honesty and fidelity have been established and their maturity developed, they can be trusted with large sums.

It is to be remembered that the law of the tithe is inextricably bound with the law of first things (Leviticus 27:26-34). It is obvious, therefore, that quality is as much a part of the tithe as is quantity. This will certainly enforce the truth that the first tenth, not the last, is the tithe, but it also indicates very strongly that a poor man may be an honest man and that the quality of the tithe increases in inverse proportion to its quantity. "This poor widow hath cast in more than they all" (Luke 21:3).

The prestige syndrome undermines some stewardship programs. How sad it is to see the unconscious grading that takes place in the church: "Do you have many 'substantial' members?" Never! "It is required in stewards, that a man be found faithful" (1 Corinthians 4:2). Not successful, not generous, not influential, but faithful! Money is the by-product of a much more important truth, and to teach less cheapens a great truth.

Public offerings with their enormous emotional pressures should be conducted very carefully. There are times when some great purpose is to be served and the accomplishment of the goal will contribute to the joy of all. If, however, this is done at the expense of demeaning the poor and exalting the rich, it is not worth it.

Furthermore, the impression given is delusory. There are some, nurtured in the atmosphere of that type of fundraising, whose sole contributions are given when they may bask in the adulation of the untutored. When the books are balanced at the close of the year and the accounts compared, another story will unfold. Some possibly less for-

tunate but consistent contributor will be found to have much more to
his credit.

The pastor has more than one responsibility in respect to stewardship. He is equally called to teach the broad stewardship of life which
includes the support of his family and a reasonable obligation to
society. Should he find a man whose impulsive and irrational
generosity is depriving his family of the necessities of life, he needs to
sit down with that man and see that he understands the whole of
stewardship (1 Timothy 5:8).

If one wishes to deprive himself of some luxury so he might be
generous, that is his privilege and joy. But if he wishes to be generous
at the expense of some merchant, that is another thing entirely
(Romans 12:17).

Stewardship is energized by generosity and nullified by *stinginess*.
Nowhere is the law of the harvest more abundantly evidenced than in
the disposition of the Lord's money. "Give, and it shall be given unto
you; good measure, pressed down, and shaken together, and running
over, shall men give into your bosom. For with the same measure that
ye mete withal it shall be measured to you again" (Luke 6:38).

Pastors complain of, and churches are criticized for, the relative inadequacy of ministerial support. Without for one moment condoning
that parsimony which keeps the pastor on the thin edge of poverty, it
must be said the pastor himself is often responsible. For one thing, he
may be fearful of talking about money lest he be thought unspiritual.
If so, the program outlined herein will soon familiarize him with
financial verities and set him free. On the other hand, he may be a
willing participant in a policy that is equally parsimonious with missionaries, evangelists, denominational support, and Christian education. He may consciously or unconsciously be fearful of depleting
funds in which he has hopes of sharing. His remedy is to insist upon
generosity to other workers in the vineyard. His officers will soon
recognize the incongruity.

Nothing is more debilitating to a tithing program than *the introduction of substitutes* for the tithe. Human nature is such that if
something will produce a comparable result, it will be substituted.
Herein lies the danger of church catering services, car washes, candy
selling, and the myriad fundraising expedients. The moment a choice
is made to utilize someone else's money, the erosion begins. If such

things are ever acceptable, it must be after the tithe has been rendered. The danger is great—thus begin those pyramiding promotions that end in the courts and on the front page of the newspaper.

Supported by Budgetary Control. Intelligent stewardship requires a rational appraisal of the funds available in relation to the opportunities offered. Waste is *anathema* to God. One soul is reckoned as of more value than the total resources of the entire world (Mark 8:36); yet it is not one soul but a world of souls which is to be reached. It is, therefore, necessary to apply those principles of estimation and economy that insure the greatest return for the amount expended.

There are many things that are better done by a coalition of resources than by individual action. Such a confederation requires organization and its attendant government. When the purpose is worthy and effective, the costs of administration become a valid charge against the project. So denominational overhead, the administrative costs of a missionary program, or the maintenance of an institution becomes a proper use of the tithe. It is at this point that the church budget becomes a necessary tool. It is not the be-all and end-all of spiritual administration; it is exactly what is implied—a tool.

Budget Planning

THE OPERATIONAL BUDGET

A budget is a statement of the financial position of an organized entity for a definite period of time based on estimates of expenditures during the period and proposals for financing them. It is a plan for the coordination of resources and expenditures and includes the amount of money that is available for, required for, or assigned to a particular purpose.

Few churches operate on true budgetary principles. What is termed "the budget" is the most recent financial report, not necessarily adjusted to estimate a like period in the future. Little attempt is made to conform to a preconceived plan. Some would argue that this is all that is necessary and, where the sums handled are so insignificant that they may be held in the mind, they may be right. However, money is slippery and from such thinking comes that hand-to-mouth existence that troubles churches and individuals alike.

Money is primarily a measuring device and, as such, it relates to almost everything. Furthermore, it is God's money and deserves worthy employment. It is hardly practical to plan a future year's program without relating it to the money available against the money required. In fact, to put dollar figures against the work to be done is an aid to faith and a check against expediency.

Essential Records. The day is past when scraps of paper tucked away in some treasurer's pocket suffice for financial records. Such haphazard methods are not only insufficient, they open the door to suspicion. Standard business practice not only guards funds but also protects reputation.

The smaller church may find it difficult to locate the expertise necessary to maintain a simple bookkeeping system. However, any intelligent person can follow a pattern, and simplified systems designed to this end are furnished by the appropriate department in most denominational headquarters. Larger churches need and have the resources to pay for more elaborate systems. Whatever the system used, it should be possible to discover exactly how much has been expended for any given purpose within the time frame examined and how much remains of the allotment. Accuracy and adequacy are the checkpoints.

The simplest form of categorization is that by which revenue is broken down into source of income, and disbursement is subdivided by relevance to that source. Each of these categories constitutes a "fund."

In establishing such funds, it is not intended there should be separate bank accounts or, for that matter, multiple treasurers. Funding as intended here is a bookkeeping device. The only possible need for a separate bank account would be to set aside surplus funds or funds held for a particular purpose, so that interest might be drawn. Any fund might show a deficit at a given time without violating standard business practice, so long as the total funds show a balance. Such a deficit simply indicates the fund needs attention, or reveals the extent of a loss that had been intended.

The *general fund* is the basic category into which all undesignated funds flow. It is, therefore, the depository of all tithes, contingent funds (interest, sales, etc.), exchanges, and miscellaneous contributions.

From this fund come whatever subsidies are required to support other funds which, by the nature of their ministry, are either deliberately overspent or cannot be expected to support themselves. Unless such subsidies are employed, there is danger of a diversion of tithes to another program by those who have a deep interest in its success. This is a contagious practice that violates the undesignated character of the tithe and will eventually erode any tithing program. Such subsidies are handled by transfer from the general fund.

All salaries are ordinarily paid from the general fund unless it is desirable to compute the full cost of a particular area as, for instance, a "plant fund" where all costs of building upkeep, including the custodian's salary, would be separately funded.

Apart from the general fund, there would ordinarily be a *missions fund* (including both foreign and home missions), an *educational department* (Sunday school) *fund*, a *women's ministries fund*, a *youth department fund*, a *music department fund*, and a *tax and social security fund*. If auxiliaries such as a coffee house or campground are operated, they would require a separate fund. Optional funds such as *debt retirement, inventory* (for the replacement of depreciating equipment), and *insurance funds* might be established. Such funds are primarily useful where the general fund requires particularly careful management.

The pastor's salary and allotments would be charged against the general fund. In addition to this base salary, the pastor usually draws allotments for housing, car expenses, entertainment, and travel expense to official conventions, seminars, etc. Denominational retirement programs are computed by deduction of a given percentage of salary which is matched by the congregation. As a self-employed person, the pastor may make his social security payments directly or, as the law now stands, have them deducted and paid through the church.

Statistics indicate that the pastor, in relation to his professional standing, is generally underpaid. He is most vulnerable in early years while he is pursuing his own education, rearing a family, and educating his children. Ancient and outmoded traditions conspire to keep him on the edge of poverty. Denominational officials and enlightened laymen can do much to alleviate this situation if they will.

The pastor is not scripturally enjoined to austerity. Like Paul (Philippians 4:12), he should know both how to abound and how to be abased. He is worthy of "double honor" (1 Timothy 5:17) and not required to maintain an average of his congregation's affluence. His salary should be sufficient to give him a degree of independence, for there are those who are not above exerting financial pressure to attain a selfish end. Whatever sacrifices a pastor must make should spring out of his own convictions and not be imposed on him.

Wherever possible a pastor should own his own home. It is reasonable, where a church furnishes a residence as part of the pastor's income, that he should build an equity in the property over a suitable period of time.

Sources of Information. A statement of assets and liabilities is foundational to any financial analysis. Assets should be realistically appraised. It is not uncommon for a church to value its building at what it cost to buy or build, plus improvements. Common business practice would completely depreciate such a building over 10 or 20 years, and the fact is the property is worth no more than what it will bring on the open market. On the other hand, real estate, depending on location, might appreciate greatly. Some system of depreciation for buildings and furniture should be employed.

Statements of receipts and disbursements for the current year and the 2 preceding years are required for comparison. This is a sufficient period to evaluate trends. Both a dollar figure and a percentage figure should be prepared. The percentage figure will prove useful in maintaining the relative position of ministries to operational expense.

There should be a schedule of debt retirement. The debt load constitutes a fixed charge that will have to be considered before adjustments are made elsewhere. If a building fund or other capital investment is being considered, there should be a schedule of capital investment.

Formulating the Budget. In formulating the budget, adjacent columns are prepared showing the experience of at least two previous years with a third column provided for the projected figures for the next year. Items are considered one by one and the best possible estimate made for the coming year. A 10-percent inflationary figure will have to be considered, although that percentage increase will apply to the total and not necessarily to each item.

The normal procedure calls for department heads to submit operational estimates prior to the preparation of the total budget. They should be prepared to explain and defend their figures. The various estimates are incorporated into a preliminary budget and prepared for examination by the appropriate board or committee.

While the pastor is the responsible administrative head and thus charged with supervision of the budget, more and more churches are finding it advantageous to employ a business manager. These men are for the most part Christian businessmen who are retiring from business and do not want full-time employment but would like to remain active in the church. Such men are extremely valuable and their work releases others who might be better employed in ministry.

New programs should be realistically evaluated since they tend to be viewed with a degree of overoptimism. Adding an assistant pastor, for instance, involves car expenses, health and accident insurance, the denominational retirement allotment, a considerable amount of secretarial expense and overhead, and some cost for attendance at seminars and conventions. Some churches have found that with a base salary of $12,000 they could expect a total cost of around $20,000.

Ratifying the Budget. The budget is provisionally set up by the administration, revised by a board or committee, and finally presented to the congregation for ratification. The annual business meeting would be the logical time for such a presentation inasmuch as it probably coincides with the fiscal year.

The presentation should certainly be more than casual and incidental. The entire congregation needs a sense of participation and involvement. It also permits those who have a strong interest in some ministry (such as, a Christian college or missionary program) to ask for its inclusion. If it is not so included, several things may happen: (1) the money may bypass the church and the church will be robbed of that ministry; (2) a precedent for the diversion of tithes may be established; and (3) control of doubtful projects may be lost.

At such a ratification meeting explanations can be made that will avoid misunderstanding. For instance, if money is being set aside on a monthly basis toward the annual insurance cost, some members may be thinking of that money as disposable. Should they see one of the funds in deficit, they may think of that deficit as a diversion of funds rather than as a bookkeeping device. When the congregation has ratified the budget it becomes official and should govern disbursements.

The inclusion and disposition of designated funds, supposing the donor wishes to avail himself of a tax deduction, must be governed by certain guidelines.

1. No contributions can be designated for a nonexempt third party.

2. Contributions must be designated for programs or projects the church has authorized in advance as part of its overall outreach and activity.

3. The church retains the right of deciding if contributions have been designated properly and in keeping with the purposes of the congregation. If contributions cannot be used within the donor's designation and the purposes of the church, the donation will be returned to the donor with an explanation of the problem.

4. If an outside agency is used to disburse the designated contribution, the church will still seek to make sure the funds are applied in accord with the wishes of the donor and the purposes of the church.

5. The church retains absolute autonomy in determining whether or not a contribution satisfies these guidelines.

Funding the Budget. The annual budget-funding program should focus attention on the ministries of the church. The vague generalization, "The church is worthy of your support," is apt to engender the question, "Why?" It must be shown to be worthy. The campaign should be built around the accomplishments of recent history and goals for the future. The intent should be to reach every constituent and obtain a commitment within a specified period of time.

The committee responsible for funding the budget should be reasonably large so as to represent the varying financial strata of the congregation. Its members should share a common commitment to the stewardship philosophy of the church. The chairman should have the confidence of the people and have some ability in organization and public relations. If the personnel assignments are rotated yearly, a widening knowledgeability can be established. The committee should enlist and outline responsibilities for every officer, teacher, and leader of the congregation.

Promoting the Budget. As much as 60 days will be required for the committee to organize, plan, and prepare materials for an intensive campaign. Precampaign publicity should be extensive and climactic. By the time a commitment is expected, the entire constituency should be reasonably familiar with the project.

All church publications, especially the bulletin and newsletter, should reflect the approaching campaign in accelerating tempo. Personalized mailings have proven their worth. Supplies designed as aids for just such programs are obtainable from a number of service companies. One such company furnishes complete programs excellently conceived and colorfully printed.[15] These materials have the further advantage of being scripturally valid. Also, one insurance company furnishes supplementary data, both in print and on cassette, particularly as concerns ministers' salaries and tax concessions.[16]

It is in the pastor's interest to be on the mailing list of as many of these service companies as possible. It is fashionable to depreciate the value of so-called "junk" mail, but it occasionally produces a good source. The collection of ideas cannot be left to the moment. It is a perpetual search.

Professional assistance is not only expensive, but also, on the whole, will produce less than the normal income of a tithing church. The service rendered is only that of supervision. Furthermore, there is the risk of confusing the stewardship philosophy of the church. Outside specialists in the stewardship ministry may provide a starting point, but they are no substitute for a consistent ministry by the pastor.

Pledging the Budget. While the preliminary lead-in may cover as much as a month, it is well to confine the actual pledging session to one Sunday with the follow-up continuing through the week and concluding on the second Sunday. Some churches prefer to use a banquet meeting for the pledging and the following Sunday for the follow-up.

The word *pledge* has some unfortunate connotations. Many sincere tithers consider that they have made a commitment to God and look on card signing as an irrelevancy. It is also true that a tithing church will almost invariably go beyond anything that might have been pledged. Because of these feelings, the euphemism "faith promise" and similar synonyms have been substituted for "pledge." It is important, therefore, that signing a committal form be looked on as a means of determining the funds available rather than as a means of extracting a reluctant dollar.

---

[15]Arthur Davenport Associates, Inc., P. O. Box 18545, Oklahoma City, OK 73118.

[16]Minister's Life and Casualty Union, Minister's Life Building, Minneapolis, MN 55416.

The stewardship program outlined in these pages makes a distinction between tithes and offerings, and it would be well if the committal card made such a distinction.

A meeting scheduled for the implementation of the budget needs to be handled with imagination. Graphs, flash cards, "pies," slides, and even motion pictures can be used. If departmental reports are furnished, they should not be read but used to provide a pertinent illustration.

A follow-up system will have to be divised to pick up those who were absent from the pledging session. Such people should be carefully allocated among the committee lest overlapping assignments give the impression of harrassment.

Collecting the Budget. A signed committal card should not constitute a legal obligation but should be prefaced with a statement like, "As God enables me . . . ." Information such as individual quarterly reports and a final annual total for tax purposes are valuable but there are no permissible pressures other than the Word of God and the atmosphere of the church. Devoted Christians pay tithes, but they are subject to circumstances beyond their control that might, for a time, make additional offerings difficult or impossible. The Lord certainly understands these occasional strictures and the church should be no less understanding.

Disbursing the Budget. The line of authority in disbursing the budget begins with the congregation, which determines the policies to be followed; it continues with the board of the church, which interprets that policy; and then it moves to the disbursing officer. The responsible executive is generally considered to be authorized to disburse funds allotted to him without further reference to the board except for overruns. At least two cautions are necessary: (1) supervision is required to avoid early affluence and late privation; and (2) it should be understood that the money does not *have* to be spent. A decision must be made whether funds unspent in one time period carry over into the next.

Routine expenditures such as salaries, utilities, and missionary obligations, being authorized as standing commitments in the minutes, do not require specific authorization. However, just as every contribution should be receipted, so every check should be issued on the warrant of an authorizing voucher. Church treasurers are officers, not employees, of the corporation and generally can only exercise supervision and make certain that guidelines are followed. Purchase orders and vouchers simplify their task.

It has become standard practice in some churches to appoint a standing committee whose duty it is to make a monthly check of expenditures against vouchers and of the minutes of the board. Whatever system is used, adequate procedures should be established so there is a distinct audit trail for every transaction.

No budget should be set in concrete and incapable of revision. Guidelines should demand adherence to the paperwork necessary to assure that all funds are properly disbursed, but they should not be so rigid as to hinder the work. Emergencies will arise, opportunities will open, and utility prices will escalate. There must be room for exceptions and for spontaneous projects. The budget should be a tool and not a slavemaster.

THE CAPITAL BUDGET

A capital budget is devised for the accumulations of assets for long-term additions or betterments. Such assets are normally invested in a manner designed to augment their worth.

Building Funds. There are things within the vision of any progressive church that cannot be financed by the operational budget. Reserves must be built up against the cost of a new building, the inauguration of a television ministry, or the purchase of a youth camp. Such reserves are counted among the assets of the church but are deliberately set aside from the operational funds. They are therefore eligible to be employed in long-term investments. How large should that reserve be? The matter boils down to the basic question, "What is a safe debt load for the church?"

This question was asked of a financial house whose officers had experience with several denominations. They came up with the following formula which has since been the basis of a successful home missions program.[17]

1. Compute 1/3 the value of church property owned;
2. Add $200 per family of active membership;
3. Multiply the annual budget disbursement figure by 5;

[17]The New York District of the Assemblies of God, Box 1, Colvin Station, Syracuse, NY 13205.

AND HE GAVE PASTORS

The average of the total is the safe debt load.

The following figures apply that formula to the circumstances of a well-established, growing, and progressive church with no debt. The membership of that church would probably not be shocked if they were asked to assume a debt load of $2 million. What are the facts?

1. 1/3 the value of church property owned . . . . $ 311,983
2. 225 active families @ $200   45,000
3. Annual disbursements multiplied by 5   1,016,975
$1,373,958

The safe debt load would be the average ($1,373,958 ÷ 3), or $457,986. Whether or not the formula is valid in every case, the fact remains that the establishment of a capital fund is important to a growing church.

Investments. The investment of capital funds for maximum profit is a highly specialized business. Unless a church has capable advisors, it will probably serve its constituents best by using certificates of deposit or government bonds. The element of risk that may be acceptable to the private investor cannot be accepted by those who administrate public funds. A church may accumulate certain stocks because there is a tax advantage to donors in contributing stocks as against the same dollar figure in cash. These constitute a legitimate reserve. In the same manner, real estate will come to the church and some decision must be made regarding it. Church-owned property that is not used directly for religious purposes is almost universally taxable. The subject of investments requires better and more immediate service than can be given here.

Whether or not a church should operate a business is a moral question each church must answer for itself. Certain types of business seem acceptable because they answer the specialized needs of the religious community or serve a benevolent purpose. Beyond that, the church enters into competition with the business community and engenders ill-will. The political climate, whether justifiably so or not, is unfavorable.

Methods of Financing Capital Projects. There is no unanimous agreement as to the best way of financing a capital project. An established congregation with a proven track record would probably opt for bonding. There are a number of advantages: (1) the debt is, for the most part, kept within the religious community; (2) a certain percentage of interest will be forgiven as a contribution; and (3) a significant quantity may return to the church as a legacy.

One very important caution must be noted. Churches are notoriously careless about observing legal restrictions and some end up in trouble with the Securities Commission. Good legal advice is imperative.

Insurance programs have proliferated in such variety that any comprehensive recommendation would be difficult. .In general, the money advanced is secured by policies written on the life of subscribing members. Almost invariably the property is also held under mortgage.

Denominational programs operate on the same principle as the conventional mortgage. Profits accrue to the religious community and are utilized to enlarge the financial base from which such loans are made. It is unlikely that denominational reserves permit wholesale financing of church buildings, but progress is being made on a selective basis.

Whatever the method of financing is, the church should realize that if the security is so tenuous that a loan is difficult, the practicality of the venture ought to be squarely faced. When the debt load is onerous, fringe supporters will fade away. It is unthinkable for a pastor to overobligate his church and then move on to greener pastures to avoid the responsibility.

Insurance

Adequate insurance is a necessity for any church. Churches are a target of the arsonist and subject to the carelessness of a congregation, all of whom assume that somebody else is watching over security. Being unoccupied for hours and sometimes days at a time, any damage may be extensive and serious. Vandalism is a common risk, and no one is exempt.

No existing building can be rebuilt at the original figure, and the situation worsens annually. A fire can have debilitating consequences to a church that is already at the limit of its resources. Church boards are tempted to insure at less than full value because a few dollars in premiums may be saved. By so doing they become coinsurers and in case of loss will be saddled with a percentage of the cost. Insurance should be thought of as a fixed charge that is part of unescapable overhead. It is immoral for a church to excuse itself with the thought that the religious community will come to the rescue.

Liability and accident insurance is a "must" in the litigious climate that prevails across the country. The courts are loaded with everything from legitimate claims to nuisance suits. Juries are granting increasingly exorbitant judgments. The crack in the sidewalk, the "attractive nuisance," and the waxed floor are invitations to disaster. Liability and accident insurance not only protects against such things but also provides for those mishaps that members may occasionally suffer.

TYPES OF INSURANCE

Basic coverage. The two basic coverages a church should have are *fire* and *liability* insurance. The policy covering fire damage should be written to cover 80 percent of replacement value to avoid the risk of becoming a coinsurer. The insurance company will appraise the property to determine that figure. If the church does not agree with the insurance appraiser's figure, it can insure at its own figure but must face the possibility of having to prove the point. The church must also submit to periodic inspections by the insurance company's engineer and the local fire department and meet the demands of both.

The fire insurance purchased should include *comprehensive* which adds storm and wind damage, lightning destruction, water damage, vandalism (usually excluding glass breakage), and other incidentals. Liability should cover all properties owned by the church and automobiles (even if privately owned) that are used on church business. The liability insurance should be coupled with an accident provision that will pay limited medical expenses.

Optional policies a church might consider are: (1) health and accident for staff and employees; (2) workmen's compensation; (3) flood;[18] and (4) burglary.

Health and accident insurance is a concession to employer/employee relationships and obligations. It should be accompanied by an explicit statement of policy. Workmen's compensation is not obtainable in all jurisdictions and, where it is, requires a minimum number of employees. It is not expensive. Insurance against flooding, particularly

---

[18]Flood plain insurance is guaranteed by the government, but the program must be accepted by the local municipality. Investigation must be made of what conditions apply locally.

for churches built on a flood plain, should certainly be considered. Burglary insurance comes at very high premiums.

AGENCY SUPERVISION

The trustees of a church are charged by law with the responsibility of safeguarding the property. In some instances they may be held personally liable for dereliction of duty if they fail. They will be helped greatly by the professionalism of a reputable agency. Variation in insurance rates derives primarily from differences in the services offered, because the base rates are subject to review by state commissions. Commission rebates and sharing are illegal in many jurisdictions. An agency may offer a variety of companies and coverages and can prepare a package suited to any situation.

GROUP INSURANCE

Some denominations or ecclesiastical divisions thereof provide group insurance at significant savings. Where such group programs have been long-established, the advantages are more obvious. In the beginning, while reserves are being built, dividends may accrue to the group plan and the savings offered seem minimal. However, as the program develops, those farsighted enough to stay with it may enjoy substantial savings.

SELF-INSURANCE

Anything less than full coverage is a form of self-insurance. To be self-insured in the popular meaning of the term requires sufficient capital reserves to meet any foreseeable loss. Such reserves are acquired by setting aside an amount equal to the premium that might otherwise have been paid. The net result, at least for churches whose reserves are earmarked for another purpose, is the church is, in effect, not insured at all while the reserves are building. The value of self-insurance accrues best where multiple units exist and where the value of any single unit is inconsequential in relation to the whole. Churches are for the most part single-unit institutions.

Conclusion

Experience and expertise are the most important single factors in any financial matter. It is a fortunate church that has laymen with abilities in this field. Yet, when all is said and done, there are spiritual laws that may under some circumstances supersede purely mundane considerations. Such are faith and generosity. The danger is to mistake presumption for faith.

The following paragraph is a fitting conclusion.

> Faith rests upon the promises of God; presumption distorts the promises of God. Opportunity comes to faith; presumption strains to create opportunity. Faith opportunities are entered with the eyes open; presumptuous action is entered with the eyes closed. Faith counts the cost; presumption expects a free ride. Faith operates *on* a strain as do the strings of a violin; presumption operates *under* a strain as does the improvident debtor. The price of faith is paid *before* the act; the price of presumption is paid *after* the act. Faith is peace; presumption is neurotic. Faith is a gift of the Spirit; presumption is a hallucination of the flesh. Faith is confident; presumption is desperate. Faith walks hand in hand with God; presumption cringes in company with pride.[19]

Suggested Reading

Brazell, George. *This Is Stewardship*. Springfield, MO: Gospel Publishing House, 1962.

Calkins, Harvey Reeves. *A Man and His Money*. New York: The Methodist Book Concern, 1914.

Davenport, Arthur S. *The Ten Best Stewardship Sermons*. Oklahoma City: Arthur Davenport Associates, 1963.

Harrell, Costen J. *Stewardship and the Tithe*. New York: Abingdon Press, 1953.

Kelley, Dean M. *Why Churches Should Not Pay Taxes*. New York: Harper & Row, 1977.

McConaughy, David. *Money—The Acid Test*. Philadelphia: The Westminster Press, 1919.

Schwarz, Ted. *The Successful Promoter*. Chicago: Henry Regnery Co., 1976.

Smith, Roy L. *Stewardship Studies*. Nashville: Abingdon Press, 1954.

---

[19] 1970 Annual Missionary Conference, Locarno, Switzerland.

18

The Pastor
and
Legal Affairs

JOSEPH L. GERHART

Render therefore unto Caesar the things which are Caesar's; and unto
God the things that are God's (Matthew 22:21).

Submit yourselves to every ordinance of man for the Lord's sake:
whether it be to the king, as supreme; or unto governors, as unto them
that are sent by him for the punishment of evildoers, and for the praise
of them that do well (1 Peter 2:13,14).

Corporate Law

The Christian has dual citizenship. He is a citizen of his country
and a citizen of heaven. Since the local assembly is made up of born-
again Christians, both citizenships are involved. This chapter deals
with legal affairs of our earthly citizenship.

To be a citizen of the United States is something for which to be
thankful. We live in and are an integral part of a nation that allows
religious freedom—freedom of worship according to the dictates of
our conscience, our heart, and our experience; and freedom of speech
in the pulpit, in the marketplace, in mass meetings, and on radio and
television.

We also have the freedom of organization with the liberty to form
nonprofit corporations that are accorded specific considerations and
exemptions by existing laws.

When Jesus said, "Render . . . unto Caesar the things which are
Caesar's," He was referring to obedience to the laws of the land. The

*Joseph L. Gerhart, D.D., is superintendent emeritus of Northern
California-Nevada District of the Assemblies of God, Santa Cruz,
California.*

Scriptures teach that we, as His followers, must conform to both systems: the laws of the land and God's laws. This is dual citizenship.

The Constitution of the United States guarantees religious freedom. Individual states interpret this freedom within the framework of the Constitution but cannot violate its basic principles. Since individual states vary in some respects in their interpretation of the law, it is advisable for members of an organization to familiarize themselves with the laws of the state in which they reside if they are contemplating incorporating or changing an existing corporation.

THE MEANING OF LEGAL CORPORATION

The corporation is a device for carrying on an enterprise as an entity entirely distinct from the persons who are interested in it and control it. The state authorizes its existence. As long as it complies with the provisions of the law, it continues to exist, irrespective of changes in its membership. It has an individual name by which it may enter into contracts; it may hold property; and it may sue and be sued. It has powers that it requests and receives in its articles of incorporation when it goes through the formalities of incorporation. It may also do such ordinary things as are necessary in conducting its business.

The classical definition of a corporation given by Chief Justice Marshall in the famous Dartmouth College case, which incidentally did not involve a business corporation, is helpful:

A corporation is an artificial being, invisible, intangible, and existing only in contemplation of law. Being the mere creature of law, it possesses only those properties which the charter of its creation confers upon it, either expressly or as incidental to its very existence. These are such as are supposed best calculated to effect the objects for which it was created. Among the most important are immortality, and if the expression may be allowed, individuality, properties by which a perpetual succession of many persons are considered as the same, and may act as a single individual. They enable a corporation to manage its own affairs, and to hold property without the perplexing intricacies, the hazardous and endless necessity of perpetual conveyances for the purpose of transmitting it from hand to hand. It is chiefly for the purpose of clothing bodies of men in succession with these qualities and capacities that corporations were invented, and are in use. By these means, a perpetual succession of individuals are capable of acting for the promotion of the particular object, like one immortal thing.[1]

The definition brings out these two points: (1) The corporation exists only by virtue of law; in other words, without a law to give it life, a corporation could not exist. (2) The corporation as a legal personality is capable of acting in many ways like a natural person. But since it is not a natural person, it enjoys certain immunities that natural persons do not. For example, it cannot commit treason. On the other hand, as an artificial being, it can act only through its members as a body, or the directors and officers who direct its affairs.

DIFFERENT KINDS OF CORPORATIONS

Basically there are two kinds of corporations. One is a corporation for profit, and the other is a corporation not for pecuniary gain, commonly called a nonprofit corporation. In this chapter we are concerned chiefly with the nonprofit corporation.

Corporations for Profit. Private corporations, according to the character of their organization, may be either stock corporations or nonstock corporations. In stock corporations the membership is represented by shares of stock. In nonstock corporations there are no shares of stock, but the membership is determined by rules and regulations set out in the bylaws. Stock corporations are organized for the purpose of profit, whereas nonstock corporations are organized as not-for-pecuniary-profit corporations, such as mutual benefit associations, fraternal organizations, clubs, churches, and the like.

The Assemblies of God position concerning ministers holding title to properties supported by funds solicited for the work of God is as follows:

> c. *Private ownership of religious institutions.* The General Council of the Assemblies of God approves the holding of title to all church buildings, schools, or other institutions that are supported by funds solicited for the work of God by properly constituted corporations. It disapproves the holding of title to such properties by the ministers of the Assemblies of God, through private ownership, corporation of sole,

---

[1]Chief Justice Marshall, Trustees of Dartmouth College vs. Woodward (1819) 4 Wheat. 636, 4L Ed 629.

closed corporation or any other type of ownership where initiative of action or final authority is not vested in a corporation of the whole.[2]

Corporations Not for Profit. A religious corporation is one whose purposes are directly and manifestly ancillary or auxiliary to divine worship or religious teaching; it is not necessarily a church in the common acceptation of the term, or even a religious society. The corporation and church are distinct bodies, the purposes of one being temporal, and those of the other spiritual. The former acquires the rights and powers of a corporation for certain purposes, without losing its sectarian and denominational characteristics.

The first requirement of a nonprofit corporation is that its *purposes* be religious, ethical, social, moral, or educational. The *activities* of a nonprofit corporation may be of the same nature. The second requirement is that any income or profit of the corporation must be used solely to carry out its legal purposes and cannot be distributed as profit to its members. The corporation cannot pay dividends or other remuneration to its members. It can, however, pay reasonable compensation or salaries for services rendered.

A nonprofit corporation may receive profit incidental to its operations, but that profit must be used for the purposes for which the corporation exists. For example, a church having tax exemption as a nonprofit corporation might receive considerable profit from some of its activities; this money could not be distributed as pecuniary gain to its members, but it could be expended for educational or other purposes, as provided for in its articles of incorporation, that would benefit its members and/or the public.

Nonprofit corporations are not exempt from businesslike responsibility. Even though city, county, state, and federal taxes may not be required, the nonprofit corporation must file all necessary exemption forms and maintain fiscal responsibility. Aside from gifts, reimbursements, remuneration, and generally accepted costs for capital improvements, equipment, maintenance, etc., all disbursements of nonprofit corporation funds must be approved in keeping with the bylaws before being made. Corporation receipts for tax purposes may be given to contributors for gifts of cash and real and personal property as provided for in the bylaws.

[2]From the *Minutes* of the Thirty-Seventh Session of The General Council of the Assemblies of God, 1977, p. 144.

WHY FORM A NONPROFIT CORPORATION?

From the standpoint of the state, a local congregation is either a society, a voluntary association of church members, or an incorporated body, the latter being a legal entity. The incorporation option has a number of important implications which should be carefully considered by any group meeting together as a church congregation.

Indemnification. An incorporated church has, in addition to attaining legal status, several distinct characteristics. Individual members are not responsible for any of the acts of the corporation. They are not liable for debts or damages caused by negligence on the part of the employees of the church.

The trustees, elected to office by the congregation, are not individually liable for debts or judgments against the corporation unless they have exceeded their authority in incurring liabilities or engaging in contracts. The nature of such authority is defined and limited in state statutes, articles of incorporation, and in the bylaws of the corporation. Protection of members of the congregation and trustees as indicated above is known as indemnification.

Title to Properties. A nonincorporated group has no legal position in most states. Consequently, it is unable to hold real estate, enter into contracts, or sue in its own name. In order for such organizations to own real estate, for instance, it is necessary for them to work through trustees, who hold the property in their names.

Perpetuation of the Organization. It is important to note that the perpetuation of the local church can be assured by incorporating. As a corporation, it has continued life. It does not cease to exist upon the death or relocation of its incorporators or leaders. This is of value in engaging in transactions requiring long periods of time for their completion, such as bond issues to build a new edifice.

Protection of the Name of the Organization. What's in a name? To most of us it is exceedingly important. It gives not only identification but it also protects reputation. Because of this, state laws will allow only one corporation in the state to have an individual name. It is not possible for any other corporation in the same state to have an identical name. Every legal name must differ from others in some way.

Insurance. Most insurance companies desire (some require) a church congregation to be incorporated before they will issue proper coverages, especially certain types of insurance. Most companies also desire to have someone designated by the corporate body as a contact person through whom the company can officially communicate with the corporation.

Legal Status With Specific Powers. Following is a "ladder of priorities of powers" for a legal corporation:

1. Constitution of the United States (supreme)
2. Civil Law (federal, state, and local)
3. Articles of Incorporation (sometimes called a charter)
4. Constitution of the Corporation
5. Bylaws of the Corporation
6. Standing Rules of the Corporation
7. Parliamentary Law (authority book chosen by the corporation)

Civil laws centered in the Constitution of the United States, as interpreted by the Supreme Court, are the source of legal powers for our nation. These powers are granted to states who then may share them in keeping with their legal stewardship of powers. States share powers with counties and cities within the state. This is known as civil law or laws that govern citizens.

Congress and the states share the powers they possess. Corporations can be recipients of certain powers upon formal request, normally to the state. When this is done, the instrument issued to the corporation by the state is called a charter or articles of incorporation. No corporation has any power other than that which has been granted to it by the state in which it is incorporated or registered. A corporate charter or articles of incorporation can be changed by the corporate body only by a legal process and through the state that granted its corporation powers.

Many corporations have binding agreements of purpose and operation called a constitution and/or bylaws. A constitution sets forth the basic purpose and organizational format and can be changed or amended only under limited circumstances. It helps to perpetuate the essentials of the corporation. Some corporations do not have a constitution but believe that the basic essentials are sufficiently included in the articles of incorporation; such organizations have only bylaws to provide details of operation. Bylaws modify the constitution (if there is one) or the articles of incorporation (if there is no constitution). As a rule, bylaws may be changed by a simple majority vote of the body that has the power to change them.

Standing rules are simply agreements, usually temporary. They have to do mainly with nonessential matters and may be established by the body in session or by any lessor body or person to whom this power may be delegated by the corporate body.

One thing to keep in mind is that this priority of powers is a flow of powers. The standing rules can use only the powers granted in the preceding reservoirs of powers as indicated on the "ladder." Also, the bylaws can in no way violate the constitution, the articles, or civil law; likewise, the constitution has no power not provided for in the articles, and the articles have only the powers requested by the organization and granted by civil law. A legal corporation, therefore, is limited in powers and amenable to civil law. Any body or person having power to establish rules also has the power to change the rules it established unless limited by a body with higher powers.

A corporation exceeding its powers is liable to forfeiture of its charter by the state. Where certain powers are designated, this implies an exclusion of all others that are not necessary to carry into effect those expressly granted.

Due to the fact that various authorities on parliamentary law differ in their recommendations and procedures, a standard book of parliamentary law should be selected, adopted, and named in the constitution or bylaws. (Usually this is done in the bylaws.) Parliamentary law is not intended to control the corporation. Its purpose is to provide a system for controlling the body according to its adopted constitution and bylaws. It is a method, adopted and placed in the constitution or bylaws, to guide the corporation in conducting and carrying out its business in an acceptable manner. It fills in the blanks where omissions in organizational or parliamentary procedure may exist in the bylaws. Its position on the "ladder of priorities of powers" indicates its relative importance.

The church as a legal corporation has a good standing in the community. It has been recognized by the civil law that granted it its legal status with specific purposes and powers to perform its rights with privilege. It has recognized fiscal responsibility which helps in doing business with banks, lending agencies, and other businesses in the community. It provides a legal platform on which to have complete insurance coverage.

These are the reasons why The General Council of the Assemblies of God will not grant full affiliation of a local congregation unless the congregation has been duly set in order or incorporated by the state in which it exists, and unless the qualified membership of the congregation owns and controls the corporation.

Alienation of Title

The question, "To whom does this belong?" is of utmost importance. Let us examine a few of the reasons.

ACQUISITION OF AND RESPONSIBILITY FOR CORPORATION PROPERTIES

Suppose a church was started in a home or rented facility of some kind. As the congregation grew and developed it was duly organized, incorporated, and set in order by the district council. The congregation now recognizes that owning a church building could be of great help in community and worldwide outreach.

Under the pastor's capable leadership, a committee is appointed to help find a suitable location in a growing area of the community and, if possible, on a busy street or highway in order to provide advertising and accessibility for the church. With the thought of future expansion, including schools, senior-citizen facilities, and adequate parking space, several acres should be considered by the search committee in areas where such facilities are warranted. In smaller communities larger acreages are not advisable except where some land can be purchased and sold to the church's advantage, providing, of course, that sufficient is kept for future needs.

Real estate should be purchased in the name of the corporation. It is advisable for the corporation to purchase land for church buildings as soon as possible after the incorporation and as soon as the congregation is sure of the location and need for the land. There are times when the corporation may not have sufficient funds to buy the land or even to put a required down payment on the purchase of the land. A temptation may arise for the pastor or someone else to purchase the land in his or her name for the corporation. This temptation should not be yielded to. If someone wishes to assist the corporation in this manner, he should do so by lending the money to the corporation with a proper note and interest for the loan. If this is found to be necessary, advisable, and approved by the corporation, then the land can be purchased in the name of the corporation. A note of warning, however: be sure the corporation is not obligating itself to the extent that it cannot meet its obligations.

When the land has been purchased in the name of the corporation, the church may then be ready to talk about buildings. A bank may not be interested in lending the corporation funds for building, even though the land is free and clear of debt, if the corporation balance sheet shows excessive liabilities, such as personal loans. It may be necessary to go to the people for more personal loans for construction or to find a lending agency or program that can help.

All loans for construction should be to the corporation. This includes furniture, fixtures, and equipment for the building, classrooms, and offices. Again, caution is to be exercised in the cost of buildings and the furnishings and fixtures for the buildings. Do not obligate the corporation beyond its ability and willingness to pay. Be sure all loans, contracts, accounts, and purchases for the corporation are made in the name of the corporation. Never mix personal business with corporate business. This is a rule that may prevent trouble and misunderstanding today, tomorrow, and in years to come.

All corporate purchases, whether for real estate, buildings, furniture, fixtures, equipment, etc. (known as nonexpendables), must be listed in the corporation audit as assets of the corporation. These items must be properly identified, showing the date and cost of purchase. Model and serial numbers of items so identified by manufacturers should also be listed with each item. In case of burglary, fire, or other loss, this information is necessary. This information is also necessary for the auditor when he figures depreciation for the corporation balance sheet and annual report.

DISPOSAL AND ACCOUNTABILITY OF CORPORATION PROPERTIES

Items of corporation-owned property should never be sold or disposed of in any way without the approval of the corporate body that owns it. Usually the body gives the official board the power to dispose of certain items or to do business for the corporation, within a limited price range. This should be defined very clearly in the corporation bylaws.

Pastors and members should avoid mixing personal money with corporate money. Again, be reminded that this is the source of many misunderstandings and causes serious friction within the body. Purchase of corporate property, or any expenditures of corporation funds, must be properly approved by whoever has the corporate power to grant approval. If personal money has been used in behalf of the corporation, do not expect a refund from corporate funds unless the disbursement has been properly approved. Accountability for corporate funds is the responsibility of the corporation and is of utmost importance to the State Corporations Commission and to the Federal Internal Revenue Service. The continued approval of state and federal agencies can depend on proper fidelity and accountability of the corporation.

When planning a church building, consider building in a fireproof walk-in vault in which corporate records, insurance policies, and other important papers can be protected. If this is not feasible, a good fireproof safe should be installed for this purpose.

Insurance

Someone has said, "Insurance is usually worthless until it is too late to obtain it." This statement is not altogether true, for there are certain kinds of life insurance that provide borrowing capability against the value of the policy. Certain insurance also is a requirement for borrowing money from banks and other lending agencies. Insurance is required should a church seek to rent, lease, or buy buildings and equipment. Among the several advantages of having proper insurance coverage is that important one of "peace of mind," knowing there is proper coverage in case of any eventuality.

BYLAW PROVISION TO NAME AN INSURANCE COMMITTEE

An adequate insurance program for the church is of such importance that an insurance committee should be appointed by the church board with the express responsibility of seeing that every possible peril is considered and that proper recommendations are made to the board for their consideration and adoption if approved. The reason for this committee of course is threefold: (1) to seek and search for the very best and most complete coverage, at the most reasonable rates, with responsible insurance companies; (2) to place responsibility in case of claims and litigations when neglect, carelessness, or poor judgment are evident; (3) to serve as the agent for the church in communication with insurance companies. The committee chairman is usually named as the contact person. This responsibility is so important that provisions for and responsibilities of an insurance committee should be provided for in the bylaws of the corporation.

In lieu of a committee, some churches or organizations have one qualified board member or elected officer who is charged with the same responsibilities as that of an insurance committee. Even though the pastor or president is normally the chief executive officer of a corporation and is ultimately responsible for all matters, he should not be involved in insurance responsibilities as a specific duty unless it is by his own choosing.

It takes a good deal of sacrifice for a congregation to construct buildings. Church administrative boards carry a heavy responsibility for the stewardship of the property in their care. Their obligation assumes a sacred character, and failure to provide adequate insurance protection could subject church leadership to severe criticism.

It is important for churches to be better informed of the many coverages currently carried by churches, including some of the important limitations contained in these coverages. Equally important are the available coverages that a church may not have. For ease of understanding, statements in this chapter are not phrased in technical language and are necessarily brief. In some of the descriptions of coverage, we have not listed every possible exclusion. The actual policies must be consulted for complete descriptions of coverages and complete descriptions of exclusions.

An insurance policy is a contract. In the case of church insurance, the contract is between the insurance company and the church. The church property is a valuable monument to the sacrifices of the faithful—quite often, generations of the faithful. Unfortunately, individual church administrators are temporary, and they rarely have an adequate understanding of the complicated and serious obligations they accept in the name of the church when they insure these valuable properties. "The building was partially covered by insurance" is an all-too-frequent report after a loss has occurred. The first rule for any newly elected pastor or administrator: Read your insurance contract (policy).

Insurance pertaining to the church is divided into two important coverages: (1) damage to church property and (2) liability. One cannot rightfully say which of these two is the more important as both have to be given complete consideration. Let us examine them briefly.

INSURANCE AGAINST DAMAGE TO CHURCH PROPERTY

Basic coverage should include the following:

1. Fire and Lightning—Provides against direct loss from these two perils.

2. Windstorm and Hail—This coverage normally does not include losses due to frost, cold weather, snowstorms, sleet, and ice (except hail) whether driven by wind or not. Nor does it include losses to the interior of the building or property therein, caused by rain, snow, sand, or dust, unless an opening is first caused by wind or hail. Losses to outdoor radio and TV antennas, trees, shrubs, or plants are not normally covered under this provision.

3. Explosion—Excluded are losses due to explosion of steam boilers, steam pipes, steam turbines, or steam engines. These excluded explosions can be covered by a separate policy.

4. Smoke Damage—Covers sudden and accidental smoke damage, except damage from agricultural smudging or industrial operations.

5. Vehicles or Aircraft—Covers direct damage caused by vehicles or aircraft, except for vehicles owned or operated by the insured or by any occupant of the premises.

6. Riot and Civil Commotion—Provides against direct loss by these two perils, including pillage and looting.

Optional coverages should also be considered:

1. Vandalism and Malicious Mischief—Covers willful and malicious damage to the property covered, including damage to the building caused by burglars. Excluded however, is damage to any glass constituting a part of the building, except where special and specific coverage for glass has been provided. It is noteworthy that vandalism and malicious mischief coverage is suspended if the building is vacant more than 30 days.

2. Glass Breakage—Provides "all-risk" coverage, including vandalism on glass constituting a part of the building. There are usually limits on this coverage. Special optional perils endorsement may be available without limits.

3. Falling Objects—Covers damage to property caused by falling objects, except personal property in the open and loss to the interior of the building or contents unless the exterior shall first sustain damage by a falling object.

4. Weight of Snow, Ice, or Sleet—Covers damage to buildings. Not included are radio and TV antennas, outdoor equipment, gutters, downspouts, fences, pavements, patios, awnings, foundations, and retaining walls when such loss is caused by freezing, thawing, or by the pressure or weight of ice or water, whether driven by wind or not.

5. Water Damage—In most states this insurance covers damage to property caused by water or steam accidentally discharged from any utility system, appliance, or baptistry, including overflow. This does not cover damages to any utility system or appliance from which water or steam escapes, nor does it cover losses from freezing when a building is vacant. Coverage is void if the building is vacant more than 30 days.

6. Collapse of Building—Covers collapse of building structure with the exception of the separate collapse of antennas, outdoor equipment, guttering, fences, pavements, foundation, awnings, or retaining walls, when such collapse is caused by freezing or the pressure or weight of ice or water. These exceptions would be covered, however, if loss occurred in a general collapse of the entire structure.

Extensions of Coverage. Other than optional perils endorsement, the church may wish to consider the following extensions of coverage. These extensions of coverage are applicable to all policies for losses by an insured peril, unless otherwise stated. Additional amounts of insurance (over policy limits) may be secured by consulting your insurance agent. The following are a few things to be considered:

1. Newly Acquired Property—This would automatically extend your coverage, with certain limitations, to additional property purchased.

2. Off-premises Property—Picnics, outings, etc.

3. Loss to Property Being Transported—Moving furniture, musical instruments, equipment.

4. Personal Property of Clergy and Others—Library, recording equipment, kitchen utensils, musical instruments, etc. Losses should be covered for any named peril when such personal property is located

on the described premise (not parsonage) and if not otherwise insured. This does not normally include loss by theft.

5. Valuable Papers and Records—Even though some valuable papers and records may be kept in a fireproof safe or a safe-deposit box at the bank, there are many such papers and records that may be left where they could be damaged or destroyed by perils. The church should consider the cost of replacing such records if they were destroyed. This should include the loss of such records incurred off the premises as well as on the premises.

There are also extensions of coverage that are included in the basic policy (usually with limits). The following are examples of such extended coverage.

1. Outdoor Signs—Located on the premises, whether attached to or separated from the building.

2. Trees, Plants, Shrubs—Covered against loss by fire, lightning, explosion, riot, civil commotion, or aircraft.

3. Extra Expenses—To defray the extra expense necessarily incurred to continue normal operations as a result of loss from an insured peril to building or contents.

4. Replacement Costs—Covers full costs of repair or replacement on buildings, with certain limitations. Does not include losses to carpeting, mirrors, air conditioners, domestic appliances, and outdoor equipment. Full-replacement-cost insurance may be available.

Other Optional Physical Damage Coverages. Where a need exists, other specific coverages may be desired or necessary. The following are some of the more common coverages needed and used:

1. Neon and Electric Signs. These may be covered for "all risks," with the exception of wear and tear, faulty manufacture or installation, breakage during repair or installation, mechanical breakdown, neglect of the insured, dampness, and extremes of temperature. Coverage is usually written on a deductible basis.

2. All-risk Glass. This coverage pays for damages to plate glass, stained glass, lettering, or ornamentation from virtually any cause. It also extends to frames, boarding-up openings, and temporary plates.

3. Musical Instruments, Camera Equipment, and Fine Arts. This inclusion is worldwide under the all-risk coverage with the exception of wear and tear, gradual deterioration, insects, vermin, inherent vice, war risks, and nuclear losses.

4. Sprinkler Leakage. This insurance covers collapses, leakage, or discharge of water from automatic sprinkler systems.

5. Boiler and Machinery. This coverage is especially important where heavy use of heating and cooling systems is required. It provides protection against financial loss from accidental breakdown of boilers, pressure, vessels, refrigeration and air conditioning, and mechanical and electrical power equipment. Inspection service is usually included in this coverage to help prevent losses before they occur. The need for this coverage is determined by the type of steam and pressure equipment used in the church. Specialized professional advice may be required to determine specific needs.

Other Information on Property-damage Insurance

1. Insurable Value. Do not consider the value of land or the cost of preparing the land for construction of buildings, parking lots, concrete foundations, or anything below the surface of the ground. Figure only those costs that can be affected by peril.

2. Amount of Insurance. The amount of insurance must at least be equal to the specified coinsurance-clause percentage (usually 90 percent) of the insurable value, at the time of loss.

3. Coinsurance Clause. This is one of the most important clauses in your contract and it is extremely important that it be understood well. Go over every detail carefully with the insurance agent. Ask him to explain the advantages and disadvantages of each option.

4. Actual Cash Value. When settling a claim, the insurance company will take depreciation into account. The general rule is that actual cash value is equal to the replacement cost new of the property, less deductions for depreciation and obsolescence. When the policy is being considered for purchase, be sure that examples, as discussed, are recorded so there can be no misunderstandings should a claim be necessary.

5. Replacement Cost Insurance. This is simply an agreement in the policy that the insurance company pays the cost of replacement with no deductions and is subject to the coinsurance agreement.

6. Donated Labor. Many churches are built either partly or entirely with the use of donated or volunteer labor. Should a loss occur to such a church, the insurance company must settle on the basis of actual cash value (or replacement cost) of the property. Therefore, when considering the amount of insurance for a church built with donated

labor, *the value of all donated labor must be considered*—as if the church had been built by paid workers at the "going" rate for such work.

7. Importance of Appraisal. The church is obligated to insure its property to a specified percentage of its value. How can property be insured for 90 percent of an unknown value? Because of improvements, additions, and fluctuations in building costs, one cannot know the value (nor prove the value) without a detailed appraisal that is updated from time to time.

Some companies or agents may provide their clients with a summary appraisal. This usually is not the detailed appraisal required in case of a loss. At best, it is nothing more than an informed guess at the value of the property. Usually it will include a statement to the effect that the valuations set forth will not be binding on the company in case of a loss. If an agent tells you his appraisal is binding, *require that your policy be endorsed in writing.*

The only correct solution is an appraisal made by a qualified appraiser. The fee you pay for an appraisal, like the policy premium, is part of your ordinary insurance costs. Once the appraisal is made, it is good for several years. Values change, of course, but these can be easily adjusted by any qualified contractor or estimator. Your insurance agent may be able to furnish a suggested contract of appraisal to be given to the appraiser of your choice.

Inventory-of-contents forms may also be available for the church in taking inventory of its personal property.

8. Deductibles. The basic policy may offer various deductible amounts. The larger the deductible, the lower the premiums. Consult your agent for the amount of your deductible. Consult the policy for any disappearing features.

Liability Insurance

Liability insurance is another essential insurance coverage for the church. Like insurance against damage to church property, this coverage is broken down into *basic* and *optional*. Liability insurance protects the church against claims arising from an occurrence (accident) on the described premises, or operations away from the premises if the operation is the result of normal and incidental church activity. Coverage is for bodily injury and property damage, for sums up to the policy limit. The church is protected against claims by the general public and members of the church, even if the allegations are groundless or false.

Note that payment for injury or damage is limited to the legal liability of the church; however, all costs of defending the church are usually covered whether liability exists or not. Coverage for injuries without regard for the church's legal liability may be secured under medical-payments insurance.

Various liability limits are available to fit the needs of a church. The small difference required between minimum limits and the amount that would fully protect the church, is the biggest insurance bargain. The bargain is most evident when one thinks of the cost of just one underinsured damage   suit—the consequences could even destroy a thriving church.

Basic Coverage

1. Supplementary expenses are paid, in addition to the limits of the policy, for the following: costs to the insurance company of investigating claims, court costs, interest on judgments, premiums for bonds, expenses for first aid for persons injured by accidents to which the policy applies.

2. Officers of the church, including the pastor, are normally protected for their personal liability while acting within the scope of their duties for the church. The policy may not protect the church, under either liability or medical, for injuries to any employee. (See worker's compensation section.)

3. Physical damage to the property of others, regardless of liability, caused by persons participating in an organized activity, on or off the premises, is covered within certain limits.

4. Products liability should protect the church for claims arising from the sale or consumption of food or other products, both on and off the premises. Examples: Church dinners and picnics.

5. Organizational activities should be automatically covered, if such organization is sponsored by the church. Examples: Sunday school classes, youth groups, Boy Scouts, Royal Rangers, Missionettes, 4-H Clubs, sports teams, etc.

6. Activities away from the premises should be automatically covered, if such activity is normal and incidental to the operation of the church. Examples: Sunday school picnics, organizational outings

of all types (such as Royal Rangers, Missionettes, senior-adult outings, temporary meetings at another location, church softball and basketball teams, and visitation programs).

7. Schools, other than Sunday school and vacation Bible schools, are not considered to be integral to the operation of a church and would not be covered unless specifically endorsed to the policy.

8. Parking lots owned by the church and immediately adjoining the church property, or directly across a street or alley, are normally automatically included without additional charge—unless a rental fee is charged for parking.

9. New properties or rented properties should be automatically covered, if the church notifies the company within 30 days and pays any additional premium, if required.

10. New construction of buildings or structural alteration of existing property on the insured premises should be automatically covered; however, the company must be notified and any additional premium paid. *Important:* Before starting new construction or structural alterations: (a) notify the insurance company; and (b) require the contractor to show evidence that he carries public liability insurance and worker's compensation insurance to include all of his employees and workers.

11. Volunteer workers for maintenance, repair, alteration, and new construction should be automatically covered for bodily injury in the course of work for the insured. Medical Payments coverage extends protection for injuries for which the church is not liable.

12. Sports teams' activities may be automatically covered. This does not obviate the need for medical coverage on the team members themselves.

13. Camps are usually not owned by the church; they are often owned by a separate corporate body. If the church does not own, rent, or control such camp, the church's liability for any normal activity of the church that takes place at the camp should be covered.

14. Additional owned or rented properties, such as a parsonage, chapel, camp, or vacant land, must be specifically designated in the policy for coverage to apply.

15. Independent contractors performing work for the church (plumbers, electricians, etc.) can involve the church in contingent liability arising from their work or operations. The church should be

automatically protected against such liability. Liability protection normally does not extend to the contractor.

Be aware of possible exclusions in a policy. Consult with the agent carefully regarding this possibility, for the basic liability policy may exclude coverage for some items listed below under Optional Coverage. Many of the following exclusions can be covered by an endorsement to the policy or by buying a separate policy: use of automobiles, aircraft, and watercraft; medical payments; demolition operations; assumed liability under contracts or agreements, except an incidental contract; premises and hazards not defined in the policy; false arrest, libel, slander, etc.; property damage to property owned by, used by, or in the care, custody, or control of the church.

Optional Coverage

1. Comprehensive personal liability extends protection to the pastor and his family for personal acts, on or off the premises.

2. Owned automobiles and buses coverage must be bought under a separate policy. The need for protection is obvious. If the church owns any vehicles, specific protection to cover the operation of those vehicles is a "must" in the best interests of the church.

3. Non-owned automobile coverage is essential for all churches; it protects the church against claims arising from anyone using his own car in the interests of the church (employees, members, non-members). Examples: The pastor and others making visitation calls, members transporting children to Sunday school, etc. If personal insurance doesn't extend to cover the church, if limits are not enough, or if a volunteer worker doesn't carry insurance, non-owned auto coverage would protect the church.

4. Hired automobile coverage protects the church against claims arising from the use of automobiles or buses hired by or loaned to the church. Examples include the hiring or borrowing of a car for an evangelist conducting services for the church, or the hiring of a bus to transport children to Bible camp. In case of accidental injuries and where medical aid is needed, someone has to pay the expenses involved. It may be the church's responsibility. Give careful consideration to this peril.

MEDICAL INSURANCE

Basic Coverage. Be sure the policy covers the following:

1. Volunteer workers should be covered for maintenance, repair, alteration, and new construction, subject to other valid insurance.

2. Sports and athletic activities, except practicing for or participating on church-sponsored teams, should be covered subject to other insurance. (A church-sponsored team is one that plays scheduled games independently or in a league.)

3. Campers medical payments should extend coverage to persons attending a church-sponsored camp (except a camp owned or leased by the church), in excess of other insurance. Any exclusions such as the following may be covered by an endorsement to the policy or by separate insurance: (1) persons residing on the premises (this excludes coverage for the pastor and his family on the parsonage premises); (2) persons practicing for or participating on any church-sponsored athletic team; (3) persons attending any college, school, or day nursery (except Sunday school and vacation Bible school), unless specifically covered by endorsement.

Optional Coverage. The following is suggested as optional medical-payment coverage:

1. Sponsored sports teams coverage should extend medical payments to persons while practicing or participating on an athletic team sponsored by the church, subject to any established deductibles for each person and in excess of any other collectible insurance.

2. School medical payments should extend coverage to persons while attending a school insured under the policy. Coverage for football, soccer, hockey, and lacrosse is usually optional. Any established deductible for each person applies to injuries while participating in physical education classes or athletic contests.

CHURCH THEFT INSURANCE

The church committee responsible for adequate insurance coverage should give consideration to theft insurance. Theft coverage, even though optional, is in most parts of the country today an increasingly important coverage for a church to have. The normal church theft policy covers any act of stealing, including burglary, larceny, and holdup. However, it may not include the following: dishonest acts of any officer, trustee, or employee; losses occurring during a fire; and loss of contents of alms boxes or similar receptacles. It may, however, include:

1. Church property within the church, money within a bank night-depository safe, and elsewhere in the custody of a duly authorized person. Losses at chapels or missions, etc., are not covered unless separate insurance is written covering that location.

2. Double coverage for loss of money on Christmas, Easter, and Thanksgiving.

3. Property of individuals if located within the premises *for the use of the church*, but only for the church's liability to others.

4. Damage to interior of premises by theft or attempted theft. Damage to a building by burglars is normally covered under the vandalism endorsement.

5. Mysterious disappearance of church property normally is not covered, *unless there is evidence of a theft having occurred.* By its very nature, a church is vulnerable to the "mysterious disappearance" or depletion of property—such as books, chairs, dishes, office equipment, and even more valuable items. Theft insurance does not, as a rule, cover losses of this nature, which actually are considered to be operating expenses.

OTHER IMPORTANT CONSIDERATIONS

1. Blanket Fidelity Bond. This insurance pays for loss sustained by the church through fraudulent or dishonest acts committed by any employee, clergy, any person duly elected, or any person appointed by the clergy or other official with the authority to appoint.

2. Worker's Compensation Insurance. Damage to church property and liability insurance do not automatically cover the church's liability to its pastor or other employees. The church definitely should protect itself by purchasing a worker's compensation insurance policy. In many states this is mandatory. Confer with an agent or attorney about this.

In states where the church is not covered under the Act, the policy pays on behalf of the church those claims of the pastor and other employees for which the church is at fault and thus liable. Even in these states, the church may always come under the Act voluntarily and purchase worker's compensation insurance. In this latter event, the policy pays the pastor and other employees the benefits of the Act. This course is strongly recommended to the church because it avoids the necessity for a pastor or other employee to prove his church to be at fault before he can recover benefits.

If a church is an "employer" and is not insured, it is vulnerable to unlimited liability claims. If it is insured, in addition to the protection of the insurance itself, the law does limit the church's liability. As an employer, your church can hardly afford to be without this protection.

3. Health Insurance (hospitalization, major medical, hospital income, disability income). This is an important area of protection for all employees of the church and is an open expression of Christian concern, as well as an economic benefit in the interest of both the employee and the church.

4. Life Insurance. This coverage is highly desirable from the standpoint of both the individual and the church. If the pastor were to die, when would the church ask his widow to leave the parsonage? Where would she go? What would she live on? The answer to many urgent and often embarrassing questions lies in a life insurance plan.

5. Retirement Plans. Federal laws now allow very favorable tax savings to church employees involved in retirement plans established under these laws. These tax savings can be a substantial factor in building a retirement income for the individual. Contact the denomination's district and national offices or banks and savings and loan offices for plans.

Deeds

Churches in many areas are growing and developing as God prospers them and as population growth continues. The growth of a church depends on several factors. First and foremost is good leadership, but there are other factors that help make this possible. One is the location of the church. In planning a new church, much attention should be given to this. The reason for being for the church should also be kept clearly in mind. Is the church to be a sanctuary only or are facilities needed for Christian education, both on Sunday and during the week? Is there a need for ministries such as children's day care or senior adult housing? Sufficient property should be acquired for present and future plans. In site selection, therefore, the amount of land needed, accessibility, visibility from main roads and arteries, and neighborhood composition and future trends should be carefully considered.

PREPARING TO PURCHASE PROPERTY

The purchase of real estate represents a major expenditure for the church. It is one purchase that does not occur frequently enough for the average individual or church to become competent enough to handle it without professional assistance. Consequently, an early consultation with an experienced attorney may be the most important step in completing the purchase. The real estate agent may be obligated to protect the interests of the seller, which at times may be to the disadvantage of the buyer.

The land should be surveyed by a professionally qualified person if there are any questions about boundaries. The owner's statements concerning this may not be exactly true, even though he may believe they are. If the land is not surveyed, any claims made by the agent or owner should be included as a part of the contract of sale. The cost of a survey should be paid by the buyer.

An abstract of title and title insurance should be acquired in all real estate transactions for the church. An abstract is a historical record of the property that states in summary everything that has happened to it as the title passed from owner to owner. It indicates whether there are unpaid taxes, pending court claims, assessments, unpaid bills, mortgages, and similar encumbrances standing in the way of the purchaser's obtaining a clear title. With title insurance, the title company guarantees the abstract is true and correct to the best available records.

Even though the seller has an abstract of title that was prepared at the time he acquired the property, the buyer should insist the abstract be brought up-to-date. This is accomplished by employing a title company, which specializes in making abstracts, to search the public records. The cost of obtaining the abstract should be paid by the seller, and he is obligated to take the necessary steps to have the title cleared before the purchase is completed.

The abstract of title and title insurance are usually written in language that is not understandable to the average layman. Sound practice suggests the buyer should take the abstract to a competent attorney who will examine it carefully and render an opinion as to whether or not the seller is passing a clear title. The cost of the attorney's opinion should be paid by the buyer.

It is advisable to have the church's attorney on hand to assist in preparing deeds and contracts. It is not wise to depend on oral agreements. All items of importance should be in writing. To be safe, contracts should include the claims and agreements made by the owner and his agent, the terms of the sale, the price to be paid, a legal description of the property, the disposition to be made of current taxes and pending assessments, when occupancy can occur, the nature of the deed, a statement to the effect that marketable title will be passed by the seller, and all other items noted by the attorney.

KINDS OF DEEDS AND CONVEYANCES

A deed, sometimes called a conveyance, is the instrument by means of which the title to property is passed from the seller to the buyer. It is a contract between the buyer and seller and must be in writing. To meet legal requirements, it is advisable to have an attorney supervise its preparation. The deed must be executed in the name of a person or an organization that has legal status. For this reason, it is impossible for an unincorporated church to hold title to property.

The most common deeds are general and special warranty deeds; deed of trust; quitclaim deed; and administrator's deed.

General and Special Warranty Deeds. The seller of the property warrants that he is the owner, that he has the right to sell it, and that there are no encumbrances against it. He may execute either a general warranty deed or a special warranty deed. In a general warranty deed he guarantees that he will defend his title against all comers; whereas, in a special warranty deed he guarantees only that he will defend his title against anyone who claims to receive title from or through him. Even though warranties are made, it may be desirable to purchase title insurance which provides that the insurance company will defend title against claimants.

Deed of Trust. In some states, a species of security resembling a mortgage, known as a trust deed or deed of trust, is given to a trustee in the form of a deed or conveyance of lands or other property as security for a loan. This normally accompanies a note or contract of sale for the unpaid balance when only a down payment is made and is not effective until the full amount of the contract of sale is paid.

Quitclaim Deed. If the seller proposes giving a quitclaim deed, be careful. This kind of deed warrants nothing, and says in effect, "I am not claiming that I own this property or that I have any rights in it at all, but whatever I do have, is yours." Such an instrument is usually given when there is some doubt or dispute over a title (although it is sometimes used when one relative is conveying to another), and should not be accepted by the corporation in an ordinary sale.

Administrator's Deed. If the deed comes from an executor or administrator of an estate, you probably won't receive a warranty deed. Instead, an administrator's deed may be used with a representation that the seller has complied with the requirements of the court. This is not a warranty of title, and some further safeguards, such as title insurance or an abstract of title, should be secured. Sometimes the administrator may not know what kind of deed is customary; if the church is in a good bargaining position, ask that a warranty deed be given.

SAFEGUARDING TITLE TO LOCAL CHURCH PROPERTY

The fact that each congregation in many religious bodies is an autonomous unit presents a problem in the handling or disposition of church property in the event of a division within the local church or the abandonment of property by the congregation. This is true because title to property is retained by the local congregation rather than placed under the ownership and control of a central authority.

A conditional deeding plan has been developed that enables the local congregation to hold title to its property and yet avoid the loss of property in case of adverse happenings. The plan calls for the insertion of a clause in the deed of the local congregation to the effect that title to the property shall remain with the local congregation so long as it exists and remains in fellowship and doctrinal unity with the parent church. If a group professing a different doctrine attempts to assume control, the property can be claimed through legal procedures by the parent body. A congregation should write to the parent body offices for legal guidance before the deeding procedure is undertaken.

RECORDING THE DEED

When the deed has been properly executed and delivered to the buyer, the church should proceed immediately to have it recorded in the appropriate town or county recorder's office. The contents of the deed are recorded in the public records, which serves notice to all interested parties as to who is not the rightful owner. Recording the deed provides protection against a subsequent conveyance by the seller or loss or destruction of the deed.

Articles of Incorporation

Unlike a partnership, a corporation cannot come into existence merely through agreement of parties or an association of persons, but must have state or federal government sanction before it can be formed and legally recognized. Although this recognition may be granted by special legislative acts, the rule is for a state legislature to provide in a general statute for certain formalities, such as filing and fee requirements, upon compliance with which individuals may secure a right to form a corporation.

States vary as to what they call this legal recognition or document—franchise; charter; certificate of incorporation; and, most commonly, articles of incorporation.

The articles serve as a bridge between civil law and the assembly corporation. The articles are next under civil law on the "ladder of priorities of power" and consist of a list of powers granted by state and civil law. The corporation has no more legal power than given to it by civil law. It is important, therefore, that the church include in its application for this legal recognition all of the general and specific powers necessary to perform its purpose or reason for being.

An organization looks to civil law as its highest source of guidance on procedures and to its articles as the next-ranking source. Articles and charters differ as follows: articles of incorporation are received from a governmental unit and charters of affiliation are received from a parent body. In legal matters, articles from a government rank above a charter from a parent body.

How They Are Constituted

The charter of a nonprofit corporation usually contains its name and business address; a statement of the purposes of the organization;

names and addresses of initial board members; the name and address of the registered agent; the name of address of each incorporator who signs the articles; the right to acquire property; how funds are to be used; arrangements for dissolution of the corporation; and the provisions and qualifications for members, a governing board, and officers.

The charter should provide for its own amendments by the membership, subject to the approval of the governmental or parent body that issued the charter. No amendment to the charter or articles of incorporation is effective until it has been approved by the membership and also by the governmental authority that granted the charter. Amendments to charters are adopted by the same rules and procedures as amendments to the constitution.

A charter may be surrendered at any time and a new one accepted; or it may be amended from time to time, provided such amendment does not alter the orginal principles or violate the fundamental law of the church.

How to Form a Corporation

In some districts of the Assemblies of God this procedure is handled through the district office. Work forms may be sent to the pastor on which he supplies the information required by the secretary of state. Using this information, the district office fills out the formal application and returns the completed form to the pastor (who usually serves as president of the corporation) for his signature and for the signature of the church secretary (who usually serves as the corporation secretary).

These forms are then returned to the district office where photocopies are made. A letter of endorsement and filing fees accompany the original application to the secretary of state. The authorities there either approve or disapprove it at this time. The district office should request a photocopy of the articles of incorporation from the secretary of state for the district office church file. State fees for filing an application and/or photocopies are very reasonable, and should be paid by the church to the district office.

A church should then do two more things. First, it should take a copy of the charter to the county clerk for filing. Next, it should file an application, supplied by the district office, to certify to the Internal Revenue Service that the church is duly incorporated. This application is to free the church from paying corporation income taxes to the federal government and needs to be filed only once.

In the event the district office has not worked out an arrangement to assist member assemblies in the completion of incorporation, the pastor should write to the secretary of state for assistance or engage an attorney.

Following is a sample copy of the articles of incorporation form developed and used by one district of the Assemblies of God. It has been updated as required by law over the years of its use.

ARTICLES OF INCORPORATION
OF

_____

I

The name of this corporation shall be _____

_____

II

The purposes for which this corporation is formed are:
(a) The specific and primary purposes are:
1. To establish and maintain a place of worship to Almighty God and for the promotion of Christian fellowship and edification;
2. To function as a local Assembly of God in harmony with the Constitution and Bylaws of the General Council of the Assemblies of God, Springfield, Missouri, and the Assemblies of God, _____

District Council, Inc., _____ (City), _____ (State). _____

(b) The general purposes and powers are:
1. To establish and maintain such departments and institutions as may be thought advisable for the pursuance of its work;
2. To contract and be contracted with;
3. To have and use a corporate seal;
4. To purchase, receive, possess, and dispose of such real and personal property as may be necessary or convenient to carry out the object of said corporation;
5. To make bylaws, not inconsistent with any existing civil law, for the government of its affairs and the management of its property; and now or hereafter may be permitted by law for corporations of this character.

III

This corporation is organized pursuant to the General Nonprofit Corporation Law of the State of _____.

IV

The county in this state where the principal office for the transaction of business of this corporation is located is _____ County.

V

The names and addresses of the persons who are to act in the capacity of directors until the selection of their successors are:

Name	Address

VI

The authorized number and qualifications of members of the corporation; the different classes of membership, if any; voting, and other rights and privileges of members, and their liability to dues and assessments and the method of collection thereof, shall be set forth in the bylaws.

VII

This corporation shall have the right to use the name "Assembly of God" or "Assemblies of God" only so long as it shall be a cooperative unit of the Assemblies of God, _____ District of the General Council of the Assemblies of God, and such Council shall have the right to restrain the use of said name in an action at law and in equity in the event this corporation at any time ceases to be a cooperative unit.

VIII

Section 1. This corporation is one which does not contemplate pecuniary gain or profit to the members thereof, and it is organized solely for nonprofit purposes; any and all assets of the corporation are irrevocably dedicated to religious and charitable purposes and no part of any net earnings or assets shall inure to the benefit of any member or any other individual.

Section 2. Upon the termination and dissolution of this corporation, after paying or adequately providing for the debts and obligations of the corporation, the remaining assets shall be distributed to the Assembles of God, _____ District Council, a (state name) nonprofit corporation, or in the event that said Assemblies of God, _____ District Council is not then in existence or has not established its tax-exempt status under Section 501 (c) (3) of the Internal Revenue Code, then said assets shall be distributed to the General Council of the Assemblies of God, a nonprofit corporation with international headquarters in Springfild, Missouri; or in the event that said General Council of the Assemblies of God is not then in existence or has not established its tax-exempt status under Section 501 (c) (3) of the Internal Revenue Code, then said assets shall be distributed to a non-profit fund, foundation, or corporation which is organized and operated exclusively for religious and charitable purposes in harmony with the purposes of the above-named corporations and which has established its tax-exempt status under Section 501 (c) (3) of the Internal Revenue Code. If this corporation holds any assets on trust, such assets shall be disposed of in such manner as may be directed by decree of the superior court of the county in which this corporation's principal office is located, upon petition therefore by the attorney general or by any person concerned in the liquidation.

IX

The name of the unincorporated association which is being incorporated is

_____.

IN WITNESS WHEREOF, the undersigned, being the president and the secretary, respectively, of _____, the unincorporated association which is being incorporated hereby, have executed these Articles of Incorporation this _____ day of _____ 19___.

_____
President

_____
Secretary

Note: The affidavit of the notary public should be attached to the articles of incorporation forms (as required by the state) to be submitted to the secretary of state.

Constitution and Bylaws

THE CONSTITUTION

The constitution is next in importance and authority to the articles of incorporation. Even though many corporations have only their articles of incorporation and a set of bylaws, it is advisable for a church to adopt a constitution as well as bylaws since this, if properly done, can help to safeguard and perpetuate the name, affiliation, tenets of faith, etc., of the church.

It sometimes happens that during the continued existence of the church there will be those who wish to change the name, doctrines, and even the affiliation with the parent body. They might be able to do this unless a large majority of the members would contend for the purpose and character that prevailed when the founders gave of their efforts and finances to establish the assembly, expecting it to remain as such. The constitution, therefore, normally contains the basic or more permanent provisions, such as the name, the purpose, the tenets of faith, qualifications for members, officers and their election, meetings, and the method of amending the constitution.

Most organizations, other than churches, have bylaws only. Earlier organizations liked the distinction, however, between a constitution and bylaws and kept them separate. New organizations today may adopt a constitution only and have no bylaws, adopt bylaws and have no constitution, or have combined instruments, a constitution and bylaws. The advantage of a church having both should be kept clearly in mind, especially in light of the "ladder of priorities of powers," as previously discussed in this chapter.

A constitution is short and compact. It is general rather than detailed. For instance, the constitution might mention something about the frequency of meetings: "at least five meetings a year," or, "a regular annual meeting in the spring." It does *not* specify dates, such as "the second Friday of each month." The constitution may indicate who appoints committees, but it does not include a detailed list of committees. It mentions qualifications for membership, since this is necessary to the continued life of the church's original purpose. The constitution confers authority to collect funds, receive gifts, and deal with nonsupporting members. Normally it does *not* specify amounts of financial support or other contributing factors leading to the disqualifying of members.

The constitution may also include general references to committees—method of appointment, distinction between standing and special committees, etc. Usually, however, this is done in the bylaws. The membership and nominating committees, and in some organizations a program committee, may be mentioned specifically in the constitution. Other committees need not be named. Even if the constitution is silent about committees, the society can always create them, and the president may nominate committee personnel. This derives from the common parliamentary law that confers such authority on all societies and all presidents, unless there is some specific provision to the contrary.

The church board, executive committee, or other high-authority bodies, should be provided for in the constitution. This may be included in the same article as the other officers, or it may have an article of its own. The body should be named, the composition indicated, and its authority made clear.

Amending a constitution is normally accomplished by at least a two-thirds vote of the qualified active members of the church corporation present after copies of the proposed amendments have been sent to each such member at least 30 days prior to the meeting where the amendments are to be considered. Amendments to the constitution (and bylaws) become effective as soon as adopted unless otherwise specified or clearly understood at the time of their adoption or unless the bylaws provide differently.

THE BYLAWS

The bylaws are next in importance in power and authority to the constitution. When a corporation has only the articles of incorporation and bylaws (not recommended for churches), then the bylaws must include all material normally placed in the constitution. However, if there are both a constitution and bylaws, then the constitution contains the organic law and the more permanent provisions and allows for the bylaws to modify or enlarge on the provisions in the constitution. The bylaws, therefore, contain the less essential provisions. This arrangement, of course, safeguards and perpetuates the life of the assembly and provides a workable method of operation.

There are seven fundamental subjects that should be contained in the bylaws. Each such subject occupies a separate article which can be divided into as many sections and paragraphs as desired. The seven minimum fundamental subjects (besides the preamble, if included) are arranged in the following logical order: name, purpose, membership, officers, meetings, parliamentary authority, and amendments to bylaws. Other articles, as desired, may be incorporated.

There is no limit either to the number of subjects that can be included in a set of bylaws or to the number of articles or sections into which the individual topics can be subdivided. Each organization decides this for itself. Many organizations include in their bylaws an order of business; dates of meetings (some states require that a certain day of the year be indicated for the annual meeting, such as the "first Tuesday in February"); place of meeting, or who has the authority to determine the place; lists of committees; the quorum rule; provisions for affiliation; means of financial support; procedural details with respect to nominations and elections; filling of vacancies of offices and committes; procedures and requirements for becoming a member; instructions about the receipt deposit, vouchering, expenditure, and auditing of funds; naming of an authority (book) on parliamentary law for parliamentary procedure, etc.

Since bylaws are less important than other powers on the "ladder of priorities," they can be changed more easily than those above on the ladder. Unlike the two-thirds majority vote with at least 30 days notice required to change the consitution, the bylaws may be amended at any regular or special meeting properly called and announced for this purpose, with a simple majority vote, unless prohibited elsewhere in the bylaws or by action of the voting body.

The articles titled "Amendments" in the constitution, the bylaws, and the standing rules should give full details as to how changes can be made.

STANDING RULES

Standing rules are merely previously adopted *main* motions that have *continuing* effect. They are usually amendable, suspendable, and rescindable by a *majority* vote (if notice has been given at a previous meeting or in the call for the meeting), by a two-thirds vote (without such previous notice), by a majority vote of the *membership*, or in a convention or annual meeting by a *majority* vote of the *registered* delegates.

Standing rules, including house rules, election or convention rules fixed annual donations, and any and all other effective motions, rules, orders, or decisions of the body or adopted *motions* of the assembly, remain continually in force (regardless of succeeding administrations in office) until they have been modified, executed, or rescinded, unless, when adopted, a specified time for their duration was included in the motion or in other rules of procedure for the body.

Importance of Securing Legal Counsel

NEED FOR FORMAL LEGAL TRAINING AND EXPERIENCE

One of California's oldest and most experienced attorneys recently stated that when he started his practice in the state, he could lay out all of California's state laws on about one-quarter of his desk. Now, he said, he cannot get all of them on one wall in his library. He went on to say that because of this fact attorneys are having to become specialists. They confine their work to only one area of law. It is totally impossible for any one attorney to know all of what California's law says, except in his specialized field. Laws are becoming so technical and complicated that a good attorney can be compared to a good surgeon. He must have the very best aptitude, training, and experience to be successful.

This rapidly growing problem requires each attorney to spend more time in preparation for his profession. It is to his advantage to be associated with a firm of attorneys, each proficient in some specific area of law. It is wise, therefore, to carefully choose an attorney who is fully qualified and preferably one who is associated with other attorneys of various specialties.

It is important when selecting an attorney to consider his years of service, experience, reputation, and time spent in the community. A worthy attorney should know the attitude of the courts and of other attorneys in the community. If he knows a particular court has a reputation for favoring churches and understanding church problems and needs, he will endeavor to have litigations and/or other legal matters handled by that court. It is also a noteworthy fact that some attorneys are more sympathetic and understanding of church problems than others.

BENEFITS OF USING LEGAL COUNSEL

An attorney can be worth his reasonable fee by saving the church much trouble and money.

Corporate Documents and Contracts. A corporation in which the writer served as an officer for a number of years was given the estate of a personal friend who provided the gift for this corporation in his will. The estate included the assets of a mission, a nonprofit corporation. Several years before his death, the friend had changed the name of the corporation and in so doing had his secretary copy the articles of incorporation to be sent to the secretary of state for the amendment.

The friend had asked for and received corporate powers for the original corporation many years before and among these powers was a provision to use some of its earnings to support foreign missions. However, when the document was copied by this secretary for amendment, she accidentally omitted a line that specifically mentioned foreign missions.

As our corporation was in the process of receiving this estate upon the death of the benefactor, the Internal Revenue Service informed the corporation that the deceased friend had been using earnings from the mission illegally. Funds were used for foreign missions and this power had not been granted to the mission by the state; therefore the IRS would have to revoke the nonprofit benefits and the widow of the deceased friend would have to pay corporation-for-profit taxes on the estate from the time of the corporation's reorganization and change of name. This small mistake cost the corporation named in the will thousands of dollars that could have been saved for the work of the church had the friend employed a competent attorney to supervise the reorganization in the first place.

Some denominational district councils today have worked with attorneys and the secretary of state to provide a way to assist churches in their incorporating and with other legal matters. In this case, one can be reasonably sure that all is done properly. If there is any doubt, a church should inquire from the denominational office if proper clearance has been given by all civil authorities and if a good attorney has approved the process before taking legal action of any kind.

Since contracts vary widely, it is wise to have an attorney approve all documents before the church obligates itself.

Financial Programs. Herein lies a grave danger to the church. There are times when an assembly is very anxious to enter into a program of raising money for buildings, improvements, equipment, etc. Someone comes along with a plan that might or might not be good for the church. Here again the attorney should be consulted. If he does not feel qualified to give an official opinion, he can refer the question to someone who can. Too many good, sacrificing, faithful members of congregations have lost their savings because of bad judgment on the part of church leadership. For the sake of these members and in the interest of good business, play it safe and seek legal aid.

Insurance and Claims. Insurance companies are in business to make a profit. In case of claims against the church's insurance company because of perils of any kind, it is wise to check with an attorney. Here again, he can protect the church against any dishonest or honest mistakes on the part of the insurance company. The attorney may recommend an interpretation of the policy by a court in case of a misunderstanding. It is advisable to ask the attorney to read the insurance policy before purchasing the policy and also before accepting a settlement of a claim. He may discover a flaw that would cost the church a great deal of money in case of peril.

Acquiring and Disposing of Property. There are sources of help to which a pastor may turn at this time, such as a title company, real estate agent, or banker. It is safest, however, to take all of the papers for acquisition or disposal to an attorney to get his opinion that all is in order. Here again is a safeguard that may prevent an embarrassment or even a disaster to an assembly. Clouds on titles, building restrictions, liens, and other problems have shown up in some cases after contracts have been signed and have caused the pastor and congregation much embarrassment, trouble, and expense. A qualified attorney can help prevent such occurrences.

Lawsuits. It has been aptly said, "We live in a 'sue-crazy' society." There are those who seem to be constantly on the alert for an opportunity to sue—even a church. It is often true that lawsuits have been lost due to an incompetent and inexperienced attorney. If a church is facing a lawsuit it should seek the assistance of an attorney who has the reputation of winning similar cases. An attorney who knows the courts and the opposition he is facing can be of great help at such a time. Even though Satan may be on the side of the plaintiff against the church, the pastor and the church will have a much better chance to win with God on their side, especially if they are doing their best by having the finest legal assistance obtainable. God expects us to use wisdom in all matters.

Wills and Deferred Giving to the Church. There are two ways in which an attorney can assist with wills and deferred giving. First, in the business taken to him and, second, in the business he may bring to the church. A definite part of good financial stewardship on the part of the church members is to have properly prepared wills. Members of the congregation should be shown by the pastor, the finance committee, and/or special committees, the scriptural admonition and the spiritual blessing provided by God for their generosity to God's work.

Before a suitable program for financial stewardship has been adopted by the congregation, it should be submitted to the attorney to be sure everything is within the boundaries of civil law. Members should be encouraged by the church to seek legal assistance in the preparation of wills and gifts. This common procedure may save large sums of money in taxes and litigations later, resulting in substantial financial gain to the church and to the heirs.

The attorney can suggest to both church members and non-church members who go to him for advice regarding wills and gifts, that they remember a church that is doing such a fine job of making the community a better and safer place to live and rear children. This is often done. The writer knows of a church that received over $1 million from one individual because of a suggestion from a friendly attorney. The attorney should be reminded of this kind of opportunity which he may have to assist the church.

Suggested Reading

Corporation Course. Englewood Cliffs, NJ: Prentice Hall, 1964.

Demeter, George. *Demeter's Manual of Parliamentary Law and Procedure*. Boston: Little, Brown, and Co., 1969.

Dillavou, Essel R.; Charles G. Howard; Paul C. Roberts; William J. Robert; and Robert N. Corley. *Principles of Business Law. Uniform Commercial Code* (alternate seventh edition). Englewood Cliffs, NJ: Prentice Hall, Inc., 1965.

Ellis, William H., and Joel H. Paget. *Legal Guidelines for Christian Organizations*. Oak Park, IL: Christian Legal Society, published in cooperation with Stewardship Commission, National Association of Evangelicals, n.d.

Insurance and Your Church. Des Moines. Preferred Risk Mutual Insurance Co., 1972.

Lavine, A. Lincoln, and E. M. Edelson. *College Business Law Revised*. Baltimore: H. M. Rowe Company, 1958.

Linamen, Harold F. *Business Handbook for Churches*. Anderson, IN: Warner Press, Rev. 1964.

Sturgis, Alice. *Sturgis Standard Code of Parliamentary Procedure* (second edition). New York: McGraw Hill, 1966.

19

The Pastor
and
Building Programs

THOMAS E. SCRUGGS

At sometime in a pastor's career, he will be serving at a church when numerical growth and God's blessing seem to point toward a need for building a new facility or enlarging a present one. Few pastors have the advantage of construction experience prior to that first project undertaken as a novice. Fortunate is the pastor who has a church board whose members have experience in working with contractors, architects, and inspectors who enforce local codes. And there is some basic knowledge the pastor can acquire to make him a more effective leader as a church enters a building program.

Preliminary Planning

SPIRITUAL AND PSYCHOLOGICAL PREPARATION

When the time comes to build new worship facilities, the pastor will face some unusual and exciting experiences, especially if it is his first building program. The Bible says, "For which of you, intending to build a tower, sitteth not down first, and counteth the cost . . .?" (Luke 14:28). While this verse refers primarily to the cost of discipleship, there are some sound words of advice the pastor needs to hear concerning planning and preparation for the construction of a church building.

The pastor must be mentally and spiritually prepared to accept the challenges of building in this complex age. This is of primary importance to both the pastor and the congregation. The attitudes

Thomas E. Scruggs is pastor of Heritage Assembly of God, Florence, Kentucky.

transmitted to the congregation by the pastor will greatly influence their total acceptance of the program and assure their full support for the project.

Many positive and inspirational portions of God's Word can be applied in the pastor's preaching during the preliminary planning stages of the new building. Times of prayer and fasting are vital as steps of faith are taken to promote a smooth and efficient program. Nothing can be a greater means of promoting unity and strength in a congregation of believers than a well-planned building program where burden and vision are shared on a dynamic and challenging basis. By the same token, many problems can arise that may result in disaster and defeat if they are not met decisively. The suggestions that follow, if observed conscientiously, will help avoid many of the pitfalls that have beset pastors who are inexperienced in building programs.

CHOOSING A BUILDING COMMITTEE

The building committee can only serve meaningfully if its chairman has the right qualifications. In some instances, he may be the pastor of the church, but in most cases a qualified layman can be a tremendous asset in this role. The chairman should be a person with a general knowledge of construction and current trends in the building business. This does not mean he needs to be a general contractor. However, if there is a successful builder in the church, he may be the best choice, if he also has the necessary spiritual qualifications.

The chairman should be a person who can devote as much time as is needed throughout the entire building program. His ability to negotiate the various aspects of the project is most important. He should be pleasant and even-tempered and have the ability to work with people. If the pastor does not serve as chairman, he should serve as an *ex officio* member of this committee, just as with all other committees of the church. The members of the committee may be the official board of the church, although this is not necessarily the best course of action. There may be persons who can contribute a great deal of assistance and strength to the project, and yet they may not currently be on the board or any other committee. Each member should be chosen on the basis of his or her ability to contribute ideas and suggestions that will cover every detail of the proposed project. Committee members should be people of vision and mature reasoning power. Five to seven members would make an ideal committee size, although a small or large church might have justification for fewer or more members.

It is the responsibility of the building committee to work with the architect and designers at every stage of planning the project. At the same time the committee will be in regular communication with the official church board to which it is amenable. In the early stages of planning, many time-consuming meetings will be conducted. The committee will be involved in extensive study regarding current trends of church construction. No doubt, the committee will visit many worship facilities as they proceed with their survey and compile the list of requirements for their particular needs. The time to eliminate costly changes and long-lasting mistakes is at this stage of committee preliminary planning.

DISTRICT AND SECTIONAL APPROVAL OF THE PROJECT

Most districts have published guidelines and adopted polices that regulate the establishment of new congregations and the building of new churches. For the sake of harmony and good relations in advancing the kingdom of Christ, these policies should be observed when entering a city or community to build a new church. Usually there is a person at the district and sectional level who can give direction and assistance when a proposal is made to open a new work.

The pastor and congregation of the established church also should be considerate of other sister churches when the time comes to relocate. Misunderstanding and potential conflicts with an existing church can arise through various circumstances. Numerical growth with no room to expand, changing conditions of environment, growth patterns of the city, or any number of reasons can result in the necessity of relocation. When this time comes, the pastor should deal fairly with his fellow pastors, maintaining a high code of ethics.

DETERMINING CONSTRUCTION METHODS

There are many methods the committee will consider regarding contracts and agreements in the actual erection of the building. Three of the most common will be named here, but treated in more detail later in this chapter.

First, the church may choose to serve as its own contractor. This is permitted by most agencies that regulate permits and codes of construction. It can work successfully on any size project. The key is proper supervision. Not everyone who has had building experience can qualify to supervise church construction. Usually church construction falls into the category of commercial building, hence the ordinary house builder may not qualify. There may be retired contractors or building foremen within the local congregation who could meet the requirements for the job. Also, such a qualified man could become a part of the church staff and be the director of development. Under such an arangement, most of the work would be done by subcontractors; the staff member or designated lay person would actually be the general contractor on the job.

The greatest advantage to the church serving as its own contractor is the savings factor. There are many fixed costs of a general contractor that can be eliminated through this method. However, certain safeguards must be taken here by the church. All subcontractors should be certified as financially responsible. This can be accomplished through performance bonds or bank guarantees. Such precautions will protect the church from liens being filed for labor and materials during the course of construction or even after work has been completed. It is important in the agreements with subcontractors that payment schedules be established and closely observed. The church should make sure adequate construction-related insurance is in force at all times during the building program.

The monetary benefits to the church that serves as its own general contractor may vary in different sections of the country. In most instances, the savings can amount to at least 20 percent of the total cost of construction. These savings come through tax-exempt purchases of materials and furnishings, elimination of general contractor's profits, and fixed overhead and special concession given to the church by subcontractors and suppliers. There will alwasy be certain items of work that can be done by volunteers within the congregation. Under proper supervision, this can result in considerable additional savings.

Second the church may elect to engage a general contractor. If the building committee decides to secure the services of a general contractor for the project, careful consideration should be given to such a choice. There are many contractors today who specialize in church construction, and experience in this field is a vital asset. The church should be completely satisfied with the contractor's credentials before a contract is drawn.

The contract is a very important document. One should never rely on verbal agreements or mutual understandings based on friendship of supposition. Many costly problems can be avoided by properly preparing this agreement. Legal counsel for the church should examine and approve all contracts. This is the time to protect the interests of the entire congregation.

We live in a time of unprecedented inflation and rising costs. Every precaution should be taken to arrive at firm prices without the possibility of exhorbitant increases. Escalator clauses are not uncommon, but they should only be allowed to cover unforeseen increases, such as unannounced wage and material hikes. Since the average span of construction time will be 1 year or less, the contractor can usually determine these factors when the estimates are made and bids are received from the various subcontractors.

The payment schedule for the contractor's services is usually regulated by the bank or institution that serves as lending agent. However, since there are other means of financing, such as bonds and private loans, an adequate percentage of the total contract should be held in reserve by the church until all work is satisfactorily completed. If the church has chosen architectural services that include supervision of the project, these items regulating the release of funds will be covered.

The church should reinforce its position of security in every way possible. Many projects have been left unfinished because of bankruptcy or insolvency of contractors. It is becoming more difficult and expensive for contractors to furnish security and completion bonds. The next best assurance the church can have is bank letters of credit on the contractor. This is not just line of credit or a statement of financial condition, but it serves as an actual bank guarantee to the church.

There should be a stipulation in every contract regarding time for completion. The only way to make this agreement work is to specify a penalty for delay beyond an agreed number of working days. This is common procedure on all large projects. Any changes in plans and specifications including those that might alter the time for completion should be acknowledged by a change order properly endorsed by all parties.

Third, the church may make use of managment and consultant services. In recent years there has been an increase in these types of services. Many companies have been formed to render services to all kinds of organizations and businesses, especially in the area of church planning and construction. They offer a variety of services including architectural planning and designing, financing, supervision of construction, and other organizational and growth-related functions.

If this plan of church development is chosen the church must realize that many of the liabilities such as insurance claims, assurance for payment of all labor and materials, and those mentioned under the area of the church serving as its own contractor, apply to this agreement. In reality the church is its own contractor, with the consultant serving as an agent for the church.

The fees for such services are usually based on a percentage of the total cost of the project. Sometimes the agreement is referred to as a cost-plus arrangement. Under this plan, the church must rely totally on the integrity of the parties involved, and the church probably has less protection from the standpoint of guaranteed cost of construction. If a management program is chosen, it is advisable if at all possible to agree on a fixed fee for these services rather than a cost-plus arrangement.

Site Location

The proper choice of the site for the new church is no doubt one of the most important decisions that will be made in this program. Someone has said God could not have given some of our churches the sites on which they have built. We need not argue the validity of this statement, but it is extremely important to receive all the help available, including divine guidance, when this choice is to be made.

FEASIBILITY STUDY

A thorough feasibility study of the site should be conducted. Utilize the services offered by local and area planning and development agencies. These planners and engineers can project the anticipated development in an area for several years to come. These projections would include new streets and highways along with other growth patterns of the area. If a church overlooks this point, it is possible the site chosen could prove of little value because of major changes occurring by the time construction is finished.

Zoning is a very important item in the choice of the site. Even though churches are allowed to build in almost any zone, some areas remain where churches are excluded. There are also areas that would be undesirable because of the permitted uses of surrounding properties. When the time comes to purchase the property or secure an option to buy, proper contingency clauses should be drawn into the contracts to assure the church that permits can be obtained for the desired use.

Public utilities must also be a decisive factor in the choice of the site. Access to adequate electrical service without prohibitive costs is a must. The local power company can furnish this information, indicating the kind of service available. Efficient heating and air-conditioning equipment must have a special size service in voltage rating. Public water and sewer are essential items to consider. In some instances, if the site is large enough for the drilling of wells, and sewage disposal can be provided, it is very possible the cost of installing and maintaining these services would be prohibitive. If a site is selected that does not have a pubic sewer, the soil should be given percolation tests to determine whether septic tanks can be installed.

PROVISION FOR FUTURE EXPANSION

Choose a site large enough for future expansion. Many churches have found themselves boxed in with no room to grow or adequately serve their needs because the original site was too small. If available, several acres should be considered. In some cases, it may be necessary to buy more than is actually needed, with the thought of selling a part of it and thus paying for the part the church really wants. If the site considered is too small, it is possible adjoining properties could be optioned for the church to purchase at a later time.

In most cases, less than a 3-acre site should never be considered. From 5 to 10 acres is preferable. Even more acreage might be important if the overall plans of the church call for day schools or other related facilities. Should these be possible considerations, the state and local agencies that regulate accredited schools and other institutions can furnish minimum land requirements.

UNFAVORABLE CONDITIONS TO AVOID

While there are many items that are a must on the list of requirements for acceptable sites, there are some conditions that render a site totally unacceptable. The foundation of the building is the most important part of all construction. Unless there are suitable soil conditions on which to build, the site is not a good one. There are areas of the country where these unstable conditions are prevalent. Proper allowance in construction costs has to be made for these conditions. Soil tests can be made before the site is purchased to determine if it is suitable for the needs of the church.

Some sites are not suitable for worship facilities because of the high noise level in the area. These conditions may be caused by air-traffic patterns, railroads, factories, and industrial complexes. Any excessive noise levels should be avoided.

Another factor to be considered is traffic congestion. Sites located in high-density areas are not only problems for the stand-point of accessibility but are also definite safety hazards. Easy access and a smooth flow of traffic are desirable.

Low elevations should be avoided. High elevations of building sites not only enhance the value of the property because of appearance, but many drainage problems and flooding hazards can also be eliminated. There can be problems in connecting to the public sewer if the site is too low. In most cities there are areas that have been declared flood zones. Such areas should be avoided.

Local Codes

Nearly all cities and communities have adopted zoning ordinances and building codes that regulate planned development. Copies of these ordinances and codes are available to persons and groups planning to build. In most areas a licensed architect must prepare plans, and blueprints if a church is to secure a permit to build. All this information is available through the city or county offices.

Maps and plats of the area under consideration will give valuable information regarding the property on which a church will build. There are specified setback lines from public streets and right-of-ways that must be observed when building. Sometimes a piece of property may appear to be large in size, but because of these setbacks the actual portion of permitted building area on the lot may prove to be inadequate. Also from these maps and plats one can locate any recorded easement on the property which may affect its usefulness.

Off-street parking requirements are most important. A specified number of paved parking spaces is usually required, based on the number of seats in the sanctuary, or the total square footage of the complex. If the site is located on a state or federal highway, special permits are required to establish new driveways from such streets. City engineers must approve ingress and egress to public streets. These guidelines promote a smooth flow of traffic with maximum safety.

SUBDIVISION CODES

When building sites are a part of a planned development or a subdivision, there may be special restrictions or codes in addition to normal regulations. In some cases, building plans and designs may require approval of the developer or a reviewing committee established for this purpose.

STATE AND FEDERAL REQUIREMENTS

All public buildings are required to meet certain safety and health standards. These items should be remembered in preliminary planning sessions with the architect. The use of approved materials can save money and assist in meeting these standards. Most states require that all church plans be approved by the state fire marshall's office. In addition to approved fire-rated materials, this agency also regulates such items as widths of corridors, proper emergency lighting and smoke signals, marked exits with doors opening in the proper direction, and a list of other things that relate to the safety of each individual served by the facility.

The architect should be current on all the Environmental Protection Agency guidelines. These are being rigidly enforced in many areas and should be considered in proper planning. If there is to be a kitchen or food-handling equipment, the Department of Public Health must approve this area of the facility. The health department also regulates the number of restrooms and sanitary facilities.

Architectural Services

CHOICE OF THE ARCHITECT

There will probably be many factors that enter into this decision. We will discuss only a few. It is advantageous to the church if the architect has background experience in designing and planning worship facilities. The steady increase of construction in this field has led many architectural firms to specialize in church planning and designing. A firm with such expertise can help a church avoid many costly mistakes. Of great value is an architect with imagination and innovative ideas who will also listen sympathetically to the desires of the building committee. Unfortunately, many firms in this buisness seem more concerned about building a reputation than building functional facilities to meet the needs of their clients. The church should establish this point of understanding very early in discussion with potential architects by noting the firm's ability to listen as well as to give advice. An open line of communication between the committee and the architect is very vital. Taking time to get recommendations from other pastors and churches can help a church avoid mistakes.

We have a tendency to be thrifty and conservative in spending God's money. But a cheap price should not be the determining factor in choosing an architect. The assumed savings here could prove to be very expensive if the architect is not a competent one. A firm that will work with the church's interests in mind can save much more than the amount of the architectural fee.

The architectural firm must meet all state and local licensing requirements. If an architect is a member of the American Institute of Architects, he may serve in any state by properly registering in that state.

COSTS OF ARCHITECTURAL SERVICES

Most architectural firms offer varied services to their clients. Naturally the costs are established on the basis of services rendered. A contract should be drawn between the church and the architect. This agreement should spell out in detail the services expected from the architect and the fee he will receive for these services.

Most architects work for a fee that is determined by a percentage of the building costs. This fee will vary in different sections of the country. Sometimes there are additional fees for engineering services. All these points should be discussed when arriving at a price.

If the project is built with the church serving as its own contractor or by a consulting and management firm, a fixed fee should be negotiated between the parties. The architect will not be responsible for putting the project out for bids and will only give limited supervision to construction. If a master plan is agreed on, a small additional charge may be rendered for this service based on the extra time involved in such preparation. The fee should be based only on the amount of construction for which working plans and specifications are furnished.

THE MASTER PLAN

After the site has been selected and the architect chosen, you are ready to get down to some specifics of planning your building program. If it is impossible for the entire building committee to be in all planning sessions with the architect, notes of all these meetings should be made and shared with those not present. The architect may give some assistance and guidelines in establishing goals, but these must be basically set by the congregation through its official board and building committee. As soon as these goals have been established, work should begin on a master plan that will serve several purposes.

Through master planning, total land utilization may be realized. Too often nice building sites have been spoiled because of improper placement of buildings. True, the placement and design of the first units of construction are important in creating first impressions in the community; but with imagination and good planning, this goal can be accomplished with proper allowance for future expansion. The master plan will create a schematic for the staged development. As this plan is followed, each stage of construction will complement the entire project.

Even though the total project is planned in stages, an artist's conception or a scaled model of the finished product can be an effective tool in promotions and public relations. The Chinese proverb, "A picture is worth a thousand words," is certainly applicable in conveying to the congregation what the facility will look like when finished.

Design and Function of a Facility

STEPS IN CHOOSING A GOOD DESIGN

The design of the building should be adapted to the community in which it is built. To do this, several factors must be considered. Here, the size of the overall project will come into focus. If the building site contains several acres, it is possible to consider a maximum of single-story planning. From the standpoint of safety and easy access for all ages, the single-story design is most desirable. For this kind of planning there are many structural designs with eye appeal which provide for such things as accessible mobility, outside lighting, and ventilation. Interest centers, courtyard areas, decorative furnishings, and many other features can complement such a design. Whenever a distinctive design is chosen, such as colonial, Spanish, or contemporary, this decor should be maintained throughout the entire project, if possible.

If the site lends itself to multistory planning and design, many of the features mentioned in the single-story design can be duplicated. One important factor to be considered in all designs is provision for the handicapped. In most states there are mandatory requirements that dictate many items to be included that heretofore have not been a part of conventional planning. Such items include wheelchair ramps, special toilet facilities, and specified corridor and door widths. The architect should be current on the requirements in these areas.

Some locations may necessitate a design for the contour of the land, particularly if the site is hilly or of uneven terrain. Through good planning, these conditions can be made to work in favor of an attractive church complex.

There is a wide range of helps in choosing the design of a facility. Most architects can display pictures and brochures of almost any design one could desire. It is also possible the building committee could actually visit a finished complex. This is always very helpful. One should take pictures and make notes of features that are of special interest. Note also any undesirable aspects.

The design of the complex is what the outsider will see first. It will make either a good or a bad impression. Through careful planning to achieve an attractive design, this can be controlled.

Landscaping and Exterior Planning

The grounds and the exterior areas of the building should receive careful study. Too often these areas are left unfinished or totally neglected in planning the project. If monies are not specified and set aside for these areas of development, a church may discover that funds are already depleted when the program reaches the landscaping or external beautification stage. If at all possible, the services of a professional landscape designer should be secured. Some nurseries offer this service. Here again, examine the company's work, get recommendations, and then make the decision.

Functional Planning

After the seating capacity of the sanctuary has been determined, there must be careful study of total utilization of space. A variety of floor plans and designs should be considered. Here again the site can be a deciding factor because of its terrain, shape, size, and elevation. Before considering educational space and other supporting facilities, let us consider two floor plans and designs for the main sanctuary.

The fan-shaped or semicircle design is very popular in contemporary planning. One of the great advantages of this design, in addition to its appearance, is the capacity to seat large numbers of people in proximity to the platform and pulpit area. This feature produces an atmosphere of closeness and personalized worship. This arrangement also contributes to better acoustics. The rectangular design is still used for smaller congregations. While this design lacks some of the advantages of the semicircle design, in many cases it is less expensive and less complicated to build.

When planning the sanctuary, regardless of shape and design, several essential matters should be remembered. The platform section needs to be large enough to accommodate all phases of special ministries besides the pulpit. Allow for choirs, orchestra, and special musical presentations. If a baptistry is planned for this area, attention should be given to proper access to dressing rooms and toilet facilities.

Supporting public facilities such as well-planned nurseries, roomy foyers, all-weather carports, and well-lit entrances are just a few areas that sometimes could be improved by better planning. Restrooms and drinking fountains should be located conveniently though not so conspicuously that they create distraction.

The Sunday school and educational buildings should be planned with a multipurpose use. Today more churches are entering into day-care and school ministries. It is far wiser to plan for these at the time of construction than to convert space at a later time. Brochures and other materials are available from appropriate government agencies to assist with proper room dimensions, lighting, and ventilation. These facilities can easily be designed to accommodate the needs of both the Sunday school and the day school.

Kitchen and fellowship areas can also be multipurpose facilities. The fellowship hall or dining room can be utilized as classrooms by the installation of folding partitions. Ample space for storage and mechanical equipment must not be overlooked. Space for heating and air-conditioning units should be provided—and not as an afterthought. The services of mechanical engineers should be engaged while in the planning stages of the building. Costly heating and cooling bills can be greatly reduced by installing the correct unit sizes and adequate insulation.

ADEQUATE FURNISHINGS

The furnishings for the sanctuary and the educational units should be chosen on the basis of comfort, durability, appearance, and functional use. Sanctuary seating may consist of pews or individual opera chairs. Neither type will affect the overall seating capacity. There are all types and qualities of both styles. The pew arrangement is probably less expensive on initial installation.

The services of an interior decorator could prove very helpful in such matters as choice of colors, fabrics, wall coverings, and carpets. These items should meet all the standards of the fire marshall's office as well as other regulatory agencies.

The right selection of chairs, tables, and other vital furnishings for the educational unit is important also. Types and sizes of this equipment are regulated by the age-group to be served. Unless proper allowance is made in the building budget for all these items, it is possible the facility will suffer by being inadequately furnished for a long time.

SOUND SYSTEMS AND ACOUSTICS

A sound system does not have to be expensive or sophisticated to do a good job. Many factors contribute to natural and adequate distribution of sound. One should think about this important feature when selecting ceiling materials, interior walls, floor coverings, and windows and doors. If all these items are taken into consideration, the acoustics in the building will be good. As in other areas of the building program, advice from people competent in this field is also a good investment.

A variety of sound systems is available. Top priority, however, should be a natural transmission of voice and music. A pleasant and distinct sound is more desirable than mere volume. Any good system can serve the need if it is properly installed. Special sound chambers should be planned as part of the building's design. Unsightly cabinets and columns containing speakers should be avoided.

In addition to the main sanctuary, other areas of the complex may require the installation of sound amplifiers. Speakers can be installed in nurseries, offices, overflow rooms, or any other section of the building. If budget and space permit, it would be well to plan a sound-and-projection room.

For the showing of films, a large screen may be installed from the ceiling of the platform area which could be lowered and raised electrically. Special outlets may be installed throughout the seating area of the sanctuary for hearing devices. These outlets may also be adapted for cassette recorders.

Should the church desire to use the sanctuary for television productions, special planning would be necessary. This would include special equipment rooms as well as special lighting and acoustics. Providing for this in the planning stage will usually mean more effective and less expensive construction than adding it at a later time.

*   *   *   *   *

It has not been the purpose of this chapter to try to cover all the details of the buliding program or to deal with specifics in given areas. It has sought merely to point out the necessity of prayerful and deliberate planning before the task is undertaken. The physical structure is an important part of a witness in any community. This is added incentive for giving much thought to both planning and construction.

Suggested Reading

Anderson, Martin. *A Guide to Church Building and Fund Raising.* Minneapolis, MN: Augsburg Publishing House, 1959.

Anderson, Martin. *Planning and Financing the New Church.* Minneapolis, MN: Augsburg Publishing House, 1949.

Burroughs, P. E. *Let Us Build.* Nashville, TN: Broadman Press, 1938.

Harrell, William A. *Planning Better Church Buildings.* Nashville, TN: Convention Press, 1957.

Morse, John E. *To Build A Church.* New York: Holt, Rinehart, and Winston, 1969.

Scotford, John R. *When You Build Your Church.* Great Neck, NY: Doniger and Raughley, Inc., 1955.

20

The Pastor
and
Pentecostal Distinctives

LELAND R. KEYS

What do we mean when we speak of Pentecostal *distinctives?* The word is defined as that which distinguishes, or as separate from. A distinctive clearly marks a person or thing as being different from others. A distinctive characteristic is an identifying feature of an individual or a group.

It should become increasingly evident as we proceed with this chapter that there are certain Pentecostal distinctives present in the lives of those who have been filled with the Holy Spirit as on the Day of Pentecost. Pentecostal people should be distinctive in today's world of self-centered and uncommitted people.

The Holy Spirit was poured out on the day of Pentecost as promised by the prophet Joel and by the Lord Jesus Christ (Acts 1:4-8; 2:4, 14-18). Peter, in his sermon following the supernatural phenomena of the outpouring, declared: "Therefore being by the right hand of God exalted, and having received of the Father the promise of the Holy Ghost, he hath shed forth this, which ye now see and hear" (Acts 2:33).

What a difference the coming of the Holy Spirit made! It is recorded that the believers served the Lord "with gladness and singleness of heart, praising God" (Acts 2:46, 47). They were a distinctive people for they had received a distinctive experience. Worship became alive, vibrant, and interesting. Marvelous things were happening. Laymen were prophesying. Ordinary people were being moved on by

---

Leland R. Keys, D.D., is a senior semiretired minister of the Assemblies of God, Los Altos, California.

the Holy Spirit in tongues and interpretation of tongues. Healings and miracles were present. There was a joyous exultation in the hearts of these Spirit-filled believers.

The apostles witnessed for their Lord with great power and boldness. When they were persecuted for their faith, they rejoiced that they were counted worthy to suffer for Jesus Christ (Acts 4:31, 33; 5:41).

This mood of joyful victory marked off the body of Spirit-filled believers from those followers of Judaism who had not accepted Christ as their Saviour and been filled with the Holy Spirit. Gone was the singing in a minor key; they were singing psalms, hymns, and spiritual songs in a major dominant. A glorious faith and victory overcame all obstacles as they went forward with God in the proclamation and spread of the gospel.

Within a century the fervency of the Early Church was replaced by formalism and ritual. The centuries that followed were marked by sporadic spiritual awakenings that restored to a place of importance the ministry of the Holy Spirit in the body of believers. Then at the beginning of this century something wonderful happened. God again poured out His Spirit as on the Day of Pentecost. The first evidences of this latter-day outpouring appeared in Topeka, Kansas in 1901 and Los Angeles, California in 1906. A full account of these outpourings is given in *With Signs Following* by Stanley H. Frodsham.[1]

Here was a movement that was truly distinctive. It was different from cold, formal religion. It was Pentecostal.

> There is such power in the preaching of the Word . . . that people are shaken on the benches. Coming to the altar many fall prostrate under the power of God and often come out speaking in tongues. Sometimes the power falls on people . . . during the giving of testimonies, or the preaching, and they receive the Holy Spirit.[2]

There were other supernatural phenomena. The sick were healed. To some were given songs in the Spirit. Here is the testimony of one so blessed:

---

[1]Stanley H. Frodsham, *With Signs Following* (Springfield, MO: Gospel Publishing House, 1946).

[2]Frodsham, *With Signs Following*, p. 34.

My joy overflowed in utterance in other tongues . . . often interpreted by friends who spoke the different languages. He also gave me the most beautiful songs in the Spirit, indescribably glorious and so different from our ordinary singing.[3]

The writer to the Hebrews speaks of our "so great salvation" which was first spoken by our Lord, and then confirmed by those who heard Him, "God also bearing them witness, both with signs and wonders, and with divers miracles, and gifts of the Holy Ghost, according to his own will" (Hebrews 2:3,4).

One Great Distinctive

The one great truth of the Pentecostal Movement which distinguishes it from other denominations is the belief that a Christian may today receive the baptism in the Holy Spirit as did the disciples on the Day of Pentecost, speaking in other tongues as the Spirit gives utterance. The experience has made this body of believers truly distinctive—truly Pentecostal. There are other distinctives, but this is the most significant.

The Assemblies of God's position is stated in part in the Statement of Fundamental Truths as follows:

The baptism of believers in the Holy Ghost is witnessed by the initial physical sign of speaking in other tongues as the Spirit of God gives them utterance (Acts 2:4).

We hold this truth to be the essential and indispensable element of the Pentecostal experience, and of the Movement which has resulted from the renewed outpouring of the Holy Spirit in our time, as on the Day of Pentecost.

Much space could be devoted to the ministry of the Holy Spirit—in the world, the church, and the individual. However, that is not the purpose of this chapter. There are many ministries of the Spirit which all Christians enjoy, but some things have made Pentecostals "distinctive" as a people; these we seek to present and to emphasize.

The experience of the baptism in the Holy Spirit is not terminal or the pinnacle of spiritual experience. This is indicated in the Scriptures in a number of ways. The experience introduces the believer into a

---

[3]Frodsham, *With Signs Following*, p. 26.

whole new realm of power and blessing. When one is filled with the Spirit he experiences an intensification of all the good things of God. The testimonies of those who have received the experience indicate this. They speak of a new sense of the nearness of God; of a Christ more real, more dear; of an intensified love for Christ; of a quickened expectation of Christ's return; and of a surprising illumination and understanding of the Word of God. Others speak of a new power for witnessing and service for God.

However, the baptism in the Holy Spirit is, as the Greek in Acts 2:4 would indicate, a crisis experience, something that happens at a particular point in time in the life of a believer. As one expositor has put it, "It is something done and finished with." In other words, there is but one Baptism. But this is not the end.

In Ephesians 5:18 we find the scriptural authority for believing in a continuing experience of the Holy Spirit's infilling: "And be not drunk with wine, wherein is excess; but be filled with the Spirit." The tense of the verb *filled* is a present tense, indicating an action taking place. There is implied the inflow to sustain the outflow. It is a picture of replenishment. One does not get the Baptism every day, but he or she can have a fresh infilling every day.

For scriptural illustrations of this principle we recall the experience of the apostles and fellow believers who had received the experience of Acts 2:4 on the Day of Pentecost. But now, persecution had arisen because of "the way." Peter and John were threatened by the Sanhedrin and released. "And being let go, they went to their own company." There they gave a report of what had happened to them. "And when they heard that, they lifted up their voice to God with one accord" (Acts 4:23, 24). Then occurred the blessed infilling of the Holy Spirit to those believers who had previously been baptized in the Spirit on the Day of Pentecost: "And they were all filled with the Holy Ghost, and they spake the word of God with boldness" (Acts 4:31).

In Antioch in Pisidia, the church faced opposition and persecution, but it found strength to go on through a fresh infilling of the Holy Spirit. The record states, "And the disciples were filled with joy, and with the Holy Ghost" (Acts 13:52). The Greek renders it, ". . . were being filled."

Nor did the apostle Paul rely only on the initial experience of being filled with the Spirit, an experience which he had certainly received according to Acts 9:17. Paul, while incarcerated in a Roman prison, made a statement that shows even an apostle needed the continuing supply of the Spirit. He wrote to the Philippians, telling them he knew the persecution through which he was going would turn out for good, depending on two things: (a) the prayers of the believers at Philippi, and (b) "the supply of the Spirit" (Philippians 1:19).

A New Dimension in Worship

The outpouring of the Spirit created a new dimension in worship among Spirit-filled believers. Jesus foretold the kind of worship that would characterize the dispensation of the Holy Spirit:

> But the hour cometh, and now is, when the true worshippers shall worship the Father in spirit and in truth. . . . God is a Spirit: and they that worship him must worship him in spirit and in truth (John 4:23, 24).

Under the Law, an elaborate ritual with set forms was indicated. Under grace, all this has been set aside, God having provided some better things for us, namely worship *in* the Spirit and *by* the Spirit.

The apostle Paul, writing many years later, states: "For we are the circumcision, which worship God in [or by] the spirit, and rejoice in Christ Jesus, and have no confidence in the flesh" (Philippians 3:3). This describes a worship that displaces cold form and ceremony, a worship that does not cater to that which is merely soulish nor resort to "fleshly" expedients to produce an effect.

There were two prohibitions in the Old Testament regarding worship which are typical and richly suggestive. First, no strange incense was to be offered on the altar of incense (Exodus 30:9). Mere form or ritual, without the heart being in it (mere lip service), would seem to be a "strange incense" on the altar. Second, no strange fire was permitted. In Leviticus 10:1 we read: "And Nadab and Abihu, the sons of Aaron, took either of them his censer, and put fire therein, and put incense thereon, and offered strange fire before the Lord, which he commanded them not." Verse 2 concludes, "They died before the Lord." "Fire out from before the Lord" (Leviticus 9:24) had kindled on the altar of burnt offering and consumed the sacrifice. Worshiping as God had directed, the people were blessed: "When all the people saw, they shouted, and fell on their faces" (Leviticus 9:24). But no commandment had yet been given as to how the incense was to be kindled. Thus, the fire was a strange fire, unauthorized by God.

Here we have a picture of worship marred by self-will; fleshly expedient was substituted for God's direction. It could be call "will worship."

Might not this suggest that any attempt to excite religious feelings by psychological methods and purely sensuous means is indeed "strange fire" in an assembly of believers? If the Lord is having His way, if the Holy Spirit is honored, there is no need to work up something. When an altar of scriptural worship is built and the living sacrifice of our bodies is placed thereon, the fire from heaven will fall. No "strange fire" will be needed or desired. In fact, it would be distinctly out of place in a congregation that is worshiping God in the Spirit.

The Early Church was characterized by a great freedom of expression in its worship services. This is brought out so succinctly in 1 Corinthians 14:26 *(NIV):*

> What then shall we say, brothers? When you come together, everyone has a hymn, or a word of instruction, a revelation, a tongue, or an interpretation. All of these must be done for the strengthening of the church.

Certainly there was a place and time for the teacher and preacher, but place was also made for the believer-priest to minister. This opportunity for the participation of all believers in worship is a distinctive of Pentecost. It represents for many a new dimension in worship.

The apostle Paul wrote, "Where the Spirit of the Lord is, there is liberty" (2 Corinthians 3:17). In the Early Church there was flexibility; a pulsating life manifested itself in a variety of ways. There was a blessed freedom in the Holy Spirit. It is true that freedom, sometimes carried too far, did turn into license. But the Holy Spirit had a solution for that, according to the writings of Paul. The apostle did not seek to quench anyone's gift or to deprive any believer of his freedom in the Lord. He strove for good and for the edification of the church as a whole.

It must have been exciting then, as it is today, to be in a church where the unexpected could and did happen. A Spirit-filled church pulsates with the life of Christ. It is a living, acting organism—a sufficient vehicle for the Holy Spirit's work and ministry.

The Gifts of the Spirit

One of the greatest distinctives of the Pentecostal Movement has been the exercise of the gifts of the Spirit as enumerated in 1 Corinthians 12:1-11. There is no reason to believe that God ever intended these manifestations of the Spirit to cease during the Church Age. We thank God they are in operation in the Chruch today. Paul wrote, "But the manifestation of the Spirit is given to every man to profit" (1 Corinthians 12:7).

Paul was referring to these supernatural ministries, for he goes on to name the nine gifts. Some are spectacular in their manifestation; some are not, "But all these worketh that one and the selfsame [the very same] Spirit, dividing to every man severally as he will' (1 Corinthians 12:11). Let us look at them in some detail.

THE WORD OF WISDOM

Through the operation of the word of wisdom, there is an impartation of divine wisdom in the solution of problems; the right application of knowledge which can only be known by special revelation.

In a General Presbyters meeting in Springfield, Missouri, some years ago, a particularly knotty problem came before the assembled brethren. More than 200 leaders from all parts of our nation were there, meeting with the executive officers elected to lead the church. After much discussion by many of the brethren, the problem remained unsolved. When it was apparent they had come up against a stone wall, the general superintendent called the body to prayer. There was much earnest prayer and seeking the face of God, as they knelt together asking God to help in the situation. After a time, the spirit of prayer lifted and the brethren took their seats. Then one of the brethren standing before the group, in a few short sentences, gave the solution to the problem. Truly the word of wisdom was exercised that day and the problem was solved.

THE WORD OF KNOWLEDGE

The word of knowledge involves the supernatural impartation of facts which could not be received through natural means. Peter's knowledge of Ananias' deceit (Acts 5:1-6) and Paul's awareness of a lame man's faith (Acts 14:9) are examples.

FAITH

The gift of faith is extraordinary faith, miracle-working faith. It is to be distinguished from "saving faith" which is the possession of all believers. However, a distinction must also be drawn between the gift of faith and the working of miracles.

> Though the gift of faith produces results that transcend natural law, it is not identical with the gift of miracles (1 Corinthians 12:10). The gift of miracles operates with immediacy in overt action as a public testimony to the greatness of God. It has an objective effective upon persons, creatures, or things (Matthew 15:36-38). In contrast, the gift of faith has its effect primarily upon the gifted believer. Its essential functions are to afford him divine protection, provide for his physical need, and aid him in his work. Unlike the gift of miracles, its outcome may be deferred—a circumstance doubtless intended to increase the gifted person's reliance upon God.[4]

GIFTS OF HEALINGS

The gifts of healings have to do with supernatural healing that is extraordinary in nature. In addition to the gifts of healings, God has also provided for extraordinary healing through the ministry of elders and believers in general.

THE WORKING OF MIRACLES

Harold Horton had described a miracle as "a supernatural intervention in the ordinary course of nature." The working of miracles may include creative as well as restorative ministry. The raising of Dorcas (Acts 9:36-43) and of Eutychus (Acts 20:9-12) are examples.

PROPHECY

The gift of prophecy is utterance in the native tongue of the believer, which results in edification, exhortation, and comfort (1 Corinthians 14:3). It is more than ordinary preaching. It is the divine impartation of truth, always consistent with the written Word of God.

---

[4]Albert L. Hoy, "The Gift of Faith," *Paraclete*, Winter 1977, p. 9.

Any prophecy that contradicts what God has written is to be rejected as spurious.

THE DISCERNING OF SPIRITS

The discerning of spirits is the God-given ability to discern whether a manifestation of any kind is of demonic or human origin rather than divine. An illustration of this manifestation of the Spirit is Paul's recognition of the demonic power motivating the maiden at Philippi (Acts 16:16-18).

VARIOUS KINDS OF TONGUES

This is utterance in a language unlearned by the speaker. The apostle Paul never questioned the reality of this gift of the Spirit, but he did seek to direct this manifestation of the Spirit in the assembly for the edification of all (1 Corinthians 14:12). One of his last admonitions to the church at Corinth on this matter was: "Forbid not to speak with tongues" (1 Corinthians 14:39).

THE INTERPRETATION OF TONGUES

The interpretation of tongues is the counterpart of the gift of various kinds of tongues. Paul's ideal was that the one who gave a message in tongues should pray that he might give the interpretation. His admonition was that a message in tongues should always be interpreted, otherwise the assembly would not be edified. God's Word gives clear directions in these mattters in 1 Corinthians 14. In the 12th and 14th chapters of 1 Corinthians we have the picture of a church in which the supernatural was in evidence. God was truly moving by His Spirit.

Three exhortations given by the apostle Paul are most relevant in connection with the manifestations of the Spirit: "Quench not the Spirit. Despise not prophesyings. Prove all things; hold fast that which is good" (1 Thessalonians 5:19-21). The manifestations of the Spirit flourish in a warm, spiritual atmosphere. As one Pentecostal has said, "They do not flourish in a refrigerator."

Herein lies the responsibility of the pastor or leader of a service of worship. While steering away from fleshly extremes, he must at the same time avoid a cold formal worship. He can encourage a warm freedom in the Spirit; he can do much to encourage the saints in their worship *in the Spirit.* "For we are the circumcision, which worship God in the spirit, and rejoice in Christ Jesus, and have no confidence in the flesh" (Philippians 3:3). The pastor's attitude and example are of tremendous importance here.

A New Dimension in Personal Devotions

For those Christians who grow to know the Lord intimately, the baptism in the Holy Spirit is the introduction to an overflowing life in the Spirit. There are some who are content to speak in tongues as evidence they have received the Baptism; then they rest there and progress no further in a walk in the Spirit. They feel, unfortunately, that they have arrived. And so they have, but at only one point of Christian experience. There is more, much more, to follow in the realm of experiences in the Spirit.

Praying in Tongues. It is a distinctive teaching of the Pentecostal Movement that one may continue to speak in tongues after being baptized in the Spirit. This physical manifestation might be called *devotional tongues* and serves an important function in personal edification. This is not a mechanical utterance; it is the overflow of the "rivers of living water." It is the outflow of the inflow of the blessed Holy Spirit.

Paul said, "He that speaketh in an unknown tongue edifieth himself" (1 Corinthians 14:4). He builds himself up. This does not refer to a message in a public assembly. It is a spiritual exercise in the devotional life of the Spirit-filled believer.

Again, the apostle says, "I thank God that I 'speak in tongues' privately more than any of the rest of you" (1 Corinthians 14:18, *The Living Bible).* In contrast he says, "But in public worship . . .," indicating that his speaking in other tongues for the purpose of personal edification was done in his private devotions. Such ecstatic utterance has an uplifting effect; it is a tonic for the soul. Surely one who is so blessed would agree with an Old Testament word from the prophet Isaiah: "This is the rest wherewith ye may cause the weary to rest; and this is the refreshing" (Isaiah 28:12). Harold Horton of England has written, "What heavenly rest in spiritual exercise has the Lord designed in these heavenly tongues! Hallelujah!"[5]

---

[5]Harold Horton, *The Gifts of the Spirit* (U. S. edition, Springfield, MO: Gospel Publishing House, 1975), p. 138.

This continued speaking in tongues as a part of one's devotions is here presented not so much as a duty but as a high privilege of Spirit-filled believers.

Singing in the Spirit. This is another distinctive phenomenon of worship in the Spirit, whether in private or in the assembly of Spirit-filled believers. How beautiful when the Spirit of God moves on a company of believers in this way; how uplifting. Note two Scripture passages in this connection: "Speaking to yourselves in psalms and hymns and spiritual songs, singing and making melody in your heart to the Lord" (Ephesians 5:19). "Teaching and admonishing one another in psalms and hymns and spiritual songs" (Colossians 3:16). These "spiritual songs" are most certainly utterances in other tongues.

The apostle Paul said, "I will sing with the spirit, and I will sing with the understanding also" (1 Corinthians 14:15). *The Living Bible* renders it this way: "I will sing in unknown tongues and also in ordinary language, so that I can understand the praise I am giving."

What is the value of prayer in an unknown language? The Word of God answers this question for us clearly. Paul says: "If I pray in an unknown tongue, my spirit prayeth, but my understanding is unfruitful. What is it then? I will pray with the spirit, and I will pray with the understanding also" (1 Corinthians 14:14,15). Again *The Living Bible* preserves the clear meaning: "Well, then, what shall I do? I will do both. I will pray in unknown tongues and also in ordinary language that everyone understands" (v. 15).

How often do we experience the reality of Romans 8:26! "We know not what we should pray for as we ought." How frequently we feel that we have prayed ourselves out. There are also times in our prayer life when we are conscious that we are face to face with demonic powers that would seek to keep our prayers from getting through. Then what a blessing to be able to pray in an unknown language as inspired by the Holy Spirit. The Spirit makes the requests known at the Throne by praying in a tongue unknown to one's intellectual comprehension. Again, the Spirit-filled Christian enjoys a high privilege.

In a sense this whole chapter may be said to be a commentary on the essential differences between Pentecostal evangelicals and other evangelicals. These differences or distinctives constitute our reason-for-being.

Pentecostal churches are theologically orthodox. On the great foundational and fundamental truths of the Word of God they are in complete agreement with other evangelicals. This includes faith in the infallibility and inerrancy of the Bible.

It is the experience of the baptism in the Holy Spirit, with the initial evidence of speaking in other tongues as the Spirit gives utterance, that has made Pentecostal people different from other evangelical Christians. These differences find expression in many ways in the services of Pentecostal churches. We mention here a few:

1. Instead of a sense of form and rigidity, one feels a warm atmosphere of freedom in the Holy Spirit.

2. The singing is spirited. Spirit-filled believers sing with a special zest and anointing of the Spirit.

3. There is no formal order of service that cannot be changed, should the Spirit so lead.

4. The prayer time may be different. One may lead in prayer while the congregation remains silent or the whole assembly may pray out loud at the same time. That there is scriptural precedent for this kind of praying is seen in Acts 4:24, "They lifted up their voice to God with one accord." This kind of praying is of common occurrence in Pentecostal assemblies.

5. The preaching can be described as "orthodoxy set on fire." The preacher himself is often so full of the Spirit and of the truth of his message that he may preach with unusually great fervor.

6. During the song service, the worshipers often lay the hymnals down and engage in the singing of choruses, lifting up their hearts to God in joyful songs. There is a spirit of joyful gladness in such singing, as they sing with grace in their hearts to the Lord (Colossians 3:16).

7. Sometimes the usual order of the service is interrupted for special prayer if an immediate need is indicated, such as prayer for the sick or another pressing need.

8. At times Pentecostal services are marked by singing in the Spirit. This unique phenomenon of a Pentecostal worhsip service brings much blessing to the congregation. Paul said, "I will sing with the spirit, and I will sing with the understanding also" (1 Corinthians 14:15). In Ephesians 5:18,19 we find this admonition: "Be filled with the Spirit; speaking to yourselves in psalms and hymns and spiritual songs, singing and making melody in your heart to the Lord." Singing

in the Spirit may be either in unknown tongues or simply singing a beautiful melody as unto the Lord under the anointing of the Holy Spirit. Both are heard in Pentecostal services. The practice sometimes involves many of the worshipers.

9. Opportunity is given for vocal praise. Frequently the pastor will call the congregation to a time of praise. The believer-priests offer to God the sacrifice of praise, the fruit of their lips, giving thanks to His name. (See Hebrews 13:15.) This is often accompanied by the lifting up of the hands as the congregation together worships God in this manner.

10. The gifts of the Spirit are frequently in evidence. Perhaps one of the most distinctive features of a Pentecostal church is the place that is given for the manifestation of the gifts of the Spirit, such as prophecy, tongues, and the interpretation of tongues. Paul warned the church at Corinth, "Forbid not to speak with tongues" (1 Corinthians 14:39). The gifts of the Spirit are for ministry and for edification.

11. The altar service is a distinctive part of a Pentecostal service. Its purpose is to give believers an opportunity to wait on God in prayer until He meets their needs and blesses their souls. It is during the altar service that many receive the baptism in the Holy Spirit. Many wonderful things take place in these services as God reveals himself to hungry souls. The altar service has played an important part in the services of Pentecostal churches from the beginning of the Movement.

These, then, are some of the features that make Pentecostal services different from services in most other evangelical and/or mainline Protestant churches.

Potential Areas of Danger

With the outpouring of the Spirit, there comes to the Spirit-baptized believer a blessed sense of freedom. He has been ushered into a whole new realm of Christian experience both personally and in public worship!

There are two things to be guarded against—and avoided: fanaticism and formalism. One is as bad as the other.

Well-meaning believers sometimes go beyond that which is seemly. Sometimes one's own spirit is predominant rather than the Holy Spirit. In the Early Church, problems arose as to church order, personal liberties, and the use and abuse of the gifts of the Spirit. This is evident from Paul's writings. However, guidance was given in solving these and other matters that concerned the early believers. We have only to humbly follow what has been written in the Word of God to avoid making mistakes. God's Word is so clear. God has given a principle to be followed by all: "Let all things be done unto edifying" (1 Corinthians 14:26).

Where there is reality, sometimes a counterfeit is present. This is not surprising. Remember that Moses and Aaron went in before Pharaoh, and when Aaron cast down his rod it became a serpent. Then came the magicians and sorcerers of Egypt. They cast down their rods and they became serpents. Now note: "But Aaron's rod swallowed up their rods" (Exodus 7:12).

The writer was subjected to a situation, during his student days, in a certain church where there was rampant fanaticism and a terrible abuse of the gifts of the Spirit. Being in great mental and spiritual distress, he went to a godly pastor for help. This good man of God referred him to Jeremiah 23:28, "What is the chaff to the wheat? saith the Lord." Wherever you find some chaff, you may be sure there is also wheat to be found. We do not eat the chaff; it is burned in the fire. We eat the wheat and give God thanks. God can take care of the chaff. The real can overcome the counterfeit.

Through the patient, kindly teaching of God's Word, sincere but often misguided believers can be helped to avoid pitfalls. Open rebuke in a public assembly may wound Christ's lambs and divide God's sheep. Private teaching and counseling is usually the better procedure in matters of this kind.

Some people, because of certain fleshly excesses, would do away with all public manifestations of the Spirit. Such a policy would rule out what God would do in an assembly of believers if given the opportunity. Some years ago a group of brethren began to legislate what the Holy Spirit could and could not do in their meetings. An aged saint of God remarked, "If they continue in this manner, soon they will have no Holy Ghost to legislate."

There is also the danger of *formalism*. Emerson tells of sitting in a church in New England on a Sunday morning. It was during the dead of winter. As he watched the falling snow, he said there was more life and movement outside the church than there was within. One wonders if the sermon that day resembled a winter's day—short and cold.

The Pentecostal movement was born in the fire of the Holy Spirit. There was power and there was glory. Let us never settle for cold formalism. The dean of a well-known theological seminary said to the writer, "You Pentecostal people are in the same place our denomination was in a few years ago. You're in danger of losing your fire." This must not happen.

The pastor is the one who largely determines the spiritual climate of the assembly, the spiritual tenor of a meeting. How important that he be truly spiritual with a present fullness of the Holy Spirit. If he is cold and formal, such an attitude will be reflected in the services of the church. If he is full of the Spirit, sensitive to the movings of the Spirit, and encouraging in his attitude of worshiping God in spirit and in truth, the congregation will sense his attitude and follow his lead.

We are Pentecostal, a Movement of the Holy Ghost. God forbid it should ever be said of us, as it was of the church at Sardis: "Thou hast a name that thou livest, and art dead" (Revelation 3:1).

Let's Just Praise the Lord

We close this chapter on a joyful note of praise to God for what He has done in the past, for what He is doing in our world today, and for what we may expect in the future, should Jesus tarry. How wonderful to be living in these days of the Holy Spirit's outpouring. Never before in the history of the world has the scriptural promise been so literally fulfilled, "I will pour out my spirit upon all flesh" (Joel 2:28).

The outpouring of the Spirit on the Day of Pentecost reached relatively few people. At the end of the first century the population was small compared to the number of people living today. Centuries passed by. New lands were discovered, new countries were established, including our own United States. Then, in the process of time, God poured out His Spirit on hungry Christians, as He did on the Day of Pentecost. The outpouring of the Spirit spread to every known country of the world until it could be called a worldwide outpouring of the Spirit.

There has been in recent years a most remarkable renewal of the Holy Spirit among many members of what we might call old-line churches. They too have received the baptism in the Holy Spirit. Nor has this been limited to Protestantism. Today many in the Roman Catholic Church have received this experience. What a day in which to be a witness for the Lord! What tremendous opportunities lie before God's servants! What wonderful means of getting the full gospel out are ours—radio, television, the printed page! More people are being saved, filled with the Spirit, and healed today than ever before in the history of the world, including the days of the apostles.

It's a great time to be alive. It's a great time to be a witness for Christ and the full-gospel message. Jesus said, "Ye shall receive power, after that the Holy Ghost is come upon you" (Acts 1:8). We have received this power in the experience of the baptism in the Spirit. Let us minister, as God gives us opportunity, in the power of the Holy Spirit.

Let us praise the Lord, for, as Martin Luther wrote in his song, "A mighty fortress is our God."

The Spirit and the gifts are ours
Through Him who with us sideth.

Suggested Reading

Frodsham, Stanley H. *With Signs Following.* Springfield, MO: Gospel Publishing House, 1946.

Gee, Donald. *Concerning Spiritual Gifts.* Springfield, MO: Gospel Publishing House, rev., 1972.

Gee, Donald. *Spiritual Gifts in the Work of the Ministry Today.* Springfield, MO: Gospel Publishing House, 1963.

Hodges, Melvin L. *When the Spirit Comes.* Springfield, MO: Gospel Publishing House, 1972.

Horton, Stanley M. *Desire Spiritual Gifts Earnestly.* Springfield, MO: Gospel Publishing House, 1972.

Ness, Henry H. *Dunamis and the Church.* Springfield, MO: Gospel Publishing House, 1972.

Riggs, Ralph M. *The Spirit Himself.* Springfield, MO: Gospel Publishing House, 1949.

Steinberg, Hardy W. *The Church of the Spirit.* Springfield, MO: Gospel Publishing House, 1972.

Appendix

THE BIBLICAL VIEW OF THE MINISTRY[1]

The Biblical view of the ministry will be presented under three divisions of thought: the vocabulary of ministry; the types of ministry; and the functions of ministry.

The Vocabulary of Ministry

A great amount can be learned about the Biblical view of ministry by studying the usage of New Testament words related to the ministry. Although the following vocabulary is not exhaustive, it does present a topical outline of the main New Testament words of ministry.

THE NATURE OF THE MINISTRY

Proclamation
Kerusso (60 times) = to proclaim as a herald.
Kerux (3 times) = preacher.
Personal
Laleo (284 times) = to talk it up, to converse, to preach.
Experiential
Martureo (78 times) = to testify from the viewpoint of an eyewitness.
Martur, martus (34 times) = witnesses (martyrs).
Marturion (20 times) = witness, testimony.

[1]Selected from *Theological and Functional Dimensions of Ordination* (Springfield, MO: Gospel Publishing House, 1977), pp. 12-27, 29-36.

Dialogical
  Dialegomai (13 times) = to hold dialogue.
Thorough
  Katangello (17 times) = to tell thoroughly.
  Pleroo (90 times) = to fill, to make full, to preach fully.
Authoritative
  Parresiazomai (9 times) = to speak openly, boldly, authoritatively.

THE CONTENT OF THE MINISTRY

Good News
  Euangelizo (56 times) = to tell, preach good news.
  Euangelion (75 times) = good message, tidings, news.
  Euangelistes (3 times) = evangelist.
Christ-centered
  Kerygma (8 times) = the proclamation, the preaching (basic gospel
  content).
Bible-centered
  Logos (about 330 times) = the Word (the divinely-given message
  from God).

THE PURPOSE OF THE MINISTRY

Evangelism
  Euangelion (75 times) = good message, tidings, news.
  Kerygma (8 times) = proclamation, the preaching (basic gospel con-
  tent).
Instruction
  Didasko (97 times) = teach, taught.
  Didaskalos (58 times) = teacher.
  Didache (30 times) = the doctrine, the teaching (content).
  Didaskalia (21 times) = the doctrine, the teaching (content).
  Katexeo (7 times) = informed, instructed.
  Matheteuo (4 times) = instruct, disciple, teach.
  Paideuo (13 times) = to train.
  Propheteuo (28 times) = prophesy (to speak under immediate inspira-
  tion of the Spirit).
  Propheteia (19 times) = prophecy.
  Prophetes (147 times) = prophet, prophets.

Growth

Parakaleo (107 times) = to call to one's side for the purpose of intimate, urgent instruction.

Paraklesis (29 times) = consolation, comfort, exhortation, entreaty.

Parakletos (5 times) = Comforter, Advocate.

Episterizo (4 times) = confirming, strengthening.

Oikodomeo (39 times) = edify, build up (the total person).

Oikodome (18 times) = edifying, building.

THE DYNAMIC OF THE MINISTRY

Truth

Aletheia (110 times) = verity, true essence of a matter. When used with respect to God's Word it bears the idea that God's power and authority are inherent within it.

Anointing

Chrisma (3 times) = the special endowment of the Holy Spirit that supernaturally enhances the entire faculties.

Demonstration

Apodeixis (1 time) = a demonstration, a pointing out.

Power

Dunamis (127 times) = power or ability based on the indwelling of the Holy Spirit.

Conviction

Elencho (17 times) = to be convicted of moral wrong by word of mouth or action.

Diakatelenchomai (1 time) = to convince strongly of moral wrong.

The study of this vocabulary and other New Testament words pertaining to the ministry indicates that the ministry is characteristically a Word-centered proclamation.

The Types of Ministry

The most popular term currently used to denote the person who is set apart for special leadership and service in the church is *minister.* Minister (from *minus* or *minor)* means one who acts as an inferior agent in obedience or subservience to another, or who serves or officiates in contrast to the master (from *magnus)* or superior.

Three New Testament words are translated minister. The most frequently used Greek word is *diakonos*. It is variously translated servant, deacon, attendant, and minister. It is translated minister in Mark 10:43; Romans 13:4 (twice); 15:8; 1 Corinthians 3:5; 2 Corinthians 3:6; 6:4; 11:15 (twice); Galatians 2:17; Ephesians 6:21; Colossians 1:7, 23, 25; 4:7; 1 Thessalonians 3:2; and 1 Timothy 4:6. *Diakonos* was used in reference to service or ministry of any kind—civil service; waiting on tables; or ministry of angels, apostles, and Christ. It finally took on a more technical meaning in reference to a particular group who served as ministers of temporalities (Acts 6; 1 Timothy 3) as distinguished from . . . ministers of the Word.

The second word for minister is *leitourgos* which means a public servant or minister. It originally applied to public service rendered by the well-to-do at their own expense. In the New Testament it is applied to angels (Hebrews 1:7); prophets and teachers (Acts 13:1, 2); Epaphroditus (Philippians 2:25); Gentile offerings to Jews (Romans 15:27); civil magistrates (Romans 13:6); Paul (Romans 15:16); and Christ (Hebrews 8:2).

The third word for minister is *huperetes* which refers to one in a subordinate position. It originally was used in reference to an under-rower in a galley. It is used in the New Testament to refer to the custodian of the sacred books in the Jewish synagogue (Luke 4:20); John Mark (Acts 13:5); Paul (Acts 26:16; 1 Corinthians 4:1); and to servants of the Word (Luke 1:2).

There is another term that refers to the minister but is not translated "minister." This is *steward (oikonomos)*. *Oikonomos* is used in reference to believers in general (1 Peter 4:10); preachers and teachers of the Word (1 Corinthians 4:1, 2); and bishops (overseers) and presbyters (elders) (Titus 1:7). "Steward" was originally used for the manager of a household or estate (Luke 12:42; 16:1, 3, 8; 1 Corinthians 4:2; Galatians 4:2) and for civil servants (Romans 16:23).

Diakonos, leitourgos, huperetes, and *oikonomos* all connote the rendering of service or ministry and convey the view of the Christian ministry as servanthood. We give service unto Christ as we minister Him to others.

The New Testament clearly establishes that, while all believers constitute a ministering priesthood, God calls and sets apart a select group for special ministry in the establishment, edification, and leadership of the Church. The divine call can be seen in the New Testament in the practice of Jesus and, in certain passages, in words and examples.

Jesus himself professed a call to preach (Luke 4:18). He called others at the beginning of His ministry (Peter and Andrew (Mark 1:16-18); James and John (1:19, 20); and Matthew (2:14)). Jesus called others in the midst of His ministry (the Twelve were chosen and ordained (Mark 3:13-19), sent to preach and heal (6:7-13), and report back (6:30, 31)). He called others at the end of His ministry (John 17:18; Mark 16:14-20; Matthew 28:16-20). Jesus called persons after His ascension (Paul (Acts 9:15; 26:15-18; 1 Corinthians 9:16, 17)).

Of the many New Testament passages that teach the idea of a divine call to preach at least the following are noteworthy: John 1:6; Acts 9:15; 20:28; 26:15-18; Romans 10:13-15; 12:1-8; 1 Corinthians 9:16, 17; 12:11, 18; 2 Corinthians 3:5, 6; 5:18, 20; Ephesians 3:6, 7; 4:11-16; Colossians 1:23, 25; 1 Thessalonians 1:4; 1 Timothy 4:14.

Certain words in the New Testament are compound words that include the meaning of being "sent." Examples include such words as *kaleo*, "call"; *proskaleo*, "to call"; *klesis*, "calling"; and *kletos*, "called." Each of these have among their connotations "the call to vocation." So does *apostello*, "to send forth," and its cognates—*apostolos* (apostle), "one sent forth." Apostle is a compounding of *apo*, "from," and *stello*, "to send." Another cognate of *apostello* is *apestalmenos*, "sent as with a message or commission," used of John the Baptist (John 1:6). Other New Testament words could be introduced to support the idea of a divine call to ministry but these will suffice to illustrate the point.

God has been pleased to give to the Church an especially gifted quartet of persons, according to Ephesians 4:11, each of whom performs a special type of ministry, and all of which complement each other and edify the Church. These are gifted individuals given to the Church, not gifts given to individuals as in 1 Corinthians 12:8-11. Every minister is called and set apart for one or, in some cases, a combination of these types of proclamational ministry. "And he gave some, apostles; and some, prophets; and some evangelists; and some, pastors and teachers" (Ephesians 4:11).

In 1 Corinthians 12:28, Paul speaks of three of these four types of gifted persons: "And God hath set some in the church, first apostles, secondarily prophets, thirdly teachers . . . ." Then Paul mentions a combination of gifts and functions of ministry. These will be discussed later. We will now concentrate on the types of ministry.

APOSTLES (Ephesians 4:11; 1 Corinthians 12:28)

The word *apostle* is from the Greek *apostolos* which is a compounding of *apo*, "from," and *stello*, "to send," and means "one sent forth." *Apostolos* appears 80 times in the New Testament, and *apostole* (apostleship) four times. Consideration of these references indicates that "apostle" was used to refer to: Christ (Hebrews 3:1); the original 12 disciples (Luke 6:13; 9:10); Paul, as a special appointee of Christ (1 Corinthians 9:1; 15:9); James (Galatians 1:19); Barnabas (and Paul) (Acts 14:4, 14); Andronicus and Junia (Romans 16:7); two unnamed ministers (2 Corinthians 8:23); Epaphroditus (Philippians 2:25); and Silas and Timothy (and Paul) (1 Thessalonians 2:6).

In reference to Christ, *apostolos* shows His relationship to the Father. In its general usage *apostolos* shows the relationship of the "sent one" to Christ, and means basically what our English term *missionary* does. However, in its more specific and technical usage—in reference to those especially appointed (the Twelve and Paul)—it means much more.

From the New Testament it can be discovered that apostleship in the primary sense required the following credentials.

The apostles were directly called by Christ himself (the Twelve (Mark 3:14; Luke 6:13); Paul (Galatians 1:1)). They were eye and ear witnesses to Christ's life, death, and resurrection (John 15:27; Acts 1:21, 22; 4:33; 5:32; 1 Corinthians 9:1; 15:8, 9; 1 John 1:1).

The apostles were delegates or ambassadors sent on a mission. This meaning of the word *apostolos* carries the sense of the Hebrew word *shaliach* which referred to an agent, delegate, or ambassador sent with the authority (power of attorney) of the sender (Matthew 10:40). They were divinely-inspired writers (John 16:13; 1 Corinthians 2:10; Galatians 1:11, 12) and teachers of doctrine (Ephesians 3:5; 2 Peter 3:2; Jude 17).

The apostles were church founders (Ephesians 2:20) and administrators. They were the top-level administrators in organizing churches, dealing with doctrinal problems (Acts 15:22-29) and church factions (Corinthian correspondence), and fundraising (Paul). The apostles were international rather than local in the scope of their vision, ministry, responsibility, and authority (2 Corinthians 11:28). They were fully charismatic and had great success (Acts 2:43; 5:12, 16; 14:8-10; 19:11, 12; 2 Corinthians 12:12).

Perhaps not in the primary (foundational) sense (Ephesians 2:20; Revelation 21:14), but in a very functional sense, the apostleship of the Church today is comprised of those top-level preacher-administrators who most nearly approximate the credentials listed above. These might include the most outstanding denominational leaders, missionary statesmen, educators, etc. The apostolic ministry is essential to the success of the Church today.

PROPHETS (Ephesians 4:11; 1 Corinthians 12:28)
(Prophecy, Romans 12:6; 1 Corinthians 12:10-31)

The word *prophet* is from the Greek *prophetes* which is a compounding of *pro,* "before" or "for," and *phemi,* "to speak." A prophet is one who speaks *before* (proclaims) and also one who speaks *for* (in the name of) God. These two meanings are fulfilled by the prophet in *forthtelling* (the will of God) and *foretelling* (future events). *Prophetes* (prophets) appears in the New Testament 147 times, *prophetis,* (prophetess), 2 times, and *prophetikos* (prophetic), once.

While every Spirit-filled Christian has the potential of being exercised in the gift of prophecy (1 Corinthians 12:10-31; 14:1, 31), it is clear from the New Testament that God designated certain individuals to specialize in this type of ministry.

The New Testament indicates that the following were prophets: Jesus (Deuteronomy 18:15-18; Isaiah 61:1; Matthew 13:57; Luke 4:24; 13:33, 34; John 6:14; Acts 3:22, 26); Agabus and others (Acts 11:27, 28; 21:4, 10); Barnabas, Simeon (Niger), Lucius, Manaen, and Saul (Paul) (Acts 13:1-3); Judas (Barsabas) and Silas (Acts 15:32); Philip and his four daughters (Acts 21:8, 9); and John, who was heavily prophetic in the Book of Revelation.

From the New Testament we can discover the following about the credentials and ministry of Christian prophets. They were the continuation of an unbroken line of prophets that began with Abraham. Some of the prophets/prophetesses who formed the continuity between the Old and New Covenants were: Simeon (Luke 2:25-35); Anna (Luke 2:36-38); and John the Baptist (Matthew 11:9; 14:5; 21:26).

The prophet was one who spoke out of immediate spiritual impulse and illumination. He spoke with greater moral motive power than others did (priests, rabbis, etc.). He had a national or universal rather than provincial or local frame of reference. He had more of an eternal than a temporal view. He was primarily a spokesman of the Word of God and spoke with a sense of the imperative rather than passive indifference.

In the Book of Acts and the Epistles, the prophetic message included forthtelling (proclaiming) and foretelling (predicting). The Christian prophet's ministry to believers was characterized by exhortation and confirmation (Acts 15:32), edification, exhortation, comfort (1 Corinthians 14:3), and revelation (1 Corinthians 14:30). His ministry to unbelievers, judging by the expected consequence, must have included condemnation of sin, the explanation of judgment, and the gracious plan of salvation (1 Corinthians 14:24, 25).

The foundational aspect of prophecy (Ephesians 2:20) that gave divine inspiration for the writing of Scripture was fulfilled with the conclusion of the Book of Revelation (Revelation 22:18) by the apostle John. But all other aspects of this type of ministry continue in the Church today. The prophets of our day are those ministers who most nearly approximate the credentials and ministry described above—the great voices, the spiritual and moral reformers, the change bringers, and the back-to-the-Bible preachers of extraordinary vision, faith, boldness, and anointing.

While preaching and prophecy are not always synonymous, a great amount of truly Pentecostal preaching qualifies as prophecy. Prophecy can be defined as the supernaturally induced proclamation of the divine purposes of salvation, judgment, and glory to be accomplished in the present and/or the future. Every minister should pray that his preaching might be characterized as prophetic as much as pleases the Lord. The Church needs prophets and the manifestation of the gift of prophecy today.

EVANGELISTS (Ephesians 4:11; Acts 21:8; 2 Timothy 4:5)

The English noun *evangelist* (from the Latin *evangelista*) is translated from the Greek *euangelistes*. It means a bringer of the gospel (good news) and comes from the same root as *euangelion* (gospel, good news) and *euangelizomai* (to announce good news). Evangelist appears in the New Testament three times. In Ephesians 4:11 we find indication that God has placed individuals in the Church who have the gift of evangelism. In Acts 21:8 Philip is the only one named as an evangelist in the New Testament. However, in 2 Timothy 4:5 Timothy is urged to ". . . do the work of an evangelist . . . ."

The verb *euangelizomai* (evangelize) is used in reference to God (Galatians 3:8); to Jesus (Luke 20:1); to believers (Acts 8:4); and to the apostles on their itineraries. It also seems that the unnamed men of Cyprus and Cyrene were evangelists (Acts 11:20, 21). They were ". . . preaching the Lord Jesus . . ." (v. 20), which meant proclaiming the gospel (evangelizing). And they won many converts: ". . . a great number believed, and turned unto the Lord" (v. 21). There is also reason to believe that Timothy, Titus, Mark, and many others were evangelists.

The nature of the evangelist's ministry can be seen in the meaning of the term itself—a bringer of good news. This leads us to believe that the content of their ministry was gospel-centered. They ministered primarily to unbelievers. They were missionaries and pioneer church starters. Consequently, their ministry was foundational.

While it is evident that every believer was to be involved in evangelism as much as possible (Acts 8:4), there were certain individuals especially called and endowed by God for the itinerate ministry of evangelism.

Their ministry was primarily to preach the gospel (Acts 8:4, 5) in the interest of winning converts, with the spiritual maturation of these converts being left to the pastor-teachers who followed them. They were to baptize converts (Acts 8:12). They were to exercise discipline (Titus 3:10). Some were to ordain elders in the cities (Titus 1:5). Some served as special assistants to the apostles (1 Thessalonians 3:1-6; Philippians 2:19-23; Titus 1:5).

The ministry of the evangelist continues today by those who preach the basic gospel in the interest of winning converts to Christ. The nature of the work of many missionaries is basically evangelistic in the style of the New Testament evangelists. Additional dimensions of evangelistic work are the healing and deliverance ministry, and the promotion of revival in local assemblies and deeper spiritual life among believers. God-called and anointed evangelists are urgently needed in the Church today. Along with this, every minister should pray for the evangelistic dimension to be added to his ministry, and every believer needs to be vitally involved in soul winning.

PASTOR-TEACHERS (Ephesians 4:11) (TEACHERS, 1 Corinthians 12:28; TEACHING AND ADMINISTRATION, Romans 12:7, 8)

The pastoral and teaching roles are joined together in Ephesians 4:11. The *kai*, "and," here forms a simple conjunction of similar things, and the absence of the article before *didaskalous*, "teachers," contributes further to this view.

However, this is not to be taken as an indication that teaching can exist only in connection with pastoring. Teaching may well stand on its own as a 5th proclamational ministerial function.

The pastoral and teaching roles are complementary and essential to each other and to the edification of the body of Christ. They are the Siamese twins of the ministry. This truth is bolstered by 1 Timothy 5:17 where the most honorable elders were teachers. In Hebrews 13:7 the rulers were teachers. Also, in 2 Timothy 2:2 Paul admonishes Timothy to appoint faithful men who are competent to teach. It will be instructive to examine the pastoral and teaching roles separately to better see how they complement each other.

Pastors

While the detailed study of the ministerial titles of bishop (overseer) and presbyter (elder) will come later, it is necessary to notice at this juncture that pastor, bishop, and presbyter all refer to the same office in the New Testament.

The word *pastor* (from the Latin *pastores*) is the translation of the Greek word *poimen*. Ephesians 4:11 is the only place it is translated pastor. In its 16 additional appearances in the New Testament it is translated *shepherd*. Pastor and shepherd mean one who feeds and cares for a flock.

Eight times *poimen* refers to literal shepherds of sheep (Matthew 9:36; 25:32; Mark 6:34; Luke 2:8, 15, 18, 20; John 10:2). Eight times *poimen* refers to Jesus, the chief shepherd (Matthew 26:31; Mark 14:27; John 10:11, 12, 14, 16; Hebrews 13:20; 1 Peter 2:25). The Hebrew equivalent of *poimen* is used frequently in the Old Testament (example Psalm 23) in reference to God as the divine shepherd.

Much can be learned about pastoral ministry from a consideration of the relationship between the shepherd and his sheep. It was a personal, intimate relationship. The shepherd lived with his sheep. He named each of them. They recognized and responded to his voice. He loved them. It was a providing relationship. The shepherd helped his sheep to find water and grass (Psalm 23:2), and guided them away from danger. He ministered to the sick and wounded. It was a protecting relationship. The shepherd was constantly watching his sheep and guarding them from the hazards of nature, fierce beasts, and thieves.

The good shepherd would retrieve any of his own that went astray (Ezekiel 34:8; Matthew 18:12). It was a sacrificing relationship. The shepherd forsook comforts and lived with his sheep in the fields. He was often required to risk his life, and some shepherds died protecting their sheep. He was obligated to account for each one and make restitution for any that were lost (Genesis 31:39), unless he could prove that the circumstances were beyond his control (Exodus 22:10-13; Ezekiel 34:8-10).

From the comparison of spiritual shepherds and their sheep with the relationships of natural shepherds, it can be concluded that pastors sustain the same relationships. Their relationship to their people is personal and intimate. Apostles, prophets, and evangelists itinerate, but pastors are committed to a given locale—they have a flock. They are to love the people to whom they minister (1 Thessalonians 1:3; 1 John 3:16). The spiritual shepherd's relationship to the sheep is a providing relationship. In Acts 20:28 Paul urges the elders of Ephesus (where he had pastored for 3 years) to "... feed [poimainein= shepherd] the church of God . . . ." This means to give to them the full provision of which the shepherd is capable—to guide, feed, and minister to the sick and wounded.

The pastor also sustains a protecting relationship. The pastor must guard the flock against "grievous wolves" who would intimidate and persecute the members from without (Acts 20:29) and against heretical pastors from within (v. 30). Pastors are also accountable for their spiritual sheep (Hebrews 13:17) as the shepherds are accountable for each of their sheep. The pastor must live a life of dedication and sacrifice in the effective fulfillment of his shepherding ministry.

In addition to what we learned about the pastoral ministry by comparing it to the shepherd, the New Testament indicates that the character of this ministry includes overseeing, superintending, and presiding over the affairs of the flock of God in all things that constitute them the flock of God (Acts 20:28; 1 Timothy 5:17; Hebrews 13:7, 17; 1 Peter 5:1-3). This oversight (sometimes translated "rule") is to be in the nature of tender, vigilant, exemplary superintendence— not as "being lords over God's heritage . . ." (1 Peter 5:3).

The shepherd does not drive the sheep, he leads them. This oversight includes guidance, training, and discipline (Acts 20:31; Titus 1:13; 2:15). More will be said about this when considering bishops and presbyters. Pastors (elders) were to visit the sick and afflicted of the flock and pray for their healing—emotionally, physically, and spiritually (James 5:13-16). Finally, pastors are to teach, as is indicated by the dual title pastor-teachers.

Teachers (Ephesians 4:11; 1 Corinthians 12:28)
(Teaching, Romans 12:7)

The word *didaskalous* (teachers) and its cognates appear many times in the New Testament. *Didaskalous* is from the Greek verb *didasko*, "to teach," and means doctor, teacher, instructor, master. It is used in reference to Jesus (Matthew 8:19; 17:24; 23:8; 26:18; Mark 4:38; 5:35; 14:14; Luke 8:49; 22:11; John 1:38; 3:2; 11:28; 13:13, 14; 20:16); the relationship of a disciple to the master (Matthew 10:24, 25; Luke 6:40); Nicodemus (John 3:10); Christian teachers (Acts 13:1; 1 Corinthians 12:28, 29; Ephesians 4:11; Hebrews 5:12; James 3:1); and Paul (1 Timothy 2:7; 2 Timothy 1:11).

In addition, numerous other passages show the teaching ministry to be a prime obligation of the pastor (bishop/elder) (1 Timothy 2:12; 3:2; 4:13, 16; 5:17; Titus 2:1; Hebrews 13:7). The pastor-teacher is to teach sound doctrine (Titus 2:1) in the spirit of love (Ephesians 4:14, 15). He is to "contend for the faith" (a body of fundamental doctrine, Jude 3) without being contentious!

The qualifications for ministers can best be seen under the study of bishops/elders which follows.

Bishops/Elders (Pastors) (1 Timothy 3:1-7; Titus 1:5-9)

In the New Testament we have two other titles that need to be considered as applying to ministers. These are *bishop* (overseer) and *elder* (presbyter).

Bishop is the translation of the Greek word *episkopos*. It came from *episkeptomai* which means "to inspect," "to look after," "to oversee," "to superintend." *Episkopos* is a compounding of *epi*, "over," and *skopeo*, "to watch" or "to look." *Episkopos* (bishop) is used five times in the New Testament: four times by Paul (Acts 20:28; Philippians 1:1; 1 Timothy 3:2; Titus 1:7), and once by Peter (1 Peter 2:25).

As has previously been observed, bishop and elder are two titles for the same person. There are two principal reasons to justify the use of the two terms. First, bishop (overseer) refers to the function, and elder (presbyter) refers to the man. Second, bishop is used mainly by Paul, who was extremely careful to use the most communicable language. He used the Hellenistic word in writing to his Gentile assemblies and leaders. They would understand "bishop" better than the Jewish idea expressed in the Greek *presbyteros* (elder). Notice that he uses it in writing to Philippi in Asia Minor (Philippians 1:1); to the Ephesian elders (quoted by Luke in Acts 20:17, 28); to Timothy in Ephesus (1 Timothy 3:1, 2); and to Titus in Crete (Titus 1:7).

That bishop, elder, and pastor are interchangeable terms can be established by the fact that they are so used several times in the New Testament. In Acts 20:17 the leaders from Ephesus are referred to as "elders" *(presbyterous)*, and in verse 28 Luke says the Holy Spirit has made them "overseers" *(episkopous)* and they are to "shepherd" *(poimainein)* the Church. So in one passage we have elder/bishop/pastor. In Titus 1:5, Paul indicates that he left Titus in Crete to appoint "elders in every city" *(presbyterous)*. Then he immediately lists the qualifications of a bishop *(episkopon)* (vv. 6-9). In none of the New Testament references to pastor, bishop, and elder is there the slightest suggestion of rank among these titles. They are all on the same level.

There was a plurality of bishop/elder/pastors in some cities (Acts 14:23; 20:17; Philippians 1:1; Titus 1:5; James 5:14). No doubt prior to the building of Christian church buildings, they congregated in borrowed buildings, such as synagogues, and in private houses. The rapid growth of Christianity would have quickly produced many small congregations (house churches) in many cities, each needing a bishop/elder/pastor. When larger places of assembly were provided, the size of some congregations would require more than one elder (a multiple staff) to accomplish its ministry. Thus, there definitely was a plurality of elders in some cities and in some assemblies (Acts 14:23) in the New Testament.

While there is no trace of a monarchical bishop and hierarchy in the New Testament or apostolic times, it was not long in developing.

Men of great ability and spiritual influence were called on to be chairman or president of the council of bishops/elders/pastors in a given locale or region (for example, James at Jerusalem, Acts 15:13; 21:18; Galatians 2:9, 12). Then with the rise of persecution, heresy, and schism, strong leadership was demanded. By the beginning of the second century the focus had shifted from charismatic leadership to carnal leadership by a college of local elders. By the end of the second century, the presiding elder of each of these groups had gained such power, prestige, and permanence as to dominate the group. This eventuated in the development of a hierarchy of command on three levels —bishop, presbyter, and deacon—with the rank and file of the laity being on an even lower level.

We can legitimize the setting up of a presidential bishop (chairman or superintendent of bishops/elders/pastors) on the basis of the ascendancy of James, the assignments given to Timothy and Titus by Paul, and the need for strong, decisive leadership in times of persecution, heresy, and schism. But there can be no warrant for a monarchical bishop or sacerdotalism. All leadership must be determined on the basis of charisma and a ministry of proclamation of the Word. There is no New Testament support or other justification for having two classes of elders—"ruling" elders and "teaching" elders. Originally the ruling (presiding) elders presided by the authority of the charismatically preached and taught Word of God. This is the only guarantee against hierarchy and sacerdotalism.

The duties of bishops include those enumerated for pastors above. Two duties that were not mentioned are: being a member of a council, with the apostles deciding doctrines and practices of the Church, and receiving financial gifts for the local assemblies (Acts 11:30) and delegating the distribution of funds (Acts 6:3). It may also be that a committee or council *(presbyterion,* 1 Timothy 4:14) of elders served as ordainers of Timothy (2 Timothy 1:6) and others.

Elder is the translation of the Greek word *presbyteros.* The adjective *presbyteros* (elder) is a cognate of *presbus,* "an old man" or "an elder," and of *presbyterion,* "an assembly of old men."

Presbyteros (elder) is used in Judaism to refer to the elders (heads) of families, tribes, the seventy who assisted Moses (Numbers 11:16; Deuteronomy 27:1), and King Solomon. Also, it is used in reference to the secular city managers (Luke 7:3), and to the elders, scribes, and chief priests who comprised the Sanhedrin (the Jewish supreme court). The New Testament uses *presbyteros* to refer to the 24 elders in heaven (Revelation 4:4, 10; 5:5-14; 7:11, 13; 11:16; 14:3; 19:4).

The Jewish synagogues were governed by a council of elders under the presidency of the ruler (presider) of the synagogue with the high priest being president *ex officio*. It seems that the Early Church adapted this pattern of leadership to fit its needs.

The word *presbyteros* (elder) appears 67 times in the New Testament. *Presbyterion* (elderhood) appears 3 times, once in reference to Christian elders (1 Timothy 4:14), and twice in reference to the Sanhedrin (Luke 22:66; Acts 22:5). If, as we have suggested, bishop was the preferred term in writing or speaking to Gentile Christian converts, elder was the best term to use with converts to Christianity from Judaism. Elder/s is so used in Acts 11:30; 14:23; 15:2, 4, 6, 22, 23; 16:4; and 21:18.

The qualifications for bishops/elders/pastors (no doubt apostles, prophets, evangelists, and teachers as well) are catalogued principally in two almost parallel passages (1 Timothy 3:1-7 and Titus 1: 5-9) . . . .

In this section of study on "The Types of Ministry" we have discovered that four principal types of charismatic individuals have been given by Christ to His church. They are the itinerant ministers— apostles, prophets, and evangelists—and the local ministers— pastor/teachers (bishops/elders). Basic to each of these types of ministry is the proclamation of the Word of God. They are evangelical. However, additional functions complement their ministries.

The Functions of Ministry

In addition to the ministerial duties noted in the previous study of each type of ministry, there are other functions that are performed by one or all of them and their counterparts in the Church today.

In Romans 12:4 Paul says: "All members have not the same office" *(praxis)*, which means "a mode of acting," "a function." Then in verses 6-8 he lists several functions of the ministry. In 1 Corinthians 12:28, he names three types of ministers (apostles, prophets, teachers) and five functions. The functions of Romans 12:6-8 are: prophecy; service; teaching; exhortation; giving (financial aid); ruling (taking the lead); and showing mercy (visiting the poor, sick, and spiritually needy). The functions of 1 Corinthians 12:28 are: works of power (miracles); gifts of healings; helps (assistance); governments (administrations); and various tongues. In 1 Corinthians 12:8-11 Paul lists nine gifts of the Spirit. These gifts are to be expressed at the discretion of the Holy Spirit through every Spirit-filled believer-priest. However, their purpose indicates that they should find optimum expression through ministers as functions of ministry.

In the light of the duties ascribed to ministers and the scriptural functions of ministry, the following ministerial functions are essential to the edification of the local assembly today.

PREACHING/TEACHING

The proclamational ministry is primary. The other functions of ministry are secondary and convey spiritual benefit only as they, in their own way, communicate the Word of God. According to Romans 10:8-17, the Word of God is requisite to faith, and faith is essential to the reception of saving grace. Only the Word of God combined with the Holy Spirit has inherent spiritual power, and only in response to faith. The nearest thing to a sacrament, as it is usually defined, is the anointed preaching of God's Word. Evangelicals show the priority of the Word over other functions of ministry in their church architecture.

> In the middle ages sacerdotalism almost smothered preaching from the Church. Evangelical Protestantism has been able to keep the communion and preaching in appropriate balance, and even indicates this in her church architecture. The communion table and the pulpit are both centered in the sanctuary to show their importance, but the pulpit is elevated above the table to show the primacy of the preached Word.[2]

(For an informative historical sketch of the place of the pulpit and altar/table in church architecture see: "Where Does the Pulpit Belong?" *Advance*, May 1967, pp. 13, 14, by Dr. William Menzies.)

The word *sacrament* does not occur in the Scripture. Sacrament is from the Latin word *sacramentum* and originally had three classical connotations. First, from *sacro* it meant "to make sacred," "to dedicate to sacred use or gods." Second, a sacred deposit or pledge

[2]Jesse K. Moon, *Principles for Preachers* (Waxahachie, TX: Published by the author, 1975), pp. 18, 19.

(monetary). Third, an oath, especially that made by a soldier to obey the orders of his superiors and be loyal to his nation. The Latin church fathers used *sacramentum* in the senses above, and also as a synonym for the Greek word *musterion*, "a mystery," hence something hidden until revealed. Thus, it came to refer to a rite, type, or emblem having latent spiritual meaning and power known only to the initiated. In the Latin Vulgate, by the use of *sacramentum*, this meaning is pressed onto Ephesians 3:3, 4, 9; 5:32; 1 Timothy 3:16; and Revelation 1:20 where the original Greek word *musterion* is appropriately translated "mystery" in the King James Version. The true sense is "the revelation of truth undiscoverable by human reason alone." The following are representative definitions of sacrament.

> CATHOLIC. A sacrament is something presented to the senses, which has the power, by divine institution, not only of signifying, but also of efficiently conveying grace.—Council of Trent, Cat. Rom., Part II., Chap. I., Q. 6.

> ANGLICAN. Sacraments instituted by Christ are not only the badges and tokens of the profession of Christian men, but rather they be certain sure witnesses and effectual signs of grace, and of God's good will towards us, by the which he doth work inwardly in us, and doth not only quicken, but also strengthen and confirm our faith in him.—The Twenty-Fifth Article of Religion.

> PRESBYTERIAN. Sacrament is a holy ordinance instituted by Christ in his church, to signify, seal, and exhibit to those who are within the covenant of grace the benefits of his mediation, to increase their faith and all other graces, to oblige them to obedience, to testify and cherish their love and communion with one another, and to distinguish them from those that are without.[3]

Protestants generally would agree with the Presbyterian definition and disagree with the Catholic definition of sacrament. Catholics have traditionally held that the seven sacraments (baptism, confirmation, the Eucharist, penance, holy orders, matrimony, and extreme unction), when legitimately administered by a duly ordained priest (regardless of his spiritual and moral state), convey the grace which they signify to every recipient. The communication of grace is not dependent on the intention or faith of the recipient but is *ex opere operato*, by the inherent grace-conferring virtue of the sacrament it-

---

[3]The Westminster Assembly's Larger Catechism, A.162.

self. Catholics further hold that the grace of justification and true righteousness is conferred through the external action of the sacraments as the sole instrumental cause. This is the essence of sacerdotalism—the belief that the substance of the rite is made efficacious through the supernatural power and grace which inheres in the priesthood.

Protestants and especially evangelicals disagree with the Catholics at this point. Not even the Word of God is *ex opere operato*. It conveys grace only on the occasions when it is quickened by the Holy Spirit and received through faith in the heart of the recipient. Thus, as it has been asserted previously, the anointed preaching of the Word of God is the *nearest* thing to a sacrament, as usually defined, among the functions of ministry. (But it does not qualify by the Catholic notion as a sacrament.)

Actually, evangelicals, following the precedent established during the Protestant Reformation, prefer to discard the use of the word *sacrament* so as to not get drawn into Sacramentarianism (sacerdotalism) and the consubstantiation-transubstantiation debates.

In Assemblies of God literature, the word *sacrament* is rarely used and never with any sacerdotal connotation intended. The term *ordinance* is preferred. Simply defined, ordinances are "those outward rites which Christ has appointed to be administered in his church as visible signs of the saving truth of the gospel" (A. H. Strong, *Systematic Theology* (Philadelphia: The Judson Press, 1907), p. 930).

Protestants accept only the Lord's Supper (often called Communion) and baptism as ordinances. It is held that the grace received through the ordinances is not conferred through the external action. Even though they are obligatory upon Christians as duties, and are means for spiritual nourishment and growth, they are not considered essential means without which justification and true righteousness cannot be attained.

These two ordinances are dramatic, visual and symbolic ways of witnessing to the gospel. All the other functions of ministry communicate the gospel in their own distinctive ways.

WORSHIP LEADING

Worship leading is a second function of the ministry that is essential in the Church today. In addition to leading all aspects of various types of worship services, under this function should be listed the administration of the ordinances—the Lord's Supper and baptism; and the ceremonies—weddings, dedications, funerals, reception of members, and ordinations.

PASTORAL CARE

Pastoral care is another function of ministry that is essential in the Church today. This includes counseling, home calling, and hospital visitation.

ADMINISTRATION

Administration is an essential function of ministry in the Church today. It includes oversight and planning for the departments, deacons, committees, staff, finances, public relations, building programs, and so on.

THE ASSEMBLIES OF GOD VIEW OF MINISTRY

The Assemblies of God view of ministry, being Bible-based, is in agreement with the Biblical view of ministry as presented above. In addition, official statements about the Assemblies of God view of ministry can be drawn from the Constitution of The General Council of the Assemblies of God.

Article V, Statement of Fundamental Truths, 11, The Ministry: "A divinely called and scripturally ordained ministry has been provided by our Lord for the threefold purpose of leading the Church in: (1) Evangelization of the world (Mark 16:15-20), (2) Worship of God (John 4:23, 24), (3) Building a body of saints being perfected in the image of His Son (Ephesians 4:11-16)."

Bylaws, Article VII. Ministry
Section 1. Ministry Described:

Christ's gifts to the Church include apostles, prophets, evangelists, pastors, and teachers (Ephesians 4:11), exhorters, administrators, leaders and helpers (Romans 12:7, 8).

In terms of maturity of ministry, three classifications of ministry are recognized, viz., the ordained minister, the licensed minister, and the Christian worker. An applicant for ministerial recognition must give testimony to having experienced the new birth (John 3:5) and to having received the baptism in the Holy Spirit according to Acts 2:4. The Spirit-filled life will enable him to fulfill the threefold mission of the Church (Article V, par. 10 of the Constitution).

Section 2. Qualifications

a. Qualifications for ordination are outlined in the New Testament Scriptures. 1 Timothy 3:1-7; Titus 1:7-9.

b. Qualifications for license shall be in two categories:

1) Preaching Ministry

First: Clear evidence of a divine call, a practical experience in preaching, together with an evident purpose to devote one's time to preaching the gospel. They shall preach at least twenty times a year, except in case of ill health and infirmity.

Second: Conformity to such provisions as are made for candidates by The General Council of the Assemblies of God in reading courses and other training.

2) Specialized Ministry

An evident purpose to devote one's time to a specialized ministry such as Christian education, youth, music, or other full-time ministries. The same spiritual qualifications shall apply as outlined in Article VII. Section 1.

c. Efficient helpers in gospel work who devote a part of their time to Christian service may be recognized as Christian workers. They shall preach at least twelve times a year except in case of ill health or infirmity.

Section 3. Licenses and Christian Workers Certificates

Licenses and Christian Workers Certificates shall be granted by district councils to properly qualified applicants.

Section 4. Ordinations

a. All ordinations shall take place under the auspices of the district councils. Applicants twenty-three years of age or over who shall have met the necessary requirements shall appear before the credentials committee of the district where they reside. No person may be ordained to the ministry until he shall have held a license to preach and shall have been engaged in active work as a pastor or evangelist for at least two full consecutive years.

b. The Scriptures plainly teach that while there is a difference between the ministry of men and women in the church, divinely called and qualified women may also serve the church in the ministry of the Word. Women who may have demonstrated a distinct ministry of evangelism and who have met the requirements of district councils may be licensed to preach the Word. Mature women of not less than twenty-three years of age who have developed in the ministry of the Word so that their ministry is acceptable generally and who have proved their qualifications in actual service and who have met all the requirements of the credentials committees of the district councils may be ordained to the ministry of the gospel and may serve either as evangelists or as pastors as their qualifications warrant. The right to administer the ordinances of the church, when such acts are necessary, shall be included in the ordination.

Section 5. Exceptions

a. It is recommended that our district councils refrain from ordaining to the ministry any preacher who may have been licensed in another district until such licentiate shall have resided in the district in which he is seeking ordination at least one year and shall have met the requirements of the district granting him license, and until endorsement be secured from the officiary of the district in which the candidate was previously licensed.

b. We disapprove of district councils granting credentials to married persons in cases where either the applicant or the married partner has a former companion living (see Article VIII, Section 5e).

c. The Executive Presbytery shall have the authority to determine whether an applicant's annulment of a former marriage is consistent with the scriptural position of the Fellowship relating to the granting or holding of ministerial credentials; or, in the case of a divorce or a dissolution whether the circumstances would more appropriately be classified ·as calling for an annulment. The application must be accompanied by clear and satisfactory evidence of an illegal marriage through deception or fraud. Appeals from the decisions of the Executive Presbytery may be made to the General Presbytery.